DECISION
AND
STRESS

To my Daughter
PATRICIA ANNE BROADBENT

"Let these words answer
For what is done, not to be done again
May the judgment not be too heavy upon us."

T. S. ELIOT, Ash Wednesday

DECISION

AND

STRESS

D. E. BROADBENT

Medical Research Council
Applied Psychology Unit
Cambridge, England

1971

ACADEMIC PRESS ◆ LONDON ◆ NEW YORK

ACADEMIC PRESS INC. (LONDON) LTD
Berkeley Square House
Berkeley Square,
London, W1X 6BA

U.S. Edition published by
ACADEMIC PRESS INC.
111 Fifth Avenue,
New York, New York 10003

Library of Congress Catalog Card Number: 76-141737
ISBN: 0-12-135550-0

Printed in Great Britain by
T. and A. CONSTABLE LTD, Edinburgh

ACKNOWLEDGMENTS

A spoken version of this book was delivered as the first Paul M. Fitts Memorial Lectures at the University of Michigan in March and April of 1969. Many thanks are due to the University for this opportunity both to honour a great psychologist and to discuss with his successors in Michigan the problems handled in the book.

Thanks are also due to the Medical Research Council for their generosity in allowing absence from my normal work for the writing of this book: and to All Souls College, Oxford, for a Visiting Fellowship which provided the best possible circumstances for doing so.

In fact, however, the production of a book such as this is not due to the apparent author, but is the product of a great deal of work by many different individuals. In particular, this is true of Margaret H. P. Gregory, whose careful and sustained efforts in searching literature, checking references, reading proofs, and other arduous tasks could not have been bettered. The same is true of Mrs Stella Mathias, who typed the manuscript. The labour of compiling the Subject Index was undertaken by Dr Laurence Hartley, Mr Graham Hitch, Dr Clive Holloway and Mr Peter McLeod. The number of those who have given me ideas in discussion or after reading preliminary drafts is regrettably too great for an exhaustive citation: it certainly includes not only the Department of Psychology in Michigan, as already indicated, but also all my colleagues at the M.R.C. Applied Psychology Unit. Special mention should however be made of detailed comments and criticisms which I have had and used from Dr David Ingleby of the M.R.C. Unit for the Study of Environmental Factors in Mental and Physical Illness, from Professor Sam Glucksberg of Princeton University, and from Professor Dan Kahneman of the Hebrew University of Jerusalem.

Although the diagrams are freshly drawn, the data on which they are based is very often taken from publications by a variety of authors: and thanks are due to them for permission to do this. The authors concerned are: Dr N. H. Mackworth, Figure 2; Dr J. J. McGrath and Dr A. Harabedian, Figure 3; Dr R. T. Wilkinson, Figures 4, 8, 38, 39, 40, 42; Dr W. P. Colquhoun, Figures 5, 6, 37; Dr J. J. McGrath, Figure 7; Dr D. M. Green and Dr J. A. Swets, Figure 12; Dr M. Loeb and Dr J. R. Binford, Figure 13; Dr P. Ladefoged,

Figures 15, 17, 23; Dr A. M. Treisman, Figure 18; Dr J. F. Mackworth, Figure 19; Dr J. M. Bowsher, Dr W. C. Copeland and Dr D. W. Robinson, Figure 21; Dr G. A. Miller, Dr G. A. Heise and Dr W. Lichten, Figure 24; Dr I. Pollack, Figure 25; Dr W. J. McGill, Figure 28; Professor L. R. Peterson and Dr M. J. Peterson, Figure 29; Professor A. W. Melton, Figure 30; Dr A. D. Baddeley, Figure 32; Professor L. Postman and Dr L. W. Phillips, Figure 33; Dr N. C. Waugh and Dr D. A. Norman, Figure 34; Professor R. C. Atkinson and Mr R. M. Shiffrin, Figure 35; Dr D. B. Yntema and Dr G. M. Schulman, Figure 36; Dr D. W. J. Corcoran, Figure 41.

Thanks are also due to Faber and Faber Ltd. for permission to quote from T. S. Eliot's poem "Ash Wednesday" which is included in their edition of the poet's "Collected Poems 1909-1962".

CONTENTS

CHAPTER V

Selective Perception

CHAPTER VI

Reaction to Stimuli Occurring with Different Probabilities

CHAPTER VII

The Speed of Decisions

CHAPTER VIII

Primary Memory

CHAPTER IX

Noise and Other Stresses

CHAPTER X

Speculations and Plans

A*

GLOSSARY

Glossary of Terms to be Used, in Systematic Order

Stimulus　　　　　One of the possible states of the environment.

Stimulus Feature　A part of such a state, which can be detected by an elementary recognition mechanism in the nervous system. E.g. a straight line in a particular orientation.

Stimulus Event　　A part of the stimulus containing a number of features which often occur systematically together, even though each of them may also occur in other combinations.

Category State　　One of the possible states of the output of the main limited capacity portion of the nervous system.

Categorizing　　　The process by which the nervous system adjusts so as to allocate certain category states to certain stimulus events. Typically, any of several different stimulus events will elicit any one category state. This may happen because some stimulus features will be treated as irrelevant, both red and green squares eliciting the response "square". It may also happen because two or more different combinations of features are allocated to the same category; as when tall broad men and short slender ones may both qualify as "well proportioned" although the other combinations would not.

Thus categorizing involves both input and output selection, determining which features shall be analysed and also which outputs shall occur.

State of Evidence　One of the possible states of the input to the limited capacity part of the nervous system. Because of errors in transmission, it may not correspond perfectly to the stimulus: either because the presence or absence of some features is wrongly represented, or because no information at all is transmitted about some features.

Pigeon-holing　　The process by which the nervous system adjusts so as to allocate larger or smaller numbers of states of evidence to each category state. Thus when a state of evidence contains no information about a certain feature, it may be linked either to the category state corresponding to the stimulus event with that feature, or to the one without it. Pigeonholing involves no input selection, and merely increases the probability of certain outputs at the expense of others.

Filtering   One of the processes by which the nervous system adjusts so as to reduce the number of states of evidence which may result from a certain stimulus. (Categorizing is another such process, because of its selective input aspects.) Filtering is a hierarchical process, in which each stimulus event is first examined for the presence or absence of some key features: only if these features are present do all the other features have a normal probability of representation in the evidence. That is, analysis of some features depends on prior detection of the presence of others.

Examples of the three main strategies of processing

Categorizing   Consider the set of eight possible stimulus events formed by the presence or absence of each of three features, thus:

		Features			
		I	II	III	
	A	1	0	0	*a*
Stimuli	*B*	1	0	1	*b* Responses
	C	0	1	0	*c*
	D	0	1	1	*d*
	E	0	0	0	
	F	0	0	1	
	G	1	1	0	Inaction
	H	1	1	1	

To these there may be allotted four responses, *a*, *b*, *c*, *d*, each being made to *A*, *B*, *C*, *D* respectively, while *E*, *F*, *G*, *H* all produce the same response of inactivity. This creates a set of responses and thus is output selective. It is also input selective because any other features of the stimuli remain unanalysed.

Filtering   If the same eight stimuli are divided in a different way, Feature I may distinguish those requiring no response from the others, thus:

Features

		I	II	III	
	A	1	0	0	a
	B	1	0	1	b
	C	1	1	0	c
	D	1	1	1	d
Stimuli					
	A^1	0	0	0	
	B^1	0	0	1	
	C^1	0	1	0	Inaction
	D^1	0	1	1	

Notice that Features II and III may, amongst the irrelevant stimuli, still give a pattern identical with one of the relevant stimuli. Thus by reversing the meaning of Feature I, a selection of the input results without any change in the vocabulary of responses. Notice also that because of the use of Feature I as a cue, amongst irrelevant stimuli Features II and III need never be analysed: even if one of the features is analysed, the other need not.

Pigeon-holing   If Feature III is imperfectly detected, there will be occasions when no evidence is received about its presence or absence. The states of evidence would then become

Evidence about Features		
II	III	Response
0	0	a
0	1	b
1	0	c
1	1	d
0	?	a
1	?	c

By assuming that Feature III is absent when there is no evidence either way, we can allot responses a and c to the doubtful cases. The opposite assumption would allot responses b and d to these cases. The adoption of such an assumption is "pigeon-holing": it changes the probabilities of the outputs without any effect upon inputs, and thus selects outputs without selecting inputs.

*Combined pigeon-
holing and
filtering*

	Evidence received from Features			
Stimulus	I	II	III	
A	1	0	0	a
B	1	0	1	b
C	1	1	0	c
D	1	1	1	d
A^1	0	0	?	a
B^1	0	0	?	
C^1	0	1	?	Inaction
D^1	0	1	?	

In this case filtering is employed to select the stimuli
A, B, C, D, which all possess Feature I. Thus if Feature I
is absent, no analysis of Feature III takes place and no
evidence concerning it reaches the decision system.

In addition, pigeon-holing produces a strong bias towards
response a, so that it occurs for any state of evidence
indicating the absence of Feature II, unless Feature III is
definitely also present. Thus stimulus A^1 produces response
a, even though it has the wrong value of Feature I. Note
however that this does *not* imply analysis of all Features of
A^1, because a will also occur to B^1, incorrectly.

The relationship between category states, evidence, and the outside world. Filtering varies
the strength of transition a (solid arrow), relative to transitions b, c and d (dotted arrows).
Pigeon-holing varies the strength of p (solid arrow), relative to q (dotted arrow).

CHAPTER I

Components of the Scene

There is a problem in the layout and presentation of a book such as this which the reader should perhaps consider. It arises from the rapid development of psychology and the tendency of the discipline to render out of date views put forward only a short time ago. The usual method of dealing with this problem is simply to state the view at the time of writing; but in this book we are going rather to show how the current view has arisen over the past ten years or so. In this way we may give an impression of the trend of research and the direction in which it is moving, rather than merely a static picture of conclusions at one instant. In each chapter, therefore, there will be a chronological development rather than an axiomatic one. In this first chapter we are going to try and justify this approach, to give some idea of the topics we are to cover in the rest of the book, and to point ahead to the conclusions we shall reach. Those who need no orientation may skip to Chapter II and the experiments; this one is general and discursive.

On Progress in Psychology

The main idea of the behaviourist approach in psychology is that we need to achieve communication, both between one man and another, and also between all men and the world around them. Such an achievement can come only from a determined effort to define our concepts of human nature in terms which are public and independent of our own experience. This is not to deny the short-term value of attempts to crystallize the landmarks of the human situation in a literary or existential way. Some approach to communication may be achieved by the use of adjectives such as "cool" or "swinging" or nouns such as *Angst*, "alienation", or indeed "communication" itself. But there are two weaknesses in such language. First, it cuts us off from those who have a different literary background, or whose minds work in a different way, and who therefore might be the most valuable source of new and profitable insights. Second, it makes it harder to interrogate nature to obtain fresh information, since concepts defined subjectively are difficult to translate into the public world. In the extreme case, we may have to wait passively for spontaneous insights because we have no way of exposing our ideas to the trial of experiments. Progress therefore should be faster and less variable if a deliberate attempt is made to keep concepts publicly defined. Psychological science changes more rapidly than does the idiom of artistic or existential expression.

Indeed, we can see a number of changes as we compare the psychological scene of the 1950's with that which surrounds us now as we near the 1970's. One may sum these up, so far as psychologists of the cybernetic persuasion are concerned, by saying that in the 1950's the preferred analogy for the workings of the nervous system was the radio or telephone channel; while now the analogy is the general-purpose computer. Similar changes have occurred in other approaches to psychology. Their impact is to shift emphasis away from an unanalysed correlation of output and input, towards a consideration of fairly complex internal processes, of observing responses, of cognitive styles, of the structure of grammatical rules, and so on. Much of this change is merely a fashionable swing of the pendulum, but to some extent it is clear that new analogies and languages have made it possible to cope now with problems which psychology had put aside as too difficult a decade and more ago.

There is however an element in the progress of psychology which is lacking in that of artistic analysis of experience; and which can be overlooked in older established sciences such as physics although it is still very definitely present in those sciences. This is the change due not to fashion nor debate but to the comparison of theory with experiment. No modern author would now write as Dickens or James Joyce did; but some of the psychological views expressed in the 1950's, including some held by the present author, are now known to be wrong in a way that Dickens or Joyce are not wrong. We have not only developed our concepts by communication between different psychologists; we have eliminated some of them because nature did not agree with them. In well-established sciences, this process may be sufficiently slow for the book of one decade to be much like that of another; and hence each may seem like a static revelation of the real world. In psychology, however, the pace of advance is such that a snapshot of the views of the present day may seem to have nothing in common with those of a few years ago. This is in truth a sign of strength and of the power of the experimental method; but it can look like frivolity and lack of sound scholarship to those who have not followed the line of thought that has led from one view to another.

Hence it seems wisest not to give simply current views on decision and stress, but to try to communicate to the reader the mode of attack on these problems. If this technique is successful, he will not be surprised to find in ten years' time that views have changed again; he may even feel that something essential to the nature of science comes through more clearly in such a developing field than it does in the well-established areas where conclusions can be taught and received on authority.

On the Topics Before Us

Words such as decision and stress are themselves labels which may have an agreed meaning in one group of people but may be woefully misunderstood in another. They have been used in this case because our subject-matter is a complex bundle made up of psychological questions which cut across the traditional chapter headings of the textbooks. These questions are linked together by the theoretical ideas which are applied to them, and in particular by two ideas. One of these concerns the way in which a mechanism, having only imperfect information about the world around it, may nevertheless select actions which increase the probability that certain events will occur. Mathematically, this is of course the central problem which statisticians have studied for many years. People may not behave precisely in the ways which statisticians would regard as ideal, but they are clearly faced in many areas of life with a similar problem, and their behaviour in such situations is certainly systematic. One needs therefore a convenient way of referring to researches concerning this idea in whatever area of traditional psychology they may appear. Similarly, one needs a word with which one can refer to researches linked by the second idea. This concerns the way in which the general state of the man, rather than the particular features of his task, may affect his behaviour. Background states of alertness or depression, excitement or somnolence, are invoked by theorists in many psychological areas, and these areas too will form part of our concern.

It may save disappointment then to be clear at this stage that this book will not reveal facts obtained from social studies of tycoons under financial pressure or of generals in the heat of battle. We shall rather be considering laboratory studies of simple functions such as the ability to detect a faint light occurring at unexpected times, or to remember a telephone number. Sometimes these tasks may be performed under alarming conditions, such as in a loud noise after a night's loss of sleep, but that is the nearest we shall come to direct study of the situations which one might in everyday life regard as those of stressful decision. Nevertheless, the mechanisms of human behaviour which we shall consider do have implications for these more dramatic situations. A man does not use one brain in the laboratory and another in the rest of his life, and if he cannot in an experiment combine information from two sources to give the same conclusion as a statistician, it is not likely that he will suddenly become able to do so when running a financial empire. Differences between laboratory and real life may indeed exist in other ways, some of which we shall mention as we go on through the book; but an understanding of the principles of human action does mean something for generals even if it is found in the laboratory.

One last link between the various areas of interest is worth mentioning at this stage. Most of them have a practical importance in their own right, although it is usually much less flamboyant and dramatic than the correctness of a general's decisions. The detection of faint stimuli is a function used by sonar operators and industrial inspectors; the forgetting of telephone numbers, through its impact on the amount of telephone switch-gear and other equipment tied up unproductively in wrong numbers, is a matter of some economic importance. Most of the problems which the author has studied arise similarly from concrete working situations, even though the reader may not always be able to recognize what they were. This use of applied problems gives our different specific areas another common tie; they tend to be areas requiring the man to receive and transmit information, as he may if working at some mechanical system. This means that the different tasks are likely to make use of the same underlying functions of the nervous system, and so to impose another kind of unity on our subject-matter. That is why the same theoretical analyses seem to arise in tasks which superficially do not have much in common; one task may fit in the "Perception" chapter of a traditional textbook, one in that on "Reaction Time", one in that on "Learning". Yet we find in our own analysis that each of them involves within the man a buffer storage, a mechanism of coding or categorization, a primary store, and so on. The common element is that of information processing, so much so that the subject matter of the book could almost be described as "psychology from the information-processing point of view". And this common element has been introduced by the common origin of the various tasks in practical situations.

This illustrates one of the reasons why we need not apologize for the applied origin of the most theoretical parts of the present book. In situations arising from technology our attention is compelled to the major variables in human behaviour, and we cannot ignore them in favour of some artificial distinction as can a theorist working purely from the ivory tower. The researcher remote from immediate practical pressures may indeed be free to study major variables in which at this instant society does not seem to be interested; but he should not use this freedom in order to study minor variables, until there are no major ones within reach of our techniques. The necessity for some relevance to real life is a worthwhile intellectual discipline.

ON QUESTIONS OF SCIENTIFIC STRATEGY AND OF PRESENTATION

The contrast of applied and theoretical research appears to the writer to be a false one; the most valid theory is one which works, and the most useful way of dealing with an applied problem is to spend ten minutes working out the answer from a sound theory, rather than ten years performing fresh specific experiments. For a lucid exposition of this view from the standpoint of the older established sciences, one cannot do better than consult Medawar

(1966). The same author raises however another issue which we had better face at this early stage. Biologists, he contends, normally report their results as if they had used undirected and atheoretic observation; they set out an array of facts and then purport to infer any theory from these facts. In reality, Medawar argues, the observation is itself often determined by theory, and it would be more honest and more instructive to uninformed readers if research were reported more in accordance with the principles of hypothetico-deductive method. The investigator sets up a theory, works out the implications of that theory, and then makes observations to verify or disconfirm the theory. If the results turn out unexpectedly, the theory has to be abandoned or at least modified.

Amongst psychologists, the fashionable mode of reporting results has for about thirty years been the hypothetico-deductive form, and the journals consist of a steady stream of papers giving hypothesis, prediction, and verification. This stream is punctuated by occasional protests from those who feel that the balance has swung too much the other way. One such protest was made by Broadbent (1958), in a book which we shall cite frequently in order to contrast past attitudes with those of the present. His argument can fairly be described as a rationalization of a felt distaste for the amount of theory current in psychology; he located the source of this distaste in the nature of the experiments used to justify theories according to the hypothetico-deductive method. Many complex theories were verified by experiments which were so simple that alternative theories would predict the same result; when predictions as specific and detailed as the theory were tried, they were usually disproved, and in that case the research led to no advance. If biologists were guilty of hiding their theories, psychologists were at least equally guilty of over-complicating them.

The answer to such a criticism could not be a return to a purely positivist tradition, for which the arguments cited by Medawar are fatal. The solution suggested by Broadbent (1958) was to take into account not only the theory which the experimenter himself favoured but also its alternatives; to treat each experiment not as a means of testing the presence or absence of a particular result, but as a way of dividing the set of all possible theories into as many classes as there are possible experimental results and then seeing which classes of theories are eliminated by the actual result obtained. We should not say simply "Our theory predicts that Task A will give fewer errors than Task B". Rather we should say "If A has fewer errors than B, we will conclude that theories of Type I are supported; if A has more than B, theories of Type II. If there is no difference, Type III." Two benefits flow from such an approach. First, we waste less experimental time because we learn something from every experiment. In practice, of course, we can only rarely reach the ideal because we may be forced to say "If A and B have equal errors, we can draw no conclusion". At least, however, we can keep the number of experiments with such possible results to a minimum. In order to do so, we shall realize the second advantage, which is to force ourselves to formulate theories only with the degree of complexity which practicable experiments can distinguish. In early stages of a science, this means that our approach will look very like the positivist approach, since the theories will be so simple that they will amount to no more than "I wonder whether Task A will be easier, harder, or the same as B?" At later stages the procedure will look more like the hypothetico-deductive method, where a very complex theory has only a fifty-fifty chance of being disproved and so is worth testing.

Like Medawar, Broadbent (1958) felt that the convention of scientific reporting is misleading, and he is still unrepentant. One of the changes in the psychological world as a whole has been the greatly reduced status of all-inclusive theories of the type so ably urged by Hull (1952), and it is fair to say that this is because of methodological difficulties like those raised here. The substitute for broad theory has however been to a great extent miniature theorizing within a particular area; and such theories very frequently become so elaborate that they outrun the ability of experiment to test between them. The ease with which the predictions of complex theories can be calculated on a computer has been a retrograde step; and it is not uncommon to hear theorists defend a policy of fitting one model to data on the grounds that no experiment can be really crucial in deciding between the model and its alternatives. This is of course the most damning indictment of the formulation of the theories. A presentation of the results of research in which the theory is given first and experiments reported only as confirming its predictions must tend to perpetuate methods of this kind.

Broadbent (1958) therefore reported a scientific area in the order which it had developed chronologically, starting with relatively undirected observations and gradually drawing to more confident theoretical conclusions. This will be the plan of this book also; but it has proved evident that such a style of presentation is hard to read, at least for some people. One of the psychological areas which we shall discuss is that of selective perception; it is clear that a man faced with a large mass of varied information cannot cope with it all, and tends to pick out some elements of it. If he does so in an uninstructed way, he may select the wrong elements and fail to make any sense of the situation at all. Consequently it may be well in a book such as this to indicate what the conclusions are going to be before the evidence leading to them is considered; the reader can then notice with especial interest those points which support the conclusion—or of course those which oppose them, according to taste. We shall therefore set up signposts at the beginning of each chapter to indicate where the argument is going, even though the argument itself will not follow the traditional line of setting up a theory and then testing it. In the remainder of this chapter we shall give a very general indication of the conclusions of the whole book.

An Information Flow Diagram of 1958

Let us start by summarizing the conclusions reached by Broadbent (1958), as a launching-pad and basis of comparison for those of this book. The *first and most general conclusion* was one which we can still support, and that was the value of analysing human function in terms of the flow of information within the organism. The concept of information had come into psychology from telephone and radio engineering, and its essential features in this application were as follows.

Suppose there are two alternative physical events *A* and *B*, such as a square flash of light and a round one. We observe that when *A* occurs a man produces an action I, whereas when *B* occurs he produces action II. It follows that at every stage of the intervening events within his nervous system there must have been two possible states of the system, one corresponding to *A* and one to *B*. It is not essential in any way that there should be an identity in any physical property between *A* and its corresponding state at any stage in the nervous system; for example, if *A* occurs it is not necessary that the image on the retina be square. It must merely differ in some way from the image of *B*. So long as such a difference exists, we may say that the retina transmits information about the occurrence of *A* and *B*. Conversely, of course, we do not need to know about the physical nature of the difference to make such a statement; the transmission of information all the way through to the responses I and II entails its transmission through the retina or at least, to be hyper-cautious, through some sensory pathway. We can therefore discuss transmission of information in the abstract, without knowledge of its physical basis, but with a clear understanding of what is meant: it is the selection of one out of an ensemble of possible states at one stage by the occurrence of one of an ensemble of states at an earlier stage. This kind of language immediately clears up certain pseudo-problems which were still current before its introduction, such as the fact that we see a three-dimensional world by means of two-dimensional images in the eyes, and the even more hoary example that the image on the retina is upside-down but the world looks right way up.

Perhaps more important is the insight that the effects of a stimulus depend crucially on the other stimuli which have not on this occasion occurred but which are part of the possible set that might have occurred. Returning to our example, if *B* had been a sound rather than a round flash of light the demands on the retina would obviously be quite different, and a consistent response of I to *A* might be practical at exposure times which would be much too short if *B* were also a visual stimulus of different shape. As soon as this point was realized, a whole variety of psychological phenomena were observed and brought under control; the perception of a word depends on the size of the vocabulary of other words which are possible at that moment, correct judgment of the pitch of a tone depends on the set of other pitches being used in the experiment, and so on. From the moment the concept of information was introduced, it became impossible for psychologists to consider isolated stimuli apart from the others which were physically absent but from which the one present was being discriminated.

Information possesses certain quantitative properties also; the size of the ensemble of states in any particular system sets a limit to the rate at which information can be transmitted through it, if the change from one state to another takes a finite time. If we suppose, rather gruesomely, that our responses I and II were flexion and extension of one finger, and that the man under observation was so crippled that he could make no other action, then he could by one response only transmit information about one pair of stimuli. He could however still cope with an experiment involving four stimuli by arranging a code in which, say, two successive flexions indicated stimulus *A* and two successive extensions *B*, while *C* would give flexion followed by extension and *D* extension followed by flexion. The cost would be one of time; to minimize this cost it would clearly be advantageous to attach particularly quick responses to stimuli which were more likely to occur. If this were done, a series of stimuli in which, say, *A* occurred twice as often as any other stimulus could be dealt with more rapidly than could a stream in which all stimuli were equally likely. If we have a system containing *n* states, and in which p_i is the probability of the *i*th state, then with the best possible coding there is a maximum average rate of transmission through the system which may be measured by

$$C = \sum_{i=1}^{i=n} -p_i \log p_i.$$

As we shall see, this logarithmic relationship to probability appears in the results of a number of psychological experiments. Its meaning is not always clear, however.

The *second conclusion* of Broadbent (1958) may be introduced at this point. He held that it was to some extent meaningful to regard the whole nervous system as a single channel, having a limit to the rate at which it can transmit information; such a limit is usually termed a limit to "capacity". This conclusion also we may on the whole support, although exceptions and qualifications are now quite numerous and of great interest. The meaning of this conclusion is that a man will be unable to manage within a fixed period of time to cope with more than a certain number of signals. The limiting number varies however with the number of possible signals from which the actual ones are drawn, and with their relative probabilities. If for example a man is doing a rapid task in which there is a large ensemble of signals, any other task he is given will suffer severely. If however the signals are drawn from a very small set of possibilities, he can respond to them and yet do something else at the same time. It is not true to say that he cannot do two things at once, since tasks with a low information content can be carried out simultaneously without too much impairment. This again is an illustration of the value of the concept of information.

Suppose that we try to formulate human limitations purely in terms of the stimuli present at one time. We might conclude, say, that auditory and visual stimuli can be dealt with simultaneously, because a man can drive and converse at the same time. But, on a familiar route, rounding one corner makes it almost certain what the next visual scene will be; given the past stimuli, the probability of any event other than the one which actually occurs is very low. Similarly in everyday casual conversation the remark one hears is drawn from a small set of possibilities and there are few other things which could have been said. Neither visual nor auditory task then conveys much information, even though both are delivering stimuli. It is not surprising that the central mechanisms can deal with both. But suppose that the driver is on a strange route with many unfamiliar traffic patterns; the visual stimulus may be the same, but it is drawn from a larger set of possibilities and conveys more information. Then suppose that the heard conversation is not casual but consists of a statement of a new form of transformational grammar. Again the set of possibilities is large, and the auditory stimulus conveys much information. It is most unlikely that the driver will be able to react adequately to both stimuli at the same time. The limit is on information, not on stimulation.

It is very reasonable that the limited capacity of the nervous system should reveal itself in practice, because in principle the amount of information provided by the senses is enormous. Large though the brain is, any conceivable mechanism which could cope simultaneously with all possible states of the eye, the ear, and our other receptors, would probably be even larger. The workings of the nervous system then are likely to incorporate a good many devices aimed at economizing on the mechanism necessary. One of these was represented by the *third conclusion* of Broadbent (1958). He held that the limited capacity portion of the nervous system was preceded and protected by a selective device or filter, which would pass only some of the incoming information. Figure 1, redrawn from the 1958 book, illustrates the arrangement. The filter operated by selecting those stimulus events which possessed some common feature, such as coming from a certain spatial location, and passing on all other features of those events to the limited capacity system for analysis. (This operation has sometimes been misunderstood as requiring that selected events should be stimuli affecting one group of sense-organs and rejected events should affect other sense-organs, but this is not the case. The common property of selected events might indeed in some cases be the stimulation of a particular group of sense-organs, but it might not.) The basis of selection could change from time to time and thus the central, limited capacity, system would be protected at any instant from having to deal with all the available information: but over a prolonged period could make use of any of it. The selection of any event was made more likely by such properties as physical intensity; and it was supposed that a change in the basis of selection took an appreciable time.

This conclusion also is still valid, but requires much more supplementation and comment than the other two. Filtering as described above is not the only mechanism by which systematic selection of information takes place at the entrance to the limited capacity system; but it is still one of the mechanisms. The question of the time taken by a change of selection is especially controversial; the author would still hold to the earlier formulation as the most probable, but there are other possibilities.

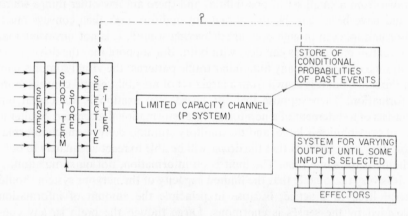

FIG. 1. A diagram of the flow of information within the nervous system, as conceived by Broadbent (1958).

The *fourth conclusion*, which too can be seen in Fig. 1, was that the filter was preceded by a buffer or temporary store, which could hold any excess information arriving by channels other than the one selected; so that if signals A and B arrived simultaneously the filter could select first A and then B even though the time of arrival of B was some way past when A had been dealt with by the limited capacity system. The information about B would however decay with time and after a time "of the order of seconds" would have become unusable. This conclusion is now very widely accepted, except that the statement concerning the time taken by the decay is usually given a smaller value of under one second.

With the *fifth conclusion* we come to the realm of doubt, modification and rejection of former views. The view in 1958 was that a second form of short-term memory came into play after information had passed through the limited capacity part of the system. This took the form of passing the information back to the original buffer store, from which it must of course be retrieved again before the period of decay ran out. That required the operation of the limited capacity system again, and so the cycle could be repeated indefinitely as long as the limited capacity system was not required to deal with anything else, such as a new input from the senses. Such a process would make the amount of interference with memory, produced by any fresh demand on the system, dependent on the time for which the recirculation was stopped and not on the number of events intervening between presentation and recall. Since 1958, the importance of some intermediate form of immediate memory has gradually won some acceptance. Such a process is conceived as requiring the limited capacity part of the system, but it is often held to operate with a fixed number of events rather than with a limited time for recycling all items. Furthermore, it is quite certain that the information does not return to the original part of the buffer store during the recycling; it may or may not return to a different part. This therefore is one of the points which will need much discussion in the present book: to conform to much recent usage, we shall call information at this stage "primary memory", reserving "buffer" for the earlier storage stage.

The *sixth conclusion* from 1958 is one which the author would now reject or at least reword very substantially. This was that the operation of the filter might be altered by motivational states or "drives". The example given was that food would have a high probability of being selected if an animal had been deprived of it for twenty-four hours. It now seems much more likely that motivational states indeed affect the probability of selection of information for passage through the limited capacity channel, but do so through another mechanism and not through the filter. (See third modification below.)

A *seventh conclusion* was that noise, the only stress systematically considered in 1958, impaired the efficiency of work by causing a shift of the filter towards itself, that is, by distracting the man. Much of the recent evidence shows rather that noise makes a man distractible, but not that it does itself distract him.

Lastly, the *eighth conclusion* was that a long-term store was kept of the information which had passed through the limited capacity system, in the form of a record of the conditional probability that events of one kind had been followed by events of another kind. The form of this store must be modified to take account of theoretical criticisms which have been levelled against any account of human learning in terms of conditional probabilities of specific events. Nevertheless, the view that long-term storage only takes place for those events which have been selected and passed through the limited capacity system remains attractive.

Current Views on Information Flow Within the Nervous System

If we turn now to the present day, we do not require any major changes in Fig. 1 to represent the changes of our ideas. This of course reflects the high degree of generality of Fig. 1 rather than the absence of error in the original formulation. Nevertheless, the main outline of the flow of information remains the same. The evidence which we are going to review points rather to new interpretations of the processes which are going on within each of the boxes in the figure, and especially within the limited capacity system.

The *first modification* is that we must consider and specify in more detail the way in which error and unreliability creep into a system of this kind and are combated. In any discussion of the transmission of information, one must of course consider the possibility of corruption of the original message by some random failure of correspondence between the state occurring at one stage of the system and the appropriate state at the next stage. At the cost of some capacity, however, this can be combated by using error-correcting codes such that any such random disturbance or "noise" gives a state at the later stage which can only have resulted from noise and which therefore requires the whole process to be repeated. In 1958, therefore, noise in the system was merely included implicitly as one of the factors reducing capacity. But in fact it is obvious that all human performance contains an occasional element of error, and that perfect transmission of information through the nervous system is not attained. Any consideration of the working of the nervous system makes it clear that there are myriad possible causes of unreliability and failure at every stage; cells may die or be refractory, facilitatory stimulation may be present or absent, and all processes such as conduction or transmission across synapses may vary in speed.

Some sources of noise furthermore lie outside the nervous system altogether. We speak of a stimulus as being a square patch of light, but unless it is viewed under very favourable conditions much the same pattern of light on the retina might be produced by a tilted oblong. The state which occurs at the retina therefore is consistent with a number of different possible states of the outside world; and because of the various unreliabilities of the nervous system the signal reaching some central point in the system is consistent with several possible states of the retina. Some of these are more likely than others, so that the position is not completely hopeless. We may speak with advantage therefore of the limited capacity section of Fig. 1 as receiving, not determinate information, but rather "evidence" about the outside world. The evidence points to state *A* of the outside world as being more likely than state *B*, or vice versa, but does not always make it absolutely certain that *A* was present.

In the output of the limited capacity channel, however, some one definite state must occur and the various uncertainties associated with the evidence have to be left behind. The state of that central box must be, say, the one corresponding to *A* or else the one corresponding to *B*. It is the incoming evidence which selects one possibility rather than the other; but it is not obvious what is the relationship between the evidence and the state which results from that evidence. It might be that the state corresponding to *A* requires far more evidence in its favour than does state *B*; or vice versa. It might be that the state corresponding to *B* occurs on a certain proportion of the occasions regardless of the evidence; or that neither state will occur unless the difference, in the degree to which the evidence points to one rather than the other, is greater than a critical amount. The precise nature of the rules relating the evidence to the states of the limited capacity system will have a large effect on the extent to which the ultimate response by the man will transmit information concerning the original state of the outside world to which he is reacting.

Let us therefore summarize the first modification in this way. There are three places in the system, at each of which a set of possible states exists. The "stimulus" is the particular one of the possible states of the environment which occurs on this occasion. The "evidence" is the particular one of the possible inputs to the limited capacity channel, which results from the stimulus. One of the possible outputs from that channel will then follow: we shall term this the "category state", and justify that term in the fifth modification below.

There will then exist rules connecting the three classes of states to each other. Such rules will determine what evidence may result from each stimulus, what category state from each state of evidence, and what category state corresponds to each possible stimulus. These rules governing the operation of the limited capacity system lead us to the *second modification* in our view of the nervous system. We shall now argue that changes in selection of information for transmission through the system take place through changes in all three kinds of rules, and not only through filtering. The first form of selection, which corresponds to filtering, links the stimulus states to the states of evidence. Filtering causes the evidence to depend to an increased extent upon those stimulus events which have some feature in common. If therefore we are listening to speech from a loudspeaker placed on our right-hand side, and ignoring speech coming from the left, sounds arriving from the right will play a large role in deciding which words we hear. The difference from the older view is that sounds from the left side are not shut out from all possibility of affecting the limited capacity system; they merely receive less weight, because fewer states of evidence can result from any particular stimulus on the left ear.

Another kind of rule links states of evidence to category states. One change in the rules is one which increases the chances of one category state occurring rather than others, by making it follow a larger class of possible evidence. Such a rule might be the example given above, of state B occurring on a proportion of occasions regardless of evidence; another might be the rule requiring more evidence for state A than for state B. In the extreme, this kind of rule means that only evidence relevant to certain states is considered at all: there may be a state C which will never occur whatever evidence arrives. This therefore acts as another kind of selection, different from filtering. The typical case of filtering is listening to hear what words are being said by a particular person; this new kind of selection is rather listening to hear whether certain words are said, regardless of who says them. In both cases, much of the information reaching the senses remains unused, but the detailed mechanism by which selection takes place is different and, as we shall see, the two processes behave rather differently in certain ways. For brevity, we may perhaps refer to the older concept as filtering and the newer as "pigeon-holing". This name is used since it refers to manipulation of the set of categories or pigeon-holes one of which must be used when any message arrives.

The *third modification* to the older view is that the role of motives and "drives" probably comes in the second type of selection and not in the first and older type. If we are deprived of food, this increases the chance of one of those category states occurring which is related to food, but it does not necessarily have any effect on the weight attached to various sources of evidence. That is, there is no effect on filtering, but there is an effect on pigeon-holing through an increased tendency to use certain pigeon-holes.

The *fourth modification* is that, as the information passes through the limited capacity system, it is not fed back in its original form to the buffer. On the contrary, it is transformed and encoded in a more drastic fashion than has been the case at earlier stages of the process. The phrase "drastic fashion" clearly requires some further explanation; as has been said, the passage of information through the system always requires some coding of the set of states at one stage into the set possible at the next stage. The image on the retina is not the same shape as the original object. Nevertheless, the set of possible images on the retina is used for transmitting information about patterns of light and not about those of sound. In the central mechanisms it ceases to be true that the set of possible outputs of the limited capacity system is used only for information derived from visual inputs. In ordinary language, when a man is shown a written letter of the alphabet, he is likely to say its name to himself, and so to transform the written input into something more like a sound or a pattern of speech movements. This is why it is now certain that primary memory does not take the form of passing information back from the limited capacity system to the same part of the buffer store as that which originally received it. A visual buffer store would no longer be appropriate once the information had been transformed.

It will be noted that the preceding paragraph is an extension of the concept of "pigeon-holing", since a set of acoustic or articulatory categories is being used to handle either a set of visual inputs or a set of acoustic ones. The *fifth modification* concerns this role of the categories or coding responses in the limited capacity system. Any one state of that system may be appropriate to a number of states of the input channels; a visual input of "2" may give the same state of the limited capacity system as will "II", and so will "two". Equally, different acoustic inputs may converge on to the same central state as each other and as a variety of visual inputs. There is a loss of information in this process, but it is rather different from the selective loss which occurs in filtering or in the use of pigeon-holing as we have so far considered it; because it cannot change from moment to moment. We can listen to one speaker now and another in thirty seconds' time: equally we can listen for any mention of food now, and after dinner listen for any mention of drink. But we cannot in this flexible fashion change the set of visual patterns which we regard as attempts to write "two"; that can only be done by long training.

Returning to theoretical language, we now have three ways in which information is lost between the outside world and the output of the limited capacity system. First, several states of the outside world correspond to each such output. Second, when the system receives evidence regarding the state of the outside world, less states of evidence can result from stimuli from some sources (filtering). Third, the relation between the evidence and the resulting state of the system may be manipulated so that certain outputs states are less likely to result (pigeon-holing). We need some brief term to refer to the first of these, as we already have words for the others; let us call it "categorizing" and refer to each of the possible output states of the limited capacity system as a "category state". (Terminology is flexible in this area, and it is unfortunate that in its everyday usage the term "filtering", for example, can be used to cover either categorizing or pigeon-holing, and probably each of those terms can be used for the other process. We will however try to be consistent in usage throughout this book, and the foregoing exposition should make it clear that there are distinctions which any one term would blur.)

Using these terms, category states each correspond not only to a class of possible inputs but also to a class of possible outputs; having categorized an input as "two" we may say, write, type, or tap a response which transmits the information in the category state. In some sense therefore the organization of response depends upon categorizing and the appearance of an appropriate category state might be described as a response by some theorists, pigeon-holing being a response bias. But this usage carries a slightly undesirable overtone. Categorizing is undeniably central and there is no one-to-one correspondence of category state and overt action even though the reverse may be true; if I write "two" I mean it, but if I mean it I do not necessarily write it.

An important difference between categorizing, filtering, and pigeon-holing lies in the speed with which each type of rule can be changed. Terminologically, let us distinguish the process of changing the rules from the process of using them by speaking of "filter-setting", "pigeon-hole-setting", and "category-setting" for the changes and "filtering, pigeon-holing, categorizing" for using the rules. Thus a man listening to a voice from the right and ignoring voices from the left is filtering; when he decides to change over and start listening to the left, this decision is an instance of filter-setting. As this illustration shows, filter-setting can be a rapid process; and the same is true of pigeon-hole-setting. Category-setting, on the other hand, is a slow process requiring long experience.

There is another possible connection of categorizing with long-term memory, and this is perhaps sufficiently separable to be classed as a *sixth modification* of the 1958 approach. In Fig. 1, information is shown as flowing into long-term store through the limited capacity system, which we can now refer to as the categorizing stage. But the main flow of the long-term store is shown simply as passing to the effector system. A problem which has become pressing since 1958 is that storage of information in a long-term store does not necessarily solve the problem of extracting the appropriate information again on some later occasion when it is needed. It is clear therefore that some specific suggestion needs to be made for the problems of retrieval; and one which has some plausibility is that access to the long-term store is through the categorizing stage, not only in input but also in retrieval. Amongst the facts which this modification is designed to handle are the facilitation and interference effects appearing in long-term memory as a result of semantic and associative links between category states. It can be represented in Fig. 1 by showing the outflow of information from long-term memory as passing only through the categorizing stage; if one adopts this course, however, one must remember that the category setting is itself a form of long-term memory.

The *seventh modification* is the last, but one of the most important. This is the introduction of stress not simply as a source of distracting stimuli, but rather as affecting general properties of the entire system. Thus a high level of excitement may cause filtering to be more extreme and evidence to be considered almost entirely from one source rather than any other. Paradoxically, this may cause a man to appear more distractible at a task, since selection of any inappropriate source of information will completely exclude information from the task itself. Such a general change in the parameters of the entire system is at least the one supported by most recent evidence; a less probable effect of excitement or "drive" might be an increase in the degree of pigeon-holing, such that category states having a temporary advantage receive even more bias when the man is excited. This view, which is related to certain classical theories of the impairing effects of high levels of personal anxiety through facilitating inappropriate error responses, does not at the moment seem probable; but it is still possible, and would also represent a change in the general parameters of the whole system.

General Summary of the Conclusions to be Reached

After an abstract and dogmatic presentation of this sort, it may be well to remind the reader that the course of this book will not be to set out predictions from this theory, but rather to follow the way in which a series of experiments has led to it. It would clearly have been absurd to set up such a view from the armchair and then to have tested it; there are many places at which it agrees with common sense, but others at which equally plausible other assumptions could have been made if one were using a hypothetico-deductive method. This formulation is the one which remains after experiment has gradually excluded whole classes of other possible theories; it would be wrong to regard it as a set of postulates. As we go through the book, we shall see some instances in which this difference in approach solves certain problems of interpretation.

Nevertheless, the goal is now in sight. The information-flow model of 1958 is to be modified largely by considering the working of the limited capacity system which formed part of it. That system is now thought of as producing one of a set of category states; the particular one is selected by the incoming evidence derived from the senses. Evidence from some sources may be given more weight than that from others; and some category states may have a bias in their favour whatever the nature of the evidence. A category state corresponds to any one of several states of the outside world, acts as a controlling centre from which several alternative lines of overt response may diverge, and is a point of access to long-term memory. The parameters governing these various relationships are changed by changes in the general state of the nervous system, which themselves may be produced by stress. With this broad picture of the eventual conclusions in mind, let us turn now to specific fields of experiment. As a start, let us consider the very simple situation of a man detecting the presence or absence of a stimulus.

Chapter II will present a large body of experimental evidence about such a situation. Readers whose interest is mostly theoretical may not wish to read it all: if so, they can safely shift to Chapter III, provided they grasp certain broad conclusions from the experiments. These are (1) that the chances of human detection of a stimulus depend upon the probability of that stimulus, (2) that they also depend upon the general state of arousal or excitement of the man, and (3) that there is some progressive change in responsiveness to a situation when a man remains in it for a long period. To establish these generalizations properly, rather than loosely, has needed much effort by many laboratories: and Chapter II is devoted to demonstrating that they are indeed valid.

It is impossible to dispense with any of them by using one of the others to explain failures of detection. Chapter III will consider further the implications of these broad factual generalizations.

Vigilance: Results with Traditional Measures

The Classic Phenomena of Vigilance

The area of research usually included under the term "vigilance" involves the study of men keeping watch for inconspicuous signals during fairly long periods. The theoretical interest of this situation is that it allows one to study, in a simple and easily controlled task, almost all the factors which one might hypothesize as controlling a man's attention. In contrast to most psychological tests, the man is left reasonably free; and by suitable changes in conditions we can hope to find out what causes him to attend to this or that feature of the surroundings.

Thus, in the terms introduced in Chapter I, we might hope to find whether failure to react to a signal was due to the operation of filtering, of pigeon-holing, or of some general change in the parameters of the process. In ordinary language, does a man fail to react because he is not looking, or because he is expecting to make some other reaction, or because he is so sleepy that he can make no response to anything? As we shall see, the distinction between filtering and pigeon-holing is too difficult for conventional analyses of vigilance experiments: but we shall show that the probability of a signal has a marked effect upon its detection, that the general state of wakefulness or arousal is also important, and that the time for which the task has been performed seems to be a factor even when these other variables are held constant. In a later chapter we shall go on to enquire whether probability, arousal, and prolonged work operate through filtering or pigeon-holing; the first step is to prove that they affect performance.

The origins of research on vigilance are however applied rather than theoretical. The whole line of research takes its origin from a group of studies by Mackworth (1950). He simulated the task of radar watch for submarines from aircraft: using a clock pointer which moved on in a series of steps. The experimental subject had to watch this pointer and to report any occasions on which the pointer gave a double step. The signals were quite easy to see when attention was called to them, but they were brief and if they were not noticed immediately there was no further opportunity to respond to them.

Using this task, Mackworth found that the number of signals reported declined after a work period of only half an hour: which was by the standards of the day a remarkably rapid onset of "fatigue". A deterioration of this sort has been found in large numbers of similar tasks since the original investigation, and it is one of the key facts which investigators seek to explain. It is of course of some practical importance, and in addition the hitherto unsuspected appearance of a decline in efficiency following a relatively small

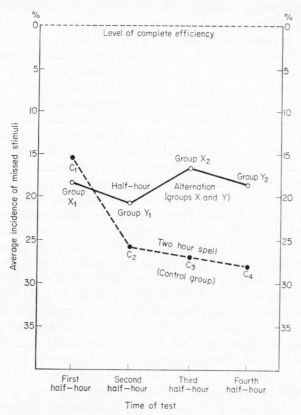

FIG. 2. Performance in a vigilance task, as shown by the data of Mackworth (1950). The control group worked for two hours with no break: the experimental groups X and Y performed half-hour spells with half-hour rest pauses in between.

number of overt actions posed a considerable theoretical problem. Mackworth showed in his original studies that the decline could be prevented by stimulant drugs, by rest pauses, and by providing knowledge of results when a signal was missed or correctly detected. As we shall see, other conditions also changed the efficiency of detection.

At quite an early stage in the study of the problem, however, it became apparent that a decrement during the work period would not always appear in tasks of this general kind, even though there were no rest pauses, stimulants, etc. Examples of such tasks were provided by Broadbent (1950), Elliott (1957) and Bowen (1964). (Bowen's work was carried out considerably before the date of publication, and was thus available to those in the field as early as 1956.) These tasks which showed no decrement during the run were usually tasks in which the signal was not transient but remained available over a prolonged period. In some cases it was simply the presence of a pointer reading a dangerous amount on a dial, which remained stationary until corrected: in others it was a signal of threshold type, which was reinserted at the same or higher intensities until a reaction was provoked. Despite the absence of decrement in such tasks, it was notable that efficiency was less than it might have been expected to be on the basis of alerted performance. The time taken to see the pointer might be 10 seconds instead of the usual reaction time of a second or so: and the strength of the sound necessary to provoke a reaction might be a number of decibels above that which could be heard at threshold. Thus the low level of performance in these situations provides a practical and theoretical problem, even where there is no decrement from the beginning of the work period to the end.

Perhaps the clearest illustration of the problems to be tackled in this field is found in two tasks used by Jerison (Jerison and Wallis, 1957a, b; Jerison, 1957, 1959). Jerison compared performance for a man watching one clock similar to Mackworth's, and a man watching three such clocks simultaneously. In the former case performance showed a decrement during the work period; in the latter case there was no decrement during the work period (at least if one analysed in fairly large units such as half an hour), but performance was at a much lower level throughout. An incidental difference is that high intensity sound present during the work period affected the latter task but not the former. The contrast between these two types of task is especially interesting, because each element of the three-clock task is the same as the one-clock task. There is no question for instance of the signal being present for a longer time in one case than in the other. The difference in decrement and in the overall level must in some way have to do with the complexity of the three-clock task. As we shall see, the difference between these two tasks has given rise to a fair amount of research.

THE STATE OF OPINION IN 1958

Broadbent (1958) divided the various theories of vigilance into four. As was clear at the time, these were not necessarily mutually exclusive, and it might well be that more than one of them was true. They do not therefore fit ideally into the scientific plan of attack recommended in our first chapter, but each of them has nevertheless had its partisans. Without undue forcing, one can classify the work done on vigilance since 1958 into the same four groups, since various investigators have planned their research in the interval in the light of their enthusiasm for one theory or another. There are a number of investigations on particular factual points, such as those of Bergum and Lehr on the beneficial effects of rest pauses, of financial incentives, of the presence of an authority figure, and so on. (Bergum and Lehr, 1962, 1963a, b, 1964). Nevertheless, most investigations can be pushed into relevance to one or other of the main lines of thinking.

The oldest approach to the vigilance decrement was that of Mackworth himself, and this is the *inhibition* theory. In essence, the idea is that some response to the display is necessary throughout the task, that this receives no reward during a typical vigilance task, and that consequently it ceases to occur just as a conditioned response becomes extinguished when it is not rewarded. In support of this view, Mackworth had cited analogies between the disinhibition effects shown in conditioning, and the disappearance of vigilance decrement following unusual stimuli. If an animal is conditioned and the response is then extinguished by non-reward, some outside disturbing stimulus may revive the extinguished response. Similarly, if for example the experimental subject received a telephone call during the watch, he did better subsequently. The most direct support for the inhibition theory comes however from the beneficial effects of knowledge of results: if successful response to a signal is immediately rewarded, then the decrement does not appear to occur.

Even by 1958, certain facts had made it necessary to revise this theory. Perhaps the most striking of these is the point made by Deese (1955) and supported in a number of studies since, that performance in a vigilance task is better if the rate at which signals occur is higher. In terms of the inhibition theory as first formulated, this suggests that the more frequently one fails to reward response to a stimulus, the less it extinguishes, which would of course be quite contrary to general principles of learning. One can however modify the theory to avoid this difficulty, by supposing that it is in some sense the response to intervening non-signal stimuli which produces inhibition, which in turn generalizes to the closely similar signal stimuli. The point which especially concerned Broadbent (1958) was that the theory seems to predict a downward trend in performance in all tasks where signals receive reaction without any corresponding reward, and that therefore it offers no explanation for the vigilance tasks which show a low but steady level of performance. Inhibition seemed therefore at that time, and indeed still seems, to be a theory of the decrement but not of the general level of performance.

The second class of theories current in 1958 was the *expectancy* view. The essence of this approach was that the response to a signal became more likely if the signal was more probable, the probability being derived from past incidence of signals. This view was first launched by Deese, although Mackworth himself noted that unexpected signals might give a poor response. The well established fact already mentioned that a high signal rate often leads to better performance is easy to understand from the point of view of the expectancy theory: and the general assumption of good performance for probable signals is itself very plausible in the light of the general considerations about the transmission of information which we outlined in the last chapter. In 1958, however, this view seemed attractive as an explanation for the low level of performance in tasks with a low signal rate, but did not seem so plausible for explaining the decrement within a single work period. The only case in which that might seem to fit in with this theory is the case in which the experimental subject has to revise his estimate of the probability of signals as the work period continues. He starts off expecting many signals, then realizes that only few will arrive, and in consequence his efficiency drops. This might indeed be the case in the first few sessions of the task: but even in 1958 it was clear that repeated sessions on a task would give decrements even in later sessions, where the observer might be supposed to have a stable estimate of the probability of a signal.

The third theory current in 1958 was that of *activation or arousal*. On this view, the nervous system requires a constant barrage of stimulation of all kinds in order to maintain itself in a reasonable level of general efficiency. If, therefore, a man works in unstimulating conditions, his efficiency will decline. This approach also was mentioned by Deese in 1955, and it fits in well with the contemporary interest of physiologists in the role of the non-specific pathways through the reticular system in maintaining alertness. A good review of such work is to be found in Oswald (1962). Briefly, it appears that states of drowsiness and sleep are likely to arise if an animal is deprived by surgical means of the general facilitation produced by stimulation of the sense organs. It might well be argued that the situation of a subject in a vigilance task is itself unstimulating, even though all the senses are still in operation.

Experiments on the deliberate withholding of stimulation from people over very long periods have become numerous since the original work under Professor Hebb in Canada (Bexton et al., 1954). It is clear that considerable deteriorations in many kinds of performance can be produced by keeping people lying in the dark in silence for long periods (Zubek, 1964 reviews the area). While there was in 1958 rather little direct evidence connecting vigilance tasks with this general effect of sensory deprivation on performance, yet the similarities in the experimental situations were obviously sufficiently great to make it plausible that arousal played some role in vigilance. Difficulties were apparent however in 1958: for example, we may try to explain the decrement in performance during a work period by supposing that the man enters a vigilance situation in a reasonably high state of arousal, having been exposed to varied stimulation outside the laboratory. When he is placed in a monotonous and unstimulating environment, however, the level of arousal of the nervous system does not drop instantaneously but takes a little time to do so. As it does so, his ability to detect signals drops correspondingly. If this were an adequate explanation, we have some difficulty in seeing why some tasks show very little decrement, notably those of the kind studied by Elliott, Broadbent, and Bowen. At first sight these seem tasks with a very low level of stimulation. Furthermore, performance at vigilance tasks may deteriorate in conditions of very intense noise: and this is hardly a condition of under-stimulation. In general, the theory of activation or arousal had received very little directly relevant experimental work in 1958, and was merely an attractive possibility: but Broadbent (1958) concluded that its importance was probably on the average level of performance rather than on the decrement or absence of decrement during the work period.

The last theory current in 1958 was that of *filter theory*. This was the personal favourite of Broadbent (1958) although he did not exclude the operation of the other theories. Briefly, the suggestion was that filtering of information was taking place during vigilance tasks as in all other situations, so that the man being studied was effectively receiving only part of the information striking his senses. One of the factors governing whether or not the source of information would be selected was the novelty of the information from that source: so that early in a task the signals from the task itself would all be selected, whereas later in the work period there would be brief periods during which the nervous system would be handling information from sources other than the task, and would therefore be inefficient at the task itself.

The main line of evidence on which Broadbent relied was not drawn from vigilance tasks at all, but rather from the measurement of continuous performance at serial reaction tasks and similar kinds of work. It has been known since the time of Bills (1931) that a man naming a series of colours at his own speed does not maintain a steady rate of work for long periods. When he has been performing the task for some minutes, he begins to show irregularities in his performance, with occasional very long intervals between successive reactions. These "gaps" or "blocks" may not at first show in the average speed of reaction, as the intervening rate of work may be as fast or faster than it was at the beginning of the period studied. Broadbent (1953) confirmed this result for a task using five signal lights, each having its own appropriate reaction and in which each reaction produced the next stimulus. The average rate of work at such a task remains reasonably constant for quite long periods, but at the end of a work session there are occasional very slow reactions. He also showed however that, if the lights were presented automatically at a fixed rate, each light going off at the end of its scheduled time and being replaced by the next one, the number of correct reactions within the permitted time period would show quite a rapid decrement after ten minutes or so of work. The two findings are of course very consistent with each other, since the fixed or paced method of presenting the task does not allow sufficient time for the very slow reactions, and equally does not permit the man to compensate by working faster between his moments of inefficiency. Broadbent therefore drew an analogy between the paced and unpaced forms of this task, on the one hand, and vigilance tasks using short and prolonged signals, on the other. He contended that decrement would be confined largely to the vigilance tasks with transient signals and would not appear in those with prolonged signals. In 1958, it was a fair division of those vigilance tasks which showed decrement and those which did not, that the latter used signals of unlimited duration while the former used transient signals. Consequently Broadbent concluded that this theory provided a good explanation of decrement during a watch period, even although it contributed little or nothing to the other problem of the low level of performance in many tasks with long duration signals. The theory also afforded a reasonable explanation for the damaging effects of high intensity noise on vigilance, since a high level of irrelevant stimulation might be expected to make selection of stimuli from the task less likely.

It will be noticed that the difference between the two tasks used by Jerison (1957, 1959) cannot readily be explained on the basis of filter theory, since in that case the task with a low and constant level of performance is one using transient signals. Furthermore, the task which was not affected by loud noise was one which did use transient signals, and which did show a decrement during the run. This casts some doubt on the interpretation of the noise effect also: and hence the research effort later directed at explaining the difference between Jerison's two tasks.

Finally, it should be noted that this theory incorporates two features which are logically quite distinct and which have since been separated by various authors. One feature is the occurrence of filtering during the performance of vigilance tasks: while the second feature is the principle that novelty in a stimulus makes it more likely to be selected by the filter. It is quite possible to accept and urge the importance of filtering, and yet to argue that the dominant variable in deciding whether a stimulus is selected will be the probability of arrival of such a stimulus at the time in question. This is a kind of "expectancy-filter" theory, which has since been held by a number of authors, usually using the term "observing response" rather than the term "filter". Such a theory differs from the formulation produced by Broadbent in 1958 in the variable supposed to control filtering, but not in the mechanism by which the variable operates. On the other hand, the principle that a key variable is the novelty or shortness of time for which a stimulus has been experienced on this occasion, is one which need not be linked to a filtering mechanism and becomes rather similar to the inhibition approach. Broadbent in fact tended to explain the extinction of conditioned responses as due to failure of the filter to select the conditioned stimulus, and thus formed a link between the inhibition and filtering theories. One can now see why these various theories are not regarded as mutually exclusive, although some parts of each of them are at odds with some parts of each of the others. Bearing these rather complicated interrelationships in mind, we may now turn to the development of each point of view over the intervening ten years.

Inhibition Theory Since 1958

The main exponent of an inhibition point of view has in this period been McCormack, who has reviewed the work conducted on this approach (McCormack, 1962, 1967). In his version, the response to the wanted signal develops an inhibition which dissipates with time, but which will be present soon after the reaction to the signal unless that reaction has been reinforced. The inhibition is, on this view therefore, not attached primarily to response to the irrelevant features of the task, but to that to the signal itself: and as we indicated previously this cannot be a completely adequate explanation on its own because of the effects of variables such as signal rate. When signals occur frequently, performance is more efficient. McCormack's theory therefore incorporates a second, motivational, variable which is supposed to increase the efficiency of reaction, and which may be supposed to be increased by factors such as the regularity or frequency of signals. It is however predicted by the theory that immediately after response to each signal efficiency should be at its lowest, and should gradually improve until the next signal occurs. The research conducted by McCormack therefore pays much attention to this factor, and also to the effects of knowledge of results.

Perhaps its most distinctive feature, however, is its concentration upon reaction time rather than probability of detection, as the measure of deterioration. In the typical situation used by McCormack a 15-watt electric lamp bulb was turned on at uncertain times, and the subject had to press a switch when he saw it. Failures of reaction normally did not occur, but nevertheless the time taken to react did deteriorate as the work period progressed. The deterioration was reduced by rests, and especially by the provision after every reaction of a lamp indicating whether the reaction was faster or slower than the one before. As the provision of knowledge of results will be discussed several times later, it is worth noticing that its role in McCormack's experiments is presumably purely motivational, and that this is rather different from possible functions of knowledge of results in tasks where some signals are undetected. It does not, for example, give more accurate information about the number of signals presented, nor does it resolve uncertainty concerning the exact nature of the signal. By showing that decrements occur in a task with an easily visible signal, and that information about one's own performance prevents them, McCormack has therefore shown that the decrement does not depend upon imperfect knowledge of the structure of the task, and that motivational effects are important. This of course does not exclude the presence of other factors in tasks where some signals fail to be detected.

Despite the generally useful results obtained by McCormack using reaction time, and the similar results obtained by other experimenters (see Buck, 1966 for a review), one cannot necessarily assume that latency will always behave in the same way as the probability of detection of inconspicuous signals. A striking counter-instance is given by Jerison (1967a), who found in his tasks that the shortest latencies appeared in the conditions giving the worst probability of detection. In general terms, we shall see later that a man who confines himself to reporting only signals of which he is absolutely confident will obtain fewer detections than one who is prepared also to report signals which he merely suspects to be present. Yet it is well known that confident judgments tend to be faster than those made with greater uncertainty (see for example Audley, 1964). Thus any condition which changes the proportion of "doubtful" perceptions which are reported will produce a slowing of reaction combined with an increase in detections.

Perhaps the most crucial aspect of this version of inhibition theory, however, is the effect of time between one signal and the next one. The longer the interval, the greater the opportunity for inhibition to dissipate, and therefore the faster the reaction should be. In some of McCormack's own experiments this was true: although in others there was no effect of the interval between the signals. McCormack's studies usually used a mixture of different values for the interval between signals, so that the experimental subject did not know whether the next signal was going to occur 30 seconds or 90 seconds after the last one. Baker carried out an experiment in which a reaction signal was presented at 10 second intervals regularly for a long series, following which a signal occurred 2, 5, 20, 25 or 30 seconds after the last of the regular series. In this case the reaction time was extremely slow at the 2 second interval and then improved until somewhere in the region of the 10 second interval which had been the average of the whole preceding series. When the interval got longer than this, however, the reaction time began to get slower again. This is not really consistent with the inhibition point of view, since although the improvement with increasing interval could be regarded as dissipation of inhibition, there seems no reason for the sudden reappearance of inhibition when the interval gets longer than the previous average amount. Baker himself, as we shall see, explained the curve as due to the expectancy of the subject, which would be greatest at the average interval he had previously experienced. [This experiment is conveniently reported by Baker (1963a) although it was available earlier in a mimeograph version.]

The obvious difference between Baker's experiment and that of McCormack is the extreme regularity of the signals in Baker's case. One can establish different degrees of uncertainty about the value of the inter-signal interval which is being used, by mixing together widely different or fairly similar intervals within an experiment. Boulter and Adams (1963) measured reaction time under medium and high uncertainty about inter-signal interval, as well as with a completely regular signal. With a moderate degree of uncertainty the reaction time decreased as the interval got longer, but with a high degree of uncertainty the response time increased at longer intervals. Similar results were found by Dardano (1962). With high uncertainty about the length of the interval being used, Webber and Adams (1964) again found reaction time to be best at short intervals between signals.

If we consider now experiments on the probability of detection rather than upon reaction time, Baker (1962) presented a series of signals at intervals ranging from half a minute to $7\frac{1}{2}$ minutes with an average of 4 minutes. A single test signal was then inserted at intervals ranging from a quarter of a minute to 10 minutes: detection improved as the interval got longer, up to $6\frac{1}{2}$ minutes, but the efficiency with a 10 minute interval was low. Once again therefore the best performance is at about the average of the previous intervals, or a little longer.

All these results on the effect of inter-signal interval must however be viewed in the light of results reported by McGrath and Harabedian (1963).

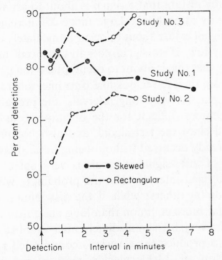

Fig. 3. The effect of inter-signal interval on performance, from the data of McGrath and Harabedian (1963). When subjects have experienced a rectangular distribution of time intervals between signals, their performance gets better as the interval gets longer: when however they have experienced a condition in which the most common interval is a short one, then their performance gets worse as the interval increases.

They compared performance in tasks with about the same average interval between signals, and with the same value of the shortest possible interval, but with a very different shaped distribution. In one case the most common interval between signals was the shortest, while in the other case different intervals were equally probable. In the latter case, the probability of detecting a signal increased as the interval increased, just as inhibition theory would predict. In the former case however the probability of detecting a signal decreased as the interval between signals got greater. (To show this result most clearly required the analysis of the time between each signal and the last detected signal, rather than the last signal which had occurred without being detected, as is perhaps reasonable.)

What then can one conclude about the usefulness of the inhibition theory in the light of these studies of inter-signal interval? It is certainly the case that response becomes slower at very short intervals between signals, in a good number of experiments. The fact that it becomes slower again at very long intervals, especially under conditions of stimulus uncertainty, must however be put down to some effect of the probability of a signal. Yet once such an explanation has been admitted, it seems also to explain the poor performance at very short intervals; and especially to explain the fact that this poor performance may actually become good performance when most of the inter-signal intervals are themselves short ones. If we attempt to tie together the various results on inter-signal interval, the best way is perhaps to think of the probability at any instant that a signal is about to arrive. If signals occur with equal probability at each of a large range of inter-signal intervals, the probability that a signal is just about to occur immediately after one has been detected is relatively low. If no signal does in fact occur at a short interval, then the probability that one is about to occur after a longer interval becomes greater since there are then fewer possible time intervals remaining in which the signal could occur. At very long intervals, the probability drops again both because it becomes difficult for the operator to assess how long an interval has elapsed since the last signal, and also because the probability that a signal has already occurred without being noticed becomes important. If the distribution of inter-signal intervals is very narrow, so that signals occur regularly at a fixed interval, then the probability will be very high at that interval and low at others; while if the distribution is such that very short intervals are far more common than long ones, then the probability of a signal will become very high immediately after one has been detected. It might be possible to produce these various complicated relationships by a suitable manipulation of McCormack's motivational factor, which is supposed to improve performance when signals are occurring at regular fixed inter-signal intervals: but the combination of the two factors would have to be fairly complicated in order to account for the result of McGrath and Harabedian, and it would seem essential in that case for the relationship between the good effects of motivation and the bad effect of inhibition to be specified quantitatively.

An expectancy interpretation of the effects of inter-signal interval does not of course allow us any explanation for the increase in reaction time occurring as the work period proceeds. With signals that are almost always detected, there is no reason why the apparent probability of the signal should change at the end of the run as compared with the beginning. This widely confirmed effect on reaction time points rather to some consequence simply of the time spent at work. If an inhibitory process does result from continued observation, however, it does not seem terribly plausible at the moment that it results from unrewarded reaction to the signals themselves, since the man is not necessarily at his worst immediately after he has performed such a reaction (McGrath and Harabedian, 1963). On the contrary, it would still seem more plausible as it did in 1958 that the inhibition results from the continual reactions to stimuli other than the signal itself.

The Expectancy Approach Since 1958

This is perhaps the approach which has given rise to the largest body of work in recent years. The main areas of research concern artificial signals, the effect of knowledge of results, the rate of non-signal events, and pre-training with different signal rates. Of these the first two areas give equivocal results, but the latter two make it clear that expectancy is indeed a factor, if not the only one.

Baker (1963a) has given the most comprehensive account of his own attitude to vigilance, which is the clearest version of the expectancy theory. As will be evident from the experimental studies mentioned in the last section, Baker considered the efficiency of reaction to depend not only on the average probability of a signal observed over the whole work period, but also on the conditional probability of a signal at a particular time interval since the last one was detected. Mackworth's original experiment was performed with a wide range of time intervals between signals: and Baker (1959) showed that the decrement would disappear if signals were presented at the same average interval but with a reduced range of intervals. With a completely regular series of signals occurring every $2\frac{1}{2}$ minutes, detection did not decline significantly as the task proceeded. We have already cited Baker's evidence that signals occurring at too short or too long an interval are less likely to be noticed: and it will be seen therefore that Baker has made a strong case for the role of the instantaneous probability of a signal as affecting the chances of its being detected.

The probability relevant to detection may also depend upon where the signal is to occur, as well as the time at which it is expected. If there are more places where a signal can occur, as well as increased uncertainty about the time at which it is to happen, performance will be worse (Adams and Boulter, 1964). If signals are more probable in one place than another, they will be detected more efficiently in the probable location (Nicely and Miller, 1957; Blair and Kaufman, 1959).

Thus far, nothing has been said which might give an explanation of the decrement during the work period. However, Baker points out that any failure to perceive a signal produces a kind of vicious circle effect, since it not only lowers the overall apparent probability of signals from the subject's point of view, but also distorts his information about inter-signal intervals. As the work period proceeds, the total number of signals missed is bound to accumulate, even if the probability of detection were to remain constant. The knowledge which the man has about the situation therefore becomes progressively more distorted, and this distortion will in turn show itself by an increased number of missed signals. In this way one might well get a decrement from an expectancy point of view. Furthermore, such decrements should be more serious if the initial number of detections is lower. Mackworth (1950) had found that a dimmer echo on a radar screen showed a greater decrement during a run than did a bright signal, and that those individuals who made few mistakes at the beginning showed less deterioration as the run went on. Baker also suggested that any stress such as the presence of irrelevant loud noise might cause an occasional failure to detect signals which would become amplified through the distorted expectancy which it would produce. This "vicious circle" type of effect therefore affords a possible mechanism by which an expectancy theory would predict a decrement.

There are some difficulties nevertheless in this point of view. The most serious of these concerns the way performance changes when one gives repeated work periods separated by rests. In each new session performance starts again as high as it was originally, but deterioration during the work period continues to occur even in highly practised people. (See for example Adams *et al.*, 1963; Binford and Loeb, 1966.) Furthermore, the effects of stresses such as noise (Broadbent, 1954a) may indeed produce a greater decrement, but often give superior performance at the beginning of the work period, so that the decrement does not seem plausibly to be explicable by a "vicious circle" induced by a few missed signals. Lastly, Baker's formulation does provide a useful explanation for the absence of decrement in those tasks which have signals of long duration (because the subject always sees them and hence knows when the signals occurred); but it does not explain the difference between the tasks of Jerison (1957) and Jerison (1959), which have been mentioned several times already. In this case the decrement was in the easier version of the task and not in the harder one. One may therefore consider the work on expectancy theory with a certain prior doubt whether it can explain all forms of decrement: but equally it seems clear that the "vicious circle" mechanism is a highly plausible one to contribute to decrement in some situations. We shall in fact consider it again later, when certain other information has been presented which will allow a more useful discussion of it. In the meantime, research based on an expectancy point of view has branched out into several sub-areas, and each of these is worth considering separately.

The first sub-area is that of *artificial signals*. If the efficiency of detection rises with an increase in the probability that a signal will occur, then in real life situations the performance of industrial inspectors or radar monitors might be improved by putting in extra signals for them to detect, not arising naturally in the task but from some artificial means. Not only would these increase the apparent signal frequency, but it would also be possible for the operator to be informed whenever he had missed one, a provision of knowledge of results which is hardly practical in a real job where nobody knows that a component is faulty or an echo present on the radar screen until the monitor reports it! As one might expect, Baker (1960a) has carried out an experiment showing that such artificial signals with knowledge of results do improve performance, and similar findings have been produced by Garvey *et al.* (1959), Faulkner (1962) and Wilkinson (1964a). The effect is not purely an increase in apparent signal frequency: thus Wilkinson (1964a) actually found no benefit at all from artificial signals unless knowledge of results about

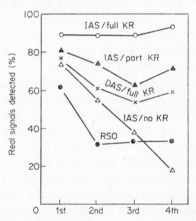

FIG. 4. The effect of artificial signals on vigilance performance, from the data of Wilkinson (1964). The various symbols are as follows:

        RSO = real signals only
        DAS = different artificial signals
        IAS = identical artificial signals, just like the real ones
        KR = knowledge of results.

Note that the best performance is given by artificial signals exactly like the real ones, with full knowledge of results, and the worst by complete absence of artificial signals.

their detection was given to the subject. The increase in signal rate by itself did not give the desired result. In view of the fairly common finding that changes in the signal rate may improve performance, this may simply have been due to the particular conditions of his experiment: but it is clear that a good part of the advantage of artificial signals is the possibility of giving knowledge of results about their detection. Another variation in the experiment, which sheds light on the way in which artificial signals have their effect, is to use signals which are different from the real ones. This clearly does not raise the apparent frequency of the real ones: and although Garvey, Taylor and Newlin found that different artificial signals were just as effective as real ones, Wallis and Newton (1957) found no advantage at all, while Wilkinson (1964a) found the advantage to be present but less than that of signals identical to the real ones. He points out that the signals used by Garvey, Taylor and Newlin, although different from the real signals, nevertheless had elements in common with them: the real signal was a pointer deflection in one direction out of a neutral zone, while an artificial signal might be a pointer deflection in the other direction. The two types of signal have in common that there is no pointer in the neutral zone. Wilkinson's real signals were occasional tones of short duration interspersed in a regular series of tones of rather longer duration. The "different" artificial signals were tones which were even longer than the neutral signals. The complete absence of beneficial effect from different artificial signals in the experiment of Wallis and Newton is perhaps to be explained by the fact that their subjects only received artificial signals following the lighting of a conspicuous red lamp, indicating that an artificial signal was about to be inserted. This might mean that the artificial signals affected monitoring performance only when the lamp was on, which would not of course alter performance on real signals.

Wilkinson in an analysis of his data more detailed than the usual reporting only of detections noticed that the different artificial signals produced a substantial rise in the number of "false alarms", that is, reports of a signal when no signal was present. Artificial signals identical with the real ones did not give such a substantial rise in false alarms, but merely an increase in detections greater even than that produced by the different artificial signals. The most natural interpretation of this is that the signals identical with the real ones provide information about the exact nature of a signal, and thus improve discrimination between signals and neutral stimuli: whereas artificial signals differing from the real ones merely increase the responsiveness of the subject without improving his ability to discriminate signals from neutral stimuli.

Perhaps the clearest instance of a beneficial effect from artificial signals without a change in the apparent probability of real signals, or in knowledge of their characteristics, is provided by experiments in which the operator has some completely different task to perform as well as his main one, and gets knowledge of results on the secondary task. He may, for example, have to watch a radar screen as his main task, but also be asked to react to a change in the general level of room illumination, and be informed about the speed of his reaction when he does do so. Studies of this type both by Baker (1961), and by O'Hanlon et al. (1965) have shown that a secondary task can act in this way as an alertness indicator and improve performance on a main task. Here the knowledge which is given to the operator is not so much about the probability of real signals as about his own state of efficiency, although one can see that it may cause him to become more reactive by a compensatory effort if he is informed that his efficiency is dropping. The effect is obviously therefore motivational rather than a pure expectancy effect, as Baker himself indicated. It seems fair to conclude from these various experiments that the effect of artificial signals has at least three components: a rise in apparent signal probability, the provision of extra information about the exact nature of a signal, and a motivational component causing the monitor to change his own performance in the light of what he learns about his past work.

More detailed studies of *knowledge of results* form the second group of studies related to the expectancy approach. As we have already seen, this factor must have some effects other than the provision of better information about signal probability. This is implied by the results of McCormack (1962, 1967) on a task in which the measure is reaction time rather than probability of detection, since when all signals are detected knowledge of results does not provide probability information. It has been shown by Adams and Humes (1963) that in such a task knowledge of results will not only improve the speed of reaction during the session in which it is given, but actually on a later session when knowledge is withheld. Furthermore, this cannot be some general arousing effect of the extra stimulation given after each response, because such stimulation given without reference to the subject's own performance was ineffective. There are certain puzzles in that the results of Adams and Humes showed no effect of knowledge of results on decrement, but rather on the average level of performance: and Montague and Webber (1965) actually failed to get an effect of knowledge of results at all in a similar task. This may however have been due to the particular form of knowledge of results used, which was relatively uninformative. In general however these effects of knowledge of results on latency cannot be due to provision of information about the signal. Furthermore, one would not expect knowledge of results to improve knowledge about the signal very much unless it was given after a high proportion of signal presentations. It has been shown not only in McCormack's results, but also in data of Johnson and Payne (1966) that beneficial effects of knowledge of results appear when less than half the signals are accompanied by such knowledge. Furthermore, if knowledge of results acted solely by improving the apparent probability of signals, then false information given to the subject that he had missed signals when in fact no signal had occurred might be expected to give as large an improvement as true knowledge of results. Mackworth (1964a) found that false knowledge of results did not change the decrement during a watch period: although it did give an overall level of performance intermediate between true knowledge of results and no knowledge at all. Mackworth points out that the false knowledge of results does not help the monitor to learn the characteristics of the signal, and that this may weaken its effect compared with true knowledge.

Perhaps the clearest way of attacking the relationship between knowledge of results and apparent signal probability is however to distinguish two kinds of knowledge. One of these is dependent upon the occurrence of some response by the monitor: that is, he is told when he has reported a signal incorrectly, but is not told when he fails to respond and thus misses a signal. This kind of feedback is relatively easy to produce in practical situations, and probably exists to some extent even when no particular provision is made for it: if an industrial inspector throws out a component which later turns out to be perfectly satisfactory, he hears about it. On the other hand, he does not hear about components which were faulty and which he failed to notice, because the complaints come back too long afterwards to bring the responsibility home to him. The other form of knowledge of results, in which the operator is told about signals which he has missed, is the one originally used by Mackworth and is essentially confined to the laboratory, to the use of artificial signals, or to training sessions. But it is only this latter form which will increase the apparent probability of signals, and provide accurate information about time intervals between them. The former version will positively decrease the apparent probability of signals, since it will prevent the operator from mistakenly thinking that his false detections were real ones. Chinn and Alluisi (1964) gave information about missed signals, about false reports, and about detected signals in all possible combinations of knowledge of results and found in fact that different aspects of performance were changed. Knowledge about false alarms reduced the number of such responses: while knowledge about correct detections reduced the number of missed signals. Curiously enough however knowledge about missed signals reduced the number of false alarms, that is, it gave the same effect as know ledge about false alarms rather than the opposite effect. Chinn and Alluis explain their results not so much in terms of apparent probability as of the good effects of reinforcing efficient responding. Wiener (1963) also obtained a paradoxical effect, by showing that response-dependent knowledge of results actually produced an increase of false reports as compared with full knowledge or absence of knowledge. The response-dependent condition produced however a large improvement in detections when the operator was transferred subsequently to performance under no-knowledge conditions.

Perhaps the fairest way of considering these two results is in terms of the effect on the operator of his own knowledge of the conditions under which he is working. When he knows that he will hear nothing about missed signals but will be told about false reports, he can get more information in doubtful cases by responding; and thus can improve his own subsequent performance. When however he knows that he will be told about misses, he might as well refrain from responding when in doubt, so as to avoid the odium of possible false reports. As in the case of knowledge about performance on some secondary task, the operator can adjust his responsiveness in the interest of some ultimate gain, provided he has the information on which to do so.

In addition to its motivating effect, then, knowledge of results does have an important action through reminding the operator of the exact nature and frequency of the signal; and this may explain why it fails to improve performance in some conditions. Colquhoun (1966a) trained operators either by knowledge of results, or by "cueing" before each signal so as to draw their attention to the signal; and found no beneficial effect greater than that of simple practice. He had, however, pre-trained all his subjects with the actual frequency of signals to be met in the task and with knowledge of results in that session; thus they were fully aware of the signal probability. They did show an improvement with practice, and thus had still something to learn about the exact nature of the signal or the best ways of keeping watch for it. But knowledge of results did not in this case seem to help with those aspects of the task.

To summarize, the evidence for expectancy theory drawn from this group of experiments is not very powerful; we need not disbelieve that knowledge of results allows the probability of the signal to have a more powerful effect, since some features of the results are consistent with that view. But it is clear that information about other features of the signal, and general motivating effects, are also involved.

Experiments on *event rate* form the next group which should be considered, and they provide stronger evidence for the importance of expectancy. The basic design of such experiments is shown by one of Colquhoun (1961); he

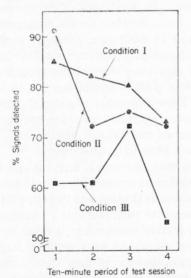

FIG. 5. The effect of signal rate and event rate varied independently. In condition I, there were 144 events of which half were signals: in condition II, 24 events of which half were signals. In condition III there were 144 events of which only 12 were signals. From the data of Colquhoun (1961).

used a task in which, as is common, the signals to be detected consisted of minor changes in a series of neutral, non-signal, stimuli. The task is then analogous to the inspection of a series of industrial products in search of any one which is defective. In all the studies we have mentioned thus far any change in the frequency of signals has left unchanged the total number of signal-plus-non-signal stimuli, and has therefore altered the probability that any particular stimulus is a signal, as well as altering the overall probability of signals. Colquhoun compared two conditions with different numbers of signals but with correspondingly different numbers of non-signal stimuli, so that the probability that a given stimulus was a signal remained constant. He also included a condition in which the smaller number of signals was combined with the larger number of total events, so that there was a drop in the probability that any given stimulus was a signal. With a design of this sort one can distinguish effects of the total number of events, of the total number of signals, and of the ratio between the two. The results were quite clear; the probability of detection was unaffected by the total number of events or signals when the ratio between them was constant, but dropped when the ratio dropped.

The importance of this result lies in its distinction between expectancy and other points of view. The older finding that signal detection is higher at higher signal rates is consistent with expectancy; but it is also consistent with arousal theory. The more stimuli of any kind arriving during the task, the more general and non-specific facilitation of the nervous system there should be. Findings on signal rate therefore do not distinguish one class of theory from another. Changes in event rate, however, ought to change arousal without necessarily changing expectancy; we have already seen that the important variable in expectancy theory is the conditional probability that a signal is about to occur given a certain location or interval since the last signal. Consequently if the probability of a signal, given that some event has occurred, remains unchanged, the total event rate should not affect expectancy. An increase in event rate will still affect arousal. Colquhoun's result is therefore a considerable blow to arousal theory.

The general finding that an increase in event rate fails to improve performance has been confirmed several times. An important group of studies by Jerison and his colleagues (Jerison and Pickett, 1964; Jerison et al., 1965; Jerison, 1967a) has varied the event rate over a wide range and had found not only that the average level of performance is worse for a greater event rate, but that the decrement during the work period is larger. It may be almost absent at low event rates. In most of these studies, the absolute number of signals was kept constant, so that an increase in event rate implied a drop in the ratio of signal to non-signal events. The result therefore agrees with Colquhoun's; but in the last result of the series (Jerison, 1967a) different event rates were compared with the same ratio of signals to non-signals. As in

Colquhoun's results, there was an effect of ratio at the same event rate; but there was also a drop in performance at the faster event rate holding ratio constant. There was also an interaction between the two variables so that the ratio of signals to non-signals had a large effect at fast event rates. Jerison therefore regards the speed at which decisions are required (the "observing response rate", to anticipate a usage we shall explain later) as the crucial variable. He has pointed out that Colquhoun's situation involved an element of visual search whereas his did not (Jerison, 1966); in Colquhoun's task a row of six circles were presented as each event, and a signal consisted of a circle of slightly different colour amongst five normal circles. The failures of detection of signals mixed with many non-signal events occurred mainly at the ends of the row, and this might at first sight suggest a change in search and scanning patterns. However, Colquhoun (1966b) has reported a confirmation of his original result with a new task having only two circles for each event, where visual scanning seems much less important. He also reported that, if six circles were used and the signal was a difference of size rather than colour, the effect of signal/non-signal ratio ceased to be greater at the edges of the display but was simply present at all locations.

There is therefore a difference between Colquhoun's results and Jerison's, in that the former shows no effect of event rate as such but only of signal/non-signal ratio, while the latter shows an effect of event rate and only finds the largest effect of ratio at fast event rates. This discrepancy cannot be explained by the visual search factor; but it is perhaps easiest to point simply to the range used for each of the variables by each experimenter. Colquhoun's fastest event rate was less than four events per minute; Jerison's was 30 events per minute. Colquhoun's signal/non-signal ratio ranged from 0·5 to 0·083; Jerison's from 0·05 to 0·0083. It would seem reasonable therefore to say that both ratio and event rate have an effect, but, from Jerison's results, that the latter comes into play at rather fast event rates and then magnifies the ratio effect.

Whatever the explanation we prefer, there is no doubt whatever that fast event rates fail to improve performance and accordingly that arousal cannot be a complete theory of vigilance. These findings do not however establish the importance of expectancy as opposed, say, to inhibition or filter theory. As the number of non-signal events increases, we might well expect the amount of inhibition or the number of deviations of the filter to increase. Some other line of experiment is needed to dispose of these possibilities.

Studies on *training with different signal rates* provide such a line of attack. The traditional way of doing a vigilance experiment is to show one or two demonstration signals to the subject, and then to give him a short practice in which signals usually occur at a higher rate than in the main test. This allows the experimenter to get adequate evidence that the subject understands the instructions and knows what a signal is like; but it does have the effect of exposing the subject to a higher signal rate than he will meet in the work period itself. As he carries on with the task then his estimate of the probability of signals will gradually be revised downward; and this indeed is the expectancy theory's explanation of decrement during the watch period.

It is possible to depart from the traditional method, and to give each subject in the experiment a deliberate pre-training session in which signals are presented at realistic rates, with full knowledge of results to ensure that a correct estimate of the probability is formed. Then by using a rate of signalling in this pre-training session which is or is not appropriate to the rate met in the main experiment one can check whether the argument of expectancy theory is in fact sound or not. This was done by Colquhoun and Baddeley (1964,

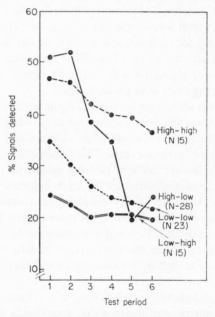

FIG. 6. The effect of training with a high or low signal rate upon subsequent performance with a high or low signal rate. The first word attached to each graph is the rate experienced before the session, and the second word is the rate experienced during the session. From the data of Colquhoun and Baddeley (1967).

1967) for both visual and auditory vigilance. Broadly speaking, their results were that a low signal rate in the main session produced a smaller decrement if the pre-training session had had a low rate than if it had had a high rate; and that the overall level of performance when the main session had a high rate of signalling was worse for those subjects who had been pre-trained with a low rate than for those with a high rate. These main findings are those which one would predict from the expectancy point of view.

Some minor points are worth noting. First, in the visual task it was found that the time of occurrence of the very first signal in the main session would affect the results. Getting the first signal quite soon after starting work seems to give good performance in the first sixth of the period as opposed to the last sixth; this is not just because one does well on the first signal itself, but on the other early signals as well. This is plausible enough if we think of the first signal as establishing a subjective probability for the general signal rate; however, as it did not happen in the auditory experiment the whole effect of pre-training cannot be due to this factor.

Second, the inter-signal interval in this experiment covered a range up to ten to one. That is, there was a good deal of uncertainty about the time at which each signal was going to appear even though the overall average rate was fixed. This is important because one can get quite different results by giving signals completely regularly in the pre-training and main sessions. In that case it is best to be trained at the actual rate to be used in the main session, and a man trained at a high rate will not do well when tested with a low one, even initially (Floyd et al., 1961). This is of course an example of the operation of expectancy for particular inter-signal intervals which we discussed earlier.

Third, in Colquhoun and Baddeley's experiments there was still significant decrement present even in those subjects who had been pre-trained with a completely appropriate signal rate. Starting out with too high an idea of the signal rate does increase the decrement during the work period, but there is still some decrement even if one has the right rate established before one begins.

At this point we can draw some general *conclusions on expectancy*. It seems to have established itself beyond all reasonable doubt as a factor in vigilance. The key experiments in doing this are Baker's on inter-signal interval, and the pre-training experiments of Colquhoun and Baddeley. Neither of these are well explained by any other theory; in the former case because performance first improves and then deteriorates with a peak at a point unrelated to any present stimulation but only to the average of past stimulation. In the latter case the crucial treatment is applied during pre-training and cannot therefore alter the arousal, the inhibition or the novelty of stimuli in the main session, at least as existing theories have been formulated.

Expectancy is a factor: but is it the only factor? One has to doubt this, and certainly Baker himself allows of other variables. The work on knowledge of results and on artificial signals shows some effects which go beyond the establishing of a correct signal probability for the subject, since they appear even with knowledge about a secondary task rather than the main one, and even in tasks where all signals are detected so that probabilities are already available. The continued decrement in repeated work-periods, and the decrement in subjects who have been pre-trained with the correct signal rate are a problem; pushing expectancy as far as it can go, we might perhaps argue that even appropriately trained subjects fail to see many signals and therefore shift during the period from a correct to an under-estimate of the signal rate. Since it is conditional probability which matters, they then learn that "there are fewer signals at the end of the run" and so go on showing decrement in later sessions. But even this argument will not deal with the experiments in which all signals are seen and reaction time rather than detection is the measure. There must be more than expectancy in vigilance.

OBSERVING RESPONSES: AN APPROACH RELATED TO EXPECTANCY

There is another approach to vigilance, which Broadbent (1958) treated as a sub-class of expectancy theory, but which its originator would doubtless prefer to be regarded as an atheoretic approach. Holland (1957, 1958) developed an analogy between the behaviour of animals in learning situations of a kind named after B. F. Skinner, and the observing behaviour of people in vigilance tasks. He pointed out that the monitor of a vigilance display can be regarded as having to emit a series of adjustments of his sense organs and receptor apparatus, without which successful observation of the wanted signals would be impossible. The "observing response" is closely similar as a concept to "filtering", but whereas Broadbent made failures of filtering depend on passage of time, Holland made failures of observing response depend on other variables. Successful detection of a signal is the aim of the behaviour and therefore each detection of a signal might exert the same kind of control over the observing responses as does a pellet of food over the preceding actions of a hungry animal. In ordinary vigilance tasks the observing responses might be unrecorded, but in a modified task one might place the subject before a display and yet allow him to see it only for a brief instant after he had performed some action such as pushing a button. The button-pushes would then be overt observing responses, and could be used to check the connection between the delivery of signals and the occurrence of observing responses.

Some of the basic findings of animal learning experiments should be recalled at this stage. There are two basic ways in which an animal may be reinforced by being given food for acting in a certain way. One of these ways is "fixed-ratio" and involves food being given every time the animal has acted in the desired way a definite number of times; for example, one might give a pellet of food every hundred times a rat pressed a bar. In this case, the bar-pressing occurs at a higher rate than it would without food being given at all, and often occurs faster the less often food is given. That is, if the rat must press a hundred times for one food pellet, it often presses faster than if it can get a pellet for only fifty presses. In the other basic schedule of reinforcement, "fixed interval", food is given only for the first bar-press following a certain time interval after the last food was given. Here the relationship to rate of reinforcement is quite different; if food arrives only once every five minutes, there is less bar-pressing than if food is available every ten seconds. Furthermore, immediately after each reinforcement there is a period of slow responding which is replaced by more intensive activity as the time for the next food pellet draws near. To get rid of this uneven rate of responding one must use "variable interval" reinforcement, in which food is given for the first press after an interval which is varied randomly from one occasion to another. An even rate is then obtained, but the speed with which the animal works depends on the average value of the variable interval, being faster the shorter the interval. If one abandons giving reinforcement, the effects depend on the schedule which has been used; with fixed ratio, after the reinforcement stops the animal goes on giving bursts of presses at its old speed, but intersperses them with periods of inactivity. If fixed interval has been used, the rate of pressing drops away slowly after the interval at which reinforcement had in the past been obtained.

Using the technique he had suggested, Holland was able to obtain all these findings substituting for bar-pressing the pushing of a button to illuminate a display; and for the giving of food the presentation of a signal on the display. It will be seen at once that the results on fixed and variable interval repeat those on inter-signal interval which we discussed earlier and which were taken as evidence for expectancy. If signals occur at a fixed rate, one does not look for them just after one has seen one; and one looks more eagerly at about the usual interval. If the interval is random, one looks more often the shorter the average interval and the higher the consequent probability of seeing a signal. It is for this reason that this approach has been treated as a variant of expectancy theory, but there are two reasons for reminding the reader that this classification is somewhat arbitrary.

First, Holland himself regards his approach as atheoretic and would object to "expectancy" as being a theoretical term. Briefly, the present author would reject this claim on two grounds. One is that an assertion that detection depends upon the instantaneous probability of occurrence of a signal is no more theoretic than an assertion that it obeys the principles of fixed ratio reinforcement; probability is just as much an observable as schedules of reinforcement are. It may be a more general assertion, but that is another matter. The other reason for rejecting the claim that a Skinnerian approach is atheoretic is that observing responses are not measured in the ordinary vigilance task, and the appeal to them to explain those phenomena which are measured is just as theoretical as, say, an appeal to filtering.

Returning to the arbitrariness of the classification of observing responses as a species of expectancy theory, we must not forget that the postulation of observing responses is logically separate from the postulate that they are controlled by the probability of signal occurrence. One might for example contend that such responses cannot be emitted at too high a rate for a prolonged period, thus turning the theory into a kind of filter-inhibition approach. As we shall see, some authors do take this line.

The history of Holland's approach since his original suggestion has been disappointing on the side of experimental technique, but successful on the more theoretical side. The technique which he suggested was seized upon by several investigators as a way of checking in detail the behaviour of the subject at times when no signal was present; but the results were unsatisfactory. To take the most obvious line first, one can measure eye movements and attempt to record natural observing responses. Baker (1960b) showed that missed signals did not parallel the frequency with which the subject in a clock test looked away from the display. Mackworth *et al.* (1964) extended this line of attack to subjects watching two clocks as well as those watching only one. They found that none of the signals missed when watching one clock occurred when the subject was looking away from the display; he was looking without seeing. If two clocks were watched, then a number of the missed signals did occur at times when the subject was looking somewhere other than the display which carried the signal; but from the results with one clock, the appearance of appropriate eye fixations is only part of the story in detecting a signal, and eye movements could not be used as a superior technique for finding out more about behaviour than the detections themselves reveal.

It could be argued that eye movements are less satisfactory than Holland's technique of linking a button into the task, which must be pressed before an observation can be made. Other authors however have found disappointing results with Holland's own technique. Jerison and Wing (1963) studied the same subjects in an ordinary and a Holland version of the clock test, and found that detection rate in the ordinary version did not correlate significantly with button-pressing rate in the Holland version. Blair and Kaufman (1959) used three sources of signals, gave different signal rates on the three, and obtained the usual result that performance was more efficient on the source with the larger number of signals; when the time taken to detect a signal was used as the measure. The number of observing responses made to each source of signals was however equal. Broadbent (1963a) used both three sources and one source, and found that in either case the time taken to detect signals increased as the period of work went on; but the rate of button-pressing was also increasing, so that subjects were going faster at the end of the watch than at the beginning. A counter specially inserted into the system revealed that initially subjects reported a signal as soon as they had made an observing response which revealed it. As the work period went on, subjects were making several observing responses before they reported a signal which had been present on the display all the time. The overt measure of button-pressing was therefore unsatisfactory as a measure of the subject's efficiency.

Following these studies the number of experiments in the literature using the technique declined. Recently, Hamilton (1967) has found experimental variables which may make Holland's technique more useful. While he confirmed Blair and Kaufman's result when allowing subjects to make observing responses at their own speed, he was able to get a difference between the number of observations on a source giving many signals and one giving few, by allowing the subject only to make observations at fixed times. The longer the intervals between these times, and also the higher the signal rate, the greater the effect of the relative probability of signals upon the relative probability of observations. One might well argue that these variables increase the probable cost of observing the wrong source, in terms of the average time for which a signal may remain present before it is detected. Although Hamilton's technique has so far only been used with relatively few subjects, and needs further extension it may well give Holland's method a new lease of life.

There is of course no logical connection between the usefulness or otherwise of Holland's technique and the usefulness of the theory that some, perhaps undetectable, observing response is being made in vigilance tasks. It might well be that the technique is unable to make the response sufficiently overt, and yet that it does nevertheless exist. The two sides of the approach do not stand or fall together; and in fact despite the relative weakness of the technique a number of authors have been attracted by the theory. Thus for example Adams *et al.* (1962) explained some features of their results in this way. They employed a task in which moving symbols were present in the field of view, each carrying a three-digit number preceded by the letter G. The signal was the change of this letter to F on one of the items visible. As the items were moving about, an index of separation could be calculated, which indicated how far the particular item carrying the signal was away from the other items present at the same time. Isolated items were given slower reactions than clustered items, but only at the latter end of the work period. Thus the decrement during the run affected more seriously signals coming from isolated items. The authors put this down to a failure of the observing response of searching or scanning across all the items present.

Similarly, Johnston *et al.* (1966) and Johnston *et al.* (1967) make use of the concept of reinforcement of the response of directing attention to certain locations. They employed a task in which a number of stimuli were simultaneously present, and the subject had to notice either additions or deletions from the array. Performance deteriorated with the ratio of signals per session to stimuli present at one time, a result like that of Colquhoun and of Jerison on event rate; but the main usefulness of the concept of reinforcement comes in explaining differences in detectability of different kinds of signal. If a high proportion of the signals came from stimuli with a certain feature (having a certain number written on the stimulus) then the disappearance of such stimuli was noticed very efficiently, and their relative advantage was greatest later in the run. It is reasonable to suppose that the subject made many observing responses to stimuli present in the field which had a feature frequently associated in the past with a high probability of disappearance. As might perhaps also be expected, the appearance of such stimuli was not especially well noticed, presumably since attention could not be directed to their location until they were present.

A particularly vigorous use of the observing response as a theoretical concept is made by Jerison (Jerison and Pickett, 1963, 1964; Jerison *et al.*, 1965). As we have already seen, his studies on event rate have shown an effect of the conditional probability of a signal being present given that an event has occurred; and he suggests that the emission of observing responses can be represented as the result of a decision about the probable value of emitting such a response. If a signal is likely to be present, then it is worth making an observation; equally if the detection of a signal is especially valuable then an observation is worth while. This view is clearly connected with Hamilton's experimental results already mentioned, that observation follows signal probability more closely if signals are more numerous or observations allowed only rarely. That is, if there is an increase in the cost of slow reactions or in the probability of such a slow reaction following an incorrect observation. Jerison does not regard only probability and value as the variables controlling the emission of observing responses, however; because of the effects of a high event rate with constant signal/non-signal ratio he also regards the generation of observing responses as producing some inhibition. This means that there will be changes in the observing behaviour as a function of the time for which the work has gone on, even though probability conditions remain constant.

A full discussion of the merits of this view must await the presentation of other data and theorizing of a "decision theory" type in the next chapter. For the moment it will be enough to say that this approach is certainly sound in so far as concerns the effects of signal probability on the scanning and searching of displays with different spatial locations. As we saw from Mackworth *et al.* (1964), such tasks certainly involve the making of correct observing responses; and from Hamilton (1967) the occurrence of such responses may follow signal frequency. In practice many forms of display may bias the part of the available information to which attention is given, and do so in an undesirable way; on an ordinary radar screen, the man will tend to look at the middle of the rotating bright sweep line and so to do badly on signals appearing at the edge of the display, that is, at extreme range. Redesigning the display can reduce this, reduce the equally unsound tendency to look away from the sweep, and so improve performance (Baker, 1958, 1967). It is therefore a merit of this point of view, as Jerison (1967b) urges, that it may lead to improvements of displays.

One of the most sophisticated applications of such principles is the work of Senders (1967). If a display is made up of many sources, each of which requires attention with different frequency, there is a problem both of finding optimum layouts for the system and of ensuring that it is possible for a man to monitor so many channels. On grounds of information theory, the output of each source can be specified by sampling it at a rate proportional to its band-width. Thus from physical considerations of the character of the aircraft or other system which is being controlled we can decide how often a man should look at each source in order to handle it adequately. The data suggest that people do in fact look at each source in the proportion which one would predict in this way, and that one can design a reasonable display by calculating the probability that any source will require observation immediately after any other, and grouping together those with high transition probabilities.

The Arousal Approach Since 1958

Whereas in 1958 there was little direct evidence for the importance of arousal in vigilance, there are now quite a few experiments stemming from that point of view. One of the earliest and still most satisfactory in its implications was that of McGrath (1963) who compared visual vigilance with a

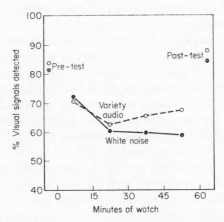

FIG. 7. The effect of varied background of sound stimulation upon performance at a visual vigilance task. From the data of McGrath (1963).

steady low level of noise and with a varied background of sound; and auditory vigilance with and without the provision of interesting visual material irrelevant to the task. In each case vigilance was better with the larger amount of irrelevant stimulation present. This clearly cannot be explained by expectancy, and is in the wrong direction for filter theory; the latter might well predict that performance would get worse in the presence of potentially distracting stimuli. Inhibition theory could only explain McGrath's results by postulating a "disinhibiting" effect of irrelevant stimuli, which itself might be felt to need explaining. There is here fairly clear evidence for the importance of some general state unrelated to the task itself and depending on the overall level of stimulation.

Other evidence pointing in the same direction is provided by Zuercherl (1965), who found that it was beneficial to make the subjects stand and stretch or converse with the experimenter during the watch; and Binford and Loeb (1963), who combined an easy auditory vigilance task with a difficult visual one. They found that increasing the signal rate on the auditory task improved performance on the visual one, although admittedly no signals at all on the auditory task were better than a few. The latter effect they explained as due to the reduction of performance due to dividing attention between two tasks at once. Adams *et al.* (1961) and Monty (1962) each left the stimulus conditions of the task unchanged and altered the response which the subject had to perform when he saw a signal. In the former case, simple reporting of a signal was compared with evaluating it as one of four possibilities. In the latter case, simple reporting was compared with a more complex but predictable motor response; and with pressing an extra button which might be one of several possibilities and which was selected on the particular occasion by an extra stimulus light. Both experiments showed beneficial effects of the more complex response instructions (though see below).

These results are not quite as convincing as McGrath's, for a variety of reasons. Zuercher's effect might be due either to a motivational change or to the beneficial effects of ceasing to respond to the display during the extra activity. Binford and Loeb's might be due to the complex interactions existing between multiple tasks, which we shall consider again under the heading of filter theory; and the two experiments on response complexity might be explained either by better registration of stimulus probability due to increased activity, or to beneficial effects of ceasing to respond to the display. McGrath's result is more convincing simply because the background stimulation was not arranged to fall out of synchrony with the task signals, and because it was irrelevant to the task. Given McGrath's findings, however, it certainly seems plausible that all these results are due to increasing arousal.

There are however certain difficulties and discrepancies when we come to consider other experiments. For example, Bakan and Manley (1963) measured auditory vigilance in subjects who were blindfolded and found that they were more efficient than those who received normal visual stimulation. Montague *et al.* (1965) varied response complexity by requiring a calculation on the numerical signal for which their subjects were watching, and found that this did not produce any improvement in performance. (They also found no improvement at a higher signal rate.) One of Monty's conditions of response complexity did not improve performance; in that case, the subjects had to make a more complex motor response and also had to make it in an unpredictable place. Lastly, McGrath repeated his experiment on varied auditory stimulation, with the modification of using a higher event rate in the visual task; and the beneficial effect of the varied sound now disappeared. All these authors suggest that conditions were already sufficiently stimulating for maximum performance, and that consequently their increases in stimulation produced too high a level for optimum performance. We shall in a later chapter see evidence that effects of increased stimulation do interact with other conditions, giving rises in performance in some cases and falls in others; so this argument is not so much special pleading as it seems at first sight. Nevertheless, it means that we cannot simply suppose that an increase in stimulation will always be beneficial. Indeed, the harmful effects of noise on visual vigilance (Broadbent, 1954a; Jerison, 1959; Broadbent and Gregory, 1965a) and of a combination of noise and vibration (Loeb and Jeantheau, 1958) would be very hard to reconcile with such a view. This point will be considered in more detail when we come to consider the effects of stress on all kinds of performance, but for the moment it will be enough to accept the doctrine of an optimum level of arousal for working efficiency.

That being so, it would be desirable to have some independent measure of the state of arousal, rather than deducing it from the rises and falls in performance. Various attempts have been made to relate physiological measures to performance, usually employing relatively peripheral measurements such as skin conductance, heart rate and muscle tension. Skin conductance usually decreases during the work period (Dardano, 1962; Davies and Krkovic, 1965, Eason et al., 1965). As these experiments were also cases in which there was a decrement in performance, it is tempting to suppose that the one decline caused the other, but this argument is not completely compelling, as both changes might be proceeding independently. Verschoor and Hoogenboom (1970) found that relatively good subjects showed no decrement within a session in detections or in skin conductance while relatively poor subjects gave a decrement in both. This provides some evidence for a link between the variables. When however Eason and his colleagues varied signal rate, they did not produce a corresponding change in any of their physiological measures; although they did note that those subjects who did relatively best under any signal rate tended to be those who had the highest skin conductance at that rate. Stern (1966) varied signal rate and found a lower detection rate at the lower signal rate, but skin conductance was (insignificantly) higher at that rate. He ascribed this to a super-optimal level of arousal resulting from reaction to irrelevant stimuli. Corcoran (1963a) found no relationship between heart rate and vigilance performance in normal subjects; but did so if the subjects had been deprived of sleep. Eason and his co-workers found no drop in heart rate while their detection rate was dropping; it is worth noting that heart rate reacts vigorously to arousing situations such as performance in a flight simulator or watching emotionally loaded films (see for example Levi, 1967). If therefore a form of arousal affects vigilance, but is not measured by heart rate, it must be a rather specialized form. Furthermore, noise, which as we have seen sometimes impairs vigilance, does increase skin conductance (Helper, 1957). Perhaps the clearest and most hopeful result is that of Surwillo and Quilter (1965) who measured spontaneous changes in skin potential rather than conductance, and found a significant relation between the detection of vigilance signals and the frequency of spontaneous changes in the period just before the signal arrived. This relation did not appear to be the result of correlation of both variables with time. With this exception, the results are obviously rather unclear and disappointing.

There are two difficulties in this group of physiological studies. First, it is distinctly possible that low performance appears at both low and high levels of arousal. That would explain some of the apparent inconsistencies in the results; and as long as we were convinced that, say, skin conductance increases monotonically with arousal, we could decide which inefficiencies were due to which cause. The second difficulty however is that we cannot be confident of these peripheral measures as being related in a fixed way to a central state. Venables (1963) has shown that in normal subjects there is no negative correlation between skin potential and the size of the interval between two flashes of light necessary to discriminate that two are present. Yet the latter is on physiological grounds likely to be an inverse measure of central arousal, since animal experiments have shown that the central response to two flashes is more distinct when facilitatory stimulation is applied to the reticular system; and Venables has also shown that the two measures do correlate in schizophrenics.

To anticipate the later discussion of arousal in tasks other than vigilance, Wilkinson (1961a, 1962) has measured both performance and muscle tension in men working after loss of sleep both with and without knowledge of results. In the relatively unmotivated condition, performance fell; in the motivated one performance was maintained but with increased muscle tension; in general, those individuals who showed little impairment of performance by sleeplessness showed a rise in tension, and those who were impaired gave no rise in tension. These results show that the effect of sleeplessness is to change the amount of tension which goes with a certain level of performance; the simplest explanation is that the sleepless man deteriorates unless he exerts some compensating effort, and this involves tensing the muscles. The peripheral physiological measure may thus show the amount of effort that is being exerted rather than the level of central arousal; indeed, more effort may be needed if the central arousal is low.

A similar appearance of effort directed by the subject himself towards compensating for lowered arousal may explain the result of Eason and his colleagues, quoted above, that different signal rates did not give overall differences in performance but that some individuals gave higher performance in the conditions where they also had the highest conductance. Baker (1960b) with his increase in general activity and tendency to look away from the display unparalleled by a drop in performance, provides another example; and so does Micko (1966), who found that subjects presented with visually projected jokes during an auditory vigilance task tended to remember more of those presented at the end of the work period. There was no close relation however between the numbers of jokes read and vigilance performance, in either direction. People may well resort in fact to shifting position, and to attending to outside stimuli, as well as tensing their muscles, in an attempt to compensate for a central drop in arousal, and thus display an increase in peripheral measures.

A more central measure of arousal might be derived from the EEG, the electrical activity of the brain as picked up from the outside of the head. Davies and Krkovic (1965) showed a decline in alpha activity as the watch period continued; alpha, the predominant component of the EEG at roughly 10 Hz, decreases as a man moves into the first stages of sleep, and this result might therefore be expected if the subjects were beginning to show short bursts of low arousal. Unfortunately, alpha also decreases when a man moves from an alert but unoccupied state to one of concentration on some stimulus or task, and this measure cannot therefore be applied automatically as an index of lowered arousal. An alternative way of using EEG is to sample the electrical activity for, say, half a second after each stimulus, and then add together a large number of such samples, say, fifty. When this is done, the various random components of the EEG present in each sample cancel each other out, and a series of waves can be seen which are apparently responses to the stimulus used as the starting point for each sample. This "cortical evoked response" has been shown to be smaller in overall amplitude for missed signals in a vigilance task than it is for detected ones (Haider, 1967). This however again must not be taken as evidence for the role of arousal, since the same group of studies has been claimed to show that the evoked response is smaller for auditory stimuli when the subject is attending to a visual task and vice versa. That is, the evoked response might be measuring expectancy or observing response effects rather than arousal ones.

The point is a doubtful one, since Näätänen (1967) has recently provided evidence that the reduction in auditory responses when expecting a visual signal may depend upon the subject knowing the time at which each kind of signal may arrive. For example, if visual and auditory signals alternate, the subject will know that the next signal after a visual one will require no response, and thus he may relax and become unaroused. This, rather than a selective exclusion of auditory information, might explain the smaller evoked response to auditory stimuli. Näätänen found that randomly mixed relevant and irrelevant signals gave equally large evoked responses. It is unclear therefore whether the overall amplitude of the evoked response reflects selective control of the input, or merely general arousal.

A possible way round this difficulty is to examine different components of the response separately. In the first 50 msec or so after the stimulus, there are various components which are to be regarded as specific to the channel by which the stimulus is being delivered, because on the whole they are best recorded over those parts of the scalp closest to the projection area where the particular sense organ delivers its information to the cortex. The parts of the response which have so far been of most interest for vigilance are rather later and can be picked up at many places on the scalp, that is, they are non-specific. Amongst these parts of the response we can distinguish a positive potential coming about 50 msec after the stimulus, succeeded by a negative potential at about 90 msec, a second positive at about 150–160, and a second negative at about 270 (for auditory stimuli: visual responses will be later). These four components are still present even if the subject is asleep, and the only one of them which changes substantially is N_2, which is considerably larger in sleep (Weitzman and Kremen, 1965). Wilkinson *et al.* (1966) used a vigilance task of the type with a fairly high event rate (one/2 sec) and a low signal rate (8/hr) requiring reaction only to signals, and averaged the evoked response over the fifty non-signal events before each signal. They found a significant relation between N_2 and failure to detect signals, the large values of N_2 giving more failures, and no relation between detection and either N_1 or P_2. On the other hand, when a high signal rate was used (event rate

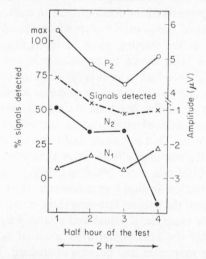

FIG. 8. Magnitude of various components of the evoked response, during a vigilance task, in relation to signal detection. In this experiment it was the component N_2 which correlated with the rate of signal detection: the rate of signalling was low, and the component in question seems to be related to level of arousal. From the data of Wilkinson (1967).

one/$4\frac{1}{2}$ sec, every event a signal) reaction time correlated with N_1 and not with N_2 (Wilkinson and Morlock, 1967; Wilkinson, 1967). In this case the smaller evoked response went with the less efficient reaction; and N_1 was increased by applying incentives. The relationship only appeared in work periods of 20 minutes or so, which contained the usual decrement in reaction time found by McCormack and others; there was no relation within runs of 50 signals separated by rest pauses. While most of the studies of the effect of attention or expectancy upon the evoked response have not distinguished various components, it seems as Wilkinson (1967) suggests that N_1 is the component that has usually been contributing most substantially to results such as those of Haider (1967) and of Satterfield (1965). In other words, when attending to vision the N_1 response to a sound seems to be reduced and N_2 appears much as usual.

These results therefore certainly show that different components of the evoked response are related to performance at low and at high signal rates, and rather suggest that the important component in the former case is one related to sleepiness while in the latter case it is a component related to expectancy or the direction of attention. If these results can be extended they may allow an objective distinction to be made between cases in which the level of arousal is sub-optimal and those in which it is high enough for some other factor to come into play, without appealing to super-optimal arousal simply because the performance deteriorates. Notice however that even in this case the meaning of the physiological measure appears only from the behavioural effects with which it is associated; it does not seem safe at present to take any physiological measure as a criterion of arousal and explain behaviour by reference to it, rather than vice versa.

In summary of the arousal approach, however, we must accept that some general state of the man, raised by stimulation having nothing to do with the task, can affect efficiency. In unstimulating conditions it is certain both that a variety of outside stimulation may increase efficiency and also that physiological measures of low arousal will be associated with poor performance. The difficulty arises at higher levels of stimulation, where outside treatments cease to be helpful and where the physiological variables change their relation to performance. It is not clear whether there is simply a deterioration due to high arousal itself, or whether at high levels arousal ceases to be important and gives way to the effects of expectancy which we agreed to be important when discussing that approach. Low arousal certainly means poor performance, but high arousal does not necessarily mean either good or bad performance.

The Filter Approach Since 1958

As has already been indicated, this approach was particularly favoured by Broadbent (1958), but it has not been the cause of as much research in the

C

interval as have the other approaches. There are three main groups of experiment which are relevant to it, and two of these give results which are at least equivocal from the point of view of the theory. The third, however, supports it fairly well, and it must still be regarded as in the field.

The first group are experiments on *unpaced vigilance*. It will be recalled that the main support for filter theory came from the contrast between the decrement shown in paced tasks of serial reaction and the absence of decrement in unpaced tasks of closely similar type, combined with the fact that many of the vigilance situations showing no decrement were in 1958 tasks with lengthy signals. The latter might be regarded as unpaced, while those tasks which had transient signals and showed decrement might be regarded as paced. One way in which the analogy could be tested was to construct a task like an industrial inspection task, in which objects to be inspected could either move past the field of view at a speed determined by the equipment, or be moved on, step by step, by the man performing the task. If filter theory were to hold, the latter task would allow the man to pause in the vigilance task during any diversion of the filter to other sources of information, and to return to the task when he was at full efficiency. He might therefore avoid any decrement in the detection of signals.

Colquhoun (1962a) tested this possibility with a version of his circle-inspecting task in which each "event", a row of circles possibly containing one defective circle, could remain visible until the subject moved it on and thus received the next event. The decrement in detected signals was just as great when the task was done this way as in the more usual situation of events occurring at a fixed automatic rate. Wilkinson (1961b) found the same result with a task in which subjects were constrained to work at a set average rate but could nevertheless speed up and slow down from moment to moment within fair limits. Lastly, it will be remembered that Broadbent (1963a), in his study of observing responses, was in fact allowing the subject to call for the presentation of a display at whatever time he chose; yet there was a decrement as judged by mean reaction time. In Broadbent's study the rate of observing responses actually rose throughout the work period, and similarly in Colquhoun's case the speed with which the subjects called for events got faster as the period continued. There is no sign whatever of the subject avoiding a vigilance decrement by stopping the inspection task when he is inattentive.

To be fair, these experiments must be taken as revealing a discrepancy between the motor task of calling for fresh events and the perceptual task of distinguishing signal from non-signal events. It is possible that the filter is producing failures of detection or slow responses by shifting away from the task, but that the man continues to call for fresh events "automatically" even though he is not selecting information from them. The argument is identical with that we advanced about observing responses themselves; we are not forbidden to believe in their existence because this technique fails to reveal them. Nevertheless, these studies provide no positive evidence for filter theory.

The second group of studies to be considered under this heading are those on *combined tasks*. The argument here is that if the man misses signals from a visual display because he is ceasing to filter information from it, he is possibly listening rather than becoming unreactive altogether. On an arousal point of view, on the other hand, one might plausibly argue that a man who is unresponsive visually ought also to be unresponsive to auditory stimulation, since it is his general state which is at fault. The argument from an expectancy point of view can go either way; if one uses an observing response version in which the man observes visually or auditorily depending on the sense from which signals are more probable, then performance will depend on the extent to which signals have been more frequent on the eye or the ear. If on the other hand one supposes that probability has some effect other than governing the occurrence of observing responses, then performance on the eye and ear will depend only on the overall probability of signals.

In fact, performance is improved if a man is required to watch for a period and then listens for a period, in alternation, rather than stick to one display throughout the work period (Gruber, 1964). This in itself however is consistent with arousal as well as with filter theory, since the change of display might be regarded as arousing. More crucial are cases in which both displays have to receive attention throughout the task, and the man is instructed to look and listen throughout. There are two ways in which this can be arranged, and both are of interest. In one case the presence of a signal on the visual display is always accompanied by one on the auditory display. Here we are actually testing performance at the same instant on both senses; and if missed signals on the visual task are due to moments of such low arousal that the man is quite unresponsive, then the addition of simultaneous auditory signals should have no effect on the number of misses. In fact this is quite untrue. Adding an auditory as well as a visual signal greatly increases the number of detections as compared with either alone (Loveless, 1957; Buckner and McGrath, 1963). At first sight this looks like good evidence for filtering, but this is not really so. What would be needed for that is an indication that the chances of the man hearing a signal were actually greater if he was not looking than if he was attending to the visual display. That is, if

P_{eye} = Probability of a miss when using eye alone
P_{ear} = Probability of a miss when using ear alone
P_{both} = Probability of a miss when using both

then filtering would be strongly supported by

$$P_{both} < P_{eye} \times P_{ear}$$

In fact, the results both of Loveless and of Buckner and McGrath show

$$P_{both} = P_{eye} \times P_{ear},$$

approximately. Colquhoun, in unpublished data, has got similar results and confirmed that they hold within individual subjects as well as on the average of a group. (This is important because otherwise the result would mean only that people have good ears, good eyes, or both, on a random basis.) Thus it does not seem that the subject *either* looks *or* listens, nor that he is *either* alert for any kind of signal *or* unresponsive to any kind of signal. Rather the eye and ear seem to detect or fail to detect in independence of each other. If there is a departure from this relationship, it is in the direction predicted by arousal theory, but on the whole the principle of independence holds.

What about the case when the man is asked to look and listen, but the signals in the two tasks are quite separate rather than always occurring together? In so far as looking is incompatible with listening, adding a second sensory channel might be expected to be harmful; but the results just discussed suggest that looking is not incompatible with listening. We might then expect an improvement by the same mechanisms as those we postulated to explain the results of Gruber (1964). In fact, neither happens; performance on the two simultaneous tasks was about the average of that on the eye and on the ear when each sense was used separately (Buckner and McGrath, 1963). But this average conceals a detailed point of considerable interest. It appeared in the original results, and has since been confirmed more thoroughly (McGrath, 1965), that the easier of the two tasks tends to get better when both are done at once, and the harder of the two tends to get worse.

The authors of this effect put forward several theories of it. Possibly doing two tasks at once is arousing, and arousal benefits easy tasks more than difficult ones. Again, perhaps the presenting of difficult signals makes the subject accustomed to reporting even doubtful and half-detected events, and he does this on the easy sensory mode as well. One might add that, if we were considering an expectancy-observing response approach, the listener might think that there were really more signals on the easy than on the difficult sense, and so might observe that display more frequently. The first and last of these theories would seem to have some difficulty with the result of Binford and Loeb (1963), which we mentioned under the expectancy approach; namely, that performance on difficult visual signals increased as the number of signals in an easy auditory task was increased. On the first and last theories, this should make the hard task deteriorate even more. (It will be recalled that Binford and Loeb did find that the addition of the first auditory signals from a base-line of zero did deteriorate the visual task, and their results are therefore consistent with those of Buckner and McGrath.) On the second theory, however, increasing the overall signal probability might well make the subject still more inclined to report doubtful signals, and so cause the effect of increasing the auditory signal rate to be opposite from that of introducing easy signals in the first place. This implies that signal probability is having an effect, not on the direction in which observing is carried out, but on some other aspect of efficient detection; in the next chapter we shall be considering a theory of this type, but at present it will confuse our review of the filter approach if we expand on this topic.

The conclusion of the experiments on combined tasks like that from work on unpaced vigilance, must be that they do not really support filter theory. They do not disprove it altogether; with the small amounts of information involved in reporting or not reporting a signal it is quite possible that observation through the eyes is compatible with observation through the ears, and that the shifts of the filter responsible for failures of detection are shifts to non-task stimuli. But there is no positive evidence for such a view. The most that can be said from the experiments on combined tasks is that they make arousal theory and expectancy-observing response theory seem a little less plausible.

The third group of experiments relevant to filter theory are on *signal duration and event rate*. It will be remembered that Broadbent's original view held that failures to select the correct task information would last only for a second or so, and that in consequence signals of long duration would not show a decrement while those of short duration would do so. This view was supported by results of Fraser (1957) in which signal duration was varied and decrement only appeared with short signals. Adams (1956) obtained a result in the same direction although insignificant. Two of the results already mentioned on the effects of varying event rate are relevant to this issue. (One must suppose, as Broadbent did for other reasons, that filter shifts can be made at convenient times and therefore at a slow event rate will occur between events.)

Firstly, consider the experiment by McGrath in which the effects on a visual task of varied auditory stimulation were tried at slow and fast event rates in the task. This study was deliberately intended to cover the possibility that the slow event rate, used when the sound helped visual performance, was allowing any filter shifts to occur during the gaps between events. As will be recalled, speeding up the event rate from one every three seconds to one event every second abolished the beneficial effect of the sound stimulation. This is what would be expected on a filter theory. However, the result cannot be regarded as supporting that theory rather than its opponents, since arousal theory will deal with the result by supposing that the higher event rate increases arousal to an optimum level even without the sound stimulation.

A second relevant experiment already mentioned is that of Jerison (1967a) on varying event rate for a constant signal/non-signal ratio. At his fastest event rates a decrement appeared during the run although it was almost absent at slow event rates. His explanation of this is in terms of an inhibition of an observing response, which is obviously closely similar to a concept of a filter failing to select information from a source which has been delivering it for a long period. It is indeed difficult to see how this result can be explained on other bases; but unfortunately it is vulnerable to Baker's expectancy explanation of decrement through the "vicious circle" mechanism, as are the original experiments on which Broadbent based his view. That is, short signals are harder to see than long ones, and so are signals embedded in faster event rates. Since the subject sees fewer signals, he thinks there are fewer, and therefore his performance deteriorates in parallel with his subjective estimate of signal probability. Since Jerison's fast event rate did give rise to lower detections originally, so far as can be decided from data so far published, the "vicious circle" cannot be ruled out.

Turning now to new experiments, one by J. F. Mackworth (1963a) studied the effect of dividing a clock face into sectors and only presenting signals in certain sectors. Since the subject knew this restriction, there were a series of "rest pauses" in each sweep of the pointer, when any inattention to the display could occur; and correspondingly there was an improvement in performance. Possibly some expectancy interpretation could be given of this result, but it is certainly consistent with concepts of excessive strain on observing responses or of a need to shift a filter away from a source which has been selected for a long time.

Perhaps the clearest result is however one by Baker (1963b) himself even though he interprets it in terms of expectancy. He studied performance on signals of various durations, and showed that decrement was greater for shorter signals. He explained this by the vicious circle mechanism, since the differences in decrement were paralleled by differences in performance on a preliminary test of the difficulty of the signals. However, during the main session all durations of signal were apparently presented in a mixed fashion. Thus the greater decrement on short signals occurred even when such signals were accompanied by long ones which themselves were showing a reduced decrement. It would seem difficult to explain this by a progressive error in the subjective assessment of signal probability, since that ought to have affected the long signals also. It is surely easier to suppose that the change in the subject as the work period progresses is one which affects his performance on short signals but not on long ones; that is, a change taking the form of moments of inefficiency interspersed by normal performance.

Parenthetically, it is a pity that experiments on reaction time in vigilance have tended to concentrate on mean latency rather than other characteristics of the distribution of response times. Faulkner (1962) has shown that variability increases with time, confirming an earlier conclusion of Fraser (1953). On a filter basis it would of course be expected that variability would be the most sensitive measure, increases in that score appearing even while the mean was still unaffected.

A last pair of studies which should be briefly mentioned here, although they will recur in the next chapter, are by J. F. Mackworth (1965a) and by Simpson (1967). These again contrasted conditions requiring a high rate of observing responses with those requiring a lower rate, and found decrement only at the high rate; using a measure not of detections but of another type to be mentioned in the next chapter. They are worth mentioning at this stage both for continuity and because Mackworth's study adopted an ingenious method of obtaining equal initial detectability in the two conditions. This of course insulates the experiment against the objection that the difference in decrement is due to the "vicious circle". What Mackworth did was to employ two flashing lights as the display, and to make a signal a slightly brighter flash from one of them. Each flash was separated from the next by a blank interval, so that the duration of the flash itself could be varied independently of the event rate. When a faster event rate was used, the duration of flash was increased to improve the detectability of the signals. Thus the difference in original detections was far less than in Jerison's experiment, and the result is much more immune to criticism on the "vicious circle" basis. (The number of detections as such was still unfortunately slightly less at the high event rate although the detectability by another measure was rather higher at that rate; the difference does not appear enough to explain the difference in decrement, and other features of the results to be explained in the next chapter confirm the view that a difference in kind of performance occurs at the fast event rate.)

Although therefore the other two groups of experiments gave no positive support to filter theory, this last group does seem to do so. It does not seem possible to explain the harmful effects of high event rates on a basis of under-arousal, and the results of Baker and of Mackworth are hard to explain on a basis of expectancy. Putting these results together with those of Fraser and Faulkner, it seems fair to conclude that Broadbent was right to draw a parallel between vigilance and the blocks appearing in continuous overt work; and to say that there is some variability of efficiency which begins to appear in vigilance when the man has been working for some time. This of course does not establish that the moments of inefficiency are due to failures of the filter to select the correct source of information; only that the failures are momentary. With this qualification however, filter theory also seems to have its area of facts which other views find hard to explain.

CONCLUSIONS FROM TRADITIONAL MEASURES OF VIGILANCE

We said at the beginning of this chapter that vigilance affords an opportunity to study the various factors which may decide the efficiency of a man's attention. What then has been learned from these numerous studies, most of them subsequent to 1958? There are four simple generalizations which seem justified.

First, it really does not seem likely that there is much deterioration in vigilance caused by the performance of the overt response itself. That is, the inhibition view does not seem very plausible in the form that inhibition arises from response to signals and dissipates with interval between signals. This in no way rules out the view that inhibition results from observing responses to non-signals, which becomes equivalent to other points of view.

Second, there does seem to be some progressive change resulting from continuing exposure to a stimulus situation without opportunity to rest or observe other things. This change takes the form of brief inefficiencies rather than a constant state of inefficiency. We do not know however at this stage whether it takes the form of a failure to select correct input information or not.

Third, the general state of the man is important, and not only the specific conditions of the task he is performing. That is, he must have sufficient background stimulation if the task is unstimulating, or he will become inefficient through being unresponsive. He may also be inefficient at high levels of stimulation however, and we do not know whether this is because of his general state or because at sufficiently high levels of arousal other variables in the task itself become of predominant importance.

Fourth, the probability that a signal is about to arrive has a definite effect upon efficiency. It is not clear whether this is exerted solely through the control of observing responses, causing the man to look when it is likely that a signal will arrive, and to look at the place where the signal is most likely. It may be due to this mechanism, or to some other effect of probability upon efficiency, arising even when the man is looking.

Both the last two factors may affect the general level of performance in a vigilance task; that is, the man may be inefficient throughout the work-period both because he is under-stimulated and also because he regards signals as improbable. They therefore provide explanations for the low but steady level of performance met in one class of vigilance tasks. In addition, both factors can produce a decrement in performance during the run if conditions are suitable; that is, if the subject has been trained with an inappropriate rate of signals or if he enters the situation with a higher level of arousal than the situation will sustain. In addition, there is a residual amount of decrement even when expectancy and arousal are appropriate initially, and this may be ascribed to the progressive change resulting from sustained observation. These factors will explain the decrement from a reasonably high to an unacceptable level of detection, found in another class of vigilance tasks.

We are left however with several problems. We wish to know what the effects of the general state of arousal are at the upper end of the scale and in particular we wish to know what the mechanism is by which probability exerts its effect on performance. At an empirical level, we wish to know why certain tasks with brief transient signals, such as that of Jerison (1959), can avoid a decrement, when a similar task having only one source of signals seems to show one (Jerison, 1957). At this stage we have probably come as far as we can with traditional measures of vigilance performance, and must turn to a different approach.

C*

CHAPTER III

Vigilance: the Approach with Measures from Decision Theory

The Need for New Measures

SOME PERSONAL HISTORY

In the first chapter, we said that the plan of this book would follow the way in which knowledge had developed historically. In discussing results on vigilance with traditional measures, however, we have been following the activities of many laboratories and consequently there has been no single process of thought to follow. One laboratory may have been pursuing the implications of expectancy, while another simultaneously was following those of arousal. In this chapter however we are going to introduce different measures of performance, and in order to see why these are desirable it may be helpful to become more personal, and to follow the process of thought which led one individual to adopt them.

We have already said that, from the point of view of Broadbent (1958), one of the principal difficulties in the literature lay in the difference between the two tasks of Jerison (1957) and Jerison (1959). Here were two tasks in which the signal was transient in both cases, and yet there was a decrement within the run in one case and not in the other. There were two major differences in the tasks, one being that the number of sources of information was greater in the task free from decrement; and the other being that the total number of signals was greater in the same task. In Jerison's original experiments, he did not reduce the number of signals from each source when he increased the total number of sources, and therefore the difference between the tasks might have been due to either factor. When there are many sources of information, it is obvious that filtering (to use Broadbent's term) or the occurrence of observing responses (to use Jerison's) may be distributed in a variety of ways over the different possible locations from which information may come. If, like Broadbent, one has the theory that decrement is due to a failure of filtering after a period of continuous work, one is very much hampered by inability to measure that process directly; one can only record what happens when a signal is in fact inserted and receives or fails to receive a response. Hence Broadbent (1963a), in a series of experiments already mentioned, adopted the technique devised by Holland and tried to get the experimental subject to reveal the distribution of his observations by pressing a button every time he wished to look at a source of signals. The experiments involved one source or three sources, because the ultimate aim was to check on the differences between Jerison's two tasks. As we have seen in the last chapter, however, this purpose was frustrated by the fact that the rate of button pressing increased throughout the work period, while simultaneously the time taken to detect each signal was also increasing. The subject would press a button, a signal would be displayed to him, and yet he would press the observing button several more times before he would report the presence of a signal. This process was happening more frequently towards the end of the work period, and manifestly made the rate of button pressing useless as a direct measure of the efficiency of attention.

A private suggestion by A. M. Treisman, however, started a new line of thought about these results. The most obvious explanation of them, as again we have already said, is that the subject presses the observing button "automatically" regardless of whether or not he is attending to the display. When there is only one source of signals, this is indeed a very plausible explanation. However, when there are three sources of signals, the man's behaviour is not quite consistent with this view. With three sources, there are of course three buttons for producing observations, and the normal behaviour is for the subject to press each of these in turn in a repeating sequence. If the sequence had become a purely motor process, independent of whether or not any intake of sensory information was occurring, then it would continue to run on after the insertion of the signal. If the man is looking at the ceiling, while pressing the three buttons one after another in a mechanical way, then the insertion of a signal on the left hand display will leave the sequence of button pressing undisturbed and it will continue to run "left, centre, right, left, centre, right" and so on. A close examination however of the actual sequence shows that something different happens. When a signal occurs on the left hand display, the sequence of button pressing may be "centre, right, left, left, left," followed by the report of a signal. Thus the sequence of observing responses does not continue automatically after the signal appears, but is interrupted and several more observations are made on the particular display which is showing the signal. In some sense therefore the signal must have produced an effect before it was reported, but the subject seemed to require additional information before he felt really justified in making a report.

This result might well of course have been due to some particular feature of the task used, such as the precise pressure needed on the buttons for an observing response, or something of that sort. However, it drew attention to another feature of Jerison's two tasks. When Jerison used one source of signals, his subjects made very few "false alarms", that is, they hardly ever reported the presence of a signal which was really not there. When there were three sources of signals, and a high overall signal rate, then there were many such false alarms. One of the tasks seemed in some way to make the subjects more hesitant about reporting, while the other made them inclined to report signals even when there was nothing there. Suppose now that the experiments

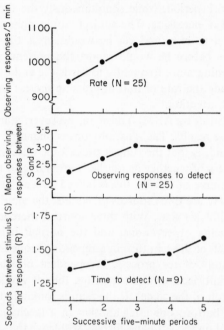

FIG. 9. Data on the rate of making observing responses in an experiment reported by Broadbent (1963a). From the top graph it can be seen that the number of observing responses per five minute period increased as the work period went on: but from the middle graph it is also clear that several observing responses were necessary before a signal was reported, late in the period. The time taken to detect a signal actually increased during the work period, even though the rate of observing responses was increasing.

on observing responses by Broadbent (1963a) were revealing some general feature of vigilance tasks rather than one specific to the particular apparatus, then the differences between Jerison's two tasks might become intelligible. Suppose it were true that the effect of prolonged work was not to abolish the detection of signals altogether, but merely to reduce the confidence with which they were seen: then a task which required subjects to report only when they were absolutely certain of being correct would show a decrement in detections, while a task which allowed reporting even of doubtful and uncertainly perceived signals would show no decrement. It might be therefore that the difference between Jerison's tasks lay primarily in the level of confidence which they caused the observer to set himself before he would report a signal.

All this however is highly speculative, and raises a series of questions about the relationship between confidence, correct detections, and false alarms. Is there really any substantial number of signals which are perceived but are so only with a low degree of confidence? In other words, does it really make much difference to the number of correct detections whether one reports only those signals of which one is certain, or also those which one suspects to have been present but of which one cannot be sure? Furthermore, if one does report signals of which one is uncertain, what happens to the number of false alarms? Presumably it will be greater if one allows reports of less than complete confidence, but how much greater? Will the probability of a false alarm rise as fast as that of a correct detection? If so, one could hardly explain the decrement in correct detections in vigilance experiments as being due to an increasingly cautious strategy of response, because the number of false alarms is extremely low. Changes in the rate of false alarms during the period of work are much smaller than changes in the number of correct detections.

EXPERIMENTS ON HITS AND FALSE ALARMS

Before proceeding any further therefore it is necessary to get some experimental evidence about the changes which would appear, both in correct detections and in false alarms, if a subject changed the degree of confidence which he thought necessary before reporting a signal. One can do this in two ways: first, one can get a man to work on one day with instructions to report signals only when he is quite certain, and on another day tell him to report any stimulus which he considers might be a signal, even though he is not sure. One can then observe the detection rates and false alarm rates under the two conditions. Secondly, one can adopt the alternative procedure of instructing the man to report any possible signal, but to report also the degree of confidence which he feels about his judgment. This can be done by giving him a rating scale on paper, or by providing him with several response buttons, one of which is to be used only when he is sure that a signal is presented, one when he is moderately confident but not quite sure, one when he is rather uncertain, and so on. The method of giving different instructions on different sessions naturally requires more experimental time, gives one only two levels of performance, and since the data are collected on different days the experimental error is liable to be large. On the other hand, it is a simpler task for the subject than is the second method, since it might conceivably be that a subject might be so worried about the task of judging his own confidence about each signal that his whole performance would be changed. The two methods therefore form a valuable check upon each other.

Whichever method one uses, one can plot the results in the form of a graph of correct detections against false alarms. With the first method one simply enters a point on the graph for performance under the cautious instructions, and another point under the less cautious instructions. With the method of a rating scale, one can obtain one point by considering only those responses of which the subject was absolutely sure, another point by adding together those of which he was sure and those of which he was not quite sure, a third point by adding to the responses already considered those of the next lower degree of confidence, and so on. It is not at all obvious from the armchair what the shape of the resulting graph is going to be. On the whole, there are two main results which one might get. First, it might be that changes in the false alarm rate produce proportionate changes in the rate of correct detections. That is, the graph will be a straight line. Second, the graph may be something more complicated than a straight line. It is important to distinguish these two possibilities, because they correspond to two major classes of psychological theory. If the graph takes the straight line form, then the assignment of confidence to any particular report about the presence of a signal is merely an additional process added on to the true perceptual mechanism, and has no intimate connection with it. If on the other hand the graph is curved in form, then the confidence which a man feels in his report truly tells us something about its perception.

Let us consider some concrete examples of the first class of theory, since they are the most serious from the point of view of our speculation that confidence is involved in vigilance. Suppose for example that the main reason for missing signals in vigilance were to be looking away from the display: and if one were looking at the display, then all signals were seen equally well. In that case, what would the subject do when asked by ourselves to rate all his responses for degree of confidence? There are really two strategies he might adopt. One would be to report every time he saw a signal, but only to put some of the reports in the category "sure", some others in "not quite sure" and so on, deciding which category to use at random. In that case, each category would contain the same relative numbers of detections and of false alarms, although no doubt the absolute number would be different in some categories than others. The graph would take a straight line form, of the type in which

$$P_D = K \times P_{FA}$$

where

P_D = probability of a correct detection
P_{FA} = probability of a false alarm

(The appearance of any false alarms at all would imply, of course, that the man could incorrectly perceive signals even when looking at the display. If this were not so, the straight line graph would still appear but would simply lie along the axis of P_D.)

There is another course of action the subject might follow: he might decide that when he saw a signal, he would report the fact in his most confident category, while on a certain proportion of occasions on which he had seen nothing he would nevertheless make a report and put it in one of his other categories of confidence. Some of these reports would no doubt be correct by chance, but once again the subject would be unaware of this. He would be as likely to assign one of these correct reports to a category of low confidence as to one of high confidence. His performance would then lie on the line

$$P_D = C + P_{FA}(1 - C)$$

where C = probability of correct detection when no guessing is occurring.

From the armchair, either of these straight line theories is extremely plausible, and the first step must therefore be to try an experiment to see what happens in a vigilance situation with ratings of confidence. Data of this sort

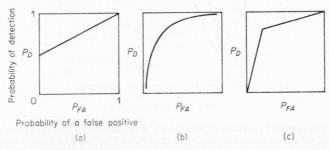

FIG. 10. Various possible theoretical relationships between detection rate P_D and false alarm rate P_{FA}. In graph (a) we see a possible relationship of the form $P_D = C + P_{FA}(1-C)$. In graph (b) we see a relationship which might correspond to $Z_D = A + BZ_{FA}$. (Or also to $P_D/(1-P_D) = \alpha P_{FA}/(1-P_{FA})$ or to $\log P_D = K \log P_{FA}$.) In graph (c) we see an approximation to graph (b), which might be produced by a suitable combination of

$$P_D = C + (1-C)P_{FA} \quad \text{and} \quad P_D = K \times P_{FA}.$$

By a suitable choice of crossing points for these two straight lines, the resulting graph is very like that in graph (b).

were provided by Broadbent and Gregory (1963a) and they showed convincingly that neither of these possibilities could apply. They used two main types of task, an auditory vigilance task in which a pure tone had to be detected at unexpected times, and a visual vigilance task in which a slightly brighter flash had to be observed amongst a series of regularly repeating flashes. Using a four point rating scale for each report of a signal, the ratio of detections to false positives became steadily greater as the category of confidence increased, and was significantly so at every step. This result is quite inconsistent with either of the straight line theories, and even with the theory that one straight line theory holds above a certain level of confidence and the other below that level.

It is worth mentioning the explosive consequences of this very simple result. Most investigators in vigilance, certainly including Broadbent, had tacitly assumed the truth of the second straight line theory. It is the more obvious of the two, since it gives a reasonable explanation for false alarms: whereas the

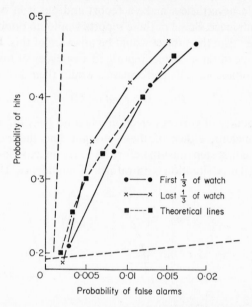

FIG. 11. Performance in a visual vigilance task, from the data of Broadbent and Gregory (1963a). The solid lines represent data, from the first and last third of a single watch period. The dotted line adjacent to them is the theoretical curve of the type labelled (b) in Fig. 10. The other two dotted lines are the two segments of graph (c) in Fig. 10: it can be seen that no combination of two lines such as this will fit the experimental results.

other theory requires that some of the perceptions be erroneous for an unspecified reason. This second theory however carries the implication that changes in P_D are never greater than the changes in P_{FA} with which they are associated. In vigilance tasks, the false alarm rate is normally low. Any changes in it must therefore be smaller still, and consequently any changes in detection rate which are produced by them might be supposed to be completely negligible. For this reason the possibility that decrement in correct detections might be due to some simultaneous change in both detections and false alarms tended to be neglected. This is undoubtedly however an example of unconscious and unfortunate domination by a theory, since even the other straight line theory would allow changes in detection rate to be large compared with their associated changes in false alarm rate. In fact, Broadbent and Gregory found that inclusion of responses made without much confidence raised the detection rate far more than the false alarm rate: the change was about ten times as great in one quantity as the other. Similar results were obtained by Colquhoun (1967) using the technique of instructing subjects to be careful on one occasion and to report anything however doubtful on another. It is quite certain therefore that any change in the level of confidence, which a subject requires before he reacts, could produce large changes in detection rate even though the associated changes in false alarm rate were relatively small. It becomes most unsafe therefore to consider detection rate alone: one must also take into account false alarm rate.

If one of the straight line theories had been true, we could have specified the line along which differences in confidence would move the performance of a subject, and we could then have found out whether changes in the conditions of a vigilance task caused performance to move along that same line or in some other way. Unfortunately, as we have seen, there is no question that the straight line theories are inadequate. We want therefore to find some simple expression for the relationship which actually does empirically obtain between detection rate and false alarm rate. The data of Broadbent and Gregory only provide four points for each of their conditions, but these seem to trace out a curve which is concave downwards, and certainly cannot be fitted by any straight line or combination of two straight lines. The simplest technique then would be to find a curve which has this general shape and which appears to fit the points we obtained with confidence ratings: there are several possibilities, some of which we shall discuss later. A straightforward technique which is often useful when dealing with probabilities, however, is to transform each probability to its corresponding z-score. If we think of a quantity which is varying in a normal or Gaussian fashion about a mean of zero and with a standard deviation of unity, then the z-score for any probability is the value which the quantity will exceed with that probability. The reason for the usefulness of this transformation is of course that a wide variety of mechanisms will incorporate some process of this sort.

In our case, then, we transform both probabilities to z-scores, and then hope that the performance under different levels of confidence may lie on a straight line of the type

$$Z_D = A + BZ_{FA}$$

where

Z_D = detection rate transformed to Z-score
Z_{FA} = false alarm rate transformed to Z-score
A, B are constants

The results of Broadbent and Gregory do lie reasonably well upon such a straight line; indeed, they do not differ seriously from an even simpler form, in which the constant B is unity, so that the equation of the line becomes

$$Z_D = d' + Z_{FA}$$

where the constant A has been rewritten as d' in order to make it comparable with a number of studies already in the literature. By getting subjects to report with different degrees of confidence, therefore, we are causing their performance to vary in a way which can be, at least roughly, described by this simple relationship. We can now examine changes in vigilance under other conditions: for example, we can compare performance at the beginning and end of a run, when there is decrement present. The change in performance will either fall on the same line, or else it will be necessary to use another value for d' in order to fit it. If the former were the case, then the change in performance is of the same type as that produced by a change in confidence, while if the latter were the case, the decrement would be of a different kind.

To give an example of the latter case, it is known that the use of a signal of different strength in a vigilance task does require the use of a different value of d', as has been shown by Colquhoun (1967). When therefore one changes the strength of a signal, one is clearly changing performance in a way different from that induced by asking the subject to be more cautious or more risky.

The whole of the argument of this chapter thus far can be summarized as a case for transforming detection rates and false alarm rates to z-scores, and then looking at the difference, d', between these transformed scores as a more satisfactory measure of performance. In what has been said so far we have not of course produced adequate evidence that this is a useful thing to do, and such evidence will come later in the chapter. The argument has been put in this bald fashion, however, in order to show its logical essentials. It should be noted, for example, that we are not necessarily contending that detection and false alarm rates do result from some process involving normal distributions: they may perfectly well, so far as we are concerned, result from any mechanism which gives the same concave downward relationship between untransformed detection and false alarm rates. For example, one might use the relationship

$$\frac{P_D}{1-P_D} = \alpha \frac{P_{FA}}{1-P_{FA}}.$$

This also, for any particular value of α, gives a concave downward relationship between detection rate and false alarm rate. For each possible value of α there is a value of d' giving a curve so similar that no existing experimental results on vigilance could possibly tell the difference. The reason for this is that the z-score for a probability P is fairly closely proportional to $\log P/(1-p)$, and this of course makes the two equations equivalent. An advantage of the alternative formulation is that it is easy to work out the value of α from experimental results without consulting tables of z-scores. On the other hand, there is only the one parameter α, whereas in the original version of the transformation to z-scores we had two constants A and B. When we suggested that B might be equal to unity, on the basis purely of one set of experimental results, we were of course taking quite a large step. If, on looking at further experimental results, we were to find that B took on some value other than unity, it would be easy to handle this within the framework of the z-score transformation. A mechanism which would produce a value of B other than unity might be, for example, if the two quantities varying in Gaussian fashion, which give rise to detection rate and false alarm rate, were to have different variances. This seems quite a possible state of affairs *a priori*, and it is as well therefore that an equation in terms of z-scores will handle it simply. The alternative equation, although it gives very similar results for the case when B is unity, cannot be altered nearly so easily to match the results when B takes on some other value. The equation using z-scores is therefore rather more general, and this is perhaps its main advantage.

Another possible curve having the necessary concave downward character would be

$$\log P_D = K \log P_{FA},$$

in which K corresponds to α and d' in the previous equations. Once again this equation might be more convenient for some purposes: for example, we could rewrite it in the form

$$\log P_D = K \log N_{FA} - K \log N_N$$
$$= K \log N_{FA} - C$$

where $N_N =$ number of opportunities to make a false report
              $N_{FA} =$ number of false reports.

This may be extremely useful when we are uncertain what is to be counted as an opportunity to make a false alarm; in many vigilance tasks, this is a little arbitrary. If a man watches a blank radar screen for two minutes, looking for a signal of one second duration, but no signals in fact arrive, how many opportunities has he had to make a false alarm? From one point of view one could say that he has had 120 such opportunities, but this is obviously rather an arbitrary assumption. By using this third possible equation, we can work simply with the number of false alarms and bypass the problem of the number of opportunities, since this affects only a constant in the resulting equation. However, once again this equation offers nothing comparable to the possibility of changing the constant B in the equation using z-scores. It agrees best with the curve one would expect from the original formulation if B has a value rather less than 1, and there is no easy way of altering it either for the case when B is 1 or for any other value.

By transforming hit rate and false alarm rate to z-scores, therefore, we are keeping greater flexibility for handling a wider variety of possible experimental results. By doing so however we are not asserting the truth of any one theory about the way in which a concave downward relationship can be obtained between hit rate and false alarm rate. We are merely denying the existence of a straight line relationship between the two, and saying that the true relationship is of a form describable for all practical purposes by a straight line after transformation to z-scores.

The importance of this line of argument comes from the fact that the use of d' originated and is widely justified on theoretical rather than on empirical grounds. As a result, the foregoing discussion will have struck many readers familiar with the field as unorthodox, and in some ways curiously wrong-headed since many of the techniques and equations employed are already widely used in other parts of psychology. In particular, they are used in psychophysics and the study of the special senses. However, in those areas their use is based on a series of theoretical assumptions, and it is perfectly possible *a priori* that those assumptions are invalid in the case of vigilance. As we shall see, some authors in the field have questioned the truth of some of the assumptions in this case, and they are certainly entitled to do so. The purpose of the preceding argument has therefore been to show that the use in vigilance of the measure called d' is based upon empirical rather than upon theoretical grounds. The line of argument is to determine the changes in detection rate as a function of changes in false alarm rate induced by requiring different degrees of confidence, and then to see whether other changes in conditions produce the same type of change or a different change. Our next step must therefore be to see what the empirical evidence is for the shape of the function, and whether or not it changes under different conditions. Before we do this however it is proper to give an account of the theoretical system from which the d' measure and the techniques for determining it were developed. This theory is known as the theory of signal detection, and a far more comprehensive and lucid presentation of it is to be found in Green and Swets (1966).

The Theory of Signal Detection

Let us consider a completely rational observer receiving evidence about the occurrence or non-occurrence of a signal in the outside world. On any given occasion, he receives a particular item of evidence. Had a signal really been present, there is a certain probability that this evidence would have arrived: had no signal been present, there is another probability that the same evidence might have arrived. The ratio of these two probabilities is known as the likelihood ratio for signal relative to non-signal, given this particular evidence. The purpose of the observer is to report signals which are present, and to avoid reporting signals if nothing is indeed there. Let us suppose that, on some scale of value, he gains G units more by responding than by failing to respond in the presence of a signal, and that he loses L units more by responding than by failing to respond in the absence of a signal. Then if he responds whenever he receives this particular piece of evidence, his average gain over a large number of occasions will be given by

$$\text{Gain} = p \times G \times P\,(\text{EV}/\text{Sig}) - (1-p) \times L \times P\,(\text{EV}/\text{Non-sig})$$

where

p = probability of a signal, regardless of the evidence received
$P\,(\text{EV}/\text{Sig})$ = probability of this evidence if a signal occurs
$P\,(\text{EV}/\text{Non-sig})$ = probability of this evidence if non-signal occurs.

This is positive if

$$\frac{P\,(\text{EV}/\text{Sig})}{P\,(\text{EV}/\text{Non-sig})} - \left(\frac{1-p}{p} \times \frac{L}{G}\right) > 0$$

$$\frac{P\,(\text{EV}/\text{Sig})}{P\,(\text{EV}/\text{Non-sig})} > \left(\frac{1-p}{p} \times \frac{L}{G}\right)$$

but

$$\frac{P\,(\text{EV}/\text{Sig})}{P\,(\text{EV}/\text{Non-sig})} = \text{Likelihood ratio.}$$

That is, he will on average gain by responding whenever the likelihood ratio is greater than some quantity which depends on the overall probability of a signal, and on the gains and losses involved in correct and incorrect responses. If a signal is improbable, or if the penalties for a false alarm are very high, he should demand a high likelihood ratio. He will thus respond only when evidence arrives which is much more probable given a signal than given a non-signal. If there is little penalty attached to false alarms, or if signal probability is high, he can be much less cautious. In any event, he will be behaving irrationally to withhold response for evidence giving more than the critical likelihood ratio, or to respond when the evidence is less than the critical ratio.

Suppose that the observer does behave rationally; what will this mean for his performance? If everything else remains unchanged, but the value of the critical ratio goes up and down, there will of course be associated changes in the observer's detection rate and false alarm rate. An interesting point which immediately emerges is that a graph of one quantity against the other will always have a concave downward form. It might take any of the three versions which we mentioned earlier in this chapter as being possible equations for the empirical graph found in vigilance: and it might take other forms as well. The precise shape will depend upon the kind of connection which exists between the occurrence of a signal and the probabilities of various levels of evidence being received by the observer. Suppose for example that the occurrence of a signal can give rise to any one of a number of states of evidence, and that the likelihood ratios associated with these states form a normal or Gaussian distribution (perhaps after transformation of scale). Suppose also that the non-occurrence of a signal did the same but with a different average value of likelihood ratio. In that case, the observer would behave according to the z-score equation

$$Z_D = A + BZ_{FA}.$$

If the distribution of likelihood ratios took other forms, the other equations would result, as we shall see.

The first major statement of this approach in the psychological literature

(Tanner and Swets, 1954) considered primarily the case where the distributions were normal, and indeed of equal variance. After a slow start, it is fair to say that this theory has revolutionized psychophysics; because as we have already seen it predicts that any change in the critical value of likelihood ratio will produce large changes in detection rate for small changes in false alarm rate, at least as long as false alarm rate is relatively low. The traditional assumption of psychophysics has been that a careful observer, with a low false alarm rate, should have a reliable detection rate: which is again an implicit adoption of a straight line theory of the kind we considered in the case of vigilance. Sometimes, people doing psychophysical experiments would use a "guessing correction" for false alarms which explicitly assumed one of the straight line theories. In fact, as soon as attention is drawn to the fact that this correction is theoretical one can do experiments to check it, using two methods which are closely similar to the two we have already discussed under the heading of vigilance. The first and most obviously suggested by the theory is to carry out threshold experiments using different signal probabilities, and different financial rewards and penalties for correct detections and false alarms. Experiments conducted in this way by Tanner and Swets and their collaborators showed that the graph of detections against false alarms was indeed very different from that of the traditional guessing correction, and roughly the one which would be predicted from signal detection with two

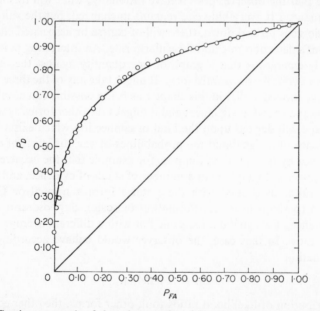

Fig. 12. Continuous graph of detections against false alarms, obtained using a sliding pointer rather than a fixed rating scale. Data from Watson *et al.* (1964), in a psychophysical experiment.

normal distributions of equal variance. More recent work has confirmed that the changes in performance produced in this way cannot be described by any theory supposing a single straight line relationship; although it is probably fair to say (Green and Swets, 1966) that the data obtained by this method could all be fitted by graphs involving a combination of two straight lines.

The second method is that of requiring the experimental subject to give a rating of confidence in his own judgment: this was introduced by Egan, Schulman and Greenberg (1959): whereas the other method places severe limits on the number of different points on the graph at which one can collect data, the method of rating scales allows many more points to be determined. In the extreme case, Watson *et al.* (1964) got their subjects to assess confidence by moving a pointer on a scale, rather than having a fixed number of categories for rating confidence. This gives a graph consisting of a very large number of points close together, and it is quite clear that the data obtained in this way cannot possibly be fitted even by a combination of two straight lines; they lie on a smooth concave downward curve. (We shall be discussing later the question whether the rating method is really equivalent to the technique of simply requiring a judgment of "signal present" or "signal absent", which some authors have questioned.)

Empirically therefore it is quite clear that the traditional subject in psychophysical experiments, with his very low false alarm rate, was extremely likely to show sharp rises and falls in his detection rate, depending upon his ideas about signal probability or his motivational state. Experimenters found indeed that, in doing psychophysical work, the same subject on different days might very often change his detection rate but lie on the same graph of detections against false alarms; and that consequently some measure was needed which would reveal whether performance had moved to a different line in the detection/false alarm plot, or whether it was still on the same line. In terms of the theory of signal detection, and assuming normal distributions with equal variances each having a value of unity, the important variable is the difference between the average values of the signal and the non-signal distributions. So long as this remains constant, other factors will merely affect the critical value of likelihood ratio and so move performance up and down along the same graph of detections against false alarms. The distance apart of the two average values was termed d', and became the measure used in many psychophysical experiments. If two experiments gave the same value of d', but different detection rates, this must mean that the false alarm rate has changed, and consequently according to the theory the critical value of likelihood ratio is now different.

Suppose one wished to specify, not merely the value of d', but even the exact point where performance was on this particular occasion. The obvious measure to choose would, according to the theory, be the value of the critical ratio. We know what this ratio should be according to the theory, namely

$(1-p)/p \times L/G$; and it is usually indicated by the symbol β for short. However, we want to know how to describe what the man actually does rather than what the theory says he should do: and sticking to our assumption of normal distributions, we can in fact do this from looking at the z-scores corresponding to hit rate and false alarm rate. The difference of those z-scores is d', as we have seen before: but in addition each z-score has corresponding to it an ordinate of the normal distribution. From the hit rate, we get the z-scores by considering what value will be exceeded with that probability by a quantity varying normally with unit variance; the corresponding ordinate of the distribution is the probability that the quantity will reach exactly the z-score rather than exceeding it. We can look this up in tables of the normal distribution, once for the hit rate and once for the false alarm rate, and the ratio of the two quantities fixes exactly where the performance is along the line of constant d'. This quantity is still called β but it is of course an obtained β rather than a theoretically predicted one.

We start therefore with empirical measures of detection rate and false alarm rate, and we obtain from them two measures d' and β. In terms of the theory of signal detection, the first of these is the shift in the average value of likelihood ratio which occurs when a signal is presented, and the second is the critical value of likelihood ratio above which the subject reports a signal. Still sticking to the theory, the estimates of these quantities are only valid if the distributions of likelihood ratio are normal and of equal variance. If for example the variances are unequal, and if we naïvely calculate d' on the assumption of equal variance, the value we get will depend upon the value of β. (The reason for this, as will be remembered, is that unequal variance corresponds to the case of

$$Z_D = A + BZ_{FA}$$

where B is not equal to unity. Consequently the two z-scores differ by different amounts as the false alarm rate varies.) The usual procedure in this case is to describe the performance by the value of d' at some particular point along the curve, such as the point where the probability of a missed signal equals that of a false alarm. This will be satisfactory enough as long as the inequality between the variances is not too great. If the assumption of normality should be false, some more complex measuring system would have to be used: fortunately, it has not in psychophysical work appeared to be seriously in error so far. Usually, there is quite a reasonable straight line relationship between the z-scores, and in many cases the assumption that the variances of the distributions are equal is fairly close to the data. Sometimes, and especially with visual experiments rather than auditory ones, it is necessary to suppose that the variance of the effects of a signal is slightly greater than the variance of the effects of a non-signal.

It will be obvious that the theory of signal detection includes a number of psychological assumptions which are very arbitrary, and which could well be questioned. We have already considered the question of the nature of the underlying distributions: among the remaining assumptions, there are perhaps three which are of especial importance.

a. It is supposed that the evidence received by an observer can be arranged on a single dimension of sensory evidence. This may not seem too implausible if we are thinking simply of the detection of a simple sound of known frequency in noise: but what about a visual signal consisting of a slightly brighter, slightly differently shaped pattern, appearing with a slightly different duration from the noise flashes, at an unknown location on a screen? What about the combined visual and auditory signals which we mentioned in the last chapter? Is it really valid in such cases to suppose that all the evidence forms a single dimension?

b. Even if the evidence does form a single dimension, can we assume that the subject knows the value of the likelihood ratio for any particular value of evidence? This seems to require that he can stand above the situation in some way and observe both the occurrences of signals and the particular value of evidence which he himself has received. If he has been trained with perfect knowledge of results, this might conceivably be true, but it is obviously asking quite a lot.

c. Even if we suppose both a single dimension of likelihood ratio, and perfect knowledge of its value by the subject, can we really assume that he is rational? That is, will he always report a signal if the evidence is above the critical ratio, and never do so if it is below? In other experimental situations, people do not behave like this. If they are guessing whether a red or a black card will turn up next in a pack, and if there are more red cards than black their best chance of success is always to guess red: but normally they guess black on a minority of occasions (see for example Restle, 1961). It seems extremely unlikely therefore that people really behave rationally in far more complicated situations of reacting appropriately to a wide range of possible values of evidence.

Other theories, different from signal detection theory, can be put forward which question these assumptions and which nevertheless give reasonably good fit to the data. We shall consider some of them later. Perhaps more serious is the fact that these assumptions might well be valid in the psychophysical case, and yet completely invalid in the case of vigilance. We cannot therefore take the success of signal detection theory in psychophysics as if it guaranteed its adequacy in the case of vigilance. There are furthermore still further assumptions in the case of vigilance: in psychophysics we are dealing with an alert observer who knows the likely time at which a signal will be presented. In vigilance, the subject does not know the time of arrival of signals, and as we saw in the last chapter it is a perfectly credible theory that he is not looking at the display for part of the time. The effect of this would be to change the distribution of likelihood ratios received by the decision mechanism. The exact nature of the change would depend on what was happening, but for example if there was a certain probability that the man closed his eyes, then on those occasions the evidence received would be identical for signal and for non-signal, and there would be a hump in the distribution at the value of a likelihood ratio of unity.

It is therefore, as we have said repeatedly, essential to check whether the results in vigilance experiments are consistent with distributions of the usual shape, before applying the measures derived from the theory of signal detection, and drawing any conclusions about them. Let us now therefore consider this evidence in the next section; after that we can consider alternative interpretations of what is happening and sum up the contributions of this approach to the study of vigilance.

Empirical Results on Vigilance

THE RELATIONSHIP OF HIT RATE TO FALSE ALARM RATE

a. Performance with different instructions. If men are told in a vigilance situation to report sounds only if they are certain, or alternatively when they have the slightest suspicion of the presence of a signal, their hit rate and false alarm rate changes. It has been shown by Egan *et al.* (1961), and by Colquhoun (1967), that the resulting changes in performance show approximately constant d'. Both experiments also show that changes in the objective strength of a signal do however give changes in performance that require a different value of d'. The two experiments differ slightly in their methods: Egan, Greenberg and Schulman, who have the distinction of being the first authors to use the theory of signal detection in this area, employed a relatively small number of highly trained subjects, and analysed the data using the equation $\log P_D = K \log P_{FA}$. As will be recalled, this avoids the difficulty of deciding what must be taken as a single presentation of non-signal, when there is a long period with no signals. They used a watch period broken up into two-minute spells, having brief rest pauses between each spell, and also employed a high signal rate of about one signal every ten seconds. They had four different levels of instruction in strictness of responding, and when they compared different signal strengths they did so at different sessions. Colquhoun on the other hand used more naïve subjects, analysed the data on the z-score assumption and assuming equal variances, and gave a lower signal rate of less than one signal a minute. Different signal strengths were mixed together within the same period, and listening was continuous for forty-five minutes. As the method of analysis was different, it was possible to calculate β, and this did change significantly with the different instructions although d' did not.

The various differences in conditions give a good deal of confidence that the result is quite a general one: and it is certainly completely inconsistent with a model based on the guessing correction. Colquhoun's results, because there are only two points, could perhaps be fitted by a combination of two straight line theories, but those of Egan, Greenberg and Schulman would require at least three straight lines. If we suppose rather that the true relationship is a concave downward curve, neither experiment really distinguishes between the different possible equations for such a curve: although the fact that d' remains constant in Colquhoun's data, when calculated on his assumptions, implies that the curve could not be based on z-scores with wildly unequal variances in the underlying distributions. The results are however consistent with more minor differences in variance, and indeed the method used by Egan, Greenberg and Schulman assumes that the curve is one which would require a slight difference in variance to fit the data perfectly.

   b. Results obtained with confidence ratings. We have already mentioned the data of Broadbent and Gregory (1963a) as an example of this method: they required the subjects to respond when they had only a suspicion that a signal might be present, but then to use one of four levels of confidence. As we have already seen, the results were compared statistically with straight line theories, and shown to be impossible to fit with any combination of two straight lines. The same authors produced later data (Broadbent and Gregory, 1965a) in which a response was required to every event, assigning it either to the category of signals or non-signals, or giving an "unsure" judgment in between. This change in conditions excludes certain possible difficulties in the original work: for instance, that subjects were not treating each stimulus event as a possible signal, but were grouping together several such events. Because of the speed at which judgments were required, the number of steps of confidence had to be reduced, and consequently like Colquhoun's experiment this one gives only two points: which are quite inconsistent with a guessing correction, but might conceivably be fitted by a combination of two straight lines. If we calculate d' from the most cautious and least cautious criteria in both experiments, it is approximately equal, although possibly slightly less (about 10%) at the least cautious criteria in the visual experiments. This corresponds to a larger variance of "signal" distribution rather than the "non-signal" distribution, and as we have seen a difference of about this size is usual in psychophysical studies using visual signals.

   An important group of experiments are those by Loeb and Binford (1964). They used an auditory task, and in some sessions they required confidence ratings while in other cases they allowed the subjects merely to report the presence or absence of a signal. This is important because it allows a comparison between performance when giving confidence ratings and those when no rating is given: it was shown by Egan *et al.* (1959) for a psychophysical situation that d' obtained in the two tasks was about the same, and that therefore the addition of the confidence rating has made no serious difference to

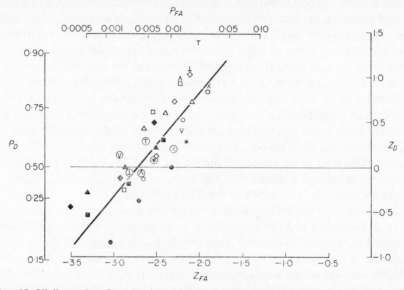

Fig. 13. Vigilance data from Loeb and Binford (1964) plotted on a scale in which probabilities have been transformed to Z-scores. The same straight line fits reasonably to all the data obtained with various degrees of confidence, with no confidence rating at all, and early and late in a work period: these conditions move performance along the line but do not shift it to a different one.

performance. We have however already seen that we are not entitled to assume in vigilance that the same assumptions hold as in psychophysics, and in consequence it is important that Loeb and Binford similarly found no change in d' in the two conditions. They also found no difference in d' between values calculated on different levels of confidence. Indeed, they applied the most severe statistical test we have considered, by transforming to z-scores the hit rate and false alarm rate for each of the levels of confidence, separately for the beginning of an 80-minute work period and for the end, and for four different groups performing at different levels of practice and after different types of training. The resulting twenty-four points were then fitted by the method of least squares with the best fitting line of the type $Z_D = A + BZ_{FA}$. The resulting line account for two-thirds of the variance in detection rate, and it is clear once again therefore that it is quite inadequate to use any model based on straight line plots of the untransformed data. An advantage of this analysis is that we obtain an empirical value for the constant B: which turns out to be 1·05. This again suggests that models based on equal variances ($B = 1$) are not far out, and indeed the departure from that value is slightly in the opposite direction to the one normally obtained in psychophysical experiments, for which B is slightly less than unity.

Binford and Loeb (1966) again compared performance when confidence ratings were given and performance when a simple judgment was required, and actually found d' to be *greater* when confidence ratings were wanted: on this occasion they did not fit the function to the different levels of confidence, although presumably any serious discrepancy in the calculation of d' from different criteria would have been observed: the same applies to an experiment by Levine (1966) in which confidence ratings were obtained.

It is clear therefore, both from the experiments on confidence ratings and from those using different instructions about caution, that performance changes roughly on the basis of a linear relationship between the z-scores corresponding to hit rate and false alarm rate, and that one will not go too far wrong by assuming that the variances are equal in the underlying distributions: although possibly the variance for the signal distribution may be slightly larger, as it has been found to be in psychophysical experiments. In most of the experiments to be considered in the rest of this section, the value of d' has been calculated on the assumption of equal variance. In interpreting it, therefore, the points we have just made should be borne in mind: on the other hand, if d' remains constant under changes in conditions which affect hit rate and false alarm rate, this is in itself some evidence that the assumption of equal variance is not far out.

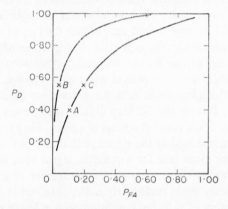

FIG. 14. A diagram of the key factual question which needs answering whenever a change in detection rate is obtained between two conditions. If the detection rate rises from that found under condition A, does this represent a movement along the same curve relating correct detections to false alarms: or does it represent a move to another curve? It is with this issue that most chapters in this book are concerned. Some variables produce movement from A to C: others from A to B. The empirical difference between them does not depend upon any particular theoretical account of the basis of the graph relating correct to false detections.

EFFECTS OF CHANGES IN SIGNAL PROBABILITY, EVENT RATE, AND MOTIVATION

Some of the experiments we mentioned in the last chapter have calculated d' and/or β for each subject, as well as more conventional measures, and have been able to do statistical analyses on the measures derived from theory of signal detection. In particular, Colquhoun and Baddeley (1964, 1967) have done so. These are the experiments in which subjects were trained with high or low signal rates, and then tested for their performance on high or low signal rates. The results were interpreted as supporting expectancy theory. In fact, training with a low signal rate caused the value of β to be higher in the experimental session than it was for training with high signal rate, in both of these experiments: but in neither case was there any significant change in d'.

Performance at different signal rates given the same event rate has been measured by Baddeley and Colquhoun (1969), using the same technique as Colquhoun (1961). They obtained no change in d' but a change in β. The latter measure was larger if signal rate was lower. It has also been found by Broadbent and Gregory (1965a) that β changed at different signal rates: in that case, the interpretation of the result was somewhat obscured by the fact that one of their conditions used three sources of signals, and that in order to produce approximately equal numbers of hits the signal intensity was increased in that condition. A difference in d' as well as in β was also obtained between conditions. On the face of it therefore this cannot be claimed as positive evidence that β changes when d' remains unchanged; on the other hand, it is not negative evidence, since change in signal strength might reasonably change d'. It should be emphasized that in fact the largest value of d' was in the lowest signal rate condition, as was the largest value of β. Thus the usual effect of a low signal probability in decreasing detections is consistent with the β change found, but not consistent with the d' change.

The effects of changing event rate for a constant signal rate have been studied by Jerison, Pickett and Stenson (1965), who as will be recalled found fewer detections for a low ratio of signals to events. They found no significant change in d', but a rise in β as the signal probability got lower. Mackworth (1965a) changed the event rate for a constant signal rate, but like Broadbent and Gregory increased signal strength in the harder condition in order to give an approximately equal performance. She obtained in fact roughly equal d', but a higher value of β in the condition with a lower ratio of signals to events. This result however was not statistically checked: it should be noticed that such a check is often difficult because some individual subjects may fail to make any false alarms, which makes a calculation of their β difficult.

Lastly, Levine (1966) maintained a constant signal rate, but attached financial penalties of various sizes to missing signals or to making false alarms. He obtained no change in d' under any condition, but found β to be larger when there was an increase in the cost either of a false alarm or, surprisingly, of a missed signal.

In the last chapter, we noticed that signal probability and motivation might well affect the average level of detections throughout a run. From what has just been said, it seems clear that there is no evidence of this change being due to a change in d', but merely to a change in β. For completeness, it may be worth mentioning the effects of high intensity noise on visual vigilance, since that is one condition which seems likely to affect level of arousal. Broadbent and Gregory (1963a, 1965a) found that the effect of loud noise was if anything to improve d': the fact that under some conditions it might give a loss of visual detections was because of its effects on β. The major effect was to reduce the number of responses assigned to intermediate levels of confidence: in noise, the subject tends to be sure that he has seen a signal or sure that he has not. This change may cause a positive increase in detections if we consider the borderline between detections that are confident and less confident, but may produce a drop in detections when we consider the borderline between confident and less confident denials of the existence of a signal. Under conditions therefore which favour rather risky performance, such as a high signal rate and the least cautious criteria, noise produces a loss in detections through its effect on β.

CHANGES DURING A WORKING PERIOD

A number of experiments have found d' to be the same size, or at least insignificantly different, at the end of a work period as at the beginning. These include Broadbent and Gregory (1963a, 1965a), Loeb and Binford (1964), Jerison *et al.* (1965), Colquhoun (1967), Levine (1966), Simpson (1967), and also Wiener *et al.* (1964). The last authors only reported detection rate and false alarm rate, but their data were re-analysed by M. M. Taylor (1965), to show that the drop in detections which they reported did not correspond to any change in d'.

Inasmuch as all the foregoing experiments showed some change in detection rates during the run, it is almost a necessary deduction that β must have changed: but this is not absolutely rigorous, because it might be possible for a drop in detections to appear by a non-independence of d' and β. For example, suppose that some subjects show a catastrophic drop in d' during the work period, associated with a drop in β; while other subjects show a rise in d' and a rise in β. It might conceivably be that the effect would be a significant drop in detections, because everybody was showing such a drop, but no significant fall either in d' or β. However, significant rises in β during the run have been reported by Broadbent and Gregory (1963a, 1965a), by Loeb and Binford (1964), by Jerison *et al.* (1965), by Levine (1966) and by Simpson (1967). One feature which is especially important is that those authors who used confidence ratings (Broadbent and Gregory, Loeb and Binford, and Levine) found the effect to be greater at the most cautious criterion and least at the most risky criterion. Indeed, Broadbent and Gregory find no consistent change in β at the most risky criterion, although the other authors do so. (Broadbent and Gregory used a rather high signal rate, over three signals a minute, so that their values of β tended to be rather lower than those for the other experimenters: there is therefore no particular discrepancy here, but it does seem that the size of the effect depends upon the initial value of β.)

At this stage, it would seem that a perfectly clear and simple relationship has been found; unfortunately, this unanimity has only been obtained by leaving out one whole group of experiments. These were started by Mackworth and Taylor (1963) and similar results have been obtained by Mackworth (1964a, b, 1965a, b). In each of these studies, d' was found to decrease during the work period. There is one other case in which this has happened, namely a study by Binford and Loeb (1966), but in general changes in d' during the work period are confined to the particular situation studied by Mackworth. The repeatability of the results both with Mackworth's task and with those in other laboratories is obviously sufficiently good for us to regard the difference as a reliable one, and not due to some accidental feature of performance in one particular group of subjects or anything of that sort. We must therefore look at the features of the tasks in some detail.

The basic task used in Mackworth's experiments was a variation on the clock test: a smoothly moving pointer was stopped for a short period in its rotation and then restarted. The task is therefore a visual one, with a short duration signal, and uncertainty about the precise times at which such a signal may be available for observation. They did not use confidence ratings, and usually did not train the subjects for very long periods: on the other hand, some subjects were used in repeated experiments, and the results do not appear to have differed very much. The experiments by Loeb and Binford, by Colquhoun, by Levine and in one of Broadbent and Gregory's early experiments used acoustic signals, and this is perhaps the most obvious difference between the two groups of studies. In 1964, Loeb and Binford suggested that this was the key factor, since d' is clearly a measure of the efficiency with which evidence is related to the presence of a signal, or the "coupling" as it has been termed by Elliott. One might well suppose that the efficiency with which the eyes are adjusted to receive a stimulus may affect coupling, while the ears have no corresponding peripheral adjustment. If then there was a failure of this peripheral adjustment when the work period continued for too long, we might get a drop in d' in a visual task but not in an auditory one. However, this explanation is not completely satisfactory, because some of the tasks used by Broadbent and Gregory were visual ones, as were those of Jerison, Pickett and Stenson and of Wiener, Poock and Steele, none of whom got a change in d' during the work period. We may however be on the right track: for each of these visual experiments used a series of non-signal events, amongst which signals were interpolated. Broadbent and Gregory used a regularly flashing light, the signal being a slightly brighter flash; Jerison, Pickett and Stenson used a regularly deflected pointer needle, a signal being a slightly greater deflection; while Wiener, Poock and Steele similarly used a discrete series of events. The Mackworth situation required continuous attention for a period of time, while the others required intermittent attention, each event being observed but an opportunity for relaxation occurring between events. At this stage we can see the importance of the experiment by Mackworth (1965a), which has already been quoted twice. She used a task in which a series of events occurred, and amongst which signals were interspersed: and she varied the event rate. At the fast event rate she increased the strength of the signal so as to give roughly equal detectability (a lower number of detections, but a higher value of d'). The fast event rate was of 200 events per minute, while the slow rate was 40 events per minute, a rate in the same region as those used by the three laboratories which found no change in d'. Mackworth obtained her usual decline in d' during the work period with the very fast event rate but no decline with the slow event rate. She did however find at that rate a significant decline in the number of false alarms, which suggests that there was still a change in β occurring even though d' remained constant. A similar experiment comparing tasks requiring continuous attention with those which do not has been carried out by Simpson (1967), although it is not at the time of writing generally available; and it seems to be a broadly acceptable conclusion that a task which allows moments of relaxation will show a constant d' during the work period, while one which requires continuous and sustained observation will give a drop in d' during the run.

How does this relate to the difference between eye and ear which we mentioned earlier? A large group of unpublished experiments by Colquhoun, on the presentation of sonar information, are relevant at this point. He studied performance in a vigilance situation of the type in which signals could occur at any time: and compared the efficiency of visual and auditory signals whose detectability had been equated under reasonably psychophysical conditions. Under these circumstances, performance with visual signals was inferior to that with auditory signals. The task could however be converted into one involving a series of neutral events, by dividing up the watch period into a series of epochs. For example, a light might flash every few seconds, and an acoustic signal might or might not be present immediately afterwards. With a task of this kind, acoustic and visual signals became equal again. It seems clear therefore that visual information is particularly dependent upon knowledge about likely time of arrival of signals and opportunity to stop observing between these times. We can fairly conclude that the d' drop found by Mackworth and Taylor and in subsequent experiments by Mackworth is due to the continuous attention required in a visual task.

We can therefore sum up the empirical results on decrement during a run by saying that decrements in detections will usually be due to rises in β, but may be due to reduced d' if the task is a visual one with continuous attention. Apart from such cases, the evidence thus far is that d' remains constant.

D

Some minor results giving changes in d'. Two other experimental variables should be mentioned, which both give changes in d'. One of them is practice at the task. It has been found by Broadbent and Gregory (1963a, 1965a) for visual signals and Binford and Loeb (1966) for auditory signals that d' increases from one session to another. The reason for this has not been explored: in terms of the theory of signal detection any increase in knowledge about the exact nature of the signal will give improvements in d', and in general terms it seems plausible that the subject's decision might be more nearly optimal when he has had practice at the task. From another point of view, we might suppose that any observing responses that may be necessary will be performed more adequately after practice.

The other variable which affects d' is the sharing of the main vigilance task with some other task: in the experiment by Wiener, Poock and Steele, the visual vigilance task was performed with and without simultaneous mental arithmetic. When the secondary task was present, the value of d' was lower, as was calculated by Taylor (1965). It is interesting to notice that the detection rate was not significantly impaired: the subjects merely made more false alarms when doing mental arithmetic, so that their detection rate remained reasonably unimpaired.

Interpretations of these Results

The experiments which we have just reviewed could be interpreted in different ways. The first and most obvious of these is in accordance with the theory of signal detection. On that theory, what is happening in vigilance is normally no change in the reliability of the evidence which the observer is receiving, but a change in the critical value of likelihood ratio which he sets himself before reporting that something is present. The critical value behaves in accordance with signal probability, as it should according to the theory and as psychophysical experiments have shown it to do: but this has nothing to do with the evidence that the senses receive. It is not altogether clear why there should be an increase in the critical ratio during a watch period, and this will be discussed again later. Nevertheless, the basic interpretation is that β changes while d' remains constant. The one exception to this lies in cases where continuous observing is necessary, and here there is good evidence for a fall in d' as the run proceeds, that is, for a failure of the signal to produce such reliable evidence for the observer. This failure might well be put down to a failure of observing responses (or a failure of filtering, if one prefers that term). It is certainly of the nature of a reduction in the sensory input to the decision, while the other changes are rather on the response side.

We have already seen that many of the assumptions of the theory of signal detection are questionable even in the psychophysical case, and perhaps even more so in the case of vigilance. But in fact the truth or falsity of these assumptions is not really essential to the usefulness of the theory. Let us go back to the terminology used in Chapter I: we said there that there were various states of the outside world, one of which will occur on any particular occasion, and that there were also a set of states of the evidence reaching some central part of the nervous system. The particular state of evidence occurring would depend upon the state which had occurred in the outside world, but there would be a certain amount of unreliability such that a perfect correspondence would not exist between the two. Given that a particular state of the evidence had occurred, it would then be succeeded by a category state drawn from a set of such possible states at a later stage in the nervous system. The strong form of signal detection theory is that the states of the evidence are arranged in a single dimension; that all states above a certain value of likelihood ratio are succeeded by a category state of "reporting a signal": and that all states of the evidence below that value are followed by the category state of "not reporting a signal".

But the first assumption that the different states of the evidence can be arranged on a single scale of evidence is not essential to the usefulness of the measures derived from theory of signal detection. So long as the data are of the form we actually observe, there are many theoretical models which do not require a single dimension of evidence to be formulated. To take a concrete example suppose there are N possible dimensions of evidence rather than one, and X levels along each, making X^N alternative states in all. Amongst these there are R^N states which will give rise to the category state of "reporting a signal" and $X^N - R^N$ which will not do so. If states of the evidence occur randomly in the absence of a signal, the probability of a false alarm is R^N/X^N. If the occurrence of a signal reduces the number of possible states of evidence to X^n, where n is some fraction of N, and correspondingly reduces to R^n the number of these which will give rise to a report, then the probability of a report in the presence of a signal is R^n/X^n. Therefore

$$P_D = \frac{R^n}{X^n} = \left(\frac{R^N}{X^N}\right)^{\frac{n}{N}} = (P_{FA})^{\frac{n}{N}}.$$

And

$$\log P_D = \frac{n}{N} \log P_{FA}.$$

This is one of the equations which we mentioned earlier as possible approximations to

$$Z_D = d' + Z_{FA}.$$

This sort of thing might happen if, for example, a signal was a flash of a particular brightness, of a particular size, in a certain place, of a certain shape, in a particular hue, with a particular duration, and so on; and if the arrival of a stimulus made the man certain that something had happened of the right shape and brightness, but gave him no information about the other qualities. With a probability that chance processes, even in the absence of a signal, will cause the evidence to indicate arrival of any one characteristic on a proportion R/X of occasions, the man will think that all characteristics have been present on $(R/X)^N$ occasions in the absence of a signal, and $(R/X)^{N-2}$ when a signal has arrived. As therefore he changes his willingness to guess on any one dimension (R/X), the graph of his hits against his false alarms will trace out the familiar concave downward curve.

It would of course be possible to imagine ways in which multi-dimensional evidence gave rise to various category states in such a fashion that the concave downward curve was not found; but empirically we do not need to worry about those. The key point is that the observer need not be aware of the relative contribution to likelihood ratio from different aspects of the stimulus, for the category states to behave in the way we know they do.

The other two assumptions of decision theory concern the subject's knowledge of the likelihood ratio corresponding to each state of evidence, and the assumption that he is rational enough to choose a certain category state consistently for every occurrence of one particular likelihood ratio. Failure of these assumptions will mean that there is no longer a sharp critical value of likelihood ratio above which signals are reported. Rather there may be some states of evidence above the critical value which fail to give the appropriate category state, and some below the critical ratio which inappropriately do give response. There may also be unreliability between any one state of evidence and the resulting category state.

These two sources of unreliability between the evidence and the resulting category state increase the unreliability of a particular category state following a particular state in the outside world: but they need not necessarily affect the shape of the relationship between the probability of the category state "reporting a signal" after a true signal as compared with the probability of the same category state after a non-signal. Precisely what will happen depends upon the distribution of probabilities of different states of the evidence, given that one knows the category state which has resulted. It also depends on the corresponding distribution of probabilities of signal or non-signal for each state of the evidence. In many cases, we may get exactly the same relationship between signal and category state from a mechanism in which all the unreliability occurs between the signal and the state of the evidence, and none between the evidence and the category state: and a mechanism in which there is greater reliability between the signal and the state of the evidence, and less between the evidence and the category state. In both cases the probabilities of detections may be simply related to the probability of false alarms, provided that both are transformed to z-scores. We shall be considering one such case later on in the chapter, in discussing the "two-state" theory, as it is called, which contends that there are only two states of the evidence rather than a complete continuum of such states.

It is not therefore necessary to suppose that the subject either behaves rationally or is possessed of perfect knowledge about likelihood ratios; and none of the experimental evidence pushes us in one direction or the other on these possibilities.

In the case of vigilance rather than psychophysics, the various assumptions of axiomatic detection theory may well be unjustified. A man watching a radar screen for long periods can hardly be receiving evidence with the alert efficiency of an ideal observer. There may well therefore be more randomness than in the ideal case, in the process linking the states of evidence both to the occurrence of signal and non-signal on the one hand, and in those linking them to the occurrence of the different category states on the other. The empirical question is whether or not this randomness takes a roughly Gaussian form, allowing the z-score transformation. So long as it does so, any change in d' must reflect a change in the amount of randomness intervening between signal and category state; while changes in hit rate for constant d' reflect a rise or fall in the number of states of evidence which give rise to the category state of "reporting a signal".

We can therefore assert a weak version of signal detection theory, in which we do not use the less likely postulates about the observer's knowledge and rationality. We merely assert that there is randomness between the signal and its corresponding category state; and that the changes in performance in vigilance fall into two classes. Some changes (signal probability, and most cases of decrement during the watch) do not reflect any alteration in this randomness. They indicate rather a change in the number of states of evidence which can give rise to a particular category state: "pigeon-holing", in the terms of Chapter I. Other changes (signal strength, decrement in visual tasks requiring continuous attention) do reflect a change in the input of the signal itself.

Two counter-interpretations can be raised however, and these should now be considered. One of them argues that there are possibly only two large states of evidence rather than a large set, and that the variability within the system lies on the response side rather than the stimulus side. This argument is worth considering in detail, to see how far it is valid, but we shall conclude that even if it is true it does not affect the weak version of signal detection theory given above. The other counter-interpretation questions our whole analysis and suggests that measured changes in β could result from changes in the intake of information and not at all from the rules connecting evidence to category state. This is of course a much more serious conflict: we shall in fact conclude that this counter-interpretation is false for most of the existing data even though it may well be true for some special cases and for other situations not yet studied.

THE TWO-STATE THEORY AND ITS RAMIFICATIONS

There are several interpretations which we want to discuss under this heading, which are slightly different from each other. It is probably simplest to begin with an elementary form of two-state theory which builds on points we have met before; it combines the two straight-line theories we mentioned at the beginning of this chapter, and so predicts two intersecting straight lines. Consider a system with two states of the outside world, signal and non-signal. There are also two corresponding states of evidence; these do not occur with complete reliability after signal and non-signal respectively, but rather the one indicates a higher probability of signal having been presented and the other of non-signal. Call the former E_s and the latter E_n for brevity. If therefore the category state of reporting a signal always and only follows E_s, there will be less than perfect detection, and there will also be some false alarms. The subject can improve the detection score if he keeps the rule that a report always follows E_s, but adds reports on a proportion of occurrences of E_n. Some of the false alarms can be eliminated, alternatively, by keeping the rule that report never follows E_n, but adding a proportion of occurrences of E_s when non-report occurs. These two possible strategies will give two straight line relations between P_D and P_{FA}, with the equations

$$P_D = C + \frac{(1-C)(P_{FA}-F)}{1-F}$$

$$P_D = K \times P_{FA}$$

where

C = probability of E_s given a signal
F = probability of E_s given non-signal

The lines will cross at $P_D = C$, $P_{FA} = F$. In combination, they will look very like a concave downward curve except for the sharp point where the two lines cross, and an experiment with a practicable number of observations might not happen to measure performance just at that point. We must therefore look rather closely at the experimental evidence before deciding whether this is an acceptable theory. For reasons which will emerge, we have to distinguish sharply between the case where subjects simply report signals under various instructions about caution, and the case where a confidence rating is given.

As we have seen, there are some *experiments on the effect of instructions* by Colquhoun (1967) and by Egan *et al.* (1961). In Colquhoun's case, subjects were told to be sure before reporting, or to report anything however doubtful, and only two points were therefore obtained. The line joining these is neither of the two lines of the two-state theory: it is too steep for one and too shallow for the other. But one might get a result like this if the point where the two lines cross was in between the two points which have been measured; if, in fact, we had measured one point on one line and one point on the other line.

So although Colquhoun's result rules out a simple guessing theory, and is perfectly consistent with detection theory, it does not rule out two-state theory. The results of Egan and his colleagues cover four points rather than two, but as has been explained above we cannot fix the point corresponding to detection of all signals because of the method of analysis they used. We cannot tell therefore where the line

$$P_D = C + \frac{(1-C)(P_{FA}-F)}{1-F}$$

would run. We can fix the other line, because we can tell where the point corresponding to zero reports of signals would be; and we can then examine the line joining the two points of highest confidence to see whether it could be the line

$$P_D = K \times P_{FA}.$$

If it is shallower than that line, then either it is the other line or the crossing point lies between the two data points. If the former, then the line joining the next two data points should be the same; so if that line is shallower again, the only interpretation consistent with two-state theory is that the crossing point is between the first two data points. We then have one last pair of data points: if the line joining them is shallower than any of the others (as it should be on detection theory) then the result is incompatible with two-state theory. Egan and his colleagues report individual data on seven subjects; the present author has calculated that the results of four of them are inconsistent with two-state theory while the remaining three are consistent with either view.

This is slightly tenuous evidence, and so it is attractive to turn to *experiments on the rating method*. If we can trust this method, we can perform similar analyses to those just described, and there are adequate data in the literature for rejecting the two-state model for vigilance. Broadbent and Gregory (1963a) tested large numbers of subjects and carried out statistical analyses specifically on this point; and the data of Loeb and Binford (1964) are also inconsistent with two straight lines. It could be argued however that the rating method is unsuitable for testing the theory (Larkin, 1965). After all, we are adding another task by getting the man to indicate his confidence in his report. Suppose that he is really functioning in a two-state fashion, but after E_s usually reports with high confidence, occasionally with moderate, and rarely with low, the particular degree of confidence used being quite random within these constraints. We might suppose also that after E_n any reports are usually given with low confidence, occasionally with moderate, and rarely with high. This would give the pattern of results which is found experimentally. In fact a wide variety of distributions of responses over the different degrees of confidence would give the same pattern; so long as the same degree of confidence can sometimes follow one state of evidence and sometimes the other, the proportions depending on which evidence has arrived.

This looks like a good argument for neglecting the rating experiments, but there is a way of countering it. If experiments using simple reports were giving performance on two straight lines, while rating data were obtained in the way just described, then it is easy to show (Broadbent, 1966) that the rating data would give higher false alarm rates for the same detection rates than would the simple reports. But Loeb and Binford (1964) found no such result and Binford and Loeb (1966) actually got *higher* values of d' for the rating method than for simple instructions. So the rating method does not introduce some extra arbitrary unreliability due to the man picking confidence values at random.

Can one save the two-state model at all? Certainly, because there was an arbitrary assumption in our original statement of it. As we put it, a man could either try to improve his hit rate or to reduce his false alarm rate; he could report after some occurrences of E_n as long as he was reporting after all E_s events, or he could remain inactive after some E_s as long as he remained inactive after all E_n. Suppose instead he tried to improve both scores, by reporting after some E_n and also refraining after some E_s. In that case his performance need not lie on two straight lines at all, and by mixing the proportions of the two kinds of behaviour he could trace out any curve including the usual concave downward one. He could also match the performance in a rating experiment, since the fact that a report can now have followed either E_s or E_n will parallel the loss of information due to the occurrence of a certain degree of confidence either after E_s or after E_n.

What has happened in this modified two-state theory is that a considerable amount of randomness has been supposed to intrude between the two states of evidence and the category states controlling response. One can represent this by regarding the appearance of one of the two states of evidence as controlling the occurrence of one of a set of states of confidence, rather as in the criticism of the rating method; but these states of confidence can either produce responses which correspond exactly to them (the rating method), or else produce simple reports by a rule such as "report if there is a higher degree of confidence than x". The shape of the distributions of confidence produced by signal or non-signal becomes an empirical matter, which from the evidence must be roughly Gaussian; and when we measure d' we are to a great extent finding out how much randomness there is in the choice of responses given the occurrence of one of the two states of evidence. The set of states of confidence however behaves just like the set of states of evidence in signal detection theory; the only change is to add an earlier stage in the process at which there are hypothesized to be two states. None of the data we have considered are able to confirm or deny this possibility, which is really a matter of whereabouts the most serious unreliability arises in the chain of events from signal to category state. Such a question can perhaps be left for future research, so long as we are clear that the answer to it, whatever it may be, does not affect the general point that d' measures the reliability of the information flowing from the senses to the category states, while β measures the bias in favour of one such category state.

There is another form of theory which should also be considered, which puts the randomness at the response end of the process, and which is called by the rather different name of *choice theory*. Like the two-state theory so far considered, it has been developed and its implications studied by R. D. Luce. The model predicting two straight lines was set out by Luce (1960, 1963); the choice model produced by Luce (1959) is quite different in its implications, and is worth considering in detail because it gives predictions very closely similar to those of detection theory while making calculations considerably easier.

On this theory, a man faced with two alternative responses such as "report" and "non-report" may choose to make one of these responses on some occasions and the other on the remainder, even when he has no evidence about the occurrence of a signal. The ratio of the probability of choosing "report" to that of choosing "non-report" is known as the *strength* of the one response relative to the other: let us call it X in the absence of a signal. Now the presentation of a signal multiplies the strength by a determinate amount to AX.

This gives, in the presence of a signal

$$\frac{\text{Probability of report}}{\text{Probability of non-report}} = \frac{P_D}{1-P_D} = AX.$$

And in the absence of a signal

$$\frac{\text{Probability of report}}{\text{Probability of non-report}} = \frac{P_{FA}}{1-P_{FA}} = X.$$

Therefore

$$\frac{P_D}{1-P_D} = A\frac{P_{FA}}{1-P_{FA}}.$$

We saw earlier in this chapter that an equation of this form gives a concave downward curve of P_D against P_{FA}, closely similar to the one derived from detection theory. The reason, as we said, is that $\log P_D/1-P_D$ is closely similar to Z_D if we choose our units carefully. The factor A corresponds to d' in the signal detection model, but is much easier to calculate from hit rates and false alarm rates. The quantity corresponding to β is also easy to calculate; it is given by

$$\beta = \frac{P_D(1-P_D)}{P_{FA}(1-P_{FA})}$$

D*

[See Luce (1959) for the derivation of this expression; he uses B rather than β; but this would create confusion here with the quantity B we have already introduced.] It will be noticed that β depends on A as well as on X; what this means is that ideally a rational man would alter the value of X even for a constant signal probability if A, the contribution made by the signal, took on a different size. If a signal is highly conspicuous, there is less to be gained by guessing that it is there when one has no evidence that it is.

In detection theory, the corresponding point is that any given value of β is located at a certain value of Z_{FA} which differs from the value for which β is one; that is, the point where the two distributions cross. As d' increases, the difference decreases between Z_{FA} for the point $\beta = 1$ and Z_{FA} for any other particular value of β. It is of course an empirical question whether people actually behave in such a way as to hold β constant; in many ways one might think it more likely that they would hold Z_{FA} constant, as is assumed by M. Treisman (1964). It would also be possible that they might hold X constant. We shall see later in another chapter that, surprisingly, the experimental evidence suggests that β is constant when d' changes.

The choice theory therefore affords quick ways of calculating parameters corresponding to d' and β; this ease of calculation becomes more than a mere convenience when in a later chapter we come to consider the case of recognizing a stimulus as one of many alternatives rather than just detecting or failing to detect one type of signal. It then becomes impossible to analyse certain kinds of data using detection theory, but possible to do so with the methods of choice theory. One of the simplifications which choice theory makes, and which produces this ease of calculation, is that it normally matches only the curve

$$Z_D = d' + Z_{FA}$$

and does not produce an approximation to the curve

$$Z_D = A + B Z_{FA}$$

when B has a value other than 1; that is, when the distributions of signal detection theory differ in variance. This is obviously a severe limitation, since we have already seen that experimentally many tasks, especially visual ones, give a function of this type. It has been pointed out by Broadbent (1967a) however that one could modify choice theory to do this by reintroducing some variability into the effects of the signal. If for example one supposes that on a proportion p of signal presentations the man is not looking and the situation remains for him identical with non-signal, then

$$P_D = p\left(\frac{X}{X+1}\right) + (1-p)\left(\frac{AX}{AX+1}\right)$$

$$P_{FA} = \frac{X}{X+1}.$$

If we now calculate from these data a value A', by assuming incorrectly that the man is looking all the time and so working out

$$A' = \frac{P_D(1-P_{FA})}{P_{FA}(1-P_D)}$$

then it is easy to show that A' will decrease as X increases. The resulting curve will be closely similar to that from a detection theory model with signal variance greater than non-signal variance. (This result should be remembered as it will be used in arguing against an "observing response" interpretation of vigilance decrement very shortly.)

Because choice theory is so similar in its predictions to detection theory, it is once again impossible to distinguish the two approaches using the experimental data considered earlier. Once again however this need not concern us; choice theory implies that there is, for any given signal strength, a pair of states of evidence each of which is determinately related to signal and non-signal respectively; it then supposes that unreliability enters between these states of evidence and the category states controlling response. For our purposes it does not matter whether the source of the unreliability lies early or late in the chain of events from signal to category state. The important question is to distinguish the measure of sensory information, d' or A, from the measure of bias X or β. Even if the simple two-state model had turned out to be justified in vigilance, it would still have been important to distinguish those variables which move performance along one pair of straight lines, and those variables which shift performance to another pair of lines. The main outcome of discussing these alternative theories is therefore that we are justified in using a d' measure, although we should remember the possibility that $Z_D - Z_{FA}$ may not be constant for all values of Z_{FA}; and that we are justified in using rating methods of determining the degree of constancy of $Z_D - Z_{FA}$. We must however beware of supposing that the variability we are measuring lies necessarily between the signal and the evidence rather than between the evidence and the category state.

THEORIES OF VIGILANCE AS A MIXTURE OF PERFORMANCE

We must now consider the more fundamental objection to our weak interpretation of detection theory. This objection is formulated in most detail by Jerison et al. (1965) although it has been summarized by Jerison (1967a, b). The origins of the criticism lie in two theoretical areas. First, let us suppose that signal detection theory is to be regarded as established in the psychophysical case, by the various data reported by Green and Swets (1966). In that case it is clear that the values of d' and β found in vigilance experiments are unusual, the former being low and the latter being high. A signal which is visible in psychophysical situations without too much difficulty is often hard to see in vigilance conditions, and this is not only because the false alarm rate is low but because of a decline in d'. Similarly, if the ratio of non-signal to signal events in a task is ten to one, and if the felt distaste for missed signals is the same as that for false alarms, then β for an ideal observer would be ten, and in psychophysical situations it turns out to be rather less. In a vigilance task however it may be much more. There is obviously therefore some difference between vigilance and psychophysics.

The other theoretical influence which makes a straightforward application of decision theory measures unattractive is the "observing response" approach discussed in the last chapter. If we suppose that it is necessary to make continual adjustments of the sense organs to receive information, that this is hard to maintain over prolonged periods, and that it is more likely that one will adjust oneself to receive information from sources which are likely to deliver it; then one would expect vigilance to be affected primarily by the probability that an appropriate observing response would be made, and one might expect performance to be different on occasions when it had been and on occasions when it had not. Jerison and his colleagues therefore suggest that the measured performance mixes together some occasions on which a psychophysical level of performance is achieved, some on which a blurred and inefficient observing has occurred, and some on which no observing was conducted at all so that neither detections nor false alarms would be recorded. They calculate the measured hit and false alarm rates which would be obtained from a mixture of these three kinds of observing in various proportions, and show that if one was then to work out d' and β in the usual way from the total, the obtained values would differ from the psychophysical ones in the way which experiment shows.

Jerison (1967b) regards this analysis as weakening any interpretation which describes the changes in vigilance during a work period as representing an increase in caution. Rather they might be due to a change in the proportion of different kinds of observing, produced by changes in the elicitation of observing responses. Such a change would, from the analysis just described, give an apparent change in β even though the true value of β in each of the types of observing had remained completely constant.

We have here an antithesis which will recur several times throughout this book. If a certain variable affects performance, does it do so by selecting the source of information which is controlling performance, or does it do so by altering the rules connecting evidence with category states and so with response? Does it affect filtering or pigeon-holing? Jerison is arguing that the changes in vigilance are due to the former; and other authors such as Mackworth (1965a) accept his view.

To the present author however it seems that this analysis is unsatisfactory for most of the experiments we have considered. The reason for this is that Jerison's model does not predict changes *only* in β when there is a change in the proportion of observations made with different degrees of alertness. It also predicts two other effects, and there is little sign of those in the literature.

First, any increase in the proportion of blurred responding or of unresponsive instants must produce a drop in d' as well as a change in β. Yet we have seen that a large number of experiments, including Jerison's own, give a significant change in β with no significant change in d'. The counter which can be made to this is that the change in d' might be relatively slight and so undetectable; but the illustrative calculations given by Jerison et al. (1965) do not support this. It seems strange that the changes in d', which should accompany changes in the mixture of alert, blurred, and unresponsive performance, have been so elusive. Only in the experiments by J. F. Mackworth are there changes in d'; those studies indeed may reflect a mechanism of the "observing response" type.

Most serious however is the second objection to Jerison's view. The analysis he and his colleagues give considers only one point in the graph of P_D against P_{FA}. His model implies however that the whole graph shall not be fitted by a detection theory analysis postulating equal variance for the two underlying distributions. We saw in the last section that, if we postulate a certain proportion of occasions on which the man fails to receive a signal and acts as if non-signal were present, then his performance will resemble that to be expected for a signal distribution of larger variance than the non-signal distribution. That is, d' measured for risky performance should be less than that measured for cautious performance. This will be even more true if we adopt the suggestion that the man becomes completely unresponsive on a certain proportion of occasions, not even showing the same report rate he produces in the absence of signal.

We can work out a similar prediction for the case in which blurred observing is accompanied by a certain proportion of cases in which the man works with the value of d' customary for psychophysical situations with the same level of signal; in effect, this means with a near-perfect hit rate and zero false alarm rate. Curiously enough, the introduction of a proportion of such near-perfect performance would change the plot of P_D against P_{FA} in the same direction as would the presence of a proportion of non-responsive moments; provided that the value of P_{FA} is reasonably low, in the range occupied by vigilance data. In this case also therefore d' should be less at the risky than at the cautious criterion.

The reason for the similarity of the two predictions is simply that each of them is in fact introducing a greater variability in the effects of signal than of non-signal. This is not surprising when one reflects on the matter, as variability in the efficiency of a postulated observing response must change greatly the effects of the signal which the response is intended to observe. Admittedly, the prediction does change if one supposes a very high incidence of perfect observation rather than blurred observing. In that case, a large P_{FA} could be due only to the moments of blurred observing. A very high incidence of perfect observing would therefore change the situation to one in which the variability of the effects of non-signal became greater than those of signal; but the point where this would happen is too high to concern us.

If therefore the decrement in vigilance is due to an admixture of different kinds of observing, we must expect d' to be less at the risky level of performance, and to become more so as the work period continues. Weak data on this point are provided by the various experiments in which changes in conditions have affected β without changing d'; we would have to suppose, in order to explain these results by a mixture of levels of performance, that the same conditions had altered both d' and β in such a way as to cancel exactly the apparent changes in measured d' which would otherwise have been found. Stronger evidence comes from those experiments which have used ratings of confidence and so plotted P_D/P_{FA} at the same time. The data of Broadbent and Gregory (1963a, 1965a) show a small drop in d' from cautious to risky ratings, of the order of 10%. This is of the size to be expected in psychophysical experiments, especially visual ones (Green and Swets, 1966): and the task used by Broadbent and Gregory was visual. More important, in neither experiment does the size of the difference increase as the work period continues; on the contrary, it seems to get slightly less, so that there is rather less evidence for intervals of non-responding at the end of the run than there is at the beginning. This is to be expected from the fact already mentioned that the rise in β is largely in that for the most cautious responses, and the more risky criteria are much less affected. The rise cannot therefore be due to an admixture of less efficient observation.

The clearest data are those of Loeb and Binford (1964), who used an auditory task. It will be remembered that they found the line of best fit to their graph of one z-score against the other, and showed that it corresponded to a model with two distributions of equal variance: or if anything with larger variance in the non-signal case. As they too found a rise in β, greatest at the most cautious criterion, it does not seem that a curve of the unequal variance type is necessary to get a change in β. Lastly, it should be added that a long series of auditory experiments by Colquhoun (unpublished) show no evidence of a consistent difference in variance.

Putting these crucial experiments against the larger background of the weaker evidence from experiments without confidence ratings, it does not seem that there is any firm evidence for the observing response approach in the vigilance tasks which we have mostly considered in this chapter. This does not mean however that there are no cases in which the theory applies, merely that there are none which have so far been studied with relevant techniques and in which it has been shown to apply. It is worth considering a few cases in which it may well prove more successful when further data have been gathered. First of these is the explanation of the asymmetry usually found in visual experiments, suggesting that there is an inequality of variance in the underlying distributions. This may of course result from some feature of nervous transmission such that the variability of a process is greater when its mean is higher; but it seems quite plausible that some of it is to be attributed to failures of adjustment of the sense organs, sometimes present and sometimes absent. There may of course be a continual gradation of efficiency of observing responses, rather than a dichotomy between perfect and imperfect observation, so that the observing response may form an extra source of randomness operative only when a signal is present. It seems reasonable that this should hold more frequently in vision, and also that there should be individual differences in the extent to which it is important; which is also apparently true of the asymmetry of the P_D/P_{FA} graph in psychophysics (Green and Swets, 1966).

A second point where failure of observing response may be important is in the case of experiments with high event rates. As we saw earlier in the chapter, such experiments are unusual in that d' deteriorates during the work period, and there is therefore some element in them which is not shared by the type of study in which the event rate is relatively low. The 1958 "filter theory" of Broadbent placed a great deal of emphasis on the intermittency of the breakdown in performance to be expected from failure of filtering; and that theory predicted decrement only in tasks with transient signals and a high event rate. It seems entirely plausible that this kind of task may indeed be vulnerable to these effects. Decrement in detections in that case may come from a mixture of moments of unresponsiveness with moments of normal efficiency. Unfortunately however no experiments with this kind of task have employed confidence ratings or any similar way of plotting the whole graph; one would predict that, if decrement in these tasks is due to this mechanism, d' would be much less at the risky level of performance than when measured at the cautious level. In particular, the discrepancy in d' should increase as the work period progresses.

A third point concerns the effects of intense acoustic noise on visual performance. We shall be considering this in more detail in a later chapter, since it involves tasks other than vigilance. However, one or two points should be made here, because the effect of noise may be in part to give failures of observation. Broadbent (1958) explained the effect of noise as due to an increased number of failures by the filter to select task information rather than irrelevant signals from the surroundings. This was in accordance with the general principle that more intense stimuli are more likely to be selected by the filter (receive attention). To support this principle, Broadbent was able to cite evidence from tasks in which the intense stimuli had overt responses allotted to them. (For example, Broadbent, 1957a.) Although this view will need some modification when we do come later to think about effects of stress, it will remain likely in general that the effects of noise are to cause inefficient filtering. Now Broadbent and Gregory (1963a, 1965a) have examined the effects of noise on visual vigilance analysed with the measures of decision theory. The effects are different from those which appeared in the same papers as a result of prolonged work. Once again, any fall in detections was due to changes in β rather than d', but noise raises β at the risky rather than the cautious level, whereas prolonged work did the opposite. Correspondingly, whereas prolonged work seemed if anything to make d'_{risky} differ less from $d'_{cautious}$, the effect of noise may possibly give an increased asymmetry of the graph. In the 1963 experiments three sources of visual signals were always used and this makes interpretation a little difficult as fixation of one source rather than another is bound to produce some asymmetry. In the 1965 paper however, one group watched only one source of signals at a high signal rate. This task showed a significant rise in the number of completely missed signals in noise, at the end of the work period. If one examines d' for the cautious and risky criteria for this group, one finds a difference of under 5% for the last quarter of the test on quiet, but roughly 15% for the corresponding period in noise. It would seem well worth conducting a more systematic study of the constancy of d' at various levels of caution in noise. Jerison's suggestion may well apply to deterioration of vigilance in noise, and if so the measured value of d' in noise might depend very much on the level of caution at which it was measured.

A last possible field of application for this approach would be in the failures of performance found in tasks with many sources of signals. As we remarked in the last paragraph, it is in such tasks obvious that observing responses will play a part in deciding whether a given signal will produce an effect in the nervous system or not; and the eye-movement data of Mackworth et al. (1964) provide direct evidence of this. We saw in the last chapter evidence that the occurrence of many signals in a certain location would improve the detection of further signals from that same location; unfortunately it has been rare to report false alarms as well as detections in these experiments, so we do not know whether this effect is a change in d' or a change in β. On the face of it, either might apply; detection theory would predict a change in β, while observing response theory would predict a change in d', possibly accompanied by a change in β if the mechanism were like that proposed by Jerison.

One experiment which did give false alarm rates was one by Colquhoun (1966a). He was using a display consisting of a row of circles, one of which might be larger than the others. As is usual in displays consisting of a straight line like this, the number of detections was greater at the centre of the row than at the ends. This was normally due to a change both in d' and in β, which looks as if the men were suffering from a mixture of alert and defective observing at the edges of the display while remaining alert in the middle of it. There were however two groups for whom β was reasonably constant with position in the row, although d' was less at the ends. These groups were those who had been trained by "cueing", that is, by the lighting of a lamp before each signal of the training session. The lamp was adjacent to the place where the signal was about to appear. It is perhaps fair to argue that these groups were more fully aware of the fact that signals were equally likely in any position than were groups given no formal training or else knowledge of results after signals and false alarms. There is the possibility here of a "vicious circle" of the kind we discussed in the last chapter under the heading of expectancy. If a man is scanning his eyes backwards and forwards over a linear display, he will spend longer in the middle than at either end: in the sequence ABCBABCBABCBABCB the letter B occurs twice as often as A or C. If therefore he observes the ends less often he may detect fewer signals there. Hockey (1970) has obtained evidence that this is indeed a factor, by using transient and non-transient signals in a spatially separated display. The latter of course are always seen in the end and so give accurate information about their own probability. In Colquhoun's experiment therefore the effects at the edge of the display might be caused by a mixture of spatial scanning and a vicious circle effect on subjective probability of signals from different locations. In the "cueing" groups, who showed no effect on β, the subjective probability effect was presumably lacking; but these groups showed as big a d' difference between locations as did the other groups. This in turn suggests that subjective probability did not affect the scanning pattern in this case, and therefore did not affect d', but only β. Further data are badly needed to see whether it is really true that locations where signals are probable are observed more frequently; or whether they are merely observed with a favourable β. On the face of it, the former seems likely, but there is no firm evidence of it as yet.

This same conclusion must serve as a summary of the whole approach of supposing that vigilance performance consists of a mixture of alert and un-alert observation. For tasks with a low event rate it is certainly untrue that decrements in detection are due to unalert moments; and it is probably untrue for all auditory tasks. For visual tasks with a high event rate, it may be true; the present author believes that it is, but there is no direct evidence. Most of the tasks studied in recent years are showing their changes because of alterations in β, that is, in the pigeon-holing mechanism and not in the filtering mechanism. We must therefore, before we leave the subject, consider what may be the underlying explanation of these changes in β. The suggestions given in the next section are complex, require further evidence, and are given largely as a means of provoking the reader to further thought about the problem. Doubts about their validity should not be allowed to obscure the central fact that pigeon-holing is responsible for many changes in vigilance tasks.

Criterion Shifts in Vigilance

The theories of vigilance derived from conventional experiments rest on expectancy, arousal, and filtering (observing responses). The last of these carries the implication that d' should change; so changes in β, unaccompanied by d' changes, ought to be related to the other two theories. In our discussion of expectancy in the last chapter, we concluded that it was satisfactory as an explanation of the experiments by Colquhoun and by Colquhoun and Baddeley, showing that the signal/non-signal ratio changed performance for a constant event rate; and showing that the signal rate during pretraining would change the average level of performance in a subsequent test. It would also produce a decrement if the test rate was lower than the training rate. In this chapter, we have seen that these same experiments show changes in β, and it seems reasonable to suppose that signal probability is controlling β as the theory of signal detection says that it should. The main contribution of the new analysis is to show that, since these experiments do not give changes in d', the effect is not an effect on observing responses or filtering, but on pigeon-holing.

We were left uncertain in the last chapter, however, about the possible role of expectancy in explaining the decrement in people who had been trained with an appropriate signal rate, and who had worked in many sessions. Furthermore the effect of background stimuli such as loud noises can hardly be due to expectancy but rather to some concept such as arousal. When β changes during the work period, or in noise, how can this be brought about by expectancy or by arousal? The data to be explained are fairly complex, and it may be helpful to summarize them again.

(a) β increases during the run, but more so at cautious levels of performance; experiments with a rather low β by Broadbent and Gregory actually show no change at the risky level. Those by Loeb and Binford or by Levine, which use higher values of β and find some effect at all levels, still show more effect at their more cautious level.

(b) In loud noise, the risky and cautious values of β become closer; that is, responses of intermediate confidence become rare. This may however happen either through an increase in confident reports or through an increase in confident denials of the presence of a signal.

(c) The effect of noise does not give the opposite change to that occurring during the run, that is, it does not give a significant drop in β; nor does the effect of prolonged work produce an increase in the separation of cautious and risky values of β.

(The apparent contradiction between this result on prolonged work and the result (a) cited above, is due to differences between individual subjects. That is, some people show more responses of intermediate confidence at the end of the run and some show less, while all show a drop in their confident reports of signals. There is therefore little significant change in the risky criterion over the group as a whole, a significant change in the cautious criterion, and yet little significant change in the separation of criteria over the group as a whole.)

(d) The effect of noise does give a rise in the risky value of β when the value is in quiet exceptionally low, whether because the individual subject uses a low β (Broadbent and Gregory, 1963a) or because the signal rate is high and the group as a whole has a low β (Broadbent and Gregory, 1965a). As is usual with harmful effects of noise on work this applies only late in the work period.

(e) The rise in β during the run, although it varies with different degrees of confidence, has not been shown to change when the signal rate changes; the experiment has only been tried for limited numbers of rates by Broadbent and Gregory (1965a), but there is an important result by Simpson (1967) which we have not previously mentioned, and which points in the same direction. Simpson actually used a signal rate far higher than the non-signal rate in one of his conditions, but β still increased during the run, that is, fewer signals were detected at the end.

Two theoretical conclusions follow immediately from these results. First, we cannot explain the effects of noise and of prolonged work by the same mechanism working in opposite directions, because they are not simple opposites. Thus if noise changes arousal, prolonged work must either change some other kind of arousal or change expectancy, if those are the concepts we have available.

The second conclusion is that some explanation is needed for the difference in effect at different levels of confidence. On the face of it, changes in subjective probability of a signal ought to affect all criteria in the same direction; so should a simple increase in reactivity causing positive responses to appear to smaller levels of evidence. We must therefore look at each of the hypothesized mechanisms to see whether they can be led to explain a difference in the changes at one criterion rather than another.

EXPECTANCY

First, let us take expectancy. This theory can only explain decrements during the run, in appropriately trained subjects, by the "vicious circle" mechanism; and that mechanism has a new element when considered from the point of view of detection theory. When β equals one, the number of false alarms is equal to the number of missed signals; if β is greater than one, the probability of a false alarm is less than that of a miss. For a signal probability of 0·5, therefore, a man who erroneously observes with a β slightly greater than one will report less often than there were signals; and if he takes his own reports as indicating the signal rate, he will be led to adopt a still higher level of β. If he starts with β less than one, the opposite will occur. When signal and non-signal are unequal in probability, as is usually the case in vigilance, an even more striking result appears. An ideal observer working with β equal to $(1-p)/p$, where p is the probability of a signal, will always report less often than signals are in fact presented for $p < 0·5$, and more often for $p > 0·5$. An ideal observer therefore who started work with an accurate idea of signal probability, and who thereafter counted his own reports as evidence of the signal rate, would gradually show higher and higher β as the task went on, provided the signal was less frequent than non-signal. Only if β was less cautious than the ideal would the total number of reports equal the initial correct estimate of signal probability.

This then is a theory which might be advanced for the tendency of β to increase during the run for "sure" responses, and to do so less markedly for "doubtful" responses. There are two difficulties in applying it to the data; first, we would have to suppose that the man uses only his "sure" responses in assessing the signal probability for making such responses in future, and uses all his responses of at least "doubtful" status in setting a criterion for "doubtful" responses. This is perhaps a little unlikely. The second difficulty is that people do not act as ideal observers, and in psychophysical situations usually set β less extreme than an ideal observer would; thus making more reports for improbable signals than would the ideal observer, and perhaps as many reports as there were signals. We cannot therefore assume that hits plus false alarms will be less numerous than signals.

The easy way round these difficulties is to examine the results of vigilance experiments and see what the total of hits and false alarms actually is. It does turn out that this total usually is less than the total of signals, and that the use of various degrees of confidence does shift the performance across the critical point where the man's own reports cease to mislead him. For example, in one of Broadbent and Gregory's (1965a) groups, for every 20 signals, there were roughly 15 hits and false alarms with high confidence, and roughly 30 including those of low confidence. It is not surprising therefore that β increases in the former case but not the latter. Similarly, one of the conditions of Loeb and Binford (1964) gives, for each 10 signals, roughly 5 reports of high confidence but 18 reports if one includes the most doubtful. This experiment also will be remembered as one of those which shows a lower proportion of confident responses as work proceeds.

This analysis therefore greatly strengthens the plausibility of the vicious circle of lowered expectancy as a factor in vigilance decrement. It would explain the deterioration even in subjects trained with an appropriate rate (as were those of Broadbent and Gregory); and if as in the last chapter we argue that a subjective signal rate could be associated with time during the work period, then repeated decrements in repeated work periods could be explained. On Run II the man thinks "There were few signals late in the last run". There are however still serious difficulties in this explanation. First, β should certainly not increase during the run when the total number of reports is more than the known initial signal rate. Yet Loeb and Binford did find significant changes even at their most doubtful criterion, for which, as indicated above, total reports were well above the objective signal rate.

Secondly, the effect should be symmetrical, so that if signals were far more probable than non-signals, β should drop during the run. Simpson's result, showing that β still increases in such a case, therefore becomes crucial; and apparently fatal to the expectancy theory.

AROUSAL

Let us now consider arousal. At first sight, one might argue that the effects of a general rise in the responsiveness of the nervous system would be to reduce randomness and so to increase d'. On this reasoning, the decrement during the run cannot be due to falling arousal because d' is unchanged except in the Mackworth experiments. Neither can the effects of noise be due to arousal, as d' does not alter (except for one rise for one criterion value in one of the experiments of Broadbent and Gregory, 1963a). But there is no obligation to accept the link between arousal and d'. One might as well argue, as Welford (1962) pointed out, that a rise in reactivity will increase the neural consequences of everything that happens. The signal would then produce a larger effect but all the random factors will also have larger effects. The d' measure represents the difference in the means of two normal distributions, divided by their (identical) standard deviation. If the standard deviation increases at the same rate as the difference in means, d' will be identical.

What happens to β under these circumstances will depend on the details of the underlying mechanism. Let us be unwisely concrete, and think of a nerve fibre firing at 100 impulses/sec with a standard deviation of 10. A signal then raises the average rate to 120, with the same standard deviation. If all rates above 110 give rise to a report, β will be equal to one; and d' will of course be equal to two. Now suppose that a rise in arousal raises the non-signal rate of firing to 110, the signal rate to 132, and the standard deviation to $1\cdot1$; the value of d' will still equal two but if the critical rate remains at 110, there will be a rise both in hits and false alarms corresponding to a fall in β. This is the type of theory which would predict a change in the same direction for all levels of confidence, and therefore is not adequate.

Let us suppose a slightly different physical mechanism; let us imagine a pair of nerve fibres rather than one, and let us suppose that in the absence of a signal, fibre A fires at 110 impulses/sec and fibre B at 100. Each rate varies with a standard deviation of $5\sqrt{2}$. In the presence of a signal, fibre B takes up a rate of 110, and fibre A of 100, the standard deviations remaining unchanged. If one now considers the difference in rates, A-B, this will have a mean of $+10$ in the absence of a signal and -10 in the presence of a signal, the standard deviation being 10 in either case. A mechanism which produced a report whenever A-B was negative would therefore have a d' of two and a β of one, just as in our previous example. The performance would not distinguish these two mechanisms. If however a change in arousal increased the firing rates and standard deviations, A-B could become $+11$ in the absence of a signal and

−11 in the presence of a signal, with a standard deviation of 1·1; d' would still be unchanged, but now a mechanism which was set to report a signal whenever A-B was negative would still have a β of one. This type of process could give opposite changes for criteria at different levels; if the reporting system had been set rather cautiously, to report only if A-B became more negative than −10, it would have reported 50% of signals when unaroused but rather more when aroused, a fall in β with arousal. Had the reporting system been set riskily, however, to report whenever A-B fell below +10, it would have had a false alarm rate of 50% in the unaroused state and rather less when aroused; a rise in β with arousal.

The mechanism we have just considered implies that changes in arousal would leave d' unchanged, and leave β unchanged when it is equal to one, but increased arousal will move all other criteria closer to the point where β equals one. That point acts as a kind of fixed zero and the distance from it to all other criteria, in terms of z-scores, expands and contracts. By supposing yet other modified mechanisms, we could place the zero point at any other value of β; for example, if we supposed that fibres A and B fired at equal rates in the presence of a signal, but that fibre A fired more rapidly in its absence, we would produce a mechanism in which changes in arousal would leave unchanged the value of β for which the detection rate was 50%. A comparison of this mechanism with the earlier one shows that in a sense the raising of the zero point corresponds to a bias of the mechanism against the signal, but in such a way that the subsequent processes can recover all the information about signal occurrence as efficiently as if the zero point were at the value where β equals one.

The particular mechanisms we have been describing are of course implausible. They are used only to explain the point that a decision mechanism reporting at a constant value of evidence may perform with the same d' and with either higher or lower β if the distributions of evidence following signal and non-signal are transformed systematically. On any such model the distance between different criteria, in terms of z-scores, will decrease as the underlying scale of evidence is expanded. This is of course the effect which has been shown empirically to result from the presence of loud noise; and we can therefore describe the effect of noise more rationally as an expansion of the underlying scale of evidence, leaving the various criteria of confidence spaced at the same intervals of evidence as they were in quiet.

If this is the effect of noise, do we need anything else to explain the data? We cannot tell in advance where the zero point of unchanging β will be. But we can examine the data to see where the zero point is empirically; since if

RN = Z-score for detections at the risky criterion in noise

CN = Z-score for detections at the cautious criterion in noise

RQ = Z-score for detection at the risky criterion in quiet

CQ = Z-score for detections at the cautious criterion in quiet
x = Z-score for detections at the zero point.

Then

$$\frac{RN-x}{RQ-x} = \frac{CN-RN}{CQ-RQ}, \text{ (assuming } d' \text{ is unchanged).}$$

Looking at the data of Broadbent and Gregory (1965a) (Table I) in this way, one sees that the zero point lies at different places at the beginning and the end of the work period; indeed, this is implied by the results already summarized. Initially, the zero point lies at the position of the most risky criterion or at a point yet more risky still. Thus, at the beginning of the run the closing

TABLE I

Performance in Noise and Quiet at Beginning and End of Watch measured as Z-scores of Detections, from the data of Broadbent and Gregory (1965a)

Group	Cautious criterion Quiet	Noise	Risky criterion Quiet	Noise	Zero point
One source, many signals					
Beginning	0·18	0·44	0·68	0·70	0·72
End	0·08	0·08	0·64	0·36	0·08
One source, few signals					
Beginning	0·26	0·61	0·88	1·18	4·18
End	0·15	0·23	0·84	0·84	0·84
Three sources, many signals					
Beginning	0·38	0·61	0·84	0·96	1·29
End	0·36	0·36	0·95	0·80	0·36

together of the criteria by noise takes place with no marked reduction in the number of detections at any criteria, but rather some sign of an increase especially at the most cautious criterion. At the end of the run on the other hand, the zero point is in a considerably more cautious position; usually in the neighbourhood of the most cautious criterion. (In one group, having a very low signal frequency, the initial position is well below that of the most risky criterion and the final position in the neighbourhood of that criterion.) Thus at the end of the work period the effect of noise is to reduce the number of detections at the risky criterion, except in the one group with a low signal frequency already mentioned. Even that group however does give a shift in its zero point in the same direction as the others. It is this shift in the zero point which causes the effects of noise to be harmful to the detection rate only at the end of the work period, and then only at the most risky criterion.

The calculation of a single zero point assumes that the effects of noise are confined to expanding the scale of evidence, and that the change during the work period is the same whether the man works in noise or in quiet. We must also suppose that the man makes his various judgments of confidence at criteria which are separated from one another by a constant amount but which are not always in the same place with reference to the zero point; at the beginning of the run most judgments are above the zero, while at the end they are often below it. This seems odd, if not completely inconceivable.

To give an analogy to show how this might happen, it is as if a man was asked to judge "loud" or "soft" of two sounds presented repeatedly in random order, and as if the two stimuli were both reduced in intensity during the experiment until, perhaps, the louder was weaker than the original soft value. As we shall discuss later, in a real experiment of such a type judgments of "loud" will continue to be given at least part of the time even at the end of the session. It is therefore possible to imagine a mechanism wherein both signal and non-signal gave rise to evidence whose average value was lower later in the work period; and nevertheless judgments of "Sure there was a signal" might continue to be given to evidence which was originally too weak to produce such a judgment.

An experiment which might shed light on this point would be to ask for a numerical estimate of confidence rather than a rating. In studies on assessing loudness of a series of stimuli, judgment is much less inclined to be relative to the mean intensity of the series if the man is allowed to use a numerical scale of response rather than the fixed framework of a rating scale. This is a point to which we shall return in the next chapter but one; for the moment, the point is that a numerical estimate of confidence might remain fixed with respect to the hypothetical zero point, and so show a more marked change in confidence during a run even than that which has been possible with rating scales.

Is there any other means of analysing these results, without supposing a zero point?

Another way to handle the data would be to suppose that the various criteria are all separated by a constant amount from each other and also from some reference point. This point cannot then be the same in quiet and noise. It might lie, for example, halfway between the cautious and risky criteria; if so, to fit the data of Broadbent and Gregory, it would at the beginning of the run need to lie at a value corresponding to lower β in noise than in quiet, while at the end of the run it would need to correspond to a higher β in noise than in quiet. Thus this approach avoids the need to have the criteria altering their relation to the zero; at the cost of supposing a different trend during the run if noise is present.

The alternatives are (a) to suppose a "zero point" which moves in the cautious direction during the watch either in noise or quiet; but which lies below the judgment criteria initially and above them finally. (b) To suppose a "reference point" always at a fixed distance from the judgment criteria. The reference point, like the hypothetical zero point, would move in the direction of increased caution as the watch proceeded. Unlike the zero point, however, it would show a more marked trend of this kind when noise was present.

At present it seems to be a matter of taste which of these possibilities one thinks more likely. Both of them explain why the decrement during the run is largely a matter of the cautious criterion: in either case the argument would be that any individuals who happened to show a drop in arousal during a run in quiet might well show a rise in detections at their most risky criterion, and thus deprive any measurement at that criterion of statistical significance. Unless there were many people who showed a rise in arousal during the run, however, the most cautious criterion should either follow or even improve upon the decrement shown by the zero point or the reference point, whichever is supposed by one's favourite theory.

A possible way of distinguishing the two models would be to introduce noise only towards the end of the work period. If the change during the run is independent of noise, and that condition merely shifts criteria towards the zero point, then performance in noise at the end of the session should be the same whether or not noise has been present throughout it. If however noise first raises and then lowers detections as compared with performance in quiet, applying the noise only at the end of the session might well give quite different results from putting it in throughout.

Whichever theory is true, however, noise must either leave the decrement unchanged or else accentuate it. Here is another argument that noise does not produce an effect opposite to that of prolonged work. We cannot therefore adopt the view that the decrement is due to lowered arousal of a kind which noise increases. Unfortunately, we do not have much evidence of the way in which the trend of the zero point (or the reference point) is affected by changes in the event rate of the task when the signal/non-signal ratio is kept constant; and very little evidence of the way the trend during the run is altered by changes in signal rate for constant event rate. This makes it hard to distinguish the possible role of expectancy and of other kinds of arousal in the decrement. For what it is worth, we have the results summarized earlier of Broadbent and Gregory and of Simpson, that the trend of β is unaffected by signal probability, and the balance of probability therefore favours the idea that the trend is not due to expectancy. More evidence is clearly needed however: data on the effects of signal probability on decrement are of little use without confidence ratings, as they may be contaminated to an unknown extent by expansion of the scale of evidence.

If the trend were not due to expectancy, and is not due to a fall in the kind of arousal which noise increases, what could explain it? We have used several times the phrase "another kind of arousal" without further explanation. So far we have confined ourselves to looking at the effects of expanding and contracting the scale on which evidence is arrayed, while holding constant the position of the decision criteria in some absolute units. The position of the criteria is however decided, according to detection theory, by the gains and losses for correct detections and for various kinds of error. In psychophysics there is evidence that altering gains and losses does move criteria in the appropriate direction, so that a large penalty for false alarms gives a higher β and so on. In vigilance, Levine has shown similarly that changing the gains and losses shifts β, although the direction of shift is not always that expected theoretically. If therefore prolonged work were to change the balance of gain and loss it might well give a trend in β on which the various complications due to expanding and contracting scales could be superimposed.

Theoretically

$$\beta = \frac{\text{Loss due to false positive}}{\text{Gain due to hit}} \times \frac{1-p}{p}.$$

It follows therefore that simple multiplication or division of gains and losses will not alter β; and experimental evidence has been produced by Galanter and Holman (1967) to show in the psychophysical case that β does remain constant if one multiplies by a constant the amounts of money given for correct and fined for incorrect responses. But if prolonged work altered the gain without affecting the loss, as was suggested by Broadbent and Gregory (1963a), then β would change. Alternatively, prolonged work might change the values of gain and loss by some other method than simple multiplication, say by altering the power to which they were raised (multiplying and dividing their logarithms). In that case changes in the general state might well cause β to shift up and down from the point where loss is equal to gain. At that point

$$\beta = \frac{1-p}{p}.$$

It will be recalled that Levine found a rise in β for *all* increases in costs, even for misses. But here again Simpson's result, on the trend in β still being an increase with a value of p greater than 0·5, becomes crucial, and seems to make a general change in both gains and losses unlikely. None of the evidence we have considered, however, rules out the possibility of a drop in subjective gain for hits as the work proceeds.

SUMMARY

To summarize the position on the changes of β in vigilance, some of them (those produced by pre-training) are clearly controlled by signal probability: and in addition there appears to be an expansion or contraction of the scale of evidence which moves different values of β towards and away from each other. Some people show an expansion during the work period and some a contraction: but loud noise typically reduces the separation of values of β. Both for that reason and because such a change might result from a magnification of neural activity, this change of the scale of evidence is probably an arousal change. It is superimposed however on a trend during the work period, which is not a change in the scale of evidence but rather a shift of the whole scale in an unresponsive direction. This shift is either unchanged or actually increased by noise. It might conceivably be an expectancy effect of the "vicious circle" type, or else a motivational change of a kind corresponding to a drop in the (relative) gain from making a hit. Because very largely of one study by Simpson, the latter seems slightly the more probable. We have now reached the borders of existing knowledge on the subject, although there are a number of clear lines for further experiment, and can go no further in our explanations as yet.

General Conclusions About Vigilance

It has long been clear that no single theory would encompass all the phenomena of vigilance; in 1958, Broadbent argued that expectancy and arousal both dictated the general level of performance during a run, but that the decrement in some tasks was due to an increase in the number of occasions on which the filter failed to select information from the task. Decrement in a task was associated with the use of a transient signal, which could come and go while the filter was occupied elsewhere. The difficulty in this view was that Jerison's two tasks both had transient signals, but one showed a decrement and the other did not. We now know that one must distinguish between transience of the signal and event rate. A signal which remains visible until dealt with does not require continuous sustained attention (filtering) to the task; but it does not follow that a transient signal requires sustained attention. If the event rate is low, it may not.

One can sum up as follows:

(1) High event rate tasks, including those with transient signals occurring at unexpected times. There will be a decrement in d' during the run, which will result in a decrement in detections unless β moves in a compensating fashion. That is, sensory information will fail to get through at the end of the run, which seems like Broadbent's original filtering.

(2) Transient signals with low event rates. These will show no decrement in d', and filter theory is therefore inadequate. There is however a general and

underlying trend to higher β during the task, which may or may not cause a fall in detections. If β is high it will do so. If β is low there may be no change in detections during the run, because a spreading of the gap between cautious and risky β may in some subjects cancel out the underlying shift to higher β of the reference or zero point of the scale. (The difference between Jerison's two tasks is to be explained by the difference in β induced by the much higher signal rate in the multi-source task; a similar comparison of one and three source monitoring, but with overall signal rate held constant, shows equal decrement for both conditions; Wiener, 1964.)

(3) Non-transient signals. These will typically show no decrement in detection rate; since brief failures of filtering will not be relevant. Equally, the rise in β will not mean that the signal has no effect, but merely that it does not at first produce enough confidence to justify response. A further observing response will increase confidence sufficiently to give a reaction, and thus detections will be normal but latency will increase.

Superimposed on these changes during the work period will be differences in β due to the probability of a signal at any given instant; these will normally affect performance throughout the run equally, but if training has been inappropriate to the conditions of performance there may be a trend during the run as the man readjusts. There will also be the effects of arousal in expanding the scale of evidence, that is, in reducing the number of responses given with intermediate confidence.

Further work seems to be needed to clarify the nature of the underlying trend to higher β during the run, and particularly whether it is affected by event rate, signal probability, and the presence of conditions such as noise. It would be desirable also for more data to be provided on the conditions affecting the filtering mechanism of decrement, the d' change, such as the extent to which it is true of other senses than the eye, the extent to which the probability of a signal in a given location alters d' rather than β, and so on.

Most of the foregoing conclusions concern the decrement during the work period rather than the level of performance throughout the watch: although we said originally that a real problem was the fact that the average level was often low, regardless of decrement. To some extent the low level of performance can now be seen to be due to a high β, itself due to low signal probability. It can also, so far as confident detections are concerned, be due to low arousal causing a large region of detections with intermediate confidence. There remains the point however that d' itself is undoubtedly much less in vigilance than for the same signal in psychophysical conditions, so that these explanations cannot be the whole story. There must also be extra randomness within the observer, reducing the effect of the stimulus. Yet, because of the rough constancy of d' at high and low values of β, this randomness is unlikely to be due to failures of observing response in tasks where intermittent attention is sufficient. In such cases therefore it seems that it must be due to a variability in β from moment to moment: which will itself appear in our calculations as a change in d'.

General Conclusions about Human Functioning

Although we may not have solved all the problems of vigilance, we have in this chapter encountered a number of features of human performance which will colour all our subsequent discussions; and this was the reason for introducing vigilance as the first topic. We have seen that the probability of response under two conditions may be related either by a straight-line function, suggesting that the two probabilities are simply being added; or by a curve which straightens out when we transform the probabilities to z-scores. The latter implies that small changes in one probability may have large effects on the other, and this makes possible large changes in correct responding from adjustments of the type which we have called pigeon-holing; that is, extending the range of evidence which will give rise to a particular category state. We have seen that one can distinguish factors which alter pigeon-holing from those which alter the reliability of the incoming information; and that in some cases performance is improved by the former and in others by the latter. The mechanism of filtering, which was important in 1958, is one of the processes altering the inflow of information and is still necessary to explain certain effects. Pigeon-holing however, which was not considered in 1958, is clearly necessary for others, and particularly is the mechanism which mediates many of the effects of signal probability.

Our next step should be to consider some of the phenomena of perceptual selection, a field in which filtering is perhaps of a greater relative importance than in vigilance; though even here we shall see that pigeon-holing plays a part. Before doing so however it may be useful to explain certain features of the auditory mechanism, of particular importance for the perception of speech, since much of the work on perceptual selection uses auditory stimulation. In addition, this allows us to give a concrete example of the mechanism of filtering at a low level of the nervous system. This will clarify what is meant by the term before it is used more widely.

CHAPTER IV

Some Necessary Preliminaries on the Nature of the Auditory System

This chapter may be regarded as a slight digression in the general line of argument. It sets out, very much in outline and without the technical detail that would be desired by specialists, some rather little known features of hearing. These may be necessary to allow the reader to follow the succeeding chapter on perceptual selection; those who are already well-informed about the auditory system may wish to skip straight to that chapter. It is however desirable to make these points available, since many elementary texts about hearing do not include them and they are consequently unknown to a number of psychologists. The main point which will emerge by the end of the chapter is that one can demonstrate at quite an elementary level of the auditory system a mechanism which operates in a way which we described in the first chapter as "filtering". That is, there is a system which groups together sensory events which possess some common characteristic, and then analyses the other features of those events before a response is obtained.

The Analyses of Complex Sounds

Let us start by considering the nature of the auditory stimulus. If we take the ordinary kind of sounds normally met in real life, such as the sound of a human voice, and apply some mechanical device so as to record the sound pressure level in the air at successive instants of time, we will obtain a very complicated and irregular looking pattern of changes. If the sound is a steady one, such as somebody singing a constant vowel sound on a steady pitch, the pattern of changes of sound pressure level will repeat itself over and over again. It is a mathematical truth that such a repeating and complicated wave can be represented as the sum of a number of simple components. The components are simple because each of them consists of a series of waves reaching the same amplitude, and each following the preceding one at the same time interval. Different components will of course have different time intervals, and may well have different amplitudes. There is however only one combination of components which will add together to make a particular complex wave: so we can specify the complex wave in terms of the *amplitude* of each of its components, and the particular time interval characteristic of each of them. (It is of course more usual to talk about the reciprocal of the time interval, namely the *frequency* of the component.) In order to specify the original wave completely, we also need to know the *phase* relationship between each of the components; that is, we need to know which components have their peaks of amplitude at the same time, and for each of the other components whereabouts their cycle has reached at that time. Unless we specify phase, we have not completely determined what the shape of the total wave is going to be, since we can take a given set of simple waves of known frequency and amplitude, and by adding them in different phase relationships we get quite different-looking total waves.

Let us labour this point a little further, by considering an example of the analysis of a complex wave. The example is not chosen randomly, and we shall in fact be considering waves of this kind on a number of occasions in this chapter. The type of wave to be considered is that produced by tapping with a ruler a wineglass containing some water. As most of us know, the glass possesses a natural frequency of vibration, and tapping it in this way will cause it to shake at that frequency and so to cause changes in sound pressure in the air around it. The result will be a wave which has the frequency of the glass, but which dies away fairly rapidly to zero since nothing is maintaining the vibration. Let us now tap the glass again: whereupon another similar burst of sound will occur. In the extreme case, let us suppose that we manage to tap the glass over and over again, perhaps 100 times a second, and that in consequence we keep producing bursts of wave at the frequency of the glass: to be specific, let us suppose that we have managed to tune our glass to vibrate 2000 times per second. The result is a wave which rises above the resting atmospheric level of pressure 2000 times per second: but which only rises to its highest amplitude 100 times per second, and following each such peak gives a series of successively smaller peaks until the next major burst begins.

We can now represent a complex wave of this sort as the sum of a number of components, the most important of which is a simple repeating wave at a frequency of 2000. (The unit of repetitions of a wave per second is now known as Herz, and abbreviated Hz.) In addition to this main component at 2000 Hz, there are other smaller components at 2100 and at 1900, others smaller still at 2200 and 1800, others smaller again at 2300 and at 1700, and so on. The various components are centred about the natural frequency of the wineglass, and are spaced out from it at steps which correspond to the frequency with which the ruler is tapping the glass. We might as well introduce two terms to which we shall refer a good deal later, and call the frequency of the wineglass the "carrier frequency" and the frequency with which the ruler is tapping the glass the "modulation frequency". One can see readily enough how these terms are derived: the carrier frequency is the basic rate of vibration, while the modulation frequency is the rate at which the amplitude of wave increases and decreases. Notice again that we have not said anything about phase; and while it is true that we can represent the wave produced by our rapid tapping of the wineglass by a series of components of the type described, it would not necessarily be true that a series of simple waves having those frequencies and amplitudes would add together to give a complex wave exactly like that produced by the wineglass. If the phase relationships between the components were wrong, the resulting wave would look different, and in particular might not have such marked changes in amplitude.

THE FREQUENCY ANALYSING MECHANISM OF THE EAR

We have taken one particular complex wave, which happens to be of interest to us, but by a similar analysis any complex sound can be split into a number of components of different frequency. Now in general a listener exposed to a complex sound made up of components widely spaced in frequency can hear a number of separate elements in his experience, and when he is presented with a simple wave at a frequency corresponding to any one of the components of a complex wave, he will then identify the sound of this simple wave as similar to that of one of the components he hears in the complex wave. In other words, the ear seems to carry out an analysis of complex waves into the components which mathematically can be recombined to give the original complex. For this reason, most research on hearing has concentrated upon simple waves, and has tried to elucidate the ways in which different properties of a simple wave are related to different aspects of the man's experience. As we have said, different simple waves can differ in amplitude and in frequency: roughly speaking, if we play to a man two simple waves which differ only in amplitude, he will say that they differ in loudness: whereas if we play to him two waves which differ in frequency, he will say that they differ in pitch. This rule is by no means absolute, since for example two waves of equal amplitude but different frequencies may often differ in loudness as well as in pitch, but it is broadly true. The aim of researchers has therefore tended to be one much in line with the general tenor of this book; they seek to find out what set of states in the ear, and in the message in the auditory nerve, corresponds to the set of different amplitudes of the original stimulus: since information on amplitude is apparently preserved in the man's judgments of loudness. Similarly, and perhaps more importantly, they seek to find out the set of states in the ear and the nerve which corresponds to the set of possible frequencies of a simple stimulus wave, since judgments of pitch preserve the information in that feature of the stimulus.

If now one considers the layout of the actual sense-organs of the ear one finds that the neural message starts at a series of receptors arranged along a membrane, the basilar membrane. As any introductory text in psychology will indicate, this membrane is contained in a spiral tubular structure known as the cochlea, and the pressure changes in the air outside the ear are transmitted through a system of mechanical linkages to the bottom end of the cochlea. Two obvious theories or classes of theories then suggest themselves: one is that loud sounds stimulate some receptors on the basilar membrane which are not stimulated by soft sounds, while high frequency sounds differ from low frequency sounds in stimulating the same receptors more frequently. The second alternative theory is that the physical structure of the cochlea and the basilar membrane somehow perform the mathematical analysis of a complex sound into its different components so that high frequency components stimulate some receptors at one part of the basilar membrane, while

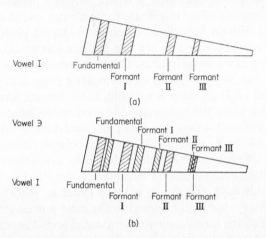

FIG. 15. The activity on the basilar membrane, when a vowel is heard. In (a), the vowel in *beet* is striking the ear; in (b), the same vowel together with another vowel such as that in *bird*. How does the brain know which regions of stimulation belong together?

low frequency components stimulate other receptors at another part. An increase in the amplitude of the stimulus could then be represented either by an increase in the width of the area stimulated on the basilar membrane, or possibly by an increase in the frequency of nerve impulses from the same receptors, as that has been found to be the nature of the coding in certain other sensory pathways. It is the latter of these two theories which is nowadays most widely presented in texts for non-specialists, and there is indeed no question whatever that a mechanism of this kind exists.

The original version of this popular theory, which was due to Helmholtz, suggested that different parts of the basilar membrane resonated to different components in the stimulus: that is, that any one part of the membrane had a natural frequency just as our wineglass did. When a complex wave was

E

delivered to the membrane the particular region would vibrate maximally to any component at its own frequency. It would thus stimulate its attached receptor organs only when such a component was present. The shape of the membrane happened to lend itself to a theory of this kind, as it is narrow at one end and wide at the other, just as the arrangement of wires in a piano or a harp is. The idea was therefore that receptors at the narrow end responded to high frequencies and those at the wide end to low frequencies. (To confuse terminology, the narrow end of the membrane is at the bottom end of the cochlea, where the sound enters: so low notes would be heard by receptors at 'he top end of the membrane, which is also the wide end.)

This theory of resonance is now untenable, because it is clear that the mechanical structure of the membrane would not allow the right kind of sharply tuned response. However, it is still perfectly possible to get more activity at the wide end of the membrane for low notes, and at the narrow end for high notes, without appealing to resonance. Direct observation by the membrane by von Bekesy has shown that the stimulus produces a travelling wave proceeding along the membrane from the bottom of the cochlea to the top, rather as one may produce a wave travelling along a skipping rope by shaking one end while the other is held still. In the ear, the wave dies away at a certain distance along the membrane, and produces its biggest displacement at a point just before it disappears. This point moves along the membrane as the frequency of the stimulus is changed. The biggest displacement of the membrane does therefore occur at the wide end for low notes and the narrow end for high notes, even though the membrane is not like the wires of a piano or a harp. In this form, this theory is better called a "place" theory than a "resonance" theory, but it still belongs to the same general class of theories. The way in which the travelling wave is produced and changed in its characteristics by changes in the applied frequency depends upon a complex pattern of mechanical properties of the solid and fluid parts of the cochlea, and a number of mechanical models have been built which demonstrate the same kind of behaviour.

In addition to the direct observations which have shown that stimulation of the narrow end of the membrane is greatest for high frequencies, electrical recording near that end of the cochlea reveals a greater response when high frequency stimuli are present than when low frequencies are; while at the other end, the relationship is reversed. Experimentally induced damage to the narrow end of the membrane, in animals, gives a deafness specific to high frequencies, as it can be shown by behavioural testing. The ears of human beings who are deaf to particular high frequencies show damage in localized regions of the narrow end of the membrane rather than the wide end. Lastly, electrical recording from single fibres in the pathways of the auditory system shows that any one fibre responds most readily to a particular frequency, with reduced sensitivity to others adjacent to it: and that this relationship becomes more firm and determinate as one moves up the line of transmission towards the central mechanisms. (See for example Whitfield, 1967 for a detailed review of recent advances in this area.)

At this point the reader may well wonder why it is worth even mentioning the opposing class of theory, since it is clear that the place mechanism is so solidly based. This is especially true since the alternative theory, that the frequency of the stimulus is encoded into the frequency of impulses in the auditory nerve, requires some mechanism at a later stage to perform a complex analysis on time intervals between impulses, which may well by that stage have become unreliable. There are however certain general reasons for dissatisfaction with a theory based purely on place, which have been set out by Wever (1950). In brief, they are that the evidence already mentioned applies largely to discrimination between one fairly high frequency and another. The direct observations by von Bekesy do not show very much of a change in the place in the membrane most stimulated when one changes, say, from 200 Hz to 100 Hz. It is a change from 3000 Hz to 2000 Hz which is more likely to be noticeable. Similarly, it is hard to produce experimental deafness to specific low frequencies, nor does one encounter patients with a deafness to specific low frequencies and damage to a corresponding localized part of the basilar membrane. They may be deaf to all low frequencies, and have widespread damage covering large portions of the membrane, but they do not have the kind of deafness frequently found at high frequencies. At the upper end of the spectrum, a man may be quite severely deaf at 6000 Hz, with fairly normal hearing at 4000 and 8000: and post-mortem examination of his ear will show a corresponding narrow belt of damage. Lastly, the specific frequencies to which units in the cochlear nerve respond are normally fairly high.

For these reasons, the typical reviewer of the subject will often suggest that there may be a different mechanism for the perception of pitch at low frequencies. This is regrettable from the point of view of parsimony, and some investigators would therefore prefer to hold that the place theory would still apply throughout the spectrum, explaining the various difficulties by reference to complex lateral interactions between the receptors at different points at the wide end of the basilar membrane. There is also perhaps an understandable feeling that a mechanism applying only when the frequency of the stimulus gets below four figures is of relatively minor importance. The region of the ear of maximum sensitivity lies at 1000 or 2000 Hz, and the low frequency end of the scale can perhaps be regarded as a rather specialist interest.

In terms of everyday experience or of musical pitch, however, this is not altogether justified. If we start considering a frequency as low when it goes below 1000 Hz, we are including pitches up to two octaves above middle C: which itself is an octave or so above the pitch of an ordinary male speaking voice. The bulk of musical pitch and the pitch of human voices lies in the region of the spectrum where the place theory has not been satisfactorily demonstrated. There are therefore general grounds for keeping a distinctly open mind about the possible importance of an alternative mechanism.

The Perception of Pitch
in Complex Amplitude Modulated Sounds

Let us now return to the kind of wave produced by our rapid tapping of a wineglass. It will be recalled that the largest component in the resulting complex was at 2000 Hz, with other components spaced out from that value at intervals of 100 Hz. If one listens to such a complex wave, the impression is distinctly different from that of a single component at 2000. In fact, if most listeners are given an oscillator of adjustable frequency, and asked to produce a simple wave matching the pitch of the complex, they will adjust it to about 100 Hz. Thus the apparent pitch of a wave of this sort is not that of the component at which there is most energy, and it may even be that there is no component at all in the neighbourhood of the spectrum where a simple wave of matching pitch would be placed. This is by no means an abstract laboratory phenomenon: most of us feel that we can hear the pitch of a spoken voice over the telephone, despite the fact that the telephone system does not pass components below about 300 Hz, and that the pitch of spoken voices is considerably below that value. We shall see later that human voices are closely similar to the amplitude modulated sounds under discussion.

An obvious explanation of this effect is that the timing of impulses in the auditory nerve is related to the times of greatest amplitude of stimulation, and that therefore the frequency of impulses preserves information about the modulation frequency. In the case of a simple wave the frequency of impulses has no modulation frequency to follow and simply follows the carrier frequency. If now perceived pitch were related to the frequency of impulses leaving the receptor organs, rather than to the particular receptors which were stimulated, the pitch of the complex wave might be the same as that of a simple wave of a frequency much below the carrier frequency of the complex.

This however would be a complete reversal of the place theory, at least for this region of the spectrum, and one must therefore consider carefully the possible artifacts in the original observation. The most serious of these is the possibility that the process of getting the sound from the eardrum to the receptors may introduce a component at a frequency which was not in the original sound stimulus, but is at that corresponding to the perceived pitch. This is in fact the explanation which has normally been accepted by place theorists for the phenomenon under discussion; since it has of course been known since the time of Helmholtz himself. The original explanation was in terms of "non-linear distortion". By this is meant the mathematical truth that unless the displacement of the basilar membrane is perfectly proportional to the pressure reaching the eardrum, the wave on the membrane will contain extra components. Suppose for example that the displacement on the membrane is partially proportional to the square of the pressure at the eardrum rather than to the pressure itself. In that case, for every pair of components in the original stimulus there will be four new components in the wave on the membrane. The frequencies of these new components will be the octave of each of the original ones, the sum of the original ones, and their difference. It is of course the latter which is of special interest in the present connection: if a whole series of components is present, spaced out at the modulation frequency, then there will from every one of these pairs be a contribution to a component at the same value of frequency, which in the case considered happens to be the pitch we hear. Still further contributions may come from other products of distortion, due to the cube of the original stimulus and so on: and it is certainly very plausible that transmission through the complicated mechanical system from the eardrum to the receptors themselves should include distortions of this sort, even though they may be slight ones. The fact that one can recognize the pitch of a spoken voice over the telephone was not therefore regarded as a major difficulty for place theory. Furthermore, some of the mechanical models devised in recent years to imitate the travelling wave action of the cochlea have the property of reintroducing components at the fundamental frequency of a series of harmonics: that is, at the frequency corresponding to the difference between a set of equally spaced components. Place theorists can therefore feel reasonably content to ignore the basic phenomenon of the perception of pitch of an amplitude modulated sound.

In recent years, however, the basic phenomenon has been demonstrated in a variety of ways which exclude completely the possibility that a new component is present in such sounds when they actually reach the receptor organs. The start of this line of work is due to J. F. Schouten, writing in 1938 to 1940 in Holland: the results have been conveniently summarized by Licklider (1956) and Plomp (1966). The core of Schouten's contribution was to present a complex sound produced by a series of pulses occurring 200 times per second: but with the component at 200 Hz removed. The resulting sound is made up of components spaced at 200 Hz intervals but with the lowest component at 400 Hz: and has a very strong pitch corresponding to 200. If now another simple wave is introduced from another generator, and adjusted in frequency and phase in the neighbourhood of 200 Hz, it ought to be possible to show interference between such a real physical component and any other real physical component which is present on the basilar membrane as a result of distortion of the original stimulus. When the frequencies are very close together for example, the two waves ought to reinforce each other at intervals and then to cancel out at other times, giving rise to a rough sound known as a beat. It did not prove possible to show such an interference between a real component at the neighbourhood of 200 Hz and any part of the complex sound with the same pitch. These results were later challenged by Hoogland in a doctoral thesis for the University of Utrecht (summarized by Licklider, 1956), but in his case the complex sounds were made up by quite separate generators producing the different components spaced out at regular intervals. Since the phase of the different generators was not controlled, the resulting wave form would probably not be sharply modulated: remember the discussion of this point in our original outline of the nature of the auditory stimulus. It is known from the work of Mathes and Miller (1947) that one can hear a difference when the phase of closely adjacent components is adjusted relative to each other, and Licklider (1956) showed that this was indeed the explanation of the discrepancy between the results of Hoogland and Schouten.

Another line of attack was employed by de Boer (1956). We have so far considered only the case in which the carrier frequency is a simple multiple of the modulation frequency. In that case, the perceived pitch is the same as the difference in frequency between the various components, and this makes an explanation due to non-linear distortion especially likely. However, there is no reason whatever why one should not make up a sound in which the various components are spaced at an interval which does not divide perfectly into the frequency of any of them. For instance, one could use a complex wave whose carrier frequency was 2030 Hz, with other components spaced out at intervals of 200 Hz at each side of that frequency. Non-linear distortion ought, with such a complex wave, to produce a new component at 200 Hz: but in fact the pitch is slightly higher than that value, and corresponds more nearly to a simple wave at a frequency of 203 Hz. This is quite consistent with the idea that the pitch is due to the periodicity of the complex wave, because if one examines the wave produced by a set of "inharmonic" components of this kind one can see that it does tend to repeat itself at an interval which is not quite 200 Hz but rather a little higher.

The most clinching experiment is however one by Licklider (1956). The essence of the place interpretation of the low pitch of these complex sounds is that a component is present at the low frequency end of the basilar membrane, even though it is not present in the physical stimulus delivered to the eardrum. It is however generally agreed that the stimulation of receptors at one part of the membrane by one sound may make it impossible to detect another sound affecting the same part of the membrane: that is, a pure tone at 200 Hz will be masked by a noise of sufficient intensity which is of predominantly low frequency and includes 200 Hz within its spectrum. Such a noise, which will mask a real stimulus at 200 Hz, also ought to be capable of masking any component at that frequency which is re-introduced into a complex sound by the mechanism of the ear before the receptor organs. If however a complex sound is composed of components well up into the high frequency region, although amplitude modulated at a low frequency, then the receptors being affected will be untouched by the noise and the high frequency components should transmit messages to the central mechanisms without any interference from the noise. One must therefore expect on a place theory that, if a complex wave made up of high frequency components is delivered in the presence of an intense low frequency masking noise, then the apparent low pitch of the complex wave will change and it will be heard at a pitch more appropriate to the part of the spectrum where most of the energy is being carried. There is admittedly a problem of the intensity necessary to produce the masking: this can be met by making the complex wave equal in energy to a simple wave at the modulation frequency, and then adjusting the noise until it completely obliterates the simple wave. It cannot be held that any extra component introduced into the complex wave by distortion will contain more energy than the total complex, and the noise must therefore be adequate to mask any such component.

The results of this experiment are quite clear and striking: the complex wave remains audible with its pitch unchanged, when a simple wave of the same pitch has disappeared completely in the noise. It is completely impossible therefore to explain the pitch of a complex wave as being due to the presence at the basilar membrane of a component absent from the original stimulus.

A number of other experiments on the perception of a pitch corresponding to the modulation frequency have been conducted by various authors, and are reviewed by Plomp (1966). He discusses in considerably more detail the implications of these findings, and presents himself an important series of studies on consonance and dissonance which point in the same direction. Broadly speaking, one must conclude from these studies that the place stimulated on the basilar membrane is important in determining pitch only at frequencies above about 1400 Hz, which as already indicated is a high pitch musically speaking. Below that frequency there operates increasingly a pitch mechanism based on the periodicity of the complex wave rather than on the frequency of its components. These experiments are of course purely behavioural, and there remains the problem of the neural mechanism which transmits the periodic character of the wave through the auditory nerve. It is likely, however, that the periodicity of the stimulus is encoded somehow into the repetition rate or periodicity of the impulses in the nerve fibre. A crude possibility would be that an amplitude modulated wave at a certain carrier frequency will stimulate receptors corresponding to that carrier frequency, and will produce a rate of firing which is equal to the modulation frequency. For the purposes of transmitting the information, however, it would of course be equally adequate if the rate of firing was, say, half the modulation frequency: which is especially likely at the upper end of the frequency range to which this mechanism applies. It would also be possible, for example, to get rapid bursts of impulses occurring in clusters which themselves repeated at the modulation frequency. Unhappily, complex waves of this type are rarely used as stimuli in physiological experiments, and consequently any suggestions on the point must be somewhat speculative: it should be noticed however that Davies *et al.* (1951) found that an amplitude modulated signal, which was rather at the borderline of the two mechanisms and which could be matched in pitch either to carrier frequency or to modulation frequency, was stimulating the region of the basilar membrane that corresponded to carrier frequency; and was producing in the nerve a rate of firing corresponding to modulation frequency.

It may seem curious that a dual mechanism of this kind should exist, and one of the minor purposes of this chapter is to indicate a sound biological reason why it should. To understand why this should be so, we must turn now to the nature of speech sounds.

The Generation of Speech

It will be recalled that we started our discussion of the acoustic stimulus by thinking of a wineglass being tapped repeatedly by a ruler. We extended this to the case in which the ruler is tapping extremely rapidly, faster than would in fact be practicable by that method. When a man speaks, his vocal chords allow a series of bursts of air to pass up into the cavities of his head. Each such burst strikes the first cavity it reaches, rather like the ruler tapping a wineglass: since a space full of air has a natural frequency just as the glass does. If therefore we imagine the rather artificial situation of a single space inside the man's head, receiving a series of pulses from the vocal chords, then we would expect the sound waves to come out with the same general structure as those produced by repeated tapping of a wineglass: they will have a carrier frequency corresponding to the natural frequency of the cavity, and a modulation frequency corresponding to the rate of pulsing produced by the vocal chords. There is of course more than one cavity: at the very least, we ought for instance to consider as separate cavities the space between the vocal chords and the hump of the tongue, and the space between the hump and the lips. The sizes of these two spaces are different, and therefore they will have different natural frequencies. If we think of them each as being activated quite separately by the pulses from the vocal chords, there will therefore be two complex waves, having the same modulation frequency but different carriers. The same process can be extended to other cavities: as they get smaller and smaller the carrier frequencies will get fairly high and can perhaps be neglected. The sophisticated reader will of course already have noticed that the simplification of supposing the two spaces to be excited quite independently is an unfair one, and that it would be better to consider the vocal tract as a transmission line being driven from one end: this is perfectly true, but does not affect the essence of the argument to be used on this occasion. Those interested in the sophisticated description of the speech process on these lines are referred to Flanagan (1965).

Returning to our simple analysis, a man producing a "voiced" sound is therefore giving two or more complex waves mixed together, and one can specify the result by the modulation frequency and the two or more carrier frequencies. These can of course change: the man can vibrate his vocal chords faster or slower, and he can, by moving his tongue, jaw and other articulatory systems change the carrier frequencies also. Which of these quantities, then, transmits the information used in speech so that we know whether a man is saying "beat" or "boot"? The answer is quite clear: it is the carrier frequencies which transmit this information, while the modulation frequency is important primarily as conveying the intonation of the voice. Sometimes this may be useful semantically: if we say "they went to the beach" with a rising intonation it becomes a question or an indication of surprise rather than a simple statement. If however somebody maintains their modulation frequency at a steady rate we can understand pretty well what they are saying and merely note that they are talking on one note, like a recitative in opera.

If intelligibility is transmitted by the carrier frequencies in the complex sound, what is the coding? The various vowel sounds can be quite well represented by looking only at the first two carriers in the voice; that is, the two lowest frequencies at which there is a lot of energy. This is the point at which to indicate that, in talking about speech, these carrier frequencies are usually known as "formants". If the first formant is at a very low frequency, and the second is fairly high, we hear the vowel in "beat", while if both are low we hear that in "boot". If the first formant is relatively high we may hear vowels such as "bet" or "bert", depending on the position of the second formant. Getting the right vowel therefore depends upon detecting the position of both carrier frequencies in combination.

So much then for the vowels, which are steady continuous sounds: what about consonants? These are of course sounds of relatively short duration, and some of them do not involve vocal chord activity. There may be bursts of noise, produced by whistling air through different parts of the system, as in the sounds we normally represent by the letters F or S: acoustically, this gives a fairly wide band of noise with peaks in various places. The formant frequencies are still important however: if one says the word "pit" as opposed to the word "kit", there is in each case an initial sharp onset of sound, followed by the same steady vowel. When one says these words to oneself, however, one can feel that the mouth starts in a different position for the two words, and then moves rapidly to the same steady vowel position. As the bursts of sound begin to arrive from the vocal chords to produce the vowel, therefore, we catch the articulators in rather different positions depending upon where the whole operation started: and correspondingly the second formant frequency is changing rapidly at the very beginning of the vowel, from a position which is different in "pit" from that in "kit". These very rapid shifts in carrier frequency are therefore part of the acoustic message which causes

E*

us to distinguish one consonant from the other: and are known as "transitions". Similarly, the transition at the start of the first formant, rather than the second, may distinguish between "pit" and "bit". A correct identification of p, t, b, and d is heavily dependent upon detecting correctly the transitions both in the first formant and in the second formant.

We need not go into all the technicalities of acoustic phonetics, but it is clear therefore that many consonants as well as vowels depend on the reception of information about different carrier frequencies; and the combination of this information in order to identify the particular speech sound that is present. Turning now to the mechanism of hearing which we have considered previously, it is obvious that the place mechanism will transmit information satisfactorily about the carrier frequencies that are present, whereas the periodicity mechanism will convey information about the modulation frequency; the place mechanism is transmitting the relatively neutral information about intelligibility, while the periodicity mechanism is conveying that about intonation. This in itself, however, does not really indicate why there should have been two mechanisms, since it would be quite reasonable to pick up intonation by a further place system detecting the first frequency at which any energy is present. We must therefore go a little further before we can find any biological utility in the double mechanism.

Fusion and Filtering of Information at Different Sense Organs

The picture we have now reached is of a nervous system which is being stimulated at two or more locations along the basilar membrane, so that by detecting which receptors are active it is able to identify the particular speech sounds that are being received. This seems a simple mechanism so long as the only acoustic stimulation present is relevant. Suppose however that one is listening to a human voice under reasonably natural conditions. It is exceedingly unlikely that the only receptors being stimulated will be those corresponding to the formant frequencies in the voice itself. There are almost certainly other sounds present, which in normal listening we do not notice, but which will cause some of the receptors on the basilar membrane to be active even though the voice is not affecting them. How then does the central part of the system know how to identify which receptors are being stimulated by the wanted voice and which by some quite irrelevant sound? If the only information being transmitted from each receptor is whether or not it is being stimulated, there is no way of telling the relevant from the irrelevant receptors. Yet intelligibility of speech will hardly be affected at all by randomly placed bursts of pure tone superimposed on a recording: and in the extreme case as we shall see in later chapters, one can even make out what is being said by one voice when another is saying something completely different at the same time. There is a limit to this process when one sound masks the other, and presumably makes unavailable the receptors concerned: but there does not seem to be any particular difficulty in identifying which sense organs are being stimulated by a wanted voice, so long as no other sound is actually making use of those same sense organs. How then does the central mechanism identify the particular receptors being activated by one voice?

The problem goes further than merely fusing together different receptors on the same basilar membrane. A similar problem arises between the two ears. Normally speaking, if one applies different stimuli to the two ears they are heard quite separately and sharply localized on opposite sides of the head. If I receive a simple wave at a frequency of 500 Hz at one ear, and one of 1500 Hz at the other ear, I hear unequivocally a low note on one side and a high note on the other. Of course, two steady waves at 500 Hz sound like a single note, localized at a position which depends upon the exact phase relationships between the two waves. If the peak of one on my left ear occurs at the same time as the peak on my right ear, then the note sounds roughly central: if the one on the left ear occurs slightly earlier in time than the one on the right ear, then the fused sound sounds more to the left. When the frequencies rather than the phases are different, however, the sounds from the two ears do not fuse.

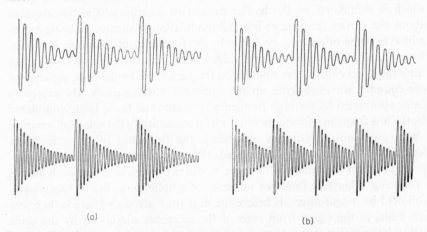

(a) (b)

FIG. 16. Waveforms which give perception of one sound when presented together (a); and others which give perception of two sounds (b). In (a) the same train of pulses is led through filters set to two different frequencies. In (b), two different pulse trains are used, although the filters are the same as in (a).

With speech sounds however the case is quite different. One can take the natural human voice, divide the sound into the upper frequencies of the spectrum and the lower frequencies of the spectrum; and then deliver one of the resulting waves to one ear and the other to the other ear. The result is a single fused percept in the middle of the head. This fact was known to Fletcher (1953), but is rediscovered from time to time, for example by

Broadbent (1955). With a natural voice, the interpretation is a little ambiguous since the voice may contain components quite close to the part of the spectrum where the filtering has taken place. Possibly therefore there may be some receptor stimulated on one basilar membrane which corresponds to the same frequency as some of those being stimulated on the other. In that case fusion might be expected, just as it occurs when we present two steady tones of 500 Hz. But one can in fact present artificially generated speech sounds, in which the components present are known, and none are in common between the first and second formants. It is still true that presentation of the first formant to one ear and the second formant to the other ear will produce a fused percept of a single voice. Apparently therefore the central mechanisms are able to identify that the low frequency receptors being stimulated on one basilar membrane are being affected by the same voice as the high frequency receptors being stimulated on the other basilar membrane. This raises yet more acutely the problem of the way in which information from different groups of receptors is combined together.

Let us now recall our earlier approach to the theory of hearing. The voice is made up of different complex waves, each possessing a different carrier frequency but the same modulation frequency. We would regard the place which is stimulated on the basilar membrane as transmitting information about the carrier frequency; but the modulation frequency is being transmitted in some other way, probably by the frequency of the nerve impulses. Since the whole wave in a natural voice results from the same series of pulses from the vocal chords, the modulation frequency will be the same for each of the complex waves making up the formants. Consequently, the receptors being stimulated by the high frequency formants and those being stimulated by the low frequency formants will both be transmitting the same information about modulation frequency: plausibly, the frequency of firing in fibres leading from them will be correlated. (We say correlated rather than supposing that the frequency is the same, to cover the case in which each fibre is producing a burst of impulses at peaks of amplitude in the incident wave, followed by longer intervals before the next peak arrives.) There is therefore available, in the signal from each of the receptors stimulated by the same voice, information that this group of receptors belongs together.

A check on this interpretation was made by Broadbent and Ladefoged (1957). They used both meaningless sounds and artificially generated speech sounds, but the sense of the results can be most clearly seen from the meaningless sounds. In brief, if we present a complex wave to the right ear and a different wave to the left ear, they are heard as a single sound even if the carrier frequencies are different, so long as the modulation frequency is the same. If however the modulation frequency is different, they are heard as separate sounds, one each side of the listener, even although the carrier frequency is the same. The latter result is especially important, because it

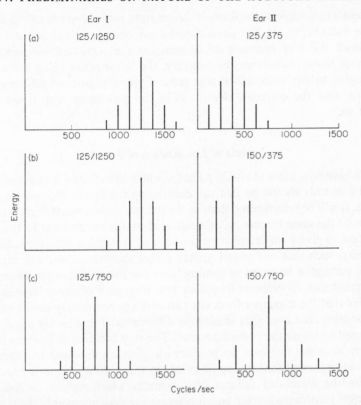

FIG. 17. Spectra of sounds which are delivered to the right and left ear, and which give perception of one voice (a) or of more than one (b and c). Notice that in (c) the greatest energy is at the same frequency in both ears, but in (a) it is at a quite different frequency. On the other hand, in (a) the wave-form is the same in both cases just as in (a) of Fig. 16. In (b) and (c) the wave-form is different, as in (b) of Fig. 16. Experiment performed by Broadbent and Ladefoged (1957).

shows that stimulation of corresponding points on the two basilar membranes does not necessarily produce fusion. The results with speech were essentially similar, and it was even possible to cause a voice presented to a single basilar membrane to disintegrate perceptually into different components, by using different modulation frequencies on the different formants.

Clearly therefore the central mechanisms do group together those carrier frequencies which share a single modulation frequency: plausibly, the mechanism is that if any receptor organ is being stimulated in such a way as to produce a pattern of nerve impulses correlated with the pattern from another receptor, then those receptors are treated as belonging together. Once the wanted pattern of nerve impulses is detected, it becomes worth while knowing which receptor was being stimulated, so that the original speech sounds can be recognized. We have here therefore a very simple and elementary example of the form of information processing termed "filtering" in the first chapter. It is of particular interest, because it is clearly not a case in which different channels of information are separated by stimulating different sense organs: on the contrary, the information being taken in as belonging to one voice has almost certainly itself stimulated different sense organs, and the common element is in the periodicity with which it has done so.

Aspects of Localization of Sounds

We have now made the main point for which this chapter is intended, but a few loose ends should be tied up, concerning the localization of sounds in space. It will be remembered that, in the last section, we noted that two sound waves of the same frequency, one delivered to one ear and one to the other, will fuse to give a single apparent sound; and that phase differences between the ears, such that one sound arrives earlier than the other, will cause the single percept to be heard as coming from one side or the other. In terms of the translation of stimulus frequency into frequency of nerve impulses, this implies that the messages from the two ears are not merely correlated with one another, but even that small time differences of lead or lag are detected and used to locate the resulting sound. The very fact that differences in time of arrival at the two ears do produce an effect on apparent localization is itself an argument that timing of events in the auditory nerve is important, despite the increasing failures of synchrony which appear as one takes electrical recordings further and further up the system towards the cortex.

Time differences between the ears are not of course the only information used for localizing sounds: intensity differences are also important. Indeed, with simple waves one could not locate unambiguously using time differences between the ears alone, above, say, 1000 Hz. The reason is that in a simple wave each successive peak is identical, so that if two successive peaks 1 and 2 arrive at the left ear separated by their normal interval, and if peak 1 reaches the right ear at more than half that interval, the brain will have no way of distinguishing this late arrival of peak 1 from an early arrival of peak 2 at the right ear. The sound might therefore be coming either from the left or the right. If the frequency is sufficiently low, the time between successive peaks is so great that this ambiguity does not arise: but it will become important at higher frequencies. In the natural state, intensity differences between the ears will not be large at low frequencies, because it so happens that at such frequencies the "shadow" cast by the head is relatively unimportant and therefore a sound approaching from the right will reach both right and left ears with almost equal intensity. At high frequencies however this is not true: and accordingly it has been usual since the pioneering work of Stevens and Newman (1936) to ascribe localization of high frequencies to intensity differences between the ears, and of low frequencies to time differences between the ears.

The classic view may underestimate the importance of time differences between the ears in real life: since natural sounds rarely consist of pure simple waves, but rather may have a modulation frequency. If we have a complex sound consisting of a higher carrier frequency with a low modulation frequency, it will be obvious that the relationship between the two ears becomes ambiguous only when the time differences become comparable with the modulation frequency rather than with the carrier frequency. If we go back to our wineglass analogy, the fact that the left ear is receiving the sound later than the right can still be detected even when the first rise in pressure on the left ear occurs after several rises and falls on the right ear. The changes in the peak amplitude provide the necessary information. Correspondingly, it has been shown by Leakey et al. (1958) that sounds in the upper part of the spectrum can be assigned to the right or left of the listener on the basis of time differences, provided that there is a low modulation frequency.

In general, a whole body of experiments by Cherry and his co-workers (see for example Sayers and Cherry, 1957) have shown that the lateralization of sounds can be represented by the working out of the correlation between the wave reaching one ear and that reaching the other, at various values of time interval between the two ears. When a maximum correlation is reached between the signal at the right ear at time t and that at the left at a later time $t + \delta t$, lateralization of the sound occurs to the right, and vice versa. With sounds containing simple components, the lateralization will shift backwards and forwards as the time delay is increased beyond the value of half a wave length, while intensity differences between the ear truncate the extent to which these swings of lateralization occur. Information concerning relative timing of the stimulation of the two ears is of key importance.

In order to keep clear this importance of timing at the two ears and the correlation of the two messages in order to form a fused percept, it may be necessary to clarify a point about stereophonic as opposed to natural localization of sounds. Under natural conditions, a sound arrives from a single point in space, and therefore reaches first the ear of the listener which is nearer to the source and then later the other ear. As explained previously, there may also be intensity differences between the two ears. In stereophonic localization, there are two sources of sound in the room, and each of these sources is heard by each of the listener's ears; for example, consider a listener who is sitting in between two stereo-loudspeakers, and who has put himself by chance one inch nearer the speaker on his left. If both speakers send out a sound simultaneously, it will arrive first at the listener's left ear from the left speaker, then at the right ear from the right speaker, then at the right ear from the left speaker, and lastly at the left ear from the right speaker. This is clearly something quite different from listening to a single source of sound but fortunately if there are no intensity differences, the pattern of stimulation described will give an apparent localization of the sound to the left of the listener, since the first pair of waves to arrive dominate the localization of the sound perceived (Wallach *et al.*, 1949). If a time difference is introduced between the activation of the two loudspeakers, by delaying the left speaker relative to the right, the difference in time of arrival of the first pair of sounds will become less, and will ultimately change to give a lead for the right ear. The time difference between the second pair of sounds will change in the opposite direction. This will stop the movement of the total percept being as great as it would be for a similar time difference between a simple pair of sounds, but nevertheless the net effect will be a shift of the apparent localization to the right. An intensity difference between the two loudspeakers will give a similar complex effect; a gain in intensity on the left loudspeaker will increase at the left ear the strength of the first sound as opposed to the second, but at the right ear will increase the intensity of the second sound to arrive rather than the first. Resolution of a complex wave into its components will show that this produces at the ears a phase difference between components, so that by producing intensity differences between loudspeakers we are actually producing time differences between the ears. The effect therefore is that time and intensity differences between the loudspeakers do not correspond to time and intensity differences between the two ears in natural listening, although nevertheless they will produce differences in apparent localization. The point is important because experiments on stereo systems will show that time differences between the loudspeakers are rather less effective than intensity differences in producing the desired effect, and a widely used commercial stereo system actually operates entirely with intensity differences between the loudspeakers. This however does not mean in any way that time differences between the ears are unimportant; if anything, the reverse, because part of the role of the intensity differences at the loudspeakers is through the time differences which they produce at the ears.

Conclusions

We may summarize this excursion into the localization of sounds, rather dogmatically, by saying that the medley of sounds reaching the two ears is not only examined to find different carrier frequencies having the same modulation frequency; but also the time differences between the peak of the modulation on one ear and that on the other are employed to give a localization to the resulting combined sound. The auditory world in which the listener operates contains therefore a number of bundles of information, each of which is characterized by coming from a certain location in space, and also possesses other characteristics. These other characteristics convey the intelligibility of speech if that be the nature of the sound, or doubtless other properties if the sound is not a speech one. The original formation into these bundles of the complicated stimuli corresponding to different frequency components is an essential basis of filtering: as we said in Chapter I, that process has sometimes been misunderstood as the switching on of some sense organs and the switching off of others, but it is clearly far more complex than that. Lastly, this formation of the auditory world into the perception of a number of sound sources provides a reasonable biological basis for the existence of two mechanisms of frequency analysis. The periodicity mechanism, strongly responsive to modulation frequency, provides the basis for forming sounds into their different sources; while the mechanism of analysis into simple components, which is presumably based upon the place on the basilar membrane, provides the other information which the listener may wish to extract from any particular source.

It need hardly be said that all we have shown here is the way in which the acoustic input is formed into a structure of different bundles of evidence coming from different parts of the outside world. We have not as yet considered the way in which selection of one bundle rather than another can act as a filter. At this stage therefore we must turn from simple consideration of the mechanism of hearing, to more complex experiments on selective perception.

CHAPTER V

Selective Perception

The Position in 1958

During the 1950's, a number of experiments were performed on selective perception in hearing; and it was from these that the concept of filtering was developed. The advantage of hearing for studies of attention was that the ear possesses no peripheral adjustments comparable to the eyelids and the fixation mechanism. The ear does, as became evident towards the end of the period, have a control of the sensitivity of the peripheral sense organs, by messages proceeding efferently from the brain to the ear. Nevertheless, an auditory signal cannot be shut out in a simple and mechanical fashion as can an unwanted visual one. Experiments on hearing therefore have the advantage of getting at genuinely neural processes rather than mechanical ones. In more recent years, it has turned out to be possible to do experiments on selective perception in vision, by ingenious variations on the use of the tachistocope. The auditory situation remains however almost the only one in which a continuous flow of information can be presented without the danger of artificial selection by the mere direction in which the sense organs are pointed.

There were three basic findings by 1958, which still stand and on which all the later work has developed.

(1) *The perceptual mechanism is of limited capacity in an information sense.* When stimuli for two tasks arrive simultaneously, the extent of the interference between them depends on the amount of information which they convey. This was found by Webster and Thompson (1953, 1954), by Webster and Solomon (1955), by Poulton (1953, 1956), and by Broadbent (1952b, 1956a). In each of these studies, the effect of an extra message to understand, while one was listening to a primary message, was more serious when there was more information in the second message. In some cases, the actual physical stimuli were identical, and the amount of information was altered merely by varying the instructions to the subject. The man then thought that other messages might have arrived; although in fact they did not do so. It seems quite clear therefore that in some sense the difficulty of dealing with too many stimuli at one time arises because some central mechanism cannot deal with too much information in a limited period of time.

(2) *Pre-instruction about the channel to receive response is better than post-instruction.* If a man receives two speech messages, and only has to respond to one of them, he does better if he knows in advance which is relevant than if he is told after stimulation, or has to pick up the information from the stimulation itself. This has been shown by Broadbent (1952a) and by Cherry (1953). It was especially notable in the latter case that, when the man has been asked to listen to one message and to repeat it as it arrived, he could tell very little about the content of the other message. He might for instance be ignorant of the language in which it had been delivered, or of the fact that it consisted of reversed speech rather than ordinary speech. He might however notice if it changed from being a man's voice to a woman's, or if the second signal ceased to be speech and became a pure tone.

The importance of this general class of findings is that the overloading of the limited capacity channel is dealt with by selection of some items only; and in particular that this selection takes place either during the time of input, or while the material is in store. (We shall consider the latter possibility very seriously later.) It does not take place at the time of response, since instruction is less helpful when it comes after stimulation but before response.

(3) *A physical cue common to all words in one message is helpful when selective response is required, but not otherwise.* When two speech messages arrive at the same listener, they are in ordinary life distinguished because each person has an individual quality of voice: referring back to the last chapter, each person will probably use a different range of formant frequencies, speak at a different larynx frequency, and so on. In addition, in normal life, different speakers will be heard in different directions. Under artificial laboratory conditions, one can deliver two messages from a tape recording both spoken by the same person, and heard through the same loudspeaker or headphones. There is considerable applied interest in the relative efficiency of listening with voices localized together or apart, because men in communication centres may receive many messages at once. It is desirable to know whether these messages should all be transmitted through one loudspeaker, or through an array of loudspeakers. In fact it is clear from results by Broadbent (1952b, 1954b), Cherry (1953), Egan *et al.* (1954), Spieth *et al.* (1954), and Poulton (1953, 1956) that separation of two messages by some physical cue is extremely helpful when only one of them is to be answered. This applies whether one knows in advance which message is to receive response, or whether one has to monitor both messages in order to find out which one is to receive a detailed answer. However, if one has an overload of messages and must nevertheless try to answer all of them, it has been found both by Poulton and by Webster and Thompson that physical separation is much less helpful. Broadbent (1958) even mentioned one unpublished experiment by himself in which a listener had to deal with a very rapid series of pairs of messages. In each pair one was relevant and one irrelevant, but it was impossible to tell which was going to be

which until they had both been heard. If spatial separation of the two streams of messages was introduced, it was positively harmful at high rates of presentation, and in particular in the case where the relevant message had just changed from one channel to the other. In ordinary language, the listener was trying to keep up with both channels, was listening to one of them, and was caught on the wrong foot by a message coming in very rapidly subsequently from quite a different place.

The methods which have been used to separate one message from another include the use of different people speaking, intensity differences, and the insertion of band-pass filters into the channel carrying one of the speech messages. The most effective cue however has normally been found to be some form of spatial separation of the voices either by using different loudspeakers arranged horizontally around the listener, or by using headphones in which one voice was heard in one ear and one in the other. Broadbent (1954b) used headphones with time delays such that both voices were in fact delivered to both ears, but one of the voices appeared to be localized to one side of the listener, and the other voice to the other side. This experiment has turned out to be of particular importance at a later time, because it shows that the selective listening is not carried out by "turning off" one ear. If that were the case, there would be no advantage with stereophonic localization of this type.

All these methods of separating the voices, however, divide the total array of stimuli reaching the ears into two classes. The relevant stimuli differ from each other in a number of ways, which characterize the particular words that are being said, as has been described in the last chapter. All relevant words however share a common feature such as larynx frequency, arrival at the right ear before arrival at the left ear, and so on. Irrelevant stimuli may also differ amongst themselves by representing different words, but irrelevant stimuli do not possess the common characteristic of larynx frequency, of time of arrival at the two ears, or whatever it may be which is characteristic of relevant words. Thus the introduction of physical differences of this kind forms the stimuli into classes or bundles much as, in the last chapter, we saw that the different components of a single voice were bound together by their common larynx frequency.

In the last chapter however there was no evidence of selective response to one bundle rather than another: the experiments just cited show that a listener can give efficient response to all stimuli possessing some common feature, provided that he is allowed to reject those stimuli which do not possess this feature. The stimuli which do not need response must be discarded before they have been fully processed, because of the role of pre-instruction before the stimuli arrive rather than merely before response. Further, the physical cue separating relevant from irrelevant must act by assisting the discarding, because it is less helpful when discarding is impossible. This is the mechanism which we have called "filtering", and from what has been said it is clear that it serves the function of protecting the limited capacity channel against overloads of information.

The three basic findings available in 1958 therefore argued for a selective process in the intake of information, based upon filtering: but there were a few other phenomena which were also known at that time and which implied that the mechanism must be more than a simple filtering process. These subsidiary phenomena can be classified as follows.

THE BUFFER STORE (S SYSTEM)

If the mechanism were a simple filter picking out some of the stimuli for response and rejecting others, then two simultaneous stimuli of high information content should not both receive a response. It was clear however from some of the applied experiments that they might do so, provided that such a simultaneous presentation of stimuli did not occur too often. That is, if two words were spoken simultaneously to a man, with a pause afterwards, he might react appropriately to both of them. The difficulty of dealing with simultaneous stimuli was much more noticeable when there were two simultaneous sentences rather than a pair of words. This leads on to an experiment which makes the point more formally, and which has been used in a number of subsequent investigations. We shall refer to it by the name of dichotic memory, or multi-channel memory when vision rather than hearing is used. In the original form of this experiment (Broadbent, 1954b) three pairs of spoken digits are presented successively to the listener. In each pair, one digit is heard through an earphone on the right ear, and one through an earphone on the left ear. After all six items have arrived, the listener has to reproduce as many of them as he can. The basic finding is that, if all six digits are reproduced correctly, then in the majority of cases the three items from one ear are reproduced before the three items from the other. It thus appears that the second set of items to produce response have been held at some point in their passage through the nervous system while the first three travelled further on: that is, there must be a stage early in the mechanism at which simultaneous processing of information from the two channels is possible. This stage is succeeded by a stage at which successive processing only is possible. In 1958, the first of these stages was labelled as anonymously as possible the S system, and the latter the P system. The S system was so called because it possesses some of the characteristics of a buffer store: while the P system might, in some usages of the term "perception", be regarded as a perceptual mechanism. As the stages were defined by the simultaneous versus successive quality of the operations, it might in some ways have been better if the letters had been used in the opposite sense, since the S system performs Parallel processing, while the P system performs Serial processing. For present purposes, we will call the S system the buffer: and its existence means that the limited capacity of the nervous system does not prevent the system from hand-ling temporary overloads of information, as long as any such overload is followed by a pause during which information in the buffer can be passed through the limited capacity P system.

It may be added that it was shown by Broadbent (1956b) that similar performance would appear if three items were delivered to the eye and three to the ear, so that the effect is not a purely auditory one. It will also appear if two recordings of the same voice are delivered through the same loudspeaker, but if a filter removes the low frequencies from one recording.

TIME TAKEN TO SWITCH THE FILTER

The phenomenon already described only applies if the rate of presentation of pairs of digits is fast, about two pairs per second. Broadbent (1954b) instructed some subjects to reproduce the incoming information in a sequence alternating between the ears, and not to group it ear by ear. While they did very badly at fast rates of presentation they improved considerably as the rate was slowed down. When a pair of digits was arriving every two seconds, their performance was as good as that of listeners at the fast rate reproducing all items from one ear before those from the other. (As we shall be discussing later, there is a logical weakness in this experiment, and it is presented now solely because later work has shown nevertheless that the conclusion is sound). The theoretical inference which Broadbent drew from this was as follows. Given that the filter system lies between the buffer store and the limited capacity channel, then there is a limit to the speed at which the filter can change the basis which it is using for selection. That is, if it is set to select items from the right ear, it takes time before it can select items from the left ear. Thus at high rates of presentation it finds it necessary to select all items from one ear, before turning to those from the other ear. At low rates of presentation however it is able to change from one ear to the other between each pair of digits.

LOSS OF INFORMATION FROM THE BUFFER WITH TIME

With a mechanism of the type described so far, there seems no reason why a man should not receive two long sentences simultaneously and deal with them both efficiently, provided that he is allowed an interval before any further stimulation. The filter could select one sentence, and, when it had been dealt with, the second sentence could pass through the limited capacity system as long as nothing else required handling at that time. This however supposes that the buffer store can hold an indefinite amount of excess information and can do so for an indefinite time. Broadbent (1957b) presented six items to one ear and two items to the other, instructing subjects to reproduce the six items first and then the two. If the two items were delivered simultaneously with the last two items of the six, performance was better than if they were delivered earlier. That is, if the excess information had waited in the buffer store for a longer period while more items went through the limited capacity system, then the items in the buffer were less likely to emerge successfully in response. It may be noted here that similar results have been obtained recently by Bryden (1966) when the items in the buffer were not necessarily both adjacent to each other; one could be early and one late in the delivery of the whole sequence of stimuli.

A result with a different technique, but pointing to the same conclusion, was that of Cherry (1953), since repeated and developed by Treisman (1964a). The technique here was to get subjects to repeat continuously a message delivered to one ear, while presenting the same message to the other ear at a certain value of time interval between the two messages. If the time interval is too great, the subjects never notice that the same material is reaching both ears. On the other hand, when it is relatively short they do notice. This suggests that the information on the ear which is not receiving response does go into a buffer storage but is lost from that store after a relatively short time. It may be added that, if the ear which receives response is the first to receive the message, rather than the second, then the time interval can be made considerably longer. In some sense therefore making a response to the message increases the time for which some stored knowledge about its content is preserved in the nervous system.

Broadbent's interpretation of these various results was that information was lost from the buffer store as time went on: neither experiment as such however really distinguished whether the loss was due to passage of time as such or to the number of items which had occurred on the other channel. In the experiments by Cherry and by Treisman, moreover, increase in the time delay also involved a larger number of items in the buffer store itself, as well as on the channel receiving response. Broadbent (1957b) showed that, if one presented six items on one ear to receive response, and two items on the other ear to be recalled after response to the first six, then the recall of these latter two items was greatly impaired by the presence of other irrelevant items on the same ear. Thus the quantity of information in the buffer store itself affects the efficiency of recall. The latter effect might be caused by the problem of selecting any particular desired information from the buffer.

We shall be considering later whether loss of information from the buffer is due to passage of time or to the presentation of other items. Whatever the explanation it is clear that the buffer will not hold any excess items indefinitely. As a result, it can be used only for brief peaks of overload in the incoming information, and cannot store a long sentence arriving at one ear while an equally long sentence is receiving attention on the other ear. The whole of this mechanism together therefore provides an explanation for the way in which two tasks may or may not be capable of being done by a man at the same time. If they involve little information, then the limited capacity system can deal with both of them: if they involve momentary peaks of load when two items arrive simultaneously, this can nevertheless be managed by means of the buffer store, which will hold one item till the other has been dealt with. The selection of items from this buffer is carried out by filtering, that is, by the selection of all items having some common characteristic. Only when long streams of high information content arrive simultaneously will two tasks become impossible to combine.

Since 1958, a number of studies have been carried out on the correctness or otherwise of the theoretical model we have been stating. Some support it, some do not; some are drawn from one kind of performance and some from another. They can therefore be classified in various ways: it may perhaps be easiest to group together researches by the tasks they study, and to discuss theoretical implications as these arise. As a guide to the reader let us outline the plan of the remainder of the chapter.

(1) First, we shall discuss studies carried out with a technique known as "shadowing". These studies revealed that the hearing of one word rather than another simultaneous one may depend upon the nature of the words themselves as well as upon the physical cues attached to them; and this shed some doubt upon the reality of filtering. More shadowing experiments made it clear that filtering does take place; but that some further process is also involved.

(2) Next, we shall discuss two main theoretical suggestions which have been put forward to explain the effect of word content upon selection: one minimizes filtering, while the other retains it but adds a mechanism of the "pigeon-holing" type, and we shall support the latter.

(3) Then, returning to experiment, we shall survey recent studies on dichotic memory. Here again, some such studies show that recall may be selective by the content of the items rather than the physical cues linked to their presentation. These results have therefore been interpreted by some authors as supporting a theory which replaces filtering by a selective recall process. We shall show however that pigeon-holing during the intake of information is a better explanation of the facts.

(4) After digressing to mention some minor results on dichotic memory, we shall then turn to vision; and describe recent studies which show a buffer store and a subsequent selective process comparable with those demonstrated in hearing.

(5) In vision, some studies on pre- and post-instruction for selection have shown that certain tasks will give little advantage for pre-selection. In terms of the mechanisms we have been discussing, filtering would show such an advantage, but pigeon-holing would show less. At this stage therefore we shall distinguish the two more carefully and show that pre-instruction does help the former but is less help to the latter.

(6) Experiments on perceptual search also show a difference between tasks allowing filtering and those requiring pigeon-holing. In addition, they make

it necessary to introduce the concept of "categorizing". Studies of reaction time in the presence of irrelevant stimuli again show differences between filtering and pigeon-holing, in that the former is vulnerable to irrelevant information while the latter is not.

(7) Next, we shall turn to decision theory and show that changes in d' but no change in β appear in selective tasks which involve filtering. The converse, that β changes in tasks involving pigeon-holing, will be left to the next chapter.

(8) As a tail-piece to this chapter, we shall mention the relationship of right-handedness and of ageing to multi-channel memory. In both cases, the distinction between filtering and pigeon-holing may be important. They are discussed here primarily however because the techniques have been considered in this chapter.

Experiments on Auditory Shadowing Since 1958

The technique known as "shadowing" is that in which the listener repeats continuously a stream of speech, while ignoring any other messages which may accompany it. It was the method used in the pioneering studies of Cherry (1953): studies since 1958 have investigated three main aspects of the process. First, there is the question of the amount which is known about irrelevant messages even when they are not repeated. Second, there are studies of the exact role of the physical cues used in filtering. Third, there are studies of the effects of content of the relevant and irrelevant messages, as opposed to the common physical qualities used in filtering.

WHAT IS KNOWN ABOUT IRRELEVANT MESSAGES

An experiment by Moray (1959) used the technique of shadowing a message on one ear while irrelevant material was presented to the other ear. He found not merely that the content of the irrelevant material could not be recalled; but even that subjects showed no advantage in attempting afterwards to learn material which had been presented to the irrelevant ear. This is of particular importance because, as we shall see in later chapters, it is now known that material which has been presented once and then apparently forgotten through the subsequent presentation of other material, may nevertheless leave a considerable permanent effect as shown by improvement in subsequent learning. Thus, to use our own theoretical terms, Moray's result shows that information lost from the buffer store without passage through the filter seems to have less effect on long-term memory than does information which has once passed through the filter even though it has apparently been forgotten. To make the contrast clear, a paper by Inglis and Tansey (1967a) used the technique of requiring memory for a complete set of items half on one ear and half on the other. They asked for recall from one ear before the other, and repeated the same sets of items at intervals throughout the experiment, separated by other non-repeated lists. The repeated lists showed an improvement on successive presentations, which was equally great both in the half-set recalled first and in the half-set recalled second. In this case of course both half-sets had been selected by the filter and this has allowed the information to produce some long-lasting effect within the nervous system. When however as in Moray's case the information receives no response within a second or two after stimulation arrives, there is no corresponding lasting effect.

There is however some evidence that certain kinds of material will be noticed even on the irrelevant ear.

In another experiment, Moray (1959) showed that the occurrence of the listener's own name in the irrelevant message would be noticed and re-membered at the end of the experiment. The longer duration of memory in this case can perhaps fairly be ascribed to some difference in the immediate effects of the stimulus when it first arrives: that is, for some reason the listener's own name does obtain access to the limited capacity channel im-mediately and is not rejected as other irrelevant items are. If this result existed in isolation, one could perhaps conceivably argue that it was still due to the filtering mechanism, but that the filter possessed a permanent tendency to select a word with certain physical characteristics. The rule governing the operation of the filter could then perhaps then be stated as "Select all words reaching the right ear, and reject words on the left ear: but any word possess-ing formant frequencies x and y, present in one's own name, is to be selected even if on the wrong ear". That is, the selection could be carried out on the basis of acoustic cues.

A similar interpretation cannot be applied however to a result by Treisman (1964a). As already mentioned, she presented identical messages on the selected and the rejected ear, and noted the time interval between the two at which the identity was noticed. It was possible for subjects to notice the identity despite the fact that the people speaking the messages were different and even if the two messages were identical in meaning but spoken in two different languages both of which the subject understood. It is difficult there-fore to see how this result can be explained if the only mechanism controlling access to the limited capacity channel is a filter working on physical charac-teristics common to all the desired words.

One can sum up these experiments as showing that the selection of one ear shuts out most of the information on the other. But if some does break through, the items which do so are not random, but are those whose content is of certain kinds.

COMPARISONS OF PHYSICAL AND CONTENT CUES DIFFERENTIATING BETWEEN SELECTED AND NEGLECTED MESSAGES

The facts just cited raise a question about the role of a physical difference, such as localization, between the relevant and irrelevant messages. If the content of a word is one of the factors deciding whether it shall receive response, one might deduce that the brain can afford to choose which message shall elicit reaction *after* the full content of the words has been analysed. Why then should we continue to believe that filtering takes place, that is, that the brain discards irrelevant stimuli once it has found that they do not possess some simple physical characteristic? The 1958 analysis placed great importance on the role of a physical cue, as providing a basis for the filter to select a stimulus for further analysis. One could conceivably argue, however, that the important point in selection is the division of the words into two classes, desired and undesired, and that a common physical feature is only one way of doing this. Perhaps a difference of content or meaning could be equally effective. It would not then be working by the mechanism which we have called filtering, even although it might still be selective. Cherry (1953) had already studied a case in which the listener was presented with two different messages mixed on the same tape recording and in the same voice. The listener could, *after repeated trials*, separate one message from the other: unless the two messages consisted of strings of clichés, in which case the attempt to separate them was likely to break down at the end of one cliché and the beginning of the next. The listener might quite well run on to the wrong message at such a point!

There is no question that listeners are aware of the successive constraints in speech which make certain sequences of words much more probable than others, and that they can use this information to perceive connected discourse correctly under conditions when a series of random words would be impossible to perceive. We shall come to this question in a later chapter. At the moment, the problem is rather whether differences in content between the relevant and irrelevant messages can be used to select one rather than the other for a response. If for example a word in the relevant message is "high" while the word in the irrelevant message is "England", then if the next pair of words are "mountain" and "expects", one of these words is clearly much more likely to belong to the relevant message and one to the irrelevant. Can listeners use this distinction in the same way as a difference in localization of the source of the sound?

Treisman (1964b) used a situation like Cherry's with two messages in the same voice and channel. However, in her case the listener was allowed only one presentation of the mixed voices and was asked to shadow continuously one message. The relevant message was always a female voice reading a passage from a novel: the irrelevant message was sometimes in the same voice, and as the localization of the relevant and the irrelevant was the same, there were then no obvious common physical cues to the relevant words. She compared the cases in which the irrelevant message was a different passage from the same novel, a technical discussion of biochemistry, a foreign language known or unknown to the listener, or nonsense of the same phonetic structure as English. There were certainly significant differences in the efficiency of shadowing the relevant message, depending upon the nature of the irrelevant material. The effect most clearly dependent upon content is that it was easier to hear the novel in the presence of a biochemical discussion than it was in the presence of another part of the same novel. When the irrelevant material was a foreign language, furthermore, it made a difference whether the listener understood that language or not, it being easier to ignore irrelevant sounds if one did not understand them. All these differences, whilst statistically significant, were however relatively small: whereas when Treisman made the irrelevant material a passage from the same novel, but spoken by a man's voice rather than a woman's, the percentage of words correctly heard increased markedly. The difference was approximately 40%, whereas when the irrelevant material was in the same female voice, the difference between a novel and biochemistry as the irrelevant material was less than 10%. When a man's voice was used for the irrelevant material, it made no difference what language the man was speaking, a point to which we shall return in the next sub-section. Lastly, when the same female voice was used for both relevant and irrelevant material, it was clear that part of the advantage of having the irrelevant material in a foreign language was due to the difference in phonetic structure of the foreign language and of English; since there was a significant advantage for an unknown foreign language as opposed to English-sounding nonsense. These results therefore show that a difference of content between relevant and irrelevant messages can be used for selection, but that it is much less effective than a physical cue marking out all the relevant words.

Another mode of attack on the role of the physical cue is to use more than one irrelevant message, and to give these either common or different characteristics while keeping the relevant message distinct from either. Treisman (1964b) tried this experiment both with spatial localization and with the difference between male and female voice. For example, she would ask the subject to shadow a voice heard on the right ear alone, while two irrelevant messages were presented as a mixture to both ears equally: the two irrelevant voices would then sound together in a central position. If one of the irrelevant voices was switched off the right ear and put in the left ear alone, the two irrelevant messages would apparently come from different positions. This produced a deterioration in the shadowing of the relevant message. This is particularly striking, because the peripheral masking of the relevant message should have been less in this case.

In the foregoing experiment, the material was always recorded by the same woman's voice: if the two irrelevant messages were mixed together apparently in the middle of the head, but if one of them was male rather than female, performance on the relevant message again deteriorated compared with two female irrelevant messages. In other words, the listener seems to take some notice of physical differences between the irrelevant messages even though it is quite unnecessary for him to notice these in order to distinguish the relevant message from either of them.

One can sum up these experiments as showing that a physical cue for separating relevant and irrelevant messages has a genuine importance of its own and is not working in the same way as a difference of content.

EFFECTS OF THE CONTENT OF THE IRRELEVANT MESSAGE

We have already noticed that Treisman (1964b) found that the language in which the irrelevant material was given made no difference, so long as the voice in which it was spoken was different from that of the relevant material. Similar results were found by Treisman (1964c), when the relevant material was localized in a different position from the irrelevant one. In that case, she used prose, and at the opposite extreme Czech spoken with an English accent to listeners who did not know the language, so that it was effectively nonsense. As an intermediate step, second order approximations to English were employed. These consist of English words arranged in such a way that the probability of any word following the one immediately before is much the same as in ordinary English; but the word two positions back is not taken into account. The whole passage is thus nonsense. No differences were found between any of these conditions: the one case in which material did produce a slightly better performance was when the irrelevant items consisted of the ten digits spoken in ascending order over and over again: in this case there was a difference of rhythm as well as of content, and the advantage was in any case less than 5%. Given a physical cue therefore the content of the irrelevant message appears to have very little effect on efficiency.

When there is no physical cue separating the messages, what is the detailed fashion in which content exercises its effect? Another experiment reported by Treisman (1964b) sheds some light on this question. She used recordings of the same person heard in the same location, and the irrelevant material was always a passage from a novel. The relevant material to be shadowed was however a set of approximations to English of different exactness, from first order to twelfth order. That is, the probability of each word was that which it would have in the language as a whole taking into account a number of preceding words which increased as the order to approximation increased. The efficiency of shadowing was of course greater for higher orders of approximation, which sound more and more meaningful: this would be true even if there was no irrelevant material present. However, at low orders of approximation, where the number of words correctly repeated was low, there were more intrusions from the irrelevant message: the subject did not say less words in all, but included more words from the wrong message.

One can then analyse the results in detail, to distinguish two different ways in which listeners might be breaking down with the low order of approximation in the relevant material. They might be shifting more often to the wrong message, and they might also or alternatively be repeating longer chunks from the wrong message once they were there. In fact, it turns out that the first of these is true, but the second is not.

Thus with a high order of approximation, a tightly organized and meaningful string of words, one is less likely to shift away to another message, but one is no more likely to shift back once one has started repeating the wrong message. If we go back to our hypothetical case therefore of one message containing "high mountain" and the other message "England expects", the way in which the difference of content separates the two messages can be clarified. It is not that the listener takes the word "high" and the word "England", and evaluates the probability of each of the next two words in relation to each of the two that have already arrived. Rather, he takes one of the first pair, such as "high", and this then settles the relative probabilities of the next two words, without reference to the word "England".

The tentative conclusion therefore is that content of a *neglected* message has no effect on subsequent performance: but the content of the *selected* message somehow sets the mechanisms to make subsequent words of appropriate content more likely to achieve selection.

Such an interpretation makes one curious whether a similar effect might not be shown even with relevant and irrelevant messages distinguished by a physical cue, provided that the conditions were suitable. In fact such an effect has been demonstrated by Treisman (1960). She instructed her subjects to shadow a message on one particular ear, and gave distinct messages to the attended and to the neglected ear: for example, she might have a passage of ordinary English text on the attended ear, and a statistical approximation to English, making no sense over the long term, on the neglected ear. (In fact a number of combinations of different types of material was used, but this particular pair illustrates the point easily.) At a certain time during the session, the two messages were changed over without warning from one ear to the other, so that the passage of prose which had previously been shadowed now continued on the neglected ear, while the ear to be shadowed was stimulated by the nonsense series of words. The subjects continued to shadow, as they had been instructed, the ear which was now receiving the nonsense series. However, just at the change from one type of material to the other a word or two might intrude from the wrong ear. Thus if the shadowed ear had received "England" just before the change, the neglected ear might then receive "expects", while the shadowed ear received some inappropriate word such as "mountain". The subject might under these circumstances say "England expects mountain". Treisman performed a control experiment in which no stimulus was delivered to the neglected ear, and subsequent intrusions did not appear in this control experiment. They were thus not due to purely random guessing, but represented a genuine response to the ear which was not receiving attention. Intrusions of this kind were more frequent if the message which was originally being shadowed was more tightly structured: that is, the more closely it approximated to normal English rather than being a sequence of random words. It does appear therefore that the words which have been perceived are controlling the words that are selected at a later stage.

One point which should be noted, as it is perhaps a little out of line with the theory we are leaning towards thus far, is that intrusions would sometimes occur from words presented to the neglected ear just before the changeover. Thus to take our familiar example, if the ear which was being shadowed received "high, expects" while the ear which was being neglected received "England, mountain" then the subject might sometimes say "high, England, expects". It seems fair to say that this is still a case of selection being governed by the high probability of some words in the context of others which have already been selected, but to argue that speech is perceived in fairly long segments, and that the perception of words on the shadowed ear after the changeover raises the probability of *preceding* words on the neglected ear, so that a complete phrase is emitted.

It seems reasonable to interpret this experiment, as Treisman did, as confirming that the physical separation of the relevant and irrelevant messages is of primary importance, since the subject does keep on shadowing the ear which the instructions have selected despite the change in content. Nevertheless, in this particular case one can see that content may cause words to break through from the neglected ear despite the difference in physical character between the relevant and irrelevant messages.

One may sum up this whole group of experiments as showing that a listener instructed to attend to one ear may nevertheless hear items from the other ear if they are probable in the context that has previously been heard; but not if they are probable in the context that has been ignored.

ALTERNATIVE THEORIES OF THE EFFECT OF CONTENT

As we have already seen, one possible interpretation of the breakthrough of particular items might be that there is a permanent setting of the filter; in addition to the selection of one channel at one time and another at other times it will always select any stimulus having a particular combination of qualities. This can most easily be applied to the perception of one's own name, as in Moray's experiment; Treisman also reports one or two instances of an apparently similar effect when subjects noticed that a passage on the irrelevant ear was about a country which the subject had just visited, or the title of a book whose author the subject knew. It seems quite hard however to explain Treisman's 1960 experiment in this way, because the class of words which might conceivably follow any given word in a connected sentence is very large, and it is therefore difficult to see how a specific rule could make the filter select any word in that class. Two alternative interpretations seem possible.

The first of these has perhaps been put most clearly by Deutsch and

Deutsch (1963). They felt that the effects of the content of the irrelevant message, which we have described, made filtering an unsatisfactory mechanism for explaining selection. (Evidence derived from the dichotic memory situation, which we shall be considering shortly, was also relevant). They therefore contended that the nature of the signal on each ear would decide which of the competing stimuli was to be selected. It might be incorrect to suppose, as the filtering theory supposed, that each stimulus was analysed first only for the possession of a desired characteristic such as localization in a particular place: and that only those stimuli possessing the desired characteristic were then analysed for other features. Rather it might be that all features of all stimuli were analysed, to give a final combined degree of "importance" for that stimulus. The stimulus possessing greatest meaning might then be selected for response and for memory, while those of lesser meaning would be rapidly forgotten. This view might explain the tendency for particularly loaded items such as the name to break through from the neglected ear: and it would still be compatible with the fact that stimuli having a certain physical cue possess a dominant weight when previous instructions have asked for such stimuli to be selected. This would itself increase their importance.

It is worth digressing a little to consider what is implied in a theory of this kind. In one sense of course all the information from the senses must be available within the nervous system, since as we have already seen there is no difficulty in dealing with two simultaneous stimuli. One is not obliged simply to deal with one and neglect the other completely. So long as there is an opportunity after the arrival of the two stimuli, in which response may occur to the one which did not receive immediate response, then all the information does seem to be preserved adequately in the nervous system. This is the phenomenon we have referred to as buffer storage. Thus the information about stimuli on the neglected ear is certainly present in the nervous system, and it may seen quite plausible that the detailed nature of the signal which has been delivered should in fact control whether or not it is selected.

There are however different ways in which information may be encoded, and there are marked quantitative differences between these ways, which must be reflected in any machinery which adopts them. For example, we saw in the last chapter that the recognition of a given vowel sound will normally involve the recognition of the presence of at least two formant frequencies in the complex sound wave reaching the ear: and the particular vowel being presented cannot be identified without detecting the presence of both. By linking together recognition devices for such isolated physical features, we can imagine that the nervous system could recognize the presence or absence of each of the forty or so phonemes of spoken English. In the more familiar visual case, recognition of the presence of a combination of lines, corners, and curves may allow the eye to detect the presence or absence of any of the 26 letters of the alphabet.

The evidence relevant to identification of a letter or phoneme is therefore the presence of a combination of many features, and the absence of many others. Each feature alone may be relevant to many combinations: there are vertical lines in several letters, horizontal lines in many, and so on: it is the combination which is unique. But the number of possible combinations expands very rapidly as one increases the number of features considered. There are 26 possible combinations making up the letters of the alphabet; but if we think of 10-letter groups, the number of possible sequences of letters is 26^{10}. If therefore the nervous system is able to make a different and appropriate reaction to each possible 10-letter string, it must contain devices capable of responding differently to each of the very many different combinations of letters; and similarly for any other patterned stimulus. If the presence or absence of all possible patterns from all the sense-organs is being analysed simultaneously, the number of possible combinations to be detected is very large; it is easy to suppose that all the features present and absent can simultaneously be registered, but very hard to imagine that all the conceivable *combinations* present can be detected at one time and distinguished from those which are absent. It is essentially for this reason that a tape recorder can store all the information contained in an hour-long speech by a politician; but a very much more complicated machine would be needed to light a lamp every time he uttered a logical fallacy. The tape can store each sound of the relatively small set of possible sounds as it is uttered, but the number of possible sequences of sounds is so vast that a very complex machine indeed would be needed to take on an appropriate state for each possible combination.

Now if we suggest that the content of any spoken message reaching the ears is sufficiently analysed to decide whether or not the item be selected, we are asking the nervous system to behave for every stimulus not as a tape recorder but as a much more complicated recognizing device. If there were really sufficient machinery available in the brain to perform such an analysis for every stimulus, and then to use the results to decide which should be selected, it is difficult to see why any selection at all should occur. The obvious utility of a selection system is to produce an economy in mechanism. If a complete analysis were performed even of the neglected messages, there seems no reason for selection at all.

Admittedly, it might be possible for analysis to extract some but not all of the information about content, and thus to produce some economy compared with a full analysis. For example, if one were to listen only to one word in ten of the conversation between two neighbours at dinner, one might notice that they were using words such as "computer", "software", "time-sharing", and so become aware that their conversation was on a topic of interest even although one had not made out the sense from any single sentence they uttered. Similar principles might perhaps be applied to the perception of individual words; and this indeed was the position of Broadbent (1958). As

F

we shall be considering in the next chapter, there is a long-standing problem that improbable or emotionally loaded words are sometimes less well perceived than probable or neutral words. Broadbent suggested that a class of undesirable words might possess enough individual features in common for a listener to recognize that a word was one of this class even before he had identified which one it was. As we shall see in the next chapter, the evidence now points rather against this view, and it is certainly a rather dangerous assumption when one cannot point out any features by which the class of words has been recognized.

We have therefore seen that general theoretical reasons make rather unlikely the idea that a large number of simultaneous messages are being analysed for content although this analysis cannot then emerge in response. The long series of experiments by Treisman have also provided empirical difficulties for it: notably, (1) the fact that selection without a physical cue is extremely difficult even with the widest possible differences of content, (2) the fact that differences in content of the irrelevant message make very little difference to the selection as long as a physical cue is present, and (3) the fact that the selection of the more probable of a pair of words seems to depend upon the word that has just been selected and not upon the irrelevant word which has been presented but not selected. Treisman (1960) therefore put forward an alternative point of view, which is in essence that which we shall support.

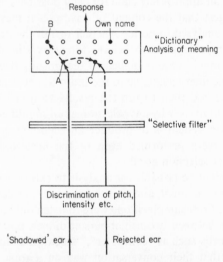

FIG. 18. The modified theory of attention introduced by Treisman (1960). Following occurrence of word A, the "thresholds" of words B and C are lowered because they are very probable following word A. If word C is activated by the "attenuated" signal from the rejected ear, it may be heard.

On her view, the nervous system contained a set of dictionary units, as they were then termed, each of which corresponded to a word. The firing of a unit represented the perception of that word. Under normal circumstances, the signals from the senses would tend to excite the particular dictionary unit corresponding to the word being delivered to the senses: and accordingly the correct dictionary unit would fire when its threshold was exceeded. Following the firing of any one unit, the thresholds of certain other units were lowered, so that the constraints within an ordinary English message would mean that units corresponding to words probable in that context in the language would be more easily fired. In the situation of selective listening, Treisman supposed that signals from all the senses would be delivered to the dictionary, but that some of them would be "attenuated". That is, if one had instructions to listen to one ear, stimuli delivered to the other ear would produce only a weaker signal applied to the dictionary. Normally speaking therefore the dictionary unit to fire at any instant would be one aroused by signals from the selected groups of inputs, but if there should happen to occur a combination of a low threshold on a dictionary unit and of an appropriate signal, even though weak from a rejected group of inputs, then there might occur firing of a unit corresponding to the word in a previously neglected message. Some units, such as that corresponding to one's own name, might be expected to have permanently lower thresholds.

The differences and resemblances between this view and others are worth noting. First, it differs from the view of Broadbent (1958) in that the filter mechanism is not absolute. That is, if a stimulus fails to possess the correct distinctive feature marking it out as a relevant one, it is not therefore blocked completely but may still produce a reduced effect. Treisman's theory rightly leaves it open whether this effect is through a lower probability of completely perfect input of information from such a rejected source (as if one heard perfectly the odd words about computers in a neighbouring conversation, and heard nothing in between) or whether it is a continuous but low intake of information (as if one knew the number of syllables in every word in the neighbouring conversation, but not what each syllable was). In either case, there is a possibility of the rejected message getting through.

Secondly, Treisman's theory adds to the filter mechanism another device for carrying out selection, namely the threshold applied to each dictionary unit. While this has the same consequence in one sense, of deciding which message shall be selected, it does not work on a common physical characteristic in all the desired signals, but rather by altering biases in the response processes going on inside the nervous system. It represents in a way a development of the view of attention put forward by Hebb (1949), in which the processes going on in the brain at one time depended heavily on those which had previously occurred. On that view neural events inconsistent with the ongoing stream of activity are inhibited. Such a view is difficult to apply to the kind of experiments which made Broadbent postulate a filtering system, but nevertheless has advantages in handling problems such as those attacked by Treisman. Such a second mechanism of selection will possess some differences from the filtering system, as we shall see later.

If we now turn to the similarities between Treisman's theory and the theory of analysis of meaning even of irrelevant messages, we can see that they possess a common element of giving a role to the content of a signal in deciding whether or not it should be selected. However, by adopting the device of the dictionary, Treisman has avoided the problem of the large number of states necessary to encode content for irrelevant messages. There is in her model only one set of dictionary units, and only signals firing one of these units can be regarded as completely analysed. Correspondingly, the lowering of the threshold for a given dictionary unit depends upon the units which have fired previously, and not upon the signals which may previously have arrived on the neglected channel without firing a unit. Thus Treisman's model does avoid the need for a duplication or multiplication indefinitely of a complex encoding mechanism. It should be especially noted that the way it does this is essentially by introduction of a probabilistic element into the theory. Both Broadbent's original model and a simple theory based on meaning could be completely determinate. The filter could look at each stimulus, decide without error whether that stimulus was appropriate for further analysis and select it if it was; an analyser of meaning could compute the properties of each stimulus event and select that with the greater priority, again without error. Treisman's theory by its introduction of thresholds into the dictionary units, and signals of different strengths, makes the mechanism a probabilistic one with the distinct possibility that a unit may fire even though the signals present do not in fact originate from an event in the outside world which is intended to represent the word in question.

We may now try to relate Treisman's theory to the terminology we have been using throughout this book so far. Her "dictionary units" correspond to the events which we have been calling "category states": there are reasons for avoiding a term such as "dictionary", because it is closely associated with words and our own approach includes the perception of speech as one amongst a number of other performances. Furthermore, the term "dictionary" has a slight association with a particular mechanism for recognition of words by linking the presented word with a definition in other words; and we do not necessarily want to imply this. The occurrence of a category state therefore corresponds to the firing of one of Treisman's dictionary units: the term "threshold" has unfortunate associations with old-style psychophysics, and we have been using "criterion" or "critical level". Her "signals" correspond to our "evidence", and when she speaks of lowering the threshold we have been terming the corresponding process "pigeon-holing". Our distinction between filtering and pigeon-holing is thus the same distinction which she makes between attenuation and threshold as methods of securing selection; we have retained the term filtering, for two reasons. First, attenuation has some physical overtones which have produced some confusion in the literature. In a physical system the attenuation of a channel containing a signal embedded in noise makes no great difference to the detectability of the signal. The form of attenuation corresponding most closely to Treisman's usage is that in which the signal is attenuated before it is mixed with the noise. Even this is unsatisfactory, however, because in the physical analogy the loss of information is random. In the perceptual mechanism, it may well be that some features of the rejected message come through perfectly although others are lost completely. By using a slightly more abstract term we may perhaps hope to avoid this difficulty.

The second reason for retaining the use of the term "filter" is that it still implies that information is given a greater priority when it is carried by stimulus events possessing some desired characteristic; and filtering is thus the result of a first stage of information processing. The term "attenuation" might carry the unintentional suggestion that the process was merely a mechanical raising or lowering of the gain on a particular sensory system. Filtering *does* involve some information processing: remember Treisman's results on the bad effects of delivering irrelevant messages from different locations rather than from the same location. While therefore it seems justifiable to continue to use the term "filtering", it should be remembered that there is an important difference between the term as used now and as used in 1958. We do not now wish to imply that there is a complete blockage of information from channels to which the filter is not directed.

Since Treisman's theory was formulated, two experiments of relevance to it have been carried out using the technique of shadowing, and as most such studies have already been considered we should perhaps give an account of these here before proceeding to experiments using other methods. In both cases, the technique was to combine shadowing of a message on one ear with a manual reaction to a signal which might appear on either ear. The first of these studies was by Lawson (1966) and in that case the manual reaction was to be produced whenever the listener heard a pure tone. The second experiment was by Treisman and Geffen (1967), and in that case the manual reaction was to be made whenever a particular word occurred. In both studies the main comparison of interest was between the occurrence in the shadowed and in the unshadowed ear of the stimulus for the manual reaction. If it were really true that shadowing required the filtering system to close off all inputs from the neglected ear, then one might suppose that the manual reaction would be less efficient on that ear. If on the other hand all inputs are analysed and allotted priorities according to the desirability or otherwise of a reaction to them, then one might, in the extreme, expect that the manual reaction would be equally efficient whichever ear received the stimulus. A theory such as Treisman's which incorporates a modified form of filtering would not expect the latter result; although it might allow for a proportion of responses to the neglected ear, since the filter does not produce a complete block.

To take the later experiment first, Treisman and Geffen did obtain a very marked difference of efficiency between the two ears, shadowed and unshadowed, which they interpreted as evidence against the idea that selection was determined by meaning. Deutsch and Deutsch (1967) are not altogether convinced by this argument, and it is certainly true that a word which is to receive a verbal reaction as well as a manual response might in some sense be regarded as higher in importance than a word which is only to receive a manual response. In Lawson's study the tone stimulus was not of course to be shadowed even when it occurred on the shadowed ear. In that sense this stimulus was more comparable on the two ears than was the verbal stimulus of Treisman and Geffen. Deutsch and Deutsch appeal to Lawson's results as being contrary to those of Treisman and Geffen, and Treisman and Geffen themselves quote Lawson's results as a difficulty, perhaps to be explained by the lower amount of information involved in reacting to a tone rather than reacting to a word. The present author however has difficulty in seeing that Lawson's results are contrary to those of Treisman and Geffen and this is why the results have not been presented until the debate about them had been made clear. Lawson performed three experiments, using different combinations of tone stimuli and key-pressing responses. In brief, all three experiments showed a faster reaction time on the shadowed than on the unshadowed ear: two of them significantly so, while the other (experiment 1) failed to be statistically significant only because six subjects were tested and one gave results in the opposite direction. It seems quite plausible therefore that a larger scale experiment would have given the same conclusion as in the other two studies. One point which should be noted is that in one of the experiments (experiment 3) the design compared performance when shadowing the right ear and making manual reactions to both right and left, and also, under other conditions, shadowing the left ear while making reactions to both right and left. In the analysis of variance on the manual reactions, the main effect of "ears" is completely insignificant, and may thus easily lead readers to suppose that there was no effect of the ear being shadowed. This main effect however refers to the difference between right and left ears, and the effect of shadowing is rather represented by the interaction "ears × shadowing instructions" which is comfortably significant.

There does not therefore seem to be any very serious discrepancy between the results of Lawson and those of Treisman and Geffen. Each of them shows a less efficient reaction to a stimulus on the ear which is not receiving attention, even though the stimulus is identical whichever ear it reaches. Perhaps the one remaining difference between the two studies is that in the Treisman and Geffen experiment many of the stimuli on the neglected ear received no response at all. In the Lawson experiment on the other hand there was a reaction even though a slow one. This may perhaps reasonably be ascribed to the fact that a tone differs from speech sounds by a clear common physical characteristic, so that the first stage of information processing, analysing such characteristics only, would ultimately throw up a tone as being something requiring a response.

Experiments Since 1958 on Dichotic Memory

In this section we shall discuss only studies aimed primarily at the generalizations already advanced. There are also a number of studies on multi-channel memory concerned with problems of cerebral dominance, and with the effects of old age, but these are logically separable and also involve visual stimulation which we have not yet discussed. They may therefore be left to a later section.

Amongst the remaining experiments, two main issues emerge. One of these concerns the speed with which the filter postulated in 1958 could change its selection: it will be remembered that the original experiment on dichotic memory span was explained by supposing that the filter could not switch from one ear to the other sufficiently fast to alternate between the ears. Several authors have questioned this interpretation. The second general issue concerns the time during the entire process, from stimulation to recall, where transfer from the parallel processing S system to the serial processing P system is performed. The basic phenomenon of dichotic memory implies that there is an earlier simultaneous stage and a later serial stage, and no alternative can be devised. Some attempts have however been made to argue that the transfer from parallel to serial organization of information takes place during retrieval for response, rather than in the original intake of information. A number of experiments have centred around this point, mostly making use of variations in the content of the information on the two ears.

STUDIES PRIMARILY ON SWITCHING TIME

Both points were raised in a paper by Moray (1960). He had two principal experimental findings which seemed to raise some difficulty for the earlier interpretation. First, he presented lists of items in which different items arrived on the two ears, but in which each item on one ear was accompanied by a space between two items on the other ear. Thus the stimuli arrived in very rapid alternation. Under these circumstances, subjects were able to reproduce the items in the actual order of arrival, just as well as if they were asked to reproduce one ear first and then the other. This seemed to suggest that a rapid shift of attention was possible between one ear and the other, and that the original interpretation of the dichotic memory experiment could not therefore be correct. The second fact of principal importance was derived from presentation of lists of the original type of Broadbent (1954b), in which pairs of items were presented in strict simultaneity, one on one ear and a different one on the other ear. Moray found that, if subjects were instructed to reproduce all items on one ear first and then those on the other, their performance improved as the presentation rate slowed down. Broadbent had used the improvement with a slower rate, when subjects were asked to reproduce items pair-by-pair, as evidence for the greater ease of switching the filter at slower speeds. Moray's result showed that the evidence was insufficient for Broadbent's interpretation.

These results in themselves challenge primarily the idea that the filter takes time to switch, but this raises a further problem. If switching time is unimportant, why does the response take the form of grouping together all items on one ear, when items are presented in strict simultaneity rather than in rapid alternation? One of the suggestions made by Moray was that, at the moment of presentation, stimuli presented in strict simultaneity had to be stored quite separately whereas stimuli presented in rapid alternation could be stored in a different fashion, preserving the natural time order of arrival. Broadbent and Gregory (1961) confirmed the general finding that stimuli presented in rapid alternation could be reproduced in time order of arrival, but challenged the interpretation that this was due to some particular form of entering the items into store. They showed that if the subject did not know at the time of presentation whether he was to be required to reproduce ear-by-ear or in actual temporal order, and was merely given these instructions after presentation, then this made no difference to the efficiency of response. Thus it did not seem that a different method of storage was necessary for the ear-by-ear response. If it had been, that form of response should have been more efficient when the subject knew at the time of presentation that it was going to be wanted. Broadbent and Gregory also showed that rapid alternation of stimuli between the eye and ear did not give the same result as rapid alternation between the two ears: the visual and auditory stimuli were grouped separately in response. The conclusion advanced by Broadbent and Gregory at that time was therefore that Moray's results did not show rapid alternation of selection between the two ears, but rather simultaneous selection of both ears, which with non-simultaneous stimuli would result in the passage of each item through the buffer store into the limited capacity P system in the actual order of arrival. Simultaneous selection of information from both the eye and the ear was however supposed impossible.

Moray's other point, that even ear-by-ear recall is improved by slow presentation, has been countered by other results.

Bryden (1962) provided evidence that a rapid rate of presentation does indeed give more advantage to an ear-by-ear recall rather than pair-by-pair recall. He employed the traditional method of presenting items in strict simultaneity, and a variety of presentation speeds and lengths of list. The subjects were left free to recall in any order they liked, and in fact a fair variety of orders was found. Ear-by-ear recall became relatively more common however as presentation speed increased. Broadbent and Gregory (1964a) adopted the alternative technique of requiring subjects to recall in a certain order, rather than leaving them free. They used ear-by-ear recall and also pair-by-pair recall, the former of which had not been used in the comparison of presentation speeds by Broadbent (1954a), while the latter had not been used by Moray. In fact ear-by-ear recall became relatively more accurate at faster speeds, thus confirming Broadbent's original argument that allowing more time allowed alternation between the channels. The original finding does therefore seem to be valid.

Another line of attack upon switching time concerns the appearance of responses in which one item from an ear appears mixed in with many other items from the other. If this happens, it seems to argue that rapid switching must have occurred.

As has been noted, Bryden found other orders of recall as well as ear-by-ear and pair-by-pair. This confirms a similar finding by Moray, and indeed there is little doubt that subjects left free to recall in whatever order they choose will very frequently give mixed orders. They may start with the first item on one ear, then give the second and third items on the other ear, and then some of the remaining items. It should be noted that this had happened even in Broadbent's original experiments, and that some confusion has probably been caused by his wording of his own results. He considered only lists in which all the items were correct, and reported how many lists of this type there were in each order of recall. At high speeds, the number of such lists in ear-by-ear order was high: but this may have obscured the fact that there were many lists having one or more incorrect items, in which subjects had attempted to reproduce the items in some order other than ear-by-ear. Mixed order of report, and attempts to report pair-by-pair, very frequently resulted in the loss of one or more items. The true finding is that ear-by-ear recall is much easier, rather than that subjects spontaneously come to use it by the light of nature. If they hit upon it, they continue to use it because their performance is better, but they often try other strategies before realizing that this is the best. The fact however that a listener could report the first item from one channel and the next two from the other suggests that he was able to shift quite fast: and this must somehow be reconciled with the greater ease of switching at slower presentation speeds.

STUDIES PRIMARILY ON CONTENT AND RETRIEVAL

The findings thus far are true of dichotic presentations consisting entirely of spoken digits. Starting in 1960, however, various experimenters began to use other types of material, and especially to employ material which fell into

F*

different classes. The earliest of these studies was by Gray and Wedderburn (1960). In one of their conditions, they used three digits and a three word meaningful phrase such as "Mice eat cheese". The meaningful phrase was arranged with the first word on one ear, the second word on the other, and the third on the first ear again. Simultaneous with each word was a digit on the other ear. They reported that subjects were just as likely in their responses to group together the words of the phrase, and keep the digits separate, as to group together the items on one ear and then give those from the other ear. Furthermore, they were equally accurate whichever they did. The general finding was confirmed in variations of the experiment reported by Broadbent and Gregory (1964a). The result still held true when subjects were instructed which order to adopt rather than using whichever they pleased. Furthermore, it was not due to guessing of the middle word of the phrase having heard the first and last words. A precisely similar result could be obtained by using three digits and three letters of the alphabet, arranged in the same mixed fashion as the digits and phrase of Gray and Wedderburn's experiment. In such a case, one could not possibly guess one of the letters from hearing the other two; it was rather that the items formed two distinct classes of content. A similar result had also been obtained by Yntema and Trask (1963), who used a number of arrangements of the two classes of item rather than simply interchanging the two middle items on the two channels. Bryden (1964a) found similar results by presenting on one ear a word which was a common associate of a word in the other ear: the two might quite well be reported together. Findings of the same kind were obtained by Emmerich and co-workers (1965). In general therefore it seems well established that a mixture of two types of items in the dichotic memory situation may result in recall with the two classes of item separate; even if this means alternation between the two ears. A similar effect does not appear if half the items are presented to the eye and half to the ear (Broadbent and Gregory, 1965b); this can perhaps be classed with the failure of stimuli to be recalled in order of arrival when they are presented in rapid alternation to eye and ear. But in the dichotic case, items of the same class can be recalled together even when presented separately.

Most of the authors cited, other than Broadbent and Gregory, adopt a broadly similar interpretation of this fact. They suggest that the grouping of items by ear of arrival in the original experiment is not a characteristic of the intake of information, but a strategy of recall. The use of non-homogeneous material rather than digits allows other strategies and so the advantage of ear-by-ear recall disappears. Perhaps the most sophisticated version of this view is due to Yntema and Trask (1963). They introduced the concept of "tagging", by analogy with procedures used in computer systems when some information is required to be stored and later retrieved. At the time of retrieval, there may be a number of items in store, and there is a problem of finding the particular one. The "tag" is an identifying feature of the stored material which enables one to find it again when the need arises. To take a hypothetical example, one might number each item successively as it came in and then place each in a store marked with the appropriate number. When later asked for, say, the tenth item, one could go to the tenth store and so find the item. In the case of dichotic listening, one could suppose that the items arriving at the right ear have been placed in a store identified by the ear of arrival, and the left ear items have gone elsewhere. When retrieval takes place, any attempt to recover an item from the right ear will produce all the items from that ear. This however might only hold true if the ear of arrival was the only possible tag, as is true with homogeneous material such as digits. If the items are of different kinds, then each might be tagged as a letter, a digit, or whatever it might be. Retrieval then could just as well be by class of item as by ear of arrival.

This kind of mechanism is one which we shall return to later, and it has interesting possibilities. It could explain failure to recall items which are nevertheless known to be stored; because they are later remembered. This is a kind of phenomenon which has always been a problem for theories of learning. In the particular case of dichotic memory, however, Broadbent and Gregory (1964a) objected to the theory on the ground that it would naturally be taken as predicting improved performance when extra retrieval tags were provided. In fact subjects remembering a dichotic mixture of letters and digits did much worse than those with homogeneous material. Mixing two classes of item made ear-by-ear and class-by-class recall equally bad, not equally good. This led Broadbent and Gregory to notice that ear-by-ear recall of such material must take the form of a sequence of response items which mixes classes; such as "A6J4L9". If such a mixture is more difficult than a sequence such as "AJL649", which groups together items of the same class, then ear-by-ear recall is labouring under a handicap. Class-by-class recall would avoid the handicap, at the cost of requiring mixing of items from the two ears. Whatever strategy the subject adopted, he would have to alternate either between ears or between classes, and so it might well be that he would do equally badly in both recall orders.

Broadbent and Gregory were able to show that a list such as "A6J4L9" is particularly hard to reproduce even if it is presented straightforwardly to a single ear without any dichotic complications. Furthermore, this difficulty depends on the rate of presentation, just as the difficulty of switching between the two ears does. When items come fast, "A6J4L9" is harder than "AJL649", but at slow rates of presentation this ceases to be true. Broadbent and Gregory argued therefore that the selection of a class of item is a process like the selection of an ear, and takes time to switch. Slow presentation allows such switching, fast presentation does not. The results of Gray and Wedderburn and their successors do not therefore show the unimportance of selection though they certainly show that the class of item is a property which can be used for that purpose. For a mechanism to explain how items of one class can be selected, Broadbent and Gregory appealed to Treisman's theory; in her terms, the threshold could be lowered for a class of units. In our present language, the pigeon-holing process could cause a class of category states all to be set to occur over a wide range of evidence, rather than states of any other class.

THEORETICAL SUMMARY ON DICHOTIC MEMORY SPAN

At this stage it may be well to summarize the position both about "switching time" and about the suggestion that the transfer from simultaneous to serial processing takes place in retrieval rather than during the intake of information. On the first point, the difficulty which many authors feel is that signals arriving in rapid succession at different sense-organs can under suitable conditions produce responses, even if slightly less efficient ones than might be possible with signals to the same sense-organ. This appears for instance in the common error found by Moray and Bryden, of reporting one digit from one ear amongst the complete set from the other ear. It occurs also in the Gray and Wedderburn situation of mixing two classes of material so that class-by-class recall requires adjacent response to two items which arrived on different ears. If we held to a strict interpretation of the Broadbent (1958) filter as excluding altogether information on one channel while selecting another, these facts would certainly require very rapid shifting of the filter. That is, if we treat the appearance of a response to a stimulus as evidence that the stimulus was selected, then switching time cannot be appreciable.

The situation is changed however by adoption of Treisman's theory with its double mechanism of selection and its filter that "attenuates" rather than excludes. The appearance of a response to a stimulus on one ear is not now necessarily evidence that the filter was selecting information from that ear, but merely that enough evidence got through to initiate the appropriate category state. This might well be consistent with the filter being set to select some other input channel, especially if the category state which finally occurred was one favoured by the pigeon-holing mechanism. Thus the concept of switching time ceases to imply that response to two successive stimuli on different senses is impossible; it merely implies that it is impossible to change the parameters of the selection system quickly. If signals on the left ear have nine chances out of ten of being the signals controlling response, that fact is consistent with the appearance of occasional responses to the right ear; the process which would take time would be a change to a situation in which signals from the right ear had nine chances out of ten of getting through. In this sense of switching time, there does not seem to be any evidence against the concept; and something of the sort is needed to explain the greater benefit which slow presentation rate confers on alternation between the ears or between classes of items.

What of the idea that selection takes place in retrieval rather than intake of information? Most of the authors who have spoken approvingly of this suggestion seem to have done so because it gives an explanation for the original finding of ear-by-ear recall, without requiring a concept of switching time; they have not provided any direct evidence for it. Such evidence could take the form of changing the conditions of performance either at presentation or at recall, and seeing whether this made any difference to the effects. If selection occurs at retrieval, then conditions at presentation should have little effect. Two main lines of argument exist here.

One concerns presentation rate. If selection takes place at retrieval, why should presentation rate affect one order of report more than the other? There would need to be some postulate in the "selection at retrieval" theory comparable with the "switching time" concept. To meet this point, one might follow an idea of Yntema and Trask, that each item is tagged with its time of arrival, as well as its ear. Retrieval in a time sequence might then be easiest if the times of arrival were more markedly different, giving more substantial tags. This idea works well for the dichotic case, and fits in with the effect noted by Broadbent (1956b), that alternation is easier if the two half-sets of the memory material are distinguished by some inconspicuous physical cue such as a difference of spectrum rather than by the conspicuous one of ear of stimulation. Bryden (1962) also showed that mixture of the half-sets was more common if the physical cue separating them was less conspicuous: he used varying degrees of separation of loudspeakers. But the suggestion breaks down on the monaural presentation of mixed material such as "A6J4L9". Here the recall is to be in time order, whether the material is mixed or not; and yet the advantage of unmixed material is least at slower speeds when the tag of time of arrival ought to be even more conspicuous and dominant. Thus the effect of presentation rate favours selection at presentation rather than retrieval.

The second line of argument concerns the subject's knowledge during presentation of the required order of report. If selection takes place during retrieval, it does not matter when before that time the listener learns his instructions. If on the other hand selection takes place at presentation or shortly after, then it may well matter whether the listener is aware at that time of what he is to do. But it was shown by Broadbent (1957b) that it does make a difference to performance in the dichotic situation when the listener is not told the order or report in advance. In subjects at normal levels of practice, performance deteriorates sharply under such conditions. In our earlier terms, the subject tries to hold all the items in the buffer store until he gets his instructions, and some of them are lost. Because of this, listeners give up such a strategy with increasing practice; they could, in terms of the model, decide at random which half-set to pass through the limited capacity system first. On half the trials they will be right by chance. If they are wrong they will have to reverse the half-sets at a subsequent stage; by the same mechanism as allows a man to repeat the second half of an orthodox memory span before the first. This will allow reasonable performance on average, but change the serial position effect; instead of the second half-set in response being much worse, because it has been in the buffer longer, it will sometimes be better and sometimes worse. This kind of performance was in fact shown by practised subjects. Thus, since instructions at the time of presentation affect response, the inference would be that selection takes place at presentation.

It will of course be noted that one part of the "selection in retrieval" model would allow effects of instructions during presentation. This part is the assignment of the tag. If the listener did not know whether he was to be asked for the right ear first, the man's voice first, the rising pitch first, or the louder first, then he might have difficulty in assigning the correct tag during presentation. It is therefore important that the foregoing experiment allowed the listener to know that selection would be on a basis of ear of arrival; but merely left him ignorant which ear was wanted first. The effects become even more dramatic if *only* one half-set is wanted in response, as we shall see in the next section.

Another and related piece of evidence under this heading is the effect of the time, during presentation of one part-set, at which other items are delivered. It will be recalled that both Broadbent and Bryden found that items in the second ear to receive response were recalled much worse if their arrival was followed by some further items on the other ear. This is readily explained if selection takes place during presentation, since in that case more items on the first ear delay selection of the second ear. It is hard to see how it can be explained on the basis of selection during retrieval. Possibly some model based on interference between items in store might be devised. But such a model would need very specific postulates to explain why an item arriving by Ear I half a second after an item on Ear II is very damaging to the latter, by comparison with an item arriving on Ear I half a second before the item on Ear II. The present author cannot see a way of doing this, and it seems simpler to take the obvious explanation.

There seems therefore to be good evidence that in some cases selection is influenced by the conditions of presentation, and therefore that it takes place during presentation (or soon after, from the buffer). This is not to deny that selection ever takes place in retrieval. Yntema and Trask's ingenious mechanism may well be real; but it is an addition to rather than a substitute for selection at presentation. As evidence for the reality of selective retrieval, let us immediately consider the case of physically alternating stimulation first raised by Moray (1960). We considered earlier, evidence provided by Broadbent and Gregory about subjects given digits in rapid alternation to the two ears. They could be asked either to recall them ear-by-ear or in temporal order, with little effect on efficiency from specifying the recall order in advance. Here the selection is at retrieval, since instructions at presentation do little good. The case differs from that of strictly simultaneous stimuli because the filter can pass the items in actual temporal order and so both kinds of tag are available at recall. We shall return later to problems of retrieval; for the present we can conclude that dichotic memory, like shadowing, affords evidence for a selection system during input as well as retrieval. But, like shadowing, it requires a selective system which may work on content. Treisman's model would handle the data, by allowing such a selective process to operate during the intake of information, much as the filter does.

The foregoing conclusions are the main ones to be drawn in this section; but there are some other findings obtained with bisensory memory which ought also to be mentioned for completeness and because of their intrinsic interest, even though they fall slightly outside the main line of argument.

(a) *Studies on methods of scoring, presentation and response.* The common element in this group of methodological experiments is that they have all been performed by Moray and his associates. (Moray and Barnett, 1965; Moray *et al.*, 1965; Moray and Jordan, 1966.) Moray and Barnett examined further the point we have already mentioned concerning scoring; namely that Broadbent had originally stated his results only for lists having all items correct, whereas other workers had scored numbers of items correct even if there were some errors. Moray and Barnett scored separately cases in which all the items were correct but not in the order required, cases in which items were left out, and cases in which items were inserted. They instructed listeners whether to recall each half-set separately or to alternate between the two; and they used fast and slow rates of presentation. The two simultaneous half-sets were not presented one to each ear, but one was in a man's voice and one in a woman's voice.

Different scores did show up different effects; first, errors of order alone were always more frequent with the alternating strategy. The size of this effect did not depend on the rate of presentation, that is, the greater advantage of slow rates for alternation found by Broadbent and Gregory did not appear using this score. Second, the other types of error did not show an advantage for the voice-by-voice strategy, but they did show effects of rate of presentation and interactions between rate and strategy. (Moray and Barnett mention only interaction in the case of commission errors, but they give the data for every subject, and it is possible to calculate that the interaction found by Broadbent and Gregory is significant for the omission errors. Slow rates are relatively better for the alternating strategy, so far as omissions are concerned.)

Thus different types of error seem to be sensitive to different changes in conditions. It is difficult to go further than that, however. Moray and Barnett suggest that order errors characterize the retrieval process and the other errors the input process, as presentation rate is presumably an input variable, and recall order is not. But this is not the only possibility, as the listeners were aware at the time of presentation of the required order of response. Thus that factor may be an input variable also. Furthermore, order errors include transpositions within a half-set and intrusions from one half-set into the other, and these might well be interpreted in different ways. Craik (1965) does indeed do so; we shall consider his results later, as they involve ageing, which is a topic worth handling on its own. There are still further complications: Moray and Barnett also showed that their results changed if the six items presented were always the digits one to six. In that case there was no problem of picking the correct items for response, and one might have expected the performance to become simply one of avoiding order errors. In fact, there were substantial numbers of omission errors, more numerous at slow speeds; in the normal condition with a full range of digits possible, omissions were more numerous at *fast* speeds. Moray and Barnett suggest that the reduction in information load produced by the restricted vocabulary removes all input difficulties. Omissions then become a measure of storage efficiency, and, if some kind of time-dependent buffer is postulated, slow presentation rates will give more errors of storage. The relation between type of error and conditions is clearly complex therefore. More studies are needed of the effects of varying information load in different ways, of giving instructions at different times, and so on. For the moment, we can draw no very firm conclusion except that the distinction of different types of errors is a very hopeful line of further advance.

Moray et al. (1965) took a step beyond the original technique by using up to four simultaneous stimuli rather than two. They employed either loud-speakers arranged in an arc around the listener or headphones giving a similar subjective impression. By this means it is of course possible to deliver, say, eight digits either as one consecutive stream from one source, or as two streams of four simultaneously, or as four streams of two. From our present point of view, the main result is perhaps that the tendency to give one channel first remained constant no matter what number of channels was used. However, when one channel had been reproduced, the remaining items recalled were scattered over the other channels. The traditional result, separating the two channels sharply, apparently depends on the fact that reporting one channel of a pair leaves only one channel from which the other items can come. As Moray et al. suggest, this seems to imply that the selection of one channel is a process performed to save time during the actual arrival of the stimuli; once the first channel has been cleared, there is relatively little advantage in producing items selectively and the strategy is abandoned

The present author would regard this as still further evidence against the idea that selection takes place in retrieval rather than in the intake of information.

Other results of Moray *et al.* are more relevant to questions of memory which will be raised later. The number of items recalled was the same when the number of channels was varied, provided that the total duration of stimulation was held constant. This implies, as was in fact true, that a larger number of channels gave worse performance if the total number of items presented was held constant. Thus, as the authors conclude, the limit on the system seems to be one of limited capacity to handle items within a fixed amount of time: putting in more items per second reduces performance even if the total amount to be stored is constant. They then, in a further experiment, show that an improvement in recall occurs if, one second after the items arrive, a signal indicates one channel only which is to receive response. The listener can get right 50% of the items on one channel only, when he could only manage 40% of the whole presentation. Thus part of the limitation must be in the response process, and a higher proportion of the input is available inside the nervous system a second after presentation than is revealed in response. The authors suggest that the limitation must therefore be in a retrieval process; but the data show that every subject did better with two channels presented than with four, even when he only had to recall one channel. While therefore one would not wish to deny the reality of retrieval processes, the rate at which information is taken into the system still seems highly important.

Lastly, Moray and Jordan (1966) departed from the usual spoken or written response, and trained their subjects to indicate which digit they had heard by pressing keys on a keyboard. The great merit of this method of response is that each hand can be used separately, so that both digits arriving simultaneously can receive response simultaneously. Quite high levels of performance could be reached by subjects instructed to respond in this way, although as we have seen previous studies have found it difficult to get subjects to respond efficiently by speaking or writing the digits in an order alternating between the ears. An incidental finding of interest was that the same subjects, when then asked to speak their response in alternating order, could do so rather better than earlier groups without the keyboard training. Presumably they were able to use their finger responses as "mediators" in some way. Unfortunately, at the time of writing no studies have been reported in which manual response was used with set-by-set recall, so we do not know whether the two response strategies have changed their relative order of difficulty, or whether both have been made easier by using a keyboard response. The former is quite possible from our present point of view, since the motor response may well be more "compatible" or undemanding. We shall return to the concept of "compatibility" later; for the moment, it will suffice that some responses are more natural and easy than other responses to particular stimuli. The decision which determines the appropriate response on any particular occasion is less complex, and there is evidence that it places less demand on the limited capacity part of the nervous system. Thus it might well be that two such decisions can proceed in parallel rather than in the serial fashion necessary for verbal responses. Although in this case the information transmitted is the same, the case is rather similar to that of two simultaneous signals which convey little information, and which can therefore be dealt with simultaneously.

(b) *Identity of an item on the two channels.* Bryden (1964a) included in his studies the interesting case of the same digit occurring on both ears in a dichotic memory task. This produced an increase in the number of crossover responses, where the double digit was preceded in response by the item which had preceded it on one ear in presentation; but was followed in response by the item which had followed it on the *other* ear. This apparently innocuous result raises a number of interesting problems. On the Treisman theory, it is reasonable that the same digit presented to both ears should give anomalous results, since the same dictionary unit is being excited from both sides; indeed, this is the explanation given for the ability of listeners to notice while shadowing that the same message is being said by somebody else on the other ear. The odd point is that Treisman's theory does not hold that the attenuating filter should then change its setting to the other ear, unless some extra postulate is put in to that effect. Nor does the firing of the dictionary unit in any way affect the threshold for the unit corresponding to the next item on the other ear. So we need some modification to the theory.

The tagging theory of retrieval also needs some extra provision for this case. If we are retrieving items by ear of arrival, there is no reason why we should suddenly change to the other tag just because there is a similar item there. In fact, on some theories we need not know the identity of the two items. This would be so for example if all access to any item was through its single tag, and the stores for each tag were separate. Bryden's result implies that the information is multiply classified. To put it another way, each item is in some way linked to any other item possessing qualities in common with it; so that retrieval of an item leads on to other items similar to the retrieved one in *any* way. On such a view we do not retrieve all items having some property in common, but rather traverse a connected network of items by the links of similarity between them.

A similar modification could be made to the Treisman theory of selection during input, for which we have indicated a preference. In such a modified theory, the dictionary unit or category state would include features corresponding to specific aspects of the input, such as its channel of arrival, as well as general features such as the digit which it signifies. The various parameters of Treisman's system would then depend upon the category state which had just occurred; the pigeon-holing would reflect contextual probabilities in speech, making certain category states more readily initiated following one previous state than following another previous state. The filtering would select further signals having elements in common with the category state just past. The effect of the last state would wear off with time, and this would give the results which we have ascribed to switching time. Far more data than Bryden's one observation are needed to establish the details of such a modification, however.

(c) *Order of report with no channel separation.* Savin (1968) performed an experiment like the original dichotic one except that all systematic differences between the channels were removed as far as possible. That is, the half-sets were spoken by the same voice, mixed onto the same electrical channel rather than each into one ear, and so on. In each pair of digits arriving simultaneously, there was therefore nothing to link each item with one rather than the other of the preceding ones. The major result is however that the response tended to give one item from each pair, then another item from the next pair, and so on; rather than to give both members of one pair before proceeding to the next. Thus the absence of pair-by-pair recall in the dichotic case is not due to the separation of the two members of the pair to opposite ears; rather the listener always prefers to deal successively with items arriving successively in time and not with those arriving simultaneously.

Once again, the interpretation of this result is not yet clear. It cannot be taken as showing that the grouping of items takes place at retrieval rather than during input, since there are reasonable grounds for supposing that even during input the listener would prefer to handle items in the way Savin shows. This argument is worth expanding.

We must, as has been said, infer a buffer store which will hold two items simultaneously before they are passed serially through some later system. From the evidence reviewed earlier, this buffer will lose items as time since their arrival increases. Thus it is important to move items from the buffer and into the later stage in such an order as will minimise the probability of loss from the buffer before the transition takes place. For a certain input condition, the average time waited in the buffer will be the same whatever the order of passage to the next stage; provided that the time taken to pass a digit from buffer to next stage is longer than the interval between the arrival of one pair and that of the next. For that case,

if $x =$ time taken to process a digit

   $y =$ interval between pairs,

then

Time waited by	Strategy Alternating	Successive
1st digit handled	0	0
2nd digit handled	x	$x-y$
3rd digit handled	$2x-y$	$2x-2y$
4th digit handled	$3x-y$	$3x$
5th digit handled	$4x-2y$	$4x-y$
6th digit handled	$5x-2y$	$5x-2y$
Total	$15x-6y$	$15x-6y$

But the *average* time in the buffer may not be the important factor in deciding the number of correct responses. It is entirely plausible that the probability of an item being recovered from the buffer decays exponentially, or at least that the probability of its being recovered drops faster at first than it does later. If so, then for the same average time in the buffer it is better to use a strategy which gives more items having a short time in store, even though this means that other items have their (already long) time in store increased correspondingly. This would mean that the successive strategy would be preferable: it contains more short times although also more long ones.

Since this is so, Savin's experiment has the following implications: (*a*) It does not disprove the existence of a buffer store before the part of the system which deals with items serially; indeed, it requires the existence of such a store just as the original dichotic experiment did. (*b*) It does not indicate whether the serial part of the system comes into play immediately on presentation or at retrieval. (*c*) On the other hand it suggests that studies of traditional type shed limited light on the problem of switching time. Such studies compare recall ear-by-ear of dichotic presentation with recall pair-by-pair. But pair-by-pair recall is difficult even when no switching between channels is involved. Such studies should rather have used, as an alternative to ear-by-ear recall, response to the first item on one ear, the second on the other, the third on the first ear, and so on. Fortunately results such as those of Bryden, on the order spontaneously adopted when no instructions are given, show that ear-by-ear recall does vary in its incidence even compared with these other alternatives as the speed of presentation is varied. Thus the conclusion about switching time already stated can be maintained.

(*d*) *Personal and other preferences for certain material.* Two studies have started a line of enquiry which is potentially most fruitful, by looking at individual differences in the kind of material most easily reproduced in the simultaneous stimulation case. Paivio and Steeves (1963) used two simultaneous voices on a tape recording, each speaking material related to a different personal value. The values used were those of the Allport-Vernon-Lindzey Study of Values, upon which each subject had been tested so that the relative interest of each individual in each value was known. They reproduced more of the material related to their own dominant value than of that related to a less dominant one. The passages involved on each voice were fairly long, and as the authors indicate it is not really possible to conclude whereabouts in the mechanism the preference exerted its effect. It could have been an effect on the original intake or on storage or retrieval. Nevertheless the result is of value as a first step in showing that the parameters of the process are individually variable.

A technique closer to the original dichotic one was used by Dodwell (1964). In his case the usual short lists of items were delivered dichotically, but words rather than digits were the items. The pair of words delivered simultaneously were different in frequency in the language, or else matched in frequency and different in rated degree of "goodness". It was quite clear that in any pair the more frequent word was the more likely to appear in response; and when a good word was paired with a bad word, the better prevailed. If, however, good was paired with neutral, and bad also with neutral, there was little general effect.

In the latter case however there was some sign of an individual difference related both to personality and to the extent to which the situation was made to seem threatening to the subject. Subjects had been assessed by questionnaire for introversion and neuroticism. When they were divided into groups for every combination of high and low scores on these dimensions, there was an almost significant difference between the groups in the extent of their preference for the better of two simultaneous words. The direction of the difference was that introverted subjects tended to show a larger preference, which Dodwell had predicted from a theory due to Inglis. The same theory held that this difference would hold only under non-stressful conditions, and that introverts would reduce their effect under stress while extroverts would increase it. Dodwell found in fact that both these changes did take place when the instructions were made more anxiety-provoking; and this time each change was safely significant. The numbers however were extremely small, only four in each group.

It will be clear that at this stage this result can only be regarded as suggestive; the theory predicting such a change under stress has several steps in it at which rather different assumptions might have been made, and the statistical weight of the evidence is not great. Furthermore, as we shall see in the next chapter, there is some evidence that difficulty of perception is associated with very pleasant as well as very unpleasant words, and this may have caused another problem in Dodwell's results. In his non-stress experiment, in order to minimise difficulties in finding words comparable in frequency of usage, he paired nice with neutral words and nasty with neutral words. The score of preference then took the nicer word in each pair; so that if the effect was truly a general difficulty in hearing emotional words whether pleasant or unpleasant the score would actually have been reduced by a large effect on nice words. The personality relationship may therefore depend upon the degree of niceness which particular personalities regard as neutral.

Despite these difficulties, this experiment is important as being one which shows advantages for some kinds of material over others, and suggests that individual biases are operating to favour some of the competing material. It also makes one last general point; the favouring of some material is not necessarily at the expense of the rest. If we compare words of equal frequency in the language, but which are accompanied by common or by uncommon words on the other ear, we find that the nature of the word in the other ear is without effect on the score for the ear considered. Thus the selective mechanism favours probable words but not at the expense of the other simultaneous word. Possibly this is to be expected from a Treisman theory of threshold being lower for probable units; in our terms, from the view that probable category states will occur to a wider range of evidence. It would certainly be quite hard to explain if a filter was selecting sounds having the features characteristic of common words, and shutting out or even attenuating other sounds. We shall come back to this kind of point in the next chapter. Meanwhile, it is clear that other studies on the relationship of personality to type of material in this situation would be valuable.

Visual Experiments in Selective Attention

We have now covered most of the research on attention in listening since 1958. If we are discussing a general psychological mechanism, however, we should not confine ourselves to one sense. One of the major advances in the last ten years has been the growth of visual research in this area.

THE ANALOGUE TO THE DICHOTIC EXPERIMENT

By a natural progression from the dichotic situation, we should consider three studies by Sampson and Spong (1961a, b; Sampson 1964) which performed the exact analogue using the two eyes rather than the two ears. The results are markedly different. If in a set of six digits each pair is delivered simultaneously, one to one eye and one to the other, the typical order of response will be pair-by-pair rather than eye-by-eye. Furthermore, within each pair the one which is seen on the left will be reproduced first. The phrasing here is important; normally the item presented to the left eye will be seen to the left of the item presented to the right eye, but not always. If the item stimulating the left eye is placed to the right of a marked fixation point, while that stimulating the right eye is placed to the left of another fixation point, then the right-eye item will be seen to the left of the left-eye item. In that case the right-eye item will emerge first in response. We have here something similar to and yet interestingly different from the auditory case. The two simultaneous items must emerge successively in response because of the nature of the speech and writing mechanisms; but these mechanisms impose no obligation on them to come out in a preferred order. At the transition from simultaneous to serial processing there seems to be a systematic selection first of the left-hand item.

Thus (a) the process is like the auditory one in that the selection for transfer from parallel to serial works on some general property of the stimuli, here spatial location; (b) the process differs from the auditory one in that it is quite capable of dealing with two spatial locations in rapid succession. How rapid we do not know, as the rate of presentation was never faster than one pair per 1·1 seconds: rather slow by the standards of the dichotic experiments. Remembering the argument we applied to the results of Savin, it would seem that with an interval as long as this, not only is there time for switching from one location to another, but also the interval is longer than the time needed to read each item out of the parallel stage into the serial one. When that is so, it becomes optimal to deal with both of two simultaneous stimuli before going on to subsequent arrivals. We shall in the next subsection find evidence that the time per item is indeed very fast in vision: but repetitions of Sampson's work with faster presentation rates would be valuable.

While the foregoing are the main results of Sampson's experiments, there are two other points which deserve attention. First, his findings showed a relationship to cerebral dominance. Although it was usual for the left-hand of each pair of items to appear first in response, which is presumably due to habits derived from reading, yet the right-hand item in each pair was more likely to be accurately recalled; provided that the subject was right-handed and especially if he was also right-eyed. If he was left-handed, this difference between the two items was reduced or reversed. We shall return later to the problem of dominance, as there are also auditory data of relevance.

The second point deserving mention is that the broad findings stated apply to visual items which would all produce the same type of response, that is, digits. In the earlier studies the visual stimuli were sometimes orthodox and sometimes unconventional digits, but the responses were always digits. The type of selection from the visual field for serial processing was always therefore that which we have been terming "filtering". In the most recent of the studies quoted (Sampson, 1964) colours were presented to one eye and digits to the other. The response appropriate on one eye was therefore drawn from a different set from the response appropriate on the other eye. In these circumstances some individual subjects reported all responses of one class before turning to the responses of the other class. The subjects were divided into two groups initially by the extent to which they did this if all colours in one list were given to the same eye; and those who did it markedly under these conditions continued to do so if one eye received, say, colour, digit, colour while the other had digit, colour, digit. The selection adopted by these subjects is that which we have been calling "pigeon-holing", and as in the auditory experiments stemming from Gray and Wedderburn, it seems that the difficulty of changing from selection of colour responses to selection of digit responses is sufficiently great to make some subjects unwilling to do so.

Rabbitt (1962) did not stimulate the two eyes independently, but rather used pigeon-holing in an ordinary visual display accessible to both eyes. In each trial he gave a series of five cards, each containing one letter of the alphabet, which might be either in red or in black. Subjects were instructed to give the five colours separately from the five letter names, that is, to use pigeon-holing as their type of selection. They were also told which class of responses to give first; and the experiment compared efficiency when the order of response was prescribed before presentation with that obtaining when the order of response was given only after presentation. Prior instruction raised performance on the first class of items recalled, and lowered it on the second. Once again therefore the effects of the selective set do not appear to be confined to retrieval, but are due to something happening during the intake of information.

BUFFER STORAGE IN THE VISUAL CASE

One of the most important advances since 1958 has come, however, not from a direct analogue to the dichotic experiment, but from a new way of using visual presentation so as to avoid difficulties over fixation and closing of the lids. If we flash a display tachistoscopically, we can present a large number of items and instruct the subject to give only a few in response. Provided the location of these is not known in advance, and provided the flash is short enough to avoid eye movements, peripheral adjustments cannot be important and the selection must be neural. Now we may give the instruction about the particular items for response either by an auditory signal (Sperling, 1960) or by a visual marker which appears next to the item which is wanted (Averbach and Coriell, 1961). In either case the instruction may be given long before the main display, or simultaneous with it, or even at a controlled time *after* it. The point of major interest is that a selective instruction given later than the display may give better performance than that possible in the unselected case; provided that the instruction arrives within half a second or so after the main display. If we give three rows of digits, and one-tenth of a second later sound a tone whose pitch indicates that only the middle row is wanted, the probability that any one digit in the row will be correct is higher than the probability of correct response for the whole three rows when no selective instruction is given. As the time between the main display and the later instruction is increased, so the performance gradually drops until it reaches a stable level at the point where it is no better than could be got without selective instruction. The time at which this happens depends of course on the precise conditions used; for example, a subsequent visual event such as an attempt to instruct the subject by a marker placed actually on top of the location of the stimulus, or a wide-spread noise field, will erase the visual information in some way and bring the performance sharply down to the unselective level. Under the best conditions however a delay of much over half a second seems to give rather little surviving advantage.

Following the same arguments we have employed several times about pre- and post-instruction, it seems here that the effect of the selective instruction cannot be in the very first stages of the neural process which follows stimulation. Rather it seems that the original display must produce some effect which is unselective, and which at first contains all the information from all parts of the visual field. Then there is a selective process which picks out some parts of this information for response, and unless this process can act within a time of half a second or so, the information is lost. In the absence of any outside instruction, the selective process will doubtless pick some parts of the display for reasons which are, from the experimenter's point of view, random. Hence some information will be available even with long delays or with no selective instructions at all.

The similarity between this conclusion and those we have already reached in the auditory case is marked; again we have the buffer store receiving items in parallel, and the selective process picking out some of them. As yet we have had no evidence that the stage after selection works serially, although it is clear that it must be supposed limited in some way. If it were not, then when instructions are delayed the whole of the buffer could be picked out for possible response and await the arrival of instructions to select some part of it at the time of recall. To fit in with our previous arguments therefore we need to know whether there is evidence for the selective process being limited in the number of items it can handle in a certain time, rather than perhaps in the absolute number of items it can select regardless of time. We should therefore consider a number of experiments by Mackworth which shed light upon this point.

Mackworth's original interest (1962a, b) lay in the effect of speed of presentation of items in short-term memory experiments of the traditional type. Many such experiments having been auditory, she tried as a variation the use of visual presentation at various speeds; and incidentally noted that a simultaneous presentation of all the items for memory was better than a serial presentation of each of them successively. She then studied the effects of changing the total time for which such a simultaneous display was available; in general, the longer the better. But for durations longer than one or two seconds the improvement from further exposure was relatively slight whereas for durations shorter than that length there was a steep improvement in recall for longer exposures. Furthermore the number of items recalled appeared to increase proportionally to the time allowed, roughly one extra digit being recalled for each third of a second increase when digits were used as the items (Mackworth, 1962c). This sounds as if some process during the stimulation is dealing with the items at a rate limited in speed; but even at short exposures of a tenth of a second or so, there were still three to four digits reproduced correctly. The subject seemed, if one supposes the input to be at a rate of three items a second, to have gained between one and two seconds of input even when the stimulus lasted objectively only a tenth of a second.

Still shorter presentations gave a break in the proportional relationship (Mackworth, 1963b) and performance at these very short durations seemed to have to do with luminance. It may perhaps therefore be left aside for the moment as being a relatively sensory effect, having to do with the establishment of items in the buffer and probably specific to vision. At the time of writing there is a good deal of study of these very rapid processes either by studies varying duration of exposure or by the insertion of interfering visual fields; and as the area is changing rapidly, is somewhat outside our main interests, and at the time of writing is rather confused we shall leave it to one side. Relevant work is that of Eriksen (e.g. Eriksen and Steffy, 1964), Haber and co-workers (Weisstein, 1966) and Sperling (1967). Neisser (1967) discusses the topic in more detail than we have done.

Returning to exposures of a tenth of a second or longer, Mackworth (1963b) asked her subjects not to wait until the display disappeared but to start responding on its appearance and continue as long as possible. The rate of response was either left free or paced at a fixed rate of three digits every two seconds. As the exposure duration increased up to two seconds, the number of digits reported increased; but the number reported after the display had gone remained constant both in the free and in the paced conditions. A key variation is now the use of items other than digits, which can only be read at a different speed. Colours, for example, are slower to name than digits. Correspondingly, the increase in the number reported from durations of different lengths is less; and the number reported after the display has gone is less. But if we calculate the time needed to read this smaller number at the slower reading rate of colours, we find that it is the same as the reading time calculated in the same way from the number of digits reported after the end of the display.

It therefore seems that there is a temporary store which continues to hold items after the end of the objective exposure, and that the time for which it holds them is constant when the nature of the items changes. For items which are slower to read, the number of items extracted from this store rather than from the stimulus itself therefore becomes less. Mackworth (1963c) extended

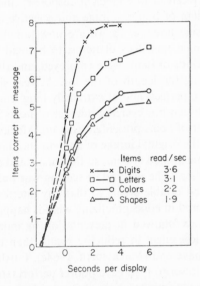

FIG. 19. The amount recalled for various kinds of material if exposures of various lengths are given. Notice that the curves all extend backwards to the same point in time: i.e. any kind of material gives performance of the level expected if it was visible for the actual exposure duration + a constant. Data from Mackworth (1963c).

these conclusions to a variety of other possible kinds of item, by giving a brief exposure and observing the linear relation between exposure duration and number of items reproduced. By extending the function backwards to the point where no items would have been correct, one finds that for all types of materials this point lies at −1·6 seconds; that is, a brief flash seems to have an effective duration of its actual length extended by 1·6 seconds, no matter which of the types of item studied was being measured.

We therefore have the evidence we wanted, that the selective process is limited in its rate of working rather than in the number of items it can pick off; that, just as we supposed in the auditory case, we have a buffer store lasting a fixed length of time, and a subsequent serial process which can extract one item after another from the buffer until the limit of time is exceeded. The speed of the serial process is less when, for example, naming colours rather than digits; and it seems therefore to have to do with the allocation of responses to stimuli. In our present terms, it is the elicitation of a category state rather than the mere transmission of evidence about the occurrence of a physical event. This however is a point better considered later in the light of findings on choice reaction time and similar topics.

Mackworth's subsequent findings are in the area of memory for items which have already received one efficient response; and are therefore less relevant to the problem of buffer storage and selective input. They may be mentioned at this stage however as we are now familiar with her general approach. She presented long lists of items, to be read aloud as they were delivered. Different kinds of items were employed, and the main interest was in the effect of varying the length of the list. At very short lengths, reproduction was of course perfect, and at extremely long lengths it was constant at a low level. In between however the number of items recalled went down linearly as the number of items presented went up (Mackworth, 1963c). Thus one could view both the original intake of an item and the recall of an item as placing a load on some limited system, so that one could only be increased at the expense of the other. (The method of scoring was only to count items in response up to the first double error, so that any interfering effects of error responses can be ignored in conceptualizing what is happening.) If a series of items of one type were followed in presentation by more items of another type, the latter had less effect in reducing recalls than further items of the original type would have had (Mackworth, 1964c). Furthermore, interpolating items which are slower to read gave poorer performance on the originally presented items than did interpolation of items which are fast to read. The effects of length of list appear also with auditory rather than visual presentation (Mackworth, 1964d).

The implication of these findings seems to be that memory even for items which have received one response, and which therefore must have been selected from the buffer and passed through later stages of the system, is still limited in some way. Recall of such items is in part incompatible with the reading of fresh ones, and the extent to which reading one new item causes forgetting of those in store depends on the difficulty of the items. But this, as has been said, takes us beyond the stage of the buffer and the selective system; so let us return to it later.

Meanwhile, the conclusion from tachistoscopic experiments on vision is that any stimulus first enters a buffer store which can hold many items in parallel; that selection from this store for later processing can then take place at a limited rate; and that any items not withdrawn from the buffer by some critical time will be lost. There is a possible difference from audition in the way the content of the buffer can be erased by following a stimulus by a noise field closely afterwards, but this difference is not absolute; in the auditory case later items do reduce the chance of retrieving earlier ones from the buffer (Broadbent, 1957b). In other ways, there seems a close similarity between the mechanisms implied by behaviour with eye and with ear. This leads us on to a closer examination of the selective process, and the extent to which it can be regarded as taking place during input of information; for there are a series of experiments on the effects of giving selective instructions before and after stimulation, and these should now be described.

PRE- AND POST-INSTRUCTION IN THE VISUAL CASE

We said at the beginning of the chapter that a firm conclusion in the auditory case was that selective instructions before presentation gave better performance than similar instructions given after presentation; and this has been appealed to repeatedly as evidence that selection is an input process. In vision however this conclusion has been challenged. The classic view, culminating in the work of Chapman (1932) was certainly that prior instruction aided selective response. By 1958 however there were some reasons to doubt this. Lawrence and Coles (1954) flashed a stimulus and either before or afterwards gave four possible verbal responses; these responses could be more or less similar to each other. If there had been some loss of information between stimulation and recall, then a more similar set of response alternatives might be expected to be more sensitive to this loss than would a less similar set. The pre-post difference in performance should be greater for the former; but it was not. Indeed, there *was* no pre-post difference in performance. Again, Lawrence and LaBerge (1956) presented two cards in a brief exposure. Each card contained several objects of the same shape and colour, so that there were six facts to be reported: two numbers, two shapes and two colours. If subjects were given "Emphasis" instructions to concentrate on one of these dimensions before presentation, performance was better on that dimension than on the others. But when the instructions simply laid down the order of recall without specifying that one dimension was more important than the others, the difference between the first and later dimensions reported was not significantly less than the difference between emphasized and unemphasized dimensions in the previous case. Thus it could be argued that the effect of selective instructions was not to alter the intake of information but rather to change the order of report.

We have here again the repeated opposition between theories of selection in input and in retrieval; perhaps recalling any one dimension causes forgetting of the others, and this is why there has seemed to be an effect of selective instructions. But this explanation is incorrect. Harris and Haber (1963) and Haber (1966) distinguished two ways in which subjects might behave in this task. One strategy, called Objects Coding, would be to observe the display and say to oneself "Three red squares, two yellow circles". This phrase could then be repeated to oneself until the recall instructions were received, and the appropriate dimension could then be reported first. Such a strategy is, in the language we have been using, a use of "filtering" to determine the order in which items pass from the buffer into the P (serial) system; information from one spatial part of the display is given priority and information from other parts is selected later. The alternative strategy would be Dimensions Coding, in which the subject would say to himself "Three two, red yellow, squares circles". In our terms, the selection here is by "pigeon-holing" rather than filtering, since the first information to be extracted from the buffer does not come from items sharing some common property such as spatial position. Rather it is information appropriate to one of a particular set of category states; number words, in the example given.

Harris and Haber found both types of strategy current in uninstructed subjects, as judged by their introspections. If subjects were deliberately trained to use one or other of these strategies, then the strategy they used made a difference to the effect of the conditions used by Lawrence and LaBerge. Pre-instruction to emphasize one dimension made a difference to Dimension Coders, but not much to Object Coders. This is reasonable; the former can pick the information to be emphasized out of buffer storage first, when there is little risk of loss from the buffer. Subjects using Object Coding would pick one spatial location first but would gain no advantage for the emphasized dimension whichever place they picked; there would always be one response on that dimension in the first material picked from the buffer, and one response in the last material picked.

With this result, there seems to be a clear picture of the effects of pre- and post-instruction in vision. The selective instruction does not operate during retrieval, in the sense of affecting only the final overt reaction scored by the experiment. Harris and Haber showed satisfactorily that different instructions about emphasis will give different levels of performance even when such a final response is in the same order. On the other hand, the instruction does not operate on the original intake of information into buffer storage. What it does do, when the task allows, is to alter the sequence in which material is taken out of the buffer during the first brief period after stimulation; if the selective strategy being used allows pre-instruction to do this, then pre-instruction will reduce the loss of desired information from the buffer. If on the other hand the selective strategy does not allow pre-instruction to alter the order of withdrawal from the buffer, it will have little advantage over post-instruction. Visual stimulation differs from auditory by its less extended nature in time, which allows all items to be present in the buffer at the end of stimulation: whereas audition may lose the first items from the buffer by the end of the stimulation, if they have not already been selected. Vision also differs because one cannot have two stimuli in the same place but of different shapes, as one can have two words spoken by the same voice but of different phonetic content; this is of course another way of putting the same point about temporal extension, and is related to the erasure of one visual stimulus from the buffer by another closely subsequent in time. For these various reasons the results of experiments on pre- and post-instruction in vision may not be as reliable as in hearing, but nevertheless it seems that the same selective processes are operating.

Stimulus Set and Response Set: Two Kinds of Selection

THE ANTITHESIS

In the last section we noted that subjects may, when the experimental situation allows it, use either of two processes for selecting material for transfer from the buffer to subsequent stages. One process corresponds to what we have been calling filtering, and one to what we have been calling pigeon-holing. The time is now ripe for looking at these two processes more closely, and trying to see whether the distinction is a clear one in behaviour or merely a rather fine point of theory. The two terms we have been using for the two processes are general ones, appropriate for all the fields covered in this book. In the case of perceptual selection, we may for the moment treat them as equivalent to stimulus set and response set. Filtering or stimulus set is the selection of certain items for analysis and response, on the basis of some common characteristic possessed by the desired stimuli. Pigeon-holing or response set is the selection of certain classes of response (category states) as having a high priority for occurrence even if the evidence in their favour is not especially high. In concrete terms, stimulus set is obtained by the instruction "Listen to this voice and repeat whatever it says, regardless of any other sounds you hear". Response set is obtained by the instruction "Listen to this medley of voices and repeat any digits you may hear". The first instruction controls the source of the stimuli controlling response, but not the vocabulary used in response; the second controls the vocabulary of responses but not the source of stimuli.

The traditional analysis of experiments on perceptual selection has not distinguished these two types of instruction, and they do of course both result in a selective response to part of the information reaching the senses. Furthermore, we have seen evidence that both take time to switch. But if we take the Treisman approach which we have found satisfactory thus far, then the two types of instruction should differ in suitable types of experiment. When discussing vigilance, we distinguished filtering and pigeon-holing by the measures d' and β. An increase in the former means that a rise in correct detections for a certain type of material has, broadly speaking, been accompanied by a constant or falling rate of false alarms for that type of material. A rise in detections produced by changing β, on the other hand, would be accompanied by a rise in the corresponding false alarm rate. In later sections we shall apply this same kind of distinction to stimulus set and response set; but for the moment let us confine ourselves to traditional measures of performance. In those measures, the two types of set should differ by the error pattern which they give.

The difference to be expected is so obvious intuitively that a formal experiment is hardly necessary to test it; nevertheless, Broadbent (1970) has reported that it is indeed true. What we expect and find is that response set shows no errors of intrusion from items designated as irrelevant, whereas stimulus set does show such errors when the stimulus to be ignored contains items drawn from the response vocabulary in use on the relevant channel. That is, when we ask a man to report any digits he hears in a medley of voices, he does not report colour names or letters of the alphabet even though such words are presented to him. When however we ask a listener to report what the man says in a mixture of voices, and to ignore what the woman says, he does sometimes report something from the woman's voice in error.

As any other result would have been surprising on almost any theory, we should perhaps look further for differences between stimulus set and response set. A valuable clue can be drawn from our general orientation, that selection takes place in order to protect a mechanism of limited capacity, the P system (serial processing system, or categorizing mechanism). Stimulus selection requires that every item be examined on arrival in order that the presence or absence of the desired common feature can be detected. If that feature be absent, no other feature need be examined. This process therefore produces a very great economy in analysis. Response set on the other hand is more complex; the arrival of each stimulus must cause evidence from it to be applied to the categorizing system and there either to produce one of the prescribed set of category states or else no state at all. It will be rare for this process to be possible by analysis of only one physical feature. If we consider the problem of picking out digits spoken by a woman's voice amongst letters spoken by the same woman, we can see that any one stimulus will need considerable analysis before it is clear that it is not a digit and therefore needs no further analysis. In some cases it may be necessary to know all about an irrelevant item before one knows that it is irrelevant; for example, a spoken "A" can hardly be distinguished from the name of the digit 8 without knowing which letter had in fact been presented. Some economy of processing can take place; for example, to distinguish letters such as B, P, T, D, from digits the final vowel would be sufficient to eliminate all digits except 3. The difference between any of the possibilities and 3 could possibly be detected by simple duration or by the behaviour of one formant alone, leaving the system in possession of the fact that this stimulus was not a digit, but not of the actual letter which it represented.

Response set then makes the rejection of irrelevant items a fairly laborious process, which may reasonably demand a sizeable share of the available capacity. Stimulus set allows easier rejection of the irrelevant. It follows that the advantage of pre-instructions should be greater for stimulus set than for response set. When it is easy to reject irrelevant items, it is better to do so as they arrive than to process them during arrival and then select only subsequently when instructions are given. Broadbent (1970) therefore performed an experiment specifically on this point. He used both visual and auditory situations, and in each case tried both stimulus set and response set. The instruction was given either before presentation or afterwards. In the latter case the instruction was delayed long enough to be sure that the buffer would have lost all its information, so as to force the subjects to pick off all the items for categorizing before they knew which were to receive response. In the auditory case the stimuli consisted of six items presented sequentially, and for stimulus set all were digits but three were spoken by a man and three by a woman. For response set all were spoken by a woman, but three were digits and three letters. In the visual case, all six items were presented simultaneously, and for the stimulus set all were digits but three were white and three were red (on a black background). For response set all were white, but three were digits and three letters.

The results in fact gave a significant advantage for pre-instruction for the stimulus set conditions but not for the response set conditions. It would be going too far to claim that response set gives absolutely no advantage for pre-instruction, however; there was an insignificant difference in the appropriate direction, the experiment was small-scale, and other studies have found pre-post differences with response set. The important point is that the advantage is greater for stimulus set. Thus there is indeed a real difference between the two mechanisms distinguished by Treisman.

Looking back at the literature, we can see that this distinction clarifies some of the results obtained. The form of instruction used by Lawrence and his colleagues was response set, and it was therefore harder for them to show any difference between pre- and post-instruction. The same is true of a similar auditory experiment by Pollack (1960) in which words were heard and possible alternatives presented later for response. We have not previously mentioned that Sperling (1960) included in his visual experiments a condition in which subjects were asked to pick out letters or digits from a mixture of both; performance with pre-instruction was so bad that subjects could do as well by selecting half the items at random for response, and post-instruction was therefore never even tried.

On the other hand, we have already mentioned that Sperling (1960) found a substantial pre-post difference using selection by spatial position on the display, that is, stimulus set. We have also mentioned various auditory experiments giving the same result, and may add that of Swets and Sewall (1961). They required detection of a tone which might be at one frequency or another, and specified the frequency either before or after each trial. This is stimulus set, and, as might be expected, gave a clear difference.

There is one discrepant result which must be mentioned for completeness, and this is that of Brown (1960). He tried selection by spatial position, by colour, and by letter/digit in a visual situation; and obtained a pre-post

G

difference only with the latter set and with all three together. Thus if anything he got more effect with response set than stimulus set. The reason for this is not all clear. Various minor features of Brown's experiment, such as the fact that his stimulus material always gave a difference in class of item between different colours even when the instruction specified colour, do not explain the discrepancy. Broadbent and Gregory have, in a number of unpublished studies, replicated these features of Brown's study and have always obtained pre-post differences for stimulus set. The explanation may lie in another point which spoils the simplicity of the picture thus far painted, but which we should nevertheless discuss.

On the theory put forward earlier, the advantage of stimulus set lies in the ease with which irrelevant items can be discarded. Generally speaking, it will indeed be true that this ease is greater for stimulus set than for response set. But suppose that the common feature which marks out all desired items is a very inconspicuous one. Suppose that we are asked to distinguish, not red items amongst white ones, but dark pink items amongst light pink ones. It is likely *a priori* that such a distinction would require more capacity than would an easy distinction; and it is known empirically that a choice reaction involving a difficult discrimination does take longer than a choice involving an easy discrimination. If stimulus set is based on some very inconspicuous feature then the rejection of irrelevant items will be slow and difficult, and there may be no great advantage for pre-instruction. Conversely, if the particular type-face used for letters and digits is one which includes clear common features for one class then rejection of that class may be quick and easy. For example, in the following sequence the digits are, on an ordinary typewriter, all larger in size than the letters: wer2tui3oas4zxc5vnm6. Less obvious distinctions may apply in other type-faces, and we shall see in the next sub-section that these differences are readily learnt. Thus the greater pre-post difference with stimulus set is not an absolute rule, but merely something which would be expected to apply in general. It certainly seems to apply to most of the literature excepting Brown's result.

EXPERIMENTS ON PERCEPTUAL SEARCH

A problem closely related to stimulus and response selection is that of a man searching a complex display in order to find the location of a particular item or items. The common domestic example is scanning down the pages of a telephone directory in search of a particular name. Here again we have the discarding of irrelevant items until a relevant one is found; but because the measure of performance must be speed in this case rather than items correctly perceived, the topic takes us into some areas of reaction time, which will be discussed in a later chapter. Nevertheless, it is so closely connected with the present problem that it is worth handling here.

(*a*) *Search by stimulus set and by response set.* Once again, in such a search task, the wanted item may differ from the other irrelevant ones in a single easily detectable feature, or it may differ only by having a particular combination of features any one of which may also occur in irrelevant items. The first of these is analogous to stimulus set, and the second to response set. As an example of the first, consider a man who is looking for a particular number on a visual display containing a large variety of similar numbers. If he knows that the number he wants is in a certain colour, the speed with which he will find it is unaffected by the quantity of other numbers in different colours which may be present on the display (Green and Anderson, 1956; Smith, 1962). If however we take a search purely by response set, in which a man searches for one of two letters of the alphabet, and there is no difference of colour; then the time he takes does depend on the number of irrelevant items present (Rabbitt, 1964a). If he is searching for a particular visual pattern amongst a number of others having no single dimension of difference from the wanted one, then the time depends on the number of irrelevant items present (Fitts et al., 1956). Equally if we have a list of items and vary the position of the wanted one in the list, the time taken to find it increases when it is further down the list (Neisser, 1963). In the case of colour selection the rejection of irrelevant items is so fast as to be the same however many irrelevant items there are; in the case of search for an item distinguished only by shape the rejection of each irrelevant item takes a measurable amount of time. Once again therefore the difference between stimulus and response set is a real and important one.

(b) *The mechanism of response selection: establishment of a group of feature analyses.* A good deal of interest attaches to the details of the way in which search by response selection operates. We can show that such a search involves the scanning of each stimulus for certain features, but does not mean a complete perception of every irrelevant item.

As the first step, consider a case in which the man looks at a card carrying several letters. All but one of these are irrelevant, but the relevant one may be either A or B. If there is an A, the card is to be put in one place; if a B, the card is to be put in another. Thus there is a two-choice reaction to every card, and by timing the sorting of a pack of cards the speed of the whole process can be measured. As already indicated, the time increases as the number of irrelevant letters increases. But the experiment can be repeated using eight relevant letters rather than two, and when this is the case the effect of increasing the number of irrelevant letters is greater (Rabbitt, 1964a). In some sense the man can be thought of as performing for each letter on the card a three-choice reaction in one case and a nine-choice reaction in the other: which relevant letter is it or is it irrelevant?

The extent to which this is true will however depend on the nature of the set of irrelevant letters. As the next step, suppose that there were two alternative relevant letters, but that these were C and O rather than A and B. If the irrelevant items are always chosen from the set AEFHIKL, then the presence of a straight line is always enough to distinguish the irrelevant items. If the irrelevant set is BDGJPQS this is no longer true. Subjects trained with the first kind of irrelevant material are disrupted by being transferred to the second kind, but not by transfer to another set of straight-line irrelevant letters. Clearly therefore they are learning to make the rejection of a letter by the simple test of presence of straight lines (Rabbitt, 1967a).

When we do not control the set of irrelevant letters so as to have one common feature, there is still some learning of the particular features present in the set; we can show this by transferring practised subjects to another set of letters, and showing that this brings a deterioration (Rabbitt, 1964a). The decrement is bigger with a larger set of relevant items, presumably because more separate features have to be learned to identify items as relevant in that case. The learning of this larger set of features might be supposed to take a longer time: at least the decrement for a large set of relevant items only exceeds that for a small set when prolonged practice is given before transfer (Rabbitt, 1967a: in this experiment the eight relevant items were divided into two groups, all members of one group receiving the same reaction. This will have a bearing on the effects of practice, since naturally more practice is needed to make the same response to four different stimuli than to one, regardless of the irrelevant stimuli present.).

We have here a useful principle, that after practice only those features of the stimulus are analysed which are necessary to allot it to one of the category states in use, including the state marked "irrelevant". Such a principle is thoroughly consistent with other discrepant results in the literature: for example, the classic work of Fitts and his colleagues (1956) on pattern perception, which was hard to handle in the framework of the time. Their studies employed patterns chosen from a prescribed set of possibilities. For example, suppose the patterns consisted of four vertical columns, and each column could have one of four heights. Any one pattern was then chosen from 256 alternatives. If the choice was restricted to a sub-set of the total population, each pattern naturally conveyed less information. If one made the restriction that no two columns in the same pattern could have the same height, then there are only 24 possibilities. As we said earlier, a stimulus drawn from a small set of possibilities is usually easier to handle; it is better perceived under difficult conditions, it is easier to perform some other task while reacting to it, and so on. When however Fitts and his colleagues gave a pattern as a target and asked subjects to find the same pattern in a group of patterns chosen from the same set, then performance was better with patterns drawn from the full set than from the sub-set. With the sub-set it is of course necessary to analyse more features of any pattern to be sure that it is not the target; with the example given earlier, the probability that the left-hand column of any one pattern is the same height as that of the target is 0·25 whether we are dealing with the full set or a sub-set. Given that the left-hand column is the same as the target, however, the probability that the next column is also the same as the target is 0·25 for the full set but 0·33 for the sub-set. Thus the proportion of possible patterns possessing two features in common with the target is higher for the sub-set than for the full set; and correspondingly a search for the target amongst patterns drawn from the same class of possibilities will be harder for the sub-set. It is the nature of the search task which makes the small sub-set of items with more common features present greater difficulty; with other tasks using the same visual material the sub-set may be no harder (Anderson and Leonard, 1958).

Another example of the same process is to be found in the work of Foster (1962). Searching for a word beginning with a certain letter, on a page of words, is faster than searching for a word beginning with a certain sequence of two or three letters; there were in the latter case irrelevant words having some but not all of the required letters, so that more features had to be analysed in order to find the target. On the other hand, instructions to search for a word which was broadly defined rather than narrowly specified gave a slow search: in this case, more features of each irrelevant word would need analysis before it could be rejected.

(c) *Serial and parallel analysis of features.* Our argument thus far has proceeded as if the examination of an item, to see whether or not it possesses several different features, must proceed in series rather than parallel. We have spoken as if a visual letter cannot be examined simultaneously for the presence of straight lines, concave downward curves, lines ascending or descending above the general height of the text, and so on. At least we have been implying that such simultaneous analysis must take longer, through loading capacity, than analysis for one feature only. But this is not necessarily so; under some conditions it certainly takes no longer to test for several features than for one. One such case comes from the type of task already mentioned briefly, in which the same response is to be given to any of a class of possible stimuli. Such a task might, for example, present digits as stimuli and require one response to odd digits and another response to even ones: there are then five stimuli for each response. It has been shown by Rabbitt (1959, 1964a) and by Pollack (1963) for visual and for auditory stimuli respectively that such tasks may give surprisingly little increase in reaction time as the number of stimuli per response is increased. The effect depends in fact on the number of possible responses as well as the number of stimuli; for two-choice reactions it makes little difference whether there are two, four, or eight possible stimuli for each response. There is some increase between the case of one stimulus per response and that of two stimuli per response, but even this disappears if one can get a situation in which subjects are highly practised. Broadbent and Gregory (1962a) found such a situation by presenting place names either in upper or lower case type; that is, the subject had to make the same reaction either to HARLOW or to Harlow. This equivalence is very highly practised, and correspondingly subjects could react as fast when the nature of the stimulus was uncertain as when all stimuli were in one size of type. Thus with small numbers of responses it seems that the man can analyse the stimulus simultaneously for the presence *either* of one set of features or for another, as long as the same response is being given for either.

This is less true, however, when there are more possible responses; with large response vocabularies, there is a definite slowing of response when the number of possible stimuli per response increases. Without too much straining one could suggest that the number of features that can be detected in strict simultaneity is limited, and thus that it is difficult to cope as easily with 48 as with 16 stimuli controlling 8 responses. One can however, as we have said, cope as easily with 48 as with 4 stimuli when only two responses are in question. To distinguish only two responses will naturally need a smaller number of features, though the exact number is unknown.

The possibility of parallel rather than serial processing is important because some variations on experiments in perceptual search do not find an increase in the time taken to reject each irrelevant item as the set of relevant items is increased. The major group of such experiments is provided by Neisser (Neisser *et al.*, 1963. Some unpublished results are also given by Egeth, 1967). In Neisser's case the subject had merely to find the wanted item in a long list, whereas in Rabbitt's there were different reactions to some wanted items and to others. Neisser found that search was as fast for ten different possible wanted items as for one, whereas as we have seen Rabbitt found that increasing the set of relevant items from two to eight increased the time taken to reject each irrelevant item; i.e. the search time. Thus Neisser did find simultaneous processing while Rabbitt's evidence is consistent with serial processing.

The discrepancy between the two cases need not be taken too tragically; Neisser's task is clearly similar to that of Rabbitt's other work and of Pollack, where several different possible stimuli can give rise to the same response. Effectively the choice for every item was simply "Relevant or irrelevant?", whereas in Rabbitt's experiment the choice was "Which relevant item or is it irrelevant?". Thus we might expect fewer features to need analysis in Neisser's case, and thus simultaneous processing to be more possible. Rabbitt (1966a) has provided another difference: the probability that any given item was relevant was low in Neisser's case but high in Rabbitt's. If one carries out the card-sorting task with two relevant letters embedded amongst irrelevant ones as before, but if one includes a high proportion of cards with no relevant letters at all, one can instruct the subject to put these cards in a separate category. In this experiment the time taken to deal with extra irrelevant letters does not depend on the size of the set of relevant ones. Thus if the presence of a relevant letter is unlikely, the man seems to test each letter for relevance in parallel; one might represent the operation as first asking "Relevant or irrelevant?" and only if the former is found asking "Which relevant?". The relative attraction of this strategy will naturally increase as the probability of relevance declines.

Others of Neisser's findings are thoroughly in accordance with our general point of view; thus the search is slower if the irrelevant items are more similar to the wanted one, and also slower if search is for the absence of a particular item rather than its presence. Both these findings imply that the system is analysing only the minimum number of features consistent with rejecting irrelevant items. In the first case, each irrelevant item possesses several of the features possessed by the target; thus analysis for several features is needed to ensure detection of the critical differences.

The case of searching for absence is especially interesting; the comparison is between a man examining, say, 50 groups of six characters searching for the one group *with* a particular character, and a man examining the same size of display for the one group *without* such a character. In this last condition, we might expect that the man could look at each character in the group in turn, and give up the group as soon as he finds the one key item; thus he should get through the groups *faster*. The fact that he does not implies that for some reason he takes longer over key items than over irrelevant ones; the plausible reason is that each key item has to be analysed for all its features in order to be sure that it is not an irrelevant one, and this takes longer than discarding clearly dissimilar items would do. The case is similar to that of Fitts *et al.* (1956).

The broad conclusion, both from Neisser's results and Rabbitt's, is that search by response set involves only partial analysis of the irrelevant items. Neisser's subjects could not introspectively recall the irrelevant items, nor recognize them amongst a similar number of items which had never been presented. Egeth (1967) rightly points out that the latter effect will presumably depend on the nature of the incorrect alternatives presented in the recognition test; but at least knowledge of the items which have been observed during the search is imperfect. Rabbitt gave in his task letters drawn from the whole 26 possibilities of the alphabet, whether two of them were in the relevant class or eight. For any given number of letters on the display, performance was faster if the relevant class was smaller; thus the man was not simply making a 26-choice reaction to every letter on the card. (This has been found also by Nickerson and Feehrer, 1964.) As we said when introducing the concept, response set may require the analysis of several features of irrelevant items; but not all features. These findings bring us yet again to a conclusion which is familiar; selection takes place during the intake of information or shortly after, from the buffer, and it is false to think of all incoming information as being analysed and then selected only in retrieval.

(*d*) *Theoretical conclusions: the distinction of pigeon-holing from cate-*

gorizing. From the results on perceptual search, we are led once again to distinguish stimulus and response set as important extreme strategies of performance, and in addition to clarify a little our ideas about response set. Taking up the language of the first chapter, we must say that the evidence relevant to the occurrence of any category state is derived from detection of the presence or absence of many features of the stimulus. In filtering or stimulus set, the detection of these features is performed hierarchically, so that if a stimulus possesses feature *A* it is more probable that the presence or absence of feature *B* in that stimulus will form part of the evidence reaching the categorizing system. In pure response set, the detection of features is not hierarchical in this way. In response set evidence regarding the presence of *B* in a stimulus is passed to the categorizing system regardless of the presence of *A*; but evidence about the presence of *B* is only passed if it is relevant to the occurrence of one rather than another category state, including the state which we may label "This stimulus requires no response". Thus the existence of a response set does have some possible effect on the evidence which is used and not only on the category state which is most likely to result. In the terms of the first chapter, response set involves both pigeon-holing and categorizing, and the distinction should be amplified at more length. Let us restate our position.

Given a mechanism for detecting the presence or absence of many features of the stimulus, there will be some unreliability in the chain of events from the stimulus to the state of evidence within the nervous system. The evidence will not always correspond exactly to the features of the original stimulus; some features may fail to be detected when they were in fact present, others may be falsely detected in their absence, and no evidence at all may be received about others. There must therefore be some rule for deciding whether a given state of evidence is to lead to a particular category state; and certain category states may become more probable by the use of rules which cause them to follow a large number of possible states of evidence. Thus suppose there is a state of evidence which indicates the detection of a heard vowel of the type which occurs in "three". For a certain listener at a certain time there may be a rule which causes the category state of "three" to occur rather than those of B, C, D or some other of the letters of the alphabet with similar-sounding names. At another time, when the listener has had different instructions or a different recent history, the rule joining evidence to category state might be just the reverse, and the category state "*B*" might occur to a state of evidence recording occurrence of the appropriate vowel. This change in the rules is the process we have been calling pigeon-holing, and it alters the number of states of evidence which will lead to any particular category state. But results from experiments such as those of Rabbitt force us to recognize that the same category state may result from different states of the outside world rather than simply from different states of evidence internally; a man can make the same response to "Harlow" and "HARLOW" with as much ease as he can perform with only one stimulus for each response. Furthermore, when he is searching for A or B, he can reject as irrelevant X, Y, or Z faster than he can choose between 26 alternatives and without knowing exactly what the irrelevant letter was. We do not even know that the different stimuli give rise to different states of evidence, although they may do so. But certainly we have to recognize a convergence at the next stage, that of "response" in the general sense whether the man is to say, write, remember or type what has been presented; that is, there is a common category state for several states of the world.

The concept of categorizing differs therefore from that of pigeon-holing in that the former changes the rule connecting a set of stimuli to a set of responses, while the latter changes only the rule connecting a set of states of evidence to a set of responses. The difference is revealed in the studies of response time already discussed, and it would also be shown in measurements of d' and β; the former, representing the contribution to response from the nature of the stimulus, would presumably be altered in categorizing though not in pigeon-holing. Pigeon-holing and categorizing differ also in their liability to rapid change; the former can be altered in a very short time of a second or so, as we have seen. The latter on the other hand seems from the results of Rabbitt to be a slowly changing process resulting from considerable practice in the particular situation. In experiments on perceptual selection therefore, where we have usually been dealing with the effects of instructions and using well-established categories such as letters and digits, we have been reasonably correct in regarding response set as purely pigeon-holing; but in perceptual search it becomes clearer that there is an element of categorizing as well. In vigilance, categorizing was unimportant because it is essentially a process arising with many different possible stimuli, and pigeon-holing was the only alternative to filtering. Equally, categorizing may be unimportant when the number of alternative category states is large, so that there is much overlap between the features distinguishing them; but this is an empirical question to which we shall return in the next chapter.

IRRELEVANT INFORMATION IN REACTION TIME MEASUREMENTS

Having touched upon questions of reaction time, we should deal also with certain other aspects of that field which relate to response set. In studies of reaction time, the stimulus which is presented may have features other than the one which is controlling reaction; if a man is to press one key for square stimuli and another for round ones, he makes the same response whether there are two squares or only one. In a sense therefore he is performing a perceptual selection and his performance becomes relevant to this chapter. With a task of the type just described, we might expect that categorizing would occur, and that the speed of a trained man would be just as great when

G*

the number of squares and circles was varying from trial to trial as when it was held constant. It has indeed been shown by Morin *et al.* (1961) and by Fitts and Biederman (1965) that reaction is as fast in either case. The result seems to depend on the possibility of ceasing to analyse the irrelevant features of the stimulus, since a slight change in the task which prevents this can give quite a different outcome. The change in question is to make the reaction still one of two, but to make the stimuli appropriate to one reaction "A single square or two circles" and the stimuli for the other reaction "A single circle or two squares". Such a task requires the analysis of both features and correspondingly takes, for unpractised subjects, much longer than does the choice between squares and circles. Results differ on the extent to which practice can overcome this; Morin *et al.* found that with practice the slower task would speed up to the level of the faster, presumably by the formation of a new category. Fitts and Biederman however never secured such a complete elimination of the effect; their fast task was more "compatible" than that of the earlier authors, a matter which we shall discuss in a later chapter. For present purposes, the point is that analysis of both features does take time, at least in unpractised subjects.

As a matter of terminology, it may be useful to note that Posner (1964) has introduced the following terms for the tasks just discussed: *conservation* tasks refer to those in which there is one response for each possible stimulus, *gating* tasks are those in which some features of the stimulus can be ignored, and *condensation* tasks are those in which the number of responses is less than the number of stimuli, but in which a feature may be appropriate to one response in the presence of another feature and to another response in its absence.

Condensation tasks clearly involve the analysis of all the features being presented, whereas gating tasks can logically be performed without the irrelevant features being analysed at all. One may well ask therefore whether such irrelevant features ever have any effect on performance? In fact there is one important case in which they do, and this is illustrated by the Stroop Test, a task largely used in research on individual differences and on effects of drugs, rather than by experimental psychologists interested in perceptual selection. Work on the Stroop Test has been thoroughly reviewed by Jensen and Rohwer (1966); the basic task requires the subject to look at a display containing a series of colour names. The names are each printed in different colours, and the ink of any one name is not in the same colour as the name itself indicates. The task is to name the colour of the ink and to ignore the word itself. This takes longer than does the naming of patches of colour or the reading of colour names. The interest of students of individual differences lies in the extent of the interference in one person rather than another; but from our point of view it is striking that there is an interference at all, since the shape of the letters of the printed word is clearly an irrelevant feature.

The distinctive quality of the Stroop Test is however the fact that the irrelevant features are appropriate to the same set of responses as those used for reaction to the relevant features. Thus response set does not allow the shutting out of these features as it does of the number of squares and circles if only shape is relevant. Intrusion errors are liable to occur, just as they do in perceptual selection using stimulus set, and it is the guarding against these errors that takes the extra time. The generality of this conclusion is shown by the highly similar effect found by Morton (1969a), who required subjects to react to the number of objects on a card and found interference when the objects were themselves numbers. Intriguing light is shed upon the mechanism by variations on the experiment; Klein (1964) used colour names which were not in fact of colours used for the inks, and found an interference which was high but not as high as for the same set of colours. Morton obtained similar results with numbers. In Klein's case, words common in the language or words associated with colour were more interfering than rare or nonsense words; and again Morton obtained rather similar results in his related situation. The use of a set of responses (category states) such as colours or digits appears to bring into readiness other related responses and features appropriate to these also may give interference.

The wording of the last sentence begs a question: is the main factor the relation of the responses now in play to those appropriate to the interfering features, or is it rather that the latter elicit previously trained responses without regard to the set now being used? It is the former explanation which seems most probable; Imai and Garner (1965) used a task in which dots on cards had to be sorted with reference to one of three possible features. Although subjects all performed under each condition, and therefore had established responses to each feature, the amount of variation of irrelevant features was without effect on the sorting time. The task was nevertheless a sensitive one, as the extent of variation of the *relevant* feature did affect the speed of sorting. It seems plausible therefore that a previously established response to the irrelevant features is only important if there is some connection between that response and the others in play in the task itself; that is, if response set is unable to operate. (For completeness, we may mention that Imai and Garner also examined the condition in which subjects were allowed to sort by any feature they liked. In that case, the use of a particular feature was more frequent when there was a good deal of variation in that feature between different cards. The use of one feature also depended on the amount of variation in other features, however; that is, the subjects tended to use the more "noticeable" feature. This task is therefore in contrast with that in which the subjects were told to select one feature for sorting.)

One possible counter-instance should be noted; Hodge (1959) for vision and Montague (1965) for hearing found effects of irrelevant features when subjects had at other times been required to react to them. These studies used however a rather special technique, which made them studies of condensation and not of gating; the relevance or irrelevance of a certain feature was unknown before presentation of the stimulus, and depended on the presence or absence of other features. To give a simplified analogy, a four-choice reaction could be set up using two pairs of keys for response, and one stimulus feature could decide whether the left-hand or the right-hand pair of keys was to be used. A second feature is then needed to decide which key is correct within each pair. This feature can be arranged to be the same whichever pair is concerned, or alternatively one feature can decide between members of the left-hand pair and another between members of the right-hand pair. In the latter case, it will be true that one of the total of three features is irrelevant to reaction, but the subject cannot tell which one until he has found out whether the left-hand or right-hand pair of keys is appropriate on this particular trial. Both Montague and Hodge used this method of introducing irrelevance, and it is certainly true that subjects take longer when there is irrelevance of this kind. We may however interpret this result as consistent with the general position that response set is unable in this case to render these features temporarily ineffective because of their relevance to certain responses needed in the task itself.

In this field also therefore we can see differences between selection by stimulus set and by response set; the former is more liable to intrusion errors, and the latter is therefore necessary to get the greatest independence of reaction time from irrelevant features of the stimulus. Just as in experiments on shadowing or on dichotic memory, the working of stimulus set does not seem to be absolute; despite the advantages which it has for pre-selection in perceptual selection, it does not bar irrelevant features completely but merely lowers their probability of securing response. The stage has now been reached where we should examine this reduction of probability in the terms we introduced in Chapter III.

Stimulus Selection and Measures from Decision Theory

THE REDUCTION OF d' BY DIVERTING ATTENTION

We have already indicated that a major change introduced by Treisman into the "filter theory" of 1958 was the idea that listening to one channel did not imply shutting off all information from other channels. Rather she suggested that there was a reduced but still real probability of neglected channels breaking through to produce response. This is essentially a theory based on the existence of some randomness in the processing of information, rather than on the completely determinate approach we have considered thus far in this chapter. Thus the measures and the concepts derived from decision theory become of importance, and some experimenters have applied them to this problem.

In Treisman's model, there are two places where selection may operate, corresponding to the terms stimulus set and response set which we have been employing. One of these would increase the amount of information entering the perceptual system from some stimuli at the expense of others; while the other kind of set would increase the probability of certain outputs from the perceptual system, without affecting the information entering the system. That is, one mechanism would affect d' and one β in the measures of decision theory. In the 1958 model of Broadbent, filtering would give an effect like that produced by failure of observing response in the approach of Jerison discussed in Chapter III. That is, it would give a rise in β on channels which were not selected by the filter; there would be no response to such channels. There would also be a change in d' and a skewing of the graph of detections against false alarms, just as in the vigilance case. (Broadbent and Gregory, 1963b concentrated upon the prediction of a change in β if the 1958 model were true, but in the light of more recent thinking it seems clear that the other predictions are also implied.)

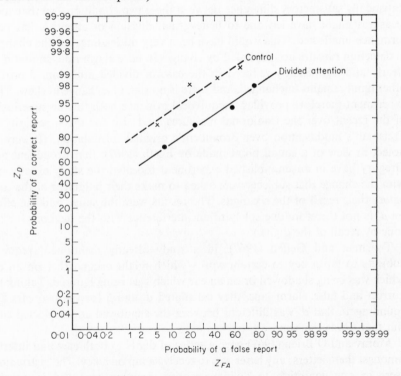

FIG. 20. The relationship between correct and false detections of a tone when attention is concentrated on the appropriate ear, and when it is divided between that ear and the other. Notice that performance shifts to another function, rather than along the same curve; and also notice that the normalized curve retains the same slope. That is the division of attention does not seem to be due to intermittent observation of each ear. Data from Broadbent and Gregory (1963b).

We can therefore check the relative merits of Treisman's modified theory and of the original formulation by analysing an experiment on selective perception with the measures of decision theory. This was undertaken by Broadbent and Gregory (1963b). They used a dichotic presentation in which six digits arrived at one ear and a burst of noise at the other ear. The noise might or might not contain a pure tone, and the subject was asked to judge whether or not it did do so. He indicated his confidence in his judgment on a rating scale, and just as in the case of vigilance a complete plot of detections against false alarms for various levels of confidence can be constructed from the data. The interesting comparison was between conditions in which the man was to ignore the digits on the opposite ear, and those in which he was to report the digits before making his judgment about the tone. In the former case he could concentrate upon one ear, while in the latter case he had to divide his attention between two ears.

Conventional measurement of the number of tones detected did not give a statistically satisfactory difference between these two conditions, so that such measures might have led one to believe that division of attention left performance unaffected. This would have been very misleading; for the changes in detection rate are accompanied by changes in false alarm rate, so that d' is clearly and significantly reduced in the case of divided attention. β on the other hand remains unchanged, and there is no sign of a change in skew. This experiment therefore provides unequivocal evidence both for the superiority of the recent over the traditional measures, and also for the superiority of Treisman's modification over Broadbent's original formulation. (It may be noted, in view of a sound point made by Egeth (1967), that Broadbent and Gregory have in an unpublished experiment repeated the study exactly but with the change that subjects were asked to make their judgment of the tone *before* their recall of the six digits. The results were the same, and the effect on d' is not therefore due solely to an interference with the memory for the tone by recall of the digits.)

Treisman and Geffen (1967), in a study already mentioned, required subjects to tap a key to certain words which might occur either on an ear which was being shadowed or on an ear which was being ignored. Taking the correct and false alarm taps, they calculated d' and β for the two ears and found again that d' was different between the shadowed and neglected ears, but that β was the same.

Moray and O'Brien (1967) gave a series of digits to both ears and inserted amongst them letters; any letter was to receive a tap on a key. The instructions were in one condition to divide attention between ears and in another condition to concentrate on one ear. Once again d' showed massive changes, being the same on both ears when attention was shared but significantly higher on the attended ear and lower on the neglected ear if there was concentration on one ear. β gave no such massive changes; Moray and

O'Brien draw attention to the occasional differences which did occur, noting that six out of eight subjects give a smaller β for the rejected than for the accepted ear in one half of the session, but this can reasonably be put down to chance. The shift, such as it is, will be noted to be in the wrong direction for the older filtering model; people are more willing to respond on the neglected ear.

At the empirical level therefore it is generally agreed that division of attention by these various means and instructions produces a change in measured d' but not in the measure of β. Moray and O'Brien raise two other issues however which are important enough to deserve sections to themselves; the first especially has implications well outside the area of selective perception.

THE CONSTANCY OF β UNDER DIFFERENT CONDITIONS

We said in Chapter III that it was an empirical question whether men actually behave with a constant β when the intensity of a signal changes. An ideal observer may certainly do so if signal probability and the gains and losses in the situation remain unchanged; even though the strength of the signal is altered. But we have seen many grounds for doubting the axioms of decision theory in their application to men; and we indicated in Chapter III that human observers might well elect to keep their false alarm rate constant or to operate at a constant point along the scale of evidence rather than to perform the complicated calculation needed to hold β constant when d' changes. Moray and O'Brien point out that their data show a set of significant correlations of $\log \beta$ and d'; that is, those people who had a high d' also had a large value of $\log \beta$, under any particular condition. This casts a good deal of doubt upon the idea that human observers actually perform with constant β for a particular set of signal probabilities and values; and it can be added that Jerison *et al.* (1965) present similar correlations for their vigilance data. While the fact has not been previously published, we may add that similar relationships appear in the results of Broadbent and Gregory.

From the point of view of our interest in the relative merits of filter theory and of Treisman's modification of it, we may well be perturbed by an indication that people do not work with constant β. If they work instead with a constant false alarm rate or a constant position on the scale of evidence, as stimulus intensity changes, then the results summarized in the last section do not mean quite what they seem to mean. A measurement of β shows that it does not change as attention is diverted from the stimulus; but if β does not change when d' does, that itself implies that false alarm rate and position on the scale of evidence have changed. Thus the results we have described by Broadbent and Gregory, Treisman and Geffen, and Moray and O'Brien only support Treisman's theory if we can confidently say that it is β rather than some other measure which reflects the bias in favour of or against responding,

Quite apart from this issue, there is of course a good deal of interest in the topic of constancy of β in its own right, and we should therefore examine the point.

The possibility of constant false alarm rate need not perhaps be taken very seriously. If the false alarm rate were a simple measure of the bias towards a particular response, then the studies of the last section would imply that attending to one ear actually *reduced* the bias towards responding to that ear. There were fewer false alarms on the selected ear. What however are the implications of the theory that position on the scale of evidence remains constant?

We have here again a difficulty which came up in Chapter III; there is no way of fixing a zero for the scale of evidence. For a start, let us take the case in which the zero lies at the point where $\log \beta$ equals zero, that is, where the underlying normal distributions cross and the evidence is as likely to result from signal as from non-signal. In that case, to maintain a constant position on the scale of evidence implies keeping a criterion distant by a constant amount C from the point where $\log \beta$ equals zero. At such a point, the ordinates of the two distributions are given by

$$\frac{1}{\sqrt{2\pi}} \exp\left(-\frac{1}{2}\left(\frac{d'}{2}+C\right)^2\right) \quad \text{and} \quad \frac{1}{\sqrt{2\pi}} \exp\left(-\frac{1}{2}\left(\frac{d'}{2}-C\right)^2\right)$$

taking the standard deviation of each distribution as unity. From which, as Taylor (1967) points out, it is easy to work out that for constant C

$$\log \beta = Cd'.$$

The correlations between $\log \beta$ and d' found in experiment are therefore consistent with the idea that people are working at a constant value of C. Furthermore, the experiments giving a constant $\log \beta$ when attention is diverted might be consistent with a bias away from the neglected ear; constant β with smaller d' implies larger C, and thus greater reluctance to respond even though the false alarm rate may be increasing.

Fortunately for our general argument, this possibility does not seem to be tenable. It might explain the results of Treisman and Geffen, and of Moray and O'Brien, because in those studies only one value of $\log \beta$ was determined under each condition. In each case, $\log \beta$ was positive, and thus it would indeed be the case that a more positive value of C under divided attention might combine with a reduced d' to give the same $\log \beta$ as under concentrated attention. But in the study of Broadbent and Gregory a whole curve of detections against false alarms was obtained, including the case when $\log \beta$ was negative. In that case, if C had moved in the direction of reluctance to respond, then for a reduced d' we would have calculated a very much altered value of $\log \beta$. The fact that $\log \beta$ remains unchanged both when the subject is saying "Sure it was a signal" and when he is saying "Sure it wasn't a signal" makes it very implausible that the underlying process is a change in C which happens to be exactly corrected by a change in d' so as to give a spuriously unchanged β. It seems much more likely that the subject does operate on a basis of β, and that he holds it unchanged when listening to one ear rather than the other. Similar arguments apply if we take some different zero for the scale of evidence; if for example we take the mean of the non-signal distribution as our zero, then

$$C = \frac{\log \beta}{d'} + \frac{d'}{2}.$$

Here again, if C is the fundamental variable, then the extent of any change produced in the measured value of $\log \beta$ will depend on the values of d' and of C with which one is working. To get unchanged values of $\log \beta$ when d' changes, both at positive and negative parts of the range of $\log \beta$, is very unlikely unless β is the fundamental variable.

We may now add yet further direct evidence that subjects operate with constant β, from a field distinct from that of perceptual selection. Ingleby (1969) has studied vigilance for auditory signals in highly practised subjects; comparing sessions in which the intensity of the signal was always fairly high and those in which it was always fairly low. This of course gives different values of d' for the two kinds of session; but $\log \beta$ remained constant. If C is calculated on the assumption that the zero is at the mean of the non-signal distribution, then it changes significantly when the signal is more intense. A particularly interesting point is that this holds true only when the subjects have had a large number of sessions with the task; initially they perform with C constant at the two intensities and show a significant difference in $\log \beta$ between them. Once used to the task however they perform with constant β. A particularly strong piece of evidence is that an extra stimulus, which changes the probability of a signal, gives a change in $\log \beta$ which is the same for both signal intensities. The change in C for one and the same stimulus must therefore be different at one signal strength from that at another signal strength. It seems clear that β is the fundamental variable in practised subjects.

What of the correlations of $\log \beta$ and d'? It should be remembered that these are correlations across individuals. Hence they mean that different people tend to work at the same point on the scale of evidence and to have values of β which depend on their d'. For any one individual however changes in d' do not necessarily leave his performance at the same point on the scale; he changes his behaviour so as to keep constant the value of β which, for him, corresponded to the original position on the scale of evidence.

More data are obviously needed on this point, from a wider variety of tasks and conditions. For the moment we may leave it that constancy of β is the most probable principle, and that therefore the experiments on diversion of attention do have the implication that they seem to have.

THE NATURE OF PERFORMANCE IN COMBINED TASKS

The other point raised by Moray and O'Brien was the interpretation of the drop in d' for one task when it is combined with another. Does this drop mean that there is a continuous steady loss of information from both the sensory systems involved, or does it mean that the man takes in information sometimes from one system and sometimes from the other? As we said earlier, Treisman wisely left these possibilities open, and it is not essential to know which is true if our purpose is simply to make clear that division of attention reduces the intake of information from each channel without abolishing it altogether. The distinction is still interesting, however.

Moray and O'Brien present two pieces of evidence on this point, which have opposite implications. First, they consider the cases in which signals were in fact present on both ears simultaneously. If the listener were truly listening simultaneously to both, then the probability of detecting each should be independent of that of detecting the other. That is, if P is the probability of detection on either ear,

Probability of detecting both signals $= P^2$
Probability of detecting neither $= (1-P)^2$
Probability of detecting one and not the other $= 2P(1-P)$

In fact for every one of the eight subjects the last of these probabilities was found empirically to be far higher than it should have been when calculated theoretically from the other two. That is, detection on one ear means that one has a lower chance of detecting simultaneously on the other ear. This seems very much as if the listener was taking his information on some trials from one ear and on others from the other ear.

The other fact produced by Moray and O'Brien is a comparison of the values of d' in the task of concentrating on one ear and in a calculation based on each ear of a shared task. The calculation is based on the following argument. Suppose the man is listening half the time to his right ear and the other half to his left ear. He only responds when he is listening. Therefore the probability of a detection when he is listening to the right ear is twice the observed probability of a detection on that ear in the experiment as a whole. The same applies to the false alarm probability. If we calculate d' from these corrected probabilities, it should be at least as high as d' for one ear when the listener is told to concentrate on that ear. In fact, it is appreciably less. Thus the assumption, that sharing performance between two ears simply halves the time on each ear, predicts a better performance on the shared task than is actually found.

For this reason, and bearing in mind the results of the shadowing experiments, Moray and O'Brien lean slightly towards the concept of true simultaneity in the intake of information. They suggest that the difficulty in reporting two signals at once might be due to a link between the two detection systems such that appearance of a signal inhibits intake temporarily from the other ear; even though normally both ears are feeding into their appropriate systems.

There is an alternative approach to the prediction of shared performance, and this is the use of d'^2 rather than d' as the measure of efficiency. It is argued by Taylor *et al.* (1967) that an information channel of limited capacity should perform in such a way that d'^2 is kept proportional to the information extracted from the signals; thus d'^2 should be proportional to the time for which the channel is operating, since information itself increases linearly with time. The measure d'^2 might also be expected to add up to the same amount if the channel is divided into parts each dealing with a separate set of signals, as the total information capacity would remain constant. (We shall discuss later the argument by which this is justified.) Both in the work of Moray and O'Brien and in experiments reported by Taylor *et al.*, it was found that d'^2 for a single task was greater than the total of d'^2 for two tasks performed at the same time. If therefore we accept the use of d'^2, some capacity has been lost by the use of two tasks at once. An attractive suggestion by Moray (1967) is that we should think of the limited capacity system not so much as a channel like a telephone or radio channel, but rather as a processor with a limited number of elements to allot to the analysis of the outside world and also to the control and combination of the various tasks it is combining. An analogy is the allocation in a computer of a fixed amount of memory storage partly to the data being handled and partly to the programme of instructions to control the handling. Any increase in the complexity of the programme reduces the amount of data which can be processed, and vice versa. One might think therefore of the simultaneous performance of two tasks as giving a constant total capacity, but nevertheless a capacity reduced by the complexity of the organization needed to control the combination.

A last argument against the concept of rapid alternation of some filtering system between the two channels of a combination of tasks is provided by Tulving and Lindsay (1967). They presented two stimuli simultaneously, one visual and one auditory, and required response either to one alone or to both. The stimulus was chosen from eight or ten possibilities, and the response was to identify it. The information in the response (in the technical sense of information) was slightly less for each sense when both responses were required, and the amount of loss of information did not alter when the duration of the stimuli was altered. Since longer stimuli would allow more time to switch from one sense to the other, the concept of a rapid alternation between senses would presumably predict less decrement for long signals.

Despite the evidence which has been brought forward against the idea of rapid alternation between the senses, we should perhaps leave the matter as an open one at this time. It is quite hard without alternation to explain the finding that detection on one ear can, at least in some circumstances, make detection on the other ear less probable. Moray's calculation of the value of d' to be expected on a model of time-sharing made no allowance for any time occupied in shifting from one ear to the other, although as we have seen such a time is needed in explaining some results in other fields. The concept of rapid alternation carries implications about the skewness of the graph of detections against false alarms, which have not been tested as yet; and above all the whole approach of calculating d'^2 rests on theoretical axioms which may not be empirically valid.

Let us consider this point further. In calculating the information corresponding to a signal of discriminability d', Taylor and his colleagues make use of the behaviour of an ideal detector, for which

$$d'^2 = \frac{2E}{N_0}$$

where E = signal energy
             N_0 = noise power density.

By entering the classical equations which relate the capacity of a channel to the power of the signals and noise, Taylor *et al.* are then able to show that d'^2 is proportional to the information transmitted in unit time. To put the matter another way, if one were to add to the original channel another channel having the same values of E and of N_0, one would expect to double the obtained value of d'^2.

But we have noted repeatedly that human beings may not act as ideal detectors. In fact the empirical evidence is that changes in signal energy give a change in performance which corresponds to

$$d' = K\frac{E}{N_0}$$

rather than to the behaviour of an ideal detector. This has been shown by Green *et al.* (1957) and in a number of later experiments of a psychophysical kind (see, e.g. Green and Swets, 1966, Chapter 7). If therefore we were to suppose that using two senses were rather like having the signal power on each sense, we might expect that the total of the two measures of d' might equal the value obtainable by a man attending to one sense alone. In fact this is essentially the result found by Moray and O'Brien when dividing attention equally between two ears. Their subjects gave values of d' on each which added to about the value of d' found on one sense alone; and when concentrating on one sense but giving responses to any signals on the other which were nevertheless noticed, they gave again a pair of values of d' which added to the same total. There is no sign here of an extra demand on capacity when performing the complex task.

We may take the point further yet. When empirical data are collected on the detectability of signals of varying duration, then indeed it is found that doubling duration doubles d'^2 rather than doubling d'. Taylor *et al.* indicate that they have verified this in a number of situations, and it appears also (at least for signals longer than 100 msec) in the results of Green *et al.* (1957). It is reasonable enough that an increase in signal duration should give behaviour more like that of an ideal detector than does increase of signal power, for the following reason. In relating d' to signal-noise ratio, the mathematics of the ideal observer assume that the noise is objective and not within the observer himself. In human beings however much of the unreliability of the process is within the detection system, as we have argued many times. An increase in signal power therefore may well have more effect on men than it would on an ideal observer, because the internal noise, which is the crucial factor, is not being increased. When however we increase the duration of a signal we are increasing the size of the sample of noise which we are taking, whether that noise is internal or external. As is well known to any student of statistics, the standard deviation of the mean of a sample of n observations is equal to $(1/\sqrt{n}) \times$ the standard deviation of one observation. Thus if d'_t is the performance on a signal of unit duration, and d'_t that on a signal of duration t, then

$$d'_t{}^2 = t \times d'_i{}^2.$$

It is therefore entirely reasonable that d'^2 should be additive over time, even though it is not additive over signal power. In that case, the calculation performed by Moray and O'Brien may be modified. They took the detection rates and false alarm rates on one ear when that ear was receiving equal attention with the other, doubled them, and regarded the result as the value of d' to be expected when the ear was receiving full attention. But since this predicted value of d' is for performance over only half the time, the value obtainable with concentration should be greater still by a factor of $\sqrt{2}$. The results given by Moray and O'Brien suggest that this prediction would be approximately correct, although it is not of course possible to assess significance.

The results to date therefore do not rule out rapid alternation, and they do not make it necessary to suppose that part of the available capacity is used up in organizing the combination of two tasks. Both these possibilities must still be considered along with the idea that strictly simultaneous processing takes place with a net loss of efficiency. There is a profitable line here for future research.

LAST THOUGHTS ON ATTENUATION

The experiments we have just discussed certainly confirm Treisman's general formulation, even if they leave some points open for further study. There seems no doubt that division of attention reduces the intake of information from one sensory channel but does not abolish it altogether. In the terms of signal detection theory, there is a reduction in d' with no change in β. This is the kind of change which can be produced within a single task by turning down the physical strength of the signal, and to that extent the term "attenuation" used originally by Treisman embodies a useful truth. As we have already said, it must be supposed that the signal only is reduced and not its accompanying noise, but this is a relatively minor point. Perhaps more serious is the rather passive overtone which is carried by the term "attenuation", inappropriate in this application since the process of filtering is certainly one requiring some processing of the incoming signal; and to that extent active. One last point which should be made is that physical attenuation of an incoming signal, when the man is trying to achieve a constant level of performance, actually imposes a greater load on the perceptual mechanism. It was shown by Broadbent (1958) that a speech message accompanied by noise produces a deterioration in a simultaneous visually guided task such as piloting an aircraft; as compared with the same message unaccompanied by noise. Now when a man is listening to one ear and neglecting the other, the change on the neglected ear presumably has the effect of relieving the central mechanism of some load. Treisman's attenuation is to that extent different from true physical attenuation, which makes larger demands on the central mechanism.

A better analogy would be with a different experiment of Broadbent (1958), in which a speech message had some frequency bands removed without the addition of noise. This reduced the number of words heard, but did not increase the errors in a simultaneous visual task. Similarly, when a man turns attention away from one ear we should not think of him as attempting to extract all the information from that ear through a greater noise level; rather he is receiving only a sub-sample of the physical signals and extracting the information from those. An interesting theoretical possibility in fact is that the listener may analyse only some features of the signals on the neglected ear, but perform as well on those features as he does on the selected ear. This is a point of view urged by Treisman (1969).

The precise nature of "attenuation" cannot therefore simply be equated with physical attenuation, even of the signal alone without its accompanying noise. It has however some points in common, and is certainly an operation performed upon the input to the system rather than a bias on the dictionary units, or category states as we have been calling them. This applies only to tasks of the kind which we have been calling stimulus selection; the alternative type of task involving response selection might be expected to give β changes without d' changes, but this kind of function has been studied mostly in tasks with only one source of stimuli. They will be discussed in the next chapter. The main points of the present chapter have now been covered; but there are two interesting by-ways of experiments on dichotic memory which should be mentioned before we leave the topic of perceptual selection.

Two Special Cases of Perceptual Selection

THE QUESTION OF CEREBRAL DOMINANCE

(a) *Auditory experiments.* The dichotic memory technique which we have discussed at length is unusual in that it shows a difference between performance on the two ears; broadly, the right ear is better than the left. Such a difference is surprising, because most simple tests of performance show no advantage for either ear. Nevertheless, this test does reveal such a difference in samples of normal subjects (Bryden, 1963; Satz *et al.*, 1965) whether performance is assessed in the usual way or by a recognition test (Broadbent and Gregory, 1964b). Probably the most crucial result however is that of Kimura (1961b) on clinical cases. Because these cases were candidates for neurosurgery, it was necessary to assess which hemisphere of their brains was primarily responsible for the efficiency of speech. This can be done by injecting sodium amytal into the internal carotid artery on one side at a time. This will usually disturb speech only when the injection is on one side, and the knowledge thus available to the surgeon justifies the use of this rather hazardous technique. In the majority of people speech is of course primarily controlled from the left hemisphere, which communicates predominantly with the right-hand side of the body. This location for speech is true even for many left-handed people; but there are some who have a reversed relationship, speech being on the right hemisphere. Kimura was able to obtain a sample of such people, and to show that the left ear was superior in the dichotic memory test for those people who had speech on the right-hand side of their brains. The link was with the location in the brain and not with handedness, as left-handed people with speech on the left hemisphere did better on the right ear.

The effectiveness of the technique does not seem to depend on the memory component, but on the presence of two stimuli simultaneously at the two ears. Thus if the listener has to ignore one ear altogether and respond only to the other ear, it is still better for the right ear to be the one selected; whereas presentation of items in rapid alternation to the two ears, after the fashion of Moray, greatly reduces the difference between the ears (Kimura, 1970).

Anatomically, each ear is connected to the temporal lobe of both hemispheres, but there is physiological evidence that the connections to the opposite side are more effective (Rosenzweig, 1951). Other studies by Kimura (1961a) make it clear that an intact temporal lobe is desirable for success at the dichotic memory task. If the lobe on one side has been removed surgically, then the opposite ear does worse in the dichotic task. The removal of the left lobe is however more serious in its effects than that of the right; as already indicated, it is the left side which is usually in right-handed people found to be damaged in cases of impairment of speech resulting from brain injury. It is therefore tempting to suppose that a crucial piece of the mechanism for speech recognition lies in the neighbourhood of the left temporal lobe, and that in most tasks either ear can communicate equally well with that mechanism. When however both ears are receiving different stimulation, the information reaching the left lobe from the right ear swamps out that reaching the same lobe from the left ear, and the latter can only reach the speech-recognizing mechanism by an indirect path through the right temporal lobe.

Such a suggestion assumes that the difference between the ears in the dichotic memory task is connected with the use of speech material; studies of the effects of brain injury have found not only that disorders of speech tend to be associated with injury to the left-hand side of the brain, but also that some other functions involving hearing are impaired by damage to the right-hand temporal lobe (Milner, 1962). Correspondingly it has been found by Kimura (1964) that when two melodies are played one to one ear and one to the other, with a subsequent recognition test including the two stimuli and two novel melodies, the left ear rather than the right gives the better performance. This effect has been replicated with humming of the melodies (Kimura, 1967) as the means of responding, and the task has also been found to be impaired by damage to the right temporal lobe rather than the left (Kimura, 1970). An advantage for the left ear in normal subjects has also been found under some conditions for the recognition of two simultaneous oboe phrases by Darwin (1969). Minor changes in conditions however may abolish the effect. Perhaps the most striking of all is a demonstration by Shankweiler and Studdert-Kennedy (1967) that even the usual advantage of the right ear for speech depends on the particular aspect of speech which is involved. When the material consisted of various consonants each followed by the same vowel, the right ear was better; when the material consisted of the same consonant preceded by different vowels, the two ears were equally good. On the other hand Darwin (1969) found that the pitch of two simultaneous speech-like sounds was better identified on the left ear.

These last results indicate that the tentative explanation put forward earlier must be an over-simplification. Not all speech tasks are better on the right, as they should be if it is easier access to the speech mechanism which matters. Not all non-speech tasks are better on the left. It must be some other aspect of acoustic performance, usually present in listening to speech and usually absent in listening to other material, which produces the difference. Possibly it may be the very rapid transitions of frequency which are crucial in the understanding of consonants; they might for some reason be analysed primarily on the left-hand side of the brain. It is worthy of note also that Oxbury *et al.* (1967) found the right-side effect predominantly when the listener was left uncertain until after the presentation which side was to be reported first. This suggests that the effect may have to do with some preliminary scanning mechanism which allots incoming signals to one analysis system or another, and which in the absence of other instructions will pass right-ear signals first to the speech system. The earlier papers cited suggest that this cannot be a complete explanation, because of the effects with a prescribed order of report known before presentation, and with report only of one ear while ignoring the other. Nevertheless, the possibility of a preliminary scan and allocation of priorities cannot be ruled out, and this is clearly an area deserving of further research.

(*b*) *Visual experiments.* We have already mentioned the results of Sampson, and these are typical of a number of other authors (see Kimura, 1970). When several stimuli are presented in a tachistoscopic flash to a subject, the order of report tends to run from left to right. Yet Sampson found that items on the right were more accurately perceived, at least in strongly right-dominant subjects. This result as such has not been typical of experiments in which items were presented simultaneously to both the right and left of the fixation point; because there is a natural tendency to do better on early than on late items reported. (It will be recalled that Sampson gave several successive pairs of items, so that there were items from left and from right both early and late in the sequence of report. The more usual tachistoscopic presentations gave all items simultaneously so that right-hand items were very much the last reported.) The tachistoscopic studies did find however that, when one item is given at a time, it was better reported if given on the right. Thus the same kind of discrepancy exists as in Sampson's results, except that in a tachistoscope it is necessary to present items on their own to reveal the superiority of the right visual field.

Left-right differences in vision may conceivably be related to other factors than to the localization of speech in the left hemisphere. The ordinary pattern of scanning in reading English is from left to right, and it could well be argued that this habitual sequence is producing the asymmetry of performance. Two methods of attacking this possibility exist: the use of subjects abnormal either in handedness or brain injury, and the use of different kinds of stimulus material rather than verbal items. Both methods show a true asymmetry of performance, although the left-right scanning pattern is equally true.

So far as handedness goes, it has been found by Bryden (1964b, 1965) that right-handers show the greater accuracy on the right side of the visual field for material presented on one side only, while left-handers do not. We may recall also that Sampson found differences between subjects of different degrees of handedness. It would seem that such differences can hardly be accounted for by habitual patterns of left-right scanning, and that there must therefore be some underlying asymmetry of a neural kind. This is supported by a result of Kimura (1963) on patients with damage to the temporal lobe; she gave an exposure of each item in the centre of the field of view and looked at the overall level of performance for different kinds of injury. Patients with damage to the right temporal lobe did worse at perceiving numbers of dots or nonsense shapes than did those with damage to the left temporal region. On the other hand patients with damage to the left temporal region did worse at perceiving familiar objects. Thus, just as in audition, it looks as if there is a separation to the two sides of the brain of mechanisms concerned with different kinds of presented material.

If we consider now results with different kinds of stimulus, we must again distinguish between simultaneous presentation of several stimuli and isolated presentation of material only in one location. In the former case, the advantage for the left appears for all kinds of material equally [see for example Bryden and Rainey (1963). Kimura (1966) reviews a number of other experiments on the topic]. In the case of isolated presentation, however, the advantage of the right side over the left depends very much on the nature of the material (Bryden and Rainey, 1963; Kimura, 1966). Letters or words are better seen on the right, while the counting of dots or other symbols is better on the left. Other material such as unfamiliar shapes gives intermediate results, and the data can be summarized as showing that familiar material is better on the right and unfamiliar on the left. This may be because familiar material usually has some verbal name available while unfamiliar material has to be handled in another way, or it may be due to some other aspect of familiarity.

An interesting minor point concerns the perception of Hebrew words, as that language is normally read from right to left and the habitual scanning pattern is therefore different. In fact the advantage of the right side is certainly less for such material and may even be reversed (Mishkin and Forgays, 1952; Orbach, 1953). One can plausibly argue that the perception of a word in a tachistoscope involves the reception of a number of letters simultaneously, and that the process therefore approximates to the case of simultaneous arrival of several items. In that case we have already seen that a scanning operation is involved which in English goes from left to right, and a word might well therefore be better perceived when the central fixation point rested on the letters at the beginning of the word. In Hebrew the reverse would apply. When the words are presented vertically rather than horizontally on the other hand, even Hebrew is better perceived to the right of the fixation point (Barton et al., 1965).

We can therefore pull together all these results by supposing that there is a real asymmetry of performance such that familiar verbal material is better perceived if it arrives on the side of the field of view which corresponds to the brain hemisphere containing speech. There is also a pattern of scanning an array of simultaneously presented items from left to right, which is probably habitual and derived from the way our written language happens to run.

EFFECTS OF BRAIN INJURY ON SPEECH

For completeness, we should perhaps amplify the brief reference given above to the fact that speech is disrupted by brain injury on one side. There are many ways in which speech could conceivably be disordered, and many distinguishable regions of the brain in which injury can occur. Examination of clinical cases and comparison of their losses of function with the places where injury has occurred suggests that different aspects of speech may be localized in different places within the hemisphere that is dominant. Various possible classifications are given for example by Jakobson, by Bay, by Luria and by Hecaen in de Reuck and O'Connor (1964). Because of the difficulty of getting enough identical injuries for statistical purposes, and the rather irregular nature of spontaneously occurring brain damage, there is some disagreement about the best classification; and when large numbers of patients have been studied with a battery of verbal tests it was found that these tests were intercorrelated (Schuell and Jenkins, 1959; Schuell *et al.*, 1962). That is, patients who were badly impaired on one test were also badly impaired on the others. On the face of it this seems to suggest that different aspects of speech are not knocked out differentially by different injuries, and thus that there is no localization of one part of the function in one place and another part in another place (always remembering the well-established point that injury to the left half of the brain, in right-handed people, is much more likely to impair speech).

From our present point of view, it is clear that listening to speech involves many sub-processes, the extremes being the intake of sensory evidence on the one hand and the biases applied to the various category states on the other. So equally utterance of speech, rather than hearing it, may involve many processes, although their interrelationship will doubtless be different in that case and in the case of listening. But straightforward tests of listening and of utterance would involve both sensory and bias components, and might reasonably deteriorate together if one or more components were impaired by an injury. To separate the components would need rather specialized tests. There is some preliminary evidence that such a separation may be possible; Howes (in de Reuck and O'Connor, 1964) analyses the speech of a number of patients and shows that they fall into two classes. In one class the number of words produced per minute is much less than that given by normal controls, while in the other the rate of speaking is rather faster than that of normals. (In all cases, speech was collected in an interview.) Whether a subject was a fast, slow, or normal speaker it is possible to count the frequency with which he used any given word, and to determine what proportion of his total speech consisted of words of more than a certain degree of frequency. It then turns out that the speech of these individuals obeys the well-established law for large samples from the language as a whole, known as Zipf's law. One way of stating this law is that

$$Z_{ut} = K \log F + M$$

where $Z_{ut} = Z$-score corresponding to the proportion of the utterance consisting of words with frequency less than F.

$$K, M \text{ are constants.}$$

Although the form of this law remains the same in the brain-injured patients, K and M are usually outside the range of normal subjects; especially M. What this means is that the patients tend to produce a higher proportion of common words than do normal people, and this is especially true of those patients who talk slower than normals. These same patients differ from the fast-talking patients very clearly in the proportion of words which are immediate repetitions of the last word said; in Howes' data, none of the fast talkers gave a proportion of repetitions outside the normal range, but just over half the slow talkers did so. Howes reports also that the slow talkers never produce jargon, in his sample, but all but the mildest cases amongst the fast talkers do so. Lastly and importantly, the slow talkers tended to have hemiplegia, that is, inability to use the muscles elsewhere on the right-hand side of the body as well as difficulty in speech, while the fast talkers did not show such a marked tendency.

There are two sub-regions of the dominant hemisphere which are often associated with disorders of speech: one known as Broca's area which is in the frontal lobes but just in front of the temporal lobe, near the centres which are known to produce movements of the articulatory organs. The other region, named after Wernicke, is in the temporal lobe and thus further back towards the projection areas where the sensory input arrives at the cortex. It is likely therefore that hemiplegia is more likely to appear when damage is in the more forward of these areas; and thus that there is a real difference of localization between the patients with the two patterns of performance found by Howes. In some sense his slow-talking patients may be suffering from a disturbance of the availability and biasing of category states, while the fast-talking ones are disturbed in the selective effect of incoming information upon those states. There are echoes here of the long-standing classification of speech disorders into sensory and motor, although as Howes indicates the slow talkers do badly at some perceptual tasks and the fast talkers at some expressive ones. As we said earlier, each type of task may well involve both types of process in various combinations.

Further study of speech disorders is needed before one can regard this interpretation as more than speculative; but enough has been said to show that it is possible that brain injury also may give a distinction related to that we have made between stimulus set and response set.

THE EFFECTS OF AGEING ON DICHOTIC MEMORY

A curious aspect of memory is the fact that the most obvious tests of its efficiency seem to agree rather badly with everyday experience of its success or failure. Thus for example an orthodox test of memory span, in which one finds out the length of the longest series of digits which a man can repeat back perfectly after one hearing, does not distinguish between old people who have defective memory in everyday life and those who do not. The dichotic memory technique, however, does do so (Inglis and Sanderson, 1961; Caird and Inglis, 1961). In the second of these studies a similar comparison was made using three visual and three auditory items, and again similar results were found; provided that the auditory items were reproduced before the visual ones rather than the other way round. Apparently therefore there is some feature of memory for items arriving simultaneously by two sensory channels which makes the performance more similar to the tasks which people have to perform in everyday life and in which they notice defects appearing. From the study of those old people who are regarded as having especially defective memory, it is a short step to considering old people as a group, and it has been shown repeatedly that unselected samples of old people will do worse than young people on dichotic memory tests even though they are quite normal on conventional tests of memory span (Inglis and Caird, 1963; Inglis and Ankus, 1965; Mackay and Inglis, 1963; Inglis and Tansey, 1967b; Inglis, 1964). From the various modifications of the experiment which have been tried, it is clear that the effect does not depend upon leaving the subject free to choose his order of recall, nor on prescribing it in advance rather than after presentation.

Similarly, it has been shown that older people do worse than younger ones when three auditory and three visual items are delivered simultaneously, with instructions to report the visual items first (Broadbent and Gregory, 1965b). The effect must therefore be connected with the general situation of using two input channels.

A plausible hypothesis, which has been urged by Inglis himself, is that this task reveals an inefficiency of the buffer store in older people. The deterioration with age is admittedly larger in the later items to be recalled, and these have presumably been in the buffer store longer than the first items recalled have been. One might therefore argue that the buffer is for some reason less able to cope with items for any extended period, and so gives impaired recall for the second channel to be reproduced even though ordinary memory span is quite normal.

There are, however, some cautions we must bear in mind and which forbid us to regard this hypothesis as completely established. First, the theory would suggest that a defective buffer store does not affect ordinary memory span. We have not yet considered memory as such in this book, but from the brief prospectus in Chapter I it will be recalled that primary memory may well take the form of passing information back from the limited capacity P system to the original buffer. The information could be stored there just long enough to allow all other items to pass through the P systems, would then be retrieved and restored, and so on. If this were the case, and if the buffer were defective in old people, one might expect ordinary memory span to show effects of age: yet such a task is relatively unaffected. Admittedly, some of the dichotic experiments do show effects on the first channel to be recalled as well as the second (Inglis and Sanderson, 1961; Caird and Inglis, 1961; Inglis and Tansey, 1967b; Craik, 1965). This is reasonable if age impairs the buffer; but why is there so little effect on conventional memory span?

Second, there is the question of the kind of error which is and which is not increased by age. Craik (1965) separated three kinds of error; those in which an item was reported among the items from the other channel, which he termed "selection errors", those in which items from the same channel were reported together but in incorrect order ("transposition errors"), and the remainder ("random errors"). Of these the second were argued, reasonably enough, to be causable only in storage and retrieval rather than intake of information. The selection and random errors, however, might be due to disturbances of perceptual selection of the kind we have many times considered in this chapter: only transposition was certainly a storage error. Yet that type of error was unaffected by age. Both the other types of error showed age effects, though the selection errors did so only on the first channel reported and at a fast rate of presentation. The bulk of the age effect was in the random errors, and Craik argued that this was an effect on the intake of information. He modified this view after performing another experiment in which the order of report was prescribed only after stimulation; in that case again the effect appeared primarily in the random errors, but such errors were greater in the second channel reported and especially so in the older subjects. Since the listeners did not know at the time of presentation which channel was to be reported first, it seems impossible to ascribe the random errors to some feature of the intake of information in this case. Thus we seem to be forced to suppose that there are two factors producing errors in storage and retrieval: whatever it is that gives transposition errors, which do not increase markedly with age, and whatever it is that gives random errors, which do increase with age. It is not clear why one of these factors should reside in the buffer store and not the other.

A third doubt about the buffer as the location of the age effect comes from a finding of Broadbent and Gregory (1965b). They used a condition in which the visual and auditory presentations each consisted of mixed letters and digits; as we saw earlier in the chapter, this experiment showed that the well-established Gray and Wedderburn effect does not appear when the eye and ear, rather than the two ears, are the channels of stimulation. That is, it is harder to recall the letters first and then the digits than it is to recall the eye first and then the ear. But the difference between these two conditions increases severely with age. The instructions to give response grouped by class of item actually gave a significant deterioration in subjects aged 26–35 as opposed to those of 16–25, a most unusual finding. It is not altogether clear why the buffer should be more strained in one case than the other, but it is obvious that responses grouped by item-class require the use of response set and thus fine control of the particular class of category states in use. After all, dichotic memory must involve other processes and not only the buffer; it is possible that it is one of these other processes which produces the effect of age.

If this were so, then age effects would presumably appear in other tasks involving the same process; and we should cite at this stage results by Rabbitt showing that the tasks of perceptual search which we have already described are performed less well by older people. That is, when a subject is asked to sort cards into one of two piles depending on which of two relevant letters is on each card, older people are slowed down more by the presence of irrelevant letters (Rabbitt, 1965). It is also true that older people are more affected by the use of several different stimuli for each of a set of responses in a reaction-time task (Rabbitt, 1964c). In general, older people are less able to modify their performance (their category states) to take advantage of any statistical properties of the situation which make it unnecessary to process all the information delivered to the senses. This is true both when one signal gives advance information about the nature of another closely subsequent one (Rabbitt, 1964b) and also when a long series of signals is repetitive and predictable (Rabbitt and Birren, 1967).

To survey the whole field of proven effects of age would take us too far afield and is in any case unnecessary since it has been done elsewhere (Welford, 1958; Birren, 1959; Welford and Birren, 1965). But effects on other memory tasks are well-known, and seem to depend on the occurrence of an interrupting stimulus after the arrival of the material to be remembered, and before it has to be reproduced. Older subjects are for example much less well able to react to a series of stimuli by making a response dependent at any instant not on the present stimulus but on the one before or the one before that (Kirchner, 1958). Welford (1958) quotes a study by Speakman in which people had to search a pack of cards in search of a particular one, and also to count how many cards they had turned before finding it. When a four-digit number was spoken to them during this operation, older subjects tended to forget either the number or their place in the pack. Broadbent and Heron (1962) required their subjects to cross out certain digits in a table of random numbers; if the digit to be marked remained the same, age had little effect on performance, but if the wanted digit was occasionally altered by a visual stimulus then older subjects tended to forget this alteration from time to time and go back to mark a digit which had been wanted earlier. The same thing happened if the wanted digit was always the next one in the ordinary series of numbers, i.e. first cross out 1, then 2, then 3, and so on.

Setting these results against the theory that age alters the rate of loss from the buffer store, Kirchner's finding might perhaps be explained that way; but is equally consistent with the idea that age increases the effects of interference on a stimulus which has been categorized and is now in primary or longer term memory. Speakman's result is rather harder to explain by the operation of the buffer, and equally in Broadbent and Heron's experiment there is no doubt that the stimulus to be remembered had passed the categorization stage (the P system) because it had already received an appropriate response before it was forgotten. Thus, whether or not age alters the efficiency of the buffer, it seems definite that age impairs primary memory when some interfering stimulus arrives between presentation and recall; and this in itself might possibly account for the special sensitivity of dichotic memory. That task does obviously involve more functions than does simple memory span, including the change from one stimulus set to another, and possibly this might act as an interference with primary or longer-term memory. It seems a little strange in that case that the effect should be larger on the second sub-set recalled rather than the first, but not completely inconceivable.

Other results on the memory of older people point in a similar direction. We suffer badly here from the difficulty that memory itself has not yet been discussed, and perhaps this section should be re-read again after Chapter IX; but there are three results on ageing which, in the light of that chapter, suggest a location other than the buffer for the effects of age. First, Heron and Craik (1964) have repeated on old and young subjects an experiment of Hebb (1961) on long and short-term memory. The technique is to give each subject a series of memory spans, and, without warning, to repeat the same material at intervals in the series; say, every third or fourth span would be the same. The repeated span improves gradually throughout the session, even though it cannot be recalled at all after the first couple of interpolated spans. Thus there must be some transfer to a long-term memory even from one presentation succeeded rapidly by quite different items. For our present purpose, the point of interest is that not one of Heron and Craik's three experiments showed a significant trend of this kind in old people. In some cases there may have been a slight effect, and the conditions were such that in one case young people also did not give the usual Hebb effect. But it seems fair to conclude that age does not affect the usual immediate recall of material presented once only; but rather the extent to which one presentation succeeds in transferring information to a longer-term store. Heron and Craik cite an unpublished experiment by Rabbitt showing similar results: and Caird (1964) has found that memory-disordered old people differ from controls by failing to show the Hebb effect.

Secondly, there is a technique we shall discuss in Chapter IX of presenting once only long lists of items well beyond the memory span and measuring the number of items recalled as a function of the items presented. (It is often arranged that the subject responds to the items as they arrive, so that this is a task involving performance for material which has passed the buffer.) When the number of items presented is less than the memory span, recall is of course equal to presentation; and at very long list lengths other factors come into play. In the intermediate range however

$$\text{Recall} = A + B \times \text{Number presented}$$

where A, B are constants.

This we shall interpret later as meaning that A is a measure of a constant primary memory while B is a measure of the probability of transfer of items to a longer-term store. Craik (1968) has found that B rather than A is affected by age.

Thirdly, we have been talking throughout of recall measures of memory, where the subject himself chooses his response from among all those in his repertoire. It is also possible to employ recognition tests, where a limited number of alternatives are put forward from which the subject must choose one as corresponding to the stimulus originally presented. We shall see later that forced choices of this kind are different in an interesting way from free response; because empirically they are found in psychophysical situations to be less affected by individual biases of response, and theoretically they can be shown by the methods of decision theory to give scores less affected by β and more by d'. Now in the case of memory it has been found recently by Schonfield and Robertson (1966) that the effects of ageing are reduced by the use of recognition rather than recall; and this is to be expected if age alters some biasing feature of the categorizing system rather than the efficiency of storage itself.

Because of the difficulty of arguing from points not yet discussed, we cannot come to a firm conclusion at this stage about the effects of ageing. In any event, such a conclusion would require the use on older people of some of the techniques we shall be describing later, for measuring category biases separately from other features of the whole perceptual-memory system. Such data are not available as yet, and the suggestion that age affects the biasing of category states cannot therefore be more than speculative. However, we have said enough to indicate that the concept of age as affecting the buffer store, while interesting and still not completely ruled out, is not absolutely entailed by the evidence.

H

Conclusions and Pointers on Perceptual Selection

We have now surveyed the available data on perceptual selection, and it is time to see what broad principles have emerged. Clearly the view of 1958 still represents a major part of the truth; sensory signals which possess some particular wanted characteristic may have a much larger effect on response than do those signals which do not share this characteristic. That is, filtering is a major strategy by which the brain protects its limited capacity against overload; and we may discount the various attempts to explain all the experimental findings by selection at retrieval or by a complete analysis of all stimuli before selection. These attempts have been highly valuable, however, not only because they have revealed other functions such as selective retrieval which are valid in addition to filtering; but also because they have compelled us to recognize that filtering is not absolute. There is some effect even of stimuli which carry the characteristics of unwantedness; which arrive on the neglected ear or in the ignored voice. This effect is statistical and partial: there is a chance of a breakthrough for such stimuli rather than a complete analysis of all of them. Once again therefore we are driven towards a consideration of the ways in which an unreliable system could achieve optimum performance. Just as in the case of vigilance, we cannot think of the man as either hearing a signal or else failing completely to hear it. There is an intermediate range in which effects of the highest importance may dwell.

One such effect is the one we have called response set. Primarily, it can be regarded as the bringing into play of a set of possible responses—when the word "response" is used in the central sense we have explained several times, which we prefer to replace by "category state". The existence of the set of digit categories or of the set of colour name categories implies the funnelling of all the evidence about presence or absence of certain sensory features (formants, transitions, bursts of noise, or straight lines, curves, corners) into the appearance of one rather than another of the possible categories. Features have importance only because of their effect on categories.

In addition to categorizing with its long-term implications, response set implies the more temporary and shifting mechanism of pigeon-holing. At one time, doubtful evidence will give rise to one of the digit categories, at another time it will give rise to one of the letter names. Here the effect may well be like that of a criterion shift or bias in the analysis of decision theory. But have we really established that it is? The answer must at this stage be "No". We have justified filtering, by the experiments on shadowing and dichotic memory and their variants and successors. We have justified categorizing, by the experiments on perceptual search. We have shown a distinction between stimulus set and response set, by studies directly on that problem; above all we have shown that the operation of filtering does *not* seem to alter biases or criteria. But we have not connected response set with criterion shifts.

To do so, we can turn away from perceptual selection to the study of perception for stimuli arriving one at a time. In such a field, there are well-known effects of the probability or desirability of a stimulus upon the chance that it will be perceived in one way rather than another. What we have to do at this point in our argument therefore is to show that such effects can be represented as biases on some category states as opposed to others; that there is no need to suppose a clearing of information channels for probable stimuli and a blocking of them for unpleasant ones. Rather the curious failures of perception to agree with the states of the outer world, or its success in doing so under difficulties which would disrupt most artificial devices, are both to be explained by the statistical nature of the process and the effects of changes in its parameters.

CHAPTER VI

Reaction to Stimuli Occurring with Different Probabilities

Psychophysical Judgments of Simple Stimuli

In this chapter, we are looking for situations where behaviour may reveal the mechanism called "pigeon-holing". That is, we are looking for the changes which Treisman described as changes in threshold for her dictionary units, and which might be expected to appear when one stimulus is more probable than another. Ultimately, we must do this by considering performance in tasks involving many alternative stimuli and responses. As a preliminary step, however, it is worth considering behaviour in very simple psychophysical tasks, such as the judgment of the heaviness of weights, of the length of lines, or of the loudness of noises. There is a large literature on performance in such tasks, and we shall not be even as exhaustive in discussing them as we have in the cases of vigilance and of perceptual selection. We shall however pick out some experiments of relevance to our own special interests. Our line of argument will take us far afield, so we should state it in advance as a guarantee that we have not forgotten our main purposes. We shall want to show first,

(*a*) that in this field also the probability of one stimulus rather than another does affect the kind of response that is elicited.

(*b*) Next, we must state a theory of this effect which appears at first sight unconnected with our concepts of pigeon-holing and filtering. This is the theory of adaptation level.

(*c*) Then we want to argue for the general importance of this theory, since it succeeds in explaining a number of effects due apparently to other causes.

(*d*) Some difficulties do arise for the theory however; and when it is modified to meet these, it comes closer to our own approach.

(*e*) We can then ask whether an appropriate application of our analyses to psychophysical judgments will reveal the effect of probability as a change in β (pigeon-holing) or as a change in d' (filtering). In fact, the former turns out to be correct.

(*f*) Lastly, we have to deal with a discrepancy: the effect of stimulus probability on β in the psychophysical case is opposite to that usually considered previously. This can be shown empirically to be due to the absence of knowledge of results in most psychophysical situations. With this qualification, pigeon-holing appears to operate in psychophysics just as our general view expects it to do.

STIMULUS PROBABILITY: THE "CONTRAST" EFFECT

(a) *Signal frequency.* In the basic situation, an experimenter might have two weights closely similar in value, and present them to a subject repeatedly in a random order. If the subject is asked to lift each weight as it is presented to him, and to say whether it is light or heavy, then the frequency with which the objectively heavier weight is given will affect his accuracy. We shall consider some specific findings later, but typically, if the objectively heavier weight is given more often than the objectively lighter weight, then the subject will make more errors of the type in which he says "Light" to a heavy weight than those in which he says "Heavy" to a light weight. Thus there is in his judgment an effect which may be called "Contrast", so that his judgments of light weights are more accurate in the presence of a large number of judgments of heavy weights and vice versa.

(b) *Anchor stimuli.* A particular form in which this experiment can often be done is to present a series of weights for judgment, differing over a whole range of values, but to precede each of them by a constant weight. The subject lifts this constant weight as a reference or anchor, and it may be regarded as an aid to him in making his judgment about the subsequent variable stimulus. The value of the anchor may, in some experiments, correspond to a point fairly high in the range of stimuli for judgment, and in others to a very low point in the range. If we consider the judgments that are made about stimuli in the middle of the range, those judgments will be lower when the anchor corresponds to a high point in the range than when the anchor corresponds to a low point in the range. The presence of the anchor has acted in the same way as an increase in the probability of a stimulus for judgment at particular parts of the range; it has produced the contrast effect of pushing the judgments away from the point at which most stimuli are occurring.

(c) *The range of stimuli presented.* Even where an experiment involves the presentation of different stimuli with equal frequency, one can detect a contrast effect from the values of the particular set of stimuli used. That is, if an experiment involves stimuli which are all of fairly low intensity, up to and including a value x, then judgments of x will be high as compared with those obtained from another experiment in which x is the lowest value of a range of stimuli going up to very high intensities. The apparent value of a stimulus is pushed away from the values which have been presented most frequently in the experiment. A particularly striking example of this effect is provided by Campbell *et al.* (1958), who used judgments about pitch on the piano keyboard. When a note was sounded, the subject had to say which note it was (using a number code for his responses, and having been taught the value to assign to middle C on the keyboard). To one group a set of notes was presented for judgment, drawn from the left-hand end of the keyboard, and performance was compared with another group of subjects who had heard mostly notes from the right-hand end of the keyboard. Then judgments of a note in the middle, presented to both groups, tended to be lower in pitch for the group which had heard mostly high notes. The reason why this experiment is a particularly interesting one is that the judgments are clearly absolute rather than relative. Words such as "heavy" or "light" make no claim to be more than relative in ordinary usage, and it is not therefore terribly surprising to find that a given weight may be called heavy in one context and light in another. Equally, if one uses a fixed set of response words or categories, instructing the subject to use only such categories, it may be reasonable for him to adopt a strategy of adjusting his categories to cover the range of stimuli presented. In the study of Campbell *et al.* however, these relatively simple explanations do not apply and it seems clear that some more basic perceptual mechanism is in play. The contrast effect can however be shown very readily in the other situations, as is apparent in studies such as those of di Lollo (1964).

THE THEORY OF ADAPTATION LEVEL

The frequent appearance of effects such as this in psychophysical situations has led Helson to develop a theory of adaptation level, in order to account for them (Helson, 1948, 1964). This theory can be presented in various forms, but for present purposes we may perhaps summarize it as follows. The various responses made in a psychophysical judgment about one dimension are not independent but themselves form an interconnected scale. Thus the response "heavy" is made to stimuli having more weight than those appropriate to the response "light". The absolute value along a sensory dimension which is appropriate to any particular point on the response scale is not constant, however: rather, the mid-point or neutral region of the response scale is attached to an objective stimulus which is a weighted average of the stimuli presented in the past. In the first judgment of any experiment the relevant adaptation level is presumably set by past experience: thus a man in a sedentary occupation will regard as "heavy" weights which a more athletic person would treat as "light". To the former, the weights are above his adaptation level, while to the latter they are below. As an experiment proceeds, the range of stimuli presented within the experiment itself exerts more and more effect upon the adaptation level. Thus the use of a range of stimuli of predominantly low intensity will cause any particular objective stimulus to elicit judgments higher on the response scale than if the experiment had involved very intense stimuli.

The precise prediction of adaptation level in a particular situation depends slightly on the assumptions one makes about the relative weights to be attached to stimuli in the experiment itself and in past history, and also to the stimulus now presented for judgment as compared with the other stimuli no longer present. One may also choose different weightings when obtaining the mean of past stimuli: a geometric mean is often employed, but other assumptions might conceivably be made. The broad conclusion however, that response is made relative to a shifting adaptation level, is quite well established.

EFFECTS OF THE SEQUENCE IN WHICH STIMULI ARE PRESENTED

The importance of adaptation level can be seen by examining other situations in which it plays a part. Thus far we have discussed only experiments in which the whole mass of stimuli experienced in the past has been different. The typical situation has been that in which middle C is judged following a series of notes of lower pitch, or following a series of higher pitch. It is however possible for similar effects to appear in a fashion which changes from moment to moment, as a sequence of stimuli for judgment proceeds.

(a) *Gradual changes in the range presented.* Thus a study on the pitch of notes may employ keys from the whole length of the piano keyboard, and yet if low notes are used predominantly at first and high notes later the judgments may be quite different from the case in which low notes are used first and high notes later. Such a contrast in fact appears both in the results of Campbell *et al.* and in those of di Lollo: when groups which had experienced different sets of stimuli were switched each to the range of magnitudes which the other group had previously experienced. A particularly clear example of the effect of sequence is provided by Parducci (1959) who required subjects to judge a series of sticks of different lengths. The sticks were presented one at a time, until the whole series was visible, before judgment began. Subjects for whom smaller sticks were laid out first showed a lower adaptation level than subjects for whom the larger sticks were made visible first. In a similar vein, Parducci and Sandusky (1965) studied the judgment whether a dot in a brief flash was on the left or the right, and altered the probability that the dot was in fact on the left. If one now looked at the detailed sequence of judgments, it was clear that judgment was more accurate when the dot had really just changed sides: that is, there was an increased tendency to say "Right" if there had very recently been more stimulation on the left. It should be noted also that performance was better for stimuli on the right when the average probability of such a stimulus over the whole sequence was lower, an illustration of the general contrast effect with which we started this chapter. It would seem in general that the contrast effect holds for the fine structure of a series of changing stimuli, as well as for the average of the whole set of stimuli taken together.

(b) *Ascending and descending methods of limits.* A similar finding can be seen in psychophysical methods which require a set of stimuli to be experienced in ascending or descending order. An example which has impressed itself on the present author is that of the kinaesthetic figural after-effect. In this effect, the subject feels a block of wood with one hand, which we may call the test hand, and gives an indication of the apparent size of the block by some means or other with the other hand. We may call the latter the response hand. If the test hand is then applied to another block of wood, say one larger than the original stimulus, and exposed to this larger block for some time, then on a redetermination of the apparent size of the original block, the response produced will be smaller. Thus it is supposed that the impression produced on the test hand has been altered by an after-effect of the larger inspection block. This effect has been used a good deal in studies of individual differences, especially between extraverts and introverts, and in consequence Broadbent (1961) conducted a number of experiments upon it. These immediately revealed certain procedural difficulties in obtaining a measurement from the response hand. The most common technique has been to require the subject to run the response hand over a wedged-shaped piece of wood until he reaches that part of the wedge which appears to him equal in width to the block on the test hand. The wedge of course may be approached either from the sharp end or from the wide end, and equally may be arranged with either the wide or the narrow end towards the subject under test. If no instructions are given for the subject to start at the wide or narrow end, then he normally begins at whichever end of the wedge is closest to himself (Broadbent, 1961). In many of the experiments in the literature it is not clear what procedure was adopted, but from those studies which do report sufficient detail it is apparent that there is little uniformity in the method between different investigators. As Broadbent (1961) became suspicious of the importance of method in determining the results obtained, he carried out two studies in which no interpolated exposure block was presented to the test hand at all: merely two successive sets of determinations with the response hand were made. In both these experiments of Broadbent the wedge was presented with its sharp end always towards the subject, and in one case he was allowed to make his judgments as he chose, which usually meant that the response hand worked from the sharp end of the wedge upwards. In the other experiment the subject was required to start alternately from the sharp and blunt ends of the wedge. Each of these experiments showed a "pseudo-figural after-effect", in opposite directions. In the first of the experiments mentioned, the measurement obtained from the response hand was smaller in the second set of measurements than in the first, while in the other experiment the value obtained from the response hand was larger for the second set of measurements than in the first.

The interpretation which Broadbent placed upon these results was that the task was revealing a contrast effect similar to the one we have already discussed. If the subject was given repeated experiences of the point of the wedge, which was naturally smaller than the width at which the response hand came to rest, then he would form an adaptation level on the response hand which was lower than the original point of apparent equality with the test hand. As repeated experiences went on, this low adaptation level would be more firmly established (di Lollo and Cassedy, 1965), and thus a smaller and smaller objective width would be necessary on the response hand to give the same subjective width. If however subjects were given experience both of the sharp and of the wide end of the wedge, then their adaptation level would presumably be somewhere in the middle region of the range of widths presented by the wedge. As the block presented to the test hand was rather smaller than the average width of the wedge, the adaptation level would therefore be larger than the point at which the response hand normally came to rest. Consequently with repeated exposures it would become necessary to give larger and larger objective stimuli to the response hand in order to give the same subjective impression of width as originally.

This interpretation was suggested by similar results obtained previously by Wertheimer and Leventhal (1958), who equally had got a pseudo-figural after-effect. It is also consistent with the direction of constant errors found by Costello (1961) who separated the descending and ascending trials on the wedge. On descending trials the subject tended to overestimate, but did not do so on ascending trials.

In more recent and unpublished experiments Broadbent and Gregory have confirmed the appearance of pseudo after-effects, and have found that even the method of starting alternately from the large and small ends of the wedge does not necessarily give consistent results. A group starting from either end in the order "Large, small, large, small" will give different results from one which proceeds "Small, large, small, large". In each case the results are consistent with the general interpretation that experience of large widths makes any given objective width feel smaller than it would have done following exposure to small widths.

(c) *The central tendency effect.* A last mention may be made, in this section on sequential effects, of the effect sometimes called the "central tendency" of judgment. This is a tendency which one can note easily in rating scale experiments: if one asks subjects to judge on a five-point rating scale five values of stimulus intensity, all presented equally often, one will often find that the ratings cluster in the middle three categories and do not occur as often in the top and bottom points of the scale. Such a tendency can readily be explained on a basis of adaptation level, if one supposes that the stimulus to be judged itself affects the level. For each stimulus therefore the adaptation level lies between the value of that particular stimulus and the average of all previous ones, and consequently each stimulus is judged more nearly in the centre of the scale of responses than it should truly be. This will give too few responses at the end of the scale.

H*

From these three fields of study therefore, we can see that the basic contrast effect explained by adaptation level may occur even from stimulus to stimulus within a series. If we wish, we may say that this is an operation of the moment to moment probability of a stimulus of any particular value rather than of the average probability over a long period. The effect is at all events for the distribution of responses to be less extreme than that of the stimuli to which they are made.

JUDGMENTS OF THE LOUDNESS OF EXTRA-LABORATORY SOUND SOURCES

If we move away from the use of artificial laboratory stimuli, we can both see the importance of adaptation level and get some foretaste of the modifications it needs from the form we stated earlier. For example, in the field of reducing noise from mechanical devices, it is common to ask panels of subjects to assess different motor cars or aeroplanes in terms of a set of response categories such as "quiet, acceptable, unacceptably noisy, intolerably noisy". As is pointed out however by Robinson *et al.* (1961) several experiments have been performed in this way for motor vehicle noise: and have given widely differing assessments of the physical intensity which makes a noise unacceptable. Looking at the details of these experiments, the study with the lowest level of unacceptability also used the lowest range of inten-

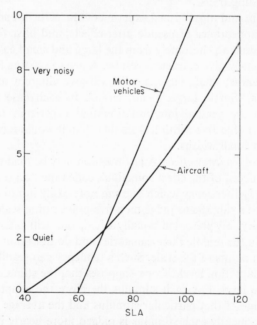

FIG. 21. The annoyance rating for various aircraft and for various motor vehicles as a function of the sound level measured with an "A" weighting (i.e. emphasizing the high frequencies). Data from Robinson *et al.* (1961).

sities of vehicle noises presented for judgment, and so on for the other experiments. Experimenters who use a range of very noisy motor cars for an experiment of this kind will end up with a much higher intensity of noise as "acceptable" than will experimenters who use an extremely quiet range of cars. Similarly, a study by Robinson *et al.* (1963) has obtained ratings from the sounds of aircraft travelling overhead, and has shown that the level of physical intensity necessary for a sound to be rated as "noisy" is greater for aircraft than it was for motor vehicles in the results of Robinson *et al.* (1961) and of Mills and Robinson (1961). The listeners appeared therefore to be more tolerant of loud noises from aircraft than from motor vehicles. A similar effect has been shown by A. J. Sanford (unpublished) in the assessment of noise produced by items of domestic machinery: an electric mixer becomes unacceptably noisy at intensities much less than those of motor cars, just as the latter become unacceptable at lower intensities than aeroplanes.

Thus far, these results with real noise sources may be taken merely as illustrating the contrast effect shown by the laboratory experiments. There are however two further points which should be noted. First, the study by Robinson *et al.* gave a result at low intensities which was opposite to that for loud sounds: *faint* aircraft noises were more objectionable than similar intensities from motor vehicles. As the authors pointed out, not only the average level but also the range of intensities in the studies of aircraft was physically larger than that in the studies of motor vehicles. There seems here therefore to be an attempt to stretch the scale of available responses to fit the range of stimuli, as well as a shift in the stimulus eliciting the middle of the scale of responses. Not only the mean is changed, but also the size of the steps.

Secondly, from the use of real noise sources we can see a possible difference between two theories of the contrast effect. Is it a passive and unintellectual shift of the scale due to the stimuli experienced in the experiment itself? Or is it an intellectual process whereby the listener takes into account the known quality of the source, knows (for example) that it is reasonable to expect cars to be quieter than aircraft, and applies the words on his response scale in an attemptedly objective fashion? In the laboratory, these two processes might give similar results, as the listener has available only the knowledge about the stimuli which the experiment itself gives him. In the field, however, one can attempt to distinguish them.

(*a*) *Different response scales for the same stimulus range.* Another study (Bowsher *et al.*, 1966) compared the ratings of the same real aircraft given by two sub-groups of subjects using different rating scales. One scale contained the response categories "very noisy, noisy, moderate, quiet", while the other contained the categories "noisy, moderate, quiet, very quiet". A comparison of the two sub-groups was made to see whether subjects were indeed fitting their categories to the range experienced in the particular experiment: or whether they were working on an absolute basis independent of the particular experiment. In fact, both factors appeared to be working.

For any physical stimulus the two sub-groups with different words on their rating scale would differ in the word most frequently used to describe the noise. That is, if we think of the words "noisy, moderate, quiet" which appeared on both rating scales, an aircraft would be rated as more noisy by the sub-group which also had the category "very noisy" than by the sub-group which had the other category "very quiet". Thus there is definitely some tendency to fill the whole scale of categories given.

On the other hand, there is also a tendency to be influenced by the general background of experience: if we consider again the comparison between the two sub-groups with different rating scales, one could forget about the words and simply convert all responses to numerical position on the scale of available categories. After such a transformation, the two sub-groups did not give identical results, their judgments differing in such a way as to increase the chances of the same word being attached to the same stimulus. The behaviour was in fact a compromise between filling the range of available categories, and assigning a judgment of "noisy" to the same physical intensity regardless of the other categories available. As is pointed out by the authors, the agreement between the assignment of the same word in two sub-groups is greatest in the middle of the scale, and it is at the ends of the scale that the judgments tend to be constrained so as to fill all available categories.

This result certainly shows that response words are used in a way which depends on experience before the experiment, but not necessarily that their use is based on anything more than a passive shift of scale. Helson's original concept would allow for the adaptation level to lie initially at a different point if pre-experimental experience was different. We need further evidence on the possible role of inference rather than passive adaptation, and some partial light is shed on this by two methods of altering the range of stimuli presented.

(b) *The near-far effect and the indoor-outdoor effect.* In the study by Bowsher *et al.* (1966), two groups of subjects were exposed to the noise of the same air display, but at different distances from the airfield. Thus the highest intensities experienced by one group were greater than those for the other, and correspondingly the same physical intensity was rated as less annoying by the former group as compared with the latter.

It has also been found by Robinson *et al.* (1963) and by Bowsher *et al.* (1966) that the same physical intensity from an aircraft will sound more annoying if heard indoors than outdoors. As in the case of the near-far effect, the whole range of stimuli experienced was naturally less intense indoors than out.

We could therefore argue that both effects were due to contrast; but equally in both cases it could be argued that the listener was inferring from the sound reaching his ears what the intensity of the source must have been. For a distant source or one heard through a wall, the same received intensity implies a more powerful source.

For the near-far effect, Bowsher *et al.* argue that the difference is established too quickly to be due to a contrast effect from the range met in the experiment. It also appears no larger at the end of the experiment than at the beginning. This is not a completely water-tight argument, since the difference in physical intensity at the two locations was also established rapidly, there being no overlap in the range of intensities experienced for the first six judgments of the session. Nevertheless, there is some reason to think that the near-far result may be due to inference.

It is likely however that the indoor-outdoor effect is due to a different mechanism from the near-far one; the former is about as great in terms of decibels for each point on the response scale, whereas the near-far effect is much greater at high intensity levels than at low levels.

There is also some direct evidence that the indoor-outdoor effect is not due to inference about source intensity. Johnson and Robinson (1967) required listeners to assess aircraft and explosive noises of various types both indoors and outdoors. They also had to assess the noisiness of sounds coming from a loudspeaker which was near them out-of-doors and in the same room indoors. Thus the loudspeaker sounds were not being transmitted through a building to reach them, and they should not have made any compensation in their judgments, as they might have done for aircraft sounds coming from outside the building. Yet there was still a difference in the assessment of loudspeaker noises heard out-of-doors and those heard indoors, the same physical intensity being judged as noisier indoors than out. It seems likely therefore that the indoor-outdoor effect is due to the low intensity levels met indoors, either within the experiment itself or in life in general.

We may summarize as follows. There is as yet no need for more than the contrast effect, known in the laboratory, to explain the indoor-outdoor effect. The near-far effect, with its greater impact at high intensities, perhaps represents some other contamination of the influence of the range of stimuli in the experiment itself by factors derived from past experience. In addition, the comparison of different rating scales shows clearly that there is some effect of previous experience, that is, that subjects are less willing to allot the top point on a rating scale to a noise of moderate intensity when that point is labelled "very noisy". The judgment is therefore rather more complicated than the simple establishment of adaptation level and the use of a response scale relative to that level, but nevertheless there is clear evidence for the occurrence of the contrast effect in these situations.

THE METHOD OF MAGNITUDE ESTIMATION

In the last of the papers quoted, we have in fact moved over from one experimental technique to another, since that study did not involve the assessment of isolated stimuli on a rating scale. Rather, a method of "magnitude estimation" was employed, in which the first stimulus presented was allotted a number 10, and all later stimuli were supposed to be assessed relative to the first one. Thus a sound twice as noisy as the first should be called 20, one ten times as noisy 100, and so on. This technique is useful in practical situations because it presses the subject to make as objective a comparison as possible of the relative magnitudes of the standard and the stimulus for judgment: and pushes him away from the formation of an adaptation level for the stimuli used in the experiment itself.

Nevertheless, it is undoubtedly contaminated to some extent by precisely the same effects as the method of rating. A comprehensive survey of such errors has been produced by Poulton (1968) and just as in the rating case we can see effects from the range of stimuli presented in the experiment itself and from those met previously in general experience. The effects which show these points most clearly, amongst the numerous ones discussed by Poulton, are those (1) of the range of stimuli used in the experiment, (2) of the value of the standard stimulus given first, and (3) of the value of the number which the experimenter assigns to this standard stimulus. Each of these effects can be seen as a tendency for the subject to spread the range of responses which he has acquired before the experiment over the range of stimuli that are given to him in the experiment itself.

(1) In the case of the first effect, that of *range of stimuli*, a particularly classic study is that by Garner (1954). He was considering the situation of fractional judgments, in which a stimulus is presented at a known physical intensity, and the observer is asked to choose which of an array of other weaker stimuli appears subjectively to be half as intense. Garner showed that the intensity of the sound chosen to appear half as loud as a given standard sound was much lower when the range of possibilities presented was centred on a lower value. Similar effects have been shown later by other workers, and a particularly striking demonstration is that by Jones and Woskow (1966) and by Poulton (1967). These authors reviewed experiments on the estimation of a variety of sensory magnitudes of different kinds. Such experiments usually conform to a relation

$$\psi = \phi^n$$

where ψ = subjective magnitude
ϕ = physical magnitude
n = a constant depending on the quantity being assessed.

Thus for a judgment of half-loudness, where

ϕ_h = physical magnitude chosen to sound half as loud as ϕ_0
$\frac{1}{2}\phi_0{}^n = \phi_h{}^n$.

From which n can be calculated.

The value of n obtained by this means differs considerably from one sense to another, being very large for quantities such as electric shock, and relatively small for quantities such as the loudness of sounds. It was shown however by Jones and Woskow and by Poulton that the differences in values of n, between different experiments, correlated very considerably with the geometric range of physical values of stimuli used in those experiments. Thus when a wide range of physical stimuli was presented, n was small, whereas when a narrow range of physical stimuli was given, n was large. In either case the range of physical stimuli could perhaps be regarded as spread over a constant range of subjective magnitudes. There may well of course be a residual difference between different sensory quantities, but it is clear that the range of stimuli presented forms a serious contaminating factor in studies of this kind.

(2) The second factor, that of *the value of the standard stimulus*, concerns a variant on the experimental technique, in which typically the subject is presented with two physical stimuli A and B, and is asked to respond with a number b corresponding to his subjective assessment of the magnitude of B. He is to use as a basis a number a supplied by the experimenter, which is to represent his subjective assessment of the magnitude of A. The second factor which we have picked out from Poulton's discussion is the choice of the value of A, given the same range of values of B and the same value of a. In general it is found that a large value of A tends in these cases to give a steeper increase of b with physical magnitude while a small value of A gives a gentler increase of b. A moment's thought will show that this means that the subject is tending to use the same range of values of b, for the same range of values of B, even although he is being given different values of A. The effect was noted by Stevens (1955) and has been confirmed by other authors.

Another form of this effect should be noted: if the same standard is used throughout, our explanation of the effect of value of standard is adequate. When however different standards are used from moment to moment within an experiment, one can no longer use the same explanation for the tendency to give intermediate values of response for extreme values of the stimulus (Robinson, 1957; Johnson and Robinson, 1967). Rather this seems like a version of the central tendency discussed earlier.

(3) The third factor, the *value assigned to the standard*, concerns the choice of a: if A and B are held constant, and a is varied, one might expect the value of b/a to remain constant. In fact however there is a tendency for it to vary inversely with a. Thus if the experimenter says that the standard stimulus is to be called by a very small number, all the subjects' judgments are larger compared with the standard than they would be if the experimenter had supplied a large number. Once again the subject is tending to use the same set of values of b, even although this is rather inappropriate to the particular experimental situation. It should be emphasized at once however that this effect is very slight compared with that of the range of stimuli presented;

Poulton and Simmonds (1963) provide the relevant data, and although the effect is normally in the expected direction it is not always statistically satisfactory. One might put it that the adjustment of the subject to the particular circumstances of the experiment is the major factor, while the scale of responses which has been built up in previous circumstances is a relatively minor one.

These different forms of error in methods of magnitude estimation all point to the same conclusion, comparable to that drawn from studies with rating scales. The set of responses which the man has available, whether constructed for this experiment or by past experience, is set relative to a kind of weighted average of the stimuli now presented and those presented in the past. As Poulton concludes, this type of judgment cannot be understood simply in terms of behaviour of the sense organs, and the mechanisms of response learning and response bias must be included to make an adequate description of the behaviour. For our present purposes, the general point is that, for a scale of responses stretching from high to low, the response given to any particular stimulus will be further in the high direction when the probability of low stimuli has been the greater.

EXPERIMENTS RAISING DIFFICULTIES FOR ADAPTATION LEVEL THEORY

Thus far the picture we have given has been simple and homogeneous: the body of stimuli experienced creates some kind of weighted average, and it is deviations from this average which control response. There is a possible qualification that the size of the deviations also may alter when the range is large: and there are various experiments which suggest that some further complication of this model may be necessary.

The first of these is only an apparent difficulty: it is the fact that paradoxical effects occur when an anchor stimulus is inserted at various distances from the range of stimuli that are presented for judgment. If we have a series of weights to be lifted, and compare judgments obtained when the weights are lifted alone and when they are lifted with a heavier anchor weight, then there is found to be the usual shift downwards in judgments in the presence of the anchor. The size of the effect is *smaller* however when the anchor is closest to the range of stimuli being judged. On the other hand, when one considers any particular position of the anchor, the contrast effect is *greatest* for those weights in the range which are closest to the value of the anchor. This effect has been studied by Helson and Nash (1960), and at first sight it seems that there is a direct contradiction between the two results. When we consider distance of the anchor from the individual stimulus being judged, the contrast effect may get larger or smaller as the distance increases.

The discrepancy is fairly readily explained however: if we remember that the adaptation level will be a weighted combination of the value of the anchor and also of that of the series itself under judgment. The more distant the anchor, the bigger the change in adaptation level which it produces. On the other hand, once the adaptation level has been produced the contrast effect is most marked for stimuli near the final level rather than those further away. Thus the apparent paradox resolves itself into the effect of the anchor upon the adaptation level, which increases as the anchor gets further away; and the effect of the adaptation level on a stimulus being judged, which increases as the two get closer together. There does not appear to be any great difficulty for adaptation level theory in this fact.

The situation is rather different when we consider another study of the effects of distance between an anchor and judged stimulus, by Sherif *et al.* (1958). This study again was carried out on the judgment of lifted weights, and when an anchor was provided at a weight much greater than any stimulus in the series, there was a drop in the general level of judgments produced. This is the usual contrast effect. When however the anchor was brought closer and closer to the range of judged stimuli, until it was actually at the same physical value as the top of the range, then the contrast effect reversed into an assimilation effect. There were actually more high value responses with an anchor equal to the top of the stimulus range than when no anchor was provided. Sherif *et al.* carried out their experiment having in mind the varying effects of propaganda which may appear in social situations; one might regard the usual contrast effect as being parallel to the consequences of presenting some wildly extreme propaganda slogan, far outside the normal experience of the person exposed. In such a case the recipient of the communication may bounce in the opposite direction: if exposed to some monstrously hostile statement about Negroes or Jews, he may positively become more favourable to those groups. A less extreme statement however might sway the recipient to agree with it, and thus give a successful propaganda effect rather than a contrast effect. Whatever the merits of this analogy with problems in social psychology, the appearance of assimilation as well as contrast in a weight lifting experiment raises some difficulties for adaptation level. The anchor weight, so long as it is never lighter than the heaviest weight of the judged series, should surely never reduce adaptation level compared with series alone without an anchor. Why then does the proportion of high value judgments increase?

We shall see later that it is not necessary to abandon adaptation level theory altogether in order to cope with this effect, but merely to modify it slightly. The modification is best discussed when we have considered one or two other discrepant findings: for the moment it may be noted that an important feature of Sherif *et al.*'s experiment lies in the instructions to the subjects. They were told that the anchor stimulus represented the top category of response out of the fixed range available for them to employ.

Another group of experiments giving difficult results are by Ladefoged and Broadbent (1957) and Broadbent and Ladefoged (1960). These studies looked at the perception of different vowel sounds, produced by an artificial process of speech synthesis. As we saw in Chapter IV, the particular vowel sound which is heard depends upon the values of the formant frequencies or resonances which are present in the speech wave. Thus for example if we analyse the speech sounds produced by one person in the following sequence of words "please, this, say, word", we shall find that the first formant increases from the first word to the last. As however different people have different sized heads, the natural frequencies of the cavities producing their voices are

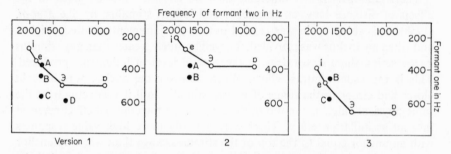

FIG. 22. The first two resonances (formants) of the sentence "Please say what this word is", are shown by the solid line, and various test-words of the form "b-vowel-t" are shown by the points A, B, C, and D. In Version 1, the introductory sentence has its natural vowel values: in 2, the first formant is lowered, and in 3, it is raised. Note that test-word B, for example, has a formant one value well below the line in 2, but above it in 3. From Ladefoged and Broadbent (1957).

also different. Correspondingly one person may use a range of first formant values which is displaced relative to that of another. In natural voices, such differences are confounded with all kinds of other differences, in second formant range, in the timing of speech, and so on. Using a speech synthesizer, however, one can produce tape recordings in which every feature of the speech is identical except that the range of formant 1 values was altered. In the sentence "Please say what this word is" the range could be made 150 to 400 Hz or alternatively 300 to 675 Hz without making the sentence unintelligible. It merely sounds as if two different people were saying it.

Following such a test sentence, one may then present a word which begins with the plosive sound written "b" and ends with that which is written "t". If the vowel between these two consonants has a second formant of about 1750 Hz, then when the word is presented in isolation it will be heard as *bit*, *bet*, or *bat*, depending upon the value of the first formant frequency. A low first formant will give the first of these responses, a medium one the second, and a high one the third. But now let us suppose that we play the test word preceded by an introductory sentence "Please say what this word is". We now find that the response given to the test word depends very much upon the range of formant 1 values used in the introductory sentence. With a physically sentence wording

test-word	sentence version	please say what this word is (60 subjects) response*			what's this (44 subjects) response			this is (44 subjects) response		
		bit	bet	bat	bit	bet	bat	bit	bet	bat
A	1 (natural)	53	7	0	10	33	1	40	4	0
	2 (formant lowered)	4	54	2	1	40	3	8	34	2
B	1 (natural)	5	55	0	2	40	2	17	27	0
	2 (formant lowered)	1	57	2	0	36	8	2	39	3
	3 (formant raised)	58	2	0	21	23	0	32	12	0
C	1 (natural)	0	25	35	0	14	30	1	18	25
	3 (formant raised)	0	48	12	2	28	14	4	34	6

* Data for the longest sentence are from Ladefoged and Broadbent (1957).

FIG. 23. The numbers of people identifying the test-words of Fig. 22 as each of several real vowels, when Versions 1, 2, and 3 are used. Note the shift in judgment when the same sentence is used in different Versions; and the relative absence of shift when the same Version is used for different sentences, even though changing the sentence varies the average value of Formant 1. Results from Broadbent and Ladefoged (1960).

identical test word, one can obtain an increase in the number of "bit" responses by having a high range for formant 1 in the introductory sentence; and an increase in the "bet" or "bat" responses by lowering the range of formant 1 values used in the introductory sentence.

This effect bears all the marks of the contrast effect with which we are familiar: and on the face of it can be explained by adaptation level. Following a series of vowels with low values for their first formant, the adaptation level is low and any succeeding stimulus is given a response appropriate to a higher first formant value than would otherwise be the case.

Broadbent and Ladefoged conducted a number of studies which showed that this effect obeyed various rules consistent with predictions from adaptation level. For example, the effect could not be abolished by telling the subjects to ignore the preceding sentence, or by presenting the sentence from one loudspeaker and the test word from another, but it was reduced by a long time interval between the sentence and the test word. Such a time interval would presumably allow the adaptation level to revert from the point resulting from a momentary burst of stimuli to one more characteristic of general experience. Even more markedly, the effect was abolished by interpolating some other sound between the sentence and the test word, or by presenting the test word before the sentence. Each of these findings argues against some intellectualist process of inference, by which the listener may be adjusting the "true" perception of the word in the light of the sentence accompanying it, and points rather to a simple passive process of adaptation to the average of preceding stimuli.

There is however one aspect of the effect which is not consistent with adaptation level as we have so far used that concept. This is the effect of changing the range of formant 1 in the introductory sentence, not by synthesizing the same words and altering the range of formant 1 used, but simply by using different words. Thus one can use the introductory sentence "This is", or "What's this" instead of the full sentence "Please say what this word is". In the shorter sentences each vowel will have the same formant 1 position as would the same word in the longer sentence. Nevertheless the range covered by the shorter sentences is different from that in the longer sentence. By the normal operation of contrast, we would expect to get more judgments of "bet" or "bat" on a subsequent test word when the introductory sentence included more instances of a low formant 1 position. But this does not happen, when the range is altered by putting in or leaving out words rather than changing the value used for a particular word. On the contrary, if anything there are more "bit" responses for an introductory sentence which has only low first formant words in it than one which does not. Thus the listener does not seem simply to be forming an average idea of first formant position and responding to deviations from that average.

Such a simple interpretation is also inconsistent with another feature of the Broadbent and Ladefoged experiments, namely that repeated experience of a particular version of the introductory sentence does not increase the effect on a subsequent test word; rather it decreases it. It is in fact as if the listener was ceasing to take into account the introductory sentence in making his judgment, rather than working from an average on which the repeated presentations had more and more effect.

A MODIFICATION OF ADAPTATION LEVEL THEORY

At this stage we may put up a simple modification of adaptation level theory, to cover these difficulties. In discussing adaptation level thus far we have supposed that the stimuli are averaged together, and that the response process only comes in at some later stage. In terms introduced in Chapter I, we have been talking as if the evidence reaching the categorizing system was evidence relevant to the departure of the present stimulus from the average of previous ones. If the present stimulus was well above the average of previous ones, then a high valued category state would be appropriate, while if the present stimulus was below the past average a low valued category state would be appropriate. This kind of mechanism for adaptation level, however, is too much derived from classical views of adaptation, and does not fit happily into the discussions we have been having on other problems. Let us rather suppose that the categorizing process is involved in the averaging itself: that the relevant factors in predicting response at one instant include, not only the average of the objective stimuli presented, but also the nature of the responses that have been made to them. In the case of our vowel experiment for example, the presentation of a vowel with a low first formant may be followed by the response "Please" or the response "Say" depending upon the other stimuli which are present, the expectations of the subject, and so on. If the low position of formant 1 results in the response "Please", then this may not shift subsequent vowel judgments because the vowel in "Please" has in any case a value at the bottom end of the range. If however the response to the vowel of low formant 1 value is "Say", then this will change subsequent responses to vowels because the vowel in "Say" does not normally have such a low first formant, and the allocation of such a category to such a stimulus implies a readjustment all along the scale.

We should not think so much therefore of a scale of responses centred on a neutral point, which point is attached to the average of all past stimuli: but rather of a dimension of response and a dimension of stimulus which can be connected together at any place. The linking together of a high value response and a high value stimulus produces no shift of scale as compared with the linking of a low value stimulus and response: but a readjustment of scale may result from the attachment of a medium response to either a high or a low valued stimulus.

To revert to the terms of Chapter I, it is not that the evidence presented to the categorizing system is evidence about deviation of each stimulus from the average of past values: rather, the evidence presented concerns the physical nature of the stimulus, and a better simple statement of the mechanism would be that each category state occurs to the average evidence which has produced that state in the past. Such a simple statement requires additional qualifications, since as it stands this would not explain why the stimuli appropriate to "bet" and "bat" are modified by the presentation of stimuli appropriate to "this is". We must therefore suppose some rule, which, whenever the evidence appropriate to one category changes, also changes that appropriate to neighbouring categories.

Let us now apply this kind of approach to the result of Sherif *et al.* In order to explain the normal contrast effect produced by an anchor stimulus, we must suppose that an uninstructed subject will, in the absence of any counter-information, give a response of intermediate value to any stimulus that arrives. As a series of stimuli builds up, therefore, the scale of responses will tend to be adjusted to a range of stimuli which is high if the physical values of the stimuli have been high, and low if it has been low. High valued responses will occur more frequently to those stimuli which are high in the range presented, but because of the centring process which we have already noticed under the heading of sequential effects, extreme high and extreme low responses will not occur as frequently as those in the middle of the range. When now an anchor is presented with deliberate instructions that it is appropriate for the top value response of the scale, the normal contrast effect will apply provided that the stimulus is very large compared with the range of those presented for judgment. In such a case, the largest of the set of available responses will be allotted to the value of the anchor, will clearly become inappropriate for even the top of the range of stimuli to be judged, and judgments will therefore be pushed further down the scale of possible responses. If however the anchor is equal in value to the top of the range of stimuli to be judged, then the existence of the anchor will provide additional instances in which that stimulus value is attached to the largest possible response. Amongst the set to be judged those stimuli which are equal to the anchor will therefore be more likely to elicit the largest response than they would have been if no anchor had been presented: since the centring effect would tend to reduce the number of top responses even to such stimuli. We should therefore get the assimilation effect which Sherif, Taub and Hovland found when the anchor was brought sufficiently close to the range of stimuli being judged.

EXPERIMENTAL EVIDENCE SUPPORTING THE MODIFICATION

Such an analysis has been put forward previously, by Parducci and Marshall (1962). They performed an experiment replicating that of Sherif *et al.*, but added conditions in which the anchor was not assigned to any particular category, as well as conditions in which the anchor was assigned to a response below the top of the range of categories. One of their results provides a slight difficulty for the interpretation we have been offering: even an anchor which was not assigned to any point on the category scale gave the assimilation effect. We do not of course know what response subjects made implicitly to the anchor: it may possibly be that they self-instructed themselves that this reference stimulus, which appeared to be equal to the heaviest in the range to be judged, corresponded to the top of the response scale.

Two other studies provide evidence in favour of our interpretation: one is by Harvey and Campbell (1963), who used the usual situation of anchors close to the stimulus range or well above any of the stimuli to be judged: the unusual feature in Harvey and Campbell's study was that they compared rating of the weights on a category scale from 1 to 5, and rating of weights in terms of genuine physical values. The latter type of response of course allows the subjects to assign the anchor a position well outside the response scale which they use for the stimuli being judged. Correspondingly, the shifts produced by the anchor were greater for the category form of response than they were for the physical judgment.

The second study is an unpublished one by Broadbent. He gave a series of weights to two groups for judgment, one group judging on a category scale and one in physical terms. Both groups were given full knowledge of results, a correct answer being assigned to each weight. At the end of the series, without warning, a weight well above the top of the series was inserted: for the group judging in categories, this was assigned the top of the category scale. For the group judging in physical amounts it was given its true physical value, well above any previous stimulus. When one compared judgments on a stimulus of medium value in the range to be judged, which was given immediately before and immediately after this interpolated heavy weight, the group judging in categories showed a marked contrast effect. The other group however showed no effect at all. These studies therefore suggest that we are right in modifying the adaptation level theory to regard the important factor as the average stimulus which has been used for each response: and that we should not regard the average of all stimuli, in an undifferentiated fashion, as being attached to the middle of the response scale.

There are still other experiments pointing in the same direction. Brown (1953) compared the effect of an anchor stimulus which was a weight looking just like the stimulus weights to be judged, and of an anchor stimulus which consisted simply of a tray on which the judged weights were presented, and which each time it was emptied, the subject had to lift and hand back to the experimenter. Although the actual stimuli experienced were the same, an anchor of the latter type had essentially no effect on the scale of judgment. In other words, the stimulus of the weight of the tray did not elicit a judgment category, and did not shift the judgmental scale at all. Davidon (1962) found a similar result by presenting a series of blocks for judgment. The blocks differed in height and in the lightness of their grey colour, and after a stable scale of judgments had been formed on both quantities, an anchor block was introduced which was tall and of a rather light grey. Each of the stimuli for judgment was compared with this anchor, but only for one of its properties. That is, half the subjects had to judge each stimulus as taller or shorter than the anchor, while the other half of the subjects had to judge it as paler or darker than the anchor. Whichever comparison had to be made, a rating of both qualities of the judged stimulus then had also to be produced. The usual contrast effect appeared in the judgment of that quality on which the variable block had been compared with the standard anchor: but not the other quality. The stimuli had of course been present; just as in Brown's experiment, therefore, it seems that only stimuli eliciting a response had affected the adaptation level.

Lastly, and perhaps most quantitatively, two studies by Parducci (Parducci et al., 1960; Parducci and Marshall, 1961) studied the extent of contrast effect produced by different distributions of stimuli. One can for example present a series of stimuli for judgment which possess the same mean, but different medians, by crowding together stimuli at the bottom end of the

scale. Similarly, one can produce different distributions of stimuli which are
the same in mean or median, but which differ in the range between top and
bottom values presented: in fact, Parducci and his associates used different
values of the mid-point half way between the top and bottom of the physical
values, while keeping mean and median constant. When now we look at the
judgments of subjects who had been exposed to these different distributions,
we find that the median and mid-point appear to influence judgment, but if
those are held constant changes in the mean do not seem to have much effect.
This was shown in the rather cognitive task of assessing numbers as "very
large, large, medium, small, very small", and also in the more directly sensory
task of judging length. Although the adaptation level for a series of stimuli
would presumably be some weighted mean rather than a direct average of the
physical stimuli, it is difficult to see how one could devise a function which
would give a constant adaptation level when the mid-point and the median
were held constant, but when the direct unweighted average was changing.
Instead of supposing therefore that some weighted average of the stimuli is
attached to the mid-point of the scale of responses, it seems more plausible to
suppose that the various responses are distributed over the various stimuli,
covering the range between the two extremes in some way which takes
account of the differing numbers of stimuli at different parts of the range.
Thus the pattern of judgments would be sensitive to changes in the mid-point
and median, but only to changes to the mean in so far as they were produced
by changes in these other quantities.

Parducci (1965) has developed a detailed model based on such an interpretation. He suggests that the different stimuli may be seen as arranged along
some single dimension, and that the criteria dividing one category of response
from another can then be viewed as located on this same dimension. Because
of the usual randomness in all information processing, the criteria are not
absolute. The presence of a stimulus at a certain point on the underlying
dimension does not therefore mean unequivocally that there will be a response
in a certain category, but merely that there will be a certain probability of
response in one category and another probability in another category. The
next crucial question concerns the positions along the dimension at which
the criteria will be located: or, in view of the randomness just mentioned, at
which the average positions of the criteria will be found. Parducci proposes
that two principles will be operative, one of which is that the criteria will be so
placed that all categories of response should be used with equal frequency.
This would not lead to an equal spacing of criteria on the stimulus scale; if it
did, and even if we were to suppose that stimuli were presented at equal
frequency at each of a number of equally spaced divisions on the underlying
dimension, and that the variance of each criterion was the same as that of
every other, then the consequences of the randomness already mentioned
would cause the number of responses in each category to be unequal. Indeed,

in such circumstances the principle of equal response frequency would mean that the criteria should depart from even spacing by lying closer to the mid-point of the stimulus scale.

The placement of the criteria will of course shift if more stimuli are presented at one end of the scale, and the amount of such a shift can be calculated. It will obviously tend to produce the usual contrast effect; if, for example, many stimuli of low value are being presented, the use of different categories of response with equal frequency can only be achieved by the elicitation of some high value responses by rather low value stimuli.

Parducci adds a second principle for the placement of criteria, namely that they are adjusted to the range of stimuli. This principle gives rise to criteria depending upon the end points of the range of stimuli and not upon the different frequencies with which stimuli are given in one part of the range rather than another. The final criterion actually used for judgment is supposed to be at the average of the two criteria derived from the two principles. Although Parducci does not in this paper provide a way of calculating the theoretical position of the criterion due to range of stimuli, he can calculate empirically where it is. He does this by observing the distribution of judgments for different distributions of stimuli, working out the theoretical placement of criteria for equal frequencies of response in each category, and using the fact that the empirical criterion is supposed to be the average of the two theoretical ones. When he analyses in this way data from various experiments on the effects of presenting uneven distributions of stimuli, he finds that the hypothetical criteria based on stimulus range remain the same for distributions of stimuli having the same end points, but change when the end points change. This certainly sounds as if the judgments can indeed be represented as a compromise between a tendency to spread the available responses over the range of stimuli presented, and a tendency to use the different responses with equal frequency.

With this approach of Parducci's we are coming close again to the approach through decision theory which we have mentioned in earlier chapters. In both cases we have the idea of randomness affecting the particular response given to a particular stimulus, and of the assignment of a response to a certain range of stimuli taking into account this randomness. Parducci's own statement of his theory is based rather in terms of the traditional psychophysical approach of Thurstone, and it is plain that it does not involve some of the assumptions of signal detection theory in its pure form. For example, there is no implication that the criterion deciding which response shall be made to a certain stimulus is set in such a way as to maximize the gains and losses for various kinds of outcome. Indeed, Parducci and Sandusky (1965) actually criticize detection theory, because their experimental results show the usual contrast effect and this is in the opposite direction to that predicted by detection theory. (The careful reader will probably have been worrying about this for some time past, as in previous chapters the criterion has moved in such a way as to make a response more probable when the stimulus corresponding to that response is more probable. The contrast effect is in the opposite direction.) Nevertheless, many of the basic elements of the approach which we have adopted in earlier chapters do appear in Parducci's model, and it is fair to say that the body of evidence we have considered here requires one to modify slightly the theory of adaptation level. It is not so much the averaging of a series of stimuli, and the attachment of a neutral response to the resulting average, but rather the adjustment of a set of output categories to a range of input stimuli. We must now consider further the extent to which this process can really be regarded as an example of the same mechanism handled in earlier chapters.

DECISION MEASURES IN A SCALING SITUATION

When we perform an experiment on the assignment of a range of stimuli to a set of response categories, we can reveal the contrast effect by picking any one stimulus and showing that the responses to that stimulus fall in higher categories when a higher proportion of the other stimuli are of low values. If however we take the number of responses in any particular category to any particular stimulus, it changes both with the size of the interval between different stimulus values, and also with the relative numbers of stimuli at one value rather than another. It is very difficult to extract a score which represents a pure effect of changes in the probability of one stimulus rather than another. The first step in deciding whether measures derived from detection theory are of use in this situation must be a familiar one: we must consider the probability of occurrence of a particular response in two conditions, and see empirically what the relationship is between them. Suppose for example that we take judgments of weight, and observe the probability of occurrence of a response "very heavy". The other responses available may be "heavy, medium, light, very light", but if we are concerned only with the topmost response we can ignore the differences between these other responses for the moment. If now we take the highest objective value of stimulus which is being presented in the experiment, there will be a certain probability that this will produce the response "very heavy", which we may call P_H. If we take a stimulus at a lower value, this also will have a certain probability of producing the response "very heavy", and we may call this probability P_h. If now we carry out two experiments in one of which the proportion of stimuli at the top value is lower than in the other, we know from what has been said already that there will be a general increase in the number of "very heavy" responses to any particular stimulus: both P_H and P_h will increase. What however will be the relationship between P_H and P_h? The simplest possible form of adaptation level theory would not tell us, but by analogy with the phenomena found in signal detection theory it is worth examining the possibility that one can transform P_H and P_h to their corresponding Z scores Z_H and Z_h. Will it then be true that

$$Z_H = d' + Z_h$$

where d' is a constant depending on the stimulus values and not on their relative frequency? If so, then the occurrence of one stimulus rather than another may be taken as producing a shift in the average value of some process of constant variance. The probability of response depends as previously on the proportion of occasions on which the varying process exceeds some critical level. This is the type of mechanism supposed by Parducci, but it is from the armchair only one of a number of possibilities. The case is in fact directly analogous to that of signal detection, which we have discussed exhaustively in an earlier chapter.

In fact, it is easiest to test this possibility by taking a relationship of the type

$$\frac{P_H}{1-P_H} = A \times \frac{P_h}{1-P_h}$$

which we have seen to be closely similar in its predictions to the equation involving Z scores. From actual probabilities of occurrence of the "very heavy" response for any given set of stimuli presented, it is however easier to work out the value of A than that of d'. We can then see whether A remains constant when the probability of one stimulus value rather than another has changed.

Data on this point have been provided by Broadbent and Gregory (unpublished). They made use of small cardboard boxes, each containing a number of ball bearings. Subjects were told to look at each box presented to them, and to assign it to one of four categories depending upon the number of ball bearings in the box. The categories were defined as objectively as possible, by giving three standard boxes, each having a different number of ball bearings in it. These marked the boundaries between the four categories, so that each stimulus presented for judgment had to be regarded as more numerous than any of the standards, as more numerous than two but less than the third, as more numerous than one but less than the other two, or as less numerous than any. Two groups of subjects were then compared, each of which had to judge the same number of stimuli. However, in one group the majority of the stimuli presented were drawn objectively from the upper two categories, while in the other group of subjects the majority of the stimuli presented were drawn from the lower two categories. The usual contrast effect appeared, responses tending to be more evenly distributed between the four categories than were the stimuli. It was possible however to calculate A for each of the category boundaries, and no significant difference was found for any category between the two groups.

It was also of course possible to calculate β for each of the criterion boundaries, by working out at each boundary

$$\beta = \frac{P_H(1-P_H).}{P_h(1-P_h)}$$

(It will be discussed shortly whether β is an appropriate score of bias, but for the present purposes it makes no difference whether β or some other score is employed because A did not change.) It was found that significant differences in β occurred at the boundary between the frequently presented and the infrequently presented categories. Thus the contrast effect already noted could indeed be regarded as the movement of a criterion over two distributions which maintained their distance from each other.

This result seems to establish the usefulness of measures derived from decision theory in this kind of situation. The fact that changes in relative frequency of one stimulus value rather than another leaves the parameter A (or d') unchanged means that we are entitled to think of a constant scale of evidence, some value on which results from the presentation of each stimulus. The effect of the relative frequency of one objective stimulus rather than another then appears in a change in the number of values on the scale of evidence which result in a particular overt response. No doubt a finer analysis might well show that it was desirable to depart from the assumptions of equal variance, and further study of this problem from this point of view is highly desirable. Nevertheless, in general it seems plausible to assign the effects of stimulus probability to "pigeon-holing" and not to any other mechanism.

It is worth reinforcing this point, since once again we meet the antithesis between filtering and pigeon-holing; between the location of an effect in the intake of information and in the linkage between states of evidence and category states. It is not at all inconceivable from the armchair that a man who has frequently been faced with stimuli drawn from the top end of the possible scale may adjust his sense organs and perceptual mechanism so as to take in more information from that part of the scale. If this were so however there should have been a change in A, and especially such a change might have been expected to appear at the boundary between the two categories of stimuli presented frequently. The fact that the value of A remained constant at that boundary suggests that in this type of situation an increase in frequency of certain stimuli does not produce increase in the intake of information from those stimuli, but merely a change in the decision rules applied once the evidence has been collected. We have seen similar antitheses before: and we shall see them again within this chapter in the more complex case of decisions between many alternatives.

Given that A (or d') remains constant when we keep the same set of objective stimuli but present some more frequently than others, what happens if we change the objective separation between stimuli? In the same series of studies,

Broadbent and Gregory compared two groups, each of which had been presented with equal numbers of stimuli objectively in each of the four categories to be judged. In one case however the range of stimuli was wider than in the other, so that the particular values presented in one category were more sharply different from those presented in the next category. Performance was correspondingly much more accurate. When A was calculated, it showed larger values in the group which had the more widely spaced stimuli. Thus A does indeed change provided that appropriate changes in the stimulus situation are made.

The point of major interest in this experiment however concerns the calculation of β. As we saw in earlier chapters, there is no need to suppose that human performance will necessarily maintain β at a constant value when d' (or A) is changed. It might equally be that $(\log \beta)/d'$ remains constant, or that some other rule connects the decision criterion to the objective probability of one stimulus rather than another. When Broadbent and Gregory showed that β changes when the stimulus probability changes, this did not prove that the criterion moves in accordance with any particular rule. In the present experiment, however, it was found that the changes in A were not associated with any change in the value of β. Thus it seems that subjects do base their decision on a constant value of β: just as we found them to do so in the data reported in the last chapter.

THE DIRECTION OF MOVEMENT OF β WITH CHANGES IN SIGNAL FREQUENCY

We must now take up the important difficulty ignored so far, that if β changes underlie the contrast effect they must be in the opposite direction from those we have met in previous chapters. If we had approached detection theory from an axiomatic point of view, it would of course be quite inappropriate to explain the contrast effect by reference to β; for a man who is working on a basis of maximization of his probable gains will adopt a value of β which gives a bias towards the more probable signal, and not one which is against it. By saying that β remains constant empirically when A is changed, we are not attempting to justify the axioms of detection theory.

At this stage in fact we reach one of the crucial points in linking the data considered in this chapter with those we have discussed in earlier parts of the book. Why is it that the judgment of stimuli arranged along a single dimension shows a contrast effect? Why does the criterion shift in such a way as to keep the number of responses in different categories more nearly equal than the number of stimuli presented in different categories? It is perhaps fair to appeal to the same principle as Parducci, that subjects given no other instruction tend to assume that they should have equal numbers of responses in each category, and that they adopt a decision rule which presses in that direction. In addition, we may remember the vicious circle mechanism which we discussed in the chapter on vigilance, and whereby unless any subject places his criterion in exactly the correct position to start with, he is likely to think that the number of stimuli in each category is less different than it really is, and so to shift his criterion further in the direction of equalizing the numbers of responses. Each of these theories supposes that the subject's placement of his criterion depends on the fact that he does not know accurately whether his response is true or false.

In most experiments on scaling, there is indeed no objective answer to such a question. In the studies by Broadbent and Gregory which we have been considering, however, it is possible to follow each judgment by an indication to the subject of whether the stimulus was objectively in any one of the four categories. Such knowledge of results was in fact presented to two fresh groups, each of which received a biased distribution of stimuli, just as in the first experiment in this section. One group received a bias towards the stimuli of low value, and the other towards the stimuli of high value. Since they were informed after each judgment of the category to which the stimulus truly belonged, they were fully aware of the objective number of stimuli in each category. Correspondingly, the two groups showed, once again, no difference in A, but a significant difference in β. The difference on this occasion however was in the opposite direction to the typical contrast effect. The value of β shifted in such a way as to give more responses in the category in which there were objectively more stimuli. Thus the motion of the criterion was in the direction predicted by detection theory, and not in the direction found in the more usual contrast effect. It is the provision of knowledge of results which produces this marked difference, and the typical contrast effect can perhaps fairly be put down to the fact that most experiments on biased presentation of stimuli for judgment involve no knowledge of results to the subject. Under such circumstances, it may well be that he adopts the assumption of equal numbers of responses in each category.

We may also note that the theory produced by Schoeffler (1965), which supposes the criterion to be set on the basis of a learning theory model, equally supposes that it will move in one direction under knowledge of results and the opposite direction without knowledge of results: the reason for this being essentially the same as the operation of the vicious circle mechanism which we discussed under vigilance.

CONCLUSIONS ABOUT THE JUDGMENT OF ONE-DIMENSIONAL STIMULI

We have now rejoined the general line of thought which has been pursued in earlier chapters. When a man is asked to judge stimuli differing upon one dimension, those stimuli produce states of evidence within him, and the category state which he adopts for any given stimulus depends upon the state of evidence that has followed it. In the absence of instructions he adopts such a rule for linking states of evidence to category states as will cause the available category states to occur with reasonably equal frequency. This has the effect that a given objective stimulus is more likely to give a high valued response when more low valued stimuli have been presented: the contrast effect. If the subject is fully informed of what is happening, by means of knowledge of results, the reverse may be the case and following many low valued stimuli he will tend to give low valued responses to more states of evidence than he would if high valued stimuli were being commonly presented. In either case however the scale of evidence is unaffected, and it is the position of the criterion upon it which is being adjusted: the effects of probability are upon pigeon-holing and not in this case upon the intake of information.

Perception of One Out of Many Multi-dimensional Stimuli

In the case of a simple psychophysical judgment, it is easy to see that the objective stimulus may produce an effect on a single scale of evidence. In real life however we are more concerned with complex and multi-dimensional stimuli: the perception of a spoken word, as we have already seen, involves the detection of different resonant frequencies in the sound wave, of changes in those frequencies, of the presence of bursts of noise, and so on. If we suppose some kind of device to recognize each such feature, are we to suppose that the outputs of all these feature recognizers are combined on a single scale of evidence? Can it be legitimate to suppose that a rise in the probability of one word rather than another increases the number of states of evidence which will produce the first category state rather than the second, if the evidence is not arranged on a single unitary scale? Furthermore, the machinery necessary to detect each feature of a complex stimulus will itself be substantial. It may well be that it is impossible to have simultaneously operative all the analysing mechanisms capable of coping with all possible features. In that case, we might well expect that the brain would have operative at any one time only those analysing mechanisms relevant to features which would be present in the stimuli most likely to arrive. If we know, to take a fanciful illustration, that a man takes exercise either by walking along the shore from his house or by going in the opposite direction inland, and if we hear him say "I have been walking on the" we may be certain that he is going to say "land" or "sand" and so have in readiness those analysers relevant to the difference between "l" and "s". If unexpectedly he said "road", we might receive no useful sensory information at all. While such an extreme case would be most unlikely, and it is plausible that several different feature recognizers are operative at the same time, yet there might still be a bias in favour of some features at one time and others at others. The mechanism of *categorizing*, which we discussed in the last chapter, indeed implies this and suggests that the adjustment of the man to a highly probable stimulus may consist in the taking in of certain information rather than the attachment of a single category state to many states of evidence.

For these reasons, it is of great interest to know what happens to human performance when complex stimuli are used, and when there are many such different stimuli possible in the situation. Do variations in stimulus probability still affect pigeon-holing only, or filtering?

The most obvious case for such studies is that of speech, and there are in fact clear effects of a probabilistic kind in speech perception. These effects can be divided into those of size of a fixed known vocabulary, those of the context in which a given stimulus arrives, and those of overall probability of a word in the language. Broadly speaking, if a stimulus is known to be one of a small fixed set it is more likely to be correctly identified than if it comes from a larger set; if it is presented in an appropriate context it is more likely to be perceived than if it is presented in an inappropriate context. Finally, the stimuli which occur more frequently in general experience are more likely to be correctly perceived than those which do not. In each of these cases it is possible to ask the question whether the effect on correct perceptions is due to a change in the intake of information from the environment or to a change of the kind we have been calling pigeon-holing. Each of them is worth considering separately.

EFFECTS OF SIZE OF A KNOWN VOCABULARY

The classic experiment on this subject is that of Miller *et al.* (1951). They presented spoken words through noise, to listeners who knew the set of alternative words, one of which was the stimulus. For the same ratio of signal to noise, the probability of correct reaction increased as the size of the vocabulary decreased. This in itself is insufficient for our purposes: clearly, if the listener had been given a fixed list of words and told to pick one at random, without any stimulus being delivered at all, the probability of his picking a particular word would increase as the length of the list decreased. Without too much violence to plausibility, we can say that

$$P_G = \frac{1}{N}$$

where P_G = probability of correct reaction in the absence of a stimulus,
        N = number of possible words.

What now is the relationship between P_C, the percentage of correct responses in the presence of a stimulus, and P_G? One plausible theory might be that the listener perceives a certain proportion of the words correctly, and then on the remaining occasions reacts as if he had received no sensory information. This would give an equation of the type

$$P_C = A + B P_G$$

$$= A + \frac{B}{N}$$

where A, B are constants. The resemblance between this equation and those met in Chapter III, but rejected as inapplicable to vigilance experiments, will be obvious. Once again, it is found in the case of speech also that this simple

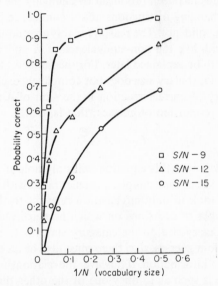

FIG. 24. A plot of correct word recognition against the probability of guessing a word correctly, when the vocabulary size is varied. Data from Miller *et al.* (1951).

theory will not hold. The actual data produced by Miller *et al.* show a relationship which is roughly of the shape

$$P_C = P_G{}^K$$

or

$$\frac{P_C}{1-P_C} = \alpha \frac{P_G}{1-P_G}$$

where K, α are constants. (See Stowe *et al.*, 1963. These authors prefer the first of these possible relationships and we shall be discussing the differences between them shortly. It is clear however that both expressions are roughly correct.) It will be recalled that both of these are relationships of the kind which were found to fit the data of vigilance, and of course this implies also that speech perception obeys roughly the rule

$$Z_C = X + Z_G$$

where Z_C, Z_G are the Z-scores equivalent to P_C, P_G, and X is a constant. In this case, we use X rather than d' because in signal detection theory d' has a theoretical meaning which does not make it equivalent to X in the multi-alternative case. This we shall be considering shortly.

We must therefore have a very considerable feeling of familiarity in looking

I

at the data from speech perception with varying sizes of vocabulary, since the empirical relationships are just like those we found in vigilance. Remember however that on this occasion the change in probability of reaction in the absence of a stimulus has been produced by changing the size of the vocabulary, and not by changing instructions about confidence or asking a subject to give a rating of confidence. The reason for this abandonment of confidence ratings is theoretical, like the non-equivalence of X and d' in the last paragraph; they will both be explained later. For the moment, the point is that the effect of changing vocabulary size does not completely exclude the possibility that the probability of correct reaction is the sum of a proportion of true perceptions and a proportion of guesses; that is, that

$$P_C = A + \frac{C}{N}.$$

What it does show is that this equation will only hold if A changes with N. This might be the case if, for example, a listener faced with a small vocabulary of possible words took in only information relevant to those words and so improved the number of occasions on which he perceived correctly. Thus *if* the effect of vocabulary size on the category states is to introduce a certain proportion of random guesses, *then* there must also be an effect of vocabulary size on the intake of information. If however the relationship between evidence and category state is such as to obey one of the other three equations, then the effect of vocabulary size can be handled entirely by changes in P_G, and the parameters K, α, or X are left to reflect the effect of the physical signal/ noise ratio being delivered to the listener. Just as the case of vigilance, experiment does show that a stronger physical signal requires a change in K, α, or X, depending upon the equation one is using. Given the same physical level of signal, however, the size of vocabulary affects only P_G. This certainly seems a tidier arrangement and one making it more possible to compare experiments using different vocabulary sizes. Let us now consider what mechanisms might correspond, in the case of speech perception, to these more successful relationships between P_C and P_G.

(a) *The exponential model.* The equation $P_C = P_G{}^K$ can be explained in a fashion closely analogous to that which we suggested in the case of vigilance. Stowe *et al.* do so: they suggest that the detection of any word requires the correct identification of each of a number of independent features, any one of which may be present or absent. If there are t features to be considered, and if the probability that a stimulus will result in a correct decision about each feature is P_O then

$$P_C = P_O{}^t.$$

We may suppose that the number of features considered is the minimum necessary to separate out the N possible words, so that

$$N = 2^t.$$

Therefore

$$t \log 2 = \log N$$

and

$$\log P_C = t \log P_O$$

$$= \frac{\log N}{\log 2} \log P_O$$

$$= \frac{\log P_G}{\log 0 \cdot 5} \log P_O.$$

$$P_C = P_G{}^K$$

where K depends on P_O.

Equally of course

$$P_C = P_O{}^h$$

where h depends on P_G.

One can regard this theory as a kind of *sophisticated guessing*. Whereas the simple theory of guessing supposed that the listener hears the word perfectly on some occasions and on other occasions guesses at random, this theory rather supposes that both guessing and stimulation play their part in each perception. The set of all conceivable words is divided into a group of those that are possible and those that are impossible, by the vocabulary provided: and the stimulus makes a similar division quite independently. If the stimulus is consistent with only half the words in the language, and if the experimenter provides a list of twenty words including the stimulus, then there are ten possibilities any one of which might be right. If however the experimenter provides only two words, the stimulus provides enough information for the listener to be absolutely sure of the correct answer.

When this equation is applied to the results of Miller *et al.* it is found to give a slightly lower value of K at large values of N. Stowe *et al.* regard this as reasonable, and one might indeed expect that small vocabularies would allow more selective intake of relevant information. At all events, Stowe *et al.* regarded this as preferable to a departure in the opposite direction, which was found on the analysis to which we shall next turn.

(*b*) *The choice analysis.* It will be recalled that the choice analysis attaches to each response a *strength*, and when two different responses are considered the ratio of their probabilities is supposed to be in the ratio of their strength. In discussing vigilance, we had only to consider the probabilities of two responses, report and non-report. We could therefore say that

$$\text{Prob of non-report} = 1 - \text{prob of report}$$

$$\frac{\text{Prob of report}}{1 - \text{prob of report}} = X = \text{strength of report response.}$$

Since therefore strength and probability were determinately linked to one another, it may have been unclear why a distinction was made between them. When we are considering a large set of possible responses, however, the value of the distinction becomes evident. It corresponds to the common sense feeling that from some points of view response A and response B remain unchanged if a treatment is applied to response C which makes it more probable. Yet a rise in the probability of C must entail a fall in the probabilities of A and B. This difficulty for common sense is met by saying that the strengths of A and B remain unchanged when the strength of C is increased. Then if a, b, c represent the strengths of responses A, B, C respectively then

$$\text{Probability of } A = \frac{a}{a+b+c}$$

$$\text{Probability of } B = \frac{b}{a+b+c}$$

$$\text{Probability of } C = \frac{c}{a+b+c}.$$

It is now clear that the probability of each response can change if the strengths of other responses change, and yet that its own strength remains constant. Clearly if any two responses are considered which each keep the same strength, then the ratio of their probabilities should be constant even though the absolute value of each changes. In the case of the intelligibility of spoken words, the question is whether the relative probability of any pair of responses, under the same stimulus condition, remains the same when the size of the set of possibilities is altered. In fact it has been shown experimentally by Clarke (1957) that this is approximately true: that is, that a constant ratio rule applies. It has been shown mathematically by Luce (1959) that whenever the constant ratio rule holds we may assign a strength to each response. This of course does not necessarily imply that the strength has any physical meaning, but at least it is a mathematical description which will hold true of any one response without changing as the set of responses changes. Luce has also shown that multiplication rather than addition is the correct rule for handling changes in strength: thus if the strength of a response in the absence of any stimulus is x, the increased strength resulting from the presentation of a stimulus appropriate to that response should be represented as ax and not as $a+x$.

For full accuracy, one ought perhaps to regard each response as having its own individual value of strength, in the absence of a stimulus: and it will also be true that a stimulus will increase the strengths of responses other than the correct one. Any response word which happens to be particularly similar to the correct one will receive some increment of strength from the stimulus, although not as much as the correct one. As a rough approximation, however, we can ignore these effects and suppose that in a small fixed vocabulary each possible response has the same strength in the absence of any stimulus. This strength can be taken as unity. The presentation of a stimulus appropriate to one response then increases the strength of that response to α. The table of strengths for each possible stimulus and each response will then appear as follows.

RESPONSES

		1	2	3
S T I M U L I	1	α	1	1
	2	1	α	1
	3	1	1	α

It is obvious that the probability of correct response in a fixed vocabulary of N possibilities is given by

$$P_C = \frac{\alpha}{\alpha + (N-1)}$$

and

$$\frac{P_C}{1-P_C} = \frac{\alpha}{N-1}.$$

But in the absence of any stimulus the probability of any one response is given by

$$P_G = \frac{1}{N}$$

$$\frac{P_G}{1-P_G} = \frac{1}{N} \cdot \frac{1}{1-\dfrac{1}{N}} = \frac{1}{N-1}.$$

Therefore

$$\frac{P_C}{1-P_C} = \alpha \frac{P_G}{1-P_G}.$$

Stowe *et al.* apply this type of analysis to the data of Miller *et al.*, and although it fits about as well as the exponential principle they point out that it departs in the opposite direction from that principle. That is, α is roughly constant for different values of N, but appears to decrease slightly for small vocabularies. They therefore argue that the exponential rule is more plausible.

It should be noted however that, as we have seen, it is only an approximation to regard all responses as having equal strength in the absence of any stimulus. If this assumption were to be invalid, then the calculations based upon it will in some cases give an apparent reduction of α as the vocabulary gets smaller. The difference between the exponential and the choice analysis is in any case relatively slight, and the important point is that either analysis accounts for the effect of changing vocabulary size almost entirely in terms of changes in P_G. Both analyses suggest that the stimulus produces a fairly determinate effect: in the choice analysis, it increases the strength of the correct response by a fixed amount, and the randomness is introduced in the subsequent occurrence of a category state, which occurs merely with a probability proportionate to the strength. In the exponential analysis, the stimulus restricts the range of possible alternatives in a fixed fashion, while not distinguishing between those which are still allowed. In both cases, changes in P_G alter the number of states of received evidence which will be followed by a particular category state.

The two analyses differ largely in the fact that the choice model allows for the correct response having a greater strength than any competitor, whereas the exponential analysis rather suggests that the correct response is only one amongst several equally probable ones. They both suppose the randomness in the system to lie primarily between the evidence and the response. There remains the possibility that the randomness lies between the stimulus and the resulting state of evidence: and this should now be considered.

(c) *The detection theory analysis.* In presenting the equation

$$Z_C = X + Z_G$$

we did not write d' instead of X. The reason for this is that the most usual analysis of multi-alternative tasks in terms of detection theory makes it inappropriate. Such an analysis says that, if we perform such a task with physical signals which have been used in a simple detection task, and for which we therefore know d', we shall find that X is not equal to d'.

The argument is as follows. In considering the case of simple detection, we supposed that a completely rational observer received evidence about the occurrence of a signal. Any particular value of evidence corresponded to a particular likelihood ratio of signal relative to non-signal. Consequently, he would behave rationally by reaction only when this likelihood ratio exceeded a certain amount. Suppose however that he was absolutely certain that a signal would occur in one of two time intervals. In that case, he would receive evidence from the first time interval, and completely independent evidence from the second time interval. Let us call the two items of evidence EV_1 and EV_2. Now suppose that, when he receives this pair of items of evidence he always says that the signal was in the first interval. His net gain from a long series of trials will then be

$$\text{Gain} = P(EV_1/\text{Sig}_1) \times P(EV_2/\text{Non-Sig}_2) \times G \times P(\text{Sig}_1\,\text{Non-Sig}_2)$$
$$- P(EV_1/\text{Non-Sig}_1) \times P(EV_2/\text{Sig}_2) \times L \times P(\text{Sig}_2\,\text{Non-Sig}_1)$$

where $\quad G =$ gain for correct response

$\qquad L =$ loss for incorrect response

$\qquad P(EV_1/\text{Sig}_1) =$ Probability of receiving EV_1 if signal was in fact in interval 1.

$\qquad P(EV_1/\text{Non-Sig}_1) =$ Probability of receiving EV_1 when there is no signal in interval 1.

$\qquad P(\text{Sig}_1\ \text{Non-Sig}_2) =$ Probability of signal in interval 1 and non-signal in interval 2.

(We know that there are no instances of signals in both or non-signals in both.)

This value of gain is positive when

$$\frac{P(EV_1/\text{Sig}_1)}{P(EV_1/\text{Non-Sig}_1)} \times \frac{P(EV_2/\text{Non-Sig}_2)}{P(EV_2/\text{Sig}_2)} > \frac{L}{G} \cdot \frac{P(\text{Sig}_2\ \text{Non-Sig}_1)}{P(\text{Sig}_1\ \text{Non-Sig}_2)}.$$

In the case when $L = G$, and the signal is equally probable in either interval, the subject should respond by picking that interval for which the likelihood ratio is greatest. If the signal is more probable in one interval than another, he should respond in that interval unless the likelihood ratio for that interval is smaller than a certain fraction of the likelihood ratio for the other interval. The analysis is in fact precisely analogous to that for the case of detection, except that in the latter case the subject worked simply with one likelihood ratio, while in the present case he works with the ratio of two ratios. It is easiest in fact to think of this as the difference between the logarithms of the original ratios for the following reason.

Suppose now that we think of the states of evidence as being distributed in a normal fashion on a logarithmic scale, with unit variance, and with the effect of a signal in a particular interval being a shift in the mean value of the distribution for that interval by d'. Then if the subject is reacting on the basis of a difference in log likelihood ratios, he will be examining the difference between a sample from a distribution with mean d' and a sample with mean zero. The distribution of these differences will itself be normal, and will have a mean of $+d'$ if the signal is in one interval, and of $-d'$ if it is in the other. Thus the subject must set a critical value for the difference, above which he regards it as drawn from one distribution and below which from the other. We could therefore think of the subject in this situation as behaving exactly like the one in a detection situation, except that his responses become "interval 1" and "interval 2" instead of "Yes" and "No". However, the distance between the means of the two underlying distributions is now $2d'$ instead of d', and the variance of each distribution is no longer unity but $\sqrt{2}$ since each is a distribution of differences derived from two distributions of unit variance. If therefore we were to analyse the data just as for a detection experiment, taking the variances of the underlying distributions as unity, then we would get the difference between their means to be $\sqrt{2} \times$ the value of d' obtained from a simple detection situation with the same signal.

In the case of two alternative states of the world, it is relatively simple to handle the possibility that the detector should respond more readily to one alternative than the other. With more than two alternatives, it becomes much harder. One can however consider the symmetrical case of equal probabilities for each possible state of the world, and equal gains for being right in identifying each of them. In that case, if we have N samples of evidence each relevant to one possible state of the world, we should pick the largest value of likelihood ratio. That has the greatest chance of being the one corresponding to the state of the outside world. Obviously however the larger the value of N the greater the chance that some one of the incorrect alternatives will happen by chance to produce evidence in its own favour which seems more convincing than that for the correct alternative. It is possible to compute the percentage of correct decisions which will result for sets of different numbers of alternatives, assuming normal distributions of equal variance, all having a mean of zero except for one which has been displaced d' by the arrival of a signal. By consulting a table for each number of alternatives, percentage correct can thus be transformed to a value of d', given the theory which we have just outlined.

At this point, we can see why it is less usual to analyse confidence ratings from speech perception experiments than it is from those on simple detection of presence or absence of a signal. In the latter case, different degrees of confidence may be taken as representing different criterion placements. In the case of experiments with many possible responses, no corresponding interpretation can be made. One might regard a high degree of confidence attached to a response as indicating that the response in question had a state of evidence far above the average of all other states; but equally one might suppose that the big factor was the difference between that response and the next closest competitor. There are many other possibilities, and one would not necessarily expect to be able to calculate d' from different confidence ratings in multiple-alternative experiments, although one can do so in detection experiments (Pollack, 1959). Rather, the theory requires us to vary false alarm rates by changing the number of alternative possible responses.

One may now turn to the facts, to see whether the values of d' calculated from forced-choice experiments do agree with those for detection experiments. The technique used for comparing the two techniques is to use various time intervals of observation, as in the examples we have been discussing. The signal can then be a tone embedded in noise, and one can compare detections of this tone when it may be present or absent, with the choice of one of N time intervals when the subject knows that the tone is certainly present in one of them. The values of d' obtained with the different methods have been found by Swets (1959) to be reasonably comparable. When Green and Birdsall (1964) calculated d' for the data of Miller *et al.* they found that it was approximately constant for each of the sizes of vocabulary.

We should perhaps consider more closely just what has been established by this evidence. The detailed mechanism suggested has not been validated, any more than it was in the case of simple detection. There are some cases indeed in which it is clearly untrue: when d' is calculated for different signal-noise ratios from the data of Miller *et al.* the increase in d' for a given increase in signal strength is not what it should be on an ideal calculation of the amount of evidence being received (Green and Birdsall, 1964). Similarly in the case of tones heard in different time intervals, the agreement between d' for a forced-choice case and that for a "Yes/No" experiment is not absolutely perfect. The discrepancy often amounts to as much as the factor of $\sqrt{2}$ mentioned earlier. This is not at all unreasonable from the point of view of detection theory itself, since as we have seen the mathematics become somewhat intractable and simplifying assumptions have therefore been made. If we adopt the point of view of detection theory, it is really rather unlikely that the distribution of likelihood ratio for all alternatives has the same zero value in the absence of a stimulus, that all the distributions are of equal variance, and that the delivery of a stimulus affects one distribution independently of all others. Nevertheless, the data rule out completely the classical guessing correction of psychophysics, which would give an equation of the type

$$P_C = A + \frac{B}{N},$$

in which A is constant. The data could only be fitted by such an equation if A alters with vocabulary size. On the other hand, if one applies detection theory, choice theory or sophisticated guessing, one can account for the effect of vocabulary size purely in terms of changes in P_G. The analysis through detection theory differs from the earlier ones in that the rule connecting evidence to response is supposed determinate and that randomness enters solely between the outside stimulus and the internal state of evidence. Nevertheless once again the effect of vocabulary size does not require any change in the intake of information.

(*d*) *General conclusions about vocabulary size.* It does not seem that there is any evidence from this type of experiment which will allow us to decide between the different theories giving a concave downward relationship between P_C and P_G. We are left with two broad alternatives: if correct responses to spoken words fall into two distinct classes, one being truly accurate perceptions and the other random guesses amongst the vocabulary provided, then the effect of vocabulary size requires an increase in the number of truly accurate perceptions. It cannot be accounted for by the greater success of random guessing with a small vocabulary. If on the other hand the effect of vocabulary size is exercised through one of the hypothetical

I*

mechanisms which incorporates some randomness between stimulus and response, then it is not necessary to suppose any change in the intake of information as vocabulary size decreases.

Each of these possibilities will recur in the other fields of experiment which we are about to consider. In each of these cases, just as in that of vocabulary size, it is possible to explain perfectly the effects of stimulus probability without supposing a change in the intake of information, so long as one adopts one of the methods of analysis which gives a non-linear connection between P_C and P_G.

THE EFFECTS OF CONTEXT

It has long been known that a word heard through a given degree of noise is more likely to produce a correct response if it forms part of a complete sentence than if it is heard in isolation. This effect can be regarded as equivalent to a change in the size of the possible vocabulary: if we hear the words "The boy stood on the burning" the set of those words which are possible as the next word is smaller than the set of all words in the language. The effect is even more subtle than this, since the words which are grammatically possible at one position are not regarded by the listener as equally probable nor are they equally likely to produce correct responses. Thus Morton (1964) has asked samples of subjects to fill in a next word following different possible contexts, and showed that a word chosen by more subjects as probable is also easier to see when presented visually as a brief flash in the specific context. Yet the more probable and less probable words may be equally grammatical: following the introductory sentences "They went out to the" and "He asked the way to the" the subsequent words "cinema" and "station" are equally grammatical but not equally likely. In some sense the probability of any particular word at an instant is affected by the sequence of words which has been received up to that point.

It is important to note that the listener cannot be basing his estimate of the relative probabilities of different words merely upon a fixed sample of past words and his experience of the relative incidence of different future words following such a sample. That is, we are not asserting that grammatical knowledge can be based upon a so-called "finite state" grammar (Miller and Chomsky, 1963). Such a theory is certainly untenable: the rules of grammar may constrain words which are separated by an infinite number of other words, and it is impossible for a listener to have experienced all such sequences in order to acquire the rule. The possibilities at any instant must rather be given by the structure of the particular sequence that has been experienced, the length of which may vary considerably and the key words in which may be situated at very different places. For example, consider the following two contexts, "The men whom we saw last week" and "The clever men". Both these contexts make it extremely unlikely that the next word will be "is" rather than "are", but the key information determining this is carried well before the end of the context in one case, and only in the last word of the context in the other. Analysis of the structural properties of grammar would take us too far afield, and reference should be made to other works such as Thomas (1966) and Neisser (1967). For present purposes, we can accept that, when one takes a sample of natural language and expects someone to perceive a particular word in it, the provision of more and more words from the sample before the particular one being perceived will give a larger and larger probability of containing an adequate definition of the structure of the sentence concerned.

Correspondingly, if an experimenter presents to his subject an increasing number of words which on some occasion had preceded one particular word in a natural sentence, and if he then asks the subject to guess the next word, there is an increasing probability that the guess will be correct. One can then perform an experiment in which various amounts of context are given before the target word is itself presented visually for a very brief period, auditorily through noise, or in some other difficult fashion. One can then observe the probability of a correct response P_C, and attempt to relate it to P_G, the probability of correct response when no stimulus at all is provided but the contextual information is the same.

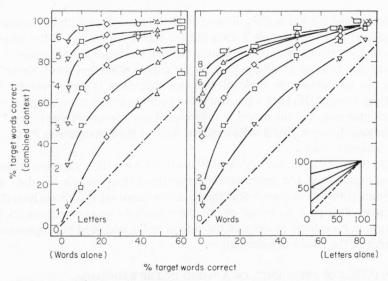

FIG. 25. In the left-hand graph the horizontal axis represents words correctly guessed purely from context. The vertical axis represents performance when the subject is provided both with context and with some letters from the correct word (each line being for a different number of letters). The right-hand graph is similar except that the horizontal axis is for performance with letters alone and the different lines are for different amounts of context. The small inset graph shows the result to be expected if the probability of correct performance due to one source is added to that due to the other source. The data clearly show a greater amount of interaction. Results from Pollack (1964).

This has been done in various ways by Stowe *et al.* (1963); by Pollack (1964), Rubenstein and Pollack (1963), Tulving, Mandler and Baumal (1964). is quite clear that the data cannot be explained by an equation of the type

$$P_C = A + B P_G$$

with A and B constant: one would have to suppose that A increases with P_G. One of the versions of this equation which has been used a good deal in such tests is

$$P_C = A + (1-A)P_G,$$

which is of course the usual guessing correction if we suppose that A is the probability of correct response due to the stimulus alone. It is more usually put forward in this field as a model of "independence" according to which a correct response will be made if the correct item is identified from sensory information, or from guessing, or from both. That is,

$$P_C = 1 - (\text{Probability of miss due to all causes})$$
$$= 1 - (1-A)(1-P_G)$$
$$= A + P_G - A P_G.$$

This relationship has certain difficulties in the case of a multiple alternative situation: how for example does a listener decide what to do if the sensory information points to one word and contextual information to another? This model assumes that he always goes for the correct word, but why? Nevertheless, we saw under the topic of vigilance that there is some evidence for independence of this kind when visual and auditory information are presented simultaneously, and the model has therefore been a favourite one to try. It is quite clear however that it will not fit the data: A must change with P_G to give an adequate result.

On the other hand, the various authors involved in these experiments have fitted exponential and detection theory analyses: they handle the data and Morton (1969b) has shown that the equation based on choice analysis does likewise. That is, if we adopt one of those analyses we can account for the change in P_C entirely in terms of the change in P_G, and need not suppose any change in the intake of information.

THE EFFECT OF FREQUENCY OF A WORD IN THE LANGUAGE

As we have already seen, the probability of any particular word varies very much from situation to situation and from moment to moment within one situation. Nevertheless, in the language as a whole some words are much more common than others, and a rough estimate of this frequency can be derived from counts such as that by Thorndike and Lorge (1944). If we present a listener with the slightly abstract task of trying to identify isolated words through noise or tachistoscopically, he will do much better on common than on uncommon words.

Two types of studies suggest that this effect of word frequency is due to a change in P_G. First, when the experiment is performed with a small set of possible words known to the subject, the effect is markedly reduced (Pierce, 1963; Pollack *et al.*, 1959). In such a case the subjective probability of each word is presumably equal, for this particular situation, even though the probability in the language as a whole may be very different. Even more convincing is a paper by Goldiamond and Hawkins (1958), who used a small set of nonsense words, which had been exposed to the subjects in a previous experiment. Some words had been experienced much more than others. In the main study, a tachistoscope was operated as if to study perception in brief exposures of the nonsense words. However, the particular word designated as "correct" on each trial was never presented, and the subjects merely received a brief flash of light. The experimenters scored them as correct if they produced the word which would have been presented if the experiment had been an orthodox one. By this standard, there were more correct responses to the words which had been frequent than to those which had been infrequent. Thus a word frequency effect had been obtained with no stimulus information presented at all: and it seemed legitimate to interpret this, as the authors did, as some form of response bias.

The difference between this situation and those previously discussed is however that we cannot usually determine P_G directly, because in the natural language the probability of guessing any one particular word without stimulus information is so low as to be unobservable. We have to estimate the value of P_G for each degree of word frequency, by observing the number of mis-perceptions which are produced at that frequency. There is of course some room for debate about the relationship between these mis-perceptions and the underlying P_G. Data on the number of responses, correct and incorrect, in each class of word frequency are provided by Brown and Rubenstein (1961) and Broadbent (1967b). The first of these studies used a list of the 6500 most common monosyllables, and divided them into successive groups of 500 from the most frequent to the least frequent. The second used only two degrees of frequency, the most common in the Thorndike Lorge Count (more than 100 occurrences per million) and a lower frequency (less than 50 but more than 10 occurrences per million). The two studies are complementary, since although a smaller range of frequencies was used by Broadbent, more subjects were studied, two-syllable words were examined in a separate experiment as well as monosyllables, and the responses in each frequency class were separated according to the frequency class of the stimulus. Some features of Brown and Rubenstein's data are analysed afresh by Morton (1968a), who reveals certain aspects not discussed in the original presentation.

In this case, unlike those of context and of size of vocabulary, we do find a linear relation of the type

$$P_C = A + B P_E$$

where P_E = probability of an error in the same frequency class as the stimulus.

For once therefore it seems at first sight as if we could account for the differences in P_C merely by the addition of a certain proportion of random guesses. Unfortunately, as both Broadbent and Morton point out, the value of B in the relation is much too large to be accounted for in this way. If we are dealing, as in Brown and Rubenstein's data, with a frequency class containing 500 words, then given that one chooses a word from the correct frequency class the probability of guessing the correct one will be 1 in 500. The obtained value of P_E will be 499 times this value, and accordingly the value of B should be 1/499. In fact it is more in the region of unity, and a theory of random guessing therefore greatly underestimates the number of correct perceptions in those frequency classes where there are also a number of mis-perceptions. We cannot therefore explain the word frequency effect as due simply to a constant proportion of true perceptions together with a selective tendency to guess common rather than uncommon words. If we suppose that P_G is related to P_C by some means of this sort, then we must suppose also that word frequency affects the intake of information and so the number of "true" perceptions as well as the number of guesses.

Although therefore we have got a linear relationship in this case, rather than a concave one, it is still true that the theory of random guessing will not explain the data without an additional effect on the intake of information. Furthermore, as we shall see, the other possible theories do predict a linear relationship in this case, because we are working with P_E rather than P_G. In the case of the word frequency effect, however, we can discriminate a little further between the different possible analyses which give large changes in P_C for small changes in P_G. First of all, let us consider the theory of "sophisticated guessing", according to which the stimulus cuts out certain possible words, context if present cuts out others, and guessing between the remaining alternatives may be biased. The experimental subject might for example always choose the most common of the words which are still possible. This type of model will give an exponential equation, and we have already seen that such a function gives an adequate account of the effects of vocabulary size and of context. Since sophisticated guessing is only between a small set of alternatives, the probability of picking the right word within the frequency class may be high (once one has arrived at that class). The constant B need no longer be very small, and could even be greater than 1 as there may only be a low chance of there being more than one word still possible within each frequency class. However, there are still two features of the data which cause this model to be rejected. First of all, it is pointed out by Morton that if we write a slightly different equation

$$P_C = A + B P_X$$

where P_X = probability of an error in the particular frequency class under consideration, given stimuli drawn with equal probability from all frequency classes

then B should still be less than 1. That is, the change in number of correct responses between two frequency classes should not be greater than the change in total probability of error responses in those two classes. If the subject is guessing between even one word in the correct frequency class and an alternative in any other class, he should distribute his responses as he does his error responses between those classes, and accordingly the difference in correct responses should not be greater than the difference in errors. But in fact it is very much larger, and the theory of sophisticated guessing will not therefore do. A related point is made by Broadbent: on the theory of sophisticated guessing, when the number of correct responses in a high frequency class is greater than that in a low frequency class, this is because some of the guesses in the former case are counted as correct whereas in the latter case they are counted as errors. There should therefore be relatively fewer common words amongst the false perceptions, when the stimulus itself is a common word. This also is quite untrue. We may therefore discard the theory of sophisticated guessing for this effect of word probability, although we were unable to do so for the effects of vocabulary size and of context.*

The analysis based on detection theory would in principle be able to handle these kinds of data: we have to suppose that for each possible word being considered there is a value of evidence, that this value is distributed in a fashion which we may reasonably take as normal, but the mean of this distribution is different for different classes of words in the absence of any stimulus. The arrival of a stimulus shifts the mean of the corresponding distribution by a further amount of d'. The perception of a word corresponds to the choice of that alternative for which the evidence happens to be strongest: other things being equal, this is more likely to be the one corresponding to the stimulus which has arrived, but it is broadly clear that those words for which the mean value of evidence is highest even before information arrives from the sense organs will have a better chance of being perceived. It is also possible that the information from the sense organs may be greater for some classes of words than others, and in principle therefore the effect of word frequency could be due either to a difference in d' between the common and

---

* This argument has been questioned. (Catlin, *Psychol. Rev.* (1969), **76**, 504-506), since the above was written. His argument depends on the plausibility of an assumption on which I disagree with him: and which in my view is also, more satisfactorily, refuted by the probe experiments described on page 262.

uncommon words, or to a difference in the initial level of evidence concerning each. (The latter difference undoubtedly exists, from the data of Goldiamond and Hawkins, and also from the difference in error rate between different frequency classes which had been noted by Brown and Rubenstein and by Broadbent.) In principle therefore we could analyse the situation to find out which was happening.

Unfortunately in practice it is very difficult to handle experimental results quantitatively by means of detection theory, in a case of this complexity. This is despite the fact that we have already made considerable simplifying assumptions by supposing independence of each distribution from each of the others, and have not mentioned the possibility that the variances might be unequal. We are forced therefore effectively to the equations of choice analysis, which we have already seen on many occasions to provide a close approximation to those of detection theory. In the present case we may imagine a table of strength of the following type:

RESPONSES

		1	2	3	4
COMMON	1	$\alpha_H V$	V	1	1
	2	V	$\alpha_H V$	1	1
UNCOMMON	3	V	V	α_L	1
	4	V	V	1	α_L

(STIMULI — COMMON: rows 1, 2; UNCOMMON: rows 3, 4)

In this table each response has attached to it a certain strength, prior to any stimulus being applied. The strength is unity for those responses which are uncommon, and V for those which are common. The arrival of an appropriate stimulus increases the strength of the corresponding response by an amount which we can call α_H for common responses and α_L for uncommon ones. (The distinction between the two types of α is maintained so as not to exclude prematurely the possibility that common and uncommon stimuli might differ in the amount of sensory information which is taken in about them.)

From the table we can calculate P_C and P_E: indeed, we can do so for the more general case in which there are $N+1$ responses in each class rather than just 2. In that case, for common words

$$P_C = \frac{\alpha_H V}{\alpha_H V + NV + N + 1}$$

$$P_E = \frac{NV}{\alpha_H V + NV + N + 1}$$

$$P_C = \frac{\alpha_H}{N} \cdot P_E$$

and for uncommon words

$$P_C = \frac{\alpha_L}{\alpha_L + (N+1)V + N}$$

$$P_E = \frac{1}{\alpha_L + (N+1)V + N}$$

$$P_C = \frac{\alpha_L}{N} \cdot P_E.$$

It will be obvious therefore that this theory is perfectly consistent with the linear relationship between P_C and P_E: provided that α_H is really the same as α_L, that is that the sensory information taken in is the same in every frequency class. In fact this has been tested and found to be so by Broadbent and by Morton for the different data they are considering, and apparently therefore the differences in correct responses for different frequency classes can be entirely accounted for by a difference in the bias factor, with no need to suppose any difference in the intake of information.

Some subsidiary points are worth making. First, notice the inclusion in the equations of the number of words in each frequency class. This is especially important when one is *not* working, as in the case of Brown and Rubenstein, with frequency classes containing known numbers of words. In some of the data produced by Broadbent, two syllable words were employed, and it so happens that there are more two syllable words of low frequency than of high. This meant that in the experiment on two syllable words the subjects actually produced more error responses of low frequency than of high. At first sight they would seem therefore not to be biased in favour of common words: but when a correction is applied for the number of possible words from which they might choose, it becomes clear that any one word had a greater chance of appearing as an error if it was a common word than if it was an uncommon word.

Secondly, notice that by using the mathematics of choice theory we are not necessarily implying its axioms. That is, we do not need to suppose that the stimulus produces a determinate effect, and that the randomness in the system occurs subsequent to that stage in the choice of the output that is made. The equations we have produced are identical with those to be expected from detection theory, with a mechanism of the type we have described, if the distributions were logistic and of equal variance. For any other case they are only approximate, and this will especially be the case if evidence concerning different alternatives is not independent. They do however provide an approximation which is for the moment reasonable.

Thirdly, it is clearly an oversimplification to suppose that the stimulus increases the strength of the correct response and has no effect upon any of the others. Any analysis of the results of an experiment on speech perception will show that the errors and misperceptions tend to have some features in common with the stimulus. One might well argue that a better derivation of the equations we have discussed would be as follows. When a stimulus arrives it increases the strength of the correct response by the factor α, and at the same time reduces to zero the strength of many other responses. The latter are chosen at random from the different frequency classes, so that the number of survivors within each frequency class is proportionate to the number in that class. In the equations we have produced therefore it is an over-estimate to use the value of N from the language as a whole, but this would merely be reflected in an exaggerated value of α as calculated from the data: the general regularity of the equation will not be altered. It will mean however that the errors would be drawn only from those words which are acoustically similar to the stimulus. Some approximation is undoubtedly introduced by supposing that within a given frequency class all the similar words have the same strength: just as an approximation was introduced by supposing that all words in the same frequency class have the same strength.

A fourth and related point concerns the kinds of similarities to the stimulus which will appear amongst misperceptions. In auditory experiments, these similarities concern individual features of the speech sound, such as the occurrence of a plosive consonant at the beginning and end, or the presence of a low first formant both in the actual stimulus used and in that which is reported. It is not by any means necessary that any letter in the response that is written down should be identical with the corresponding letter in the experimenter's list of stimuli. In the visual case however it is more common for individual letters of the response to be identical with letters of the stimulus: in our own experiments it was always the case that some such letters were perfectly reproduced. This means, as was pointed out by Broadbent (1967b) that visual experiments may give results which cannot distinguish between various possible theories of the effect. For instance, the number of words possessing certain letters in common with the stimulus may be much smaller than the number of words possessing certain acoustic features in common with the stimulus. This may mean that there are only very few words in each frequency class eligible to be produced as errors, and this in turn would mean that the number of errors in a given frequency class would be less when the stimulus was one of that class. Thus the data might appear, in a visual experiment, to be consistent with some aspects of sophisticated guessing even although they are also consistent with the more complex or detection theory approach.

Another snag of the visual situation is that it may, for this very reason, tend to induce in the subject an attitude of writing down isolated letters rather than complete words; this means that the category states being used as a vocabulary of possible responses are those corresponding to letters rather than those corresponding to complete words. The point at issue will then become whether one letter is more frequent in the language as a whole than another, rather than whether the words made up by the letters are more or less frequent. It is possible to find words which are common in the language but made up of uncommon letters, although by the nature of things there are bound to be few such words. It is also possible to find rare words made up entirely of common letters. The perception of such words visually may well reduce to the perception of the individual letters forming them, and little of use about the biases of whole words could then be concluded from such an experiment.

Lastly, and stemming from the points already made, there is the possibility that the stimulus selects from the correct frequency class proportionately more words as possible errors than it does from other frequency classes. Morton's analysis of the data of Brown and Rubenstein shows that there is a discrepancy in their results which could be explained in this way: the total number of misperceptions which are nevertheless of the correct frequency class is too great. A similar modification would be necessary if one adopted a theory of random guessing combined with a genuine improvement in the intake of sensory information of relevant common words. (The modification has to be rather more complicated in the latter case, however, as it is necessary to suppose that the amount of information about frequency class conveyed by the stimulus even when correct perception has failed is greater for common words than for uncommon ones. In an analysis based upon detection theory, the amount of information about frequency class can be supposed constant for all frequency classes.) Inherently, there is no reason why some mechanism of this sort should not exist, and it raises an interesting field for research in the effects upon word perception occurring with words containing common and uncommon component letters or features. At present however we are not compelled to adopt such an explanation, since the discrepancies explained by Morton might conceivably be due to some of the approximations and roughnesses already mentioned in the model, such as the assumption of equality of bias from all members of a frequency class. In addition the data of Broadbent (1967b) did not require any such modification.

GENERAL CONCLUSIONS ON THE WORD FREQUENCY EFFECT

Because of the disappearance of the effect in forced-choice conditions, and because of the manifest absence of a stimulus contribution in an experiment such as that of Goldiamond and Hawkins, many authors have tried to assess the extent to which a bias of responding could explain the effect. On the whole the verdict has probably been against such an explanation in its simple form of adding a proportion of guessed common words to a number of correctly perceived words which was constant whatever the frequency of the stimulus. The size of the effect is, as we have seen, much too large to be explained in this way. Furthermore, the effect still persists when care is taken to reduce guessing by such means as assessing a threshold only when the subject has given three successive correct responses rather than merely one (Zajonc and Nieuwenhuyser, 1964).

With this conclusion we can agree: and we can even reject the modification of guessing theory which we have called sophisticated guessing. A number of authors such as Solomon and Postman (1952), Newbigging (1961a), J. T. Spence (1963) and Savin (1963) have leaned towards this view. In most cases, they are influenced by the direct evidence for biased guessing which we have mentioned earlier, taken together with the fact that the errors are manifestly not random but have components in common with the stimulus. Despite the superior virtues of this theory however we can reject it also: it will not account for the word frequency effect without the extra supposition of some "genuinely perceptual" effect of stimulus probability. On the other hand, the word frequency effect can be explained without supposing a preferential intake of information from frequent words, if we suppose that the process linking category states to the incoming evidence is of the broadly statistical kind which we have discussed in earlier chapters. If it is, then the effect of word frequency is entirely due to pigeon-holing, and not at all to filtering.

We cannot be said to have ruled out the possibility of selective intake of information, because a combination of selective intake with random guessing might give an adequate account of the results: as Morton (1968a) has shown. The disadvantage of this model would be its greater complexity, since some degree of response bias must be assumed in any case to explain the imbalance of errors, and we therefore need to argue that word frequency affects both intake and output processes. There is also the inherent improbability that the statistical model would be able to account satisfactorily for all the different phenomena we have described, without supposing any change in the intake of information, if indeed there were some such change. Broadly speaking therefore it seems a fair conclusion that pigeon-holing rather than filtering is the mechanism involved in reacting to probable rather than less probable stimuli.

The probe experiment. A postscript should be added to the above conclusions, based on experiments which are at the time of writing still in progress. Although therefore they can hardly be included in the body of the argument, they seem already to have reinforced most strongly the general conclusion and closed some of the weaknesses in the argument. These studies involve the "probe technique", which is closely similar to one used by Norman and Wickelgren (1965) in the study of memory. It derives from the method of recognition memory introduced by Egan, in an unpublished technical report, of which an account is given by Green and Swets (1966). The basis of the method is that a word is presented under difficult conditions to an observer, and is then followed by a much stronger and clearly perceptible stimulus. The task of the subject is to indicate whether the original weak stimulus was the same word as the subsequent probe or was a different word. He can assign a confidence judgment to his answer, and we may therefore apply the usual analysis of confidence judgments to the data. By taking only the most confident "Yes" responses, we can determine the probability of such a response when it is correct (P_C) and when it is not (P_F): by adding in the "Yes" judgments of lower confidence we can get new values for the two probabilities, and so on until we come to the point where all responses are included except the most confident rejections of the probe.

This experiment can be conducted with a mixture of common and of uncommon stimulus words: the probe in each case being of the same frequency class as the stimulus, to avoid the complication of partial transmission of information about the class to which the stimulus belongs. In the current work of Broadbent and Gregory, visual stimulation is employed, the inadequate stimulus being obtained by typing a word with an electric typewriter through many sheets of carbon paper in order to produce a smudged version. The probe is then typed normally. It is no longer necessary therefore, as it was in acoustic experiments,, to equate the physical intensity of the stimuli by means of a forced-choice control experiment.

These experiments already allow three clear conclusions: first, the relationship between P_C and P_F is not linear, but is rather that which would be expected for a linear relationship between Z_C and Z_F. Thus we now have direct evidence for the need of a statistical model in the perception of words just as in that of simpler stimuli.

Second, the value of P_F is greater for high frequency words than for low frequency words. That is, the acceptance of common words is greater even when they are incorrect: this is the usual response bias or pigeon-holing effect as that which we found previously in the open-ended task.

Third, and perhaps most strikingly, the value of d' is *smaller* for common than for uncommon words. Thus the better performance on common words (which has been shown with the same physical stimuli in an open-ended situation) is not due to superior intake of information, and indeed the actual physical information is inferior for common words. It is by no means surprising that the language should have adjusted itself in such a way that uncommon stimuli acquire especially conspicuous shapes and sounds, since such stimuli are the ones which are likely to be difficult to perceive. Thus in general, as we have already noted, there is a higher proportion of polysyllabic words amongst uncommon ones. It is not implausible therefore that even for words of controlled length the actual sensory information should be superior for uncommon words: this was not revealed in earlier studies, because of the equation of the acoustic recordings by a forced-choice experiment. (Recordings of spoken stimuli have to be equated in this way rather than physically, because there is a large range in the physical intensity of different speech sounds; and a distinct danger that a human speaker will articulate common and uncommon words with unequal care.)

The probe experiments seem therefore to point yet more clearly to the unsatisfactory nature of any guessing theory of the word frequency effect, even if such a theory has added to it an effect on the intake of information. They rather suggest that speech perception is indeed statistical, and that the word frequency effect is entirely due to pigeon-holing.

At this stage we have completed the main argument of the chapter; there remain however two related topics which should be discussed before we move on to the question of the speed with which these various processes can occur.

THE PROBLEM OF EMOTIONAL WORDS

There is a persistent link in the literature between the effects of word frequency and those of the emotional quality of a word. It is widely agreed that socially unacceptable words are harder to perceive in a threshold experiment than are acceptable ones (McGinnies, 1949). From some points of view this might be explained by supposing that such words are lower in probability, either in the language as a whole or in the context of an experiment, than are control words. Such a difference in probability would give poorer performance for obscene words by the ordinary process we have discussed, which we would ascribe to pigeon-holing. In addition however the axiomatic approach to detection theory, as we have seen, includes the gains and losses for right and wrong responses as a factor determining the criterion or bias associated with any response. If missed signals cost less than false alarms, β will be high, and if the reverse, then it will be low. It would not be implausible that a loss might be attached to the use of certain unpleasant words; thus increasing the penalty for responding incorrectly with those words and decreasing the reward for responding correctly. If so, there might be a detectable effect on response even by comparison with control words of the same probability.

Such a mechanism has advantages which might be described as stylistic. If there were a true effect of emotional tone regardless of word frequency, it might at first sight be explained by a scanning of the input messages at one stage of the nervous system in order to exclude the passage of some of them to a later stage. This is the sort of process we considered in the last chapter in connection with the theory that the content of a signal decided whether or not it should be perceived. The same objections apply; if the information is being analysed at one stage, what is the advantage of stopping it going further? If the selection of some signals avoids the need to analyse others, then selection economizes in mechanism; but if selection were itself based on a complete analysis, it would have no apparent function. Our conclusion in the last chapter was that there was no evidence for a complete analysis of rejected signals, and that the effect of content lay in a pre-existing bias of the category states independent of the incoming signals. In the case of word probability, we have in this chapter supported this conclusion.

By supposing therefore that the category states corresponding to emotional words carry a negative bias, so that only very strong incoming evidence will be sufficient to overcome this bias, we have a conceptual mechanism which would allow such words to be harder to perceive but would not require complete analysis even of unselected items. It is quite another matter whether this mechanism does indeed exist, and for this reason we require direct data on the point. The results need to be in the form which we have considered under the heading of the word frequency effect, that is, we need to know the numbers of misperceptions of various types when subjects are listening and looking for emotional and neutral words; and unfortunately therefore most of the large literature on the subject is unsuitable for our particular purposes. Perhaps the most relevant paper is that of Minard (1965), which not only reviewed earlier results but also provided fresh data on correct responses and on misperceptions within a small fixed vocabulary of which half the words were emotional and half neutral. Minard concluded that the effect on emotional words could not be explained purely by a difference in P_G, the probability of response in the absence of stimulus information. He had two main reasons. One was that the effect on correct responses found in the literature was larger than that observed in error responses or in the absence of a stimulus. The second reason was that in the fresh experiments he described, the bias amongst errors was actually opposite to the effect found on correct perceptions. (The latter was small and different in different classes of subjects, men doing better at perceiving emotional stimuli and women worse. Whichever way the effect was, the bias on errors was in the opposite direction.)

These arguments are not from our point of view decisive. The first assumes the implicit theory that

$$P_C = A + (1 - A)P_G$$

which we have seen to be untenable. It is perfectly possible for a difference in P_G to cause a much larger difference in P_C, if one discards the idea that P_G exerts its effects only by the addition of a proportion of extra responses scored as correct. The objection to the second point is primarily to the use of a forced-choice method. As we have seen, such a method tends to reduce the word frequency effect and even in psychophysical situations minimizes the role of bias towards one response rather than another. Furthermore, in small known vocabularies there is a property of the statistical theory which we have already noted when considering the relative merits of visual and auditory experiments: even in the absence of bias the number of errors in the same class as the stimulus is $N/(N+1)$ times the number of errors in any other class, because one of the possible words in the same class as the stimulus is the correct response. This does not matter if N is large, but with small N it may make the errors systematically greater in the class to which the stimulus does not belong. Lastly, in a small fixed vocabulary there may be a tendency for the subject to avoid repetition of the last response used, thanks to the trial-to-trial operation of the contrast effect; and this too may cause a bias on errors running counter to that on correct responses.

For these reasons one may be cautious about accepting data from forced-choice experiments, and a fresh study was needed in which the subject was left uninformed about the words which he might receive. The use of obscene words is undesirable both because one is uncertain of their true frequency in the language, which we have seen to be important, and also because it is quite possible that subjects perceive them but are unwilling to say or write them. In our terms, it may be that a category state occurs but that its translation into an overt action is interrupted by processes outside our present concern. It seems better to use words which are current in ordinary speech and perfectly acceptable, but whose meaning is rather more emotional than that of other words.

One way of doing this is to employ words which, when used as stimuli in an association test, do not produce a response for a long time. This technique has been successfully used by Brown (1961) and by other authors reviewed by him, to show that emotionality affects perception. It suffers from the snag however that its theoretic basis is a little obscure; one may show empirically that words of agreed emotional quality give long association times, but it does not follow that all words with long association times are emotional. Theoretically, we can suppose that words with little connection to the routine affairs of life might have few associations and so give long latencies; but it might reasonably be that words so unemotional and non-specific as to have very many associations might also have long latencies because of the difficulty of choice between the competing possibilities (see the next chapter). As Brown brings out, several investigators have obtained a non-linear effect with this measure of "emotionality", very long or very short latencies going with better perception than medium latencies. This is hard to interpret when we do not know what the criterion means in terms of some outside assessment of emotionality.

Fortunately, it has been found by Johnson et al. (1960) and by Newbigging (1961b) that one can show effects of emotionality on perception by using stimuli which have simply been rated for degree of pleasantness by human assessors. Accordingly, Broadbent and Gregory (1967a) prepared lists of words from the same frequency class of the Thorndike-Lorge tables, had them rated for degree of pleasantness by panels of subjects of the same type as those to be used in the main experiment, and then prepared tape recordings covering the whole range of pleasantness-unpleasantness. The tapes were equated by a forced-choice technique, and then presented to listeners who did not know the words being used. From the results, one selects the misperceptions of the same frequency class as the stimulus, and then has these also rated for pleasantness. Lastly, a sample of words of the same frequency class from the language as a whole is rated. One can then analyse the correct perceptions and errors at each level of pleasantness, just as with words of different frequency.

The results however are quite different. There is indeed an effect of emotionality; words at the unpleasant end of the rating scale are always markedly and significantly harder to hear than words in the middle of the scale, even though the same tapes have given equal performance under forced-choice conditions. The extremely pleasant words are in an equivocal position; among common words nice as well as nasty words were harder to hear than neutral ones. Among uncommon words, nice words were no worse than neutral ones. But to the discomfiture of the original hypothesis the number of misperceptions was exactly proportional to the number of words of each type in the language as a whole; there was no evidence for a response bias, let along enough of a bias to explain the effect on correct perception.

What does this result mean? First and unequivocally, it means that word emotionality is not like word frequency in its effects. If, say, the frequency count had been an over-estimate of the frequency of emotional words in the language, so that the difficulty in perceiving them was really due to their being less probable than other words in the same class of the Thorndike-Lorge count, then the pattern of performance would have been the same as in the experiments on word frequency. Emotional words should have been rare as error responses as well as correct responses. The difference implies that, for whatever reason, emotionality is different from probability in its effects. In this we are supported by a finding of Newbigging (1961a, b); he counted the number of letters in common between misperceptions and correct responses, and found that the effects of emotionality and of frequency were different. The emotional words gave fewer letters breaking through to the misperceptions, and just as in our own experiments therefore it would seem that an emotional stimulus seems to cause a shut-down in the intake of information.

Next, are we forced to the conclusion that all stimuli are completely analysed before the selection of some to give rise to a category state? It would seem a pity to adopt such a theory purely for this one experiment, when results on word frequency and in so many other fields seem rather to point against it. There seem two main alternatives which are plausible, and which deserve exploration before we fall back on the theory of a complete analysis. First, we might suppose that the intake of sensory information depends on a general state of the system, and may be cut down if the general level of arousal is high. Arousal might then rise, not only if a category state of emotional type occurs, but even if evidence arrives falling in a very broad class which might under suitable conditions elicit such a category state. For example, suppose it were true that, say, the sound corresponding to "k" occurred in more emotional than unemotional words. Any detection of that sound might then give a shutting-down of the intake of information before any particular category state had occurred.

Unfortunately, examination of the stimuli used by Broadbent and Gregory does not support such a simple theory, and both their neutral and their emotional words contained a wide range of possible speech sounds. One can however imagine a sophistication of such a view with the same general consequences; speaking in Treisman's original language, one can suppose that each dictionary unit receives a gradual inflow of excitation, and that a rise in the level of any "emotional" unit may produce an attenuation of the intake of signals even though the threshold for that unit has not been reached. (We use Treisman's terms to bring out the point that it is the fact that evidence is beginning to indicate an emotional word which causes the intake to change, rather than some property of the evidence itself.)

Such a view is supported by a result of Hardy and Legge (1968). They presented emotional and unemotional words to one sense at a very low intensity while simultaneously the subject was attempting to detect a signal on another sense. That is, the word might arrive at the ear while a visual flash was being detected; or the word might be visual while a tone was being detected. Although the subjects remained unaware of the presence of a word, in the presence of an emotional word their detection rate went down for the signal which they regarded as their main task. Most important, this drop in detection was not due to a change in β but to a change in d'. Thus the presence of the emotional word, even when it was not itself detected, seemed to alter the intake of information.

Nevertheless, the present author is not completely happy that the effects are the same. It seems very odd that, if the system has detected the presence of an emotional word, this information is not used even if fresh information is shut out. That is, we might expect the number of misperceptions which are themselves emotional words to be greater when the stimulus is an emotional word. It is not so; the shutting out of fresh information neither prevents nor enhances the use of emotional words as false responses.

Perhaps therefore we should look at the last possibility. That is simply that the mathematical model is wrong because our simplifying assumptions are unjustified. We supposed that the variances of the distributions of evidence, on which decision is based, were all equal. Suppose this were unjustified, and in particular suppose that the emotional words had a larger variance than the neutral ones. Then since d' is measured relative to the standard deviation of the distribution, the same numerical shift of the mean of the distribution might give a smaller value of d' for those words which had a larger variance. Ingleby has shown by a theoretical calculation that the experimental data could indeed be produced by a mechanism of this type, in which the shift in the mean of the distribution of evidence was always the same but the variance of "emotional" distributions was greater. It is necessary to suppose in that case that those distributions have a mean in the absence of stimulation which is rather below that of neutral words; i.e. there is a bias against emotional words after all. But this calculation of Ingleby's merely shows that a difference in variance *could* be the explanation, not that it *is* the explanation.

The probe experiments mentioned under the heading of word frequency should provide the answer. From such data we can calculate the variance of the underlying distribution as well as its other properties; and at the time of writing such studies are well under way. What would it mean if the variances are different? Perhaps that the bias for or against an emotional word changes from moment to moment with the context and the mood of the listener, whereas that for neutral words does not; perhaps that the bias for or against an emotional word depends more upon the individual than does that for a neutral word. It is worth noting also that our assumption of a constant penalty for using an emotional word is unjustified; it may indeed be that the use of such a word when there is no appropriate stimulus might cause some subjective penalty, but equally the use of such a word when correct might have a considerable gain. One might speculate that the gains and losses attached to such words are exaggerated rather than being biased against response. Such an exaggeration would not affect a strictly rational observer, placing his criterion only by the ratio of the two. But we have often urged that the rational observer is psychologically unreal, and perhaps the increase of gains and losses might give something comparable to a rise in variance.

Remember the expansion and contraction of the scale of evidence which we met in vigilance in noise; something similar occurred in the results of Hardy and Legge also. At all events, the probe technique should show whether the assumptions of the model are satisfied, or whether more thought is needed.

In the meantime, the problem of emotional words must be recognized as something distinct from that of probable and improbable words. It is the latter with which we have been most concerned, since most of the evidence concerning response set in perceptual selection was derived from the use of stimuli of varying probability. We can remain content that response set demonstrated in that way does involve pigeon-holing, and does not alter the intake of information.

A NOTE ON THE ANALYSIS-BY-SYNTHESIS THEORY OF PERCEPTION

Throughout this book, we are leaving aside most of the problems of pattern perception as such; there is a substantial difficulty in tracing out the mechanism by which, say, triangles of different size and shape give rise to evidence pointing to the same category state. But our concern lies elsewhere and we have simply taken it for granted that somehow this process is achieved. Some of the evidence considered in this chapter is however cited from time to time as supporting a theory of pattern perception known as "analysis-by-synthesis", and we ought therefore to make clear how our own approach relates to that theory.

Several important distinctions must be made between different versions of the theory, because some are much more plausible than others. The whole complex can be approached through the motor theory of speech perception; in a crude version, this can be described as the theory that a listener generates movements of his own articulatory system, matches the feedback signal from those movements with the sensory input he is receiving, modifies the motor output if there is a discrepancy, and perceives that element of speech for which there is no discrepancy between the input and the matching articulation.

The basis for this theory rests on three main lines of argument. First, the role of context, of fixed vocabulary, and of word probability which we have discussed, implies that perception is not tied to the physical stimulus. Rather the listener is bringing a contribution of his own to the situation. Second, if one tabulates the acoustic cues which, when presented to a listener, produce perception of the same speech sound, they may differ quite widely. The formant transition associated with the perception of "g", for instance, may be quite different if the following vowel is that in "game" from that which appears if the vowel is the one in "girl". When however one examines the articulation of "g", one finds a closer correspondence between the way the sound is articulated and the way it is perceived. Thirdly, if one presents a range of speech-like sounds to a man and requires him to discriminate between them, he shows much better performance at those points in the range which, for him, correspond to meaningful differences in ordinary speech. That is, he might be said to be perceiving better the difference between two sounds which he can articulate differently.

Manifestly, it is not essential to speak aloud in order to listen (although some listeners may mutter) and accordingly the motor theory would normally propose that some short-circuiting takes place. The comparison between input and matching self-generated signal takes place internally; a message need not actually flow out to the muscles, but can be picked off for comparison once the articulatory sequence has been decided, or even earlier, at the point where the phonetic content of the output has been selected. As the latter distinction may be unclear, let us draw the following fanciful analogy.

An eager business man decides to depart from his usual practice of despatching salesmen to those towns from which he receives orders. Such a practice does not allow him to take advantage of the fact that more orders come from some towns than others. Rather he decides to send out his salesmen in advance, to the most likely place. He then compares any order with the actual location of the salesman, and modifies the latter if necessary. Such a method will allow him to get a salesman to a customer with a very short delay, and thus be very satisfactory.

How should he compare the incoming order with the location of the salesman? One way would be to get the man to telephone at intervals from wherever he has reached, and thus to compare directly the present position with that desired. This is analogous to a comparison by a listener between the sound he hears and the noise of his own muttering. At the opposite extreme, the business man might compare the place given on the order with the place to which he told the salesman to go. This is analogous to a comparison of input with the phonetic control signal for speech. The intermediate stage would be for the business man to obtain, for comparison with his incoming orders, information about the type of railway ticket sold to his salesman. This would be analogous to a comparison at the articulatory level. Just as the same instruction given by business man to salesman might lead to different tickets being sold, depending on the train schedules and other factors affecting the route used, so the translation of a phonetic instruction into articulatory terms might vary. Either the phonetic or the articulatory command signal would do, however, and there would be no need to obtain a complete translation of the articulation into action. In fact Liberman (1957) and his associates at the Haskins Laboratories (Liberman *et al.*, 1967a; and Liberman *et al.*, 1967b) lean rather more to the articulatory view and the M.I.T group (Stevens, 1960, Stevens and Halle, 1967) to the phonetic one.

The crude motor theory of speech cannot be maintained. There is first the conceptual difficulty that a mechanism capable of matching an articulatory command and an acoustic input would be capable of carrying out a complete analysis in any case (Fant, quoted by Morton and Broadbent, 1967). Second, there is direct evidence that speech can be understood by those who cannot articulate (Lenneberg, 1962). Third, the basic arguments apply as well to visual perception as to auditory, and in that case it cannot be supposed that the perceiver is executing, even minimally, a motor process which would create what he sees. To be specific, the role of probability has long been known to apply to visual stimulation, (Bartlett, 1932) even for non-speech stimuli. The perception of articulation as constant even though the acoustic signal varies is similar to the perception of a surface as of constant brightness even though the light reflected from it varies with the illumination. Lastly, the greater ability to discriminate stimuli when distinctive reactions have been attached to them is demonstrable with visual stimuli; it does not depend upon the reactions being of a kind which would themselves produce a similar physical stimulation. Lane (1965) discusses this point in particular, and some data are provided by Cross Lane and Sheppard (1965).

One cannot therefore hold the view that perception takes place through the generation of a response which would produce the same stimulus. But one could still hold a more abstract theory of analysis by synthesis; one could argue that the system generates a possible response which would be appropriate to a complex combination of features of the outside world, compares the received input with that combination, modifies the response if necessary, and "perceives" when no mismatch is detected. Here we have abandoned the idea that the response would *produce* a similar stimulus, and merely supposed that it would be *appropriate* to a certain pattern.

Two difficulties then appear. First, such a process would be incredibly slow when applied to large vocabularies. It may seem plausible when applied to a small set that the listener could try out the words in that set rather than listening passively; but if he is given merely the context "They went out to" and tries out every possible next word, the process would be very laborious. The second difficulty is that such a mechanism would surely imply that the main intake of information would be primarily about those features relevant to the responses first generated. Thus the word frequency effect ought to reveal a selective intake of information relevant to probable rather than improbable words. As we have seen, it does not. Thus even this version of analysis by synthesis fails to hold water.

The theory is however widely held, and as is usual for a popular theory it embodies valuable elements. The aspects of it which appear also in our own approach are several; the most important is the emphasis on perception as, in our terms, being the occurrence of a category state and not the detection of a feature. Neisser (1967) discusses analysis by synthesis as an alternative to other perceptual theories; one of these is the idea that perception of a pattern occurs when the input matches an internal template, and the other is the idea that perception occurs when the input contains certain features. Each of these is certainly inadequate.

The first has the difficulty that an input pattern may produce perception despite changes of size or orientation; the second may escape that problem, but still faces the difficulty that different percepts may occur to a constant input. This happens for example in cases of reversible perspective. In our terms, when the evidence is inadequate to select one rather than another category state, either may occur in alternation but not simultaneously. The occurrence of categorization is a positive act of the system and not passively determined by the input. Furthermore, the particular category chosen is certainly determined partly by context and probability rather than solely by stimulus information. All these are sound points in the theory of analysis by synthesis, and we may certainly agree with Neisser in supporting it in opposition to the alternative theories which he discusses. Our disagreement is rather with any interpretation of analysis-by-synthesis which supposes selective intake of information about probable words, or which regards perception as resulting from successive corrections of misperceptions.

For those who wish to emphasize the distinction from template or feature theories, and so find it desirable to speak of synthesis, we may describe our view as an analysis-by-synthesis theory with the following features. First, it does not require the category state to be a command signal for a response which would produce the same stimulus. It may well be the command signal for some other kind of response, but that is a different matter. Second, the process of matching is not a successive one with modification of unsuccessful matches. Rather there is a parallel process of matching the stimulus with many different categories simultaneously; and the perception is of that category which makes the best match bearing in mind the biasing effects of context and probability.

FINAL CONCLUSIONS ON REACTION TO STIMULI
OF DIFFERENT PROBABILITY

In our progress through this book, we have now reached the following position. The process of reacting to a stimulus has been shown to be a statistical one, involving a good deal of randomness between input and output. There is sound evidence, which has not been overthrown, that the system economizes on mechanism by selecting for analysis primarily those events in the environment which possess some characteristic in common; that is, there is filtering of the input. There is also evidence that perceptual selection does tend to be affected by the content of one of two stimuli competing for attention. This however was plausibly put down to a bias on the statistical process, such that more evidence was demanded from the input before a category state would occur which was unwanted. In this chapter, we have seen that the probability of an event does indeed produce a bias of this kind. Indeed, we have found no evidence that people tend to select by filtering those channels from which information is likely to come. All we have found is that they are biased in favour of responses they are likely to have to make. Pigeon-holing is a real mechanism of response set.

Two lines of advance are possible from this point. One is to consider the effects of the general state of the system upon these processes. This however should come better after we have dealt with memory; and in addition, the study of performance under abnormal conditions often involves measures of speed of performance. The second line of advance calls directly for a discussion of speed; for if the process of selecting one category state rather than another is performed by a mechanism of limited capacity, it should do better given more time. This is on both grounds therefore the stage at which to enquire what is known about the time taken to react to stimuli of different types.

CHAPTER VII

The Speed of Decisions

In discussing the speed with which a man can make one appropriate response rather than another, we have several different aspects of our general purpose in mind. First of all, one can regard reaction time as a field in which one might discover further evidence for the statistical and indeterminate character of information processing which is one of our general themes. As we shall see, there does seem to be reasonable grounds for finding this a useful approach in this field also. Secondly therefore we shall be looking, as so frequently in the past, at reaction to signals of different probability. As always, the more probable the signal the more efficient the reaction to it, and it will be of some interest to see whether we can distinguish the roles of pigeon-holing and of filtering which we have found in previous chapters. In this case we shall be disappointed, although there is some tentative evidence that the effect of signal probability is through pigeon-holing in this case also. Lastly, we want to know as much as we can about the general nature of the decision process which can be inferred from reaction times, so that we can see possible parameters which might change under abnormal conditions or stresses.

The Position in 1958

INFORMATION THEORY AND THE LIMIT OF CAPACITY

The position in 1958 was that reaction time had recently come into favour as a serious subject of study, after a long spell of neglect. The greatest single factor in this revived interest was possibly some work by W. E. Hick (1952) in which he linked choice reaction time to the amount of information (in the technical sense) transmitted through the man reacting. As we saw in Chapter I, for any given physical system there are a limited number of possible states which it can take: and the transmission of a message through the system requires some code which makes a series of states correspond to the particular message being sent. If we are organizing a system as efficiently as possible, then the length of the series which will just allow us to be sure which message has been sent will depend upon the probability of the message. For a fixed set of messages, all equally likely, we have to have a series of states of the transmission system which is sufficiently long that there is a different series for every possible message. That is,

if $\quad$ X = number of possible messages

$\qquad$ Y = number of possible states of the system

$\qquad$ T = number of states in the sequence corresponding to one message,

then $\qquad$ $X = Y^T$

$$\log X = T \log Y$$

$$T = \frac{1}{K} \log X$$

where $\qquad$ $K = \log Y,$

and is therefore constant for any particular system.

One can see therefore that the transmission system will have to take on a series of states which are proportional to the log of the number of possible messages. If we suppose that the time taken by the occurrence of a sequence of states in the system goes up by one unit for every extra state needed to transmit the message, then the time taken to transmit any one message will be proportional to the log of the number of possible messages.

Thus far we have spoken only about equiprobable messages: if some messages are more probable than others, then a short code can be devised for those messages and thus less time will be taken on average for transmitting messages. A practical example of this occurs in the British telephone system, where a person dialling long distance to London is only required to dial 01, whereas a person dialling long distance to Cambridge has to dial 0223. Once within each city however the relationships are reversed as there are far more telephones in London than in Cambridge.

In general, the average time taken by a system to transmit a long series of messages will be proportional to

$$\sum_{i=1}^{i=X} -p_i \log p_i$$

where $\qquad$ p_i = probability of ith message.

This will only hold true of course if we are dealing with a single system, in which the coding is so designed as to take advantage of the probabilities of one message rather than another. If, therefore, the speed of human reaction shows a similar relationship to the probabilities of input signals, it might suggest that our brains are reacting to any one signal only with reference to

K

all the other possibilities which might have occurred: and have adjusted in the best possible way to take advantage of the probabilities of one signal rather than another. This was the apparent implication of Hick's results, which we mentioned as reviving interest in reaction time.

He required subjects to make an appropriate reaction to the occurrence of one of a set of possible stimuli, and confirmed earlier indications in the literature that time taken to react varied with the log of the number of possible stimuli. He also asked subjects to speed up by making more errors, which reduces the amount of information successfully transmitted in their responses. The speeding up of the reaction corresponded satisfactorily to the loss of information. Other investigators such as Hyman (1953) and Crossman (1953) extended the result by modifying probability in other ways than by the size of the possible set of stimuli. In considering the perception of speech, we distinguished two other methods: the occurrence of some stimuli more frequently than others, and the presentation of context. Both methods apply also to experiments on reaction time. One can keep the size of the set the same and yet make some stimuli more probable than others, and equally one may have a constant average probability and yet have certain sequences more probable than others. The latter technique is analogous to the case of context in the perception of speech: by constructing various sequences of stimuli one can alter the probabilities of signals at any instant even though their average probability over the whole sequence remains unchanged. In each of these methods it was broadly true that the average speed of reaction was proportional to the average information per signal.

This result shows clearly that reaction time to any one stimulus is not determined solely by the stimulus itself, but rather by the whole complex of possible situations of which this particular stimulus is only one. The result shows for example that we cannot think of the nervous system as working like a typewriter; when we press one of the keys on the typewriter, an appropriate symbol is marked on the paper. The linkage for each key is quite separate from that of each of the others, and the time taken between the pressing of the key and the printing of the character does not depend upon the nature of the text which is being typed. An analogous imaginary system in the brain might consist of links between each possible sensory input and the appropriate motor action: each such link being independent for the others. The basic facts of choice reaction time make such a mechanism impossible. This remains true even though we shall see good reason to be sceptical about the doctrine of optimal coding which at first sight seemed to be the explanation for the dependence of reaction time upon stimulus information. It deserves emphasis at this point, before we come to the criticisms, that the work of the fifties was of the utmost importance in overthrowing the concept of separate unrelated linkages between each stimulus and its response, and rather establishing that the decision mechanism acted as a whole adjusting itself to the particular set of possibilities in play in the particular situation.

REACTION TIME AS A MEASURE OF CAPACITY

(*a*) *The form of the relationship.* It was said above that reaction time was proportional to stimulus information: but this statement was deliberately made generally and without a specific equation. In Hick's original work he fitted his data by an expression of the type

$$RT = A \log (N+1)$$

where N = number of equally likely signals

    A = a constant.

If we recall the equation we wrote for the time taken to pass equiprobable messages through a physical system, it will be obvious that the new slope constant A corresponds to the constant $1/K$ of the previous equation. K was a measure of the number of possible states of the system, that is, of its capacity. In the reaction time data we might therefore regard the slope constant A as an inverse measure of the capacity of the nervous system. If this interpretation is legitimate, that capacity was in Hick's results something of the order of five equiprobable binary choices per second.

The puzzle in Hick's equation is that the number of signals has to be increased by 1 before the logarithm is taken, whereas in the previous equation it was quite sufficient to take the log of the number of possible messages entering the physical system. Hick made the suggestion that, in experiments of this kind, the signals being presented are not the only possible states of the world which the man is considering. At any moment the possibilities include not only the set of signals, but also the possibility of no signal at all. This being so the number of possible "messages" is actually one more than the number of signals. It will be obvious that the probability of no signal at all is different from that of each of the other signals, and consequently one might expect the value which needs adding to N to vary depending upon the exact way in which the experiment is done.

One different way of conducting it is provided by Crossman (1953). In his studies, a series of signals is presented, and each follows the response to the previous signal without any interval. For example, the subject may be given a pack of playing cards to sort, turning up each one, looking at it, and putting it in an appropriate pile. As soon as one action has been completed the next stimulus is certainly present, and correspondingly the speed with which a pack can be sorted varies according to $\log N$ rather than $\log N+1$. In Hick's experiment one stimulus was presented at a time, in the classical style of reaction time studies. Surprisingly enough, there has been little experimental attempt to vary the probability of non-signal and study the effect on the shape of the relationship between reaction time and N, apart from a rather unsatisfactory study by Broadbent and Gregory (1965c). We shall return to this point later.

An alternative way of fitting the experimental results is to use the rather different expression

$$RT = B + A \log N.$$

In this case one supposes that part of the reaction time is a constant, depending purely upon the time taken to send messages along the sensory nerves to the brain, or from the motor areas to the muscles. This time cannot reasonably be supposed to adjust itself to the number of possible signals or actions in play, and behaves much more like the typewriter which we used as an analogy earlier. Only the central part of the process should be considered as adjusting itself to the most efficient possible code, and hence the equation falls into two parts. It is convenient that this allows us to use $\log N$ rather than $\log N+1$ in order to fit the results. But it means that any effects on reaction time found by changing the probability of "no signal at all" can be incorporated into the constant B rather than acting like a change in the effective number of alternatives.

The second form of the equation was favoured by Hyman, and has probably been the form preferred by most workers in the field: although Welford (1960) gives some reason for holding that the data are better explained by Hick's original formulation. Whichever equation is preferred, it is the slope of the reaction time which is related to the hypothetical channel capacity. That is, we infer a small capacity for the system if the time taken for a choice between four alternatives is very much longer than the time taken to choose between two alternatives. We do not infer a small capacity from a slow reaction at one degree of choice alone. This becomes important when the reaction time is extremely slow for various degrees of choice and yet there is little difference between them. On the face of it, the slow reaction time suggests an inefficient mechanism, and yet the smallness of the difference between the two-choice time and the four-choice time should be taken as evidence for a channel of large capacity. One might conceivably explain this kind of effect by supposing that there are different mechanisms in play, some efficient and some inefficient: and it is worth considering the implications of this.

(b) *Restrictions on input and output.* There are obviously factors which determine reaction time other than the simple number of choices involved or the probability of each. We have used the illustration of a set of lights and a set of push buttons: but suppose that, on receiving a reaction signal, the subject had to run 100 yards before he could reach the keys. Manifestly this would increase the time for each reaction, and in addition it might well affect the slope of the graph relating reaction time to the number of alternatives. There are two ways in which it could do this: first, there is the straightforward point that the difference between a two-choice reaction and a four-choice reaction is only of the order of a fifth of a second even with the usual laboratory equipment. The time taken to run 100 yards would not of course be absolutely constant, and its variability might well be much greater than a fifth of a second. Consequently it might be impossible to detect the tiny difference in decision time amongst the large variability of the actual motor performance. With enough data however it still ought theoretically to be possible to find the difference: and this makes the second possible mechanism even more crucial. The second mechanism is that the subject might start his run as soon as the warning signal came, but look over his shoulder at the lights, and carry out his observation of the lights during the motor performance. Changes in duration of the perceptual and decision process would therefore disappear from the results, because they would be simultaneous with the running.

Of course nobody would seriously carry out an experiment in which the subject had to run 100 yards: but different ways of instituting reactions do take different lengths of time. A finger hovering over a push button takes very little time to press, but a long arm movement may take a substantial period. It has been shown by Leonard (1953) that such a movement can be combined with the taking in of information, and consequently it is really possible for an experiment to be arranged in such a way that the differences in decision time disappear because of the long time occupied in the motor movement.

At the opposite end of the process, the time taken to react appropriately to one of two signals will also be affected by the discriminability of the signals themselves. Two lights can readily be distinguished from one another, but what of two lines of different lengths? As the lengths become more similar, the reaction time will increase even while performance is still fairly perfect. One would naturally like to know whether this difference also can prevent the effect of a number of alternatives from appearing, but there is a technical difficulty in the way. Each time we add an extra stimulus, there is an extra difficulty of discrimination between that stimulus and each of those already being used. So if we wish to compare, say, four-choice and two-choice times at a high and at a low difficulty of discriminability, we must have some way of measuring discriminability. Without such a method, we may introduce an enormous difficulty of discriminability by adding one particular signal. A number of attempts have been made to produce measures of discriminability, following a discussion of the problem by Crossman (1955). He himself felt that, in choosing between two lines of different lengths, the best relationship was to suppose

$$t = \frac{K}{\log x_1 - \log x_2}$$

where x_1, x_2 are the lengths, K is a constant, and t is the time.

However, one could make some sort of case for a relationship

$$t = K \log x_1 - \log (x_1 - x_2):$$

the problem is discussed by Welford (1960), Shallice and Vickers (1964) and by Laming (1968). It is fair to say that at present there is no really convincing evidence for one expression rather than the other, and indeed it has been suggested by Shallice and Vickers and by Laming that one expression may hold for one kind of experiment and the other for another. Until one has a clear understanding of this problem, it is impossible to say whether the effect of a number of choices remains or disappears when the discriminability of the individual signals is altered.

(c) *The distinction of lag and working rate.* There is a possible confusion at this point which we must avoid. One could readily suppose that the system handles information by passing it successively through three stages, of identifying the stimulus, deciding upon a response, and executing the response. Each of these stages would as a physical system have a capacity for handling information, but that capacity need not be the same in each case. One might well say, therefore, that the capacity of the entire system would be equivalent to that of the most limited stage. Thus we might suppose that the decision mechanism had a true and constant capacity, but that experimental measurements of it might be obscured by having a very difficult motor response, or a very difficult sensory discrimination: so that the capacity of the central process no longer affected the capacity of the entire system. If traffic is flowing through a narrow street into a multi-lane highway, and then out again at the far end through a narrow street, the number of cars handled by the system will be restricted by the streets at each end and not by the highway in the middle. If, however, we apply a similar argument to reaction times, we shall be falling into a confusion between usages of "time". In the analogy of the highway, one may speak of the number of cars per hour using the system, and this is indeed limited by the capacity of the access roads. If, however, we speak of the time taken for any individual car to proceed from the entrance to the exit, this is a quite different measurement. It could be increased by removing the multi-lane highway from the middle of the system and substituting an inadequate street throughout. To put the matter another way, because 4000 cars per hour may use a road it does not follow that it takes each car 1/4000th of an hour to get from the beginning of the road to the end.

We have to distinguish carefully therefore between measurements of the time taken by any given signal between insertion to the system and emergence, and the rate at which signals can be admitted to the system. Only the second of these is a true measure of capacity in the ordinary sense of information theory; and only the second of these would depend on the most limited part of the entire system. The former type of measurement would always change if there was a change in the capacity of any part of the system, provided that the various stages were successive rather than simultaneous.

Now reaction time as usually measured is certainly a quantity of the first type. In the classic type of experiment, a single isolated stimulus is delivered and the time is measured until a response occurs. Even in the continuous type of study introduced by Crossman, a fresh stimulus is not delivered until the response has occurred to the previous one, and although the man is therefore in constant activity his total time for carrying out the task is the sum of a number of measurements of the interval between delivery of a stimulus and execution of an action. Reaction time is therefore a measure of the lag between input and output, and not a measure of the rate at which the system can handle information continuously. If therefore any extra difficulty of discriminability or of motor response were superimposed on performance, we would still expect difficulties of decision to increase reaction time.

To return to our analogy of the highway, repair work in the middle of the length of road will not affect the number of cars per hour using it, as long as the repair work does not restrict the road more than the entry and exit points already do so. However, repair work can make a large difference to the travel time for any individual car.

For this reason we might still expect that one can measure the capacity of the central stages in the system by using various numbers of alternative signals and measuring the changes in reaction time which result. Whatever the difficulties of input and output, the length of the sequence of central states which forms the code corresponding to each possible signal should still affect the overall reaction time. As we shall see in the next section, the slope of the relationship is not constant but depends very much upon the particular stimuli and responses in play. In some cases there is no change at all. Where this is true, the argument just concluded implies that we cannot appeal to limited sensory and motor processes as an explanation. Rather, such a result argues against the whole conception of taking reaction time as a means of measuring the capacity of the central mechanisms.

Furthermore, even if the lag between input and output of information is an indirect measure of capacity, it ought to be possible to obtain a more direct measure. That is, we ought to be able to present signals to a man at an increasing speed and observe the maximum rate at which he can respond. When this was done by Alluisi et al. (1957) it was indeed found that a man could respond perfectly up to a certain rate of presentation of signals, but not faster than that rate. We seem at first sight here to have got a direct measure of the capacity in the true and original sense, that is, the rate of intake and output of information rather than the delay between one and the other. However, if one alters the number of alternative signals used in such a task one alters the information per response, and ought therefore to find that a man can follow the input up to a different rate of signalling. If his task is simplified from reacting to one of eight stimuli to reacting to one of four, he should be able to keep up with the signals coming at a faster rate, and he should be able to speed up by the same amount again when the task is reduced to reacting to one of two signals. In fact however the maximum rate of work was constant in terms of responses per second rather than information per second: so that the direct measure of the capacity of the nervous system fails to give any support for the idea that the system adjusts its coding to handle information at a constant rate.

We therefore reach the following position. (*a*) The fact that reaction time increases with the number of alternatives rules out any theory of separate and independent connections between each stimulus and its corresponding response. In that sense, the system is a single integrated channel. (*b*) On the other hand, the size of this slope is not a direct but only an indirect measure of the information capacity of the nervous system. (*c*) To be a satisfactory indirect measure, it should continue to appear despite restrictions at the input and output ends of the system. It certainly does not do so with restrictions at the output end, and there is some evidence that it does not do so at the input end. Certainly the slope found is different in different tasks. (*d*) A direct measure of capacity by finding the maximum rate of signals to which a man can react satisfactorily does not show a dependence upon a constant rate of handling of information, but rather a constant maximum rate of responding.

All these points make one somewhat doubtful of the value of the original analogy with the speed at which messages could be perfectly encoded in our limited system. We have however passed over rather rapidly the empirical evidence that the effect of changes in the numbers of alternatives upon reaction time depends upon the type of task considered. This subject has been worked upon considerably since 1958, and deserves a section to itself.

Stimulus Response Compatibility and Its Effects upon Reaction Time

Broadly speaking, what we shall argue in this section is that the degree of naturalness or obviousness of the response appropriate to a particular signal alters the effect of number of signals. Terms such as obvious or natural are themselves exceedingly vague. Perhaps the best attempt we can make at a definition is to argue in the following way. If we take any particular task, with an array of possible signals and an array of possible responses, a random sample of people might be asked, without other instructions, which response they would regard as correct for a particular stimulus. Two tasks may well differ in the extent to which people can guess the correct response. For example, if we have a horizontal row of lights and a horizontal row of keys, a random sample of subjects are likely to guess that the left-hand light goes with the left-hand key, and not likely to guess that the left-hand light goes with the third key from the right, the right-hand light with the second key from the left, and so on. Correspondingly, if we bring in a different group of experimental subjects and get them to perform reaction time tasks with the two arrangements, they will perform faster with the arrangement which most people would guess. This ability of the subject to pick the correct response easily is known as "compatibility".

The definition of compatibility we have just given avoids circularity: that is, it avoids our saying simply that a task is more compatible because people do it faster. Unfortunately, it is not a perfect definition as can be seen by considering differences between subjects brought up in different cultures. American subjects will normally guess that an upward movement of a switch will turn on a light, whereas British subjects will guess that a downward movement of a switch will produce the same result. Clearly the ability to guess a correct response in the absence of instructions is related to past experience with similar situations, since the convention of electrical switches on the two sides of the Atlantic is in fact opposite. This need not worry us in the particular example, since we can describe the order of compatibility for different tasks by using groups of people drawn from the same population as those whom we mean to use in a reaction time experiment. However, the difficulty is that once we have started our experiment the subjects are getting experience of that particular arrangement of stimuli and responses. When they have practised it many times, they are clearly in a rather different state: in many ways, one would now wish to say that the set of responses was now more compatible with the stimuli than it had been originally. We are now however extending the use of the term, since groups of people practised to different extents on the same task may both be able to indicate perfectly which response is correct for which stimulus. Perhaps the most cautious principle would therefore be to reserve the term "compatibility" for tasks in which the experimenter has not previously practised subjects, but to say that practice within an experiment may produce changes very much like those of compatibility.

The concept of compatibility was introduced by Fitts (Fitts and Seeger, 1953; Fitts and Deininger, 1954). At first it seemed to be a matter only of practical importance, valuable for those concerned with the layout of controls in aircraft, power stations, and similar situations: and its theoretical importance did not make itself felt. At that time, most studies of reaction time had found that an extra fifth of a second or so was needed for every doubling of the number of alternatives used in the experiment. In the second half of the 1950's, however, several exceptions were produced to this rule. Perhaps the first was that of Crossman (1956): but others were provided by Griew (1958), Mowbray and Rhoades (1959) and by Leonard (1959). In each of these cases, the task was one of a highly compatible nature. For example, Crossman made use of a row of keys corresponding spatially very closely to the row of signal lights: whereas Hick's experiment and the earlier work of Crossman himself had used rather arbitrary relationships. Hick had employed a circle of stimulus lights for a row of response keys, and Crossman's experiments on the sorting of cards required each card to be put in a different place depending

K*

upon the nature of the symbol on the card. Leonard used as stimuli vibration of the fingertips, with the response being pressure of the same finger as was stimulated, and this again is a highly compatible situation. Mowbray and Rhoades simply practised their subjects to a very high degree. Each of these experiments found that doubling the number of alternatives gave a very small increase in the reaction time, and in some cases no increase at all. Putting together this body of evidence, it is immediately tempting to suggest that the ordinary dependence of reaction time on the size of the possible set of responses depends upon a certain degree of incompatibility. One might argue that as compatibility gets greater, the reaction time falls towards a constant value no matter what the size of the set of alternatives may be.

This conclusion however required considerable change in thinking, if one regarded the slope of the reaction time function as an inverse measure of the capacity of the nervous system. If it were possible, as for example in Leonard's results, to get a reaction time which was absolutely constant for different numbers of alternatives, then the capacity of the nervous system might be inferred to be infinite. Such a finding seems absurd. Consequently alternative explanations had to be ruled out: in Crossman's experiment for example it might be that a substantial movement time was overlapping with decision time, in the way described earlier. Such an explanation could not be used for the results of Mowbray and Rhoades: but then perhaps some other explanation could be used in their case also. Highly practised subjects, working sometimes with a larger set of responses and sometimes with a smaller set, might conceivably adjust themselves to the larger set and react effectively to that set even when working under the condition where part of the set only was being employed. If one has had a lot of practice at reacting to one of ten possible stimuli, it may be hard to forget about eight of them when working in a two-choice condition. Mowbray (1960) covered this possibility by training completely separate individuals on each number of alternatives, and found that the average reaction time in a group was the same regardless of the number of alternatives used. On the other hand, Mowbray used numerals as his stimuli, and in the two-choice condition asked subjects to react to the numeral 4 and the numeral 8. It may well be that practice in everyday life has made it difficult to ignore the other numerals in favour of this particular pair: Fitts and Switzer (1962) in fact demonstrated that a task of reacting to numerals would give a faster reaction time to two-choice than to eight-choice, when the two-choice consisted of the numerals 1 and 2 but not when the two-choice consisted of the numerals 4 and 7. The numerals 1 and 2 form a familiar sub-set, while the other pair form a set which people have not usually used in their everyday lives apart from the larger set of all the numerals. Leonard's experiment is difficult to explain in this way, but one might resort to the ad hoc hypothesis that reaction to tactual stimulation is a peculiar and almost reflex form of response, not passing through higher centres.

Other experiments again showed the same result, but were perhaps open each to some *ad hoc* explanation. Davis *et al.* (1961a) showed that people repeating back words which were spoken to them showed no dependence of reaction time upon the number of alternatives; conceivably they might be reacting phoneme by phoneme, uttering the first sound of their response when they heard the first sound of the stimulus, the second response sound to the second stimulus sound, and so on. If so then they would be reacting under all conditions with the same set of possibilities, the forty phonemes of English. Brainard *et al.* (1962) found no effect of number of alternatives on a task of naming numerals: but again used unfamiliar sets of numerals for the smaller numbers of choices.

Gradually however more and more results were collected for which escape clauses were difficult to invent. For example, Fitts *et al.* (1963) varied the probability of one stimulus rather than another, instead of changing the size of the set. As had been found originally by Hyman, the more frequent stimulus normally elicited a faster reaction: but not in their most compatible task, which required subjects simply to touch one of a number of lights which had come on. The distances to be moved being short, and opposite to one another, it does not seem plausible that the movement time had been overlapped with the decision time in this case.

One of the neatest demonstrations was that of Conrad (1962a), who required subjects to read lists made up of ordinary words, or of nonsense syllables of varying association. The rate of reading familiar English words does not depend upon the size of the vocabulary being employed: whereas the rate of reading nonsense syllables does. Furthermore, the amount of extra time taken for a larger set of alternatives depended upon the kind of nonsense syllables that were used. Syllables of high association value gave a relatively small increase of time with increasing numbers of alternatives, whereas syllables of low association value gave a larger increase. The association value of nonsense syllables is determined by the number of associations which subjects can call up when presented with the meaningless sequence of letters: but it is known that this value is closely related to the probability of that particular sequence of letters occurring in counts of natural English such as that prepared by Baddeley *et al.* (1960). Thus Conrad's results on reading rate show that the effect of the number of alternative responses depends upon the amount of experience which the subject has had with the sequences of letters used in the particular sets of responses. The result cannot be explained away by the argument used for the data of Davis *et al.*: if the subjects were reading letter by letter when reading words, they could apply the same technique to the reading of nonsense syllables. Furthermore the fact that the effect of number of alternatives can be varied in size rather than abolished altogether makes it very difficult to suppose that subjects were adopting some strategy of this kind.

Results provided by Broadbent and Gregory (1965c) also showed that the effect of number of alternatives can be reduced in size without being eliminated altogether. They employed a modification of Leonard's technique, in which the finger tip was stimulated and reaction had to be made with the same finger (as a compatible condition) or with the corresponding finger on the other hand (as an incompatible condition). In the compatible case the effect of different numbers of alternatives was present, but much smaller than in the incompatible case: since it was still present, one could hardly explain the result by the *ad hoc* hypothesis suggested for Leonard's original one, that the reaction was a completely reflex one by-passing the central mechanisms. The fact that in this case the number of alternatives did have some effect even on the compatible task was probably because the stimulus was a less clear one than Leonard's, and also because the subjects were less practised.

Broadbent and Gregory (1962b) also provided evidence that the compatible version of Leonard's task would show no difference between the time taken for a two-choice reaction and the time taken to react whenever one stimulus was presented but to refrain from reaction when another one was given. It has been known since the time of F. C. Donders (1868) that the latter of these situations is faster for most tasks: but the difference apparently applies only to incompatible relationships. Once again it is difficult to see how this result could be explained if Leonard's situation was a purely reflex one: and in addition Broadbent and Gregory found that a compatible verbal task equally showed no difference between a two-choice reaction and the situation of reacting to one stimulus but ignoring another. An incompatible verbal task gave the more traditional result of a difference between the two situations.

Still more evidence is provided by Hellyer (1963), and by Costa *et al.* (196 6) It may be taken as established therefore that an increase of compatibility in a task reduces the effect of a number of alternatives, or of the relative probability of one alternative rather than another.

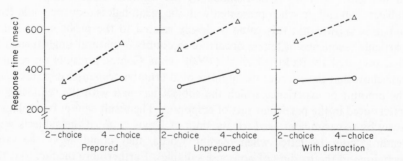

FIG. 26. The time taken for 2-choice and 4-choice reactions under compatible (solid line) and incompatible (dashed line) conditions. Notice that time uncertainty and distraction both have greater effects on incompatible reactions. Data from Broadbent and Gregory (1965c).

There are certain other effects of compatibility, shown by Broadbent and Gregory (1965c), which are worth noting at this stage although their theoretical significance is still unclear. First, the reaction signal may or may not be preceded by a warning signal, and it is well known that the latter condition produces faster reactions. The effect is greater when the task is incompatible than compatible.

Secondly, if a man is asked to perform a memory task at the same time as a reaction time, his performance on the latter is impaired: and the extent of the impairment is greater if the task is an incompatible one. In addition, the memory task is performed worse if the reaction time is being measured on an

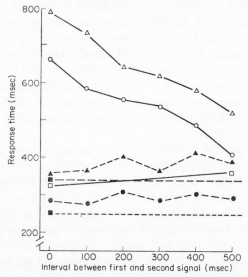

Fig. 27. Choice Reaction times to a second signal following a first after various intervals are shown in the two upper graphs. The open triangles are for those second reactions which follow the slower of the two first reactions. The next lower line shows the second reaction following the faster of the two first reactions. The various horizontal lines are the control reactions and the first reactions. Clearly there is more delay following a slow first reaction, even when the subject knows perfectly the time interval between stimuli. These data from Broadbent and Gregory (1967b) are discussed on page 310.

incompatible task than a compatible one. Broadly speaking therefore it seems fair to suppose that the processes which select the appropriate response occupy more of the general pool of available resources when the response is an incompatible one: and thus leave less of the system available for the simultaneous handling of other tasks.

Recent Theories and the Importance of Errors

From what has been said, it is clearly unsatisfactory to regard reaction time as the period required for the occurrence of a sequence of central states which encodes perfectly the information transmitted by the stimulus. That was the approach of the 1950's. Rather one has to suppose that the arrival of a stimulus starts some process which ultimately selects an appropriate output: a category state in the terms we are employing in this book. Lack of compatibility increases the time taken for this selection to occur. We have also tried to define lack of compatibility as a low probability that the subject will guess the correct response for a particular stimulus in the absence of specific instructions. From the most abstract point of view, the arrival of a stimulus must be followed by a succession of events preceding the occurrence of a category state: and in keeping with our general approach we must suppose that this succession of events is not completely determined by the signal but that the latter alters the probability of some events rather than others. That is, the arrival of the signal produces evidence in the nervous system, which in turn leads to a category state. The definition of compatibility implies that, for a given exposure to a signal, the reliability of the evidence will be higher for a more compatible task. We have already seen in earlier chapters that a longer exposure to stimulation will also improve the reliability of evidence: and thus in general terms it is reasonable that a rise in compatibility should mean a fall in the decision time.

In this very general analysis we have changed from the determinate approach of communication theory in the 1950's to a more probabilistic attitude. The reaction time is now seen as the time necessary to accumulate enough evidence to allow correct rather than incorrect action, although no doubt there is still a certain chance of error. Empirically it is perfectly obvious that increasing the speed of reaction increases the frequency of errors. Hick's original study showed this, and similar findings have been provided by Snodgrass et al. (1967), Fitts (1966) and Schouten and Bekker (1967). In the analysis based on information theory, one might suppose that pressing subjects to react fast would cause the coded sequence of central states to be restricted in length, so that there would be fewer different possible codes than there were stimuli, and some inaccuracy would result. This would on the face of it imply that the reactions most likely to be affected would be those with especially long codes: that is, the infrequently used ones. It should also be the case that error responses should be substantially faster than correct ones, since they would result from the use of a short code failing to distinguish between all the alternative stimuli. Beyond this point it is difficult to get specific predictions from information theory; although we shall see that other approaches do allow such predictions. It is already clear from what has been said, however, that the speed with which errors are made rather than correct responses, and the nature of the particular responses which are in error, are important questions for observation.

If we return to considering reaction time as a matter of accumulating enough evidence to allow accurate response, there are a large number of different ways in which we might from the armchair imagine the processes taking place. As a start, we might simply suppose that the subject fixes a time for which he will allow evidence to accumulate; and at the end of that time he reacts in the direction which the evidence favours. We might suppose that the length of time is adjusted so as to keep the probability of an incorrect reaction reasonably constant regardless of the number of alternatives in play or the compatibility of the task. As a rough illustration of what would happen, let us apply the mathematics of choice analysis rather than those of decision theory: then if the man waits for one unit of time after the arrival of a signal, the table of strengths for the various possible responses will in the usual way take on the following form.

		RESPONSES			
		1	2	3	4
S					
T	1	α	1	1	1
I	2	1	α	1	1
M	3	1	1	α	1
U	4	1	1	1	α
L					
I					

and the probability of correct response will be

$$P_C = \frac{\alpha}{\alpha+(N-1)}$$

where N = number of alternative reactions.

Thus to keep a constant probability of being correct, α must be a constant fraction of $N-1$. In order therefore to keep the same level of accuracy when N is increased, the subject must wait several units of time so that α increases to an appropriate value. The difficulty is to decide what the rate of increase of α with time is likely to be. Purely hypothetically, let us suppose that after a fixed time (t) units, α increases to α^t. In that case we have

$$\alpha^t = K(N-1)$$
$$t \log \alpha = \log K + \log (N-1)$$
$$t = A + B \log (N-1)$$

where both A and B are inversely proportional to $\log \alpha$.*

That is, there will be a roughly logarithmic increase in time as the number of alternatives is increased, but both the slope of the line and its value for

---

* Another interesting consequence of this assumption for the rate of increase of α is that $t \log \alpha - \log (N-1) = \log (P_C/P_E)$. That is the trade-off of speed and accuracy will be such that $\log (P_C/P_E)$ increases linearly with time. This relationship has been suggested empirically by R. Pew in *Attention and Performance III*, North Holland Press, Amsterdam.

$N = 1$, the simple reaction time, will depend upon the value of α. In other words, the less information one gets in unit time about the correct response, the slower the reaction time and the greater the effect of number of alternatives. Thus we are roughly on the right track in considering models of this kind, although we have no real reason for supposing that the strength of the correct response will increase exponentially with time, and in any case we have only obtained a logarithmic relationship to $N-1$ rather than to N or to $N+1$.

A more accurate account of a fixed sample model of this type, using methods based on detection theory, was put forward by Stone (1960) in a most influential paper from which many contemporary approaches to the problem have stemmed. He showed that the length of the sample which the subject would need to choose for a constant error rate was indeed closely similar to the classic logarithmic relationship. There is one very unfortunate feature of a fixed sample model, however, which means that it cannot possibly be a correct one. The length of the sample has to be fixed in advance: therefore the time taken for the reaction cannot depend upon the stimulus which is in fact delivered, nor on the response which ultimately is selected. It is easy to show experimentally that this is untrue: if one stimulus is more frequent than others, response to that stimulus is much faster. By itself therefore the fixed sample theory cannot be correct, and its interest is primarily as showing that the general approach is on the right lines. We have to consider rather some process which would allow evidence to build up for a time which is shorter in the case of a probable stimulus-response combination, and longer in the case of an improbable combination. Stone himself, followed and extended very thoroughly by Laming (1968), applied an analysis based on detection theory to this case also, the idea being that evidence builds up until the weight of that pointing to a particular alternative exceeds some criterion which could depend upon the particular alternative being considered. As we have already said however this is only one of several possibilities: so let us rather try to set out the different ways in which the process conceivably might occur.

A classification of the kind we want has been put forward by Audley and Pike (1965). They distinguish three general classes of possible theory.

ACCUMULATORS WITH PERFECT MEMORY

The first idea is that each instant of waiting after the arrival of the stimulus produces evidence in favour of one or other of the alternative reactions: and that all the evidence in favour of any one particular response is totalled up and preserved. There is a critical value for each reaction, which might for instance be less for probable than for improbable reactions. As soon as the evidence for one reaction reaches its own critical value, that response occurs regardless of what the state of evidence may be concerning other possible reactions. This kind of model has the advantage of requiring only a fairly simple mechanism and yet allowing for decision times to be different for probable and improbable reactions. On the other hand, it has been shown by Laming (1968) that theories of this class imply that the same response will have a longer average reaction time when made incorrectly than when made correctly. Audley and Pike give a prediction for reaction time as a function of the probability of evidence favouring one alternative in any instant, which appears to give a similar deduction. This offers a chance of comparing this class of theories with experiment, and as we shall see the prediction is certainly falsified in some cases.

ACCUMULATORS WITH DEFECTIVE MEMORY

The assumption of the last class of theories was that all the evidence in favour of one response was totalled, no matter how long the whole process went on. It is also possible that some of the earlier evidence is lost, and there is a very large class of models which could be made with different assumptions of this kind.

(a) Zero memory accumulators. A particularly interesting variety is the sub-class of theories in which the determiner of reaction is the state of the evidence at any instant. If it points firmly to one reaction, that reaction is made: if it is insufficient to decide between the reactions it is discarded altogether, and a fresh start made at the next instant. One could obviously alter the fixed sample theory in this way, by supposing that a sample of fixed length was taken but that the subject was not compelled to decide in favour of any one alternative at the end of a sample: in doubtful cases he could discard the sample and take a fresh one. This might allow the reaction time to improbable signals to be longer than that to probable ones. Suppose for example that at any instant following a particular signal we had the probabilities: p = probability of sufficient evidence for a correct response, q = probability of sufficient evidence for an incorrect response, r = probability of insufficient evidence for any response. For some other signal, the values could all be different. Then the probability that a correct response will take place following a sequence of t units of time is given by

$$P_C(t) = r^t p .$$

The mean value of time for a function of this sort is $r/(1-r)$. As r can be different for different signals, the mechanism can be so adjusted that an improbable signal gives a large value of r. The mean response time would then be greater for such signals. It is worthy of note however that the probability of an error occurring after a sequence of t instants is given by

$$P_E(t) = r^t q$$

and the mean of this is exactly the same as the mean for correct response. Thus the response time will depend upon the nature of the signal; and incorrect reactions to a particular signal will be made with the same speed as correct ones. As we shall see later, these predictions also are contrary to fact.

(b) *Partial memory accumulators—runs model.* The sub-class of models just discussed involves complete failure of memory for anything before the instant now present. Another class of theories would be that the reception of evidence favouring one alternative allows one to go on receiving and storing any further evidence favouring the same alternative. As soon however as some instant produces evidence favouring a different alternative, everything stored until that time is forgotten and the process shifts to the new favoured alternative. Models of this type were introduced by Audley (1960) and are sometimes called "runs" models, since they can be thought of as requiring a run of identical internal responses before the external response is made.

The behaviour of this model depends upon the length of run which is necessary before a reaction occurs. Laming (1968) shows that, as the duration of the whole process increases, one reaches an approximation to the model with zero memory, that is, the time to respond depends only on the signal and is the same for correct and for incorrect reactions to the same signal. Indeed one can see this in intuitive fashion, since if the probability of favourable evidence at one instant is P, the probability of a sequence of R such events is P^R. As in the previous analysis therefore, for constant R, the average speed of response will depend upon $1-P^R$, the probability that the particular stimulus will produce insufficient evidence for any action. Since the value of P depends on the stimulus, probable stimuli could give faster responses than improbable stimuli.

There is in this model however the possibility that R, the run length required for response might be different for probable and for improbable reactions, and in that case the setting of a longer run for improbable reactions might cause those reactions to be slow even when made incorrectly to probable stimuli. In so far as the reaction time depends upon the run length required for a particular response, it will be the same for a certain response whether that response is made correctly or not: but in so far as the probability of getting individual elements of the run will depend upon the stimulus, the speed of reaction may depend upon the particular stimulus and may tend to be faster for all reactions to one stimulus whether those reactions are correct or otherwise. Thus in this model the speed of reaction depends both upon the nature of the stimulus and on that of the response.

COMPARATIVE CRITERIA: THE RANDOM WALK MODEL

The third general class of models is that in which one ceases to suppose a system considering only evidence related to each response separately. Rather one supposes a system which takes the difference between evidence in favour of one alternative and of each of the others. The process is most easily conceived (and mathematically much better understood) in the case of two alternatives: if at one instant evidence arrives favouring alternative A, and then at another instant evidence arrives favouring alternative B, the final state is represented by the difference between the two values of evidence. Thus one can think of a process starting from a central point and moving first in one direction and then in the opposite, in an irregular and oscillating fashion, of which the average gradually drifts further and further one way. A critical value can then be set for the distance which the average has to drift, and when this value is exceeded reaction occurs in the direction in which the drift has moved. The critical value need not be the same for each of the two alternatives: which is exactly equivalent to supposing that the whole process starts from a point which is not symmetric between the two positions at which decision will take place. In the case of more than two alternatives, one has to think of a process moving in a multi-dimensional space rather than simply up or down on a simple scale of numbers. In principle the result may be the same, but in practice it is very difficult to work out what one might expect reaction time to be in such a situation. It can however be proved, and has been by Stone and more generally by Laming, that the time taken to reach a decision will depend upon the position of the final critical value, and not upon the stimulus which is giving rise to the incoming evidence. We have here therefore a clear prediction that the speed of reaction depends upon the particular response, both errors and correct responses occurring with the same latency provided the action is the same: and latency does not depend upon the particular stimulus.

We can see therefore that the many different possible mechanisms, by which reaction time might be mediated, fall into fairly clear broad classes of theory. They can be distinguished by looking closely at the reaction times for correct and for mistaken responses. For one class of theories, the reaction time for the same stimulus will be the same regardless of whether the reaction is correct or in error. These include the theories in which adjustment to the probability of one signal rather than another is carried out primarily by altering the strength of the evidence which results at any instant from a signal. A second class of theories will predict that, for the same response, reaction time will be longer when the response is in error than when it is correct: these are theories which hold that evidence is accumulated about each possible alternative without reference to the other possibilities. The third class of theories supposes that reaction time will be the same for the same response whether it is correct or an error. This is the type of theory which supposes that adjustment of reaction time to the probability of one event rather than another takes the form of altering the evidence needed for one response rather than another.

An intermediate category, theories which use some but not all of the past as well as the present evidence, is exemplified by the "runs" theory: such a view might expect the reaction for a certain response to be affected both by the nature of the response and also to some extent by the nature of the signal. It is now worth looking at the facts and to see what we can decide about these classes of theory.

REACTION TIME FOR CORRECT AND FOR ERROR RESPONSES

There are three broad findings which can be asserted with some confidence from analysis of the reaction times to errors.

(a) *Probable signals get fewer errors, probable responses occur as errors.* If one has a situation in which there are two stimuli A and B, and two corresponding responses I and II, then it is possible to present A more frequently than B and correspondingly one will find that I occurs more frequently than II. Amongst the errors, one will find that the probability of response II given stimulus A is less than the probability of response I given stimulus B. This has been found by Fitts *et al.* (1963), by Falmagne (1965), and by Laming (1968).

Such a result is consistent with the possibility that, if one knows only which response a subject has made, one has a constant probability of being wrong in asserting that the stimulus was the one corresponding to that response. This is of course a more specific prediction than the general one that the more frequent response will occur more often as an error: Laming tests his data against this relationship, and finds that it fits adequately. It is important that people do behave in this rather precise way. It means, in a sense, that when a reaction occurs there is a constant *a priori* probability that it is correct. As Laming points out however many decision processes could lead to this relationship. The result does not imply exactly what the correct theory of reaction time is. But it eliminates theories which, for example, suggest simply that one examines first the possibility that the most probable signal is present, then the possibility of the next most probable, and so on: guessing amongst the remaining possibilities when time becomes short. Such a process would give more errors amongst the *less* common responses: and thus is impossible. We may recall the last chapter and the doubts we expressed there concerning some kinds of analysis-by-synthesis. Here again, it seems unlikely that probable alternatives are examined first and improbable ones later. Rather, just as in the last chapter, adjustment to the stimulus probability results in a greater tendency to make the probable response even if the stimulus is an inappropriate one.

(b) *Stimuli giving a faster reaction also have a smaller probability of error.* This has been shown systematically by Laming (1968), and can also be deduced from the differences in error rate mentioned above, combined with the well known effects of stimulus probability on reaction time. It implies that the faster reaction to probable signals is due to a response bias and not only (if at all) to a better sensory input from the improbable signal. It can probably, as Laming points out, be deduced from any theory which incorporates a response bias and is not very discriminative between theories.

(c) When a response occurs as an error, its speed is affected by the nature of the response and not solely by the nature of the stimulus. This is a weak statement of the facts, but unfortunately we cannot say that reaction time is completely unaffected by the stimulus. Laming (1968), in a series of two-choice experiments with varying probabilities of the two alternatives, showed that an increase in the probability of a given stimulus produced an increase in the speed with which the corresponding response would be made even as an error. This is quite a powerful argument in the favour of something like the last of the three classes of theory considered by Audley and Pike. However, Laming did find in these same experiments that a given response was consistently slightly faster when occurring as an error than when occurring correctly, so that the full prediction of random-walk theories fails to be verified. Snodgrass *et al.* (1967) similarly found that reaction time depended primarily upon the nature of the response, but that it was affected to some extent by the nature of the stimulus. Rabbitt (1966b) also found that errors were faster than correct responses. Thus the only safe statement is that the nature of the response does affect the speed of reaction.

IMPLICATIONS FOR THE VARIOUS THEORIES

We now have some evidence for deciding between the different classes of theory distinguished by Audley and Pike. It seems clear that an accumulator theory with perfect memory cannot apply to all situations, since errors would then be slower than correct responses. Laming did find this to be the case in some situations, but only when he was using many alternatives rather than two, and requiring subjects to discriminate as stimuli lengths of line which were quite easy to confuse. The pattern of errors for any one stimulus was then extremely biased, towards those stimuli which were closely similar in length; and as the physical length of the line stimuli was perfectly correlated with the probability of occurrence, the most probable stimulus was always one with only one other stimulus close to it. Stimuli of intermediate probability had more than one similar stimulus. The situation appears therefore to be rather an unusual one and subject to its own principles. It may conceivably be that an accumulator theory with perfect memory might be useful in some situations; but it certainly cannot be used in the cases where errors occur faster than correct responses.

Turning to the case of accumulators with imperfect memory, we can be even more confident about rejecting those models that have zero memory. In that case the speed of response would depend upon the stimulus only and not upon the nature of the response, and this is clearly untrue. Models having a partial memory for some of the previous events may be tenable, since they would presumably involve dependence of the reaction time upon the response as well as the stimulus. As we saw, we cannot rule out completely the possibility that the stimulus affects speed as well as the response doing so. There is some slight evidence against the effect of the stimulus: in Laming's experiment showing that an increased probability of one alternative increased the speed of the corresponding response, he found a constant difference between error and correct responses at each level of stimulus probability. If there was a tendency to get better sensory evidence about probable stimuli one might reasonably have expected that an increase in stimulus probability might be slightly less beneficial to an error response than to a correct response, even though speeding up both to some extent. This is however a quantitative prediction for which one does not have a sufficiently precise theory. Partial memory models cannot at this stage be ruled out.

There remains the random-walk model based upon decision theory: this also is unsatisfactory as it stands, because responses do not occur with exactly the same speed whether correct or error. However, it is at least true that response times are heavily affected by the nature of the response whatever the nature of the stimulus. Laming himself has produced a modification for the theory, to which we will now turn, but before doing so it may be well to sum up the result of this comparison of the different classes of theory with the data. We do not seem to have enough information to narrow the possibilities down to one class of theory: but we can at least exclude those which depend purely upon stimulus effects without changes of response bias. To pick up again our usual terms, pigeon-holing seems to be involved in the adjustment of reaction time to stimulus probability, whether or not filtering is also so involved.

The Effects of Time Uncertainty upon Reaction

We saw a long time ago, in the discussion of vigilance, that simple reaction time in the absence of a warning signal was faster when the signal was at that instant more probable. In the case of simple reaction time there is of course no problem of choosing the correct reaction, but merely one of launching the response at the correct time. When we are dealing with reactions involving choice between several alternatives, however, the question immediately arises whether the probability of arrival of any signal at that instant has its effect through the same mechanism as does the probability of arrival of one signal rather than another. We discussed this point in considering Hick's formulation of his results. He fitted his data by a line of the type

$$RT = A \log (N + X)$$

where X was a quantity representing the effect of no signal at all, and in his data was equal to 1. Other authors have used an equation of the type

$$RT = B + A \log N$$

where the effect of time uncertainty is included in the variable B. If this second equation is correct, then the difference between a two-choice reaction time and a four-choice reaction time should be the same whether the uncertainty about time of arrival of a signal is great or small. If on the other hand Hick's formulation were correct, then an increase in the value of X should reduce the difference between the two-choice time and the four-choice time, although increasing both of them.

Broadbent and Gregory (1965c) attempted to test which of these was correct, and as was said earlier their results were unfortunately equivocal. They compared two-choice and four-choice reactions with a warning signal, or with no warning signal and a gap of ten seconds or so since the last signal. This increased reaction time considerably, but there was no significant change in the difference between the four-choice and two-choice times. The unsatisfactory feature of the results was that the difference did decrease, but did so insignificantly. Thus it was not really satisfactory as disproving Hick's formulation, merely failing to support it.

Another line of attack is to change the relative probability of one signal as opposed to another, rather than changing the number of alternatives in the experiment. Bertelson and Barzeele (1965) did this, and found that increasing time uncertainty had a larger effect on probable rather than improbable signals. This is consistent with a flattening of the effect of probability on reaction time, that is, with something of the nature of Hick's formulation. Purely temporal uncertainty does have some effect on the mechanism of selecting one response rather than another, whether or not later research may show this effect to be important when one varies the number of equiprobable alternatives.

Let us now return from the data to our general theoretical approach. The various models of the man as accumulating evidence concerning the occurrence of one signal rather than another have all tended to assume that he starts the process of collection at the instant the signal appears. This however begs the question: how does the brain know that the signal has appeared until it has detected some consequence of it? We must suppose therefore that the stimulus breaks in upon a continuous activity of the perceptual system, and our theories of the latter must include some way in which this can happen. Shallice (1964) in an important paper distinguishes a number of possible mechanisms which might meet the case. For example, it might be that the system takes a series of samples of the incoming information from the environment, so that everything arriving before the beginning of such a sample was discarded. A theory of this kind is often known as the "perceptual moment" hypothesis, and the present author has in irreverent moods dubbed it the "lavatory cistern" theory. The reason for the latter name is that the operation of the nervous system is conceived as rather similar to that of a flushing system, which takes in a steady flow of water, which can be emptied at intervals, but once emptied requires a certain length of time to fill up before it can be emptied again. This analogy has another property which is often associated with the theory of perceptual moments, namely that they can be extended in length, but cannot be reduced below a certain critical time. One might suppose therefore that the occurrence of a warning signal would allow the man to adjust the end of one perceptual moment so as to occur at the best possible time with reference to the reaction signal. If however there was no warning signal, and a state of high temporal uncertainty, then the reaction signal might occur at random with respect to the start and end of perceptual moments, and a delay might therefore ensue if the signal occurred at an unfortunate point in the cycle.

We shall discuss this theory again later: it has its attractions, but from our present point of view the main snag is that it seems to be a zero memory model of the type that we have already excluded by the data.

Another form of mechanism discussed by Shallice is one in which the incoming information is averaged over a certain length of time, but in which the mechanism does not discard all the input contained in one average before forming another average. That is, at any instant the average is of the input during the preceding K instants. At the next instant a new item of incoming information is taken into the average while the item at the most distant past end is dropped out. The process is not therefore intermittent but continuous. This kind of theory can be called the "moving window" theory, since it supposes that the process of taking in information is somewhat like that of a railway passenger looking out through the window of his carriage. As each new piece of visual information moves in one side of the window, a piece of old information moves out the other. This theory therefore contrasts with that of the "lavatory cistern" model, which would be more analogous to a series of snapshots, with the presence of an item in one picture meaning that it would be excluded from the next picture.

On a "moving window" view, temporal uncertainty does not affect the time at which sampling of the input begins, because sampling of the input is always going on continuously. The effect of temporal uncertainty therefore has to be in the setting of the criteria against which the running average is measured, and which result in reaction when the average exceeds an appropriate criterion. When no stimulus is present, the value of the average will fluctuate to a minor degree: when a stimulus arrives the average will begin to indicate its presence to a greater and greater extent as the amount of random non-stimulus input in the average decreases with time. If the occurrence of a stimulus at any instant is improbable, it would be rational to take no action until the value of the average became rather extreme, whereas if a stimulus was probable the chances of a given change in the value of the average being due to random changes in the input would be smaller. It would therefore be rational to react to smaller values of change. Such smaller values would be achieved sooner after the time when a signal was turned on.

There are several varieties of this type of theory: we should perhaps mention the possibility that the moving average is not based equally on the last K instants, but rather gives a gradually decreasing weight to every instant of past history, which will effectively mean that events in the remote past will make no contribution whatever. Such a form of the average would probably be the one most likely to occur to an engineer, since it could result from simple mechanisms such as the charging of a leaky condenser: it is interesting that the psychologists have tended to think more naturally of mechanisms of the intermittent type. The evidence for an intermittent theory rather than a moving average one is however rather slight: it is merely that the latter did not occur to people who were faced with, for example, errors in the perception of the order of arrival of successive stimuli.

Even on the moving average model, the process would naturally be supposed to restart after a critical value has been reached and an action made. One interesting variation on this class of theories is to suppose that "absence of signal" is itself a possible decision. If this were so, there would be some criterion value for the average, beyond which there would be a definite decision that a signal was absent, and a restarting of the process.

Let us think of a concrete though speculative illustration, to clarify this idea. Suppose a man were reacting with one of two keys, the left-hand one to a rise in the general level of illumination and the right-hand one to a fall in its level. A running average would be kept of the input from his eyes, and in the absence of a signal this average might swing about a mean of 100 units, with a standard deviation of ten units. Then the rules governing the man's behaviour might well be that a rise in the running average above 120 would cause left-hand reaction, and a fall below 80 would cause right-hand reaction. If however no reaction had taken place for the past 20 instants, and the average was between 90 and 110, the man might decide that no signal was present, discard all past information, and start averaging again. Under certain circumstances such a strategy might be advantageous, since a great amount of information known to be irrelevant would be excluded from the new average: whether this was a useful strategy or not would depend upon the exact arrangement of the situation.

On such a theory, the effect of temporal uncertainty would be to change the criteria associated with the "no signal" decision. When a signal was very probable, those criteria might be set to make this decision unlikely: when a signal was improbable, the criteria for "no signal" could be set so as to make that decision occur frequently. The difference between this kind of theory of temporal uncertainty and the form first discussed for running average models is in their effect on the predicted distribution of reaction times. The latter theory suggests that a change in temporal uncertainty will change the average value of a single distribution of reaction times: whereas this new version suggests that there will be a series of distributions, corresponding to reaction after zero, one, two, three, etc. "no signal" decisions, and that temporal uncertainty will change the relative numbers of reactions in each of these distributions rather than affecting the average of each of them. We shall come back to this point when discussing distributions of reaction times later in this chapter, but for the moment we can say briefly that the evidence is rather inadequate to decide between the possibilities, and both are of interest.

Perhaps the most important distinction between different varieties of these theories is the following. One could suppose that the man keeps a watch on the running average to decide whether or not there is a signal present, and when the evidence indicates that there is, discards all the input accumulated up to that time and starts a fresh sample to decide which alternative reaction to make. The other possibility is that the evidence accumulated over the last K instants is examined all the time to see which signal may be present, as well as whether there is no signal at all. The antithesis is rather like that we discovered in discussing theories of perceptual search, where we had to decide that either process could occur depending upon the details of the situation. From our present point of view, there are interesting differences in the predictions about reaction times to be obtained from these two modes of functioning.

The most obvious difference between the two is that a successive process, in which one first decides about the presence of a signal and then decides which signal, involves less random irrelevant input present in the sample that is being used to decide on the particular reaction to be made. This in turn means that the successive strategy implies all the predictions given earlier for theories in which sampling starts at the time when a signal is presented. That is, the time for a particular response when that response is a mistake should be the same as or longer than the time for the same response made correctly. If however the other theory is true, then the choice between alternative signals is made on the same evidence used to decide whether a signal is present or not. The decision to make a particular reaction will then include some random input occurring before the start of the signal itself. Laming (1968) points out that under these conditions the theory no longer predicts that an error reaction takes the same time as the same response made correctly. On the contrary, error reactions will be faster than correct ones, because they will include some made on the basis of the irrelevant non-signal input included in the sample purely because of temporal uncertainty.

There is therefore an escape from the problem of fast error responses: we may ascribe them to the operation of temporal uncertainty. This escape does rest however on the assumption that the process of choosing an action goes on continuously and is not started only when evidence is received that a signal is present. In support of this assumption, Laming cites two pieces of evidence. The first is that one of his experiments varied the interval between each of the subject's responses and the onset of the next signal. A longer interval would presumably induce greater temporal uncertainty. With a very short interval, there would be hardly any such uncertainty. Correspondingly, the difference between error and correct responses was greatly reduced when the uncertainty was reduced. The second piece of evidence is that, in Laming's experiment, the variance of choice reactions is no larger than that of simple reactions: although, if the process of choice was an extra one superimposed on detection of the presence of a signal, one might expect an increase in variance due to the variability of this extra process. These lines of argument certainly make the theory plausible, although perhaps not completely entailing its truth. We can also recall the evidence given earlier that time uncertainty affects the process of choosing between reactions and is not simply an extra delay imposed before the choice process begins.

It is worth noting that the speeding up of error responses compared with correct ones could be predicted, not only from an effect of time uncertainty, but also from any process which caused random variation from trial to trial in the positions of the criteria of the random walk model. For example, consider the possibility that a subject is less worried about errors at one part of the experiment than at another. At the first part, he will set his criteria to give decisions at lower values of evidence, so that a faster reaction will result with a higher proportion of errors. When he is more cautious, he will require more evidence for an action, and so gets slower reactions with a lower proportion of errors. The overall average reaction time for error responses will then be faster than that for corrects, even although in each phase alone the errors take the same time as the corresponding corrects. A higher proportion of the error responses however will come from the faster distribution.

In fact Laming presents evidence that the speed of response is correlated with the speed of responses closely adjacent in time to the one considered, so it is certain that subjects are changing their criteria from one part of an experiment to another. This alone would therefore result in speeding up of error responses. Another mechanism pointing in the same direction would be any preference for a given reaction when that reaction had just occurred, that is a systematic movement of criteria depending on the immediate past history. This again would act overall like a random changing of criteria, and give faster error responses than correct responses. We shall be considering shortly the fact that such tendencies do occur within the sequence of reactions. Thus there is no need to assume Laming's theory of temporal uncertainty in order to explain the differences between error and correct response times: but his experiment showing that this difference changes with degree of temporal uncertainty is still some support for his way of considering the problem.

THE EFFECT OF REPETITION OF RESPONSES

If we wish to lower the average amount of information in a sequence of, say, two signals, we can do so by arranging that the probability of a signal B (and therefore also a signal A) is different following A and following B. For example, we can arrange a sequence of signals in which both signals occur equally often, but in which the occurrence of A makes it four times as likely that A will be the next signal as that B will be: whereas when B occurs the reverse is the case. We would naturally expect that under these circumstances reaction time will be faster over the sequence as a whole, and this is indeed usually true. On the other hand, we can arrange exactly the same reduction of information per signal, by having a sequence in which, following A, B is four times as likely as A, and following B the reverse is the case. The difference between the two situations is simply that in one case we have increased the proportion of repetitions and in the other the proportion of alternations. It has been shown by Bertelson in a series of papers that repetition tends to give faster performance than alternation. The basic effect was published by Bertelson (1961), and it is also shown (Bertelson, 1963) that the size of the effect depends upon the amount of S-R compatibility. An incompatible response shows a larger effect, by a greater slowing on alternations. The size of the effect depends upon the interval between each response and the next signal (Bertelson and Renkin, 1966). When there is a largish interval, the effect is not noticeable. The effect appears even in a categorization task, where two signals each produce the same response, if one compares repetition of the same signal or use of a different signal when the response remains the same: although there is also some effect from repetition versus alternation of the response as such.

One must conclude from this group of studies that the effect of repetition is not solely one on the detection of signals (especially because of the compatibility effect) but nevertheless there is some tendency to be more ready to detect the same signal when it is repeated. Shaffer (1965, 1966, 1967) used tasks in which there were two signals, one of which indicated the appropriate coding of responses to be used for the other. In this case it is possible to have the same final response resulting from a different stimulus and a different coding, or from the same stimulus and the same coding: or of course to have a different response from the same stimulus and a different coding, and so on. The broad conclusion was that a repetition effect did occur both for repetition of the same coding and for repetition of the same response within that coding. On the whole a change in the meaning to be attached to the stimulus was more disruptive than a change in the stimulus itself: but there were a number of variations in the pattern of results depending upon the arrangement of them as a set of discrete reactions, as a continuous reaction task, with the coding changed randomly from stimulus to stimulus as opposed to being delivered in blocks of the same type, and so on.

One interpretation of this result would be to maintain a statistical theory but to argue that the criterion for a particular response is moved so as to increase the probability of that response immediately after such an action has been demanded. Suppose we adopt, as we have been doing, the approach that criteria for decision depend upon the probability that a response will be required. This approach implies that there must be a mechanism for shifting the criteria to fit in with the statistical structure of the outside world. It is not implausible therefore that every occurrence of a response should create a bias in favour of that particular action. If this were the case, then the effect of a time delay before the next signal came in would simply be to allow the *status quo* to re-establish itself: in assessing probability for the setting of criteria, the most recent events have a disproportionate weight which gradually disappears with the passage of time. A rather interesting though speculative variation on this theme would be that the decision process was *not* reset to zero every time a decision was reached, but that there was a continuous moving average of the input information so that the effect of one signal had to be washed out of the system before the mechanism could have an even chance at a new signal.

It is fair to notice that Bertelson and his colleagues have introduced a rather different line of attack which concentrates rather on the need for preparation of a response before the mechanism of choice can operate. That is, there are processes going on before the arrival of a signal which must be completed before the signal itself is analysed. When one signal follows hard upon another response, that same response is already prepared but the alternative one is not: the passage of time allows the alternative also to be prepared. The concept of preparation is an important minor theme in work on reaction time: most authors have probably ignored it too easily, because it complicates theorizing, but it may well be that some mechanism of this type needs to be introduced.

Finally, one should notice that the repetition effect itself creates the possibility of an artifact in most of the findings about reaction time and stimulus information. If for instance one has a number of equally probable alternative reactions, then as the number of alternatives increases the chances of two successive repetitions of the same response fall. This factor undoubtedly contaminates most experiments on the subject, and especially those done before Bertelson announced his findings. It does not account for the full effect: Kornblum (1967) varied the number of repetitions and the number of alternatives, and found that the reaction time for an alternation remained reasonably constant for the same number of alternatives as the probability of alternations was changed, but changed steeply when the number of responses used in the experiment was changed. Thus the effect of changes in stimulus information produced by changes in the number of alternatives still seems reasonably sound. We may have some doubts however about the effects of changes in the structure in the sequence of signals, maintaining the number of alternatives constant.

Last of all, it will be noted that this mechanism, which is well established, is one of those which would tend to give error reactions faster than correct reactions and thus allow us to continue to believe a random walk theory.

TIME TAKEN TO CORRECT ERRORS

There are two further points concerning errors which must be mentioned because of their impact on the theories we have already discussed. First, all the models we have considered seem to imply that the decision to launch a response is taken on a certain amount of received evidence, and that there is no way in which the man performing the action can tell whether that evidence has in fact resulted from a correct or from an incorrect signal. Yet in practice subjects are immediately aware of the vast majority of occasions when they have made an error (Rabbitt, 1966b). This is so even though the equipment gives no indication whatever to the man that his response was wrong, and immediately withdraws the stimulus to which he was reacting. Some provision therefore has to be made in the mechanism for a further process in addition simply to that which leads up to the action itself.

The second fact which needs emphasis is that we can measure the time taken to detect an error, by asking the subject to make some extra response if he does so: or we can get the subject to correct any error he makes immediately. In either case the interval between the error response and the appearance of the detection or correction response is shorter than the average of correct reaction times (Rabbitt, 1966c). We cannot suppose therefore that the subject is simply going through the entire process of deciding on a reaction all over again after he has made the error response. Rabbitt (1967b) distinguishes a number of possibilities, which we can group into three broad classes: (1) that a complete second decision process goes on but partially overlaps with the original process, (2) that the action finally chosen is fed back to an earlier stage in the system and compared with the input at that stage, thus detecting errors appearing in late stages in the system, (3) that some part of the original decision process continues on past the point where action is launched, and may result in an outcome at variance with the one which was chosen. (Rabbitt actually considers the special case of two decision processes operating independently and parallel, but there are other mechanisms of simpler type which might fall in this class. For example, on a theory of random walk the evidence might pass a critical value and then if allowed to accumulate further repass it in the opposite direction and exceed some other criterion with a higher degree of confidence.)

Some attempt at distinguishing these hypotheses can be made by changing the task so as to change the basic reaction time. If the original reaction is a difficult and slow one, obviously any complete repetition of the process will also be difficult and slow. A matching of the action chosen against some earlier part of the process would only take longer if the source of the difficulty was at the response end of the system and not if it was at the input end. It is a little hard to know what prediction to make from the theory of a continuing process: crudely one might suppose that if the source of difficulty was in the early stages of the process then the extra time needed to get a correct decision after an error would not alter, but this is by no means a rigorous deduction.

In fact, the evidence available at present (Rabbitt, 1967b; Rabbitt and Phillips, 1967) shows no change in the time taken to detect errors when the original response is made more difficult by changing the compatibility, the number of alternatives, or the number of stimuli appropriate to each response. At least this is true at high levels of practice, although relatively untrained subjects may take longer to detect errors when the task itself is more difficult.

It is worth noting at this stage that, at the time of writing, Rabbitt's published evidence on the effect of task difficulty concerns only the time taken to *detect* errors, and only in a two-choice task is there evidence concerning the time to *correct* them. This point may be of no ultimate importance; but we shall see when discussing the psychological refractory period that there is a curious discrepancy between Rabbitt's findings and those on refractoriness. In the latter case, difficult reactions produce an interference with other reactions demanded immediately after them, whereas easy reactions do not. It will be tempting to regard this extra delay as due to the same mechanism as that which detects and corrects errors, and if so it is odd that it is affected by task difficulty in refractoriness and not in error correction. The subjects in experiments on the psychological refractory period are probably at Rabbitt's earlier stage of practice, however, so that the discrepancy may be more apparent than real.

From the lack of effect of task difficulty on error detection time, we can rule out the theory that errors are detected by a repetition of the original process, even one starting before the error has occurred. We cannot distinguish so readily between the other two theories, except that perhaps the theory of a comparison between the feedback of action at an earlier stage in the process is slightly less likely than the theory of a continuing process.

From our survey of the speed of error responses and of correction of errors and of the effects of time uncertainty, and repetition of responses, we seem to have reached the following point.

(*a*) It is not possible to hold a theory of reaction time based on a mechanism of zero memory for past evidence. That is, we cannot think of a reaction as based on a series of independent samples, with no action on those samples which provide insufficient evidence, and action ultimately on the first sample which does provide such evidence.

(*b*) A process which starts at some arbitrary point in time and then possesses perfect memory for all evidence received after that time is consistent with the data. One must however incorporate the effect of uncertainty about the time of arrival of a signal, not by supposing that a decision is taken first that a signal is present, followed by a decision about which signal it is; but rather by supposing that the various alternative signals are all considered in parallel with the possibility of no signal.

(c) One must also suppose that the criteria for decision between the different alternatives vary from time to time and in a fashion dependent upon the detailed structure of the sequence of signals: and that following each reaction there is either a continuation of the process or a feedback of the action for comparison with an earlier stage to allow the detection of errors. With these modifications we can handle the fact that error responses are usually faster than correct ones.

(d) A model in which the evidence used for decision is a running average of the input over some past time, maintained continuously, is also reasonably tenable. The same points about structure of the sequence and about error correction apply as to the model with a fixed starting point: the main difference is perhaps that this theory does not require a series of "no signal" decisions.

We have therefore reached an understanding at least of the general type of process which is going on in a choice reaction time. The point which we have not considered however is the extent to which one such process is incompatible with another. The approach of information theory, regarding the mechanism as a single communication channel, naturally implied that the simultaneous performance of two reactions was bound to slow up each. By changing our model to a statistical and indeterminate one, we have lost the automatic prediction that one reaction will interfere with another, although the parallel with the data on selective perception would suggest that it is most likely to do so. It is now time to turn to an important sub-group of experiments aimed specifically at this point.

The Psychological Refractory Period

THE POSITION IN 1958

The basic effect to be considered in this section is that one may present in rapid succession the signals for two reactions. When this is done, the second reaction tends to be delayed. There is an important class of exceptions to this rule, when the first reaction instead is slowed down, and both reactions occur together. This type of behaviour is known as "grouping" and is of considerable interest in itself although it has been rather little studied. Researches have tended to concentrate rather upon the case in which the first reaction is normal or fairly so, and the second reaction is then slow.

The dominant theory in the 1950's, which as we shall see still seems the best, is that of *limited capacity* and was put forward by Welford (1952). Reviewing the data available at the time, he suggested that the phenomenon could best be understood by supposing that the process of decision for the first reaction occupied the same mechanisms as that needed by the second reaction, and therefore that the second could not start until the first was over.

Since there were some cases in which delays occurred with the second stimulus arriving even after the end of the first reaction, Welford suggested that feedback about the first response also occupied the decision mechanisms, holding up the processing of the second stimulus even longer. He also suggested that the second stimulus might possibly get priority over the analysis of the feedback information, if it happened to arrive just at the opportune moment before the feedback information had started to come in, and Welford was able to point to some features of the literature which supported such an effect. Since Welford first published his theory, Davis (1956) has shown that very highly practised subjects would show delay only with the second stimulus arriving during the first reaction, and not after it, but this is quite consistent with Welford's view if one supposes, as he did, that the analysis of feedback is only important to unpractised subjects.

Broadbent (1958) listed four other theories of the effect, of varying merit. One need not detain us here: it is the view that, in a continuous performance, *output is deliberately withheld* at intervals so that the system can observe the changes of the environment independent of any action of its own. This may conceivably be a strategy adopted by subjects in, for example, the following of rapidly moving targets with a "compensatory" display, where one's own action is liable to blur the movement of the target. Most of the work since 1958 has been done with situations in which such a strategy would not be useful, however, and this approach has not been used by the numerous workers whose results we shall have to consider.

A third possible theory is still a very definite contender, but remains as it was in 1958, somewhat *ad hoc*. This is the view that the mechanism responsible for taking the first decision becomes inoperative for a brief period after it has completed the decision process. Such a *period of inaction* would of course explain easily those cases in which there is delay to a second stimulus arriving shortly after completion of the first response. This however is not the only result which makes this view attractive: the fact that delay occurs with stimuli arriving shortly before the first response is in fact a difficulty for Welford's theory. That theory, ascribing the phenomenon to limited capacity, would surely suggest that only the decision mechanisms are occupied by the first reaction, and only those mechanisms are unable to handle anything further while coping with the first reaction. The sensory nerves and the motor nerves could, as far as we can see, work quite satisfactorily while other processes were going on. Thus there would seem no reason why the conduction of a second stimulus from the sense organs to the brain should not be proceeding, while at the same time the conduction of a motor command for the first reaction from the brain to the muscles was also being carried out. These two processes together occupy quite an appreciable time, and yet there is delay to the second stimulus, even in Davis's experiment, if it arrives before the first response is completed. There is therefore some time left over, within

L

the first reaction time, which can hardly be explained by supposing that the decision mechanism is occupied elsewhere.

Davis (1957) made this difficulty yet more acute by pairing an auditory first signal with a visual second signal, and showing that delay to the second reaction occurred with the same value of inter-stimulus interval as when both stimuli were visual. Because of the faster conduction time in auditory reactions, the first reaction was faster in that case, and one would suppose therefore on Welford's view that delay to the second reaction would occur only at smaller values of inter-stimulus interval. These types of phenomenon are readily explained by a period of inactivity of the central mechanism, and it is only obscure why such inactivity should occur.

The next theory which should be considered is that of *expectancy*. This theory was not favoured by Broadbent (1958) but it could not be ruled out at that time, and other authors have continued to support it since. The doctrine is in general that reaction time at a particular instant is known to be affected by the probability of a signal at that instant, and that when one has an experiment in which there is a sequence "warning signal—first reaction signal—second reaction signal" with a variable interval between the first and second reaction signals, then the probability of a second signal is low immediately after the first signal and rises as the time interval increases. Thus subjects are bound to show slow reaction for short values of inter-signal interval, and a faster reaction at larger values. The tenability of this theory has been due to the universal use, up to 1958, of simple reactions rather than choice reactions in experiments on the refractory period. In a task of simple reaction time, the analysis of incoming information from the environment need only occur if there is some uncertainty about the time of arrival of a stimulus. Indeed, if the time of arrival of a signal is exactly known, practised subjects will be able to eliminate reaction time altogether and make their responses synchronous with such an accurately predictable stimulus. Correspondingly, it was found by Adams and Chambers (1962) that an experiment using simple reaction times with a fixed time interval between first and second stimulus showed no delay in reaction to the second stimulus. This is indeed consistent with the idea that the normal delay is due solely to the low probability of signals at short intervals; but the absence of refractoriness is to be expected also on Welford's limited capacity theory. Where there is no analysis of incoming information, there need be no delay in reaction on that theory. Hence experiments with simple reaction time and a fixed interval between signals do not distinguish the theories; nor do experiments with a range of time intervals between signals. Thus expectancy theory was hard to disprove on the evidence available in 1958.

The last theory discussed by Broadbent (1958) was one of the *perceptual moment* type: the postulate was that the environment was sampled for a time which had a minimum duration, the decision was based on the contents of such a sample, and that after a sample was complete the information in it was discarded and a fresh sample formed. If two stimuli were both contained in the same sample, they would then produce grouped responses: if the first stimulus was within one sample, while the second lay in the next, the first might produce a reaction at the end of the sample in which it arrived, while the second would have to wait until the end of the next sample. The attraction of this idea was that the minimum length of the sample would not be connected with sensory or motor conduction times, and if it happened to be of the same length as the visual reaction time one might well therefore obtain the effect that a second stimulus was delayed if it arrived within one reaction time of a first: whether the first stimulus was visual or auditory. The delay could well be longer than the time taken by central decision processes, or indeed longer than the first reaction time itself if that were a fast auditory one. Hence this view was attractive, at that time, as providing an answer to some of the difficulties of Welford's theory.

THE ELIMINATION OF EXPECTANCY THEORY

Two lines of attack on expectancy theory have been pursued since 1958. First, even using simple reaction time it is possible to manipulate the range of time intervals so as to examine the question of expectancy directly. One line of attack is to allow the subject to press a button in order to start a time interval after which a reaction signal will appear. The time intervals can then be arranged in the same distribution as has been employed in a refractoriness experiment. This has been done by Davis (1965) and by Koster and Bekker (1967). In both cases there is no evidence for refractoriness, although the effect of expectancy on the efficiency of reaction to the signal should have been the same as that on the reaction to a second signal in a refractoriness experiment. Another line of attack, still using simple reaction time, is to alter the distribution of inter-signal intervals in a refractoriness experiment, so that the probability of a second signal at any instant remains constant as the interval increases. This means giving more signals at short intervals than long ones. Such an experiment has been performed by Nickerson (1967a), and yet refractoriness has been observed as usual.

The most effective onslaught on an expectancy interpretation of refractoriness comes however from the use of choice reaction times and a fixed interval between stimuli. The first studies of this kind (Borger, 1963; Sanders, 1963; Creamer, 1963) were bedevilled by individual differences, very long reaction times, or both: as we have already indicated, grouping of stimuli may occur with both responses emerging together, after a long delay before the first response. This strategy can be deliberately induced by instructions (Sanders, 1964) and appears spontaneously in some subjects. When a fixed interval is used between the first and second signals, as is possible with choice reactions, this strategy gives more trouble than in orthodox experiments on refractoriness. It was found by Broadbent and Gregory (1967b), however, that this behaviour could be controlled by giving the subjects knowledge of results about the length of their first reaction times but not about their second ones: they then produce first reactions of normal speed. Even so, Broadbent and Gregory were able to show convincingly that significant delay occurs to the second reaction. This has been confirmed by Bertelson (1967), who also compared the case of fixed inter-signal intervals with that of variable inter-signal intervals, and showed that the effect of the latter was relatively slight. There seems no question whatever therefore that the role of expectancy in explaining this particular effect is negligible. This is by no means to deny the importance of temporal uncertainty in affecting reaction time in general, which we have already seen in other applications. It does mean however that we need some other explanation for the psychological refractory period.

THE ASSAULT ON A THEORY OF PERCEPTUAL MOMENTS

Studies of choice reaction time also allow a check on the last of the hypotheses considered by Broadbent in 1958. That is, the theory that the delay is due to the basing of reaction upon a succession of separate samples of the environment. The attraction of this theory is that it allows one to explain why the delay to a second signal remains constant when reaction to the first signal is faster for sensory reasons. Suppose however that, using choice reactions, one were to introduce conditions which slow down the decision about the first reaction. If the delay to the second were due to the need to gather a new perceptual sample, and not to the time for which central mechanisms were occupied, then the delay to the second reaction should be the same whatever the length of time taken by the first reaction. If on the other hand Welford's theory were correct, then reaction to the second signal should be delayed for a longer time if the decision about the first signal is more complex. Broadbent and Gregory (1967b) tested these theories, first by varying the compatibility of motor reactions, and then by changing the relative frequency of one rather than the other of the two alternative signals used for the first reaction.* The second of these methods is perhaps more rigorous than the first, since it requires no change whatever in the second reaction, whereas the other technique required the second reaction as well as the first to be incompatible. Furthermore, when the probability of a signal was varied the subject could not decide in advance whether his first reaction was going to be long or short and consequently could not adopt some preliminary adjustment which might affect the second reaction time. Whichever method was used, however, slower first reactions gave longer delays in reaction to a second stimulus at a fixed inter-stimulus interval: and also gave significant delays at larger values of inter-stimulus interval. Thus there is no question that the

* See Fig. 27 on page 287.

prediction of the fixed sample theory was incorrect, and that from the original Welford theory was fulfilled.

We may add, as further elements in the destruction of the theory of fixed samples, the fact that the length of sample needed to explain the psychological refractory period would have to be greater than that most tenable as a duration for the perceptual moment, even supposing the latter to be a correct view. To explain refractoriness, the sample of incoming information would need to be something like a quarter or a third of a second, like a visual reaction time. In 1958, it was just plausible to argue that the sample might be as long as this, because of a result by Cherry and Taylor (1954), in which they interrupted speech by switching it on and off at a regular rate, and showed that the disruption of intelligibility was greatest when the switching rate was 3 Hz. This might conceivably be regarded as the rate which gave the greatest loss of information for any one of the perceptual samples. A slower interruption rate would allow some samples to be full even though others were empty, while a faster rate might allow each sample to contain more than one burst of speech and thus restore its adequacy. It has since been shown however by Huggins (1964) that the result found by Cherry and Taylor holds only for a given rate of speech: speeding up the speech speeds up the interruption rate which has the greatest effect upon intelligibility. Thus the rate must be connected with the size of important units in the incoming speech sounds, such as syllables, and is not related to a unit imposed by the listener. This removes the only positive evidence for suggesting that the sample was as long as a third of a second.

On the other hand, there is positive evidence for perception being based upon an extended temporal sample of the input. Yet this evidence comes from studies in which the appropriate time is much shorter than a third of a second. One can, for example, show that people may confuse the order of arrival of stimuli which are in fact successive: Broadbent and Ladefoged (1959) presented short sequences of tone and noise, and showed that untrained listeners could not tell the order in which the tone and noise occurred even though they could detect the presence or absence of either. But this held true only for times of the order of a tenth of a second. (Practised listeners could learn to distinguish the order at much shorter times, but this may be due to a different mechanism.) Again, if one presents a burst of noise followed by an artificial vowel sound, one will hear a consonant vowel sequence which depends not only on the frequency of the burst of noise, but also on the particular vowel which follows (Cooper *et al.*, 1952). This is because of the importance of transitions, which we mentioned in Chapter IV. But this is an effect extending again only over a time of the order of a tenth of a second rather than a longer period. Again, if one presents a succession of lines spaced out at regular intervals on a cathode ray tube, one can by adjusting the speed with which the lines follow one another reach a point at which several lines are seen simultaneously. By counting the lines present for a given speed, one can then measure the span of apparent simultaneity: and when this is done it turns out to be rather shorter than a tenth of a second, and certainly nothing like a third of a second (Allport, 1968).

One may add to these arguments the fact that the evidence for separate and independent samples of the environment is in any case now weak. We have already seen that a theory of this type predicts that reaction times will depend on the stimulus which is delivered and not upon the nature of the response, correct or incorrect, which is made to that stimulus. As we saw, the facts are that reaction time depends upon the nature of the response, so that a probable reaction occurs rapidly even when it is made to an improbable signal. It is hard to reconcile this with a theory of perceptual moments, although it would of course be quite consistent with a theory of running averages: we are pressed towards a moving window theory rather than a lavatory cistern theory.

Another line of evidence comes from the work of Allport mentioned above: suppose that one presents in rapid succession ten lines on a cathode ray tube, starting by showing a line at the bottom of the tube, then turning it off and showing one just above it, and so on till one reaches the tenth line and returns to the bottom line again. After adjusting the rate of presentation to the point where all the lines appear to be present simultaneously, one can then slow down the presentation slightly, and nine lines will be seen simultaneously, with one missing. The missing line will move gradually across the face of the screen. Now a theory of perceptual moment would predict that the missing line would move in the opposite direction to the order of objective presentation of lines. This can be seen by considering the case in which all lines but the top one fall within one perceptual sample. The next sample contains the top line, the bottom eight of the display and leaves out the second line from the top. The next sample contains the top two lines, the bottom seven, and leaves out the third line from the top. One would therefore expect the missing line to move downwards across the display. A moving window theory, on the other hand, predicts that the missing line will move in the same direction as the objective order of presentation. The missing line, on that theory, is always the one which occurred longer ago than time t, and this line moves upwards across the display.

In fact, subjects report seeing the missing line move in the direction of objective presentation, and in this situation therefore the apparent simultaneity is due to a moving window mechanism and not to perceptual moments. A similar set of predictions, and empirical conclusions, can be derived from the technique of leaving a gap between the presentation of the top line and the bottom one equal to the length of time occupied by presenting all the lines. The interval between presentation of the bottom line on the display and the top line on the display is then no longer equal to the interval between successive presentations of the bottom line on the display. The theory of perceptual moments would suggest that simultaneity should depend upon the first of these intervals, while a moving window theory would suggest that it should depend upon the second. In fact it depends upon the second, and again therefore a theory of perceptual moments is inadequate.

We must conclude that the perceptual moment, in the sense of a fixed sample of the environment independent of earlier or later samples, is no longer a tenable hypothesis in the areas we have been considering. Conceivably it may apply in other areas, but we have considered no data which cannot be better handled by a "moving window" (running average) theory. In particular, perceptual moments offer no competition to limited capacity in the explanation of refractoriness.

RESIDUAL DIFFICULTIES IN THE THEORY OF LIMITED CAPACITY

(a) *The problem of delay after the response.* Since the theories of expectancy and of perceptual moment have been put out of court, we are thrown back against the same difficulty in Welford's theory which provoked the suggestion of perceptual moments. That is, why does a second stimulus arriving after the end of the first reaction still get delayed? In the results of Broadbent and Gregory (1967b), it was especially interesting that an increase in the first reaction time produced an increased delay for second reactions which was actually larger than the difference in the first reaction. That is, when the first signal was probable rather than improbable the reaction time might differ by 75 msec or so: but the reaction time to a second stimulus closely subsequent to the first might differ by 150 msec or so. With the fast first reaction, there is no delay to a second stimulus provided that it occurred after the first response: whereas with a slow first reaction, there was a delay even to second stimuli arriving when the first response was over. We cannot therefore explain all the delay to the second reaction merely by preoccupation of the decision mechanism with the first reaction.

Welford's original explanation of such delays was that the subject was analysing feedback about his first response. In view of our previous discussion of the time taken to correct errors, some theory of this sort is quite attractive: particularly if we generalise it to include the possibility that the extra time is spent in some continuation of the original decision process, giving a more reliable conclusion, rather than necessarily in a comparison of the actual action with the intended action. There is the difficulty however that it is hard to see why this extra function, of the general nature of checking against error, should only apply to the slower of the two possible first reactions. In Welford's original theory, practised subjects ceased to check against errors, and hence showed no delay after the first reaction. This explanation is harder to adopt when fast and slow reactions are mixed indiscriminately within the same task. The suggestion put forward by Broadbent and Gregory was that the process of checking against errors was really present in all cases, whether the first reaction was slow or fast and whether the subjects were practised or not. With practised and fast first reactions, however, the process of checking was also itself fast: it still occurred, but it occupied only a time of the same extent as the sensory and motor conduction times. It could therefore act as an explanation for the fact, noted above, that Welford's theory really has some difficulty in accounting for delay lasting the whole of the first reaction time rather than simply that part of the process which is occupied in decision rather than peripheral nerve conduction. When the first reaction was slow and difficult, however, Broadbent and Gregory argued that the process of checking would also be slow and difficult and hence the delay to subsequent reactions would continue after the first reaction was over. The only independent evidence which they were able to produce for this suggestion was that, even with compatible first reactions giving no delay beyond the end of the reaction time itself, the occurrence of any error in the first reaction disrupted the second reaction considerably. Thus the subjects must still have been aware of their own errors, and one could not suppose that they had abandoned any checking mechanism.

There is a difficulty in this interpretation, in that we saw earlier that Rabbitt found the time taken to detect errors to be constant no matter what the difficulty of the first reaction. This difficulty may not be insuperable: it may be due to differences in level of practice, or to differences between the particular tasks used. If it can be overcome, then the mechanism of checking against errors provides a reasonable explanation for the delay of a second reaction beyond the end of the first reaction.

(b) *The possibility of splitting into two sub-channels.* Given that the ability of the decision process to handle more than one decision at once is limited, it does not follow that speed of response to one signal must depend upon the presence or absence of some other reaction. It would be quite possible for the decision mechanism to be capable of splitting into two parts, each operating independently but at a lower speed. In the analogy with a communication channel, the existence of a limit on capacity does not mean that messages must be dealt with one by one, but merely that any arrangement of the channel to handle parallel streams of messages will reduce the speed at which each can be processed. If we take the more up-to-date analogy of a computer, the available facilities for storage and other functions may either be devoted to one program or shared between several, and the possibility of sharing is perfectly consistent with the existence of a limit to the scope of the machine. It is still an open question whether such a process can take place in human beings: one might well imagine that particular tasks might be so arranged as to encourage the decision mechanism to adopt a strategy of operating as two independent systems of less power than the usual total system. There has been an attempt to find evidence for such a mechanism, in a group of studies by

Elithorn (Elithorn, 1961; Kerr *et al.*, 1963, 1965; Elithorn and Barnett, 1967). The main advance of technique in these papers is the consideration of individual pairs of reactions. Most other studies have considered only average reaction times, and it is quite clear on reflection that this is inadequate. When for example we said earlier that a second signal gave a slow reaction even when arriving after the first reaction was over, we would have been committing a fallacy had we based this statement solely on reactions arriving after the average first reaction time. Many of the first reactions will take longer than the average, and consequently when the second signal arrives there will be a proportion of trials on which the first reaction will still be in progress. In fact, Broadbent and Gregory considered individual cases rather than averages, so that the conclusions we have given earlier do stand. Nevertheless it is apparent that a general occurrence of delay might be consistent with some cases in which fast reactions occurred to both first and second signals. The papers by Elithorn which we have quoted do argue that a certain number of pairs of responses can be detected in which both the first and the second reactions are within the normal limits for isolated reaction times. The reactions were in this case made one with one hand and one with the other, thus perhaps encouraging the nervous system to operate as two separate hemispheres, and one might therefore cite these instances of paired fast reactions as evidence for some processing that was independent.

Unfortunately, the technique normally used in these studies has been a rather special one, which may not allow us to conclude that independent processing is occurring. The subject was faced with two possible signals, one for one hand and one for the other, and did not know which would be the first to occur. If however the first has occurred, then it becomes certain that the other stimulus will be the second one to arrive. Thus in one sense the first reaction time is a two-choice task, and the second is a simple reaction: provided that the subject has made use of the information that the first signal has arrived. Thus the occurrence of a fast second reaction may be evidence, not so much for independence of the two processes, but for the rapid use of information about the first signal as advance information concerning the second (Leonard, 1958). In the experiment by Broadbent and Gregory, this ambiguity does not occur since the appearance of the first signal gives no information whatever about the nature of the second. In their experiment a detailed analysis of the reactions to pairs of signals, not included in the published version of the paper, showed no evidence whatever for the occurrence of independent processing by Elithorn's criteria. One cannot therefore feel that there is any evidence for independent processing at present, although it may nevertheless be possible that some evidence for it may be produced in the future. A point which should not be neglected is that the existence of fast pairs of responses has been found by Elithorn's group to depend upon the personality of the experimental subject. This information may be of impor-

L*

tance whether the speed of the second reaction is due to dissociation of the two processes or rather to their effective integration.

(c) *Stimulus versus response factors in the interference.* A last point which needs clarification is the precise portion of the first reaction which interferes with the second reaction. Is it the arrival of the stimulus, the organization of the response, or some intervening stage? One can modify the ordinary experiment on refractoriness so as to shed some light on this point, for example by instructing the subject to ignore the first stimulus and react only to a second one. Some delay can be shown in reaction to the second stimulus under these conditions (Fraisse, 1957; Davis, 1959; Koster and Bekker, 1967; Nickerson, 1967b). The first signal can under some circumstances be without effect (Borger, 1963; Rubinstein, 1964): intuitively this seems reasonable enough, since in the last extreme one might imagine a situation where the first stimulus could be shut out by fixating the eyes in a suitable direction. The interesting thing is however that in some cases a stimulus which has no reaction required by the instructions may nevertheless sometimes give an interference.

Another way of modifying the experiment is to present one signal only but to ask for two responses, and this has been done by Sanders (1967a, b). Thus three lights might be used as stimuli, arranged in a column, and three buttons be given for response with the left hand while a second set of three buttons were provided for response with the right hand. The lighting of a lamp then called for an appropriate action with each hand. If one of the reactions was compatible with the stimulus, the top button of a column corresponding to the top light of a column, then there was no difference in the response time from having to do two responses at once. This was true even if one of the responses was an incompatible one. Suppose however that both responses were incompatible: for example, that a vertical column of light stimuli controlled a horizontal row of keys to be pressed with the left hand, and a vertical row of keys for the right hand in which the bottom key was controlled by the top light, and so on. In this case, the two responses each took longer when both had to be made than if one alone had to be made. As Sanders suggests, these results look as if the compatible reaction to a stimulus is an immediate and unavoidable stage, with a further translation process to produce the incompatible response. The two translation processes can interfere with one another, and clearly therefore the interference shown in experiments on refractoriness is not purely an interference between the detection of two stimuli.

It is worth noting also that the after effect of one reaction upon another depends upon the particular limbs concerned in the two reactions. This was pointed out by Fraisse (1957) and by Broadbent and Gregory (1967b): if one has to react with the index finger of the right hand, there is more delay on a closely subsequent reaction with the middle finger of the left hand than on one with the index finger of that hand also. Blyth (1963, 1964) tried various combinations of hand and foot reactions, and found that the second reaction was faster if one used the hand and foot on the same side, or the two hands, or the two feet, than if one had a reaction with one limb followed by a reaction with the other kind of limb on the other side of the body. This sort of effect continues to apply even when the first reaction has been over before the second stimulus arrives: Rabbitt (1966d) showed sequential effects in a serial task of the same kind as those found by Blyth.

In general therefore we have to admit that interference between two successive reactions can be shown to depend partly upon the stimuli used, partly upon the responses, and partly on the translation process between the two (because of the compatibility effects). The part of the reaction time which is taken up by a process of limited capacity is not simply a mechanism for detecting signals, nor one for executing responses: it is easiest and in line with our standard approach to think of it as the mechanism which selects one category state rather than another. Category states are not necessarily tied to overt actions, and may be brought into being by the occurrence of a stimulus which merely requires discrimination from the wanted signal: the first of two rapidly successive light flashes, as in the experiments of Davis. On the other hand, the category state is the point from which various overt actions are controlled, so that the nature of the muscular movement which is going to be required, or the compatibility between reaction and stimulus, could all affect the complexity of the process.

In summarizing the findings in this way, we are harking back to the discussion of categorizing which took place in the last chapter. We indicated there that the occurrence of one of four reactions would take much the same length of time whether each response were elicited by two or by four possible stimuli. The key factor was probably the number of the features of the stimulus which had to be detected to allow efficient reaction. Thus one cannot say that the time taken for a choice reaction is a function purely of that to identify a stimulus, nor to select the appropriate overt response, but rather of the time taken to identify enough features of the stimulus to bring about the appropriate category state.

We can add as supporting evidence at this stage the study by Bertelson and Tisseyre (1966) who carried out a two-choice reaction with two possible stimuli for each response. One of the four stimuli was frequent in the experiment, while the other three were of low and equal probability. There was no difference in the reaction time to the three rare stimuli, even though one of them was eliciting a more probable response than the other two. The common stimulus however gave a faster reaction time. As Bertelson and Tisseyre indicate, this result will depend upon the particular set of stimuli that is used: in this case, they were letters, which naturally possess well established category states. If as in certain earlier work some feature were in common to groups of stimuli, the results might well be different.

Another group of studies of similar import are those of Audley and Wallis (1964), Wallis and Audley (1964). These authors found that time taken to make a judgment about the relative brightness of two visual stimuli depended upon the instructions and the range of stimuli. If two rather intense stimuli are used, the response "brighter" is faster than that of "darker", while if two fairly dim stimuli are used the reverse is the case. It seems fair to suppose that in this particular situation relatively intense stimuli both elicit to some extent the category state of "bright" while relative weak stimuli do not do so to such an extent. The response which is overtly correct according to the experimental instructions is therefore being helped or hindered by an "implicit response" which cannot be directly observed, and which is best called by our name of category state.

The conclusion from these other studies, as well as from those on refractoriness, must therefore be that the reaction process is not a simple function of the overt stimuli or the overt responses: rather it is a matter of selection of one of many internal states, using evidence derived from a variety of features of the stimulus, the particular nature of the process depending exactly upon the task being demanded. The selection of the category state is an operation which loads the capacity of the system, and which therefore cannot be carried out as fast for two simultaneous processes as for one. This, as Welford suggested more than fifteen years ago, is undoubtedly the explanation of the delay to the second of closely successive reactions.

The Distribution of Response Times

In everything that has been said thus far, we have considered only the average reaction time obtained under one condition rather than another. This however has been an arbitrary limitation: given our conception of reaction time as spent in a gradual accumulation of evidence, one can easily see that a change in the average time might result from several different changes in the process, all quite distinct in their meaning. The time taken to react would vary from trial to trial, through the chance variations in the incoming evidence: but an increase in the average time might result from a constant extra time added to every trial, or perhaps from a rise in the minimum time to reach a decision with no change in the maximum time. Yet again, it might perhaps result from a constant minimum time with a rise in the maximum. Equally and especially alarmingly it might be that some changes in the process would leave the mean unaffected while changing the variability or some other feature of the process. Most of these possibilities have been ignored by experimentalists: but a good deal of theoretical study has been devoted by mathematical psychologists to considering possible distributions which might be obtained. The point has been well made by Taylor (1965) that there has been singularly little contact between theoreticians and experimentalists in this field.

One of the points most obvious about reaction time distributions is the fact that they are not of the usual Gaussian form. The model reaction time, the most obtained in a series of trials, is considerably nearer to the shortest value obtained than it is to the longest value obtained. Perhaps the most usual approach amongst theoreticians has therefore been to explore the possibilities of heavily asymmetrical distributions: we have already touched on one of the most common approaches, in our discussion of perceptual moments. If we think of a reaction as an event which has probability of occurrence p at any instant, then the probability of obtaining a reaction after a time $t+1$ is given by

$$P(t+1) = (1-p)^t. p .$$

The mean time which would be obtained from a distribution of this sort is $1/p$, and as will be recalled one has to conclude that this will be the same for any given signal whether the reaction is correct or not. For this reason we rejected earlier a simple zero-memory theory of reaction time. Let us, however, explore this model further.

The distribution of reaction times to be expected on this model would be heavily asymmetrical, with the most common value of reaction time being the shortest. It would also be discontinuous, that is there would be reactions only at certain possible times with none at all between them. However, it can be shown that the same equation can be approximated by a continuous distribution of the form

$$P(t+1) = \lambda \exp(-\lambda t)$$

where λ is a constant corresponding to p in the previous form. (See McGill, 1963 for a detailed exposition of this approach.) This will allow one to get a continuous distribution of reaction times, but on the same general assumption that one was waiting for some event whose probability was constant.

A particularly interesting property of this kind of process is that it can be easily extended to cover a series of events rather than one single one. Thus one can think of a process in which a certain time has to go by before event A occurs, that there is then a similar wait for a next event B, another wait for a third event C, and so on. This begins to sound less like a perceptual moment theory and more similar to our conception of a steady flow of evidence arriving to push the decision in one direction or another. Yet if we take the total time for the entire series of events, it can still be approximated by an equation of the type

$$P(t+1) = \lambda \exp(-\lambda t)$$

with a different value of λ.

This then allows an interesting way of analysing distributions of reaction times: for if the process is really of this type, then the probability that a reaction time will be greater than any given amount t is given by

$$P(RT>t) = \exp(-\lambda t)$$

and by taking logs we obtain

$$\log P(RT>t) = -\lambda t.$$

DECISION AND STRESS

From an experiment one can therefore plot a graph against time of the log of the proportion of reactions which take longer than that time. The resulting graph should be a straight line with a slope of $-\lambda$. In fact the results of experiments plotted in this way do look reasonably straight, although with some discrepancy at the end corresponding to shortest reaction times. The most common reaction time is usually not the shortest, and there are a few reactions still shorter, which makes the graph bend to a flatter shape at the end corresponding to short reaction times. With this exception, the relationship is reasonably good.

We now have a way of distinguishing some of the possibilities mentioned at the beginning of this section. If the average reaction time were changing without any change in the shortest possible time, then the graph just discussed should give a straight line with different slope but with the same value of t at the point where all reactions are faster than t. This would correspond to a change in λ, and this might indeed be the most plausible way in which any condition might affect such a mechanism. If on the other hand a constant time were being added to all decisions, then the slope of the graph would remain constant but the value of the fastest possible reaction would change. It would also be possible to get both effects, if the shortest reaction were increasing without any change in the longest possible time.

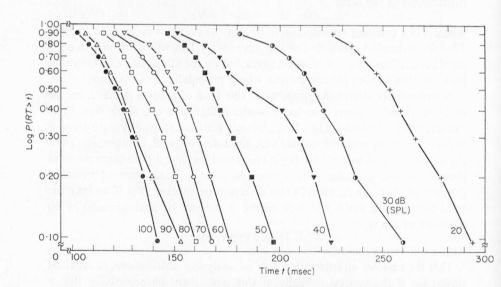

FIG. 28. Reaction time to sounds of various intensities, plotted as a cumulative distribution on a scale which should give a straight line if the distribution is exponential. Notice that, broadly speaking, changes in intensity alter the starting point of the distribution, but not its slope. This suggests that stimulus intensity affects some process other than the supposed exponential one. Data from McGill (1963).

At this stage we encounter the irritating lack of contact between experimentalists and theoreticians. McGill has provided some data on simple reaction times to sounds of different intensity (conveniently available in McGill, 1963). In general, it has long been known that weak sounds give slow reactions. McGill's results show that the change in average reaction time does not affect the value of λ but rather is of the kind one would expect from addition of a constant extra time to all reactions. He rightly points out therefore that one cannot regard reaction times as explained by a single mechanism of the type we have discussed, in which λ might be changed by various conditions: and the analysis in these terms by Restle (1961) needs some supplementation to be an adequate account of the facts.

Once, however, we allow more than one process, there are considerable difficulties in analysing data. It would be fair to suppose that the second process, the one responsible for the effects of signal intensity in McGill's results, does not really produce a fixed constant delay to reaction but rather one which varies in some way. This is not only reasonable *a priori*, but also allows one to explain why the fastest reaction time is not also the commonest: the variation in the second, different, process may well be of Gaussian type. If so, then we would have to suppose that amongst those reactions which took the shortest time on the exponential process described by

$$P(t+1) = \lambda \exp(-\lambda t),$$

a minority would take an exceptionally short time on the second Gaussian process. Thus they would take a time shorter than would be predicted from the exponential process, and cause the departure from linearity at short times.

If, however, we are dealing with a combination of an exponential and a Gaussian process, analysis of the results becomes difficult. A rare attempt to analyse distributions in this way has been made by Hohle (1965), who reports results of experiments on temporal uncertainty and cites earlier findings of his own on the effect of stimulus intensity in a visual reaction. Unhappily, his results appear flatly contradictory to those of McGill: he finds that signal intensity alters the exponential part of the process while time uncertainty alters the normal part. As we have seen, McGill found that signal intensity left the exponential part unaffected and altered the part which was added to it. At present there is no way of telling whether this discrepancy is due to the particular experimental techniques employed, to the difference in methods of analysis, or conceivably to some basic difference between vision and audition.

Whatever the resolution of this uncertainty, it seems quite clear that reaction must be made up of different processes with different distributions, so that the final distribution of reaction times is really a convolution of these underlying elements. The various papers we have reviewed earlier in the chapter make no attempt to distinguish one from another, and this is bound to leave us in a position of some uncertainty about the proper handling of reaction time.

Matters would be even worse if we start to consider (as is indeed likely to be necessary) complications such as the introduction of a γ distribution or general γ distribution rather than a simple exponential: one may consult Laming (1968) for a general account of such complications, or Christie and Luce (1956); Restle (1961); McGill (1963); McGill and Gibbon (1965) for more detailed discussions. There seem, however, to be so many theoretical possibilities that some experimentation to narrow down the possibilities is badly needed. Unfortunately, as we have already said, the theoreticians have conducted few experiments; while the experimenters have remained content with simple averages, which are incapable of distinguishing the interesting classes of theories. There is a moral here for the progress of research.

Pending the collection of experimental data in such a way as to distinguish interesting classes of theory, we may draw attention to one possibility. At various points in this chapter we have discussed the possibility that a choice reaction with time uncertainty is to be represented by a decision process in which "no signal" is one of the alternatives considered. The evidence accumulates until there is sufficient to decide which alternative is present, or that none is present at all: and after this stage is reached the entire procedure starts again. If the probability of a decision of "no signal" is $1-P$, then an experiment will include a proportion of P reaction times which are obtained on the first decision after the onset of a signal, $P(1-P)$ which result from one decision of "no signal" followed by a subsequent decision of "signal", $P(1-P)^2$ following two decisions of "no signal", and so on. The total distribution would then consist of several subsidiary distributions, each having the shape produced by the original decision process, but each centred on different times. The distribution centred on the shortest time would contain the larger number of responses, and there would be a gradually decreasing tail of responses going out to long reaction times. Such a distribution would possess a broadly exponential property, while nevertheless allowing differences in response time for different responses even made to the same signal, because of the underlying decision process. The important point to notice, because of its connection with later data, is that any change in the criterion for "no signal" would produce a change in the tail of the distribution rather than in the mode: it would change the number of very slow responses rather than the fastest or more common response times.

The truth or falsehood of such a possibility, and of the other classes of theory, must await the provision of further evidence.

Conclusions About Reaction Time

This survey of the speed with which different actions can be chosen leaves us with less definite conclusions than we have been able to reach in previous chapters. There are however a few clear gains, which are worth restating.

First, there seems adequate evidence in this aspect of performance also that the underlying mechanism is one of unreliable transmission of evidence about the nature of the outside world. We cannot maintain the view of the 1950's that changes in reaction time are due to differences in the length of code necessary to get perfect transmission of information. Rather it seems more appropriate to think of the latency of the reaction as the time necessary for unreliable evidence to accumulate to a point where error falls to an acceptably low value. The recent concentration on the probability of error, the time taken to make errors when they occur, and the relation between this time and the time to make correct responses, are all symptomatic of the shift of theorizing towards a probabilistic system rather than a determinate one. There is no reason in reaction time to find our general approach unsatisfactory.

Second, the probability of a stimulus has an important effect upon reaction time just as it does on other aspects of behaviour. Whether one uses a small set of probable alternatives, or increases the probability of one signal rather than another, or whether one looks at the microstructure of a sequence of signals, the probable signal gets the more efficient reaction in terms of speed as well as of accuracy.

Third, we can ask our usual question, whether this distinction is due to filtering or to pigeon-holing: is it because of a better intake of information concerning probable signals, or because of a setting of the criteria for response so as to favour those alternatives? Because of the gaps in knowledge about reaction time, we cannot rule out the possibility of filtering. There is no doubt however that, within the framework of this approach to reaction time, probability does affect criterion placement. That is, pigeon-holing is certainly operative, whether or not filtering is also occurring. This is shown by the tendency to make as errors those responses which occur most rapidly.

Lastly, we have seen that general characteristics of the process may well affect speed and accuracy of decision. If the criteria for decision are set to lower levels of evidence, faster performance will be obtained at the cost of accuracy. If the criterion of "no signal" is set to require less evidence, there will be an increase in the number of occasions when several successive decisions have to be made before a reaction occurs: and thus there will be an increase in the tail of the distribution of reaction times. Both speed and accuracy will be sensitive to general changes of criterion placement.

CHAPTER VIII

Primary Memory

All processes we have considered thus far in this book have extended only over very short time intervals. In a vigilance task or an experiment on divided attention, whether or not one detects a signal is a matter decided during a second or so after the delivery of a stimulus: so is the efficiency of one's reaction to an improbable signal, or the speed with which one decides between one alternative and another in a choice reaction experiment. In some cases we have had to suppose that there are processes which might be called "memory", especially in the case of successive response to two simultaneous stimuli, or in the case of delayed response to the second of two closely successive stimuli. We have had, that is, to suppose a kind of buffer storage between the sense organs and the limited capacity system: to use the old terms, an S system and a P system. To use a more current language, there must be a stage of simultaneous processing followed by one of serial processing.

But very short storage of this kind is manifestly inadequate to deal even with some of the situations we have been describing. When a man is presented with a dichotic memory span, there must be a delay before he writes down the various items he has heard. This delay may in fact be considerably longer than the critical time intervals we have been able to infer. Indeed it is obvious to common experience that one can give a man a telephone number and ask him to repeat it: and that, so long as he is left undisturbed during the time interval before he repeats it, it makes little difference whether that time interval is half a second or thirty seconds. We must therefore give some account of the way in which information is held over periods of a minute or so rather than a fraction of a second. The title of this chapter is intended merely to indicate this area of interest.

The Position in 1958

Broadbent (1958) followed a suggestion put forward by Brown (1955; some of the work contained in that thesis was published by Brown, 1954, 1958).

The suggestion was that memory for periods greater than a few seconds could be handled by a combination of the limited capacity system and the preceding buffer storage, even though the latter alone could last only a very short time. If a series of items were fed from the buffer through the limited capacity system, and if the latter then delivered the information back to the buffer storage, a limited number of items could be kept in circulation indefinitely. Each item need only stay in the buffer storage long enough for all the other items to be passed through the limited capacity system, and each in turn could then be extracted from the buffer and fed back into it. In introspective terms, this might correspond to "saying a telephone number over to oneself" when one has heard it. The limitation on such a process is that the preservation of the information depends in part upon the same limited capacity system as is used in perception. Thus if any fresh action is required, the recirculation (rehearsal) of the items in memory must be interrupted to deal with the fresh incoming signal: or if the memory is preserved, the external signal must be ignored. In the everyday example, a telephone number can be remembered indefinitely by saying it over to oneself, but if somebody asks one a question during this time one must either ignore the question or else forget the number. Thus memory working on this basis would be very vulnerable to any intruding activity carried out during the retention period. Gradually there would be a transfer of information from this recirculatory type of storage to a more permanent long-term store: and when this process had been completed the perceptual system could be diverted on to other tasks without loss of the long-term memory. During the rehearsal period, however, the man would be unable to cope with other tasks.

The evidence for this theory was almost entirely confined to the group of experiments performed by Brown himself. He showed that the recall of a list of items, presented once only, could indeed be severely impaired by requiring subjects to react appropriately to some other stimulus during a retention period. The amount of interference depended upon the amount to be held in memory and on the number of interpolated stimuli: if there were few items to be recalled, many interpolated stimuli could be handled before interference appeared, and vice versa. Over the range he studied, it made no difference whether the interpolated activity occurred early in retention or late; and there was little effect of the degree of similarity between the interpolated stimuli and the ones which were to be remembered. Lastly, he showed that the recall of one set of items impaired the subsequent recall of other items which were still being held in memory: this confirmed a finding by Kay and Poulton (1951).

All these findings were consistent with the theory of "rehearsal and fading trace", or "recirculation from buffer store to limited capacity system back to buffer store". The findings were not particularly consistent with most other theories of learning at that time, which had primarily been devised to deal with long-term memory and had not been elaborated to consider the problem of primary memory. Furthermore, the existence of a buffer store and the limited capacity channel seemed well established even by 1958, and for reasons of parsimony therefore it seemed appropriate to Broadbent to explain primary memory by those mechanisms only. Even then, however, it remained open whether information which had passed through the limited capacity system was fed to the same buffer store as that receiving the original intake of information: or whether possibly it was fed to another rapidly decaying store elsewhere. Again parsimony seemed to suggest the former.

In the context of the time, there was one apparent difficulty in such a theory, namely that the speed with which each item could be recirculated through such a system ought to depend upon the amount of information per item. As the P system could deal faster with an item of low information content than with one of high information content, it should in a fixed period of time be able to recirculate more items when each of them conveyed less information. Suppose for example one conducted an experiment on the largest number of items which could be recalled following a single presentation, and compared two vocabularies of items differing in size. If the smaller vocabulary was of such a size that each item conveyed half as much information as an item from the larger vocabulary, then the person memorizing should be able to remember twice as many items from the small vocabulary as the large one. Yet in fact this is not true: it is rather more true that a constant number of items can be recalled regardless of the vocabulary from which they are drawn (Miller, 1956). Even this is not strictly true, since items such as letters drawn from a large vocabulary tend to be worse remembered than items from a small vocabulary, but as we shall see, there may be reasons for this other than the information per item. Broadbent (1958) had therefore to consider this difficulty, but was able to claim that there were various possible ways of escaping it. One might suppose that the time for which the buffer would hold an item varied with its information content: or one might adopt a suggestion by Brown that the information contained in the order of items was lost more readily than information on their nature. Although it was unclear which possible explanation should be adopted, the difficulty could certainly be evaded in one way or another, and the theory could therefore be maintained.

Basic Advances Since 1958

In the intervening period, an enormous number of publications have appeared on the subject of primary memory. It is probably easiest to see the main lines of development by following the theoretical arguments which have given rise to the work. Before we do this, however, it will clarify issues to set out certain points on which everybody is agreed, leaving the areas of disagreement to stand out by contrast. There are three of these areas relatively free of controversy, which we shall consider in this section: they concern the techniques available to study primary memory, the acceptance of the buffer store and the categorising system, and the acceptance of a considerable degree of transfer to long-term memory even in one presentation.

TECHNIQUES OF EXPERIMENTATION

(a) *The use of unpredictable tasks during retention.* This technique is included here only for completeness as we have already stated it. It is in fact the one used by Brown. Between the presentation of material and its recall one may require a subject to perform some task such as looking at digits and deciding whether they are odd or even, or copying down a series of arrows each of which points in a different direction. Such a task requires transmission of information through the man, but does not involve any learning. As Brown found, it will nevertheless produce very rapid forgetting of items which have been presented immediately previously.

(b) *Predictable activities during retention.* The main technique to mention

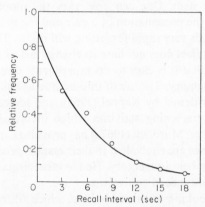

FIG. 29. Recall of items retained for various times filled by irrelevant activity, from the data of Peterson and Peterson (1959).

here is that of Peterson and Peterson (1959). They presented the material to be remembered, and then asked subjects to count backwards by threes during the retention interval, starting with a high number. Again this method will show very rapid forgetting of the item presented before the counting begins, and from some points of view it may seem unnecessary to distinguish the method from that of Brown. However, it is of some theoretical interest that forgetting can occur even through an activity which involves no outside stimulus to elicit each response. A particularly striking case is that of Conrad (1958), who showed that the accuracy of recall of a telephone number was impaired by requiring a subject to give the digit zero before each response, as people do in the British telephone system when dialling long distance.

(c) *Use of other learning during retention.* In the methods so far mentioned, presentation of an item for later recall is followed by activities that have nothing to do with learning. This was the feature of these methods which made them most strikingly different from older work on long-term memory. Classic studies of learning had shown many times that forgetting might occur through the learning of other material before or after the items being tested on a particular occasion. It was interference from activities other than learning which made short-term memory seem unusual: but it is perfectly possible to apply in short-term memory the same techniques as in long-term, by presenting a number of items before or after the one of interest, and seeing how they affect memory on that particular item. A clear concrete example is provided by the technique of Murdock (1963). This method consists of a presentation of a series of pairs of items, in each of which the second of the pair is to be 'earned as a response to the occurrence of the first item of the pair. At an unpredictable point in the sequence, one of the stimulus items which has already occurred is presented, and the subject is required to recall the corresponding response item. One can now vary the number of other items intervening between the presentation of a pair and the first recall, and just as with the other methods very rapid forgetting will occur. The attraction of the method is that the subject does not have to change tasks in a rapid and rather confusing way, and that it is easy to do experiments directly comparable to those in long-term memory. The use of this method as equivalent to the other methods has been criticised by Keppel (1965), and logically there is a clear difference between intervening activities which involve learning and those which do not. However, Murdock (1967a) has provided experimental evidence that the two techniques are equivalent in their results, provided that the same total amount is being held in memory. He therefore argues convincingly that the two techniques are indeed equivalent.

Another way of looking at this technique, which Murdock brings out, is that one is inserting a "probe" into the subject to obtain recall of part of the material in memory: whereas in the other techniques one is merely distracting the subject before recall. Selective probing of memory allows us both to demonstrate and to eliminate a fact mentioned above as implicit in the results of Brown and of Kay and Poulton. This fact is that recall of one item from memory produces a deterioration in the recall of any other items that are elicited subsequently. Consequently when one tests memory in the traditional style, by giving a list of items and then requiring recall of the whole list, performance at any one point in the list is a complicated mixture of harmful effects from other items which have been presented subsequently to the learned item, and of harmful effects of recall of other material before the recall of that item. Suppose however that we present a list of paired associates, and then test the subject by applying the stimuli in a different order from that of presentation. The first item tested may be one which was presented early or late in the sequence of presentation: so by comparing early items with late ones we can measure the effect of subsequently presented items with no interference due to recall. On the other hand, if we compare the performance on the last item presented, on occasions when it was tested immediately and occasions when it was tested only after some other item had been tested, there have been no other items subsequently presented in either case. Thus we shall obtain a pure measure of the effects of recall. This technique has been used by Tulving and Arbuckle (1963, 1966). It is not necessary however to use paired-associates to show this kind of effect: one can also present a serial list of items, in which the subject has to remember the order rather than pairing response items to stimulus items: and then give an instruction by light signal or some similar method for the recall only of the last part, the middle part, or the first part of the list (Anderson, 1960). One may also present the subject with a single item from the serial list, and require him to recall the next item on the list, as in an important paper by Waugh and Norman (1965), to which we shall refer again.

All these techniques agree in showing that, when one tests for memory of a single item which has been followed by the presentation of other items for memory, there is a very rapid forgetting of the tested item as the number of other intervening items increases.

THE ACCEPTANCE OF A BUFFER STORE AND A CODING PROCESS

Since 1958, Sperling's technique has produced a very widespread acceptance of the existence of buffer storage, lasting only a very short period under a second or so in length, and decaying with time. Strong support was provided by the studies by J. F. Mackworth, which we mentioned in a previous chapter; they show that visual memory gives a number of items recalled which corresponds to a fixed time duration for the original visual information, even when one changes the kind of material being remembered. If an item has been presented, it will enter this early stage of buffer storage, but unless some further process takes place within the first second or so, the item will be lost.

What now are the characteristics of the further event which must take place? One important piece of evidence is that memory for items presented visually may show patterns of error which are acoustic rather than visual. Thus for example if we present the letter B, the man may produce in his recall the letter V, which does not look like the stimulus but which does sound like it when spoken. This type of error has been noticed by Sperling (1963) and studied intensively by Conrad (1962b, 1964). In a fixed vocabulary, such as the names of letters, one can show that the matrix of errors in memory corresponds closely to the matrix of errors obtained by listening to the same items presented acoustically through noise and attempting simply to perceive them rather than to remember them. Clearly therefore the processes within the nervous system resulting from visual and from auditory stimulation must converge at some point on to a common set of events: the presentation of a visual or an auditory B must end up with a consequence at some point in the brain which is the same. Indeed of course the consequence must be the same whether the visual stimulus is capital B or italic *b*, or a handwritten version of the same stimulus. The process in question is therefore the one we have named categorization, and must have occurred as soon as one can obtain a response to the stimulus. Broadbent and Gregory (unpublished) have shown that it does not occur in the buffer storage: they used an experiment on perceptual selection in which letters of the alphabet were presented, in two different colours, and subjects were required to pick out items of a certain colour. In a brief exposure, some errors of perception naturally occurred in which the error was acoustically similar to the relevant stimuli. However, such errors were no more common when the irrelevant items, visually present but in the wrong colour, were in fact acoustically similar to relevant items. Thus these irrelevant items did not seem to have been analysed to the point where their acoustic similarity to the wanted items became important: a result thoroughly in accordance with the views we formed about perceptual selection earlier. If on the other hand the visual display was presented, and only later was there given an instruction indicating which colour of item was to be recalled, then acoustically similar irrelevant items gave an increase in the number of intrusion errors. Thus the acoustic quality appears to become relevant as the information passes from the buffer store to the later stage. It is a property of the category state, the internal response to the objective stimulus.

All this seems now quite well established, and although it is partly consistent with the views put forward by Broadbent (1958), it does require at least some modification to them. The view then was that incoming information might pass from buffer storage, through P system, back to buffer storage: but if the essence of the P system is categorization of the incoming information into a form which may have acoustic properties even for visual inputs, then the stage of parallel processing to which the information is returned after categorization certainly cannot be the same buffer store as that which received it originally. It may conceivably be a different region of the buffer: it might be that the acoustic buffer is used both for acoustic inputs and for storing information originally visual in nature after it has been categorized. Certainly however some change does occur in the information as it goes through the stage of categorization.

Some evidence pointing in the same direction is provided by Turvey (1966), who presented a visual array of items, with instructions to remember these items until after certain intervening events. There were then a succession of visual presentations of the Sperling type, in which a large array of visual symbols were presented and part were to produce response, the particular part being selected by a signal given only after the flash. After these presentations, the original visual input was reproduced. The result of interest was that the information being extracted from buffer storage was as well preserved when other material was being held in memory as when it was not: the argument being therefore that the material being held in memory was held in acoustic storage rather than in some process which made use of the visual buffer. This result is however not altogether clear in its implications. If we suppose that visual information, after categorization, is held in memory by recirculating continuously between the categorizing system and a buffer other than the visual one, it is certainly true that the visual buffer will be free to handle some other information. The categorizing system itself, however, might also be expected to be needed for this extra visual input, and so it is rather surprising that there was no interference between the tasks. We cannot, therefore, place too much reliance on this result alone, but at least it is consistent with the other evidence pointing to important differences between categorized and uncategorized information.

TRANSFER FROM PRIMARY TO LONGER-TERM MEMORY

The third point which has become generally accepted, and which we should make, is that even one presentation of a list of items produces some effect within the brain which is still detectable after a good deal of intervening activity. This is not altogether consistent with the idea of recirculation from a categorizing system to buffer storage and back: since any occupation of the categorizing system by some other demand would cause the recirculating information to be lost for ever. At some stage, information must be transferred to a longer-term store, since certainly there are many things which we have learned which we continue to remember even after performing other activities. Since there must therefore be some form of storage other than the recurrent circuit from a categorizing system to buffer store and back, the important question is the amount of transfer to the longer-term store which takes place each time a stimulus is presented or information is passed through the categorizing system: and whether the latter is necessary or only the former. Sanders (1961) attacked this problem by requiring subjects to rehearse aloud information which they had received, on the assumption that silent rehearsal would be faster and therefore more effective than overt rehearsal. By delaying the time at which the overt rehearsal had to be carried out, he showed an improvement in performance, suggesting that the silent rehearsal was transferring information effectively to a longer term store and making it more resistant to the interfering effects of overt rehearsal. Quantitatively it seemed likely from his results that quite a substantial amount of transfer to long-term memory occurred even from one presentation.

A very dramatic illustration of the transfer to long-term memory was shown by Hebb (1961), in the following way. He presented lists of digits for immediate recall, a whole series of different lists of digits being used. Unknown to the subject (at least originally) the same list of digits was repeated at intervals throughout the experiment. Other lists had been presented between each such repetition, and if the whole recall of a digit list was carried out by a recirculating system, then certainly that system would have been cleared and refilled two or more times between each presentation of the repeated list. Nevertheless, performance on that list gradually improved throughout the experiment. Thus the single presentation of a list must have left some record which has survived the presentation and recall of other lists in between.

There is little evidence on the interesting question whether this transfer to a longer-term memory does or does not depend upon the occurrence of categorization. In Hebb's case, the stimuli were objectively repeated, and some at least of the digits were correctly recalled on each presentation so that they had certainly been categorized. One would like to know whether there is any trace left in the nervous system from items which were not categorized at all. We quoted in an earlier chapter a result of Moray (1959) showing that items which were presented to the neglected ear during shadowing did not give longer-term memory. This suggests strongly that uncategorized stimuli have no effect on long-term memory. There is also a pioneering study by Turvey (1967), in which a Sperling-type experiment was performed with the same visual display appearing at intervals during the experiment. On one presentation the subject might be instructed to respond to the top line of the visual display, on another presentation to the bottom line, and so on. There was no indication of improvement in performance on this repeated display, and one might therefore conclude that the stimuli to which the subject had not responded on any one occasion produced no permanent effect within the nervous system. Further work on these lines is desirable, because there are many technical difficulties of practice, easier and harder stimulus material, and so on, which need to be explored: and it is in fact quite surprising that there was no beneficial effect on the repeated display in Turvey's conditions. In that experiment the same items would actually have received response sufficiently frequently for one to have expected some sign of the Hebb effect, even if there was no effect from uncategorized stimuli.

THE AREA OF AGREEMENT AND DISAGREEMENT

From these general advances of the past ten years, we can see that there is certainly rapid forgetting of items presented once, if some activity immediately follows presentation. We can also see that items which elicit no response of categorization fade away very rapidly with time, and that the type of category which is used will certainly affect any later memory. We also see that, even though rapid forgetting has occurred, after one presentation there has certainly been some transfer to a form of storage which resists intervening activity. The point of argument which is left unclear by these results is however the nature of memory once a stimulus has been categorized, and while it is vulnerable to intervening activity. Is memory at this stage to be explained by the recirculating process championed by Broadbent (1958), albeit with a change in the recirculating information from its original sensory form to its new transformed and categorized version? Or is it possible to argue that, once a stimulus has been categorized, the information enters a single memory system whose principles remain the same between periods of a few seconds and periods of days or weeks? Throughout most of the last decade there has been considerable discussion of this issue, and the facts discovered have (as is perhaps usual) required both sides to modify and relax their views. As we shall see, the answer is that memory does not shift sharply at, say, 30 seconds from being of one form to being of another quite different one, and that the same mechanisms can certainly be shown to be operative both in experiments of very short duration and in those of much longer term. There is equally no doubt however that memory involves many functions and systems, and that some of these operate over shorter time periods than others do. The meaning of this cryptic distinction will appear as we go through the arguments.

Memory for Categorized Information Soon After Presentation

THE CRITIQUE FROM INTERFERENCE THEORY

(a) *Long-term forgetting as due to interference.* During the 1950's, the understanding of forgetting in long-term memory had advanced considerably: and in particular the analysis of the mechanism by which one memory could suffer interference from other memories. As we shall see, this mechanism had been shown to account for a great deal of forgetting, and it was questionable whether long-term memory any longer required the idea that some engram or trace of the original stimulus decayed gradually with time in the absence of other interfering memories. For this reason, on grounds of parsimony interference theorists tended to resist the idea of simple decay over time even in short-term memory, and to argue that the same principles established in the long-term would apply also to the short-term. We must therefore consider now the lines of argument which they could bring forward.

The full analysis of forgetting through interference is too complex for us to give completely, and it would be impossible to improve on the reviews by Postman (1961, 1964). We may however give a brief and simplified account of the advances of the 1950's in the field of long-term memory. According to interference theory, the learning of one association between a particular stimulus and response, say, S_1 and R_1, could be interfered with by a subsequent learning of some other combination S_2 and R_2. The most obvious mechanism of this interference was that some part at least of the stimulus was the same in the two situations, so that in fact this common stimulus S was being attached first to R_1 and then later to R_2. Suppose then that only one response can occur, two kinds of interference would then appear: first, performance of R_1 would be poor when tested after the learning of R_2

(retro-active inhibition, or RI for short). Secondly, the learning and retention of R_2 might be worse than they would have been if R_1 had never been learned (pro-active inhibition of PI for short). Experimentally both retro-active and pro-active inhibition can easily be shown: but it has been clear since some classic work by A. W. Melton (Melton and Irwin, 1940, Melton and von Lackum, 1941) that retro-active inhibition is not a simple transfer of a new response to supersede the one originally learned. If one varies the degree of practice given on R_2, one varies the amount of interference with subsequent testing of R_1. The more learning of R_2, the worse subsequent performance of R_1. However, this is not only because the subject gives R_2 when he is being tested for R_1, because the number of such intrusion errors rises as practice on R_2 increases to a moderate degree, but then falls again if R_2 is practised even more. There is therefore part of the forgetting of R_1 which can be ascribed to intrusion errors of R_2, but a further part which continues to appear even when R_2 has been practised to the point when intrusions become rather rare. This second factor in RI is transient; that is, it appears only on the first test of R_1 and not on measures of relearning. If we take a man, teach him R_1, then give him a great deal of practice on R_2, and then put him back on relearning R_1 he will do very badly at first and then suddenly improve to a high level of performance.

There are therefore definitely two factors in retro-active inhibition, one due to the switching of responses and the other to some unknown cause. The tempting hypothesis put forward by interference theorists however is that the second factor is due to the weakening or extinction of the associations between stimulus and response; any intrusion of R_1 during the learning of R_2 is an error, is subjectively punished, and thus weakens the link between S and R_1. Thus there is not only a strengthening of R_2, but also a weakening of R_1. It would be expected that this latter process would tend to have less and less effect at longer retention intervals, since conditioned responses which have been extinguished tend to show spontaneous recovery over an interval. Thus the transience of the second factor in RI is a support for this hypothesis.

It is easy to show that PI also is found experimentally: and again an analysis of the effect supports the same kind of two-factor theory. To some extent the learning of R_2 is poor because R_1 occurs as an intrusion. When one has learned R_2, however, R_1 ceases to occur as an error. If one now waits for some time before testing, one finds that performance of R_2 has deteriorated far more seriously than would have been expected if R_1 had not been learned: and again one can explain this as due to the recovery of R_1 from the extinction which it suffered during the learning of R_2. The behaviour both of RI and PI fits therefore with this dual theory.

There is direct evidence for the theory in work by Barnes and Underwood (1959), which used an experimental situation in which subjects had to give *both* R_1 and R_2 when presented later with a common stimulus S. They showed not only that R_2 was better and better recalled with increasing practice upon it, but also that R_1 tended to be recalled less. The deterioration in performance of R_1 in an ordinary RI experiment, therefore, is linked not only with fiercer competition from R_2 but also with a decreasing availability of R_1.

Perhaps however the key advance in interference theory was made by Underwood (1957), in showing that PI was of crucial importance in ordinary processes of forgetting. Most traditional experiments on long-term memory had reported substantial forgetting over intervals of time: but equally most such experiments had been carried out using people who learned many lists, and were tested on the forgetting of each of them. This seems a sensible way to accumulate a lot of data. Underwood showed that an inexperienced person, given a list of nonsense syllables to learn without previous experience on that material, will show very little forgetting of the list once he has acquired it. If he learns another list subsequently, his forgetting of that new list will be faster, and so on. It became from this time on a rather doubtful point whether any forgetting at all would occur in the absence of some previous or subsequent learning of similar material. The whole process of forgetting might therefore be ascribed to the two-factor interference mechanism we have been describing. Part of it might be due to competition between a new and an old response, and part of the process of extinction and recovery of an old response.

(b) *Short-term forgetting as RI and PI.* If one now turned with this approach in mind to the studies on short-term memory current about 1960, it is clear that such researches always involve some interfering activity. As we have said, the presentation of a telephone number will usually ensure that it can be recalled perfectly for an indefinite period of minutes so long as the experimental subject does nothing else in the meantime. We can only show the rapid forgetting, which is used as evidence of a fading trace, if we insert some interfering activity after the presentation. On the views of Broadbent (1958), this later activity occupies the limited capacity system and stops the recirculation; but equally on the interference theory it could be regarded as providing RI. One should also notice that, without making any extra assumptions in interference theory, one would expect PI to increase with time between presentation and testing. In so far then as the experiments on short-term memory used experienced people, one might expect a gradual development of PI through any interval between presentation and response. It was shown by Keppel and Underwood (1962) that the rate of forgetting of single items in short-term memory (using the counting backwards technique) increased as experimental subjects got more and more experienced with the type of material being used.

It was particularly noticeable that the forgetting depends on the nature of the items. If a subject is used in an experiment where he receives a group of three letters and then has to name colours during an interval before his memory is tested, he forgets very little on the first trial, and the rate of forgetting builds up in successive repetitions of the experiment. If however he is then changed to a similar task in which he has to remember three digits rather than three letters, the rate of forgetting becomes very low again, and the whole process repeats itself (Wickens *et al.*, 1963).

Thus similarity of the preceding items to the present ones is important in producing this kind of PI: as again interference theory would predict that it should be. In the simplified account we gave earlier, there was a common element S between the two stimuli S_1 and S_2 employed in two successive tasks. Unless this were so, R_1 and R_2 would not be competing with each other. Thus the degree of similarity between the tasks ought to be important in deciding the amount of PI and RI: a point to which we shall return. In any event, PI is clearly apparent in short-term memory, and one may therefore argue that interference theory is applicable to that case also.

(c) *Degree of learning from one presentation.* It might conceivably be argued that the rate of forgetting in experiments such as those by Brown, by Peterson and by Murdock is so very much greater than has been found in long-term memory, as to suggest some quite different mechanism. To this the interference theorist could reply that the degree of learning produced by a single presentation is unknown and probably very slight. The fact that perfect performance can be obtained before the forgetting period starts may not reflect the underlying strength of the associations that are built up. The degree of learning produced by a single presentation is likely to be slight, and hence the rapid forgetting.

(d) *Continuity of long-term and short-term memory.* Another line of attack by interference theorists can make use of the demonstrated continuity between processes which are certainly long-term memory and processes studied by the techniques mentioned earlier. Melton (1963) performed the same experiment as Hebb (1961), in which a list of digits is repeated at intervals during an experiment apparently on memory for single presentations. Melton however varied the number of intervening lists between repetitions of the same list: and found that the Hebb effect was essentially absent when too many lists were interpolated, becoming gradually stronger as the distance apart of the repetitions was reduced. There was no sign of a sharp break between performance wholly with a kind of short-term memory and performance wholly with long-term memory. (Incidentally, the number of intervening lists at which the Hebb effect disappears is about seven or eight, which happens also to be the number of items which can be held in a memory span: this may well be coincidence, but we shall return to the point later.) A similar continuity between short-term and long-term memory is shown by Hellyer (1962), repeating presentation of a stimulus in a short-term memory experiment, and finding a progressive lessening of forgetting during the short period of retention as the stimulus has had more and more previous presentations. Once more there is no sharp break between one process and another.

(*e*) *Effects on short-term memory from previous long-term experience.* Lastly, it is easy to show that previous long-term experience is highly relevant to the efficiency of short-term memory. Even if we consider nonsense syllables made up of meaningless combinations of letters, the frequency with which a particular sequence occurs in samples of meaningful English will determine the efficiency with which it can be handled by long-term memory: this is true not only within syllables (Underwood and Schulz, 1960), but also when associations between different syllables are being formed. That is, if we have two syllables QEN and POG, to learn them in that order is easy because P occurs frequently following N in the English language, but to learn the same two syllables in the reverse order is much harder because Q does not often follow G in ordinary English (Baddeley, 1964a). Equally in short-term memory it is found that sequences of letters which are probable in the language are easier to recall than those which are improbable, even after one presentation (Baddeley, 1964b, Baddeley *et al.*, 1965). Thus the efficiency of short-term memory is clearly affected by the general background of experience which the person concerned has had in his ordinary handling of English, and thus is involved with long-term memory.

It is not merely the level of recall under some one particular condition which is affected in this way, but even the rate with which forgetting takes place. Murdock (1961) showed that a group of three letters making a meaningless combination was forgotten fairly rapidly during a process of counting backwards, but a meaningful word was not. Three meaningful words were

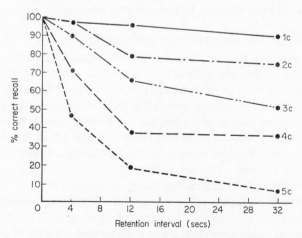

FIG. 30. Recall of various items presented in groups of 1, 2, 3, 4 or 5, and followed by various periods of irrelevant activity. Notice that the rate of forgetting is greater for larger numbers of items in memory: and the ultimate level lower. Data from Melton (1963).

forgotten about as fast as a three-letter nonsense syllable, so that the speed of forgetting seems to depend upon the number of independent units, formed by previous experience, which are present in the material to be remembered. Melton (1963) varied over a whole range of values the number of independent items being remembered, and found very little forgetting when one item alone was being remembered, but exceedingly rapid forgetting when eight items were being stored. That is, when eight items are being remembered, even counting backwards by one step is sufficient to cause severe forgetting. This result is similar to those of Brown, which we mentioned earlier: but it seems clear that the speed of forgetting in short-term memory depends very much indeed upon the extent to which previous long-term memory has associated the various items into strings or chunks. A particularly direct indication of this process is provided by Tulving and Patkau (1962), who examined the number of items correctly recalled from a single presentation of a long list of words. If one looked at the responses, there were some cases in which adjacent words were written down which had in fact been adjacent in the stimulus presentation. Counting any such group of words as a response unit, one finds that a single presentation produces seven or eight response units, even though it may consist of a number of words much larger than seven or eight.

Putting all these facts together, the interference theorist could well be sceptical about the need to postulate some new principle for forgetting in experiments lasting 30 seconds or a minute. The principles found satisfactory in older experiments with a longer time scale might well be applied in these new studies: RI and PI were clearly present, the degree of learning was unknown but probably low and thus might explain the rapid forgetting, there was continuity with longer-term memory, and there was obvious evidence of the role of long-term memory in these shorter processes.

DIFFICULTIES OF THE INTERFERENCE APPROACH

In the previous section we have put forward a case for interference theory, without either noting the difficulties inherent in it, or comparing it with experimental evidence. In the next few sections we shall look at experiments which shed some light upon it, but in this section we may first note some of the snags in the arguments of the last section. First of these is the fact that all interference theory requires some two-factor process: not merely competition between responses, but also some weakening of the first response which then spontaneously recovers. This second factor with its spontaneous recovery makes a provision for changes due solely to passage of time. When PI is operating, the simple lapse of time will produce forgetting no matter what the nature of the activity which fills the retention interval. Such a theory is more similar than one might have expected to a theory that the trace of the stimulus decays with time: to explain the changes with time by an appeal to spontaneous recovery from extinction does not really add very much, since one may well argue that the reappearance of extinguished conditioned responses is itself a phenomenon requiring some explanation. The explanation could well be in terms of decaying effects of previous stimulation.

Furthermore, some of the phenomena explained by interference theory appear to be over-explained: spontaneous recovery is postulated both to explain the transience of RI, and to explain the increasing effect of PI as retention interval increases, but each of these can also be explained by another concept of interference theory which we have so far left unmentioned. This concept is that of "generalized response learning", by which is meant the attachment of responses not merely to the stimuli which the task specifies as appropriate for them but also to generalized features of the situation. When S_1 is linked with R_1, and S_2 with R_2, it must also be supposed that R_1 is associated with general stimuli such as the appearance of the room in which the experiment takes place, the internal state of hunger or muscular stiffness of the experimental subject, and so on. Any of these stimuli will change progressively in time: hunger will increase as the experiment goes on, the illumination from the window may decrease throughout an evening experiment, and so on. Consequently the response R_1 has links with various characteristics of the time at which S_1 was first delivered and the association set up; and if some later response is learned, even though the nominal stimulus S_2 has no component in common with S_1, yet there may be some interference between R_2 and R_1 depending upon the interval of time between the learning of the two responses. When they are close together in time, there will be some minor stimulus component S in common (the degree of hunger or daylight) while when they are widely separated in time this will not be true.

This concept of generalized response learning has been introduced into interference theory because of experiments such as that of Newton and Wickens (1956). In this case two sets of material were learned, in which the stimulus sets S_1 and S_2 appeared to have nothing in common, and so also did the response sets R_1 and R_2. Under these circumstances the amount of RI shown by a test of R_1 at a fixed interval after the original learning depended upon the time at which the association of S_2 and R_2 was built up. A greater amount of RI occurred when S_2 and R_2 were learned immediately before the time of testing by presentation of S_1. Furthermore, when the association of S_1 and R_1 is relearned, the serial position effect becomes abnormal: it is usual in studies of long-term memory to find the first items in a list doing better than those in the middle, but in the relearning of material which has been subject to RI of this kind, the first items do relatively badly. Thus the pattern of results is consistent with the idea that a response R_2 is associated not only with S_2 but with the time at which the interpolated learning took place, and that therefore if one tests for R_1 at a time close to the time of interpolated learning one will get strong competition from R_2, even though S_1 and S_2 have nothing in common.

M

With such a concept of attachment of responses to the time at which they were learned, one can explain the same phenomena as those which spontaneous recovery was intended to cover. Because of generalized response learning, an experiment in which S_1 is first attached to R_1 and then to R_2 will show worse and worse performance of R_1 as the interval of time before testing increases, that is, as more and more time is spent on practising R_2. Equally the increase in effects of PI with time might be predicted, since if temporal stimuli (hunger, daylight, etc.) have changed slightly between the learning of R_1 and R_2, they will be still in roughly the latter state if we test memory immediately after the learning of R_2. After a prolonged retention interval however the temporal stimuli at the time of testing will be considerably different from those during either the learning of R_1 or that of R_2, and consequently the relative strength of R_2 will suffer more than that of R_1 by an increase in retention interval.

It would not therefore seem that one really needs both the concept of spontaneous recovery and that of generalized response learning. If the former is in some ways similar to a concept of decaying trace, however, the latter is almost more so. The association of a response with the time at which it was learned, and the suggestion that progressive changes take place in such stimuli as the retention interval proceeds, mean effectively that a response will become less available as time goes on regardless of the nature of the intervening activities. Interference theory is not therefore altogether an alternative to decay theory, but contains some elements which are a restatement of decay in other terms. Interference theory does however make the point that decay and the passage of time should only produce their consequences if the material being retained is vulnerable to competition from other previously learned material. That is, broadly speaking there must be some elements of similarity with other material learned at some other time.

Another difficulty within interference theory is the question of degree of learning. If a single item has been presented once, it is essentially certain that it will be perfectly recalled before any intervening activity such as counting backwards takes place. Nevertheless, we have seen that it may be rapidly forgotten when an intervening activity does start, and interference theory might explain this by the low level of some (hypothetical) degree of learning. Yet many of the phenomena described as evidence for interference theory depend upon taking the probability of response as an index of degree of learning. For example, Underwood's important demonstration, that forgetting is faster once PI is present, depends upon starting all items from the same degree of learning before the forgetting is measured. Therefore each list is learned for a number of trials which will just attain a particular criterion of correct performance. Yet the number of trials necessary to do this is fewer in practised than in unpractised subjects. If therefore one was to regard as a measure of learning the amount of exposure to the material, rather than the probability of recall, then the experienced subjects were forgetting from a lower degree of initial learning, and would naturally do so more rapidly. In fact it has been shown by Warr (1964) that subjects exposed to the material for the same amount of time when naïve and when experienced forget at much the same rate. Thus to explain forgetting by PI one must regard the probability of recall as the correct measure of degree of original learning, rather than the amount of exposure to the material. Yet to explain rapid forgetting in short-term memory, one has to regard the amount of exposure to the material as the correct measure, and not probability of recall. This problem is not necessarily insoluble, but it is nevertheless serious. The assumption was specifically made by Broadbent (1958) that a given criterion of performance could be attained partly from material in primary memory and partly from material in a longer-term store, and it was pointed out then that most experiments on long-term memory do not take this possibility into account. We shall see an instance later (Baddeley, 1966a) in which the conduct of an experiment in long-term memory by a method which eliminates any component of short-term memory makes an important difference to the results.

A third difficulty in the application of interference theory to short-term memory lies within the field of PI. We have already quoted the result of Keppel and Underwood, showing that PI did occur in short-term memory just as it does in long-term memory. There are however certain differences in the way PI behaves in the two cases. First, it is wry to note that Peterson (1966) actually quotes Keppel and Underwood in support of the existence of forgetting *not* due to PI in short-term memory. This is because they obtained some forgetting even in subjects who had learned nothing previously. It might perhaps be argued that the subjects were showing some PI from past experience with similar kinds of material, outside the experiment. Yet it has been shown by Loess (1964) that if one carries out a repeated experiment on more than one day, the PI builds up afresh each day and does not appear to carry over from one day to another. PI should increase with time rather than disappearing, and there seems here to be some phenomenon which is not quite the same as that found in long-term memory.

The fact that short-term PI depends only on a very few items before the one being recalled shows up very clearly in a study by Wickelgren (1966a). He presented a single letter for recall, which was preceded and followed by various numbers of other letters, not for recall. He found a steadily increasing effect of increasing numbers of letters after the desired item, that is RI went on increasing with more interpolated material. There was also a PI effect shown by a difference between zero and four letters preceding the desired item: but no further deterioration as more and more letters were put in before the one to be recalled. As Wickelgren pointed out, this strongly suggests a difference between PI and RI, and it seems reasonable to follow him and regard the important point about increases in RI material as being the fact that they increase the interval of retention without rehearsal. Increases in the PI material have no such effect, and when that is so PI builds up to a maximum over a very few items.

A slightly different point about PI is provided by Murdock (1963, 1964). The Keppel and Underwood finding applies to a group of items which are presented and then followed by a "distracting" task. Murdock made use rather of his probe technique, in which paired-associates are presented and recall of any one response is tested after a certain number of other pairs have been presented during the desired retention interval. In general he did not find that forgetting increased as the subjects got more experienced, but indeed if anything the performance improved when they had performed more trials. The most that could be said was that within any one trial the very first pair was perhaps retained better than the later pairs; but even this was less true at long retention intervals. This is the exact opposite of the PI effect discussed previously. As subjects got more experienced, the first item in the list deteriorated, with a corresponding *improvement* on later items. Murdock therefore concluded that the evidence for PI of the classic type was with this technique rather scanty, and that the evidence was more consistent with the idea that a fixed limit existed for the number of items which could be held in memory at any one time. This limit could be divided up in different ways, and experienced subjects tended to favour the later rather than the earlier of the items which they were supposed to be handling.

The antithesis here between Murdock on the one hand and Keppel and Underwood on the other is sufficiently clear to make one confident that it is the difference between the two techniques for assessing memory which is responsible. It is not some accidental feature of either experiment. PI appears in the Peterson technique and in the rather related method used by Wickelgren where the desired items are associated only with general features of the situation. Yet it does not appear in a paired-associate task where a distinctive stimulus exists for each response and we test for recall by providing that stimulus. (The absence of PI in paired-associates does not apply if the *same* stimulus has been associated with two different responses, and Peterson (1966) reviews evidence showing that normal interference effects apply in that case. It is also possible, from one result of Goggin (1966) that the absence of PI in paired-associates applies only within trials and not between trials.) We shall come back to this curious feature of PI in short-term memory: for the moment, it will suffice that PI certainly can occur in the short-term case. Yet the principles governing its operation seem to be a little different from those expected from experiments of longer-term.

There remain to be considered two points urged by interference theory: the existence of effects on short-term memory from previous long-term experience, and the continuity which seems to exist between memory at long and short periods of time. The first of these must be admitted straight away, and is perfectly consistent with a view of short-term memory as due to recirculation into and out of a decaying buffer storage. The effect of past experience in setting up various category states in the limited capacity part of the system would naturally make long-term training an important factor in any process occurring after categorization. As was indeed already urged by Broadbent (1958), one would expect to find effects of such training even in experiments of very short duration. In general one must beware of concluding that the appearance in short-term memory of an effect known from longer-term studies is evidence for identity of the two situations. So far as is known, there exists no theorist who would contend that long-term memory plays no part in the short-term, and consequently demonstrations that the principles of long-term memory hold in short-term do not discriminate between theories. Only the success or failure of attempts to show *differences* between the two situations is of interest in distinguishing the theories. In a similar way, the fact that there is no sharp break between performance by one mechanism and performance by another is perfectly consistent with the position of Broadbent (1958): that position is that an experiment on retention over a few seconds and one on retention over some hours will both involve the same mechanisms, but at one extreme will place the greatest weight on buffer storage and recirculation, while at the other extreme the greatest weight will be placed on the long-term store. No sharp transition between the two extremes would be expected, any more than a sharp transition is to be expected as an aircraft takes off, between the extreme states of its weight resting primarily upon its wheels and of its weight resting primarily upon its wings.

Despite the great steps forward which have been taken by interference theory therefore it is not without its own difficulties, and a demonstration that its principles hold even in short-term memory experiments does not possess any value in deciding between theories. There is therefore little point in checking that the predictions of interference theory apply even in short-term memory, which would be expected on either view; but rather one ought to examine those cases in which the two approaches make opposite predictions. This is the main purpose of the next few sections. As we shall see ultimately, a number of variables seem to operate differently in short-term and in long-term experiments. From the basis of the theory, however, there is one particular group of variables which might be expected to show such differences. These are variables concerning the nature of the task with which the subject is occupied during the retention interval in short-term memory. According to interference theory, forgetting is primarily a matter of the attachment of incompatible responses to some common stimulus in the original and in the interpolated activity. Variation in the number of common elements between the remembered item and those which interfere with it should therefore alter the amount of interference, and in experiments on long-term memory it has been shown to do so. On the theory of rehearsal and fading trace, or recirculation into and out of a decaying buffer storage, the key feature of interference is not its similarity to the material being remembered, but the extent to which it loads the mechanism of limited capacity and prevents rehearsal. In interference theory therefore we expect similarity of activities to be the major variable in forgetting, while on the decay theory we expect the sheer time for which rehearsal is prevented to be the key variable. In a modification of this latter prediction (to take into account the fact that immediate memory seems to be limited by the number of items rather than the amount of information), we may make the alternative prediction that short-term memory will deteriorate as a function of the number of events dealt with between presentation and recall of an item, and not perhaps so much with the sheer time taken in dealing with those items. Both decay theory and "limited items" theory would however expect that forgetting would occur even in the absence of any similarity between the material now being retained and any other which has been learned before or after.

THE EFFECTS OF SIMILARITY

We have already mentioned the results of Brown, showing little effect upon memory from changes in similarity between the material to be remembered and the material involved in a task performed during the retention interval. Studies using the "distraction" techniques, where the retention interval is filled with some task requiring no learning, frequently show forgetting when the degree of similarity between the memory material and the distracting task is extremely low. Some instances of this are worth mentioning. Broadbent and Gregory (1965c) required subjects to listen to spoken letters occurring every five seconds, and once a minute to indicate which letter had occurred twice. The letters were used as warning signals for a choice reaction task in which vibratory stimulation was applied to the tips of the fingers. Shortly after each letter, therefore, such a stimulus would arrive and the subject had to make a reaction by pressing the finger that had been stimulated, or, in other groups of subjects, the corresponding finger of the other hand. The efficiency of recall of the letters was less in the latter condition than in the former, and in both cases was less for a four-choice reaction than for a two-choice reaction. It is very difficult to see that there is any similarity whatever between the interpolated task and the memory task, and still less to see that differences of compatibility or degree of choice should affect the degree of similarity. It is extremely hard therefore to understand, on a basis of interference theory, why these conditions should differ in degree of forgetting. But on the basis of rehearsal and fading trace, it is clear that the more complex reactions will place greater demands on the categorizing system, and will leave it less well able to cope with the memory task.

Similar arguments apply to an experiment by Conrad (1966), in which subjects had to indicate their memory for a series of digits by pressing keys on a keyboard: and a difference in the compatibility of the arrangement of keys produced a deterioration which was apparently one of memory rather than of accuracy of key pressing. Again it seems reasonable that the extra time taken in choosing the correct key made it difficult to store other digits meanwhile.

Some of the clearest groups of experiments however are those of Posner and Rossman (1965) and Posner and Konick (1966). In these experiments, a group of items such as consonants were presented for later recall, and during the retention interval the subject worked at tasks of varying complexity. At one extreme he might simply be asked to record a series of digits, and at the other extreme to classify each of the series of digits as high or low, and also odd or even. The more complex the interpolated task, the greater the forgetting of the other material in memory. This again could hardly be due to changes in the similarity of the interpolated task and of the remembered material. Indeed some of the differences are in the wrong direction, memory being slightly better when a simple task involved similar material than when a difficult task involved quite different material. The particularly interesting feature of the results is that the effect is not due solely to the extra time taken to deal with each stimulus in the more complex tasks: even if the number of items handled in the more complex tasks was reduced so as to keep the total amount of time constant, it was still true that greater forgetting occurred with a more complex task.

Yet another illustration comes from the experiments by J. F. Mackworth (1964c), mentioned in Chapter V as leading on from her work on buffer store. She presented a series of letters followed by a varying number of other items, which in some cases were digits and in other cases were colours. It is known from other experiments that the rate of reading colours is less than that of reading digits, and they therefore presumably place more load on the limited capacity system. Correspondingly, the total number of items which could be correctly recalled was less for letters followed by colours than it was for letters followed by digits, when the number of items presented and their rate of presentation was held constant.

It will be remembered that Mackworth scored only items reported up to the first error, so that her score of correct reports is a measure of the number of recall events intervening between the end of the presentation series and the first error. As the length of the presentation series went up, there was a drop in the number of recall events. This drop was not large enough to keep the total number of presentation events and recall events constant, and on the whole about two and a half extra items had to be presented in order to produce the loss of one item in recall. A point of particular interest is that the size of this "trade-off" relationship was the same whether the extra items added were digits or colours, so that adding an extra item seemed to give the same effect whether that item were a complex or a less complex one. It was simply the total level of performance which was changed, and not the effect of each extra item. In the same way, if she compared performance with a varying number of letters followed by a fixed number of digits in one condition and of colours in another, the effect of adding extra letters was the same whichever type of subsequent item was to follow. However, for the same number of total items, performance was better with digits than with colours.

This relationship is important, because in its absence one might attempt to explain away these results as due to some form of interference theory acting on unknown similar elements in the task. One might argue that, in some unknown way, colours and letters are more similar than letters and digits are. But on such a view it would surely be expected that the deterioration from each extra item of interference would be different. On the recirculatory theory with a limited capacity system putting information in and out of a buffer store, Mackworth's results mean that changes in the nature of the items being handled do not alter the rate of decay in the buffer store, but merely have some effect on the limited capacity channel.

All these experiments therefore agree that it is possible to get RI in the absence of any obvious similarity between the material being learned and that in the interpolated task. They also agree that it is possible to get changes in RI with changes in the interpolated task: when such changes are apparently not varying the dimension of similarity but rather that of complexity, the demand which the interpolated task makes upon the limited capacity system. So far as they go therefore these results support the doctrine of rehearsal of a trace which dies away with time in the absence of rehearsal.

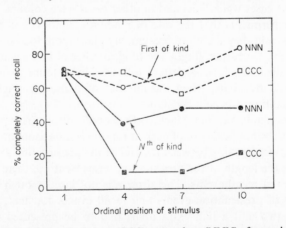

FIG. 31. Recall of a group of trigrams (CCC) or numbers (NNN) after various numbers of preceding experimental trials. The solid curves show recall when the earlier trials had been of the same kind of material, and the dotted curves for recall when the earlier trials had been for a different kind of material. After Wickens *et al.* (1963).

(a) *Experiments showing the effect of similarity in primary memory.* There is however some evidence that changes in similarity do indeed affect the amount of RI and PI. We have briefly considered one such line of evidence already, in the result of Wickens *et al.* on PI. The rapid forgetting of three-letter material, which develops after several trials of such material, disappears when the nature of the material is changed to three-digit groups and vice versa. In the case of RI from an interpolated task which uses digits without requiring their recall it makes relatively little difference whether the material being remembered is digits or consonants (Posner and Konick, 1966). We have already quoted the similar conclusions of Brown. There is, however, one type of similarity which does produce a massive effect on the amount of RI and indeed that of PI also. This is the acoustic similarity between letters or words which sound alike, such as B C D V etc. Wickelgren (1965a) showed that the copying of letters from one acoustic class (such as PTB) makes an earlier presentation of letters from the same class (such as DCV) harder to recall than would be the case if the letters copied had been from another class (such as FSM). This result has been confirmed in a variety of other experiments.

Perhaps the clearest demonstration of the effect is that by Wickelgren (1966a), which we have already cited. [This was the experiment on recall of single letters, preceded or followed by other irrelevant letters, which showed that the number of preceding letters did not matter once there were at least four of them, whereas the number of subsequent letters went on affecting recall over a much wider range. That is, PI reached its maximum very rapidly, while RI went on increasing.] In the same experiment, Wickelgren varied the number of preceding or of following letters which were acoustically similar to the one for recall. He found that increasing the proportion of acoustically similar letters gave a deterioration in recall, whether the acoustically similar material was in that producing PI or in that producing RI.

It was noticeable however that it made a difference in each case whether the other material was similar or not: that is, if the letters after the desired item were quite different in acoustic nature, the recall depended very heavily on the acoustic nature of the letters preceding it. If, however, the letters after the desired item were acoustically similar to it, it made little difference whether those before were similar or not. The same applied in the reverse case, the nature of the RI material making little difference when the PI material was acoustically similar to the desired item. One could sum this up by saying that a few acoustically similar items produce the maximum effect, and beyond that point adding any more makes little difference. If this summary is fair, it sounds as if the acoustic similarity belongs to the type of interference produced by PI, and not to that which is peculiar to RI: since PI, like the effect of acoustic similarity, reaches a maximum with a few items, while RI goes on increasing as more and more items of interpolated activity are given.

From the point of view of interference theory, it is reasonable that activity

M*

interpolated between presentation and recall should have two functions. It might produce associative interference: and it might also allow PI to increase due to recovery of those earlier irrelevant responses which had been extinguished during presentation of the relevant material. In so far as activity during the retention interval is simply allowing time for PI to develop, the nature of the interfering activity is unimportant. For PI to have an effect, however, there should be some element of similarity between the preceding and the remembered material; and equally there should be a proportion of RI which is due to associative interference rather than simple lapse of time, and which thus should depend on similarity. The results concerning acoustic similarity are thus very reasonable from the point of view of interference theory. They are much less so from that of recurrent circuit theory.

(b) *Divergences in effects of similarity between long-term and short-term tasks.* Studies already mentioned show that acoustic similarity does affect the size of RI and PI: but they are not completely comparable with studies in long-term memory, since the classic literature on RI and PI normally involves the interaction of two sets of learning material. It does not usually involve the interpolation, during a retention interval, of irrelevant material which is not to be learned at all. One group of studies exists however in which exactly similar techniques have been used in short-term and in long-term experiments. Baddeley and Dale (1966) used paired-associate learning in an RI situation, of the type in which an association between S_1 and R_1 is first formed and then followed by training on an association of S_2 and R_2. In one condition S_1 and S_2 were adjectives of similar meaning, while in the other control condition they were adjectives of very different meaning. In either case R_1 and R_2 were adjectives which were different in meaning both from each other and from the stimuli concerned. When this type of material had been presented for eight trials both on the original and on the interpolated learning, the retention of the association of S_1 and R_1 was much more impaired if S_2 had been similar to S_1 than if it had not. If however the same material was used but presented in a short-term situation, each pair being presented only once, no effect on the retention of R_1 could be shown from similarity between S_1 and the interpolated S_2.

There are two differences here from preceding experiments: the use of paired-associate learning, and the use of semantic similarity rather than acoustic. The latter factor is certainly important: because similar divergences can be shown when memory is for lists of items rather than for paired-associates. Baddeley (1966b) studied memory for sequences of words, where the entire sequence had to be reported after only one presentation. If the list of words consisted of items which were all acoustically similar to each other, they were harder to remember than a list made up of words which sounded different from each other. Using a list made up of items which had similar meanings did produce an impairment, but one which was considerably less than that from acoustic similarity. When the word lists consisted of different words, performance was at a level of 70-80%; for semantically similar lists it was a little over 60%, for acoustically similar lists it was under 10%.

This by itself means little, since we have no way of saying whether a given degree of acoustic similarity is greater or less than a given degree of semantic similarity. When however the same type of material was used in another experiment by Baddeley (1966a), he was able to show that the acoustically similar lists were no worse in long-term memory than control lists: indeed, by the end of learning they were rather better than control lists. The semantically similar lists, however, did very much worse in long-term memory, retention being under 60% correct after an amount of training which gave nearly 90% for the control lists.

The fact that semantic similarity is of lesser effect than acoustic similarity in a short-term experiment cannot, therefore, be simply because the resemblance of the acoustically similar material was greater than that of the semantically similar: because under long-term conditions it is the semantic material which shows the greater impairment. Thus the effect of semantic similarity seems to be much less than that of acoustic similarity in short-term memory, while the situation is reversed in long-term memory.

This does not mean that the semantic features of the material are completely unimportant in short-term memory: because there was a small significant effect even in short-term memory. A similar small effect has also been found by Dale and Gregory (1966), using a technique in which three similar items were presented for memorising, and followed by six items merely to be read aloud, which were either similar to or different from the material to be recalled. Acoustic similarity again had a much larger effect than semantic similarity, even though the latter had some influence; and there were other minor differences between the two ways of varying similarity. For example, with both kinds of similarity there was a reduction in the number of responses to items present in the original material and reported in their correct position in the sequence of items. With acoustic similarity there was also a reduction in the number of responses which had indeed been in the original material but which were reported in the wrong position. With semantic similarity this was not so, and it was only responses in correct order which showed a reduction by similarity. Complete omissions of response were reduced by semantic similarity, and were increased by acoustic similarity.

Nevertheless, it must be admitted that semantic similarity does play some part in increasing interference even in short-term memory. This is reasonable enough, even on the recirculatory theory, because of the involvement of long-term memory in the categorizing process which we have already noticed. Is it also true that acoustic similarity has an effect in long-term memory? In straightforward experimentation of the classic type, it is certain that it does (Dallett, 1966). Such experiments normally involve the presentation of a list of items, their testing, their presentation again, and so on until a criterion of attainment is reached. There may then be a pause of relatively long duration with a retention test at the end of it. On a recirculatory theory, during the original learning some of the items will be held in the recirculatory system and only the remainder will be in a longer-term store: and if we apply some treatment which reduces the efficiency of the recirculatory system, the criterion of learning will only be reached when the long-term system contains sufficient information. Baddeley (1966a) did in fact find that, in an experiment of traditional type, acoustic similarity in the material slowed down original learning, but paradoxically gave practically no forgetting between the end of learning and a test twenty minutes later after an interval on another task. This

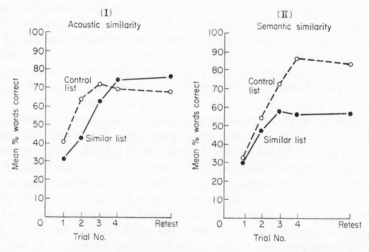

FIG. 32. The learning and retention of word sequences when short-term memory is eliminated by an irrelevant activity between every trial. Acoustic similarity then has no effect; but semantic similarity impairs performance. Data from Baddeley (1966a).

is odd, since traditional experiments usually do show a loss over an interval of this length, and the control conditions of Baddeley's experiment did so as well. On the view however that there are separate long-term and short-term processes, and bearing in mind that acoustic similarity impairs short-term memory, the difficulty with a classic technique might be that the acoustic similarity was causing performance to be based purely on long-term memory, while under control conditions there was a substantial component of short-term memory as well. Baddeley was able to show that the addition of another irrelevant task between each trial of the experiment and its corresponding test abolished all differences between the control conditions and the acoustically similar ones. It also meant that the twenty-minute retention interval ceased to produce any forgetting under any condition. Lastly, it was only by an elimination of the short-term component in this way that the effect of semantic similarity, already mentioned, could be revealed.

This point of technique is clearly therefore a highly important one: if we do adopt the view that there are several processes at work in memory (for which the most convincing evidence is still to come), and if we are attempting to study long-term processes, we can only regard evidence as satisfactory if it is derived from experiments which interpose some other activity between every trial and its corresponding test. Experiments of the classic type on long term learning, even though they may extend over a considerable period of time, clearly involve some processes which occur also in short-term experiments, but which cease to play a part if the long-term experiment is intermittent rather than continuous in time. This is evidence much more congenial to the theory of rehearsal and fading trace than it is to a unified interference theory.

(c) *Theoretical interpretations of similarity.* We started our discussion of similarity with an over-simplified antithesis: interference theory supposes that responses to one stimulus will interfere with responses to another similar stimulus, but not with those to a quite different stimulus. Therefore interference should vary with similarity. There is no obvious reason why it should vary with other properties of interpolated tasks such as their complexity. The recirculatory theory on the other hand suggests that items simply decay with time in the buffer storage between each recirculation, and that therefore the key factor is the time taken by any outside task during retention rather than the similarity of the task to the material being remembered. Clearly neither of these views is adequate. The complexity of intervening activities does make a difference, and so does their similarity to the material in memory. But the operation of similarity is demonstrably different in short-term and in long-term experiments: in the former case it is similarity along simple sensory dimensions of acoustic quality which counts most, while in the latter case it is similarity of meaning or content.

Once we admit that similarity does play some role in short-term experiments, we encounter a fresh problem. The experiment by Baddeley and Dale (1966) varied the semantic similarity of stimuli which were to receive different responses. The other investigations mentioned have made use rather of similarity between the different items in a learned sequence, or between a response item to be recalled and other irrelevant items before or after it. When a sequence rather than a paired-associate is learned, we can only apply the analysis in terms of stimulus and response by supposing that each item is the stimulus for the next item. Thus in acoustically similar lists it is not only the stimuli which are similar but also the responses. In the other technique, where a single relevant item is preceded or followed by other irrelevant items, we are varying similarity of the relevant response to irrelevant responses, not similarity of the stimuli. Yet in our simple presentation of interference theory, the interference was produced by the common elements or similarity between stimuli rather than between responses.

Now in classic presentations of interference theory, similarity of responses does indeed play a part: while similarity of stimuli determines the amount of interaction between two associations, similarity of responses determines its direction. In one extreme case, to learn an association of S_1 with R_1 and then to have further practice with the same pair will produce strengthening of the association: at the opposite extreme, if the interpolated learning uses the identical stimulus S_1 and a response R_2 which is completely incompatible with R_1, then the extent of PI and RI will be maximal. Thus for a given degree of stimulus similarity, PI and RI should reduce as the response similarity increases. This is the classic approach of Osgood (1949), and with suitable modifications to include backward associations, response availability, and similar details, still appears reasonably satisfactory (Martin, 1965). In so far as a study such as that of Wickelgren (1966a) is presenting responses in close temporal proximity to the correct one and which are similar to it, it should, therefore, improve performance rather than deteriorate it. It is, therefore, perfectly true that classical interference theory, of the type we have considered, would predict an effect of similarity upon the size of RI and PI in short-term memory as in long-term: but it is not at all clear that it would predict the direction of effect which is in fact found.

Wickelgren (1965b) suggests a more sophisticated and up-to-date version of interference theory, in which each stimulus sets up an internal representation having a number of features corresponding to features of the stimulus. When a second stimulus is presented, each feature of the first is associated with the various features of the second: so that if one presents a list for memory, and then an acoustically similar list of interpolated material, the features in common between the relevant and the irrelevant material will become associated with more than one set of other features. This type of theory works well if, say, one is asked to remember BCG and then to copy out VTP before recalling the original material. The features in common between B and V might cause one to respond with B first and then erroneously T rather than C. But it is still difficult to see why, if one is presented with a single letter B, it is harder to recall that letter when it is followed by C and G than when it is followed by X and F. Yet this does happen (Wickelgren, 1966b). The only way in which one can explain this is by supposing that the feature common to B C and G ceases to be so closely associated with the unique features of B as it was before C and G were presented. That is, the association suffering interference is within one item, not between items. It still remains exceedingly unclear why the presentation of an instruction to recall should not simply be associated with the features unique to B and not to those common to B, C and G. The associative theory will only explain the effects of acoustic similarity on recall of a single item if we suppose that the chain of association leads from the cue for recall, through the feature common to several of the stimuli presented, and then to other features.

A particularly clear illustration of the difficulty is provided by an experiment of Baddeley (1968). He presented lists of items in which, say, the even-numbered items in the list were acoustically similar to each other while the odd-numbered ones were different. If Wickelgren's theory were correct, the odd-numbered items should be badly recalled, because each of them was a response to a stimulus closely similar to the stimuli appropriate to quite different responses. In fact however it was the even-numbered items, the ones which were themselves similar, which were hard to recall.

It seems necessary therefore to modify Wickelgren's theory by supposing that, when information is stored about a stimulus containing several features, one or more of these features is used as a means for locating information about the others. It cannot be that there are independent links between the cue stimulus and feature 1, feature 2, feature 3 etc. of the response: but rather that the cue stimulus elicits feature 1, which in turn elicits features 2, 3 and 4. Any other item in memory which possesses feature 1 will then produce difficulties of retrieval.

As an analogy, think of the visual field as divided up into a matrix of small squares, forming rows and columns. Then by specifying a row and a column one can enquire what object is visible in that part of the field. If however there are several objects in the same square, the problem of distinguishing them will remain. The analogy is chosen deliberately, because it will be recalled that Averbach and Coriell (1961) found that the visual buffer storage behaved in ɑ fashion very like that we have described. If they presented a series of items in a brief flash, and then indicated one location in a visual field by a marker pointed towards it, the subject could retrieve that item from the visual buffer. If however they put the marker too close, directly over the location of the original item, it erased it from the buffer. Thus the visual buffer appears to store information organized by spatial position: the stored item can be extracted if its spatial position in the field is known, but if some other signal is in the same spatial position the storage breaks down. A rather analogous phenomenon has also been mentioned in hearing: in discussing the results of Broadbent on a man listening to digits on one ear and subsequently recalling some items which have been delivered to the other ear. The ability to retrieve in this way from auditory buffer storage is greatly impaired by the presence of any other irrelevant item spoken in the same voice and on the ear which has carried the items desired.

In general and abstract terms, it is common for modern computer storage to be divided into a number of separate locations, and arranged in such a way that the insertion of some information in one location erases whatever has been stored there previously. In modern computing, the particular location which is chosen for storing certain information may itself be significant: for example, if a series of multiplications of the type $a \times b$ was being performed, the current value of a might always be stored in the same part of the memory and replaced by a new value when a fresh calculation is being performed. The reason for this is precisely that which we have given in our simple analogy of blocking out objects in the visual field: the computer program needs to find the correct number again when it is needed. It is not unreasonable therefore nor inconsistent with the facts we have already considered about buffer storage that the buffer store should be organized in a hierarchical way. For any stimulus, some features are more fundamental than others because the possession of these features indicates the region of buffer storage in which the stimulus is located: and retrieval from the buffer takes the form of extracting all items possessing some one feature in order to analyse their other features. Indeed, this is the process which we have termed "filtering" or stimulus selection. Filtering takes place between the buffer store and the later stages of the system, and in one sense is a strategy of retrieval from the buffer rather than a direct process acting on the input.

The foregoing description applies to the buffer store; but even after categorization there is still a problem of retrieving particular stored information from amongst the other and irrelevant items also in the post-categorial store. Indeed, this problem is in some ways more acute than that of selection from the buffer, because longer-term storage must contain very many items most of which are at any instant irrelevant. The organization of retrieval from post-categorial storage may be handled in various ways; but the evidence about acoustic similarity, which we have been considering, requires a process of retrieval which is rather like the filtering we have considered previously. In this case however the filtering is directed inwards towards memory rather than outwards towards the outside world.

However, once we have supposed such a system, is it really necessary to maintain the theory of recirculation into and out of a very transient buffer storage? Could we not simply assume that the interference in short-term memory was all due to the arrival of fresh stimuli with features in common with those already present? Thus far the only evidence we have seen for a distinction between short-term and long-term processes is the different role of acoustic and semantic similarity in the two cases.

The Two Processes of Memory

EVIDENCE FOR THE TWO PROCESSES

(*a*) *The phenomena of free recall.* In most of the techniques we have mentioned, the number of items presented has been relatively small. As we have seen, this means that the retention of any particular item is very much dependent upon the number of other items which follow or precede it. It is also possible however to give a single presentation of a relatively large number of stimuli, and to ask the subject to reproduce as many of these as he can. Since he is likely to lose a fair number of the items, he need not attempt to preserve the order, but can recall in any order he wishes. Under these conditions, the effects of preceding and subsequent items upon the recall of any one item reach a constant value, and a stable relationship seems to hold over quite a wide range of lengths of list. This relationship is

$$\text{Total words recalled} = K \times L \times T + M$$

where

L = number of items presented

T = time of presentation per item

M, K are constants.

That is, for a steady presentation rate any extra item added to the list has a constant probability of being recalled. Naturally this relationship breaks down with short lists, where every item is remembered, and equally it may well break down with exceedingly long lists; but there is a substantial area between these extremes where the relationship holds. The total amount recalled seems therefore to be divided into two sections: one number of items (M) which is recalled whatever the length of list, and one number ($K \times L \times T$) which is a constant proportion of the length of the list (Murdock, 1960).

If now we plot the probability of recall of an item as a function of its serial position in the list of stimuli, we see that these two components of the total recalled are linked with different parts of the series of stimuli. Throughout most of the list there is a constant probability of recall of an item, which of course means that the total number recalled will increase with the length of list. As items approach the end of the list, however, their probability of recall rises, until the probability of recall of the very last item of the list is almost unity. The probability of recall of these items near the end of the list is constant whatever the length of the list, and depends only on the number of other items succeeding the particular one being measured. Thus the number of items recalled from this part of the list is constant (Murdock, 1962). The probability that, say, the last item but one will be recalled does not depend upon the length of the preceding list, and this is true for the last, say, five or six items of the list. A little calculation will show that the total recalled can then only maintain a proportional relationship to the total length if changes in length produce a slight change in the probability of recall for items before the last five or six: and indeed longer lists give a slightly reduced probability of recall at these earlier positions.

There is also a slight difference in the probability of recall between items at the very beginning of the list and items in the middle: but this "primacy" effect behaves differently from the "recency" effect at the end of the list. Whereas the probability of the last item but one being recalled successfully is the same whatever the length of list, the probability of recall of the first and second items drops as the list length increases. This remains true even though the first item may be better recalled than the second for any particular length of list. In the same way, presentation time affects the probability of recall of early and middle items in a list, but not that of the last five or six items.

(b) *Variables affecting different parts of the recall differently.* We have already seen that presentation rate and length of list were shown by Murdock to affect one part of the curve of serial position in free recall, and not the other: from the equation

$$\text{Total words recalled} = K \times L \times T + M.$$

Other factors have a similar effect. For example, Glanzer and Cunitz (1966) confirmed the effect of presentation rate on the early part of the serial position curve, and also showed that repetition of items affected that part of the curve only, rather than changing the "recency" effect. The addition of a subsidiary task during a memory experiment (Murdock, 1965a) changed the early part of the curve and not the late part. One may well ask whether any variables affect the late part alone and not the early part: there are some such, of which the one with the clearest effect is the insertion of some other activity between the presentation of the list and the occurrence of recall. If when the list has stopped, the subject is occupied for 30 seconds or so in a task of counting or of some other irrelevant activity, then the value of M in the equation drops to zero, and the serial position curve shows no effect of recency (Postman and Phillips, 1965; Glanzer and Cunitz, 1966). This is the clearest example of a variable in free recall which has this effect: we shall at a later stage see some less striking evidence on the effects of modality of presentation, and on effects of time intervals between items, but these are obtained using techniques other than free recall and must be deferred until we have explained those techniques.

(c) *Probe technique with short and long retention intervals.* From the data on free recall, then, we obtain a picture of two processes operating for items at the end and at earlier stages of the list. That is, for items within the last five or six events and for items succeeded by a large number of events. It becomes of interest therefore to look back at the techniques for studying primary memory with which we started this chapter. Possibly with those techniques also, rather than with free recall, one might find that some conditions of experimentation would affect recall after short intervals, and other conditions would affect recall after longer intervals. This question can particularly be examined using the probe methods where, for example, paired-associates are presented in a series, and then one of the stimuli is given with instructions to produce an appropriate response. Peterson (1966) reviews a number of studies of this type, which again confirm that different factors are operating when the number of items between presentation and test is small and when it is large. With a long retention interval, for example, the effect of presentation rate agrees with that found in free recall: slowly presented items are better recalled

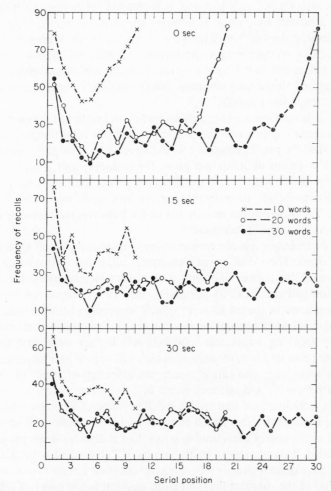

FIG. 33. Free recall for items presented at various points in a list, after intervals of 0, 15, or 30 sec of irrelevant activity. Notice that changes in list length leave recall of the last three or so items unaffected. They do however change the probability of recalling earlier items. Changes in retention interval have the opposite effect. Data from Postman and Phillips (1965).

after a number of other events have intervened. At short retention intervals, the effect of a slower presentation rate is certainly not helpful, and in some studies it has been found to be harmful. (This is a point to which we shall recur, as it has to do with the question whether buffer storage decays as a function simply of passage of time or of number of intervening events.)

Another factor affecting performance at long retention intervals is repetition of an item within a list: if an item has occurred more than once, and there is then an interval before it is tested, it is recalled better than an item which has been presented only once. If however the repeated item is tested after a short interval, it does no better than a non-repeated item. With such repeated items, one can of course vary the interval between repetitions, and again Peterson points out that longer intervals between repetitions give improved recall measured after a long retention, but (if anything) worse recall measured after short retention intervals.

Peterson also notices another curious feature of length of retention interval, which similarly requires two mechanisms to explain it, although it is not at all clear what the two mechanisms would have to be. The phenomenon is as follows: if a group of items are given for memory, and a quite different task is then interpolated before the items are tested, the last of the presented items will deteriorate considerably as the irrelevant interpolated task is extended. The earlier of the memorized items, however, may actually *improve* as the retention interval increases.

(d) *Probe technique and the greater effect of intervening recall upon recently presented items.* The use of probe technique, unlike that of free recall, allows one to control the number of events of all kinds which intervene between the presentation and recall of any particular item. In free recall, we know only that the last items of the list have no *stimuli* intervening between their presentation and recall, but we do not know whether *recall* of other words intervened. (Normally speaking, experienced subjects will in fact recall first the items which were presented last, for reasons which will appear in a moment.) Using the probe technique, one can compare the efficiency of recall of the same presented item with and without recall of other items before it. When we adopt this technique, we find that a recall of some other item, interpolated before the recall of the item which interests us, has much more effect on items presented at the end of the stimulus series than it does on items presented at the beginning. This was shown by the results of Tulving and Arbuckle (1963), which we have quoted already: there was an effect on retention not only from the position in the stimulus list, and from position in the order of recall, but also from interaction of the two. It made more difference to recall an item late if it had been presented late. Similar results have been shown by Howe (1965), and a greater vulnerability of the last items presented was also implicit in the results of Anderson (1960).

THE NATURE OF THE "RECENCY" EFFECT

If we are attempting to divide recall into a component consisting of the very recent items, and a component consisting of those presented earlier, the nature of the "recency" effect becomes crucial. The items at the end of the list are often said, following a remark by an experimental subject of Nancy Waugh, to be contained in an "echo box". What decides whether an item can be recalled from this echo box? When we test at a particular time, it might be that a fixed earlier period of time is in the echo box: or it might be that a fixed number of items are available in this way. It might also be that the loss of an item from the echo box depends upon the nature of the subsequent items. Using a probe technique, one can control the number and the nature of events between presentation and recall, and attempt to answer this question.

(a) *Effects of number of items as opposed to time.* Waugh and Norman (1965) presented digit lists, and tested for particular items within them by providing an item which had actually been in the list and asking the subject to produce the next item. They varied the speed at which the digits were presented, so that one could compare recall after the same number of interpolated digits taking a different time, and after the same time with a different number of interpolated digits. It was clear from their results that recall was less efficient at a fixed time interval if there were more events occurring in that time. Thus we have to say that the content of the echo box is at least in part restricted in number of items.

The results of Waugh and Norman are usually quoted as if they carried the opposite implication that the echo box was unaffected by the time over which the items were delivered; but it has been pointed out by Shallice (unpublished lecture) that this is not the case. Their results do show an effect of time. The reason why this has often failed to be noticed is that the average

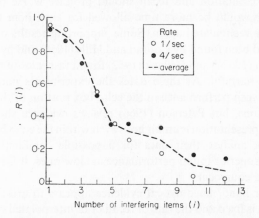

Number of interfering items (i)

FIG. 34. The probability of recalling a digit from the shortest-term memory, as assessed by probing with an item after the presentation is complete. Notice that recall for slowly presented items is better after few intervening events, but worse after many. Thus there does appear to be an effect of time in increasing the forgetting-per-item. But there is also a difference in recall after constant time, depending on the number of intervening items. Data from Waugh and Norman (1965).

360 DECISION AND STRESS

performance with slowly presented items is about as good as the average performance with rapidly presented items. But the speed of presentation affects the efficiency with which items are taken in by the system, as well as the speed with which they are forgotten: a slowly presented item is easier to perceive. (It will be recalled that rate of presentation has an effect on the other component of free recall, the recall of items presented more than five or six items before recall.) Correspondingly, slowly presented items tested immediately after presentation are rather better retained than rapidly presented items are. When a fixed number of slowly presented interpolated items have followed some particular item, retention of that item has fallen lower than after the same number of rapidly presented items: thus the average performance is the same at the two rates, but it is made up of a better performance with slow rates at short retention intervals, and a worse performance with slow rates after large numbers of items. Shallice in fact calculates that forgetting is influenced both by numbers of items and by time, one item corresponding to about one second of time. Similarly the results of Norman (1966) appear to show a slightly greater rate of forgetting per interpolated item when the rate of performance is slow, and there is some indication of a similar effect in the echo box part of the curve in the results of Murdock (1962).

This double effect of slow presentation, giving better registration of the stimulus on the one hand and a faster rate of forgetting per intervening item on the other, probably explains why experiments on rate of presentation have tended to give ambiguous results. On the recirculatory theory, in the version where the buffer storage loses information purely as a function of time, a slow rate of presentation and recall should produce worse performance in memory. There would be more time allowed for each item to decay away before it can be recirculated again. Some supporting results on presentation rate have indeed been found by Conrad and Hille (1958) and by Fraser (1958): but Mackworth (1962a) and Pollack (1952) found fast rates of presentation to be if anything harmful. At these dates the experiments naturally did not distinguish between performance in the echo box portion of the material and in earlier portions, but Peterson (1966) reviews evidence showing that the effect of rate of presentation is ambiguous even within the echo box. Since these studies did not analyse their data for a possible combination of greater forgetting and superior initial performance at slow rates, it is reasonable that the results were equivocal.

On the other hand, unequivocal evidence appears to arise when the rate of presentation is fixed and the rate of recall or of interpolated events is slowed down. This was true in some of the conditions of Conrad and Hille (1958), and also may perhaps be said to hold for a study by Murdock (1961) in which recall of the first item of a list was studied as a function of the number and rate of later items. In this case the number of items was relatively unimportant, and the crucial variable was the time taken by the whole list. Broadbent

(1963b) varied the rate with which a predictable interpolated activity had to be carried out between presentation and recall of learned material, and found a just significant deterioration when the interpolated activity was slower. There does seem therefore to be a detectable effect of sheer time, when the efficiency of original intake of information is held constant. Equally there is a definite effect of the number of intervening events holding time constant.

(b) *Effects of changes in the nature of the intervening items.* When we come to the nature of the events, the evidence is even more scanty. Waugh and Norman reviewed a number of experiments in the literature, and were able to predict performance in the echo box reasonably well on the assumption that recall of an item was determined solely by the number of events intervening between presentation and recall. This involved, for example, treating one recall event as equivalent to one presentation event. While this might be roughly true, the experiments were not intended to answer the type of question in which we are now interested, and it would be rash to assume that the nature of an interpolated event has no effect whatever. It will be recalled that in the studies by Mackworth (1964c) it was found that a single recall item counted for more than a presentation item in determining performance, so that increases in length of presented list gave increases in the total of presentations and recalls. Admittedly the performance here is not analysed into echo box and other components of recall, and may indeed be biased away from the echo box by the method of scoring. Nevertheless, for what it is worth the evidence is against regarding one recall event as equivalent to one presentation event. Similarly, although Mackworth found no difference in the trade-off between recall and presentation items as different kinds of presentation item were added, she did find that the addition of items of the same class as those tested gave a faster drop in recall for each item added. The question of the nature of intervening items in the echo box, as opposed to the earlier portion of the curve, is one which requires more experimental evidence.

CONCLUSIONS ABOUT THE EXISTENCE OF TWO PROCESSES

We have now seen a formidable array of variables, each of which gives different effects immediately after the presentation of an item, and at longer intervals. To summarize, at short intervals the number of intervening events between presentation and recall is a factor, and an increase in the time per event is if anything harmful to retention. So also is an increase in the interval between repetitions of the same item. At longer retention intervals, slow presentation rate is helpful, so are repetitions of an item, and so is an increase in the interval between such repetitions. The total length of list, as distinct from the number of subsequent items, has an effect at these long intervals and so does the presence of a subsidiary task. To go back to earlier sections, semantic similarity is more important over long intervals, whereas acoustic similarity is more important at short ones, and the role of similarity in short intervals does not seem to be the same as the classic effect of similarity in long-term experiments. Although it is certainly true that PI and RI occur in short-term memory as in long-term, they can only be regarded as the same processes if we simply define each of them as a drop in performance caused by preceding or subsequent events. The detailed functional relationships seem to be rather different.

Parsimony is a valuable goal: but it would seem unreasonable in the face of these facts to adhere to the view that all memory obeys the same principles. We are not necessarily compelled by this evidence, however, to hold that there are quite separate storage systems operating over short-term and long-term. There are really a number of theoretical possibilities, and at this stage we should perhaps set out the different alternatives as they seem at this time.

The Nature of the Echo-box and of Longer-Term Memory

To recapitulate, it is accepted that a stimulus on first arrival enters a buffer storage of short duration, which decays primarily with time. If the information is retrieved from this buffer storage and gives rise to a category state, it may then be held indefinitely by a rehearsal mechanism, but in the absence of rehearsal forgetting may occur. There appear to be differences between the recall of items which have been categorized only recently, and those which were put through that stage more than five or six items or four or five seconds ago. We now have to consider different possible explanations of these differences.

THE CONCEPT OF TWO POST-CATEGORIAL STORES, EACH SEPARATE FROM THE BUFFER STORE

This theory is perhaps the most obvious explanation of the facts we have considered. It can be regarded as the view held by Waugh and Norman, at the date of their paper, and in a more extended form by Atkinson and Shiffrin (1967), in an extremely comprehensive account of memory. This view considers two separate stores, following the buffer store. The first, the primary memory, will hold categorized information up to a certain number of items. As fresh items are received and categorized out of buffer storage, they displace items in the primary memory, and each item in primary memory therefore has a certain probability of being lost as each new stimulus occurs. On the other hand, each period of time during which an item remains in primary memory gives rise to a certain probability that that item will be entered also in a secondary memory. This second store has no limit on the number of items it will hold. Recall of a particular item will, therefore, occur if it is in primary store, secondary store, or both: there will be a marked recency effect, when recall takes place without any intervening stimulation, because the last items presented will be in the primary memory. There is

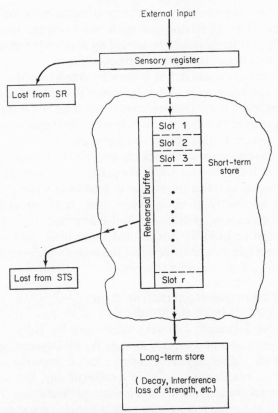

FIG. 35. A typical theory involving two stores after the "sensory register" or buffer store.
After Atkinson and Shiffrin (1967).

likely also to be better performance at the beginning of the series of
stimuli presented, because the first items to arrive will remain in primary
memory for longer before the content of primary memory is full and items
get knocked out. Accordingly, the first items to arrive will have a greater
chance of being transferred to secondary memory. One can have different
versions of this theory, several of which are discussed by Atkinson and
Shiffrin, in which different principles are applied for the transfer from primary
to secondary memory, in which the retrieval model for extracting items from
secondary memory is different, and so on. This broad class of theories can
easily explain why the echo box behaves differently from the items presented
earlier, why recall from the echo box is so much affected by presentation of
later items, and so on.

An example of the kind of experiment which is suggested by the model may
be taken from Brelsford and Atkinson (1968). They gave subjects instructions
to rehearse or not to rehearse items after they were presented: which on this

view should alter the probability that the most recent items would knock out the older ones. Thus the relative ease with which one can recall recent and more remotely past items should be altered by rehearsal: and it is. This type of study confirms the general value of the analysis.

In the form we have stated it, this newer view differs from that of Broadbent (1958) in the following ways. First, information extracted from the buffer store and categorized is not then returned to the same buffer storage. Second, the system of storage to which it passed is not quite the same as Broadbent's recirculatory system. It does appear to involve the categorizing system, in as much as subsequent events will knock out items in the primary store. It is not however so much the *time* for which the categorizing system is occupied by some other process, as rather the *number of fresh items* which it has to handle, which determine loss from the primary store. It is not quite clear how complexity of operations, as in the work of Posner and Rossman and Posner and Konick, can be included in this model, but there are various possible postulates that might be added. Some of the points which require expansion will appear as we consider other theories.

THE CONCEPT OF DIFFERENT RETRIEVAL CUES
IN THE SAME POST-CATEGORIAL STORE

An alternative approach, following suggestions by Tulving (1968), is to hold to the conception of a unitary storage for all information once it has been categorized. Admittedly information recalled from the echo box and from earlier presentations is *recalled* in a different way, but nevertheless all kinds of information are stored in the same general mechanism. The difference between recent and more remote memories is on this view supposed to lie in the retrieval processes available for extraction. We have already touched upon the difficulty that, when many items are present in perception or in memory, retrieval for response must operate on some characteristic or characteristics which mark out the relevant from the irrelevant items. In a single memory storage, there must be a very large number of items. When therefore one seeks to retrieve those items, one may do so by features which have been stored as basic addresses, in the same way that location in a visible field may act as the address of a particular item of information. Thus for example some items in a free recall experiment may be retrieved because they are associated with preceding silence, if they were at the beginning of the list: others because they are linked with items that have already been retrieved. One class of features used for retrieval may be primary sensory characteristics, such indeed as the acoustic features which we have already mentioned. A particular class of these are temporal features; and the scale of time no doubt starts from the present and moves backward, so that one may attempt to retrieve the last item heard, the last item but one, and so on. On the normal principles of Weber's Law, such features will become non-discriminative when the time passed becomes large. Thus the echo box is unique because it consists of those items which can be retrieved using information based on time, and not because the items themselves are stored in any different way.

The importance of availability of cues for retrieval is well demonstrated by Tulving and Pearlstone (1966) who gave lists of words which varied in length, and in which the words could be assigned to various categories by content. The number of words belonging to any one category was also varied, for each length of list. If the subjects were given a cue indicating the category to which some of the words presented had belonged, recall of those words was improved: the extent of the improvement being greater for longer lists and for smaller numbers of words in each category. This experiment caused Tulving and Pearlstone to make a distinction between the "availability" of words and their "accessibility". The former term means that the words are in some sense stored, and the latter term that they can be produced for response. The distinction between the two concepts is necessary, because subjects could produce the word when given the category cue, but not in its absence.

This experiment establishes quite clearly that the recall of a word is a probabilistic process, rather than an all-or-none one. We must beware of thinking that a word which is not recalled is therefore absent altogether from storage. The same implication can be drawn from the experiment by Hebb, in which some saving was shown on the second presentation of a list of digits which could not at that time be recalled. Thus one must think of the storage in memory not merely as being present with a certain probability, but also as having a certain strength which is related to the occurrence of a response, but is not identical with that occurrence. Adding extra retrieval cues will increase the strength and may thus produce the response. It may well also be held that the retrieval cues most effective for recent stimuli are different from those most effective in the long-term: in fact, this is almost a description of the various differences we have discussed.

Having admitted this, however, it is not clear that we ought simply to speak of all items as being in one store with different retrieval cues. First, as the same items are at one time recent items and at another time remotely past items, the retrieval cues for the same information are of one kind at one time and of another kind at another time. It is quite difficult to see how this can be arranged if the information does not pass from one physical store to another. The question whether the different process requires a different physical mechanism becomes perhaps a somewhat philosophical one: certainly the process itself is different.

More serious than this is the point that, if differences in retrieval cues are the only differences between the echo box and more remote information, it is not at all clear why factors which improve the recall of remote information fail to improve the recall of items in the echo box. One can see that retrieval cues available for recent items are not available for remote ones, but one cannot see why conditions which improve the recall of remote ones do not improve the recall of recent ones. In general, this fact is exceedingly surprising, and is for example inconsistent with the formulation given for the last theory, that an item would be recalled if it was in long-term or in short-term store or both. Any improvement in long-term storage ought to improve recall of items which were in the echo box as well as of items elsewhere in the list: and yet examination of the data provided by Murdock (1962) shows that items in the echo box are if anything rather better recalled under conditions which deteriorate performance earlier in the list. In terms of the Tulving approach, this seems perhaps to suggest that items can be retrieved by one cue or by another cue but not by both: in terms of the theory of separate storage systems, it suggests that one can retrieve items from one store or from the other store but not from both. There is rather little experimentation directed explicitly at this point however, and more is badly needed. For the moment, we must simply note it as a difficulty for the retrieval point of view.*

THE ECHO BOX AS A RETURN OF INFORMATION TO THE ORIGINAL BUFFER

This view takes an apparently paradoxical approach, by suggesting that items in the echo box have been returned after categorization to a buffer store of the same kind as that through which they passed on arrival. The number of items which have occurred since then is relevant, because buffer storage can be wiped out by a mechanism similar to the erasure found by Averbach for visual stimulation; and the larger the number of items which have occurred the greater the possibility that one of them has been delivered to the same area of the buffer storage which already contains an item.

Thus the effect of number of items, found by Waugh and Norman, is intelligible; and so also is the effect of rate of occurrence of items, because information will be lost from the buffer by lapse of time. Unless rehearsal takes place, the categorized items will decay in the buffer, just as uncategorized information decays in it unless categorization takes place. Only the last few items therefore, the echo box, will be available in the buffer. More remotely past stimuli can only be recalled if they have been passed to some other long-term store.

One may well wonder why such a view should be entertained at all: since we have already noted that visual stimuli undoubtedly show acoustic confusions, and categorization clearly therefore modifies information once it has arrived. There is however one group of experiments which is awkward for theories which identify the echo box with a non-sensory memory rather than with the sensory buffer. This group of experiments shows that items arriving to the ear survive longer in the echo box than do items arriving to the eye.

* Since the above was written, McLeod, Williams and Broadbent, *Br. J. Psychol.* (in press), have shown that a pair of retrieval cues will interact, thus increasing the difficulty mentioned.

Thus the echo box is affected by the nature of the raw stimulus as well as by that of the category state elicited.

In one of these experiments Murdock (1966) showed with paired-associate learning and probe technique that retention of the last two items presented was better for hearing than for vision, while for earlier items in the list the reverse was the case. Murdock (1967b) repeated this result in a number of forms, and it seems completely clear. An interesting point arose when lists of mixed visual and auditory items were used: if the item being recalled was auditory, it was necessary for the preceding probe item also to be auditory for the benefit to appear. On the other hand, it made no difference whether the next item was auditory or visual. This means that one cannot very well explain the result by, for example, adopting the "retrieval mechanism" approach, and supposing that there is something especially distinctive about acoustic retrieval cues. In that case, the presence of a later acoustic item should surely reduce the advantage of such cues.

A similar difference between visual and auditory presentation has been found by Corballis (1966) using the serial position curve of a complete serial list rather than probing individual items: both Murray (1966) and Conrad and Hull (1968) have compared the serial position curve when items are read aloud during visual presentation, and when they are merely observed visually. In both cases the last item or two is more likely to be correct when the list is read aloud. There does seem therefore to be some quality of acoustic stimulation, even that arising from one's own response to the original stimulus, which makes more reliable the recall of the last items presented. We may note that the original buffer storage for auditory information has a longer duration than that for visual signals: Posner (1967) reports an experiment on bisensory memory, half the items being presented visually and half auditorily, and notes that performance was better when visual items were being reproduced first than if the auditory items were to be reproduced first. Broadbent and Gregory (unpublished) have carried out an analogue to the Sperling experiment, in audition: they presented different items to the two ears, required response only to one ear, and gave the cue indicating the ear for response at various times from before presentation until well after. Performance was significantly better even with an instruction given one second after the end of stimulation than it was with the signal given four seconds after. Thus there must still be some buffer storage available in audition even one second after stimulation. In vision on the other hand Sperling and other workers have found that the limit is considerably less than a second. The data of Moray et al. (1965) can be cited as evidence supporting Broadbent and Gregory's result. It is quite reasonable therefore that auditory stimulation should give better performance on the last items presented, if we imagine that they are held in the buffer storage for a time.

Indeed, the very name of "echo box" suggests introspectively that these last items come from a form of storage which copies very exactly the physical characteristics of the stimulus. When the stimulus itself is acoustic, the same buffer storage might be used as that employed for the original uncategorized information. When the stimulus is visual, the categorization might be postulated as being articulatory and so to pass to a different region of the buffer from that entered by the original stimulus.

Another line of attack on the nature of the echo box develops the method of inserting one redundant item between presentation and response. This method was devised by Conrad and has been mentioned already. We may for example require the subject to respond with a zero before reproducing a series of digits. It is equally possible to present a zero stimulus, immediately after the string of digits, and require the subject to ignore it in his recall. It was shown by Crowder (1967) that this produced a marked difference in the serial position effect: when the subject responded with a zero before any digit, the harmful effects were spread evenly throughout the whole of the stimulus list. When however a stimulus zero followed the list, the harmful effects were concentrated upon the last few items. Acoustic stimulation, incidentally, was used in this case. Thus an event of the sensory type, between stimulation and response, seems to have a more harmful effect than an event of motor type: and it is the echo box rather than the other component of memory which shows the effect. Morton (1968b) has confirmed that the same number of completely predictable irrelevant events, alternating with stimuli to be recalled, will produce more effect if the series ends with an irrelevant event than if it starts with one: and that the deleterious effect will be primarily in the last positions of the sequence. This in itself is not inconsistent with the Waugh/ Norman theory, provided that the irrelevant events are regarded as items: but it is certainly true that their importance in this instance is primarily sensory, and Morton therefore argues for the importance of the sensory buffer in echo box memory. At all events, because of the discrepancy between a redundant recall item and a redundant presentation item, occurring at the same point of time, it is clear that all items are not equivalent.

INPUT BUFFER, OUTPUT BUFFER, AND REHEARSAL

The facts considered in the last section compel us to make some sort of distinction between input and output processes, even though they are no doubt intimately interwoven. The theory we must note in this section comes from Sperling (1967), and its essence is the following. Arrival of sensory information enters a buffer storage, as all theories agree: this buffer is different if the incoming signal is visual from that which would be used if the input is auditory. The new feature of Sperling's view is that the information is then transferred to another store which can hold several items simultaneously, but in which the signals stored are instructions to execute in sequence the internal representations of a series of articulations. Thus this store (the "output buffer" as one may name it) will produce the sequence of events which we have called a sequence of category states elsewhere in this book: each such state will produce a signal which is fed back to the auditory buffer, whichever buffer was used originally. From the auditory buffer, the process may be recommenced.

The reason for Sperling's adoption of this extra complication is this. When a visual display is presented, it may be erased at any desired time after presentation by a noise field which eliminates all signals from the visual buffer. As we saw in Chapter V, information is normally categorized from a visual display in a sequence starting on the left and moving across to the right. Sperling observed however that if the time between visual presentation and erasing field was gradually increased, the probability of correct recognition for items at the right hand end of the display began to rise well before perfect performance had been attained at the left hand end. Thus some simultaneous processing of the information into a form which will survive erasure of the visual buffer is going on, even although categorization must proceed successively. Hence Sperling's assumption that a set of command signals is set up partially in parallel, even though they are to be executed successively.

Such an approach obviously forms a new class of theories rather than any single one, since there are a number of different specific assumptions that could be made. It would presumably be necessary to suppose that the output buffer cannot hold information indefinitely, any more than the input buffer can do so. If this were not so, there would be no need for rehearsal at all. It might be that the output buffer is limited by number of items which can be held, rather than by the time for which signals remain in it, and in this case the theory becomes slightly similar to the last one we considered. The divergence lies in the fact that primary memory in the last theory was not necessarily an output process, while in this case it is so. It may be worth noting that the patterns of acoustic errors found even in visual memory could quite well be confusions amongst command instructions in an output buffer, rather than confusions in a store of input: since the articulations would tend to resemble each other in the same way as the sounds produced. The merit of identifying the part of the system which is not "echo box" with an output process is that it allows us to incorporate evidence such as that of Crowder on the difference between redundant outputs and redundant inputs. In general however this theory is still too undeveloped to be measured very much against experiment: and further repetitions of Sperling's original observation are desirable.

The preceding theories exhaust most of the alternative possibilities, but there are two further modifications either or both of which might be combined with any of the preceding variations.

ACID BATH THEORY

This theory has been stated most clearly by Posner (1967), and it can be summarized in this way. When items are placed in memory, the importance of subsequent activity is simply to prevent rehearsal and therefore to allow passive processes of change to take place with time. To this extent the theory is similar to the early approach of recurrent rehearsal and decay. However, in this theory when items resemble each other, the rate of mutual deterioration is greater. It is as if all items were in an acid bath which gradually removed the differences between them: and therefore similarities between items in store would be important as increasing the effect of retention interval, although they do not produce transfer of a stimulus from one response to another in the classic interference way.

The evidence for this view comes from results such as those of Posner and Konick (1966), showing that similarities or differences between the material used in an interpolated activity and the material being remembered had little effect upon the recall of the latter. When however the items being remembered were acoustically similar to each other rather than acoustically different, there was an increased amount of forgetting. The suggestion was therefore that the effect of similarity applied only between items being recalled, and not between these items and those in the interpolated activity.

This suggestion has a good deal in common with an idea we have already been led to suggest; namely, that each stimulus may be stored in a location which depends upon some of its features, so that if another stimulus arrives subsequently and possesses those same features, the two items will interfere with each other. If we were to put the acid bath theory in this latter form, we should have to add the postulate that the materials being stored must be similar in certain features, those which are used for retrieval. Similarity in other features may be relatively unimportant. Indeed this does appear to be the case in the results of Posner and Konick, since it was only acoustic similarity between consonants which was effective, and there was no difference between the lists consisting solely of consonants on the one hand and lists of mixed consonants and digits on the other. It seems likely to be the use of acoustic or of other features which is important in producing or preventing effects of similarity, rather than the fact that material is supposed to be remembered or is supposed to be part of an irrelevant task. As will be recalled, we have seen evidence that similarity between material in memory and material to be ignored will produce a deterioration in performance, provided the similarity is acoustic. Yet it is quite hard to show effects of similarity of other kinds. Thus the acid bath suggestion must be modified to suppose that the acid is rather selective in its operation! With this qualification, this view could be applied to any of the stores suggested in any of the previously mentioned theories.

CONSOLIDATION AND AROUSAL

There is one group of experiments which certainly show a difference between recall over short retention intervals and that over long ones, but which lie well outside most of the approaches mentioned thus far. These studies are those originated by Kleinsmith and Kaplan (1963) and reviewed by Walker and Tarte (1963), on the relative performance of subjects on items which do or do not produce some emotional response. In a task of learning paired-associates, it can be noted that individual items give galvanic skin responses of different magnitude as they are presented: if one tests retention immediately after presentation, or only after a very considerable delay filled with other activities, it will be found that the items with a large emotional response are relatively better retained over the long interval than over the short one. This effect is undoubtedly due to the arousal of the subject at the time the material is learned: as we shall see in the next chapter, there is evidence that bursts of noise presented with individual items will produce the same effect. The effect appears on various types of material, and it appears both in the case when different types of item are mixed in the same presentation, and also in cases where all the items given on one trial are of the same degree of emotionality. That is, it is not due to selective rehearsal of some items rather than others within a single presentation, or anything of that sort.

The theoretical explanation which is given for this effect has to do with the concept of "consolidation". The idea here is that items which have been presented to a man produce a trace within the nervous system which at first is temporary and vulnerable. One might compare it to a footprint in wet concrete, which can be erased simply by wiping some other object across the surface of the concrete. As time goes by however, and assuming that nothing occurs to wipe out the original vulnerable trace, it hardens into a more permanent and durable trace. In terms of the analogy, once the concrete has hardened the footprint is preserved even if one rubs over the hard surface. One must add to this model the assumption that, during the process of hardening, the vulnerable trace is protected against disturbance by being to some extent unavailable for recall.

We may now explain the effects of arousal on short-term and long-term retention, by supposing that a heightened state of arousal increases the intensity of the consolidation process. This means that the temporary trace is protected yet more vigorously against any disturbance until it is consolidated: while the quality of the ultimate permanent trace is superior to that produced by any impression in an unaroused condition. Thus when a word is presented in a learning task which produces an emotional response, that word is less available for immediate recall than a less emotional word would have been. In long-term recall, however, the emotional word is better remembered.

The affinities of this theory are with physiological interpretations of learning rather than with the types of model we have been considering in the immediately previous pages. In those models, the main distinction was between the echo box on the one hand and the recall of items presented more

N

than five or six events in the past. In the experiments cited by Walker and Tarte, the distinction is rather between the immediate testing of a whole series of paired-associates, and the testing of the series at a very much later time. Furthermore, in the models considered earlier the variables under discussion were activities of the man himself: interference theorists hold that forgetting is due to transfer of responses from one stimulus to another and to extinction of some responses, while decay theorists also invoke the effects of occupying the categorizing system with some other activity. In the present theory, however, we are talking about general states of the entire system.

This line of theorizing has affinities rather with a substantial body of work in physiological psychology, concerning the effects of electro-convulsive shock, freezing, and similar drastic physical treatments upon memory. We shall not be considering these studies here, although a general account of some of them was given by Gerard (1963) and they are also referred to in the symposium edited by Kimble (1967). Broadly, the point is that an animal can be taught a response by repeated reinforced trials of that response: but will fail to learn if each trial is followed within a certain time interval by ECS. If a long enough interval is allowed between the learning trial and the shock, the latter does not prevent learning. Furthermore, stimulant drugs applied to the animal shorten the period within which the shock must be given All these results suggest that some process of consolidation of the learning takes place, and that until this consolidation has been completed ECS will disrupt the memory. This looks very much like a physiological attack upon the same process of consolidation which is postulated to explain the effects of arousal upon short-term and long-term recall.

However, in tasks which require an animal to learn complex responses for reward, such as those cited by Gerard, the time interval during which ECS will abolish learning is quite long, of the order of half an hour or even more. The echo box which we have been considering earlier is a far more transitory affair and it would again seem therefore that the evidence from ECS, freezing, and related physical treatments, does not refer to the distinction between the echo box and the next stage of the memory process, but rather has to do with the mechanism by which the latter stage becomes permanent. Because of the different approaches of the two classes of investigation, it is difficult to relate them perfectly one to the other: but it would seem possible to combine a belief in consolidation over periods of half an hour or so with any of the models we have earlier discussed for the course of events over the first few seconds after presentation.

One may add that most of the physiological mechanisms which had been suggested for this consolidation (Gaito and Zavala, 1964) suggest that some structural change in the nervous system makes permanent a trace which carries the same information as the temporary trace which has preceded it. For example, it may be suggested that stimulation of a nerve cell under certain circumstances may produce protein synthesis which makes that cell more likely to respond in future. The studies we have described earlier, however, rather suggest that the echo box and later forms of memory differ in the extent to which they are organized along acoustic, semantic, or other lines; and in the variables which affect one rather than another. The neural processes involved in recall over short durations would seem to be rather different in kind from those for recall over longer periods, rather than merely being temporary versions of the same trace.

In general therefore, although we can distinguish shorter and longer-term processes in the experiments on human learning we have considered so far in this chapter, and although there seem to be shorter and longer-term processes found in experiments on physiological psychology, it would seem wise to be cautious about identifying the two. The scales are different, and the variables involved do not seem to be the same. For the moment it might seem more reasonable to keep the two sets of phenomena separate, and to think of the process which makes memory invulnerable to ECS as being something which happens considerably later in time than the transfer of information from the echo box to the next stage.

Before leaving the question of consolidation, however, we should note the important point that the nature of the task involved alters the size of the effect. In animal experiments on ECS, it is possible to reduce the period during which learning is vulnerable to shock down to a matter of seconds: by using the task of learning to inhibit the very simple and natural response of stepping down from a pedestal on which the animal is placed. It is still obscure why behaviour of this sort is more resistant to shock, when other forms of learning are not, but we shall see in the final chapter certain other evidence suggesting that the inhibition of positive responses involves rather different processes from the acquisition of such responses. At all events, experiments of this kind still provide no evidence linking the consolidation process to any intervening activity of the animal itself, and still do not tie the effects of physical treatment to the distinction between the echo box and the next stage of memory.

In the case of human learning and arousal, the experiments reviewed by Walker and Tarte concern paired-associate learning. It has been shown however by Maltzman *et al.* (1966) that similar effects do not appear to be found in the learning of serial lists. Once again the implication of this finding is not clear, and it needs further exploration. Superficially however it seems to suggest that the effect of arousal is on the retrievability of individual items in response to an appropriate stimulus, rather than upon the production of an entire sequence to a single retrieval signal. We have already considered several times the possibility that retrieval may take place by different strategies, such as the retrieval of items possessing some common physical feature, and we shall return to this distinction again. If the effect of arousal were to change the way in which the learner organized the material for retrieval, one might have an explanation for the effects of arousal upon short-term and long-term memory which was alternative to the consolidation theory. At the least, the consolidation theory must be modified so as to explain why some tasks only show the effect of arousal. However it is modified, it is likely to be capable of combining with any of the echo box theories, rather than being alternative to them.

CONCLUSIONS ABOUT THE ECHO BOX

From what has been said, it is clear that we cannot yet explain completely the nature of the echo box and of the next stage of memory. It might be that the memorizer has some information available in a buffer store, and the rest in another non-sensory storage: it might be that he has some information in a store holding a fixed number of dependent items, and some in a store of unlimited capacity. It might even be that everything is in one store, with different methods of access to it. This remaining uncertainty, however, must not obscure the broad conclusion that the processes operating immediately after a stimulus has been received are different from those occurring later after three or four intervening events have occurred since the stimulus.

An Attempted Synthesis

THE PRESENT POSITION AND ITS DIFFICULTIES

From what has been said, we have clear evidence for some kind of distinction between short-term and long-term memory processes. On the one hand, we have an array of variables which do not affect the echo box (or recency effect) portion of the retention curve: but which do affect more remote regions of memory On the other hand, we have the greater importance of acoustic similarity in short-term memory and of semantic similarity in long-term memory: even though neither kind of similarity is completely without effect in either situation Yet the apparently satisfactory nature of this position conceals a number of difficulties, which are implicit in the results we have reviewed, but which have not been emphasized as we mentioned them. This is the point at which to bring them into the open.

First, then, it is not at all clear that the acoustic/semantic distinction takes place over the same part of the retention curve as does the echo box/longer-term distinction. If we consider for example the data provided by Baddeley (1968), we see an acoustic similarity effect in serial learning of lists containing six items, where the correct reproduction of each item has been separated from its presentation by at least five events. Yet the acoustic similarity effect is substantial, and seems just as large at each portion of the list. Studies of the recency effect in free recall, or the probe technique introduced by Waugh and Norman, show that the recency effect has pretty well disappeared after six items have intervened between presentation and testing. Thus the recency effect is confined, as the name implies, to the last few items. Yet the effect of acoustic similarity applies to material which has been presented once, and which the subject is still supposed to be trying to remember, but where the presentation and recall have been separated by quite a large number of intervening events. Baddeley (1968) does plot in detail the recency effect when visual presentation is used, and it appears to be of the same size both for acoustically similar and for acoustically different items, except that the whole level of performance is shifted upwards for the acoustically different ones. Thus although we have a distinction between the echo box and longer-term memory, and between acoustically and semantically encoded memory, the two distinctions do not appear to be the same.

Secondly, the distinction between the echo box and longer-term memory does not give a completely adequate explanation of the limits on amount of material which can be handled within a single trial. As we all know, there is a substantial chance of completely correct recall for lists of items of lengths about seven: and we have already noticed the finding of Tulving and Patkau that the number of words reproduced in free recall seems to maintain such a limited number of units; provided that one measures the amount recalled in terms of "adopted chunks", where each chunk consists of words reproduced in response in contiguity just as they were in presentation. Thus it does not seem satisfactory to suppose that memory for items which are not in the "echo box" is simply and without qualification a long-term memory. In some way a limitation of short-term memory applies even to words recalled from the earlier portions of a 50-item list presented for free recall.

Thirdly, the problem of complexity remains strange and orthogonal to most of the formulations of the nature of the echo box. In some way the efficiency of recall is decided not merely by the number of events which intervene between presentation and recall, nor solely by their similarity to the material being remembered, nor by the time which they take, but by their nature in some other sense.

We seem then to need two distinctions within post-categorial memory, and not only one. While it is difficult to sum up briefly the reasons for this, we seem to have one cluster of effects which differentiate the last few items within the present memory trial from earlier items in the same trial: and another cluster of variables which distinguish items presented on this trial from items presented recently but in a separate learning trial. The latter clause is intended to cover the acoustic/semantic contrast, the limitation on numbers of adopted chunks, the effects of complexity of intervening tasks, and so on.

One way of making the two distinctions would be to suppose that there are genuinely three post-categorial stores, rather than the two postulated by an approach such as that of Atkinson and Shiffrin. This may indeed be the case: on such a point of view the original uncategorized information would be held in a buffer, then categorized and passed to the "echo box" store, from which after a fixed number of intervening events it would be lost. During its period in the echo box, however, it might or might not be transferred to the second post-categorial store: once there it would remain there for the duration of the experimental trial, with a certain probability of transfer during that time into the third or genuinely long-term memory. At the end of the experimental trial the second post-categorial store would be wiped clean.

At this stage however even the present author begins to feel that parsimony would favour some other approach. Let us see if anything can be done by keeping the number of post-categorial stores to two, but supposing also that there are limitations on the other parts of the system. In particular, let us suppose that there are limitations of control or retrieval from the two stores.

AN ANALOGY: THE IN-BASKET, THE FILE, AND THE DESK-TOP

As an introduction to such a concept, let us take the analogy of an office desk. When the mail comes into an office, it arrives successively in an in-basket, where the last item to arrive is clearly visible, the next is fairly readily accessible beneath it, the next a little less accessible beneath that, and so on. When a substantial number of papers arrive and have not been dealt with, however, the in-basket becomes an inefficient method of storage and many of its contents are better removed to a more permanent filing system. In the in-basket, there is a limit to the number of items that can be held simply because there is no organized method of retrieving them selectively, rather than merely by their recency of arrival. In the more permanent file, items are classified under various sub-headings and thus an appropriate enquiry will retrieve the correct paper from amongst the large number in the file.

We are left therefore with a clean desk containing an in-basket with the last few items, while in the corner of the office is a file containing all the items that have entered the system. On any one day however the user of the office may well wish to carry out a certain series of jobs, or to do a single job which requires a number of different items of information. Since he is generating this requirement himself, he cannot rely upon outside enquiries containing signals which will guide him to the correct item in the file or the in-tray. Thus he needs to assemble on his desk some rough notes which remind of the sequence of jobs he has to perform. He may place on his desk-top a piece of paper bearing the cryptic messages "1. George's salary. 2. Arrange transportation for equipment. 3. Revise publicity handout. 4. Write to Smith regarding committee meeting. 5. Pay today's bills". The purpose of these notes is not to provide sufficient information for adequate performance at each stage in the sequence of jobs, but rather to direct attention to that part of the file or the in-basket where the relevant information is to be found. (In the example given, for instance, the very last item is presumably in the in-basket while the others need access to the longer-term files.)

In one sense the desk-top can itself be regarded as a store, like the in-basket and the file, but differing from each of them in its limitations. In the file the number of items is unlimited and the only problem is retrieving one item rather than all the others: in the in-basket it is the number of subsequent items which matters. On the desk-top the limitation is rather the number of separate headings or notes which can be accommodated in the space available: but each of them can refer to a very large amount of information in the other storage systems. The desk-top is primarily therefore a control or retrieval system rather than a store.

A MORE FORMAL STATEMENT

The foregoing analogy has the attraction of relating the problems of short-term memory to everyday experience: but the analogy does break down at certain points, and we must also attempt a more formal statement. The suggestion is then that the system contains three components.

(a) *Store of buffer type*. Following categorization, information is returned to a store with the characteristics of the original sensory buffer. That is, it will decay with time, perhaps more slowly than the original sensory buffer because the categorized information will have a better signal/noise ratio. It will also be erased by the presentation of subsequent items possessing the same features. Thus this storage will have available the last item to have been categorized, and with decreasing probability items less recent than that.

(b) *The longer-term store*. All items which have been categorized pass also into a longer-term storage. An item is from this point of view an organized structure of features, and the subsequent presentation of incompatible associations of the same features may cause "forgetting" of the material. That is, this part of the system proceeds much according to the principles of interference theory. As we have already indicated, this does involve some element of forgetting due to passage of time, because of the greater influence of PI at long retention intervals. We shall return to this point in the final chapter, but for the moment let us merely keep this store as acting according to classical association theory.

(c) *The address register*. In addition to the two stores, there is also a component which will hold indefinitely the addresses of a fixed number of locations in the two stores. By an address is meant the necessary information to select, out of all the material stored, a particular item. The items being selected may be either in the buffer store, or in the long-term store. The limitation on this component is the number of addresses which can be maintained, and there is no element of time involved; but the information stored at a particular address may, especially in the long-term store, be extremely voluminous. The techniques of addressing used will be extremely important on this view, and we shall discuss them later.

IMPLICATIONS OF THIS FORMULATION

This formulation seems to avoid some of the difficulties we have mentioned earlier. First, it is clear that limitations of short-term memory will extend to material presented further in the past than those sharing in the recency effect. The amount reproduced even from a list of 50 items will be restricted by the number of items accessible through the fixed number of locations available in the address register. Thus the finding of Tulving and Patkau that a constant number of "adopted chunks" can be recalled becomes reasonable. It is also reasonable that there should be a fixed memory span, with a determinate number of items that can be reproduced in their order of arrival.

Conceptually, the suggestion of fixed number of items is rather similar to that of Waugh and Norman on the one hand or of Atkinson and Shiffrin on the other. There are however certain differences: there have to be, because the early part of a memorized list does behave differently from the later part. The theories of Waugh and Norman or of Atkinson and Shiffrin are postulated to explain the recency effect, and they hold that a fixed number of items are held in memory but that early items may be displaced by subsequent ones. In long lists however the early items are not greatly disturbed by the arrival of subsequent items, and hence the theories of the recency effect suppose these items to be in longer-term memory. From our own point of view, we would have to hold that the address register will accept fresh addresses until it reaches the limited number which is its maximum. After this stage it does not throw out items to make room for fresh ones, but on the contrary accepts fresh ones only if they can be associated with items already addressed. If such an association can be formed, the two words can be regarded as a single item, and reached through the same address. There would then be a constant probability that this can be done for each new incoming item, and hence the increasing total number of words which can be recalled as the number of words in the stimulus list is increased. Nevertheless the total number of groups of associated words which can be reproduced remains constant.

A point which may be related to the last is the effect of the nature of the items upon the length of the memory span. We have carefully avoided thus far indicating how many addresses can be held in the address register: perhaps the fashionable figure would be to say seven. When we examine data on memory span, however, it is notable that there is a slight effect of the nature of the material being remembered, the span being slightly longer for digits than it is for letters of the alphabet. This discrepancy seems to apply primarily, however, to the span as usually measured; that is, the point at which 50% of lists can be recalled correctly. Perfect recall is available for about three to four items, pretty well regardless of the nature of the material being presented. (See for example Cardozo and Leopold, 1963.) One possibility is that the number of addresses in the address register is only three or four, and that longer sequences are retained only if clusters of items can be associated in the longer-term store. The chances of such clustering would depend on the nature of the material. This, however, is taking us into realms of uncertainty which will only complicate the present statement.

We mentioned another difficulty for existing echo box theories; namely, the role of complexity of activities intervening between presentation and recall. From our present point of view, a complex intervening activity has its effect because it requires the use of several different positions in the address register. For example, the instruction to add 2 whenever a digit is presented requires that the system have available the address of the digit, of the instruction, and of the result of the operation. Simply to repeat a heard digit does not take up so many spaces in the address register. In consequence, complex tasks interfere more than simple ones do with the recall of material presented before the task began.

Certain other features of memory, which are hard to fit in with other views, harmonize fairly easily with the present formulation. For example, there is the phenomenon observed by Tulving and Pearlstone, that items could be recalled if a retrieval cue was given although they were unavailable to free recall. This experiment will be remembered as having given rise to the distinction between availability and accessibility. Another set of studies which have not been mentioned earlier are those of Shepard and Teghtsoonian (1961): in these studies a series of items are given, and for each the subject has to say whether the item has occurred previously in the series or not. These studies do show a deterioration as the number of items intervening between the previous and the present presentation increases: but an interesting point for our present concern is that quite high levels of performance are available at fairly long retention intervals. The recognition technique, like the provision of category cues in the Tulving and Pearlstone experiment, reduces the problems of retrieval. Thus the implication of these experiments, like that of the Tulving and Pearlstone one, is that a single presentation may leave items in store for quite long periods, if the problems of retrieval can be overcome. It is for this reason that our formulation has suggested that all categorized items go into this form of storage, and not merely a proportion of them as in the Waugh and Norman/Atkinson and Shiffrin type formulation.

Other results which can perhaps be interpreted by our present formulation are those on the effect of itemization or chunking upon rate of forgetting: it will be remembered that Melton (1963) showed that the rate of forgetting increased as the number of items being remembered increased. The more locations occupied in the address register, the fewer the remainder left for an intervening task. With seven or eight items, forgetting was immediate. Similarly, Melton studied the Hebb effect, of improved reproduction of a list when it was presented several times amongst other lists presented only once. The Hebb effect disappeared when the number of intervening lists was about seven or eight, and conceivably this might be the point at which the

N*

address of the whole list was finally lost from the register. We may also note the apparent absence of PI within an experimental trial, found by Murdock: provided paired-associate materials are used. Here again, a retrieval cue is provided, and hence the limited number of locations in the address register become less important. There are in each of the above examples however certain difficulties which can perhaps be left as an exercise to the reader!

Amongst the various difficulties which provoked us to attempt the new formulation, the one which we have not yet discussed is the role of acoustic similarity, and its importance over time periods greater than the recency effect. This raises a sufficiently large question to deserve a section of its own.

FILTERING AND PIGEON-HOLING IN RETRIEVAL

We have said so far only that the address register contains enough information to select certain items out of the stores. We have not considered the way in which this selection could be conducted. Yet we have on a number of occasions in this chapter pointed out the similarity between problems of retrieval and those of perception. Indeed selective perception itself is now viewed rather as selective retrieval from the short-lasting buffer, admission of information to the buffer being unselective. Thus we ought not to be surprised to find useful in retrieval analyses and principles similar to those we have discussed in selective perception. Categorizing perhaps becomes irrelevant, since the material in memory has already been categorized: but filtering and pigeon-holing do not. Filtering, we may recall, is the selection for response of items possessing a particular feature; while pigeon-holing is a bias towards responding with certain category states, ignoring input signals which are inappropriate to the chosen states. In the present connection, one can suppose that retrieval of memory material might either rest upon single common features appropriate to all material which was wanted and absent in that which was not; or on the other hand one might suppose that retrieval was of that information appropriate to any one of a small set of possible responses, while information inappropriate to any such responses would not be retrieved.

The distinction may become clearer when we consider the operations usually carried out in memory experiments. Typically for example we ask the subject to look at some items, then say them aloud, then to count backwards for a fixed period, and then to recall the items. When he has done this once, we ask him to do it again, and so on. In the middle of such an experiment, he is attempting to retrieve certain items which have in common the time at which they were presented, but which are drawn from the same general vocabulary of items as those used throughout the experiment. This is a form of retrieval analogous to filtering.

On the other hand, if we present a large series of words in a free recall experiment, and then subsequently tell the subject that we want the names of articles of furniture, we are asking him to use in his response items chosen from a particular vocabulary, where the corresponding stimuli may have had no single feature in common. This is an example of response selection in retrieval from memory, and more analogous to pigeon-holing than to filtering.

If this analysis is correct, the instructions in any memory experiment require the subject to act selectively upon his memories. The instructions may require him to use one vocabulary for response rather than another. Alternatively, the instructions may leave his vocabulary of responses unchanged but ask him to produce responses within the vocabulary for material possessing some other feature, such as arriving at a certain time. These two kinds of instruction may produce different patterns of performance. Admittedly, some of the differences which appear in the perceptual case can hardly apply in the memory situation. For example, we can hardly contrast selective instructions before presentation with those given afterwards, since by definition we are speaking always of selection applied at the time of retrieval. We can however look at the pattern of correct responses in relation to error responses: at a simple level, we would expect intrusion errors only when selection is by a filtering mechanism rather than by a response set mechanism. That is, we would expect errors of intrusion when the subject is recalling the material presented on the current trial rather than on any earlier one in this session, if the vocabulary of items has been the same throughout the session. We would not expect intrusion errors if he is asked to give the names of items of furniture from amongst a list of mixed words. As in the case of perception, this experiment hardly needs to be done.

There are however a few interesting further applications. For example, if we are studying a situation where intrusion errors occur, and where difficulty of recall is resulting from them, then a change in the instructions so as to allow response selection rather than stimulus selection should produce a marked improvement in performance. It will be recalled that Wickens et al. (1963) showed just such a change, under the heading of release from PI. If a series of trials have been performed using letters of the alphabet as stimulus material, and if one then turns to digits, the first trial on the new material will show dramatically improved performance. Incidentally, this will hold true even if the change in the set of responses in use leaves the stimulus characteristics closely similar to some of those in play in the old set of responses. Thus Wickens and Eckler (1968) showed no PI for a group of subjects who, having had trials on letters, now had to remember the words JAY, ARE, SEA. These words of course are acoustically very similar to the letters J, R, C. The availability of response selection however prevented the preceding trials from creating any difficulty for performance on the test trial.

The experiment last mentioned raises the question of acoustic similarity: since, when no change of response set occurs from trial to trial, we might well expect acoustic similarity between two items to increase the difficulty of recalling one of them rather than the other. The problem will only arise in our view, however, if the acoustic quality of the item is being used as a method of retrieving it selectively. Thus it is reasonable that acoustic similarity should affect experiments such as those of Wickelgren cited earlier, where the subject is asked to retrieve a single item preceded and followed by other items from the same general vocabulary. The time of occurrence of the key item is a rather weak feature which may be used for its retrieval, but if the key item differs in acoustic quality from the irrelevant items this will provide another alternative means of retrieval. On this view, acoustic similarity will produce difficulties only when the similarity is between the item to be retrieved and other items which are in memory but are not to be retrieved.

Many of the experiments on effects of acoustic similarity, which we have discussed earlier, clearly fall into this heading. The material to be remembered is preceded or followed by irrelevant material, and the experimental variable is the degree of acoustic similarity between the relevant and irrelevant items. At the same time, there are some experiments such as that of Baddeley (1966b), in which it is the similarity of one remembered item to another which matters. In these cases however the recall appears to be usually required in a fixed sequence rather than a free order; consequently at any one point in recall the same problem of selection exists, and the subject has to select which of the items recently presented to him is the correct item for retrieval at this particular point in the remembered sequence. The acoustic similarity of items will create problems in such a case.

The relationship between errors of order and errors of reproduction of items is one which has given rise to much discussion in the literature: it has for example been suggested that a separate storage of information is required for the order in which items occur, as well as for the nature of the particular items being remembered (Crossman, 1960). On the whole however this view has been relatively little urged since Conrad (1965) showed that the incidence of order errors depended upon the nature of the particular items involved. That is, if it is especially likely that item (a) will be forgotten and item (b) recalled in its place, and vice versa, then it is especially likely that the sequence (a) (b) will be recalled as (b) (a). This is strong evidence against the idea of a separate storage for order, and rather suggested to Conrad that apparent errors of order could be completely accounted for by the occurrence of two independent intrusion errors at different points in the sequence.

From our present point of view, two aspects of Conrad's analysis are especially important: first, he showed that acoustic similarity was especially relevant to the occurrence of order errors. If two items were acoustically similar to each other, the chances of their being recalled in inverted order were very greatly increased. There was also a substantial increase in the chance that one of them would be recalled at the point in the sequence where the other was appropriate, even though the one replaced did not appear at the position from which the intruder had come. Both these facts, and especially the latter, argue strongly against the independence of item and order errors. Conrad was therefore able to suggest that the acoustically similar letters transposed more frequently because there is a greater probability that each of them will be recalled in error in place of the other. The second point, however, which should be noted in his analysis is that he does suppose that items which have not occurred in the sequence at all are less likely to be recalled at any point in it than those which have occurred: that is, the important factor is acoustic similarity between items within the sequence, rather than between each of them and unpresented items in the underlying vocabulary.

Conrad's results, therefore, support the suggestion that acoustic similarity impairs performance within a learned sequence, even where no other irrelevant items have been presented, because it impairs the ability to reproduce the items in order. That is, it impairs the ability to select out of the remembered items the one which is correct at this particular point in the sequence. We shall see evidence later, derived from an analysis by decision theory, confirming this general conclusion. On this view therefore the importance of acoustic similarity which was found in short-term memory has been due to the fact that selective retrieval has been emphasized in the appropriate experiments. Correspondingly, as we have pointed out earlier, it is similarity in the response item which creates a difficulty in short-term memory, and not similarity of the stimulus as it should be on an associative theory. Acoustic similarity of the stimuli in a paired-associate experiment gives no impairment of performance even in STM (Dale and McGlaughlin, 1968).

Semantic similarity, however, is in a different position. The semantic aspects of a word may be expected to be related to its associations with other items, and correspondingly the experiment by Baddeley and Dale (1966), showing that semantic similarity was important in long-term memory, varied similarity of the stimuli rather than the responses. Such similarity had no effect in short-term memory, and this is perhaps reasonable since the variation of similarity in this task did not affect the nature of the items being retrieved but only that of the stimuli used to elicit them. Thus it could not affect retrieval either by the filtering strategy nor by that of pigeon-holing. The absence of effect of semantic similarity in the results of Baddeley and Dale for short-term memory may therefore have been because the particular task did not allow similarity to affect selective retrieval.

In other situations, however, one might expect an effect upon retrieval from semantic similarity. The establishment of a response set causes the subject to be ready to produce any one of a vocabulary of responses, and such a vocabulary can well be regarded as a set of semantically related or similar items. If, for example, the materials in memory fall into two separate groups, and the instruction to respond with names of articles of furniture allows the selection of one of these groups rather than another, one might expect semantic differences to be helpful to memory. Indeed, we have seen evidence in the experiments of Dale and of Baddeley that semantic similarity does affect short-term memory for sequences of words, and for materials followed by other irrelevant items. The fact that the effects have been rather slight, as compared with those of acoustic similarity, may reflect the lower efficiency of pigeon-holing rather than filtering: but their existence does suggest that pigeon-holing is a possible strategy for retrieval.

Because the theoretical issue had not arisen at the time of the experiments,

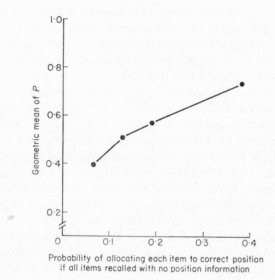

Probability of allocating each item to correct position
if all items recalled with no position information

FIG. 36. Results from Yntema and Schulman (1967), for memory of the item last presented in a certain position. The various points are obtained by using the same item vocabulary for all positions, a different vocabulary for each position, and two intermediate arrangements. Thus a benefit is clearly obtained by reducing the need for specific memory of the position in which an item has occurred; item memory alone is less demanding than item + position.

most of the studies of semantic similarity in the literature could however be explained by associative processes operating even in short-term memory. An experiment by Yntema and Schulman (1967) is of particular interest as separating the two possibilities. Their experiment required subjects to keep track of the last item placed in each of a series of boxes. Each box was labelled with a letter, and periodically the subject would be asked for the last item in a box of a certain letter. It has been shown by Yntema and Mueser (1960, 1962) that performance was much better on this task if each box contained only items drawn from its own small vocabulary of possibilities, rather than using the same vocabulary for all boxes. That is, when items in Box H were always names of animals, while those in Box K were always names of countries, performance was much better than if both boxes could have animals in them. In terms of our current approach, this would be because response selection could be used to identify the item held in memory which was appropriate for a certain box.

The result could also be explained however on a basis of associative interference, because the condition in which the same vocabulary was used for all boxes would allow the occurrence of an item in one box to have been preceded by its occurrence in another box, and so produce PI. In the experiment by Yntema and Schulman, subjects were given a condition in which each box had its own set of items: but these were chosen arbitrarily, and the subject did not know the members of the set chosen for any particular box. So far as he was concerned, any item could occur in any box: but in fact associative interference could never have occurred, because the same item, if it had occurred previously in the experiment, had always occurred on the same box. The experimental results for this condition were just the same as those in which the items had no special association with any box. That is, the results showed an effect of response selection and were not consistent with an associative interpretation.

From this analysis, we have to take a rather different view of the differences between short-term and long-term memory in effects of acoustic and semantic similarity. The two kinds of similarity can both affect selective retrieval, but one of them affects primarily filtering and the other pigeon-holing. Semantic similarity can be heavily involved also in the associative interference found in long-term memory. In cases such as the release from PI, semantic differences may be sharply beneficial even in short-term memory. Thus the distinction between acoustic and semantic similarity is not so much one of different portions of the retention curve, but rather that the two kinds of similarity are associated with different strategies of retrieval. It so happens that the experiments which have been performed emphasize primarily the filtering form of selective retrieval, in short-term memory, and hence the greater role of acoustic similarity in that case. In experiments such as that of Yntema and Schulman, however, or in that of Wickens and Eckler, semantic distinctions play an important part even in the case of short-term memory. There may perhaps be a greater bias towards semantic factors in long-term memory, because of the greater importance of association. Nevertheless, the major distinction is on this view between the same two strategies of selection which we have considered so many times in perception.

At present, the formulation we have given is merely one suggested by the difficulties of the data, which does at least have the merits of helping us to bear in mind features of the results which tend to get left out by other interpretations. Certainly, the evidence for the use of filtering on the one hand and of pigeon-holing on the other, in selective retrieval as in perception, is less convincing than one would wish. As we said earlier, some of the differences in performance which characterize filtering and pigeon-holing in perception cannot be examined in the case of memory. We need, therefore, to concentrate entirely upon the changes in correct response which occur when the probability of an incorrect response changes. In the case of perception, we saw that a function could be derived relating the probability of correct response and the probability of incorrect response; and we saw also that pigeon-holing produced a movement of performance along this curve without motion to another curve, while filtering produced a change to a different curve. In the terms of decision theory, filtering changed d' while pigeon-holing changed β.

Similar types of analysis can be applied in the case of memory. In the experiment by Yntema and Schulman, it will be remembered that the subject was asked to identify the last item placed in one of several boxes, and performance was compared when the vocabulary of items associated with any one box was unique to that box, was shared with one or two other boxes, or was common to all the boxes. Yntema and Schulman analysed the probability of correct response as a function of the proportion of items in memory which could be eliminated by giving the name of the box about which the test question is asked. From one point of view, this can be regarded as a relationship between P_C and P_G, the correct response probability and the guessing probability, just as in the various experiments considered in Chapter VI. Yntema and Schulman showed that the results were fitted by the curve $P_C = P_G{}^K$ which is of course one of the relationships we have met in the perceptual case. For each level of retention interval, the value of K was constant as the degree of uniqueness of the responses for each box was changed. That is, the use of selection by response set changed P_C purely by the amount of change in P_G, just as in response set in the perceptual case.

(Parenthetically, one should notice that in this instance P_G, the guessing probability, represents the probability of guessing from amongst items which have been presented and are in memory, and *not* from amongst all items in the total vocabulary possible. The distinction is important in Yntema and Schulman's experiment. Thus if the subject knows that Box H includes animal names, and guesses one of the six animal names at random, he is equally likely to be correct whether or not animal names are being used also for other boxes. If, however, he remembers the last six items which have been said to him, his probability of choosing one of them correctly for box H is much greater when box H is the only one associated with animal names.)

We have here some tentative reason for extending to memory the decision analyses used previously for perception. Our ultimate purpose will be to see whether we can find changes in d' associated with filtering operations, and of β associated with pigeon-holing ones.

Analyses of Memory in Terms of Decision Theory

APPLICABILITY OF THE APPROACH

Earlier in this book, we first introduced the measures derived from decision theory by drawing attention to the problem of false positives. In perceptual experiments, people occasionally see or hear stimuli which have not in fact been presented. As we showed in Chapter III, the number of correct perceptions is affected by various variables which also affect the number of false alarms. Many factors, such as changes in the degree of confidence which we demand of the subject before he makes a judgment, will give an increase in the number of detections as the number of false alarms increases: and the relationship between the two is given by the equation

$$Z_D = d' + Z_{FA}.$$

Other variables, such as a change in the intensity of the stimulus, give a change in the number of correct detections with a constant false alarm rate, that is, they change the value of d' in the above equation. When we turn to the field of memory, we find once again that classical experiments have paid relatively little attention to the problem of false alarms. In the case of memory, these false alarms take the form of items recalled despite the fact that they were never presented. Such false memories certainly occur, and are emphasized in studies of memory under complex conditions such as those of Bartlett (1932). In the laboratory, false alarms have however rarely been considered, save in the particular case of intrusion errors from other interfering learning. The distinction of introducing d' measures into the field of memory belongs, as with many techniques, to Egan (1958), but for our own purposes of presentation it will be convenient to depart from chronological order. Rather let us present a series of experiments which show that the probability of correct recall does vary with the probability of a false report, in such a way as to make appropriate the same kinds of measures which we have been employing in the case of perception.

RECOGNITION FROM SEVERAL ALTERNATIVES

In the ordinary textbooks of learning, it has long been pointed out that correct memory may be demonstrated by a recognition test even when unassisted recall is improbable. The man who is asked to recall a nonsense syllable presented three weeks ago may be unable to do so, and yet may be able to pick the correct syllable if it is presented to him together with three completely new ones. Of course, in the latter case there is a substantial probability of guessing a correct item by chance even if it had never been earned. Yet in many cases it has been possible to show that a man given a recognition test performs higher than the guessing rate. That is, it is not possible to explain his performance by an equation of the type

$$P_C = R + (1 - R)P_G$$

where P_C = probability of correct response in recognition test

R = probability of correct response in free recall

P_G = probability of correct response in recognition test if the item had never in fact been experienced, i.e. the guessing rate.

Some similarity is evident between this fact and the perceptual situations considered in Chapter VI, in which the subject is given a small fixed vocabulary of possible responses. There too the effect of a small set was greater than could be accounted for simply by adding a guessing probability to the level of performance obtained without the fixed alternatives. Whereas, however, there has been much experimentation in the field of perception upon the precise relationship between the size of the fixed set and the level of performance, there has been rather less corresponding work in the field of memory. Davis *et al.* (1961b) hit upon the idea that the advantage of recognition tests over free recall tests was due to the smaller amount of information required in memory in order to secure correct performance in the recognition test. As recognition experiments have usually been performed, a number of items are presented and the test then consists again of several correct items mixed with an equal number of incorrect items. It is quite difficult to derive a measure of information for this situation, but Davis *et al.* found one and applied it to some experiments of their own with this technique. In general the results fitted fairly well the idea that a constant amount of information was held in memory, with a corresponding better level of correct performance on tests involving choice between few alternatives. When two-digit numbers were used as stimuli, it was possible to give a recognition test which includes all the possible numbers that might have been used, and in that case recognition performance fell to the level of free recall performance.

The informational approach, while an advance over traditional methods, is still inadequate: because it considers only the size of the set of possibilities and not the degree of confusability between them. It is easy to show (Dale and Baddeley, 1962) that a very difficult recognition test can be made up out of the items which are frequently given as errors in a free recall test, whereas a recognition test containing only the correct item and some others which are rarely given in a recall test will be very easy. This is again a kind of dependence of correct recall upon the probability of the same response occurring incorrectly, which is not considered in ordinary informational analyses.

Furthermore, even when we present a recognition test consisting of the entire set of possible items from which the memorized material was drawn, there may still be differences between the recognition performance and that in free recall. Such differences depend upon the nature of the particular material being used: suppose for example that the items are drawn from a set which the subject knew perfectly before the experiment ever began, and in which there are no items which are unfamiliar to the subject. Such a set of alternatives is provided, for example, by the set of two-digit numbers. With material of this kind, as we have indicated, the performance by free recall is about the same as that for a recognition test which actually presents the complete list of two-digit numbers and requires the subject to pick out those which have been presented. If however we use a class of material such as the names of English counties, in which some items are far more familiar to the subject than others, then he may do worse at free recall of a list of twelve counties than he will at recognizing those twelve amongst a complete list of all the possible county names (Dale, 1967). The difference occurs primarily upon those county names which are rarely recalled when subjects are asked simply to produce every possible county name which occurs to them.

Once again, one can consider these effects as examples of the probability of correct recall varying with the probability that the particular response will be given even in the absence of earlier experience with that item. While these findings therefore suggest that it is unprofitable simply to look at the information extracted from memory by recognition tests with a given number of alternatives, they do suggest that we should look more closely at the relationship between correct and false occurrences of response. The literature does not provide however much information about the details of this relationship, from recognition tests involving several alternatives and requiring choice of the correct one. Let us turn rather therefore to another kind of recognition, in which a single response is suggested to the subject and he is asked whether or not this item has previously been experienced. This again may be called recognition, but there is no longer the problem of the particular alternatives from which the man must choose, only of the probability of acceptance of this particular item. Once again, he will accept the item with a certain probability when it has indeed been presented previously, and also with another, usually lower, probability when the item has never occurred before. Now we may look more closely at the relationship between the two probabilities.

THE METHOD OF RECOGNITION MEMORY WITH A SINGLE PROBE

Two papers which appeared in the same issue of the *Journal of Experimental Psychology* (Murdock, 1965b; Norman and Wickelgren, 1965) may be taken as our reference experiments in this case. The study by Norman and Wickelgren corresponded exactly to the method outlined in the last paragraph: a string of digits was presented to the subject, then he was required to copy a series of irrelevant items, and then a digit was presented to him with the question whether or not it had occurred in the material to be remembered. By requiring the subjects to indicate their degree of confidence in their response, we can obtain responses "Yes" and "No" with varying degrees of confidence, just as in the case of detection of a sensory signal. For any degree of confidence, we, therefore, have a value of P_C when the suggested item had in fact been presented for memory: and P_G when it had not. We can, therefore, examine the relationship between them and see what its general form may be.

In fact, it was found by Norman and Wickelgren that the relationship was not of the form

$$P_C = A + BP_G$$

but rather roughly of the form

$$Z_C = d' + Z_G.$$

Thus, just as in perception, large changes in P_C can result from small change in P_G. In discussing any phenomenon in memory, therefore, we must immediately ask the same question as in perception: is the change in correct responses accompanied by a change in false responses in the same direction, or by an opposite change? Simple reporting of correct responses can no longer be regarded as adequate.

As in the case of the perceptual experiments, it is important that the difference between the two Z-scores is roughly constant and does not change as the false alarm rate changes. In perception this fact meant that we could exclude the possibility that subjects were failing to look at the signal on a certain proportion of occasions: in memory it means that we can exclude the possibility that items are either perfectly in memory or completely missing, with a certain probability. Rather, they seem to be present in memory with a given degree of strength which varies continuously. The contrast can be seen in the case when Norman and Wickelgren carried out their experiment with two-digit numbers rather than single digits. In that case, the data seemed rather to show that the pair of digits sometimes failed to be stored. This point probably requires considerably more examination, since there are a large number of cases of memory in which "stimulus selection" is supposed to be important. That is, the subjects are regarded as concentrating on some parts of the list and ignoring others. Such cases could well be examined using the analyses of decision theory. At the moment, the important point is that there are at least some tasks for which the degree of evidence about items in memory varies continuously; rather than taking the form of information which is in store or not with a certain probability, but perfect provided that it is in store.

Murdock's experiment was closely similar, but had important differences. He used paired-associates rather than digits, and following a series of six pairs he presented one of the stimulus terms with a suggested response term. Thus there are two major differences from the Norman and Wickelgren technique: there is no intervening activity between presentation and test, and the test refers always to a particular location in the series of events. If we present an item which has not previously been presented, and give with it no particular stimulus, we do not know whether the subject's incorrect recognition of it means that he thought it was a very recent item, or a more remotely past item.

Murdock's results, fortunately, agree with those of Norman and Wickelgren in essentials. One can however add two important points. First, the four earlier paired-associates in the series all gave the same value of d'. That is, there is no sign of a drop in the level of evidence in store about past items, as the time since they were presented increases. Secondly however this is not true of the fifth pair, which gave a larger value of d': and performance on the sixth, as might be expected, was pretty well perfect since it was being tested immediately after presentation, without intervening events. Thus the usual superior performance for items in the "echo box" appears using this method also. (Norman and Wickelgren, because of the irrelevant activity intervening between presentation and test, had not examined this point. We shall see shortly that later experiments by them give conclusions similar to Murdock's, but with their rather different technique.)

Before we go on to other methods of assessing d' in memory, we should notice one important point. We have already emphasized that in both experiments the difference between Z_C and Z_G is roughly constant for all false alarm rates. In the echo box portion of the curve, however, Murdock's results do *not* establish this. For the last item in a series performance was effectively perfect and thus the relationship could not be tested: and for the last item but one, there was some indication that the difference of the two Z-scores changed for different false alarm rates. Thus we can reject an "all or none" view of memory for items retained over a moderately long interval, just as we can reject the theories of perception which place all the emphasis upon observation or failure of observation. In the echo box itself, however, Murdock's experiment leaves it distinctly possible that items are completely present or completely absent. We shall see that other experiments have similar implications.

COMPARISON OF SEVERAL METHODS OF MEASURING d' IN MEMORY

Since 1965, a number of studies of memory have appeared making use of the analyses of decision theory. Although therefore many of them may report measures of d' in memory, they differ in important aspects of technique, and comparison of the results obtained by different means is itself of considerable interest. A paper which is logically basic, but chronologically fairly late, is that of Kintsch (1968), who presented four-letter combinations as items, giving five-item lists and then following them by subtraction sums. His methods of testing memory always involved the presentation of one or more test items: but in some cases he gave a single item and asked whether or not it had been in the memory list. In other cases, he presented several alternative items, one of which had been in the list, and required the subject to identify which one it was. It is then possible to ask whether d' calculated from the Yes/No method is the same as that from the multiple-choice tests, on the lines which we discussed in Chapter VI. In fact, for three subjects Kintsch found that it was: although the fourth subject gave less satisfactory results. (d' derived from the Yes/No experiment underestimated the effect of vocabulary size in the multiple-choice tests, for this subject.)

The score of percentage correct responses naturally varied considerably from one method of testing recognition to another: and in so far as d' was at least roughly constant with the different methods, we have, therefore, confirmatory evidence that the measurements derived from decision theory are a useful way of analysing the results of memory experiments. They may provide a means of separating the strength of the underlying memory from the interfering factors introduced by the method of testing memory. The major gap between one method and another comes however between recognition methods and recall methods. Norman (1966) studied memory for digit strings, testing either by presenting a digit and asking for a decision about its presence in the string, or by presenting a digit which had definitely been in the string, and asking for recall of the next digit. The first of these is the method considered in the last section, while the second is that of Waugh and Norman (1965). Since the items were digits, it was possible to regard the recall as being selection of the response from one of ten alternatives, and calculate the value of d' on that basis. The value obtained was lower than that found for the recognition method: but although this is disappointing it is not conclusive evidence against the use of the calculation of d'. As Norman points out, the association of each item with the one immediately preceding is rather different from the association of an item with the list as a whole, and the values of d' might well be expected to be different. Furthermore, the calculation of d' assumed that error responses were equally likely to be any of the nine incorrect digits, and this was manifestly untrue. It remains the case however that d' has not been demonstrated as equal in recall and recognition conditions.

A second feature of the experiment of Norman (1966) is more hopeful. With each method of testing, he plotted the value of d' as a function of the number of items intervening between the presentation and the test. He also compared various rates of presentation in the recall technique, and various types of material (single digits, double digits, and backwards digits) with the recognition technique. These various conditions produced quite different forgetting curves as measured by the conventional score of correct response: but in terms of d', the fall in d' was at approximately the same rate for all conditions, although its initial value was very different. For example, listening to backwards digits gave poor performance even when one was tested for recognition of the last item: but the relative drop in d' between the last item and the next to last was about the same as the drop for listening to ordinary forwards digits. Similarly, a slow rate of presentation gave substantially better performance on recall of the last item than did a fast rate of presentation: but d' dropped by at least as large a proportion between the testing of the last item and of the last but one. (As will be remembered from our discussion of presentation rate in the echo box, the rate of fall of performance per item is actually slightly greater when the time between the items is longer.) Once again therefore a score in terms of d' gives more regular and meaningful results than a score simply in terms of correct responses.

The relationship assumed by Norman between the value of d' and the number of intervening items was in fact exponential. That is, he supposed that each item subtracted a certain proportion of the value of d' existing when that item arrived. This general relationship was established in some experiments by Wickelgren and Norman (1966), using solely the technique of presenting a single item and asking whether it had been present in the list. They were able to show that this assumed relationship of d' to the number of intervening items fitted the data reasonably well: they used lists of varying lengths, and were able to show that the rate of decay of d' as a function of subsequent items was independent of the number of preceding items. On the other hand, the initial level of d' from which forgetting occurred was different for different numbers of preceding items. Once again, conventional curves of forgetting appeared exceedingly complex, and the simplicity of the relations in terms of d' is a great point in favour of the latter measure.

The results of Wickelgren and Norman (1966) also provide evidence that the relationship between correct responses and false responses is not of the form

$$P_C = A + BP_G.$$

They plot a relationship between the two quantities for each subject and each position in the list. As in the studies by Murdock and by Norman and Wickelgren, it is clear that the relationship is more of the form

$$Z_C = A + BZ_G.$$

Furthermore, in most cases B is approximately 1.

On the other hand, this is only established for items separated from testing by more than one or two intervening events. For the last item or the last but one, performance is of course extremely good, and consequently it is in many cases impossible to plot the relationship between P_C and P_G. In the few cases where it can be plotted, it does not seem to fit very well to a relationship of the type

$$Z_C = A + Z_G.$$

If the relationship between the Z-scores is linear at all, B must be very different in value from unity. That is, it may well be that memory in the echo box is "all or none". Possibly items are perfectly recalled if they are in the echo box, but only enter that part of the system with a definite probability.

It is worth noting here that the results of Norman (1966) on recognition tests also provide little information about performance when fewer than three intervening items have occurred between the presentation of an item and its testing. Thus these two studies, like the others considered previously, tend to establish the usefulness of d' for items presented fairly remotely in the past, but not for the "echo box" portion of the curve.

We may sum up as follows these various experiments using different methods of testing recall. They establish quite satisfactorily that the chances of a correct response may rise and fall with the probability that the subject will make an incorrect response of the same kind. If we wish to eliminate this factor, then we can measure performance by the difference between the Z-scores for correct and for false responses, provided that (a) the item was not presented very shortly before testing, that is, it was not in the echo box. (b) he test involves presentation of the item either on its own for acceptance or rejection, or amongst a number of other alternatives.

We do not know for sure that the same kind of measure can be applied in the echo box, nor do we know whether it is legitimate to treat recall as equivalent to recognition from the complete vocabulary of responses used in the experiment. From the results of Dale mentioned earlier, and from the general approach that items may be in store but may be difficult to retrieve, one might suspect that recall will be equivalent to many-alternative recognition for vocabularies of items which are firmly established before the experiment. That is, for items such as numbers, months of the year, days of the week, letters of the alphabet, and so on. When however one deals with more loosely established vocabularies such as the names of the English counties, or words from the language as a whole, then there may be an additional difficulty in recall. Whereas in recognition the difficulty of memory lies solely in comparison of the strengths of each item with that of the others, in recall there may be an additional difficulty of retrieving the particular item.

These points however await further experimental investigation. For the moment, it is clear that the measures of decision theory may be applied with reasonable confidence provided that we avoid the echo box, and that we use some form of recognition test. Not only *may* these measures be applied: it is highly desirable that they *should* be, because in their absence one may confuse poor performance due to the decision mechanism with poor performance due to a low value of the underlying strength of memory.

FILTERING AND PIGEON-HOLING AS REVEALED BY DECISION MEASURES

Given that parameters such as d' and β may be applied in memory as in perception, we may now look for evidence of the selective strategies of filtering and pigeon-holing in this field also. As in perception, we would expect filtering to affect d', and pigeon-holing to affect β. From the argument we put forward earlier, filtering will take place in memory where there is a problem of selecting for response one or more items from a whole series of presented material: and where the items to receive response possess some feature in common which is not shared with any of the irrelevant items. Thus the introduction of a sharp acoustic difference between relevant and irrelevant items will allow filtering, and give an increase in d'; or to put it the other way round, acoustic similarity of relevant and irrelevant items will give a fall in d'. On the other hand, the use of semantic or response classes to distinguish the wanted from the unwanted items would be an instance of pigeon-holing, and should affect β. When therefore there is a high probability that the item to be retrieved belonged to a certain response class, we might expect a fall in β for any item in that class.

(a) *Filtering and acoustic similarity.* In the case of filtering, the experimental evidence is unfortunately rather inconclusive. This is partly because most of the experiments have been performed from a different theoretical point of view, and the relevant data are therefore not available. Wickelgren (1966b) has shown changes in d' in a task where the subject is presented with an item, which is followed by other irrelevant items. Subsequently a single probe item is given and the subject asked if it is the original one. When the intervening irrelevant items include some acoustically similar to the stored item, d' is less. So far as it goes, this result is satisfactory: but it still allows certain possible alternative explanations. To discuss these, we must look at points of technique in some detail.

The major difficulty of technique in this case is to decide upon the tactics to be adopted with respect to probes other than the correct item. If these probes are acoustically different from the correct item, they will naturally be easier to distinguish from it than would incorrect probes which are acoustically similar to the correct item. Wickelgren very reasonably therefore analysed only performance using incorrect probes which were acoustically similar to the correct one. However, when the interfering irrelevant items were acoustically similar to the correct one, this meant that the incorrect probe was sometimes itself one of the irrelevant items, whereas this never happened if the irrelevant items were acoustically different from the correct item. The fall in d' in Wickelgren's results might, therefore, not be due to our "filtering" interpretation, but rather to a tendency to accept as correct any item which has in fact been presented even though that item was one of the irrelevant ones.

To clarify this point, J. D. Ingleby (1969) tried variations on Wickelgren's experiment in which the incorrect probe never appeared in the intervening material. Changes in d' did appear, but were only of borderline significance.

In the light of our present discussion, this may be because Ingleby also changed Wickelgren's procedure in another way. He used pairs of items to be remembered, and the intervening activity was always similar to one of the items but not to the other. This meant that the degree of similarity being varied was that between the probe item (correct or incorrect) and the intervening activity, rather than between the intervening activity and the original presented material. This has the technical advantage that presentation of the intervening activity cannot give advance information about the item to be probed. But it also means that the relevant items are never marked out from the irrelevant items by a single common factor of acoustic class, and this might be expected to discourage the use of filtering as a strategy. In so far as there is any d' change at all, it can presumably be put down to the fact that one of the irrelevant items can be distinguished from the irrelevant ones by its acoustic class: but the other cannot, and the memorizer may therefore frequently use other strategies of performance.

A rather different technique used by Ingleby (1969) avoided some of these difficulties by having the irrelevant material always digits to be shadowed, while the relevant items were always letters. The variation of acoustic similarity was then between relevant items: for example, in one experiment a pair of letters was used as the items to be remembered and might be either acoustically similar to each other or acoustically different. This change of similarity produced no significant effect on performance, provided the presentation of a probe item was accompanied by the question whether or not this item was one of the relevant ones. The situation was very different however if the probe question took a different form: asking specifically whether the probe item was the *first* of the two relevant ones or not. Here selection amongst the relevant items is involved, and correspondingly acoustic similarity does show a number of significant changes in performance. These are more marked for the "retroactive inhibition" rather than the "proactive inhibition" condition, that is, for questions about the first of the relevant items rather than about the second. In that case conventional calculations of d' give a significant deterioration with acoustic similarity in each of two experiments using rather different kinds of material.

β also shows some significant changes, which are actually in the wrong direction for explaining the drop in correct responses in retroactive inhibition. That is, the significant changes in β are in the direction of increased rather than decreased responses. The position is complicated however because it seems clear that the value of B in the equation $Z_C = A + BZ_{FA}$ changes when acoustic similarity is present. Furthermore, there is no significant change in d' for the "proactive inhibition" case, where questions are asked about the second item presented: even though there are some significant changes in correct responses in that case.

The results therefore do not provide overwhelming evidence that acoustic similarity produces a drop in d'. However, inasmuch as the experiments have not been testing a case where the relevant items are marked out uniquely from the irrelevant by possession of a given acoustic quality, it is not too surprising that changes in d' may be relatively unreliable. At least acoustic similarity does not produce any significant changes of β in a direction suitable to explain the rise in incorrect responses. Furthermore, these experiments do show that the primary importance of acoustic similarity between one relevant item and another is in the assignment of that item to its correct position in the sequence of relevant items. This confirms the results of Conrad mentioned earlier, and also those of Wickelgren (1965b).

The usefulness of the concept of filtering in memory has not therefore been clearly established, but it does seem sufficiently hopeful to make future work on it worth while.

(b) *Pigeon-holing and changes in* β. By analogy with the case of perception, we might expect that a fruitful area to examine for evidence of pigeon-holing might be the role of the probability of one stimulus rather than another. In perception we saw that probable words tend to be perceived more easily than improbable ones, because of changes in β: and in memory also it is the case that word frequency has an important effect upon performance. In free recall, common words are more readily reproduced than improbable ones (Deese, 1960, and Sumby, 1963). This beneficial effect appears predominantly in the portion of the list which has been earlier presented, that is, *not* in the echo box. From our point of view it immediately becomes interesting to know whether the effect of word frequency is due to a difference in d' or in β: that is, do common words tend to occur unduly often as false memories, or unduly rarely?

In the free recall situation it is a little difficult to get a good measure of false recall rate. A suitable technique has however been devised by Ingleby (1969), using the device of presenting short meaningful stories in which the characters are identified by ordinary English surnames. Memory can then be tested by presenting the story with a blank for the name of the character, and asking the subject to recall the name. The frequency of occurrence of English surnames can be assessed from the telephone directory, and it is found as in free recall experiments that common surnames are recalled correctly more often than uncommon surnames are. False recalls can readily be provoked in this situation, and the frequency of usage of these names also can be determined from the telephone directory. The latter book also gives some indication of the number of different surnames to be found at each degree of frequency of usage.

Analysis of a recall experiment conducted on these lines was shown by Ingleby to reveal a high proportion of common names amongst the false recalls. That is, people were inclined to "guess" common names. The value of d' was certainly no greater for common names: indeed, it appeared to be less to a significant extent.

Ingleby repeated this experiment using a probe technique rather than a free recall technique. That is, he suggested a name for a character in a previously presented story, and obtained a judgment as to whether it was or was not the original name, together with a degree of confidence in the judgment. It is then possible to examine the relationship between P_c and P_g, the acceptance rate for correct and for incorrect names: once again the familiar result occurs that a single straight line cannot fit the relationship which is found. For common words, β is lower and this explains the greater success which people have in correctly recalling such words: indeed, once again d' is actually less for common than for uncommon names.

In Ingleby's results therefore we have a completely clear demonstration that β changes can account for some of the phenomena well known in memory: and in particular that the better recall of an item on a particular occasion, when that item is one that is probable in general usage, is to be put down to β rather than to d'. In terms of our general analysis, therefore, it is the result of pigeon-holing rather than of filtering.

GENERAL CONCLUSIONS ON FILTERING AND PIGEON-HOLING IN MEMORY

In this field also therefore we have seen evidence that some changes in performance appear to be associated with changes in d' and other changes with β. Because most experiments have been conducted from a rather different point of view, in this area we can only regard our theoretical approach as a guide line for the future, rather than one which is already well established. Nevertheless, we have found little that is positively inconsistent with it, and it does clarify a number of confusing results in the field of memory. As in so many areas, it is the evidence for pigeon-holing or response bias which seems the most clearly established: yet in the field of perception we found evidence that filtering was certainly occurring in addition to pigeon-holing, and so also in the field of memory we have some effects which cannot be explained by pigeon-holing.

General Conclusions on Primary Memory

This field of research is not, at the time of writing, in a state which lends itself to simple and tidy conclusions. We can say with some confidence that there was truth in the 1958 conjecture of distinguishable processes in short-term and long-term memory. That is shown both by the echo box phenomenon, in which the last few items presented behave differently from those more remotely past; and by the different effects of acoustic and semantic similarity. Beyond this conclusion, there are several alternative lines of theory; with less confidence, we have concluded that the most probable is a mechanism rather like the original one of 1958. That is, a combination of the sensory buffer store and of a longer-term store, with memory for intermediate periods carried by repeated transfer of information out of and back into different parts of the sensory buffer. We have added however a controlling system which holds a small fixed number of addresses, referring either to the buffer or to the long-term store, or both. There are alternatives to this point of view, but none which seems to cover so wide a range of phenomena.

Given that a major problem of memory is the selection for retrieval of some out of the many items in store, strategies of selection become very important. Just as in perception, selection may be through the choice of all items possessing one particular feature; or it may be by the setting up of an output vocabulary only members of which will be used, and which should be distinguished by complex combinations of features. The first is a filtering mechanism; the latter corresponds to pigeon-holing in perception. At this point the same decision mechanisms as in perception apply to the relation between correct and false responses. The data show clearly that memory is not completely all or none, but rather is based on partial and incomplete evidence. Some phenomena in memory are due to changes in this evidence; but some to changes in the response biases.

As filtering and pigeon-holing, the strategies of selective processing, acquire a general importance beyond even the field of perception, it becomes important to know whether they operate unchangeably and to the same extent. Can they change with the general state of the system, or are they purely cognitive processes with no emotional components? To answer these questions, we should look at men performing tasks which remain unchanged while the background conditions are varied. This is the next and last field to which we shall turn.

CHAPTER IX

Noise and Other Stresses

Thus far we have considered features of the tasks which a man may be asked to perform; and we have seen how different tasks may cause him to adopt various strategies of information processing. But we have not considered effects which may arise from his general state rather than the nature of his task. In this chapter we shall do this; and it will emerge that filtering rather than pigeon-holing reflects most sensitively the state of the man.

The Position in 1958

The general conditions under which a man works have been an interest of industrial psychologists since the beginnings of their discipline. Until World War II, however, the majority of investigations of such conditions were carried out in factories themselves. Occasional laboratory studies were made, but nevertheless examination of the effects of noise, prolonged work, high temperatures, and so on was predominantly centred upon the analysis of genuine industrial output. The war however brought a change. In part, this was because the circumstances of battle made it necessary to secure the best conditions immediately, rather than to observe the degree of success in operations for some time before taking any steps to improve efficiency. In addition however a good deal of the work carried out before the war had emphasized the importance of social organization, suggestion, and other factors in performance independent of the actual conditions of work. There was, therefore, a mood of some scepticism about results derived from field experiments, and it was felt that laboratory studies were necessary in order to hold such factors constant and to be sure that any changes in performance were due to the changes in the environment itself.

Consequently, laboratory studies of heat, noise, sleeplessness, and other conditions blossomed in the 1940's and 1950's. Of these only one, noise, was considered by Broadbent (1958). He argued, as will be remembered from discussion of vigilance, that filtering took place in all situations and that efficient work could only be carried out by selection of stimuli from the task and exclusion of irrelevant information. One of the conditions governing the selection of the stimulus passing the filter was supposed, however, to be its degree of novelty. Consequently, when a task was continued for some time the stimuli from that task would gradually lose priority: hence towards the end of a prolonged work period there would be moments of perceptual failure due to the filter selecting irrelevant stimuli rather than task stimuli. Since another factor governing the selection of a stimulus was its physical intensity, the presence of an intense stimulus such as noise would increase the frequency of such failures. Broadbent was able to argue that the effects of noise upon performance supported this argument.

A detailed review of the effects of noise up to that time is given by Broadbent (1957c). There is, therefore, no need to repeat this detail, but an outline of the argument should be given so that we can see the weak points at which it has been modified by more recent research. First, it is easy to show that the onset of a sudden and unfamiliar noise impairs a very wide variety of tasks. The effect wears off within a matter of minutes, however, and also applies to the sudden ending of a noise which has become familiar. Thus it appears to be a reaction to change of stimulation rather than to prolonged intense stimulation, and has been relatively little studied. A possible reason for this lies in the lack of practical importance of any effect which occurs only for a second or so and which disappears with familiarity. The industrial or military implications of such an effect are obviously slight. Once this transient effect has gone, it has been shown by a wide variety of experimenters that many tasks are performed as efficiently in loud noise as in quiet conditions. Such studies included work at Tufts College (1942) by Stevens *et al.* (1941), Viteles and Smith (1946), and so on. Other more recent studies confirm this general conclusion (Oltman, 1964; Park and Payne, 1963; Reiter, 1963; Samuel, 1964 and Weinstein and Mackenzie, 1966).

The tasks used in these various researches were tests of psychological function which were in common use. It was pointed out by Broadbent (1958) that these tests all have certain features. They require information from the surroundings to be handled at rates which are fairly low, and with crucial information arriving at times which are fairly predictable and which are separated by intervals with no crucial information. Thus, for example, in tests of judging distance, or performing choice reactions, each signal occurs at a time which is roughly known to the subject. This crucial time is preceded and followed by intervals in which little or no task information reaches the sense organs. In tests of continuous tracking of targets, the point at which the crucial information arrives is less clear but it is known from studies such as those of Poulton (1952), or Poulton and Gregory (1952) that eye blinks or momentary interference with visual display will not impair the efficiency of tracking. Most psychological tests of this traditional type would not be sensitive to any mechanism which produced brief impairments of the intake of information.

The most obvious example of a task which would be sensitive to brief interruptions of perception is the vigilance task: and it was shown by Broadbent (1954a) that a vigilance task was indeed sensitive to noise: other confirmatory results have been quoted in the chapters on vigilance. Another case in which continuous intake of information from a task would be necessary is that of serial reaction, where a new stimulus appears as soon as a satisfactory response has been made to the previous stimulus. Broadbent (1953) showed that such a task did indeed show an effect, which was not an effect on the average rate of work but rather took the form of occasional mistakes. This pattern of performance can really only be explained by supposing that noise produces brief failures in intake and analysis of information. If noise had no effect at all, then the effects on vigilance and on serial reaction would be unintelligible: if the effect were a sustained lowering of efficiency, then it would be hard to explain the lack of effect on the average speed of serial reaction, on performance of intelligence tests, or on many other tasks. Thus the effect must be one of brief periods of inefficiency, which become more frequent in noise. If such periods were due to a failure of response it would be hard to explain the observed possibility of continuous repetitive work in noise; and indeed to explain the fact that the errors made in serial reaction were co-ordinated but incorrectly chosen actions. The effect must therefore be one of increasing the frequency of the brief periods of inefficiency on the perceptual side of the system.

As Broadbent recognized, this does not necessarily imply that the failure of perception in the task is due to the intake of information from some other source. Almost the only supporting evidence for that hypothesis came from a study by Broadbent (1957a), in which high and low pitched noises were used both as background for a serial reaction task, and also separately as stimuli themselves for unprepared reaction time. The high pitched noise, which gave the faster reaction time, also gave the greatest increase in errors when it was presented as background for a visual task. Thus one could hardly argue that the high pitched noise gave a general depression of efficiency, since it was actually a source of greater efficiency when itself a stimulus for the task. It was tempting to interpret this as "the stimulus which is easy to react to is hard to ignore", and to regard it as evidence supporting the distraction theory of effects of noise.

The Effects of Other Stresses

While the effects of noise were being demonstrated in the laboratory, so also were those of a variety of other conditions. Vigilance tasks showed effects of high temperatures (Mackworth, 1950; Pepler, 1958), and of sleep deprivation (Wilkinson, 1960). They were also sensitive to drugs such as hyoscine and meclozine (Colquhoun, 1962b) to cold and rain (Poulton *et al.*, 1965) and to effects of the time of day at which the measurement is made (Colquhoun, 1962a). In general indeed this type of test would be recommended by any experienced investigator as likely to be sensitive to changes in the general conditions of work. Tests of continual serial reaction are also sensitive in this way: in addition to the effect of noise, they show effects of high temperatures (Pepler, 1959a) of loss of sleep (Wilkinson, 1959) of working at high altitudes (Gill *et al.*, 1964) and of working in high pressure air (Poulton *et al.*, 1964). They also show a difference between the performance of a man breathing high pressure air and one breathing an oxygen enriched mixture with helium at the same total pressure (Bennett *et al.*, 1967). Some of these stresses do also affect a wide variety of functions: for example, Baddeley (1966c) showed effects of high pressure air upon dexterity and tactile sensitivity, tests which do not possess those properties which Broadbent (1958) regarded as crucial for showing the effects of noise. Baddeley and Flemming (1967) showed effects of pressure on tests both of dexterity and of addition: and indeed even showed detrimental effects on those tests from breathing an oxygen-helium mixture. Similarly Blake (1967a) showed effects on a variety of tasks of the time of day at which the task was performed. It is not therefore absolutely necessary to use noise-sensitive tests if we want to show effects of other stresses. On the other hand, the effects of loss of sleep are relatively slight on many tests (Wilkinson, 1964b), and it is certainly possible to find tests which show no effect of hyoscine and meclozine (Colquhoun, 1962b). Thus it seems that the tests which show effects of noise are also on the whole those which are most likely to be affected by other unpleasant conditions of work.

Yet if we explain the effects of noise on these tasks by supposing that noise acts as a distracting stimulus, it is a little unclear why some of these other stresses should act in the same way. Heat no doubt is itself a stimulus which might demand attention: just conceivably, the abnormal conditions associated with breathing high or low pressures of air might work in the same way. But why should sleeplessness or drugs be regarded as producing intense competing stimuli, causing the filter to shift selection away from the stimuli of the task itself?

Furthermore, in some cases it is possible to show that the same test, with similar experimental subjects, shows a different kind of deterioration in one stress and in another. One test which has been used in this way is the pursuit meter, in which subjects follow a target pointer with another pointer controlled through a lever. The target oscillates with a mean frequency of 0·5 Hz, and the whole display is viewed through a diffuser which makes it very difficult to see. The discrepancy between the two pointers is integrated over time, and by this measure performance is worse in heat (Pepler, 1959a, 1960)

O

after loss of sleep (Pepler, 1959a) in glare, and under the distracting condition of hearing a faintly spoken passage from a thriller (Pepler, 1960). A second score can be obtained from the same task, however, by counting the number of times the controlled pointer changes its direction of movement; this provides some indication of the extent to which the subject was in fact attempting to follow the target. The experiments cited show that glare and distracting speech decrease the number of reversals of this type: loss of sleep gives no change: and heat gives an increase. So also does noise (Broadbent and Gregory, unpublished). Thus although all the stresses give worse performance, it seems obvious that they are not doing so in the same way. In addition, it would be natural to describe the effects of glare and of quiet speech as interfering with the intake of task information, and thus making performance worse without the subject himself realizing that he was doing less well. In noise and heat however the subject was aware of his own deterioration in performance, and was attempting to compensate for it. This argues against the interpretation that noise produces this effect by being itself a distracting stimulus, like glare or speech, and it also implies that more than one process is operating in the effects of stress.

This becomes even more clear when we consider results on a widely used test of serial reaction, the one employed to study noise by Broadbent (1953). As we have already said, this test delivers a new stimulus every time the subject makes a response: it consists of a panel of five lights arranged in a pentagon, one of which is alight at any time. Response is carried out with an electrified stylus, which is touched to one of five contacts arranged in the same pentagonal pattern. The touching of a contact turns off the last stimulus and presents a fresh one. The average rate of work on this task remains constant for a period of half an hour under normal conditions, as was shown in Broadbent's original experiment and confirmed by Pepler (1959a) and Wilkinson (1959). As the work period proceeded, however, there were an increasing number of slow reactions, taking more than one and a half to two seconds. These were interpreted by Broadbent as due to diversion of attention, and hence as consistent with the effects on vigilance which we discussed in chapters II and III. In noise he found again that the average rate of work was the same as in quiet, but that the number of mistakes increased. He put these down also to diversions of attention, and explained the fact that the moment of inattention produced a mistake rather than a slow response by the fact that the noise experiment necessarily involved prolonged practice. As we have seen, studies of anticipation and skill show that the practised subject will continue motor action during momentary interruptions of the sensory input, and consequently a practised subject on the serial reaction task would continue to attempt to respond according to his own subjective probability of the likely next signal. Unpractised subjects have no basis on which this uncontrolled motor performance could operate, and hence the fact that slow reactions were sensitive to fatigue effects within a single session, whereas in repeated sessions errors were sensitive to noise.

This explanation was destroyed by fresh evidence within a very short time of the publication of Broadbent (1958). It was found by Pepler (1959a) and Wilkinson (1959) that the effect of sleeplessness was to increase the number of slow reactions. This stress did not in those experiments increase the number of errors. Thus the idea that errors and slow reactions were both signs of distracted attention, but that errors happened to be the form in which distraction revealed itself in practised subjects was clearly untenable. If such a view were correct, sleepless subjects, should show errors just as much as those exposed to noise. As a final blow, it was found by Pepler (1959a) that high temperature did in fact increase the number of errors on this same task, but, unlike noise, heat produced its effect at the very beginning of the work period rather than late in the session. Whereas it had been tenable in 1958 that errors appeared only when the task stimuli had lost their novelty, the effects of heat were clearly inconsistent with this.

We thus have, on this test, a different pattern of breakdown for noise, for heat, and for sleeplessness. The first produces errors but does not do so until the work period has proceeded for some time: the second produces errors but does so immediately: the third produces slow reactions and does not do so until work has proceeded for some time. These differences do not necessarily mean that the three stresses are affecting completely different mechanisms It is conceivable that the same process might be operative in any kind of stress, but that the kind of score which reveals its operation may be different depending upon the extent of the stress. We cannot be sure that the severity of one night's loss of sleep is equal to that of 100dB noise, and indeed it is likely to differ. We shall be discussing later the effects of partial sleep loss, of different temperatures, and so on. It would be quite conceivable that a mild stress might produce an increase in slow reactions, and a more severe stress a compensatory effort which would result in errors rather than slow reactions. At the very least however it is clear that one must examine the possibility that different stresses are affecting different mechanisms, and so we must find some way of looking at this possibility.

The Interactions of Stresses

One method of attack which commends itself is to apply stresses in combination. If two conditions are producing impairment by quite separate mechanisms, each should produce its effect independently. If condition A gives a 10% increase in errors, and condition B a 10% increase, then the two together should give 20%. If on the other hand both stresses are affecting the same mechanism, then more drastic impairment may well appear: if each condition on its own lowers performance from a perfect level to one of 10%

error, then the addition of the second stress to the first may produce far more than 20% of error. This is to be expected because the effect of one stress alone will be partly taken up in overcoming the safety margin of the mechanism concerned. When the second stress is applied, there is no longer any margin left within the mechanism which is being affected. This kind of argument can be used to elucidate the mechanism of action of drugs: as for example in the study of Colquhoun (1962b) on the combined effects of alcohol with hyoscine or meclozine. The combination of a pair of drugs produced far more impairment than twice the effect of either alone. Thus alcohol and the other drugs appear to be affecting the same mechanism in the control of behaviour.

To put this principle in connection with our own problem, let us suppose that sleeplessness gives slow reactions rather than errors merely because it is a milder stress than noise but not one whose mechanism of action is essentially different. Then if we take men working in a noisy situation, and compare the performance of those who have slept normally and those who have not, sleeplessness should increase the stress yet further and produce an increase in error. By the same argument, if heat produces errors early in the work period because it is a more severe stress than noise, adding noise to heat should accentuate the deterioration yet more.

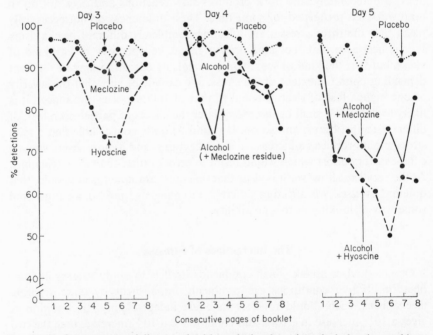

Fig. 37. Performance at a vigilance task with meclozine, hyoscine, alcohol and a combination of the latter with either of the former. Notice that the combination is worse than a summation of the two effects, suggesting that the various drugs strike in part at the same mechanism. Data from Colquhoun (1962b).

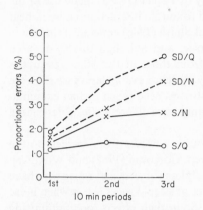

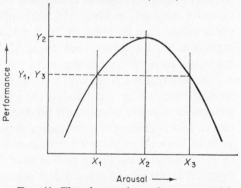

FIRST TWO WEEKS

FIG. 38. Errors in a serial reaction task with sleep (S) and under sleep deprivation (SD). Noise (N) and quiet (Q) conditions differ in their effects dependent on the other condition: for the sleepless, noise improves performance. Data from Wilkinson (1963a).

FIG. 39. The number of slow reactions in a serial reaction task under sleep (S) and no-sleep (NS) conditions. With the exciting conditions of knowledge of results (K), there is little effect of sleeplessness. With no knowledge of results (NK), NS becomes much worse than S. Data from Wilkinson (1961c).

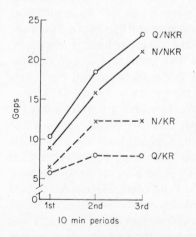

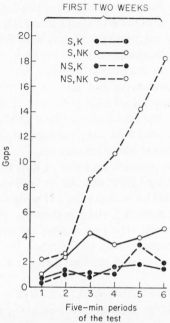

FIG. 40. Slow reactions in noise (N) and quiet (Q) with knowledge of results (KR) and without (NKR). In the motivated state, noise is harmful; but under NKR, N is better than Q. Data from Wilkinson (1963a).

FIG. 41. The changes in performance which may be produced by changes in arousal. A rise in arousal may give a rise in performance if it corresponds to a movement from X_1 to X_2; performance will rise from Y_1 to Y_2. But the same rise in arousal will give a fall in performance if arousal is already at X_2; a further rise to X_3 will give a drop from Y_2 to Y_3.

Unfortunately, there has been relatively little work on the combination of heat with noise or sleeplessness. One study by Pepler (1959a) made use of the serial reaction task already described, and found no interaction between heat and sleeplessness. The study by Viteles and Smith (1946) concluded that there was no interaction between heat and noise, and although this study used different tasks and samples of subjects from those in the other researches cited, yet it seems at present to be the only evidence available. As we shall see later, the interactions of heat with other stresses need much further examination, since high temperatures almost certainly have different effects depending upon just how high they are.

The clearest evidence of interaction comes however from studies on the combined effect of noise and of loss of sleep. Corcoran (1962) and Wilkinson (1963a) have tried effects of noise upon sleepless subjects and those who have slept normally, and it is clear that the effect of sleeplessness is less when noise is present. The two stresses are antagonistic in their effects, one minimizing the consequences of the other. We have here clear evidence against the idea that all stresses produce the same kind of effects but do so to different degrees.

INTERACTIONS WITH INCENTIVE

All the findings discussed so far have been obtained with subjects working under normal laboratory conditions. Their motives in performing the task are the usual, rather complex, social ones involved in fitting in with the instructions of an experimenter. They have no particular personal involvement in success or failure, although they would doubtless wish to avoid seeming uncooperative. From a practical point of view it can well be argued that studies of this kind might be misleading, because in real life there are far more powerful motives involved. In the military case particularly successful performance may be essential for a man's own survival. Consequently the argument has frequently been raised that performance in real conditions might be much better than that met in the laboratory.

For these reasons, there have from an early stage been attempts to vary the level of incentive in such studies (Mackworth, 1950; Pepler, 1958). These changes in incentive were usually produced by applying knowledge of results: that is, by informing the experimental subject at frequent intervals during his work of the level of his performance, and by publishing the performance of each individual in the group at the end of the experiment. Since subjects lived together, this produced a good deal of competition between them. Although doubtless the level of incentive produced was less than that of battle, it was nevertheless real. In the case of high temperature, such an incentive certainly improved performance, whether the man was tested in heat or in normal temperature. The extent of the improvement was, however, about the same in each case: so it might be true that a man in heat could, by the application of incentive, be brought back to the level which he could attain at normal temperature without incentive. He would however have done even better at normal temperature had he had the incentive then. Thus one would conclude that the effect of incentive was simply overlaid or added to that of heat, and that there was no evidence of both conditions striking the same mechanism. (This conclusion rests unfortunately on performance with tasks other than the serial reaction one, and this qualification should be borne in mind.)

In the case of sleeplessness, however, the result is quite different. Application of incentive improves the performance of sleepless men, but does so far more dramatically than it does the performance of men who have slept normally. Indeed, there appears to be little difference on the serial reaction test between men who have and have not slept, providing they are working under incentive (Wilkinson, 1961c). So the effect of incentive does seem to strike at the same mechanism as that of sleeplessness, but in the opposite direction, reducing the consequences of loss of sleep just as noise does (Fig. 39, p. 407).

In view of some of the results reported earlier, a possibility which comes to mind is that this particular method of manipulating incentive may be having its effects for reasons other than motivational ones. We saw earlier that sleeplessness was a condition which gave greater error on the pursuit meter but did not give an increase in compensatory movements of the controls. That is, sleeplessness appeared to produce poor performance and also a lack of awareness of this deterioration. Conceivably therefore the provision of knowledge of results might be substituting for the normal degree of self-awareness. This explanation however seems untenable, firstly because Williams et al. (1959) have studied effects of knowledge of results without a very strong incentive character to the latter: and found no interaction with loss of sleep. Secondly, Corcoran (1963b) used other forms of incentive, such as allowing subjects to leave the experiment at the conclusion of a fixed number of responses. This also reduced the effects of sleeplessness, although it provided no knowledge about the man's own performance until the end of the session. Thus it seems definite that the important factor in reducing the impact of loss of sleep is motivation.

There are other indirect lines of evidence which point the same way. Wilkinson (1961c) repeated his experiments on loss of sleep two or three times, on the same subjects, and the effects of sleep deprivation became greater on each repetition. It seems reasonable to suppose that this is a matter of lowered motivation as the task becomes more and more familiar. Again, Wilkinson (1964b) showed that a serial reaction test involving ten alternative choices showed more effect than one with four choices, and a similar result was found by Williams et al. (1965). In general therefore one might hold that the more information involved in a task the greater its susceptibility to sleep loss: yet a highly complex simulation of a battle situation by Wilkinson (1964b) showed no effect whatever. It seems plausible to ascribe this insensitivity of the battle situation, as Wilkinson did, to the interesting and motivating character of the task. The effects of sleeplessness are hard to show on a really interesting job.

Returning now to the general question of interactions with incentive, we see that we have evidence that sleeplessness is opposite both to noise and to incentive in its effects. This does not necessarily mean that noise and incentive are similar, since the effects of sleeplessness might be multiple and it might be different aspects of the stress which were involved in the interaction with noise on the one hand and with incentive on the other. However, it is a tempting possibility: and it is supported by the demonstration by Willett (1964) that a high incentive state may itself produce errors on the serial reaction task just as noise does. (The incentive in Willett's case was obtained by administering the test to candidates for entry to a desirable apprenticeship scheme, and comparing their performance with those who had successfully passed the selection test.) If noise and incentive were really similar in their impact, then it might be expected that incentive would increase the effect of noise: and this has indeed been shown by Wilkinson (1963a). Noise and incentive do appear to reinforce each other, and therefore to be hitting the same mechanism in the same way (Fig. 40, p. 407).

We shall see other supporting evidence of this similarity later. For the moment, it should be noted that it makes sense of certain discrepancies in the literature. For example, Broadbent and Little (1960) studied the effects of noise reduction in an actual industrial situation, the purpose being to confirm in a realistic setting the results of laboratory studies showing that noise affected error rate without altering speed of work. It was clearly important to know whether this effect held true for realistic tasks, and over a prolonged period of acclimatization to the noise which could not be achieved in the laboratory. In fact the study showed no effect on rate of work when adequate controls were taken: there was indeed an effect of noise reduction on rate of work, but it altered speed in rooms which had been left untreated as well as in those which had been made quieter. It was therefore presumably an effect of suggestion or morale. The error rate however was reduced, as predicted: but the authors were somewhat embarrassed to find the reduction was far greater than would have been predicted from the laboratory experiments. In this research the workers being studied were being paid by their performance. There was therefore a very genuine personal incentive to do well. With the benefit of hindsight, one may suggest that one might attribute to this incentive the large effect of reduction of noise. The same explanation probably holds for the clear effects of noise found by Weston and Adams (1932, 1935), which again have usually been held to be suspiciously large by comparison with laboratory studies. We cannot put down to this fact the general difficulty of finding noise effects in the laboratory, when factory studies are often positive, because the factory studies themselves are usually badly controlled. Nevertheless in the cases mentioned there do seem to have been adequate precautions against contaminating effects of morale and suggestion, and the demonstrable effect of incentive seems to be a plausible reason for the large size of the effects in industry.

INTERACTIONS WITH RATE OF SIGNALLING

We have already quoted the result by McGrath on effects of varied auditory stimulation on visual vigilance. He found that there was an interaction between the event rate in the task itself and the effects of the irrelevant acoustic stimulus. With high event rates, irrelevant sounds were if anything harmful, while at low event rates they were beneficial. A similar result has been found by Broadbent and Gregory (1965a) for signal rate rather than event rate in a vigilance task, and using high intensity continuous noise rather than moderate intensity varying noise. They found a deterioration in vigilance under noisy conditions when signals were frequent, but not when they were infrequent. On the other hand, Corcoran (1963a) studied effects of sleeplessness on a vigilance task with a high and low event rate. Sleeplessness produced deterioration primarily with the low event rate: that is, once again the effects sleeplessness were opposite to those of noise.

The Arousal Theory of Stress

From these various results on combining stresses, incentives, and signal rate, we obtain a general picture of heat as distinct from the other stresses in its effects. Sleeplessness and noise appear consistently however to be opposite to one another. It seems clear that we cannot therefore maintain the 1958 view that noise has its effect by being a distracting stimulus: rather it must be taken as changing some general state of the organism, just as sleeplessness does. Noise moves this state in one direction, and sleeplessness in the opposite direction. Whichever way the state moves from normal conditions, performance becomes worse. Incentive and an increase in the signal rate both move the state in the same direction as noise: thus they too are antagonistic to sleeplessness, but increase harmful effects of noise.

Harking back to our discussion of theories of vigilance, it seems tempting to call the general state of the system "arousal". We would then say that low arousal or high arousal produce inefficiency, and performance is best at an intermediate level of arousal. In ordinary terms, a man can be too drowsy for efficient work, or else over-excited and "flap" (Fig. 41, p. 407). As we saw on the earlier chapter on vigilance, there is a good deal of evidence from neurophysiology that wakefulness depends upon a constant supporting flow of messages from the reticular formation at the base of the brain. This general barrage of facilitation is kept going by the arrival of stimuli at the sense organs, and each stimulus produces a general non-specific waking effect by

o*

this route through the reticular formation. Thus stimuli have this non-specific action as well as conveying specific information to the projection areas of the cortex, about the particular events in the outside world which have given rise to this stimulus rather than some other. If the pathways through the reticular formation are damaged, sleep may result.

Thus we have independent evidence for a general state, which can lead to inefficient performance when its level is low. Physiology however does not give us the opposite end of the function, inefficiency at a very high level of arousal, and this is clearly essential to explain behaviour. Without it, we cannot handle the fact that noise as well as sleeplessness can impair performance and yet that each opposes the other. There is also an ambiguity in fitting psychological results to the physiological concept of arousal: which way round should the fitting be done? At first sight it seems reasonable to hold that noise, which is certainly a form of stimulation, should be regarded as raising the level of arousal, and sleeplessness as lowering it. However, all we have shown is that the two stresses are opposite: one might equally contend that sleeplessness, which keeps a man exposed to a continual barrage of stimulation, is over-arousing. In that case we would also suppose that intense continuous noise blots out the ordinary background of varied stimuli from the environment and thus lowers the level of arousal. Such a view might be urged from the results of Malmo and Surwillo (1960), who found that some physiological measures showed after sleeplessness a change in the direction of increased arousal. That is, heart rate, respiration rate, skin conductance, and the tension in certain muscles all showed increases after sleeplessness.

Despite these reasons for doubt, when we look into the matter more closely it still seems most plausible to stick to our first guess, that noise increases arousal. It is hard to hold that incentives or an increase in signal rate should lower arousal, and yet we have seen that those conditions reduce the effects of sleeplessness and increase those of noise. Again, the rise in physiological indices reported by Malmo and Surwillo is not universal: Corcoran (1964) found a drop in heart rate after loss of sleep, the most obvious difference in his situation and that of Malmo and Surwillo being that his subjects were lying down to perform a vigilance task, while theirs were visually performing a tracking task with a distinctly painful stimulus as the punishment for error. The results are in fact consistent with those of Wilkinson (1962) which we have already described under the topic of vigilance. As Wilkinson found, sleepless subjects who were under no incentive might show poor performance with normal or reduced muscle tension: subjects under incentive increased muscle tension and maintained performance longer. In addition, those subjects with the highest muscle tension were those who showed the least impairment of performance by sleeplessness. One can reasonably hold that sleeplessness will give a fall in arousal as measured by the peripheral indicators, when the task is unstimulating and demands little; but will show increased peripheral activity when the task is demanding. Wilkinson (1965) reviews a large number of studies on physiological measures after sleeplessness which confirm this generalization.

We can therefore conclude, first, that sleeplessness does lower arousal rather than raise it, and second, that physiological measures of the peripheral kind are revealing something of the nature of compensatory effort which may or may not be applied by the experimental subject when his performance becomes impaired by this lowered arousal.

We can then say that the general state which is being affected by sleeplessness and noise is one of arousal, but we must be clear that in the present state of knowledge we are defining it as such on the basis purely of behaviour and not of physiology. The physiological concept of arousal is certainly of interest and of ultimate relevance to the one we have found from behaviour, but at this stage the connection of any suggested physiological measure and the psychological state is too remote to make it practical to attach one concept directly to the other. We have just been reminded that the peripheral physiological measures, which display the level of activity of the autonomic nervous system, can be shown to behave inconsistently and thus probably to reflect at least two states, arousal and effort, rather than one. We saw in our discussion of vigilance that more central measures such as those of EEG activity are equally suspect. The effects of certain drugs and of lesions of the nervous system are known from animal experiments to change the relationship between EEG measures and behaviour: and consequently one cannot be clear whether a change in the EEG measures reflects a change in arousal or merely a change in the validity of the measure. We have therefore no satisfactory physiological reference for the general state which we are discussing, and which we have revealed purely from behavioural studies. In some ways it might have been better therefore to avoid using the term "arousal" for this behaviourally defined concept, but this would probably do too much violence to the common usage in the literature. The reader should remember however that we are working solely on the psychological level, and that the existence of a physiological concept of arousal is merely an interesting parallel, with no direct contact at present.

Detailed Aspects of Specific Stresses

The picture we have drawn so far is one of excessive simplicity. We have been talking as if there was a single scale on which the general state of the organism could be placed, with inefficiency at high and low points on the scale and efficiency at moderate points. A closer examination of each of the stresses involved reveals certain snags and difficulties in this concept. It does contain a reasonable element of truth, and hence the fact that we have bothered to present it. Before we go on to think about a mechanism by which high or low arousal impairs performance, we ought however to mention a few of these difficulties and discrepancies. They can best be revealed by considering each stress separately.

NOISE

Thus far we have referred to "noise" without analysing that term more precisely. Clearly however noises may be of different intensity and of different nature. One of the most important distinctions is that between continuous and interrupted noise: we have already seen that there is a distinction to be drawn between the onset of a noise and the effect when it has been present for some time. There are widespread effects from an unfamiliar sudden noise, which disappear as the subject gets used to it. (See Broadbent, 1957c for a review of the earlier work on this point.) As we have mentioned already, this effect is a reaction to the change in the environment rather than to a high intensity of stimulation, and the same effect can be produced by turning off a noise which is present. The size of the change is important: Teichner *et al.* (1963) show that the disturbance is greater for a larger rise or fall in noise level.

If a varied noise is continued for some time, can one regard each change in the level as producing a fresh disturbance? The harmful effects disappear completely as measured by conventional tests, which average performance over long periods of time: but Woodhead (1958, 1959, 1960) has shown that one can still find an effect from bursts of noise if one analyses performance more closely. With a continuous task accompanied by occasional one second bursts of noise, she found that the half minute of performance immediately after a burst was inferior to a corresponding half minute under control conditions: even though performance over the test as a whole was the same when bursts were present as when they were absent. This effect depends upon the intensity of the burst, and is just significant at a level of 95dB, but insignificant below that value. Furthermore, it is abolished by the wearing of ear defenders provided that the burst of noise is at a part of the spectrum which the ear defenders reduce. This point is of theoretical as well as of practical importance, because the ear defenders naturally reduce the background noise as well as the burst, and show that this effect is not simply a reaction to the size of the change in stimulation but rather to the intensity of that received at the ear.

If the analysis of the task is made even more closely, effects can be shown with stimuli of lower intensities. Thus with a continuous serial reaction task, S. Fisher (unpublished) has shown that bursts as low as 80dB will produce a slowing of the particular reaction which is in progress when the burst arrives. We thus have an effect which is lasting something under half a second, rather than the half minute or so found by Woodhead, and it seems fair to regard these as rather different processes. The effect found by Fisher is comparable in its size and in the intensity of the stimuli which produce it to the delays discussed under the heading of the psychological refractory period, and in view of our discussion of that subject it seems reasonable to ascribe it to simple overload of capacity of the nervous system at the moment when two stimuli are being handled. The Woodhead effect is longer in duration, and there must be some further reaction to the intense stimulus rather than a distraction at its time of arrival.

Woodhead (1964) applied her intense bursts of noise to an arithmetic task in which problems were presented for 5 seconds and the man was then left free to calculate from memory till he could produce an answer. If a burst arrived while he was taking in information for a problem, accuracy was reduced: if it arrived during calculation accuracy was unaffected. There was a relatively minor effect on the speed of work in that case, insufficient to change the average level over the run as a whole, but showing a significantly greater *improvement* during the experiment for those problems accompanied by noise as opposed to those which were not. Thus the main harmful effect of the intense bursts studied by Woodhead seems to be perceptual, on the intake of information, rather than on processes operating on information already received. Even if the effect of the intense burst of sound is more than a simple loading of perceptual capacity, it is still due to some change in that part of the system.

If we consider beneficial rather than harmful effects on performance from intermittent noise, then it is possible to find them at much lower intensities. The results by McGrath, showing that acoustic stimulation improved visual vigilance, were obtained at an intensity of only 72dB. The sound which improved vigilance was a varied mixture of thumps, traffic noises, music, etc., and it was certainly its variability rather than its intensity which improved vigilance since the control condition was a steady continuous noise at the same intensity. Berlyne *et al.* (1966) delivered bursts of 75dB noise during certain items in a paired-associate learning task: and those items were better remembered in a retention test after an interval, even though they were not better recalled in a test of retention immediately after learning. This last fact is particularly useful because it links the effect of noise again with that of motivation or arousal: the same effect can be shown by accompanying particular paired-associates by electric shock or giving five cents reward for correct performance, again no difference appearing in an immediate test of retention (Weiner and Walker, 1966). These studies grew out of earlier research (Walker and Tarte, 1963) in which it was found that those items which gave a larger skin response showed relatively better long term retention. Thus it seems fair to explain this effect, no matter what its detailed mechanism, as due to a change in arousal produced by the bursts of noise. This was the same explanation which we had already put forward for the results of McGrath.

We then have the problem of explaining why the effects of bursts of noise become harmful at 95dB. We have a choice of supposing either that arousal increases uniformly with intensity but that the optimum level of arousal lies below 95dB: or perhaps that some harmful effect tends to appear at that intensity and to be superimposed on rising efficiency due to increased arousal. The difficulty with any attempt to distinguish these possibilities with bursts of noise is the way in which the effects reduce with increasing experience of the bursts. This is the point therefore at which to consider continuous and unchanging noise.

The studies by Broadbent, Wilkinson, and Corcoran which showed the differences between noise and loss of sleep were conducted with such a steady intense noise. As we have already noted, the effects of such a noise are distinct from those of sudden unfamiliar noises, because they actually increase as the work period continues. A short test in which a man can pull himself together to maintain performance does not show any deterioration. With vigilance tasks it may be necessary to go on for more than an hour of work before deterioration appears, while even with a serial reaction task it may be necessary to continue for half an hour. Furthermore this type of effect, as was shown by Broadbent and Little (1960), still appears even in industrial workers who have experienced the noise for a very long time. It appears therefore to be due to some process which only develops after a fairly prolonged period of work, and which does not decline with repeated experience of the noise.

In this case also, the intensity necessary to get detrimental effects has again always been greater than 95dB: there is one modern experiment in the literature, by Hörmann and Todt (1960), where the learning of paired-associates showed a deterioration in noise of 75 phons as opposed to 55 phons, but this appears to be a unique case possibly due to an unusual spectrum of noise, to some special feature of the task, or perhaps to an unusually susceptible sample of subjects. With this exception all deterimental effects have been found with intensities of over 95dB. Direct studies such as that of Broadbent (1957a) have found that the serial reaction task which is impaired at 100dB shows no difference between 90 and 80dB. With continuous noise therefore there does appear to be an effect of intensity as such, coming in reasonably consistently at a particular level. Beneficial effects mostly occur at lower intensities, and to that extent we seem to be justified in sticking to our view that an excessive level of stimulation or an absence of stimulation are both bad for performance.

There is however one difficulty which is created by these results on continuous intense noise. It is natural to suppose, and we have done so implicitly in the last few paragraphs, that changes in stimulation are arousing. One might, therefore, expect that, at the start of a task, a man would be more aroused than later in the work period. One might, therefore, reasonably have expected that the harmful effects of intense noise should appear early in the work period and then wear off; as indeed the effects of unfamiliar noises do.

If one uses varied sounds, it is not surprising that, for example, McGrath's beneficial effect on vigilance from changing acoustic stimulation should be greater when the task has been going on for some time. In the absence of varied sounds, arousal has become low, and a change in the acoustic environment keeps the level reasonably high. Since however the effects of prolonged intense but continuous noise also appear largely at the end of the work period, we cannot satisfactorily explain them by a single state of arousal. There has to be some effect of prolonged work which is different from that of noise, just as we concluded when discussing vigilance. The single dimension of arousal is not sufficient: nevertheless, it does embody a certain amount of truth since a mild level of stimulation may improve performance and a high level may cause deterioration.

HIGH TEMPERATURES

Just as with noise, we have discussed heat as if it required no further specification. In fact of course we can find environmental temperatures which differ by any degree from that of a normal room. Not only may the temperature itself be mildly warm, distinctly hot, or so high that collapse will occur after a reasonably short exposure: but also there may be changes in the humidity. In the studies quoted earlier, as showing that the effects of heat were rather different from those of noise or sleeplessness, the conditions were usually 105° F dry bulb, and 95° F wet bulb. This was a reasonably practical condition, allowing subjects to continue working for long periods and yet being uncomfortably warm. It is by no means certain that our conclusion, of the independence of heat from other stresses, would hold true if other conditions had been used. In a wide variety of studies (Mackworth, 1950, Pepler, 1958) it has been found that performance tends to deteriorate when men are put in surroundings at a temperature greater than roughly 80-85° F. Under very extreme conditions however, which a man could not sustain indefinitely, there may be much less marked effects on performance up to the time when collapse occurs (Pepler, 1959b, Poulton and Kerslake, 1965). Furthermore, at the intermediate levels of heat from which most of our results were derived, there will be an attempt by the physiological mechanism which is responsible for temperature regulation to maintain the body temperature constant. This will be successful to a greater or lesser extent in different individuals; and it was found that the correlation between deterioration in performance and rise in body temperature was somewhat unreliable in the earlier studies where environment was made hot and a man placed in it.

In a more recent study by Wilkinson *et al.* (1964) a different approach was adopted, of applying heat to the body until the temperature was raised to a desired degree and then maintaining the environment such that the body temperature remained constant at its new value. Under these circumstances performance at a vigilance task is slightly worse when the body temperature is less than a degree above normal, but actually improved when the body temperature is raised by nearly 3° F. It seems clear therefore that, if we measure severity of heat stress by the degree by which body temperature is raised, then the state of efficiency is not moving constantly in one direction as the temperature moves up. If we take the leap of supposing that the general state which is altered by changes in body temperature is the same state of arousal which we have discussed in connection with sleeplessness and noise, then one might argue that the effect of a rise in body temperature is to produce a fall in arousal at first and a rise in arousal under more extreme conditions. (There may also be, as Poulton and Kerslake suggest, a rise in arousal at the very beginning of the exposure to an extreme of heat, when there is probably an initial drop in body temperature. This occurs as the compensating mechanisms respond before the full heat load has had time to give an effect.) This kind of change would be perfectly consistent with the failure of Pepler and of Viteles and Smith to find any interactions between heat on the one hand and sleep or noise on the other: because the effect of heat would be to throw some subjects into a lower state of arousal and some into a higher state. Averaged over a group, therefore, there would be no consistent rise or fall in the state of arousal.

Although heat has been more studied than any of the other stresses, therefore, it seems clear that still more work is required to disentangle these effects. It is quite possible that such further work might link heat with the same mechanism as that underlying effects of sleeplessness and noise, but at present there are insufficient data to do so.

SLEEPLESSNESS

Once again, we have referred thus far to loss of sleep as if it were a single simple entity. All the studies mentioned previously have involved complete loss of at least one night's sleep: in some cases of two nights. Yet it is known from electrical recording that there are two quite sharply distinguished types of sleep, usually called REM and non-REM; because the former involves rapid movements of the eyes while the latter does not. There are other associated differences, since in REM sleep there is low muscular tone in the facial and neck muscles, and the EEG shows a pattern of fast asynchronous low voltage changes. In non-REM sleep there is higher muscular tone, and an EEG showing more marked changes from the normal waking pattern. When a normal night's sleep is taken, it is usual for non-REM sleep to occupy the first period, for this to be followed by a period of REM sleep, and then for a series of alternations of increasing frequency to take place. Subjects awakened during REM sleep are more likely to say that they were dreaming, and the direction in which their eyes were last pointing before awakening shows some correspondence with the direction of regard last remembered from the dream.

One cannot assume that these two kinds of sleep serve similar functions,

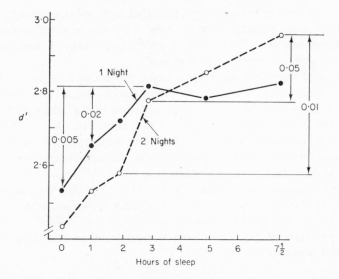

FIG. 42. The value of d' in a vigilance task when a man is allowed varying amounts of time asleep. On the first night, d' ceases to improve if at least three hours sleep have been taken, although it is unlikely that dreaming has occurred in that period. On the second night, a longer sleep is necessary for maximal d'. Data from Wilkinson (1969).

and indeed it is likely that they do not. When a man is kept without sleep completely for a night, he loses both kinds of sleep, and while we may say that part of the effects are a lowering of the general state labelled "arousal" it is not clear whether this results from one or both forms of deprivation, and what other consequences may flow from loss of one or the other kind of sleep.

There have been a number of studies of the consequences of awakening a man whenever he begins to take REM sleep. These studies have employed measures of the emotional state assessed clinically or by various psychometric means. (See Wilkinson, 1969 for a review.) The results are not completely clear-cut, but suggest that being awakened from either kind of sleep gives disturbances of emotion or mood, and that these disturbances are not quite the same in the two cases. Within our present context the one study using measurements of skilled performance is that of Wilkinson (1969), who did not measure the incidence of REM or non-REM sleep directly, but simply woke up experimental subjects after varying amounts of sleep and required them to perform tasks. It may be assumed that subjects who had slept for only three hours had spent the bulk of that time in non-REM sleep, and had had relatively little REM sleep during the night. Wilkinson tested such subjects using a vigilance task and applying the measures derived from detection theory: he found that they showed a significant drop in false positives, but no significant change in d'. That is, the effect of losing primarily REM sleep was to change β rather than d'. When however subjects were allowed only one hour of sleep or less, and therefore began to lose non-REM sleep, they showed a significant drop in d'.

If the same treatment was repeated on a second night, then effects on d' appeared even with subjects allowed three hours of sleep. This is not surprising, even if we wish to make a firm assertion that d' changes only after deprivation of non-REM sleep, because it is known that loss of REM sleep on one night causes that type of sleep to occur more frequently on succeeding nights, and therefore the three hours taken on the second night would involve some loss of non-REM sleep to allow time for REM sleep.

These results show clearly that it is an oversimplification to think only of a single level of arousal, reduced by loss of sleep. There must be some other factor as well. This need not stop us, however, from considering changes in the general state of arousal so long as we remember that there are other additional factors to be considered.

OTHER CONDITIONS AFFECTING THE GENERAL STATE

(a) *Time of day*. When results have been given previously about the effects of loss of sleep, they have referred always to measurements taken at the same time of day in people who had or had not slept a prescribed amount within the last 24 hours. The reason for prescribing the time of day is that performance does not depend simply upon the length of time for which a man has been awake. If he has been in the habit of sleeping at night, and is for some reason unable to do so, then his performance early in the morning after his sleepless night will actually be worse than his performance in the late afternoon of that same day. Thus he might even appear to have improved with a longer period since his last sleep. The reason is that the effects of sleeplessness are superimposed upon a rhythm of working efficiency which normally proceeds throughout the 24 hours, relatively low performance appearing at, say, 6.00 a.m. and relatively high performance later on in the day. The rise in performance appears in a variety of tasks and continues until, say, 9.00 p.m. It is paralleled by a daily rhythm in body temperature (Blake, 1967b). The latter point is not in itself necessarily meaningful, since there are 24 hour rhythms in many physiological quantities, which are all in step in people living under normal conditions of sleeping at night, but which it is known may separate into different rhythms when there is a shift in the time of day at which sleep is normally taken. However, the rhythm of body temperature does seem to have a closer connection to the rhythm of working efficiency than a simple chance link: Colquhoun *et al.* (1968) studied shift workers who were working at irregular times of day, so that they did not shift their hours of sleeping to a new and consistent point in the 24 hours. These men maintained the usual rhythm of body temperature, and performance corresponded to it.

When however they were put on shift work which allowed them to sleep at the same point of the 24 hour cycle in each successive day, but at a time which was different from the conventional one, their rhythm of body temperature shifted to the new cycle, and the rhythm of performance did likewise. Thus it does appear to be the rhythm of temperature rather than of other quantities which is associated with the rhythm of performance.

We have here therefore another indication of a general state which rises and falls and affects efficiency at work. It is not clear whether the general state is to be regarded as the same one affected by noise and by sleeplessness: although we know that performance after loss of sleep continues to show a diurnal rhythm, we do not know whether the difference between normal and sleepless subjects is larger at 8.00 in the morning than at 8.00 in the evening, or whether the two effects merely add. It may seem hypercautious to raise the possibility that diurnal rhythm represents a different change of state from that produced by sleeplessness. Nevertheless, Wilkinson (1963b) has noted that a disturbance of performance appears after an experiment on sleep loss, even when a night's sleep has intervened: he suggested that this might be due to disturbance of diurnal rhythm, and noted that the effects did not increase with work period as those of sleeplessness do. Thus the effects of diurnal rhythm may be rather different from those of sleeplessness. Some of the other results to be described below imply that one should not assume the identity of sleeplessness and of disturbance of diurnal rhythm until it has been shown more conclusively.

(b) *Introversion-extraversion.* The topic of time of day leads on readily to that of personality: since there appears to be a clear connection between time of day and the personality picked out by the introversion scale of tests such as the Heron Personality Inventory (Heron, 1956). This was first suspected from results by Colquhoun (1960), who analysed the results of 17 vigilance experiments carried out at different times of day, and showed that the morning experiments gave a positive correlation between introversion and efficiency, while those in the afternoon gave a negative correlation. Colquhoun and Corcoran (1964) found a similar relationship for the task of cancelling particular letters in English prose: provided that the men concerned were working alone (as they had of course been in the vigilance task). If subjects were tested in groups, the correlation between introversion and efficiency disappeared even in the morning. Blake (1967b) recorded body temperature at different times of day for a number of individuals, and found that there was a significant positive correlation between introversion and body temperature at 8.00 a.m., but significant negative correlations at 9.00 p.m., 11.00 p.m., and 1.00 a.m. The pattern seems to be that both groups show a rapid rise in body temperature between 5.00 a.m. and 10.00 a.m., followed by a slow rise between 10.00 a.m. and 9.00 p.m., and a rapid drop during the night. The introverts differ by showing their rapid rise a little earlier than the extraverts, and similarly their fall in the evening. Averaged over the 24 hours there was no correlation between temperature and personality.

This result on body temperature is theoretically important. The results on performance might be explained by supposing that introversion and time of day both represent differences in level of some state of arousal. On this view the effects interact because the chronically high arousal of introverts is helpful when the total level is sub-optimal, but harmful if other conditions give a high level. If however there is no difference in body temperature on average between introverts and extraverts, it argues against the view that this personality dimension represents a chronic difference in level of arousal. It rather argues that introversion has something to do with the *change* of level of arousal as conditions are changed.

A similar argument can be derived from the performance measurements themselves: if we supposed that the results of Colquhoun and Corcoran were to be explained by a chronically high level of arousal in introverts, together with an increment in arousal either from working in a group or from working in the afternoon, then we might expect the correlation of introversion and efficiency to be more negative when working *both* in a group *and* in the afternoon than under either condition alone. In fact it is not. Thus again it seems difficult to represent the effect of introversion as being a chronic high level of arousal. We rather have to think of it as being a condition which will result in higher arousal under certain circumstances.

So long as we stick to this rather cautious way of interpreting the relation between introversion and arousal, there are a number of other facts which support it. Thus for example it has been found by Bakan (1959) that an increase in signal frequency has a greater beneficial effect on extraverts than upon introverts. Corcoran (1963b, 1965) has found greater effects from incentives upon extraverts than upon introverts. In the realm of noise, Blake (unpublished) has found that noise improved the rate of work of extraverts early in the morning but not later in the day, while having no such effect on introverts. Davies and Hockey (1966) have found that noise gives an improvement in vigilance for extraverts under low signal frequency conditions but not under high signal frequency conditions, while introverts showed no effect of noise in either case. Davies *et al.* (1969) found a more beneficial effect from varied auditory stimulation upon vigilance in the case of extraverts than in introverts. In the case of sleeplessness, Corcoran (1965) has found some evidence that extraverts may show larger detrimental effects. All these results are consistent with the idea that extraverts may be at lower levels of arousal than introverts, in the particular conditions being tested.

The picture is not, however, completely clear. As regards noise, Broadbent (1958a) obtained some evidence that the detrimental effect of noise was actually greater in extraverts than in introverts, which would hardly suggest that their state of arousal was chronically lower than that of the introverts.

More recent unpublished repetitions of this experiment by Broadbent and Gregory have shown that the correlation is in fact rather unstable, and was due to the use of a sample of subjects who happened to have a low value on the other main personality dimension used in the Heron inventory, namely neuroticism. Amongst groups with a low level of neuroticism it may be true that extraverts are more impaired by noise than introverts, but in groups with a higher level of neuroticism this is not necessarily true. The direction of the correlation may reverse depending upon the value of the other personality dimension. Similar interactions between dimensions have been evident in published data on introversion, although not always commented upon: for example, in data by Claridge (1960) on decrement in a vigilance task, it is clear that extraverts show a greater decrement during the work period only if one compares neurotic extraverts with neurotic introverts. Amongst those at a lower level of neuroticism, the relationship is exactly the opposite. Again, Wilkinson (1965) makes the point that his own experiments have not normally shown greater effects of sleeplessness in extraverts, even though we have noted from results of Corcoran that such a relationship does sometimes appear. These points, like those we considered earlier in this section, make it clear that one cannot regard a difference in degree of introversion as corresponding simply to a difference in level of arousal, whatever the other conditions in play. Rather it would seem that introverts are more aroused than extraverts under some conditions, and that there is no difference under others. With this complication however we can regard the dimension of introversion as linked to the sleeplessness-noise system discussed previously.

(c) *Effects of pressure.* We have already mentioned that the breathing of compressed air causes a deterioration of performance. This is probably an effect of the nitrogen present in ordinary air, since its replacement by helium causes the compressed mixture to be breathable at greater pressures without loss of consciousness, and with rather greater working efficiency (Baddeley and Flemming, 1967). Again one cannot assume that the effect produced by nitrogen is the same as any of those we have discussed previously, but one would certainly not expect it to increase the level of arousal or alertness. Yet from that point of view the conditions in which the effect most readily appears are rather surprising. It has been found by Baddeley (1966c) that the effect of breathing compressed air is less when the experiment is conducted in a pressure chamber, than when one measures the performance of real divers in the open sea. In a pressure chamber there may be a deterioration of less than 6%, while there may be a difference of 20% between performing a task just below the surface of the water and performing it at depth. There must therefore be some other stress associated with depth which, in the way we have noticed previously, is exaggerating the effect of the nitrogen. In so far as there is some effect even from breathing a helium mixture, the same relation applies and the deterioration is greater in the open sea than in a pressure chamber (Baddeley and Flemming, 1967).

The nature of the stress involved in diving, as opposed to breathing compressed air on land, can perhaps be seen from a study by Baddeley *et al.* (1968), which failed to get the interaction. Although deterioration appeared with divers at depth, the effect in the sea was no greater than the effect found in a pressure chamber. The difference between this experiment and the previous ones was that the diving was done from the beach rather than from the deck of a boat in the open sea. It is plausible that open sea diving carries some element of anxiety, and that this was exaggerating the effect of the nitrogen. If so, it seems curious that a rise in anxiety, which is presumably a change in the direction of increased arousal, should actually increase the deterioration due to breathing nitrogen under pressure. The effect is working in the same direction as the increased impact of noise when incentive conditions are present: so that one would almost have to regard nitrogen as an arousing stress. We may regard this relationship as evidence for the generality of interactive effects between incentive and other stresses, but nevertheless there is something curious in it.

(*d*) *Alcohol.* We have not previously mentioned the effect of small doses of alcohol, except to note that they accentuate the effect of those drugs which relieve motion sickness. There have of course been very many studies of alcohol, showing that it impairs performance at quite low dosages (see for example, Drew *et al.*, 1959). The point of particular interest from our point of view is that a study by Wilkinson and Colquhoun (1968) has examined the interaction of alcohol with incentive on the one hand and with sleep deprivation on the other. The serial reaction task used in the other experiments by Wilkinson was employed in this case also. Incentive *increased* the adverse effect of alcohol. This again is a curious result, since physiologically alcohol must be regarded as a cortical depressant and not a stimulant. Yet by our previous arguments we would have to argue that alcohol was acting like incentive, and therefore like noise, high signal rate, and other conditions causing the system to reach a high level of arousal. There is therefore some discrepancy here between the behavioural and the known physiological mechanisms.

The interaction of alcohol with sleeplessness was slightly less clear, as it seemed to vary in different individuals. Because a fixed dose of alcohol was given to all individuals, the resulting blood alcohol level was higher in some people than in others: on the whole, larger men get a lower blood alcohol from the same intake through the mouth. Men with a relatively low blood alcohol showed a reduced effect of loss of sleep, while men with a high blood alcohol showed an increased effect. This result also is consistent with the idea that, at least in small doses, alcohol raises the level of arousal rather than lowering it. It is worth noting one other puzzle under this heading: Wilkinson

(1965) mentions that he has data, for which no details are available as yet, that hyoscine shows no interaction with the effects of sleeplessness. Yet as we have seen earlier hyoscine increases the effect of alcohol.

CONCLUSIONS FROM A DETAILED EXAMINATION OF STRESSES

All these lines of evidence show that one cannot be satisfied with the simple theory that a single state of arousal can vary from low to high levels, and that efficiency is poor at the extremes of this range and high in the middle. There must be some other factor coming in. (1) Prolonged work is necessary both before noise and also before sleeplessness show their effects, even though the effects are opposite when they do appear. (2) Different degrees of temperature rise have different implications for performance. (3) Loss of sleep includes at least two different mechanisms. (4) Time of day changes the general level of performance, but may possibly fail to interact with length of work period in the way that sleeplessness does. (5) Introversion is closely related to the effects of time of day, but only tenuously and unreliably to sleeplessness. Even though this dimension of personality shows some interaction with signal rate, with incentive, and with noise, the details of the interaction suggest that introversion is not a chronic increase in the level of arousal. (6) The effects of high pressure nitrogen, and of alcohol, interact in the opposite direction from that which might have been expected.

Yet although these results show that some extra factor must be considered, they do also support the general idea of a general state of arousal, higher in level for some conditions and lower in others. The extra features that are needed for an adequate theory cannot be stated confidently at this time: we shall make some attempt at suggesting a possible mechanism in a later speculative chapter. For the moment we must be content with our demonstration that there is a considerable common element in the effects of various working conditions, and that some stresses oppose each other. We can now ask what the detailed nature of the mechanism might be through which these changes of arousal result in deterioration of performance.

The Mechanics of Over-Arousal

There is no difficulty in explaining inefficiency due to under-arousal: response simply fails to occur on occasions when it should do so. The typical decrement produced by sleeplessness is that of the pause in which no reaction occurs. The decrement due to noise, on the other hand, is typically an error rather than a pause. If the effect of noise is to raise a general level of arousal, to increase a widespread facilitation throughout the cortex, why should this produce inefficiency? There is no problem to explain low performance at the bottom end of the arousal scale, but there is a considerable problem in explaining poor performance at the top.

If we recall the analysis of reaction time in Chapter VII, we saw that reaction is delayed until there is sufficient evidence to exceed some critical value and cause one of the possible actions to occur. The uncertainties in our theory of this mechanism concern the way in which incoming evidence is accumulated, the provision for temporal uncertainty, and so on, but the general picture seems sound. The efficiency of response will then depend on the precise setting of the criteria. If criteria for all reactions are set rather cautiously, performance will be slow but accurate. If the criteria are set to allow response on relatively little evidence, performance will be fast but inaccurate. At the cautious end of this scale, the main effect may be the occurrence of a few very slow reactions, due to the decision to react having been preceded by an earlier decision that the evidence was inadequate. As the criteria move from a very cautious to a very risky position, they will pass through some optimal point where the elimination of slow reactions is balanced by the increase in error reactions. Any shift of the criteria in one direction or the other from this optimum point will produce a deterioration of performance, but the type of change will be different.

If therefore one were to link the degree of caution in the placement of criteria with the level of arousal, we should have the desired explanation for deterioration through over-arousal. The whole structure of statistical decisions implies that there should be an optimum criterion placement, just as the data on performance under stress imply that there is an optimum state of arousal. Appealing and attractive as this identification seems, we need some independent line of evidence to confirm it. It is in essence an explanation of the effects of arousal which puts them down to "pigeon-holing"; it contends that arousal increases the biases in favour of reaction, at the expense of those for inaction. Such an emphasis on pigeon-holing is perhaps in tune with the importance of that concept throughout all the fields we have been considering: but it is not the only possibility. For example, arousal might be cutting down the intake of information, a possibility which we touched upon in discussing the perception of emotional words. It could be affecting filtering rather than pigeon-holing. We must therefore look for more direct evidence.

Because the theory of reaction time contains too many residual uncertainties, one cannot examine speed of reaction in relation to errors and see if changes in arousal produce the type of change predicted by a criterion shift. One can however study the relative number of errors of different sorts, regardless of the time taken to produce them. Many theorists have adopted the principle that a bias towards one response rather than another will be increased when the general state of drive or arousal is increased. Broadbent (1965a) formulated such a relationship mathematically in terms of Luce's choice analysis. His particular version of the principle suggested that the biases in favour of particular responses would follow the probability of those responses being correct (as we have several times seen that they do); and further would do so to an extent depending on the degree of reward for correct action. When the consequences of these assumptions are worked out in a specific form, it appears that an optimal level of incentive will appear.

The principle is however a much older one investigated in considerable detail by Spence (for example, 1956). In its older formulation, the principle originated from a modification of Hull's learning theory. The particular feature of the theory was made necessary to incorporate one class of animal experiments. These were studies in which learning might take place under a fairly low level of drive, without much consequent effect on performance: until drive was increased, when performance of the animal would improve much more steeply than that of control animals without the earlier training. This result made it impossible to regard the probability of reaction as an additive function of the degree of training and the amount of drive: roughly speaking, the correct response would occur if training had occurred and also drive was present, but not in the presence of one of these factors without the other. Thus it was necessary to regard the probability of correct response as depending upon the product rather than the sum of the two factors. If then the probability of an action depends on the product of the drive level and of the strength of the habit, any increase in drive will increase the difference in probabilities of two responses differing in initial strength. Increases in drive would thus cause the stronger of two competing responses to become stronger still. This might be expected to increase the efficiency of performance in tasks where the desired response had no close competitor: for example, in simple conditioning where the problem is merely one of acquiring a certain response to a particular stimulus. If, however, one was considering some task in which a correct response had to be discriminated from some other strongly competing response, then increase in drive would make the error response yet stronger compared with the correct response, and increase the difficulty of the task.

In the original Hull-Spence application, this theory has been tested by examining performance under high and low states of drive, and in people who score high and low marks on a test of personal anxiety; with tasks involving no competing response or else strong response competition. Responsa competition is usually varied by using paired-associate learning, with items possessing initially strong or weak association between the stimulus and response. Thus it may be hard to learn the response "stream" to the stimulus "table", if "chair" is a response to be made to some other stimulus in the same experiment. There are technical problems in this kind of study, since as learning proceeds the new correct response will obviously increase in strength compared with the competitor, and the theory itself would predict that high drive will give better performance as soon as the correct response has overtaken its competitor.

The results are not completely clear-cut. Increased drive or anxiety in the individual seems usually to give better learning in the absence of response competition; but it is not always possible to get worse performance under stressful conditions, or by anxious people, even in tasks which seem to involve strong response competition. It is usually fair to say however that there is an interaction between the personality of the subject and the degree of stress, on such tasks (Spence, 1956).

Turning now to the stresses which we have been discussing, Woodhead (1964a, 1966) has examined performance in two complex tasks while bursts of noise were occasionally presented. In one task, the subject examined a sheet of digits while crossing out any instances of a particular digit: at relatively infrequent intervals the subject would encounter some other digit which was already marked on the stimulus sheet and from then on he had to search for instances of this new digit rather than the one he had been searching for thus far. There are thus two elements to this task: looking for digits, and noticing that one has got to change to a new digit. In scoring one can distinguish cases of failing to notice a digit from cases of failing to notice that one should have changed digits, and the latter became more frequent in intense noise while the former did not.

In the other task studied, the subject had to look for letters, cross off five instances of each of two letters, then change to a different pair of letters and cross off five of each of those, change back to the original pair, and so on. Once again one can distinguish errors of the type in which the subject fails to notice a letter which he should have done, and errors of the type in which he crosses out too many or too few letters of one kind before changing to the other. In the first case he had failed to see something, and in the second to keep an adequate count in memory of his actions. Instructions could emphasize one aspect of the task or the other: this did not alter the total number of errors, and under quiet conditions it did not affect the proportion of errors which were of one kind rather than another. In noise conditions however instructions to emphasize memory had a bigger effect than they did in quiet. To put it another way, the condition emphasized by the instructions tended to improve in noise. Thus both these studies are consistent with the general idea that a noise increases the stronger of two concurrent activities.

With matters at this stage, an important study was published by Glucksberg (1962), within the framework of the Hull-Spence theory. In the experiment which most concerns us, Glucksberg measured thresholds for words under the following condition. He presented two words in different colours, the instruction to the subject being to perceive the word of a certain colour. (In terms of our earlier distinction, this was stimulus set.) One word was much easier to see than the other, both because the physical stimulus was stronger, and also because it was a common rather than an uncommon word. Subjects instructed to look for this easy word did better when competing for a financial reward. Subjects instructed to look for the difficult word did worse. This result is completely in accordance with the Hull-Spence theory.

Broadbent and Gregory therefore conducted a number of variations on this experiment, mostly using noise as the experimental variable rather than incentive. In the first place, they repeated Glucksberg's experiment simply applying intense continuous noise to the subjects rather than offering a reward. The uncommon word was harder to perceive in noise, while the common word was slightly but not significantly easier to see. This result is important in two ways: partly because it provides a detailed situation for studying competition between two simultaneous task elements, and partly because it adds another link to the evidence connecting noise with incentive. In previous work we have seen that (1) noise resembles incentive in reducing the effects of sleeplessness, that (2) each of them increases the errors in the serial reaction task, that (3) incentive increases the harmful effects of noise, and that (4) noise acts to improve long-term memory at the expense of short-term memory just as incentives do. With the addition of the present effect on perceptual selection, it does seem that we have a fairly clear case for arguing for a considerable common element between the effects of noise and those of incentive.

The Glucksberg situation however is particularly useful, since as a task involving perceptual selection it allows us to distinguish the relative roles of pigeon-holing and filtering. As in all the previous chapters, we can look at the probability of occurrence of certain responses when they are correct and also when they are incorrect. If a certain response occurs as an error more frequently than other responses do, there is a bias or pigeon-holing effect towards that response. From the extent to which the response becomes more frequent still when correct, we can work out the intake of sensory information from the corresponding stimulus. If information from certain classes of stimuli is being preferentially filtered, that class will show a larger intake of information. Thus by considering the pattern of errors and correct responses we can see whether the degree of pigeon-holing or filtering has changed when we change conditions.

Broadbent and Gregory's further results showed in fact that the effect of noise on Glucksberg's task could not be put down to pigeon-holing, at least of the type predicted by Hull-Spence theory or by Broadbent (1965a). In his original report, Glucksberg had suggested that the same results would have appeared even if one word had been presented by itself: that is, the threshold for a common word presented on its own should have been lowered by incentive and that for an uncommon word increased. He argued this quite logically on the ground that the correct perception of a word implied that the appropriate response had been selected from other competing responses, and that with an uncommon word these inappropriate responses would be relatively stronger. Broadbent and Gregory, however, performed three experiments using single isolated words; and they found no evidence for an interaction between the probability of a word in the language and the effects on its threshold from noise or from financial incentives. Perhaps even more important, they analysed the misperceptions and counted the number which were common and which were uncommon words. They were unable to find any change in the ratio of common to uncommon misperceptions either when noise was applied, or when financial incentives were given. Thus there is no evidence for noise or incentive changing the bias in favour of one response rather than another in these perceptual tasks.

Broadbent and Gregory carried out some further experiments on perceptual selection in noise, to demonstrate that indeed there was a deterioration of this function even when response biases were not apparently involved. In one study they used a mixture of red and white digits, giving a fixed exposure and scoring the number of digits in a prescribed colour which the subject was able to identify. Once again therefore the task is one of stimulus set, but in this case the relevant and irrelevant material should have equal biases. Neverthe-

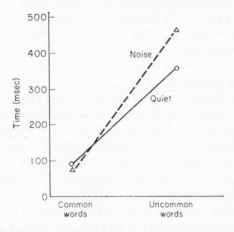

FIG. 43. The threshold for common, heavily printed words, and uncommon, less visible, words, each in the presence of the other. Noise impairs the less visible words but, if anything, improves the easy ones. Unpublished data by Broadbent and Gregory.

less there was deterioration in performance in noise, equally great whichever colour was being chosen even though it was harder to see red than white. A similar deterioration appeared when a mixture of digits was presented with instructions to pick out those digits that were underlined: the point of this variation of the experiment being to eliminate the possibility that the effect is due to a change in colour vision. Thus noise does genuinely seem to impair tasks requiring perceptual selection.

Lastly, two experiments of apparently similar type were performed in which the task was altered slightly in ways which should eliminate the effects of noise, if it is indeed due to perceptual selection. In one case, the same stimulus material of red and white digits was presented, but the subjects were told to write as many digits as possible ignoring the distinction of colour. No deterioration in noise was found, and if anything performance was slightly better under that condition. In the other variation in the task, a mixture of letters and digits was presented and the subject was instructed only to produce items of one category. In this case response set rather than stimulus set was involved, intrusions were therefore unimportant as a source of error, and correspondingly there was no effect of noise upon performance.

All these results confirm that the difficulty in noise is one of selecting one of the stimuli present for reaction and ignoring another, and not one of changes in response bias causing performance to be inefficient. To be fair, we should record one negative result found by Broadbent and Gregory: they presented a mixture of red and white letters of the alphabet, rather than digits, with instructions to give the items in one colour only. This task was one of stimulus set, and should have shown a deterioration in noise. Nevertheless, there was no effect of noise. Explanations are hard to find in this case, but it may be that the level of difficulty of the task was responsible.

Our position thus far is as follows. Noise certainly behaves like incentive, and each of these conditions appears to affect perceptual selection, as had been predicted from the Hull-Spence theory. However, neither of them does so by affecting response biases, as that theory would suppose, and it seems clear that the noise effect only occurs when there is a competing stimulus from which the reaction stimulus has to be discriminated. Possibly therefore the effect of stress is upon filtering and not upon pigeon-holing: or at least only upon pigeon-holing in a way which has been left unconsidered thus far.

EXPERIMENTS ON SPATIALLY DISTRIBUTED SOURCES OF SIGNALS

An unusual study of heat was carried out by Bursill (1958). He required subjects to perform a tracking task, while reacting at the same time to an array of lights stretching out from the tracking task to the periphery of vision. Whenever a brief illumination of one of these lights occurred the subject had to report it. The effect of temperature was to impair detection of the peripheral lights more than those in central vision. The result was confirmed by Poulton and Kerslake (1965). It was found by Bahrick *et al.* (1952) that a similar effect was produced by incentive, but although this is immediately suggestive that there is some connection with arousal, incentive itself naturally changes the gains and losses for different parts of the task and this confuses the picture somewhat. It is also unclear whether the effect is a peripheral one due to changes in the sensitivity of the edge of the eye, or a more central process. Webster and Haslerud (1964) showed that the addition of an auditory task to a task of reacting to lights also impaired performance at the edge of a display, and it does not seem very likely therefore that it is a peripheral sensory effect. Nevertheless the possibility still remained in play.

G. R. J. Hockey repeated Bursill's experiment but using noise rather than heat. He found a marked deterioration in performance at the edge of the visual display when noise was present. By changing the task, he was able to prove that the effect was not a simple retinal one, but depended upon the subject's estimate of probability of signals from one part of the visual field rather than another. The effect was only found if the task was carried out in the way just described, that is, with signals disappearing after a very brief exposure. If signals were left on indefinitely, and the latency of reaction was measured, then noise affected the edge of the display no more than the middle. In both cases the probability of signals in the middle of the display or at the edge had been equal: but when the lights remained on only for a short time, the subject remained completely unaware of those which he did not detect. Since there were more failures of detection at the edge of the display the probability of signals was subjectively higher in the middle of the field of view. If the experimental technique was changed, so that more signals were delivered objectively from the middle of the display, then noise would affect performance even for signals visible indefinitely. It increased the reaction time at the edge of the field of view. Thus the effect seems quite clearly to be one of improving reaction to probable signals at the expense of improbable signals. Because reaction time remained unaffected at the edge of the display when signals were equally probable throughout, it seems very difficult to explain the result as due to some change in the retina, and it must rather be a change in central processes.*

The obvious way of formulating this result is that noise increases the tendency to select information from sources which deliver more rather than fewer signals. It will be recalled from the discussion of vigilance that Hamilton (1967) has found a way of obtaining a count of observing responses in tasks involving many sources of signals. He allows the subject only to look at one of the several displays at a time, as in Holland's original method for recording observing responses. But Hamilton only allows the subject to make observations at a fixed slow rate. When this latter precaution is taken, the subject chooses to make more observations from sources from which the probability of signals is higher. Hockey repeated this result, and demonstrated that the relative number of observing responses to a probable source was even higher if the man was working in noise. Thus it is confirmed that noise causes the system to select information more frequently from sources which are likely to be delivering signals.

For completeness, it may be noted that Hockey has studied the effects of sleeplessness both in the Bursill situation and in the Hamilton one. In each case, sleeplessness has the opposite type of effect to that of noise, the edge of the field of view becoming relatively improved, and observations being made less often from probable sources of information.†

These results therefore confirm the view that arousal effects filtering, and

---

* These results are now published by Hockey, *Q. J. exp. Psychol.* **22**, 28-36, and 37-42.
† This result is now published by Hockey, *Br. J. Psychol.* **61**, 473-480.

make it essentially unshakeable. The type of effect produced is that the aroused system devotes a higher proportion of its time to the intake of information from dominant sources and less from relatively minor ones.

Some Related Views and Results

It is worth noticing that the Hull-Spence theory has not been the only one in the field, and that some other authors have suggested that the effects of over-arousal were due to perceptual rather than response processes. One notable example is Easterbrook (1959), who reviewed a number of studies up to that date. His general conclusion was that stress showed itself in a narrowing of the range of cues used by the person stressed, and he was able to give a plausible account of the phenomenon in those terms. The facts which we have added extend his view by distinguishing detrimental effects due to low arousal from those due to high and by making the distinction of input and output processes more clearly.

Another analysis of stress effects with a similar interpretation is that of Callaway (see Callaway and Stone, 1960). He has made use of the Stroop test in work with drugs, on the view that stimulants should give accentuated filtering and so improve performance, while depressants would give the reverse action. (This view is said to derive from Broadbent, 1958, but it is hard to find so clear a statement in that book.) Some of Callaway's results do confirm the view: they have been reviewed by Venables (1964). There is the odd and unexplained difficulty that the score on the Stroop found most sensitive is not the difference in time on the interference and control tests, but their sum: which Jenson and Rohwer (1966) suggest to be rather a measure of general speed than of resistance to distraction. Part of the difficulty may be that drugs act differentially on several mechanisms to a different degree at various dosages: we shall in the next chapter see that atropine, one of the drugs used in these studies, may have quite complex effects. The point of view adopted by Callaway in this different field is however the same as ours.

Another line of work which should be mentioned is that Hörmann and Osterkamp (1966) have studied effects of noise upon memory, and have found evidence for a change in performance rather different from any we have mentioned. They found that noise induced a fall in the amount of "clustering" in free recall. That is, the words reproduced fell less often into groups associated together. The effect was greater in those individuals who suffer most interference on the Stroop test.

It is very unclear how this result links up with the others we have mentioned; possibly as we said in the last chapter the strategies of pigeon-holing and filtering may apply to retrieval from memory as well as to perception, and an increase in the use of filtering may induce a change in the incidence of clustering since that is presumably a "pigeon-holing" strategy. The line of study is one well worth pursuing, and might conceivably provide a way into the analysis of the various retrieval mechanisms.

Final Loose Ends

The broad conclusion from this chapter must be that filtering is more sensitive to stress than pigeon-holing is. Yet there are some loose ends needing to be tied up before we can leave the subject. They fall in two main classes. First, we have left some theoretical points unclear. If arousal increases the emphasis on selecting certain sources of information, what becomes of the tempting analogy, which we drew earlier in the chapter, between the optimum level of arousal and the optimum placement of a decision criterion? And if noise increases the effect of probability upon one mode of information processing, namely filtering, why does it *not* have an effect upon pigeon-holing, since that mode is the one most usually affected by probability?

The second class of loose ends is factual, and concerns our long discussion of vigilance many chapters ago. In reviewing the evidence from that field, we found some effects of arousal upon tasks which involve no obvious perceptual selection. Furthermore, some of these effects were ascribed to pigeon-holing. In particular, the separation of criteria was found to be less in noise, so that fewer "doubtful" responses were recorded; and most effects of noise on vigilance were put down to this effect. Admittedly, the possibility was raised that more detailed studies of noise might show a change of A in the equation

$$Z_D = A + BZ_{FA}$$

and if this result was so, it might be evidence for an effect of noise on the intake of information. This was regarded at that stage however as minor compared with the effect of noise on pigeon-holing.

A clarification of theory will however help to deal with the factual point. Both the theory of Hull and Spence, and that of Broadbent (1965a), accepted too blithely the view that an increase in motivation should always increase the bias towards one response rather than another. Such a relationship is not in fact really necessary in the field which first gave rise to it: the interaction of learning and motivation to produce performance of a learned response by animals. It is true, as we said, that a hungry rat who has in the past received food pellets for bar pressing when a light flashes will have a high probability of pressing the bar when the light next occurs. Without training or without hunger the probability of reaction will be very low: the effects of the two conditions together are more than additive.

$$P(HT) > P(H\overline{T}) + P(T\overline{H}) - P(\overline{HT})$$

where

$P(HT)$ = Probability of reaction when hungry and trained.
$P(H\overline{T})$ = Probability of reaction when hungry but untrained.
$P(T\overline{H})$ = Probability of reaction when trained but not hungry.
$P(\overline{HT})$ = Probability of reaction when neither.

Thus Hull-Spence theory supposes that $P(HT)$ is a multiplicative function of H and T, where these are some measures of the hunger and the training. The particular formulation produced by Broadbent (1965a) was of similar type, and can be put in the form

$$Z(HT) = (HT) + Z(\overline{HT})$$
$$H = Z(H\overline{T}) - Z(\overline{HT})$$
$$T = Z(\overline{H}T) - Z(\overline{HT})$$

where $Z(HT)$, $Z(\overline{HT})$ etc. are the Z-scores corresponding to the respective probabilities.

But from our many previous discussions it will be clear that

$$Z(HT) = (H) + (T) + Z(\overline{HT})$$

would be just as consistent with the original inequality stated in probabilities, since in this formulation also the rise in $P(HT)$ for a given increase in H will depend upon the value of T, and will be very small when T is very small. It would be possible to distinguish these formulations by fresh animal experiments, but the original observations are insufficient to do so.

However, the implications of the two expressions are quite different when it comes to examining biases in favour of one response rather than another: say, comparing two responses with different levels of training (values of T). Whereas the first implies that the difference in Z-scores between two such responses, the bias, will increase with H, the latter does not. The difference in *probabilities* will increase with increasing H, provided that the probability of the less-trained response is low; just as the probability of a correct detection in a vigilance task will rise rapidly for small rises in false alarm rate, or just as the correct perceptions of common and uncommon words differ much more than the misperceptions in each class. But as we have seen these large changes in probability do not necessarily mean differences in d'. Equally it may be true that a general increase in motivation may leave unchanged the relationship between the strengths of two responses, even though in one part of the range it increases the probability of one response more than that of the other.

Suppose now we return from this digression into the theory of animal learning, and think again of our analysis of human performance as a serial decision with criteria whose placement may be cautious or risky. It is not necessarily the case that a general increase in error rate, by moving all criteria in a risky direction, will always give an increase in the bias towards any one reaction.

If we simplify the random-walk model by thinking only of the evidence received at a single instant, on which a decision may be made "React to A" *or* "React to B", then we can represent the process by the usual pair of distributions with unit variance and means $+d'/\sqrt{2}$ and $-d'/\sqrt{2}$. With a decision

P

criterion placed asymmetrically by X units from the mid-point between the two means

$$Z_{FB} = \frac{d'}{\sqrt{2}} + X \qquad Z_{FA} = \frac{d'}{\sqrt{2}} - X$$

where Z_{FB} = errors of reacting B when A was presented,

            Z_{FA} = errors of reacting A when B was presented.

If now the alternative is introduced of allowing a third possible outcome "refrain from reaction and collect more evidence", that can be represented by introducing two criteria symmetrically placed by C units on either side of the original one. Evidence falling between these criteria would then lead to the outcome "collect more information". In that case,

$$Z_{FB} = \sqrt{2}d' + X - C$$
$$Z_{FA} = \sqrt{2}d' - X - C$$

But $Z_{FB} = Z_{FA} + 2X$

Changes in C will therefore leave the difference between the two Z-scores unchanged, and merely cause the difference in their corresponding probabilities to change in accordance with the familiar curve. So if increases in arousal reduce the probability of suspended judgment, they do not necessarily give a bias towards the most common type of error.

We can therefore maintain our attractive analogy, and still think of arousal as changing the balance between reacting quickly and reacting accurately An absence of overall effect on response bias is quite consistent with a "pigeon-holing" effect of this restricted type: where the only category state affected is the usual one of "insufficient evidence: get more". We can also recall and re-emphasize our results on the effects of noise on vigilance. They now fit well with the idea of arousal: increasing the chance of a moderate degree of evidence producing a definite reaction. In vigilance, that was just what we found. Noise reduced the proportion of "doubtful" or "unsure" responses.

Can we link this theoretical analysis with the effect of noise on filtering? It would be desirable to do so because of the puzzle that probability alters the effect of noise but usually affects pigeon-holing rather than filtering. But the data are really insufficient. Two points may however be noted. First, on the factual side, the same disappearance of doubtful and unsure states seems to occur in those \f Hockey's experiments on noise which used observing responses rather than vigilance. It will be remembered from Chapter III that observing responses distributed over several channels may sometimes be made twice running on the same channel, even when a signal is present; and this observation started us on the long path of examining degree of subjective confidence in judgments. Hockey has found that such repeated observations became less frequent in noise.

Secondly, on the theoretical side, there is an important logical distinction between the selection of stimuli and the selection of responses. If there is insufficient evidence for the latter, response may be withheld or fresh information sought. In the case of stimulus selection however, the process has to go one way or the other: if there is too little to guide it, then it must be based on chance. Concretely, in the Hamilton observing response technique subjects have to observe one channel or another at every epoch, and cannot withhold observations. Any particular observing response may therefore be the result of a definite decision to observe that channel, or of a random choice between channels because there are inadequate grounds to choose. If the former class of responses become in noise a higher proportion of the total, and if the definite decisions are biased towards channels with a high signal frequency, noise would give a higher proportion of choices of such channels. But the effect of noise in producing greater frequency of choice of the probable channel would be due to the disappearance of doubtful judgments, rather than to a direct effect of probability. The point needs far more evidence however.

Conclusion

In this chapter we have for the first time encountered an area where filtering has become more rather than less important since 1958. Whereas pigeon-holing has become increasingly evident in signal detection, in perceptual selection, in reaction to signals of different probability, in reaction time and even in memory, the effects of stress seem rather to be on filtering. There are manifestly many further points to be studied however, and a last section of this book must be devoted to the open questions still remaining. To this we shall now turn.

CHAPTER X

Speculations and Plans

A Last Glance at 1958

We have now completed our account of the new experimental work which has, since 1958, compelled a revision of the views held at that time. As we said in the first chapter, some of the early formulations have turned out to be still defensible; others have needed modification. The main success has been for the general method of attacking psychological problems in this fashion. An account of behaviour in terms of information processing allows theories to be objective and public in their content without oversimplification of the complexities of mental life; and it maintains the advantages gained by behaviourism. That is, it provides a means for the elimination of erroneous views, not by oscillatory changes of fashion, but by building on the achievements of the past.

With this theme in mind, we ought to spend our last pages considering the lines of development which now lead on to the future. Our emphasis has been throughout upon the process of discovery and not upon the static view of truth attained at one instant. The process does not stop now at this stage; indeed, even while these pages were written many new results were coming in, and there is no doubt that important findings have been omitted simply for the sake of drawing to a conclusion within a practicable time. We should therefore continue to look ahead and foresee the coming trends.

One last feature of 1958 is relevant in this connection. At that time, it was possible to include in the same book all the fields we have covered in this one: the detection of signals, selective attention, the effect of probability on performance, short-term memory, and a certain amount of information on stress. In addition it was perfectly practicable to include, in a book much smaller than the present one, a number of other and wider-ranging topics. The principle of selective intake of information by the brain was applied to a number of problems in human and animal learning, on the grounds that nothing could be learned if it was not first selected. It was argued that many of the phenomena known in the field of learning could be explained in this way, including even possibly the effects of reward upon learning; since events of biological importance were supposed to be especially likely to be selected, the conditional probability of their occurrence, given any particular antecedent event, is more likely to be stored than is the corresponding probability of some event which is only rarely selected. Individual differences received a whole chapter to themselves in 1958; and there were discussions of the motor side of performance, of the ways in which a long-term memory could react to changes in the statistical structure of the outside world, and many other topics.

These other fields have not stood still since 1958. If they have been left out of the present book, it is merely because they have been pursued by other and more able investigators, and that all areas of research have so expanded in the intervening decade that,it is no longer reasonable to cast so wide a net. Thus the reader must go elsewhere if he wishes to pursue the ways in which men faced by complex learning situations select only part of the available information (Underwood et al., 1962; Hunt, 1962). Similarly we have not had space to spare for an account of the evidence that animals also select only part of their surroundings as a basis for action, and that changes in this selection explain a number of curious features of their behaviour (Sutherland, 1966; Mackintosh, 1965). The existence of these important areas of research must at least be mentioned, however, because it is distinctly possible that the key lines of development for the future may come from them. In particular, we should emphasize again the interest which attaches to the role of biological importance in the selection of incoming information.

In 1958, with filtering as the sole mechanism for carrying out selection, one could only explain such facts as the tendency of hungry men to see food in ambiguous stimuli, by postulating some common physical characteristic in all stimuli connected with a biological drive. With the advent of categorizing and pigeon-holing, it is much easier to see how motivation could affect the selective process; the axiomatic development of signal detection theory supposes that gains and losses affect criterion placement just as probabilities do. In Chapter VI we saw that a start is being made upon the analysis of the effects of word emotionality on perception, using these concepts. The broader implications of these motivational effects upon the intake of information remain unexplored, however. In the theories of animal learning current in the 1950's, selective perception could play a part through the concept of the "anticipatory goal response", R_g. Only if a feature of the situation gave rise to an internal response could it have further effects upon learning. But, for reasons of parsimony, theorists of that era tended to assume that the principles governing the acquisition of R_gs were the same as those governing other and overt responses; they should be better established if followed by reinforcing (rewarding) states, and so on. We still do not know whether it is adequate to apply the same principles to R_gs and to overt responses: to the learning of a certain action and to the learning to attend to a certain feature of the situation. The Sutherland-Mackintosh approach requires certain differences between the two, especially in the rate of learning and unlearning. (If an animal is trained to make a response to one feature of a pair of complex stimuli, it may under certain circumstances learn to reverse the response more readily than it can learn to react to a new feature of the stimuli. That is, it seems to take longer to acquire a new attentive habit than to reverse an old overt response.) In the field of motivation however we might expect more fundamental differences between overt and covert learning. Crudely, it pays to do things which bring reward and avoid doing things which bring punishment. But it pays to notice *either* stimuli which indicate that reward *or* those which indicate that punishment is imminent. Thus it would be adaptive for the principles governing perception to be rather different from those governing overt action.

The line of future advance may come therefore from a return to the study of effects of motivation upon human and animal learning: or from one of the other fields which are allied to the ones we have considered but which, since 1958, have been crowded out of consideration by the general expansion of research. Having made this clear, and also explained that the lack of any account of these areas is not due to their unimportance, we should neverthe- ess try and construct some signposts to the future from the areas we have covered. At least these may have the merit of revealing certain underlying biases which may not have emerged in earlier parts of the book. Three lines of possible development suggest themselves, each with its associated specu- lations and possible experiments. One concerns the elaboration of the concept of arousal; one the establishment of the detailed decision rule which underlies the effects of probability and motivation which we can now roughly discern; and the third line of development points to analysis of long-term memory and the central control of behaviour.

The Complication of Arousal

WEAKNESSES IN THE EARLIER STATEMENT

It will be remembered that, in Chapter IX, we passed somewhat hastily over certain difficulties in the concept of a single general state of arousal, producing inefficiency of performance either when there was too low or when there was too high a level. To summarize these difficulties very briefly, they all take the form of interactions appearing between two environmental conditions when a unitary concept of arousal would suppose that they should not.

(i) Both noise and sleeplessness have their greatest harmful effect late in the work-period, and are thus similar in this respect. On the other hand, they tend to cancel each other out if applied together, and are thus opposite in that respect.

(ii) The personality dimension of extraversion interacts fairly consistently with time of day, as if it corresponded to a state of low arousal. On the other hand, it does not behave consistently in relation to noise or sleeplessness.

(iii) Alcohol interacts with incentive in the way one might expect if it produced high arousal, rather than being a depressant.

These difficulties require some sort of complication of the theory, but it is not clear exactly what sort. The speculation to be advanced here is that we are dealing with two mechanisms rather than one; probably any theory to explain the difficulties would take this line. The more risky step however is to specify the differences and relations between the two mechanisms. We shall suggest that one is a lower-level one concerned with the execution of well-established decision processes, and that the other is at a higher level, monitoring and altering the parameters of the lower level in order to maintain constant performance. For brevity we may refer to the two mechanisms as Upper and Lower from now on.

In these terms, it is the Lower which is affected by sleeplessness and noise. Those conditions shift the decision criteria between a very cautious and unreactive extreme and a very risky and hyper-reactive extreme, on the lines suggested in Chapter IX. So long as the Upper is in an efficient state, however, the consequences of Lower inefficiency do not become evident. If we suppose that the Upper is efficient at the start of a work-period and becomes less so after prolonged monotonous work, then it would follow that noise and sleeplessness would show their effects only at the end of the work-period. The effects of those two conditions would however be opposite once they did appear. Similarly, if alcohol affects the Upper rather than the Lower, it might appear to increase the effects of incentive even though it is known pharmacologically to be acting as a depressant. Lastly, if extraversion is a quality of the Upper rather than the Lower, the interactions of that personality dimension with sleeplessness and noise might be expected to be inconsistent, since they would oppose the effect of one of those conditions when the level of arousal was sub-optimal; but accentuate it when the level was super-optimal.

We can thus account, *post hoc*, for the difficulties raised by the present state of experimental knowledge. There are however other reasons for adopting this particular complication of theory; they come largely from physiological psychology, and are as follows.

TRANQUILLIZERS AND TASK PACING

We have several times mentioned in passing the fact that serial reaction tasks can be given either "paced" or "unpaced", that is, either with each signal given at a fixed time after the previous one, or with each signal waiting for the previous reaction and then following it immediately. In the first case, any reaction which is especially slow will be too late and there is no opportunity for subsequent faster work to compensate for the failure. In the latter case, an abnormally slow reaction holds up performance temporarily, but this can be balanced out by faster performance at other times. Thus unpaced tasks will only show a deterioration if mechanisms in charge of compensation are out of action; but paced tasks may show effects despite attempts at compensation. Indeed they show serious decrements in performance with increase in the work period, whereas unpaced ones may not (Broadbent, 1953). On the other hand, it is certainly true that paced tasks involve more environmental stimulation, and on general grounds therefore one might expect them to be more arousing (in some sense) than unpaced tasks are.

The same task was given in both paced and unpaced forms by Mirsky and Rosvold (1960) under a variety of pharmacological and other conditions. They noted that barbiturates, which are depressants, showed an effect more readily on the unpaced version; a fact which agrees with the suggestion that paced tasks are in some way more arousing. On the other hand, tranquillizers gave effects primarily on the paced version. The authors suggested that the difference in the task affected was linked to a difference in the locus of action of the drugs; the barbiturates being supposed to affect first cortical centres, while the tranquillizers were rather seen as lowering the activity of regions in the brain stem. Some caution has to be exercised in accepting too restricted a view of the geography of drug action; barbiturates may certainly depress the brain stem if given in large doses, and the various tranquillizers do not all act in the same way. Nevertheless, there would be much agreement that tranquillizers such as chlorpromazine and reserpine might be especially likely to reduce brain-stem activity, in so far as the transmission of neural messages across synapses in that region involves transmitter substances of the adrenaline-noradrenaline type. The tranquillizers interfere with this transmission either by blocking the transmissions or, in the case of reserpine, by depleting the store of the transmitter substance so that less is available for release when a neural message needs transmission. In regions where transmission is dependent rather on acetylcholine than adrenaline, the tranquillizers would have less effect although the barbiturates might well do so.

A rather different line of evidence comes from considering the combined action of the barbiturates and amphetamine. The latter drug is related to the adrenaline-noradrenaline group, and may substitute for transmitter in synapses of the appropriate type. Yet a combination of amphetamine and barbiturate does not simply cancel out, but rather may be regarded clinically as having the desirable effect of reducing anxiety without causing sleepiness. Animal experiments confirm the usefulness of such mixtures (Rushton and Steinberg, 1963). Thus it seems clear that the barbiturates have a region of action distinct from that of the tranquillizers and amphetamine, the latter lowering or raising the activity of one mechanism while the barbiturates depress a second mechanism. In terms of the distinction between paced and unpaced tasks, one would have to argue that the mechanism affected by barbiturates is the upper one, which keeps average performance constant.

But tranquillizers show their effect first on paced tasks, where the compensatory effect of the other mechanism cannot interfere.

In terms of the stresses we have already considered, one result of Mirsky and Rosvold is especially important. They confirmed with their task that sleeplessness affects the paced rather than the unpaced version; that is, it resembles tranquillizers in its effect rather than barbiturates, and is in our terms a reduction of efficiency of the Lower system.

ACETYLCHOLINE AND INTERACTIONS IN ANIMAL EXPERIMENTS

A rather different line of evidence comes from some animal work using substances likely to alter transmission at synapses where the transmitter is acetylcholine rather than a compound of the adrenaline-noradrenaline group. Mechanisms which are cholinergic may often act in antagonism to those which are adrenergic; for example, in the peripheral emotional reactions familiar from introductory psychology texts, the adrenergic reactions of sweating, accelerated heart rate, dilation of the blood vessels, and so on are opposed in part by cholinergic processes having the opposite effects. One might therefore expect that substances blocking the transmitter action of acetylcholine (such as scopolamine or atropine) might act like those which can substitute for the adrenergic transmitter (such as amphetamine mentioned above). A number of experiments have been carried out on this point and are conveniently reviewed by Carlton (1963).

To some extent the results are in accord with expectation, just as in our own studies on the unitary concept of arousal. Thus an animal taught to alternate between two responses, or to respond at a prescribed slow rate, may be disrupted either by the administration of amphetamine or of scopolamine. In both cases the task requires the level of reactivity to be held down, and both drugs presumably increase reactivity. Again, atropine and amphetamine may interact to produce a measurable effect on responding when the dose of one drug is too low to show any effect by itself. In one sense therefore both kinds of drug are "stimulants".

On the other hand, the same kind of failures of interaction appear in this case as in our own human studies. If reserpine is given to an animal, the resulting low rate of responding can be counteracted by amphetamine. Here a depression of arousal is being cancelled by an arousing condition. But if atropine or scopolamine are used instead of amphetamine, the response rate is not increased. Thus in this case the drugs reducing the efficiency of the acetylcholine system do not act as "stimulants" in the same way as the drug which raises the activity of the adrenergic system. From our brief mention above of the action of reserpine, we can see why this should be; amphetamine substitutes for the stock of adrenergic transmitter, depleted by reserpine, but the blocking by atropine of any cholinergic control or inhibition over the

P*

adrenergic system does not in itself increase the activity of the latter, when there is too little transmitter substance.

From this group of experiments therefore we see again that a single dimension of arousal, or of stimulant-depressant, is insufficient; and that one system which is based on adrenergic transmission seems to be controlled by another which is not. Some uncertainty remains however about the meaning of "control": in the human case we were speaking of the maintenance of an average speed of response over a long period, whereas in the animal case the control seems rather to be the damping down or inhibition of response when that is desirable for other reasons. There is further evidence which goes a little way towards clarifying this issue.

STABILIZED AND UNSTABILIZED PERFORMANCE

A popular way of representing the role of the cholinergic systems is to suppose that they prevent reaction when reward fails to appear. On this view, the original learning of response might be adrenergic, but if the experimenter ceases to give food whenever the animal presses the bar or jumps the hurdle, cholinergic systems produce extinction of the response. Such a view, which is related to that set out by Carlton, is consistent with the fact that an animal which has extinguished a previously learned response is not thereby returned to its original state. The extinguished response will appear again with lapse of time, or if some novel stimulus is applied together with the one which previously elicited the learned reaction; and therefore there is still some storage of the original connection between the response and reward. Furthermore, such an account is consistent with the difficulty of extinguishing responses in animals when they have been given drugs which block the cholinergic system (Russell *et al.*, 1961). It also fits the particular nature of the tasks (alternation and slow responding) which Carlton cites as being disrupted by weakening of the cholinergic system. There are however a wider variety of tasks which can be used in animal experiments, and not all of the results on these fit the simple generalization that the cholinergic system mediates the effects of non-reward.

Gerbrandt (1965) draws up a generalized view of the results which is a development of Carlton's, with modifications. Like the latter, he treats the cholinergic and adrenergic systems as partly antagonistic, so that the balance between the two is the aspect of the animal's state which is of greatest interest. The level of the cholinergic system is taken as indexed by the level of cholinesterase, which breaks down the transmitter after its operation; and thus one can regard the animal's state as varying from one extreme of high adrenaline-low cholinesterase to another extreme of low adrenaline-high cholinesterase. The former state is regarded by Gerbrandt as favouring one group of tasks which he calls "stabilized" and the latter a different group of tasks called "unstabilized".

The nature of each of these two kinds of task can best be illustrated by example. Stabilized tasks include simple conditioned responses, simultaneous discriminations (where the animal chooses the correct one of two alternatives present before him), and positive avoidance responses (where the animal does something to avoid a punishment which will arrive if he does nothing). Unstabilized tasks on the other hand include negative avoidance responses (where the animal has to withhold a previously acquired response because the latter is now punished), extinction of previously learned responses, and reversal learning, where the previously correct alternative is now incorrect and vice versa. The difference between the two groups of task does not seem therefore to be simply in the role of non-reward; consider the appearance of simultaneous discrimination in the first group. Nor is the difference purely one of response versus non-response; consider the appearance of reversal learning in the second group. Nor is it the presence of punishment rather than reward; consider the appearance of positive avoidance learning in one group, and of negative avoidance learning in the other.

Perhaps one might sum up the distinction between the two kinds of task by saying that the former represent the original recording of some statistical regularity in the environment, while the latter require the animal to be aware that a recent departure from that regularity is at this moment in progress. The cholinergic systems seem to mediate a kind of "usually, but not today" performance. Such a function was discussed at length by Broadbent (1958); it is very desirable for any device responding to regularities in the environment to have some means for changing its rules when the environment changes. If no special provision is made, a man who has found for three years that breakfast is ready when the clock says 08.30 will take another three years to adjust to a new situation in which breakfast appears at 08.00. One simple means of dealing with this problem is to weight more recent events more heavily when counting numbers of concomitant associations, so that yesterday's breakfast time carries more weight in predicting today's than does the time of breakfast last year. A system operating on such a weighted count of past events will adapt reasonably quickly to changes in the environment.

On the other hand, a mechanism of this kind has an intriguing side effect. Suppose that the circumstances have recently changed so as to invalidate some old rule about the environment; suppose for example that a man's wife, after serving breakfast at 08.30 for three years, started last week to produce it at 08.00. By today he has adapted, because recent events have a greater weighting. But suppose tomorrow he goes into the Army and is away for a year. By the time he returns, the experience of the last week before his departure will be far in the past, and will have no more weight than any other week before he left. He will therefore revert to 08.30 as the hour at which he will expect breakfast. Such a reversion, as was pointed out by Broadbent (1958), is very like the recovery of an extinguished response.

If we adopt both the hypothesis that animal learning gives greater weight to recent experience, and also Gerbrandt's classification of tasks, it would seem that cholinergic mechanisms are responsible for the handling of relatively recent information and adrenergic mechanisms for reaction based upon more remotely past information. The use of separate mechanisms would suggest that the distinction of the recent and more remote past is more than a difference in the magnitude of the record held within a single memory store, but rather corresponds to one or other of the distinctions between components of primary memory which we considered in Chapter VIII. If a guess were made at this time it would be tempting to identify the Upper level, cholinergic, system which handles the particular features of recent events, with the "desk-top" mechanism of our account of memory. That is, it would be the system which holds in store the addresses at which are to be found material relevant to the task now in hand.

Such a view is certainly too crude; and it will not have escaped the careful reader that several different antitheses have been surreptitiously confused together in this account. It is illegitimate to make a simple identification between upper and lower levels of the nervous system, cholinergic and adrenergic transmission, reaction based on recent and that based on more remote learning; even if we have distinguished these pairs of opposites from others, such as learning by punishment and by reward, sensory and motor learning, action rather than inhibition, which are only slightly more tenuous in their link with our Upper and Lower levels. Indeed, we might almost have linked our Upper level with the hippocampal region, whose loss has little effect on new learning in animals (Kimble 1968) although perhaps more harmful to the "unstabilized" tasks of Gerbrandt; and we ought certainly to have linked the distinction of Upper and Lower levels both to the two major kinds of sleep and to the various methods used in experiments on sensory deprivation. (In some cases sensory deprivation means literally a reduction in the intensity of stimulation, but in others it can refer to a monotonous and unpatterned stimulation at an intensity which is quite high. In the former

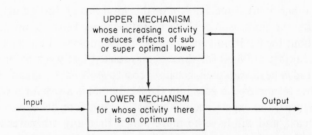

FIG. 44. A modified mechanism for interpreting effects of stress. Abnormally high or low arousal through noise or sleeplessness affect the lower mechanism; and do not alter performance unless the upper mechanism also is impaired.

case earplugs and darkness are appropriate, but in the latter steady noise and translucent goggles. The latter in particular has sometimes been reported as producing a disruption of behaviour which takes the form of excited but uncontrolled activity rather than unarousal. Upper inefficiency with Lower activity unimpaired?)

Our Upper and Lower levels are then no more than a speculation intended to indicate the way in which research will possibly develop in the next ten years A simple unidimensional theory of arousal is inadequate; to improve upon it will probably require the collaboration of pharmacologists and physiological psychologists, as well as those who study simply the psychology of information processing. One purpose of choosing this particular suggestion for this chapter is to correct any impression that the entire effort of psychology should be concentrated upon the study of behaviour. The nervous system must be studied also by the more traditional biological techniques, and if we have mentioned them little in the body of this book, it is merely because the problems discussed have been ones on which they have as yet little to say. The attempt to link physiology and psychology can be disastrous when it is premature; as for example we have regarded attempts to treat as criteria measures of arousal indices such as skin conductance or percentage Alpha in the EEG. But it would be equally disastrous to go on for ever treating the brain as an abstract and ideal construct having no biological reality. Once we understand the functions which the nervous system performs, then the structure and the details of the mechanism can be unravelled and will provide explanations of many psychological phenomena. From this point of view, the importance of understanding function is to state problems for physiology or biochemistry; a machine intended to carry out filtering or pigeon-holing could hardly be understood if we were under the impression that it was a machine for associating a response with stimuli recently presented. Equally, in complicating the theory of arousal we shall need to know more about the functions involved in various tasks; behavioural studies and the physiological attack upon the brain must go hand in hand.

A Rule for Decision

THE INADEQUACY OF EXPECTED VALUE

In the last section, and indeed in Chapter IX, we favoured the idea that changes in the general state of the nervous system would produce changes in "pigeon-holing". That is, if a man is aroused reaction might occur to less adequate incoming evidence than might be required if he is unaroused. Such a suggestion implies that human decisions are not based on the maximizing of the net gain to be expected from a series of decisions. As we saw in Chapter III, on such a basis there is a single definite point separating states of evidence which should receive reaction and those which should not. If the probabilities and values in a situation remain unchanged, then the bias in favour of a certain response should also stay the same, and be unaffected by the general state of the mechanism.

It might be argued, as a counter to this point that the general level of arousal may change the subjective gains and losses to be expected in a situation. An unaroused man might care little about missing signals or making false reports, while an aroused one might care very much. In that case, might there not be changes in the theoretical value of β, the likelihood ratio at which the man should change from non-response to response? Thus the obtained experimental changes in β could still be consistent with the notion that the man calculates the net gain to be obtained from responding with a certain degree of caution. But even this suggestion will not work simply. Theoretically, for the case of detecting a signal

$$\beta = \frac{1-p}{p} \times \frac{L}{G}$$

where
p = probability of signal
G = gain to be expected from a detection
L = loss to be expected from a false report

then we have to make some assumption about the way in which changes in arousal change values of L and G. The simplest would be to suppose that a given change will multiply or divide both by the same amount; but in that case the theoretical value of β will remain unchanged. Another possibility would be that a change will add or subtract the same amount to both L and G; but subtraction would create the problem that β might become negative, which is impossible. The only possibilities seem therefore to be that arousal multiplies the gains and losses, but does so differently for gains and for losses; or that it adds to them above some minimum value of each. In the case of multiplication, furthermore, the direction in which β moves for a certain change should be independent of its original value. But we saw in Chapter III that changes in arousal seem to give inconsistent movements in β, high initial values decreasing and low initial values increasing.

To avoid pursuing these complications further, it may be well at this stage to indicate that there are a number of reasons for thinking that men do not work on a basis of maximizing expected value. These can be summarized as follows.

(a) If a man is asked to make one of two responses, and is rewarded with a higher probability for choosing one rather than the other, he will objectively obtain the highest probability of reward by *always* choosing the response more frequently rewarded. (If his probability of choosing that response is P, and of choosing the other is $1-P$; while the probabilities on a given trial that each response will be rewarded are p and $1-p$ respectively, then his net gain over a series of trials is $Pp+(1-P)(1-p)$. But for $p>1-p$, the net gain increases with increasing P and is therefore greatest when $P = 1$.) Empirically, men do not choose that response all the time, but rather make $P = p$ approximately. (See Restle, 1961 for a discussion.)

(b) In a signal detection task where the experimenter arranges that the objective penalties for missed signals and false reports are the same, the empirical value of β is found to be 1 when $p = 0.5$. Thus the subjective gains and losses do appear to be equal as the objective ones are. Yet if the value of p is changed, the empirically measured value of β departs from 1 less than the theoretical one does (Green, 1960).

(c) In a signal detection task, if we conceptualize the various possible values of received evidence as lying upon a single dimension, then there is a single point upon that dimension where the theoretical value of β lies; provided that the values of evidence received following signal and non-signal are normally distributed *with equal variance*. But the observed graphs of correct responses plotted against false reports are inconsistent with this assumption, although they are consistent with distributions of unequal variance. When the variance is unequal, however, there is more than one point on the decision axis where a given value of β holds. The whole analysis therefore becomes unreal.

(d) If a man is given the choice between two alternatives, each of which is a gamble or bet with specified probabilities of rewards of known size, his choice is not in accordance with the expected value of the bet. For example, if alternative A provides a reward of 6 cents with probability 0.10, and alternative B a reward of 1 cent with probability 0.50, he ought rationally to choose A ($6 \times 0.10 > 1 \times 0.50$). The actual choice seems however to depend on preferences for certain probabilities, overestimations of large rewards and low probabilities, etc., in a way which shows individual differences and is very complex (Edwards, 1954).

For these reasons it seems implausible that human decision actually proceeds exactly in the way which decision theorists would approve; yet the whole tenor of our argument throughout this book has been that the rules connecting states of evidence to category states do change in the *directions* which decision theory would predict, even though they may not do so to the predicted *extent*. If pigeon-holing favours probable responses, as we have argued that it does, this is the type of change which would be favoured by the maximization of expected value. And although in the areas we have covered we have seen little evidence that β rises with increased L and falls with increased G, yet in psychophysical experiments there is ample material on this point (Green and Swets, 1966). Even in the case of choice between bets, the various biases and preferences for certain kinds of gamble are superimposed upon a general tendency to choose the gamble with the higher expected value if all other things are equal.

An example from animal experimentation may illustrate the importance of expected value, despite its inadequacies. Steiner (1967) devised a situation in which a monkey had to press a panel to obtain a reward, but would only be rewarded at certain times. If a stimulus light indicated the times at which reward was possible, the animal learned to confine its panel-pressing to those times, and not to respond when another light, indicating non-reward, was illuminated. A second pair of lights was also present, and the pressing of a bar would light one of this pair, depending on which of the main stimulus lights was illuminated. So long as the main lights were clearly discriminable, the bar was not much used; but an increase in the difficulty of discriminating the main lights increased the tendency to press the bar and bring on the easily identified secondary lights.

Some gain to the animal is therefore rewarding the bar-pressing; perhaps the uncertainty-reduction which is provided by the secondary lights? If this were so, the bar-pressing should be greatest when the uncertainty reduction was greatest. That will be the case if panel-pressing is rewarded about half the time on the average; there would be less uncertainty if the probability of reward was greater or less than that. For good measure, we could make a different prediction from behaviour theory. From classical theories of secondary reinforcement, bar-pressing should be greatest when the probability of reward for panel-pressing was high, since in that case the pressing of the bar would be most likely to be followed by the secondary light associated with reward. But Steiner (1964) found the exact opposite; the animal presses the bar most when the probability of reward for panel-pressing is *least*. Roughly speaking, the monkey is doing what it should on the basis of expected value; it presses the bar when so doing is likely to save it the extra cost of a panel press, and does not use the bar when the cost of panel presses is likely to be balanced by reward. (The cost of panel presses is not the overt exertion, as Steiner (1967) found that a classical rather than operant main situation gives similar results.) Whatever the detailed inadequacies of expected value theory, it does agree with the direction of behavioural changes better than theories of reward based on secondary association with primary reward, or those based on the reduction of uncertainty.

AN ALTERNATIVE BASIS FOR SETTING CRITERIA

We need therefore some other way of fixing the probability that a response will occur to a given state of evidence, when the probability that the response will be correct is fixed at p, and the size of the reward the man will get when it is correct is fixed at G. That is,

$$P = F(pG)$$

where F is some unknown function. Decision theory specifies this function axiomatically by saying that P is 1 for the largest value of pG and 0 for all other responses. We ought rather to look at the data and see what seem empirically to be likely forms for F. It will make the task easier if we consider strength S rather than probability P, where

$$P = \frac{S}{\Sigma S}$$

ΣS = sum of strengths for all responses.

As will be recalled, this is the form of analysis used by Luce, and it has the great advantage that it allows the probability of one response to change when some treatment such as reward is applied to another response, without it being necessary to change the strength associated with the first response. Thus we want a function relating S and pG for any one response, and need not consider other responses.

The function required must always give a positive value for S, even if G becomes negative, and should get more and more positive with increases in the expected value of the response. The obvious function which fits these requirements is the exponential, so we are led to suggest that

$$S = \exp(pG)$$

sr
$$\log S = pG.$$

This function meets the requirements; as the expected value increases, so does the strength of the corresponding response, but even a markedly negative value of G (corresponding to a strongly punished response) still has a very small but positive strength.

How does this suggested function fit the facts? The predictions it makes are somewhat flexible, because there is no good way of scaling G for any concrete situation. Consequently one can rather readily choose values of G such that the data do fit the function, and this is in itself trivial. But there are general properties of the function which are more distinctive and interesting.

(a) *Frequency matching behaviour.* First, let us consider what happens when a choice occurs between two responses one of which, but not both, is rewarded on every trial. If S_1, S_2, are the strengths of the two responses and p_1, p_2, the probabilities with which they have been correct,

$$p_2 = 1 - p_1$$

$$\frac{S_1}{S_1 + S_2} = \text{probability of response 1.}$$

$$\frac{S_1}{S_2} = \frac{\text{probability of response 1}}{\text{probability of response 2}} = \frac{\exp p_1 G}{\exp p_2 G}$$

$$= \exp G(p_1 - p_2)$$

$$= \exp G(2p_1 - 1).$$

Thus the chance that response 1 will be chosen increases with increases in the probability of it being correct, but the choice will not swing completely to the more rewarded response as the maximization of expected value would predict. The suggested function is therefore more in accord with the facts; and by choice of a suitable value for G we can arrange for the probability of the choice of each response to agree with its probability of being correct; the behaviour usually called "frequency matching".

(b) *Departures from frequency matching.* As already indicated, it is trivial that one can choose G so that, say, response 1 will be chosen 80% of the time when it is correct on 0·8 of trials. However, this apparent looseness of the formulation is a positive advantage in one way; the data only rarely show that human choices frequency-match exactly, only that they do so approximately. Other theories of the effect, which put it down to some postulated mechanism of learning, are too strong because they cannot account for the *departures* from frequency matching. For example, consider the stimulus sampling theories, according to which each presentation of reward conditions the response that has just been made to a sample of the stimuli present in the situation. When a steady state has been reached, the proportion of stimuli attached to the more rewarded response should correspond to the proportion of occasions on which it has been rewarded, and the probability of its choice should do likewise. If the choices are less frequent than the frequency of reward, this can be put down to incompleteness of learning; but it is seriously embarrassing that the man may choose a given response *more* often than it has been rewarded, though still not every time. Restle (1961) gives an account in terms of series effects which attempts to explain this phenomenon, but it is certainly quite a difficulty for stimulus sampling theories. From our point of view the extra frequency of choice will depend upon the exact value of G, and can as easily depart by exceeding the frequency of reward as by falling short of it.

One may add that it is known directly and empirically that the frequency of choice *does* depend on the level of motivation and that a high level of motivation will cause behaviour to approximate more and more to that which would be predicted by the maximization of expected value (Edwards, 1956; Siegal and Goldstein, 1959; Siegal and Andrews, 1962). Thus any adequate formulation must allow changes in motivation to play a part in at least approximately the way in which they do so in our suggested one.

(c) *Probability differences and probability ratios.* One particularly interesting point arises when a choice is being made between responses for which, on any trial, there is not necessarily one and only one correct choice. That is,

$$p_1 \neq 1 - p_2.$$

It will be remembered from (a) that the probability of choosing response 1 depends on the difference of p_1 and p_2. This difference could well be the same size even when the absolute value of each probability is varied very considerably. Thus on our formulation we should predict the same performance when $p_1 = 1 \cdot 0$, $p_2 = 0 \cdot 9$; $p_1 = 0 \cdot 55$, $p_2 = 0 \cdot 45$; and $p_1 = 0 \cdot 1$, $p_2 = 0 \cdot 0$. Other formulations would suggest that these three situations would be very different. Specifically, stimulus sampling theory predicts that the probability of choice will depend not only on the difference in probability of reward, but also on the ratio. Rather few data have been collected on this point, apart from an animal experiment by Brunswik (1939) and one on humans by Brand *et al.* (1957). Both are equivocal; Brunswik found no significant effect of ratio although he felt that the direction of the insignificant differences in his results gave some promise of such an effect. Brand *et al.* only tested their results for significant departure from stimulus sampling theory, rather than for the presence or absence of an effect of ratio. Inspection of their graphs suggests that there was no clear trend with ratio, except possibly in the case where the difference in probabilities was so large that high ratios caused p_2 to reach zero in that case; in that case high ratios gave a greater incidence of choices of the more rewarded response. There is a possible post hoc explanation for the effect of ratio in this case, which we shall mention below, when discussing mechanisms for underlying our suggested decision rule.

Our suggested rule is therefore reasonably supported by the tenuous evidence on the relative effects of difference and of ratio of probabilities. At least there is a research area here which deserves to be explored further.

THE EFFECT OF STIMULI, AND OF OVER-AROUSAL

In order to test our formulation more widely, we need to incorporate into it the changing evidence which may be received by the decision system and on which choice is based. It is only rarely that a man is asked to choose between two responses without even a faint and inadequate stimulus to indicate which of them is correct, at least in the type of experiments we have been discussing in this book. If a stimulus is provided and is correctly identified, then the probability that one response will be correct is usually unity, and the probabilities for all other responses are zero. If on the other hand a stimulus is provided but is invisible or otherwise unavailable to the man, the probability that a certain response is correct will correspond to the probability of presentation of the appropriate stimulus. How can we deal with the intermediate case when a stimulus is presented but gives imperfect evidence?

In the paper which first suggested this formulation (Broadbent, 1965a), this problem was met in the following way. A given response has a certain reward associated with it if it is known to be correct: say, G. If there is no stimulus information to say which response is correct, the expected value of the given response is pG, where p is the probability that the response is correct. Let us now suppose that the presentation of an imperfectly detected stimulus gives the response an intermediate expected value, between G and pG. It lies closer to the former if there is more stimulus information, and closer to the latter if there is less; its location can be specified as a proportion ϕ of the distance between the two values. The final value of the expected value is therefore $pG + \phi(1-p)G$. When $\phi = 0$ this corresponds to the case with no stimulus, and when $\phi = 1$ to the case of a perfectly visible stimulus. It then becomes possible to work out what will happen to the proportions of correct and incorrect responses as p is changed with constant ϕ.

We have already mentioned an experiment which varied signal probability in a detection task and found that the empirically obtained β was less different from 1 than it should theoretically have been (Green, 1960). On the present formulation the empirical β will depend on the value of G; but if we use one of the data points given by Green to fix the value of G, the other data points are well fitted by the predictions of the formula we have been considering. That is, the change of β with change in probability is of the right extent to fit our formula. A failure to fit this relationship would have been a serious drawback and it is therefore satisfactory that the hypothesis has survived this test.

On the other hand, one of the main purposes of Broadbent (1965a) was to derive an explanation for the impairment in performance which over-arousal produces; and for the Yerkes-Dodson Law which states that there is an optimum level of motivation for tasks involving discrimination, the level being lower for harder discriminations. It is indeed the case that the formula predicts deterioration in performance as G rises beyond a certain point, provided that p, the probability of one of the two alternative stimuli, is not 0·5. The optimum value of G depends upon ϕ, as it should to explain the Yerkes-Dodson Law. Although this result was satisfactory in 1965, it is very much less so at the present time. The reason is that it is essentially an explanation of the same kind as the Hull-Spence explanation discussed in Chapter IX; it predicts that rises in motivation will increase the size of response bias in the absence of a stimulus. As we saw in Chapter IX, the experimental evidence is against any such changes in bias; rather the effects of arousal seem to be an accentuation of the difficulties in selective intake of information. Thus at this point the formula is clearly incorrect. The difficulty may lie in the basic assumption that $\log S = pG$, in the way in which the role of stimulus information has been incorporated, or in the postulated effects of arousal; and further experiment is needed to decide between these alternatives.

(a) *Possible modifications to Log* S = pG. As we said in Chapter IX, the assumption that training and motivation interact multiplicatively is not really necessary to explain the phenomena for which Hull originally postulated it. The fact that a probability of response may rise far more, under the combined influence of training and motivation, than the sum of the changes induced by either alone, does not imply that the two conditions multiply. Similarly, it may be that we assumed too much even in supposing that we were searching for an unknown function of the *expected value* of a response. Perhaps we should have sought, not $F(pG)$, but rather $F(p, G)$, in which we do not even know that the probability and size of reward are multiplied before entering our unknown function. Suppose for example we had tried

$$K \log S = p + G,$$

where K is a scaling constant. Such a formulation would have many of the advantages of the one we have been favouring. It would give frequency matching, by a suitable choice of K, would depart from frequency matching as K was varied, would give performance dependent primarily upon probability difference and not on probability ratio, and so on. But it would not give changes in response bias as G was varied, since the difference in strength between any pair of responses would not depend on G. Thus it would not have the embarrassing property of predicting a change with arousal which is found not to happen.

To test such a modification to our formula would require experiments in which the size of the effects of changes in signal probability were compared at different levels of motivation. We could then check whether the effects on response strength are indeed additive or multiplicative. Pending such tests, the modification seems rather an unlikely one, because (i) it does not of itself explain the fact that motivational changes alter the degree of departure from frequency matching, unless K is made inversely related to level of motivation. If so however, we are back at an expression which predicts changes in response bias with motivation. (ii) There is no provision for a deterioration in performance at high arousal, which was at least a merit of the original formula, even if in detail the latter is unacceptable.

(*b*) *Possible modifications to the role of the stimulus.* It is obviously somewhat arbitrary to describe the effect of the stimulus by the ϕ parameter. One possibility which comes to mind is that we ought rather to consider every possible state of evidence which might result from the stimulus, and to consider what the probability of each response being correct is *given that state of evidence*. For a signal detection task, and assuming the usual single dimension of evidence with two normal distributions upon it describing the probability of occurrence of each value of evidence following signal and non-signal, it is clear that the probability of a detection response being correct rises as the value of the received evidence increases. We might well suppose that a man would, at normal levels of motivation, frequency match and say "Yes" about as often as signals have in the past occurred with the particular level of evidence he has just received. As the level of motivation rises however he would be more and more inclined to say "Yes" all the time to any state of evidence which points on balance to the presence of a signal. Such behaviour would not necessarily give an apparent increase in response bias, as it would be accompanied by a tendency to say "No" more frequently to states of evidence which point against the presence of a signal. Some computer simulations of such a model have been run by J. D. Ingleby and confirm that it would result in apparently reasonable observed values of d' and β, and that the changes from rises in G would be complex. One difficulty is that there would almost certainly be rises in d' as G increased, and we have already seen that empirically these are rarely observed. However, it is probably not worth intensive theoretical research on the predictions of such a model under various conditions, as the argument would be complicated by uncertainty about possible effects of arousal upon parameters other than G. It is simpler to change the situation to eliminate sensory factors, and to require men to take decisions under varying conditions of arousal but with known evidence before them. Such experiments are already in progress.

(c) *Possible modifications to the incorporation of arousal.* Lastly, it may well be that we are wrong in trying to represent the effects of arousal simply by an increase in G. Perhaps, with an eye on the earlier sections of this chapter, we ought to represent arousal as a change in the value of ϕ, the degree of effect which the present situation has in modifying the stored probability that a certain response will be rewarded. Another possibility is to hark back to Chapter IX and to remember the idea that arousal speeds up reaction by decreasing the amount of evidence needed for any certain outcome of the decision process, at the expense of the outcome "Uncertain, I require more evidence". In that case, it would be possible to have an optimum level of arousal without the need to suppose an increase in response biases as arousal rose. Let us restate the view given at the end of Chapter IX, in a rather different way.

Consider a symmetrical decision made between two alternative responses, with no third possibility of suspending judgment. Then in the usual way

$$\text{Probability of correct response} \quad = \frac{\alpha}{\alpha+1}$$

$$\text{Probability of incorrect response} = \frac{1}{\alpha+1}.$$

Then let us introduce the possibility of suspending judgment. If we suppose that there are states of evidence which are insufficient to produce a decision in either direction, these modify the probabilities to

$$\text{Probability of correct} \quad = \frac{\alpha}{\alpha+C}$$

$$\text{Probability of incorrect} = \frac{1}{\alpha C+1}.$$

where C is a factor which increases as the number of "Uncertain" responses rises.

But these two probabilities are related in the same way as the detections and false alarms in the usual detection situation. That is, as C varies, the graph of correct responses against incorrect ones traces out the familiar concave downward curve. There is therefore an optimum point at which the difference between correct and incorrect responses is a maximum and beyond which it decreases. On the other hand any bias in favour of one type of error rather than the other would give

$$\text{Probability of error of one type} \quad = \frac{V}{\alpha C + V}$$

$$\text{Probability of error of other type} = \frac{1}{\alpha C V + 1}$$

and the ratio of these probabilities would decrease as C decreased. Thus there would be no need to expect the apparent response bias to increase as arousal increases, but rather to decrease.

It is, of course, a difficulty that experiment showed no trend for the response bias to *decrease* with arousal, any more than the opposite result. It is also a difficulty that in the theory reduction in C always gives an increase in the absolute number of correct responses, even though there is an optimum value for the difference between corrects and errors. Both these difficulties can be met by, for example, supposing that in many real situations the responses of "Uncertain" are divided at random between the available responses.

On balance therefore the best way of dealing with the effects of over-arousal seems at present to be by supposing that arousal has its effect by decreasing the number of suspended judgments, rather than by increasing G. Experiments to check the other possible modifications will shed light on the alternative also.

THE MECHANISM UNDERLYING THE FORMULATION

In suggesting that $\log S = pG$, we have been hazarding a generalization about the facts of behaviour, not putting forward a mechanism which might explain these facts. The approach is quite different from that of decision theorists, who postulate the principle that the response is chosen to maximize expected value, and infer what the observed probabilities of response should be from this axiom. We are rather trying to find a convenient way of describing the observed response probabilities, before considering what principle the organism must be using to give such a pattern of behaviour. As we can hardly be regarded as having established satisfactorily the truth of our generalization, it would be previous to put much effort into the further search for a mechanism to underlie it. It is just worth indicating the lines which such a mechanism might take, however, for two reasons. First, we should try to defend our generalization against the possible criticism that no mechanism is conceivable which could behave in this way. Secondly, if we suggest a basis for the generalization, it may clarify the distinction we have just made between a law governing observations, and a hypothetical mechanism explaining that law.

We have on numerous occasions emphasized the equivalence between the various equations describing the concave-downward curve of correct versus incorrect response; the equation in Z-scores, the exponential equation, and that in terms of response strengths. Our suggested generalization is in terms of response strengths, but as previously one can translate it into the other formulations. If two responses have strengths X and Y, this can be regarded as equivalent to the existence of two quantities of evidence, one supporting one response and one the other, whose average numerical values are proportional to log X and log Y. Each varies from trial to trial however in a normal fashion; and the response occurring on any one trial is decided by which response is, on this trial, supported by the greater quantity of evidence. The probabilities of response obtained in this way will be the same as those derived from the formulation in terms of strengths.

Our formulation for response strengths in terms of expected value can be equivalent therefore to the suggestion that each response has corresponding to it in the brain a stored representation of its expected value, but that the exact number in this store is variable. The response chosen on any trial is that which happens to have the greatest stored expected value at that instant. How could such a stored representation be built up? If the occurrence of a reward increased the value in store by an amount proportional to the size of the reward, and if every occurrence of the response decreased the size of the amount in store, then after a succession of trials the size of the amount in store would represent the expected value. It is interesting to note that, to give a stored value related only to pG and not to the number of trials, it would be necessary for the amount stored to be *divided* by a fixed amount for every response, rather than having a quantity subtracted from it. Thus the decay of response strengths since the last rewarded response should be exponential rather than linear.

Such a method of building up a stored representation of expected value would be sensitive to the variance of the distribution of rewards, as well as to its average. The same overall proportion of rewards will give a larger stored representation if the rewards had been evenly spaced rather than clustered with some long and some short intervals between them. It is this fact which might explain the effect of probability difference as well as probability ratio, in the experiments mentioned in an earlier section. As probabilities approach unity or zero, the variance of a series of observations becomes less. Correspondingly it is likely that response strengths appropriate to probabilities of unity or zero will be built up more rapidly than those for intermediate values, and the choice of the more frequently rewarded response may be more probable in such cases than in others with the same difference of probabilities.

Changes in variance may introduce complications however. If we present a sequence of choices between responses 1 and 2, in which the correct response is 112112112112112112 and so on, it is likely that the subject will ultimately become aware of the pattern and succeed in being correct every time. In this case the probability of reward for each response is dependent on the situation at the time of choice; a choice when the last two trials have been 11 is different from a choice when the last two were 21. This is, once again, the problem of the modification of the response strength by stimulus information which may or may not be received. The mechanism to be supposed here must depend upon the correctness or otherwise of the ϕ formulation; if it is correct, we have to suppose that information from the senses communicates with the stored expected values for each response, changing them towards the values appropriate for the stimulus which has occurred. If the stimulus is undetectable, no change occurs. If the stimulus information is perfect, the change is complete. If the evidence of the senses is imperfect, it is given a weight proportional to ϕ and only changes the stored probabilities by that proportion of the full amount.

This leads on to the question of combination of information from various sources, which forms a whole area of research in itself. It will suffice to say that a series of experiments largely associated with Edwards (Phillips and Edwards, 1966; Dale, 1968) have shown that in the presence of fresh evidence men revise prior probabilities less drastically than they should. This is perhaps the best method of attack upon the question whether incoming evidence should be incorporated into our formulation by means of ϕ or in some other way. For example, the stimulus might produce behaviour in perfect agreement with the expected values which it implies, but do so only on a proportion of trials; or it might modify the strengths of the various responses by only a proportion of the change in strength which a perfectly visible stimulus would produce. (ϕ represents a proportion of the change in underlying evidence, which is related to log S rather than S.) Each of these would predict rather different forms of behaviour, and experiments on combination of evidence appear to be a convenient way of studying such problems.

IMPLICATIONS FOR FURTHER RESEARCH

We have seen a number of lines of experiment emerge from this line of speculation. Work is clearly needed upon the effects of probability difference and probability ratio, upon the combination of evidence, and upon the effects of changes in probability of reward at different levels of reward. It is also needed upon the effects of arousal on decision made with clearly specified evidence, rather than on sensory tasks in which the uncertainty is introduced by the malfunction of the senses. There is however a general lesson to be urged here, just as there was in the part of this chapter which suggested more complicated theories of arousal. In that section, we suggested particular lines of advance as a way of propagandizing both for the importance of physiological psychology, and for the necessity of using highly sophisticated tasks and measures in any study which hopes to elucidate brain mechanisms.

In the present section, we have obviously been urging the importance of mathematical psychology. But there is a corresponding caution. The usual approach of mathematical psychologists has been to assume a simple mechanism for a psychological process and then to derive the predictions of that mechanism. The consequence of this approach has been to leave a number of glaring gaps in the experimental evidence. In psychophysics, we know that d' is constant over a large number of experimental conditions; but we do not know whether the bias towards one response rather than another behaves so as to hold constant β, to hold constant response strength in the absence of a stimulus, or whether some other possibility is true. For reasons considered in earlier chapters, it seems likely that β rather than some other quantity is the constant. But the matter requires far more evidence. We need to know whether the probability and size of a reward should be multiplied or added to give simple relations to behaviour; whether, if they are multiplied, it is the probability of a response, its strength, or the log of its strength which is affected. All these are questions of fact rather than theory; and until they are known there is little chance of guessing the correct axioms from which to produce an adequate mathematical model of behaviour.

The general thesis which we have argued in this section therefore is not merely a case for more mathematical psychology. It is for a line of attack which tries to find the simplest and most consistent mathematical relationship between observed variables, and only then considers the families of axioms which might produce relationships of the kind found empirically. The axiomatic approach has achievements to its credit; one can hardly deny the value of the research which has stemmed from the axioms of signal detection theory. But it is instructive to note the weaknesses which have shown themselves even in that field because of the axiomatic approach. When it became clear that quite different axioms would predict closely similar observations (such as the axioms which give rise to the exponential and strength versions of the relation between correct and false detections) then this tended to produce a nihilistic distrust of the value of the theory at all. The key achievement of the theory is the disproof of the traditional guessing correction with its linear relation between correct and false responses. By emphasizing the axioms, this achievement was underplayed. Furthermore, the axiom that criterion position was decided on a basis of maximizing expected value has led to a lack of interest in the actual point at which the criterion does appear to settle. Even this theory then has suffered from its axiomatic character. This is the message which this section is intended to urge; mathematical psychology should work from data towards theory and not vice versa.

Central Control and Long-Term Memory

After suggesting lines of advance on the physiological and the mathematical wings of psychology, we come now to possible developments of a different kind; perhaps a kind more central to the field, in so far as it concerns the way in which information is processed within the brain without reference either to abstract mathematical expressions or to underlying physiological mechanisms. In this third area, there have been two aspects of the work considered in this book which point to further advance.

One of these is the recurrent mention of the problems of long-term memory, and of retrieval of information from that region of store. When only a small amount of material has been experienced within a certain category, there is no problem of retrieval since all of it can be reproduced. When however there is a large amount of material in memory, recall on any particular occasion creates a problem of selecting the particular items which are wanted out of all those in store. Thus the organization of and retrieval from long-term memory provide a challenging problem for further research.

The second feature of current knowledge which calls for more work is the problem of central control. We have discussed at length the various strategies of information processing which the brain may adopt in selecting amongst the available stimulus information, in adapting to consistencies in the environment, in reacting fast or accurately, and so on. The emphasis has been on an organism which contributes greatly to the behaviour which it shows in a certain situation; and we can in no sense think of the brain as like a typewriter reacting always to the same input with the same output.

But we have nowhere mentioned the way in which it is decided within the brain that this rather than that strategy shall be adopted in any given situation. The various techniques of filtering, pigeon-holing and categorization have appeared like the tools in an automated assembly plant, each doing its job when it is needed but with no visible hand to bring it into operation. The cynic can well ask whether we wish to appeal to an invisible little man, sitting somewhere in the higher nervous centres, who calls on each strategy when he sees that it is needed.

In fact, the problem of central control is closely linked with that of long-term memory and both should be considered together. In discussing them, the analogies of human libraries and computers will both be useful, since such devices have the same problems of storage and retrieval as brains do. In considering the link between memory and control, however, the computer is the more convenient analogy, and we may start with that.

STORAGE AND CONTROL

Even contemporary computers share with the nervous system the property of exercising a central control upon the behaviour which they will show when presented with any particular input. If a series of numbers is fed into the computer the first may be placed on a region of storage, the second may be added to a number already in store, the third compared to a number already specified, ignored if it is smaller and printed out if it is larger, and so on. Thus the treatment accorded to each input is different and depends upon the whole task in progress. Inputs are selected or rejected, memorized or reacted to, under the influence of a control within the computer rather than anything to be found in the inputs themselves. There is correspondingly nothing mystical or unscientific in the notion of central control as such, and indeed the facts of behaviour require us to suppose something of the sort in the brain.

When we examine the basis for such control in computers, we find that it lies in the program which has previously been inserted into the machine. In the simple case, this consists of a series of instructions which is inserted through the same input device as that subsequently employed to put in the numbers on which the machine is to calculate. Each instruction in turn is placed in a separate part of the machine's memory storage. Once the program is in, and the data for calculation available, the machine goes in succession to each location in memory where instructions are stored, and executes each instruction in turn until the end of the series is reached. Thus an outside observer who knew the program and the number of operations that had been performed could predict the way in which a new input would be handled.

Even a predictable sequence of this kind may not unroll simply as a simple chain of instructions. There may be some parts of the series which need to occur more than once. For example, a long and complicated calculation may require a square root to be found several times. Instead of listing the same sequence of instructions at each point in the whole program where it is needed, it is simplest to store this sequence only once. Then each time the sequence is needed the operative part of the computer, the processor, is referred to the same part of the program, goes through the same series of steps, and then continues with the main program at the point where it left off. Thus the processor does not simply take its instructions from a row of memory elements, moving on to the next each time it has finished a part of the task. Rather it has a whole region of memory devoted to the program, and may jump backwards and forwards within it. It follows of course that each distinguishable part of the region of storage possesses an address by which it can be located, and that the processor is directed to the appropriate address after each operation.

This arrangement means that more complex programs can become unpredictable in their effects for somebody who merely knows the original program and the history of inputs. The reason is that the program can include provision for carrying out one sequence of operations if a calculation gives one result, and a different series if it gives another. To give a simple example, the program might call for the processor to add each of a series of input numbers to the sum of the previous ones, but after each addition to examine whether the sum was yet larger than 1000. If it was not, the next instruction to be used is the start of the addition sequence for the next input number; but if 1000 had been exceeded, then the next instruction is to come from some other part of storage. It is even possible for the address of the next instruction to be chosen randomly from a number of alternatives; and consequently it can rapidly become impossible to say what the computer's next action will be, without following through every step of its previous actions.

Thus the problem of control in a computer becomes the problem of selecting a particular region of memory storage out of all those which contain possible instructions for the processor. The selection is carried out by the address of the region, a brief symbol which specifies one region rather than others but does not itself contain all the instructions.

We can now see why the problem of central control in brains is linked with that of long-term memory. It is obvious that no animal, let alone man, carries out a simple and predictable sequence of operations on the inputs which stimulate it. We must suppose therefore that the control exercised over the brain's operations is one which varies not only with the nature of the input but also with the results of past operations. Furthermore, although each control operation may be determinate and precise, the choice of one operation rather than another may well be random. The fact that a man hears all the information on his right ear and none of that on his left does not exclude the possibility that it was (even in principle) unpredictable whether he would listen to right or left. Thus there must be many possible instructions within the brain, some one of which exercises control at any instant. The specification of the particular one can be carried out by an address, and the provision of that address passes control of the system from one set of instructions to another.

It should be noted that the logic of this situation does not depend upon the controlling instructions being themselves previous inputs, as they are in computers. They might be built into the brain at birth; but still one rather than another needs to be selected at any instant. More probably, they might themselves be the result of earlier operations and thus represent a complex interaction of past inputs and of an original built-in program. Again, for the metaphysically inclined it might be noted that the instructions need have no particular physiological basis, although it seems quite probable that they do; but any consistency and reliability in the control of behaviour, such as that shown by a saint, must require the regular selection of particular behavioural strategies as the result of outside circumstances and past deliberation. The whole set of available strategies must therefore be formed into an organized body, from which one part can be found when it is required.

The essence of control therefore is the system of addresses, which implies an organization of the whole body of information. It is possible that human long-term memory for facts is organized on a different basis from that used for control instructions. On the other hand, the logical problems of finding one part of a large body of material are common to both central control and long-term memory. In computers the same memory storage is often used for both functions, a particular location serving sometimes for program and sometimes for data; and there seems no compelling reason why brains should not do the same. At all events, the study of the organization of long-term memory provides a promising start for the investigation of the problems of control.

SYSTEMS OF ADDRESSING: THE LIBRARY ANALOGY

At this point it may be helpful to consider the more homely analogy of the library, which has many aspects in common with the computer, but may reveal some features more clearly because of its familiarity and the difference in its time scale. In practice, for example, the computer very often takes all its input data into store, and only then carries out upon them the varying program operations which we described. This is because of the difference in the speed of the input devices on the one hand and the internal operations of the machine on the other. Even in computers each input may be dealt with separately in the way we have described if the machine is controlling a process "on line". The speed of the machine is generally much greater however than events in the everyday world. In libraries however the speed of the librarian is more comparable with that of the suppliers of books and we can therefore see certain parallels with the information processing which takes place in the human brain.

We can think of the world's output of books as pouring past the entrance to the library, much of it being on sale for only a limited time and then being lost for ever. From the vast amount available at each instant, a proportion is selected by any particular library, acquired and indexed. (The presence of a book in the shops corresponds to the presence of a state of evidence in the buffer store; its purchase and indexing to the occurrence of a category state).

Purchase of a book may be decided by various strategies; sometimes all books possessing certain common features may be acquired, as when all books by particular authors or from a certain publisher are bought as a routine (Filtering). Sometimes the books bought may be those appropriate to certain index categories, regardless of the fact that these may include some of the books of an author or publisher and exclude others (Pigeon-holing). Any strategy of selection must involve some examination of every book, even though it may be very formal and cursory in most cases; filtering strategies are obviously easier on the librarian than pigeon-holing ones, because in the latter he needs to read more of the book to decide which index is appropriate.

Following indexing, the book is often displayed on a shelf of recent accessions, organized only by date of arrival. This is convenient since such recent books may be of lively interest, but can only be limited because the flow of fresh books will displace those already on display. (In human beings, it is as we have seen unclear how far the recent accession shelf is limited by time since arrival, and how far by number of subsequent items.) At some stage either of time or of arrival of fresh books, a particular book must go from the recent accessions to the main shelves of the library.

Once a particular book is on the main shelves, there will be a problem of retrieval in finding it again when it is wanted. The date of publication alone becomes of rather little importance, and it is necessary to use some other method based upon the information about the book which was found out during the process of indexing. One frequent method is the use of an alphabetical index, usually by the surname of the author. This method allows an enquirer to consult the index knowing one feature of the book, the author's name, and to determine an address which indicates the particular shelf on which the desired book has been left. Another frequent method of locating books is to classify them by topic; in this case the books dealing with a certain subject may be physically placed together on the same shelves, and separated from those on other topics which may have come in at the same time. The enquirer wanting information on a subject can then merely go to the appropriate shelves, which he can find from another index such as the library catalogue. Of course, both methods can be used in the same library, so that the address found from the alphabetical list of authors may in fact refer to a particular part of the shelves dealing with a certain topic. It would be possible, though perhaps less usual, to imagine an opposite arrangement where the arrangement of books was by author, but a separate index was kept by subject-matter so that the enquirer was given the authors who had written on the topic which interests him.

Whichever system is used, it is clearly necessary for the enquirer to be given the address in some brief and usable form. Very broadly, there are two main methods which can be used; codes peculiar to the physical layout of the library, and codes related to the nature of the books in a certain region. In the former case, the enquirer may learn that the book he wants is in the Anderson Building, North Tower, Third Floor, Stack Six; in the latter case that it is in the Physical Sciences Section, Sub-Section Computer Methods, Sub-sub-section Programming Techniques. Each of these methods has its merits. The former is easier if the enquirer is going to get the book himself; the latter may be easier to remember if he is merely going to get a librarian to fetch it for him. In particular, the latter method is very useful if the library staff keep changing the physical location corresponding to particular topics, or if the enquirer wants to send information about the book to somebody who works near a different library with a different physical arrangement but the same index by topics. One can think of the two methods as Private and Public respectively; the first is meaningful only to people in the particular library, while the second is suitable for communication between libraries or with enquirers from outside.

In the last two paragraphs, we have been unable to follow the practice of the earlier stages of the library analogy, and indicate in brackets the corresponding human functions. The reason is that most experimental work on human beings has not gone beyond the stages of indexing and of recent accessions, except in a very superficial way. It seems clear, however, that the brain must meet problems similar to those of a library, when dealing with the main mass of material in store. It is also plausible that the methods adopted to meet the problem would have to be similar, because of the nature of the difficulties involved. It is likely, therefore, that retrieval will in some cases be through particular features of the material from which the location of the stored representation of other features can be determined; while in other cases retrieval will use certain topics and areas of interest. In either case, the classifications of addresses employed may be private to the person concerned or may be public and common to many people. The latter would be especially suited for communication between different people. It becomes interesting therefore to know how far human memory is organized by topic or by common features of the material; and how far the organization is public or private. In the library however the balance between these various methods of addressing is not decided by the physical buildings available, although those may bias the choice one way or another. Equally the system in one library is not necessarily the same as that in another with similar buildings. In the human case therefore we should expect that individuals will differ in their methods of retrieval, and our aim cannot be to find the one true method which all men use. Rather we should be searching for the advantages and disadvantages of different kinds of organization, for methods of diagnosing the methods being used by any particular person, and for knowledge about the experiences which may have biased his choice one way or another.

At this point however the analogy of the library begins to lose its attraction. The books stored within it represent merely information about the world; not instructions for action. Yet as we have seen in the case of the brain we do wish to consider the selection of one set of instructions rather than another, and not simply the retrieval of static information which has come in previously. Again, the arrangement of books in the library remains reasonably fixed until a particular book is wanted again, whereas in the human case the action called for in a new situation, although it may be based on past experience, is rarely a mere regurgitation of what has been passively absorbed in the past. At these points, the computer becomes more attractive again as a source of ideas. As we have seen, some regions of its storage may contain instructions to act while other regions store data; and as a result either of those instructions or of others coming from outside it may well operate upon its own memory, modifying what is stored at a certain address, moving it to another address, and so on. We ought now therefore to return to the computer analogy.

COMPUTER INSTRUCTIONS AND THE COMPREHENSION OF SENTENCES

As we said earlier, the computer meets the same problems as the library in that particular items have to be found amongst a much greater quantity of stored material; and at any instant the item which is wanted is found by an address which selects one of the regions of the machine's store. In the simple case, the various possible regions of the store are simply numbered, and the address of one region is the number assigned to it. This arrangement corresponds to the private system of addressing in libraries, and is of course only usable on one particular type of machine which has a certain arrangement of storage. Programming on this basis means the learning of a "machine language" which bears little relation to the human meaning of the tasks the computer is carrying out, and which cannot be used to program some other type of computer. For a number of years therefore, special public languages have been devised which avoid these disadvantages. To use one of these languages, the particular computer has to be given a preliminary program, the "compiler", which instructs the machine to act appropriately when given each of a series of further instructions in the public language. The programmer can then make up his own sequence of main instructions using a vocabulary which will work on any machine which has a compiler for the language he is employing. This allows him also to make his instructions more meaningful to human beings.

The technique becomes clearer in a concrete instance. When writing a program in, say, ALGOL, the human programmer starts with certain formal instructions which merely indicate to the computer that a program is coming. He then gives a series of words which he intends to use in his program. The computer, under the instruction of the compiler, takes each of these words and associates it with a region of its storage; from that point onwards, use of this word by the programmer is taken to refer to the appropriate region of store. Thus if the program is to concern the calculation of the area of a number of rectangles, the programmer may indicate that he proposes to use the words "length, width, area" and each of these will then be linked to a region of storage. The programmer does not know where it is, but for his purposes he does not need to do so.

Having thus defined his own terms, the programmer can then instruct the computer using these terms in combination with certain standard instructions. Thus if he tells the machine "length: = (read)", this tells it to read the next number on its input and to place it in the region of storage designated by the word "length". The instruction "area: = length × width" tells it to take the number in the region of storage indicated by the word "length", multiply it by the number in the region indicated by "width", and put the answer in the

Q

region called "area". The instructions thus make a certain amount of sense to a man without much knowledge of the particular computer, and also are sufficient to produce the correct result from the machine. They are public rather in the same way as a description of a library stack by the topic it contains is public. But unlike a library, a computer receiving a series of instructions in a language of this kind can operate upon its own memory, or take actions according to the nature of the content of certain parts of its memory.

The use of the word "language", in describing the various formats through which instructions may be given to the computer, points out the most natural next extension of our analogy between brains and computers. Human language is public, rests upon the existence of an agreement between different speakers and talkers about the meaning to be attached to the words they employ, and requires that the words be presented in particular syntactic sequences if they are to produce the desired result. That result may be an action, or a modification of the memory of the person receiving the message, such that he will later answer questions or take fresh actions in a fashion different from that he would use if he had never had this message. So one is tempted to view human language as having similarities to the public languages used in instructing computers. On this view, some words in a language serve the purpose of selecting a region of memory, whose content may be used in a variety of ways; such as controlling direct action, preparing for some future action, or acting as the data on which will be performed some operation controlled by other words.

Again an example may clarify the analogy. When we hear a sentence such as "Mary is blonde" the first word is a name, and can be regarded as a label indicating a region of storage, within which is contained all the information that has yet been gained about Mary. Similarly, the word "blonde" refers to a region of memory in which there is a fresh array of information. Some of this may be purely factual, referring to likely apparent colour of hair; some may be instructions for further action under appropriate circumstances. The complete sentence is an instruction to the listener or reader to transfer to the region labelled "Mary" the content of the region labelled "blonde", without deleting what is already entered under "Mary". If the same name occurs on any future occasion, the person who has received this sentence will refer to the "Mary" region of store and will find there the information related to blondness.

This account is recognizably over-simple, and other kinds of sentences would operate in different ways. For example, on this view a sentence such as "A boy was whistling in the garden" must be interpreted as an instruction to open a new region of storage, labelled "boy", as well as entering in it the information about the boy's location and activity. A later sentence, such as "The boy hit the ball", can then refer to this labelled area of storage and add to its contents some further items. In this latter case, furthermore, the sentence involves two nouns, "ball" as well as "boy", and it could well be argued that it stores information under the heading of each and not only of one. We shall return to this point, but at this stage one can simply accept that this account of the function of sentences covers only some of the instances in which they occur. However, although incomplete it can still be correct so far as it goes; and the view that words select regions of storage in the memory has certain advantages over other ways of thinking about language.

For example, the abstract logical view that a word stands for the object it represents leads to the paradox that a sentence such as "Richard Nixon is President of the United States" can in some cases be informative even though the two names in it both refer to the same entity. Viewed as a transfer of information in memory between two previously labelled regions of memory, the sentence serves a clear function.

Even the more behaviourist view that a word represents an object by eliciting the reaction which the object would produce, has well-known difficulties. Skinner (1957) recalls Whitehead's example of the sentence "There is no black scorpion on this table", in which it is clear that the words elicit changes in the listener which are definite but are not those which would be the dominant reactions if actually shown a scorpion.

Again, a third view, that words acquire meaning from the other events associated with them, leads to the paradox that the most common associate of "Beauty" may be "The Beast", and that this is certainly not what most people would call the meaning of "Beauty". Thus we cannot universally regard words either as equivalent to the objects which they name, nor as eliciting the same reaction as those objects, nor as eliciting the most common associate met in past experience. Each of these views has some instances in which it is correct; but it is more general to hold that the function of names (and of other words and phrases acting in the same way) is to select certain stored information whatever it may be. In some cases that information may represent perfectly the object named, in some cases it may represent instructions to perform an action which the object would also elicit, and in some cases it may refer to another name representing a previously associated event. So also in the computer the label of a region of storage may guide the processor either to a number needed for its calculations, or to the instructions for some operation, or to the address of another region of storage. The key feature of names is their selective function. They extract other information not contained in the name itself, but stored previously within the brain. Sentences are instructions to the brain to manipulate the information elicited by the names in the particular sentence; the manipulation depending on the syntactic structure of the sentence and the presence or absence of certain functions words such as "the, a, in", from the examples given earlier.

Such a view is not so much a definitive account of language, as a starting point from which to mount an attack. The lines which such an attack can take can be illustrated by two examples of existing work, which can be mentioned at this point.

AN EXPERIMENTAL ATTACK ON COMPREHENSION

(a) *The use of undeclared variables.* In the examples of computer programming mentioned earlier, it will be remembered that any instructions referring to a certain region of store had been preceded by a preliminary input to the computer. This earlier input indicated that a certain name was going to be used, and caused an area of storage to be set aside under that name. In such simple programs as we have discussed, it is unlikely that the programmer will make an error and fail to "declare a variable" by making sure that the name he is going to use has been made known to the computer. In more complex programs however a certain name may be used only in parts of the program and not be used in others; and as we have seen an advanced program may involve control passing from place to place within the whole array of instructions in a fashion which jumps large sections, returns on itself, loops over and over, and so on. It is by no means unknown in practice therefore for a programmer to use an undeclared variable; or perhaps to fall into some other error resulting from the sequence in which the operations are performed. For example, if a long calculation involved the working out at separate occasions of a number of areas, for each of which a width and a length were provided, then it might happen that an oversight of the programmer might cause the stores labelled "width" and "length" to contain the numbers corresponding to the previous area to be calculated rather than to the one now in hand.

If our broad analysis is correct, we should be able to show something similar in the human case. That is, one ought to be able to find errors of English style which correspond to programming errors of the kind involving undeclared variables. As we have seen, human language includes provision for opening a new region of store simply through the occurrence of a name in a sentence, as in "A boy was whistling in the garden". Nevertheless, we saw in Chapter VIII that primary memory of the desk-top type may have difficulty in holding simultaneously more than a fixed number of addresses. If therefore too many fresh areas of storage are opened without reference to existing information in memory, the incoming information is likely to be inefficiently handled.

Let us take an example from the description of a family structure. If we hear the sentence "John Smith is a friend of mine", this introduces to us the label "John Smith" and stores under it information already available in the brain concerning friendship and the speaker. If now another sentence is heard which says "Mary is John's wife", the new label "Mary" is similarly used to act as the future address of information which has already been received. The same process can then go on with "Jill is Mary's sister" and so on. Suppose however that a series of sentences describing a similar family had been received in a different order. The sequence might then run "Jack Robinson is a friend of mine. Pat is Greta's sister. Bill is Tom's son." and only then go on "Greta is Jack's wife" and so on. Experiment shows (Broadbent, 1965b) that a sequence of the first type, in which each name is referred on its first appearance to existing stored information, is better recalled subsequently. The same is true of a story made up of sentences each involving two noun phrases. The series of sentences can be arranged in two ways. In one case each new noun phrase is introduced in a sentence with one that has been met previously. In the other case the sequence is mixed so that a whole series of new noun phrases occurs before any one is linked to those already linked by earlier sentences. The latter series of sentences is harder to recall than the former is.

Such an experiment may seem almost too simple to need doing. Yet many authors do write passages of English in which the reader is expected to understand a series of sentences in each of which several new terms are placed in relation to each other with no reference to pre-existing knowledge. Such an error is easy to commit, because the writer already has stored information in his own brain under each label, and thus the sentence is perfectly clear to him. In the same way the programmer can mistakenly write "Area: = length × breadth" when some of these terms are unknown to the computer or else refer to inappropriate information. In both human and computer cases the communicator has forgotten the present state of the store of the system with which he is communicating.

(b) *The operations performed by various types of sentence.* We said earlier that it might be inadequate to think of an ordinary sentence such as "The boy hit the ball" as storing information under "boy"; it might also do so under "ball". Nevertheless, it is tempting to take the structure of the basic English sentence, with a noun phrase followed by a verb phrase, and to regard it as parallel to the basic computer instruction; an address and an instruction concerning the operation to be performed at that address. In a computer, the operation may be, for instance, to store at the designated address a reference to another address; just as the English sentence may contain a second noun phrase as the object of a transitive verb in the verb phrase.

If there is anything in this parallel, the first noun phrase is rather different from the second. The first is the label under which something is stored; the second is part of the content which is put in store. Thus sentences of the same logical meaning ought to differ in their effect on human listeners, depending on their structure. "The boy hit the ball" ought not to be equivalent to "The ball was hit by the boy" so far as its interpretation by a listener goes, even if some outside agency might regard the two sentences as meaning the same. The point is of some general interest, because in linguistics rather than psychology the contemporary preference would be to derive both sentences by transformation from the same original kernel string (Thomas, 1966;

Q*

Neisser, 1967). If one were to argue that the simplicity of the linguistic description corresponds to a real psychological process, then one might argue that the listener to either sentence would store the same kernel information, possibly together with an indicator of the transformation present in the original sentence; and that the form of the original would have no effect on the relative ease of different methods of retrieval.

The usual method of testing memory is to ask questions; so one might ask the listener "What did the boy hit?" or "What was hit by the boy?". Immediately one finds something which is odd, if it is the kernel which is stored; for the first question gives better results with the first original sentence, and the second question with the second sentence. That is, it is better to have an active question for an active original sentence, and a passive question for a passive original sentence (Wright, 1969). This in itself means only that the original sentence is in part stored as a simple string of words with rather little processing; so that a question phrased in as similar a way as possible to the sentence will give better recall. The result tells us little about the organization of the memory for a sentence which has been understood and whose meaning, rather than whose wording, has been stored. For memory of that type, our view would predict that an active sentence would give better memory for subsequent enquiries about the boy, while a passive sentence would prepare one better for being asked about the ball. Suppose for each type of sentence we call the first noun in the sentence the subject, and the second the object; and suppose that in both types of sentence we call the noun whose activity is described by the verb the "agent" and the other the "patient". That is, the boy is the agent and the ball the patient in both types of sentence, but the boy is the subject of active sentences and the ball of passive ones. Then our view suggests that the subject will be the better recall cue in both types of sentence, regardless of whether it is the agent or not.

In the question and answer technique used by Wright, the question includes both the agent (or patient) and also the verb, which complicates the picture. A rather different technique used by Tannenbaum and Williams (1968) is to provide a test sentence with blanks for all items except one; such as "The boy ... the ...". In this case, when one balances out the relation between question and sentence form already mentioned, it is indeed true that provision of the subject gave better recall than did provision of the object. Thus the two kinds of sentence do seem to result in memory organized in different ways, as our interpretation requires.

When the verb is included in the question, as in Wright's results, something rather different happens. In that case, the dominant effect is that it is better to be asked *about* the agent than *about* the patient, for both types of sentence. So it is better to be provided with the label of the subject in passive sentences, but that of the object in active sentences. The reason for this effect is obscure, but presumably has to do with the function which verbs perform in sentences.

We have glossed over the role of the verb, which in our examples ("X is Y") was merely an instruction to transfer information from one store to another. When the verb itself describes a quality of its agent ("The boy whistles"), the information going into store may plausibly be regarded as linked more closely with the agent than with the patient. But there seem to be inconsistencies here, as the surface structure of sentences such as "The boy is hot, the boy is running, the boy is pursued" seems very similar. Wright's result implies in fact an effect of the deep structure, which transformational grammar describes by the concept of the kernel.

Further studies of this kind would seem to be extremely promising. Their general technique might be described as the presentation of sentences to people, and subsequently the examination of the changes which the sentences have produced in the people. In particular, one wants to know how memory may differ in its organization if the same set of data is presented in various ways.

THE ORGANIZATION OF A SET OF ADDRESSES

From all that has been said, it is obvious that the efficiency of memory and of the central control of human performance may depend crucially upon the form of the set of addresses which is used by the brain of each person. The availability of an address may decide whether information in the memory can be found, may make available other relevant information, may ensure that a sequence of actions is executed smoothly, and may determine whether a sentence is comprehensible. In simple computer programs each label used may represent a quite independent region of storage, so that the finding of the information in a certain region depends on the occurrence of the corresponding label in the instructions. But as we have seen it is perfectly possible to store under one label the address of another region of store where other items are to be found, and then to repeat the process, so that the occurrence of one label may elicit information originally stored under another, because of the interlinking of the systematic set of labels. Thus this interlinking itself becomes important in understanding the performance of the program.

In the human case, we have already chosen to regard sentences as instructions to modify the arrangement of addresses through which certain information can be reached. In our account of the understanding of a family structure, we described how links were established between the name of each member of the family and the names of those who had already been mentioned. We cannot therefore imagine that the system of addressing used by human beings is only like the alphabetic index of authors in a library; in such a system, the various possible labels are arranged in a regular order, and against each is stored the physical whereabouts of the relevant information. We must also think in terms of cross-references, of broader and narrower categories of label, and so on, if we are to understand human memory.

Libraries provide interesting analogies at this point. An alternative to the author index is the subject index, in which a general label such as "Non-Fiction" may include several labels of smaller inclusiveness such as "Physics" or "Biology"; and within each of these there may be others such as "Mammals" or "Arthropods" before we finally find a physical address where the books are to be found. There is however a characteristic of such subject index systems which can be very misleading. This is their hierarchical nature. If a book is about dogs, and is classified under "Mammals", then it must be both "Biology" and "Non-Fiction". Some terms have broader reference than others, and thus refer to wider regions of the library's shelves, but there is no provision for overlap or for the multiple classification of a single book. In general, this works well enough; but it may create difficulties for books on topics such as "Science Fiction" or "Molecular Biology". The first of these examples may not cause too much trouble in practice, because likely enquirers at a library may not look under "Science" for their preferred form of art; but the latter may be quite serious, because an enquirer about molecular structure might approach a problem either through the physical or the biological path. If he happens to choose the one which the librarian has not chosen, he will miss important information.

In the human case, some hierarchical inter-relation between labels undoubtedly exists. If we have learned that "All Americans are hospitable" and then learn that "Mr. Jones is a Texan" we shall probably expect hospitality from him. More dangerously, if he happens to disappoint us, we may be heard subsequently saying "All Americans are unreliable". That is, the storage of information under a broad label makes it available also when an included narrower label occurs; and in some cases information stored under a narrow label may erroneously be retrieved when there occurs a broader label which includes the narrower. But it can well be questioned whether such hierarchies are the only basis of organization in the human case; when we learn that the hospitable Mr. Jones has red hair and a bad temper, do we infer that such a temper is a property of red-haired Texans, of red-haired people who are hospitable, or of some other class selected out of the total population of human beings? Mr. Jones can be regarded as one element in a classification based hierarchically on nationality, and if he is a Texan he is certainly not British. But his hair and temper place him in a different classification, because red-haired Texans are a sub-set of Texans, but there are also red-haired Englishmen.

In libraries, this kind of difficulty may be met by elaborate cross-referencing; one may proceed downwards through the hierarchy "Psychology; Experimental; Cognitive Processes; Memory" to a list of books and at the very end meet the ominous words (see also under Biochemistry, DNA; under Computer Science, Storage; and under Librarianship, Indexing and Retrieval). An alternative line of attack is to abandon the hierarchy altogether, and use a rather different system of labels. In this different system, each book may or may not have any of a large set of descriptive labels. Thus a book on molecular biology might be assigned the labels both of physics and of biology, since it is relevant to both. Any enquirer seeking information on a particular subject can then ask for the books which possess a certain set of labels but do not possess certain others. Depending on the nature of the books in the library, one will in practice find that some combinations of labels will not occur; indeed, the traditional hierarchy is based on the assumption that labels in one branch of the hierarchy will not occur in combination with labels in another branch. In so far as books on biology are never books on physics, the traditional hierarchy is satisfactory. It has the advantage, moreover, of making indexing much easier and of allowing the physical storage to correspond closely to the classification in the index. When it breaks down however the use of a number of independent systems of classification, assigning many labels to one book, may save the situation (Vickery, 1965).

In the human case, we are almost completely ignorant of the degree to which either or both of these systems is employed. One system can be distinguished from the other by the mistakes which it would make; for example we mentioned earlier an unpublished study by Broadbent and Gregory in which subjects who had seen a mixture of letters in two colours were asked to recall the letters in one colour only. If the wanted letters were acoustically similar to the unwanted, there were more intrusions of the unwanted items in recall. This suggests that the stored material was not held in memory in two quite different regions of storage, distinguished by the colour in which the letter was originally presented. If that were the case, similarity between the items in one region and those in the other could hardly affect recall. Rather the stored information must be in a region labelled both by the colour of the stimulus and the acoustic quality, so that items similar in the first respect could nevertheless confuse with each other in the second.

This result indicates the kind of experiment which could practicably be employed on this problem; but as yet it has not. We are left therefore with only a plan for future research, rather than a definite conclusion. One point is clear, however. The systems of retrieval from storage which occur in libraries, and which we want to distinguish in the human case, can be summed up in this way. At one extreme there is the strategy of selecting items out of the total in store, by their possession of some label or property which is common to all the desired items and to none of those which are irrelevant. At the other extreme, there is the strategy of selecting the items which are appropriate to a certain combination of features, any of which may also occur in different combinations amongst the irrelevant and unwanted items in memory. This distinction is yet again the same which we have seen so frequently in the field of perception; the antithesis of filtering and pigeon-holing. In the analysis of these strategies in long-term memory, and of the other characteristics of long-term storage, lies the most tempting field of advance for the 1970's.

Towards the Unknown

We finish then on a note of fresh enquiry, and without a static resting-place. That is as it should be. At the beginning of the book, it was made clear that one of its main purposes was to illustrate the steady revision and change of ideas which the empirical approach allows in psychology. The idea of a perfect vision of human nature, which can merely be confirmed by observation and will survive it unchanged, is an illusion. Furthermore, it is a dangerous illusion, for it leads those who believe in it into polemic and conflict with each other. When we appeal to observation we are upholding a belief in the possibility of reaching agreement between different psychologists; because observation unites those of different views, even when their verbal statements tend to drive them apart. It is necessary then to welcome change and the clash of data with concepts. Nevertheless, it may be profitable to ask where the whole enterprise is tending.

One view which might have been held in the 1950's would be that the study of behaviour is leading us ultimately towards structural explanations in the brain; that psychology would ultimately be explained by physiology, just as many physiological problems are now being explained by biochemistry, and many chemical problems by the physical characteristics of molecular structure. Intuitively, psychologists have always felt uneasy about the validity of such an idea, but have found it hard to resist conceptually; physiologists have perhaps been even more disturbed by it, and the last chapters of certain books by neurophysiologists are notorious for suggesting that the explanations of human behaviour may lie outside the province of science altogether. One merit of the climate of opinion in the late 1960's is that we now have a clearer analogy for the relation of psychology and physiology. This analogy may help us to understand the validity of the arguments of those who have always urged that psychology introduces new principles into science. But it may also help us to see that the subject is not therefore beyond the reach of science.

The analogy is that of the computer. The hardware of any particular machine limits its behaviour, and it is impossible to run certain programs on certain machines because they do not have large enough memory, or cannot use certain systems of addressing. The engineering aspects of computers provide baffling and important problems. At the same time, the programming of the machines produces problems which may well be equally challenging intellectually, and may remain unsolved even when the hardware is perfectly understood. In much laboratory practice, it is the problems of programming which cause experiments to be "held up till the computer is working properly"; and even if a program works, it may be the subject of fierce debate directed at establishing whether it is really carrying out the desired aim by the fastest and most elegant method. Perhaps the calculation of the desired quantities in this order, rather than that, exposes the system to the danger of searching for a non-existent quantity under certain unlikely conditions; perhaps this other sequence of operation, though reliable, will be so slow that the machine will be outpaced by the problem in the outer world which it is supposed to be handling. An understanding of the structure of the computer is irrelevant to much of the discussion of such problems. Specialists in "software" can spend much of their working time without considering the physical nature of the mechanisms which actually implement their programs. It is true that in principle the behaviour of a machine which has had a program loaded and is running could be predicted from a perfect knowledge of the physical state of every part of it; though even this may have its exceptions, as when the program is made to use some random input quantity to control which action is next performed, in the fashion discussed earlier. But even when such perfect prediction is in principle possible, it is never in fact performed, because the major intellectual problems of programming are of a quite different kind.

If we turn to the human case, there are certainly many aspects of behaviour for which the most satisfying explanation is physiological. Within the topics we have discussed in this book, one obvious example is the fusion of different sounds in perception into a single voice. The factors which determine why some sounds will do this and others will not probably lie in the structure of the ear and the auditory pathways. At the opposite extreme however the explanation for the appearance of this sentence in English rather than French lies in the particular program which was fed into the author in childhood, and it is certain that no physiological explanation is relevant.

In the intermediate ground, it is still a matter for controversy whether the structures of both English and French share certain features which are to be explained by innate physiological mechanisms (Chomsky, 1968). Although the particular point at which the dividing line should be drawn is uncertain (and indeed it may be more proper to speak of a region rather than a line, because there may be a substantial area in which, say, either factor may produce a particular result if the other does not) it is nevertheless clear that there is a substantial area of human behaviour where the major problems are the sequence in which operations are performed, the types of addressing that are used, and so on. Even given a perfect knowledge of the mechanism of the brain, these will continue to be problems. Although the basis of long-term memory may be, say, growth of connections at synapses, and although it is very important to understand what the basis actually is, a perfect understanding of the synapse will not enable us to judge the relative merits of Old and New Mathematics as a means of educating the young.

In past chapters, we have distinguished various stages of information processing. Some of these stages may correspond to structural features of the nervous system. At a guess, the layout of the brain itself probably determines the existence of the buffer store and of a selective pick-off from that store through a categorizing system. Similarly, it is likely that physiological structure decides that some filtering will take place, and probably some pigeon-holing. The influence of spatial location as a basis for filtering seems remarkably strong, and the structure of the eye obviously lends itself to it. The effect of probability on pigeon-holing suggests equally that a mechanism exists for translating the frequency of one experience rather than another into a bias towards one response and away from the other. However, it is obvious that the particular set of category states employed by a man is determined by his experience (French words rather than English ones) and it seems plausible that software rather than hardware factors may be the major influence on the relative amount to which filtering and pigeon-holing are used. When we come to the organization of long-term memory, it is even more probable that physiology has little to say about the use of one strategy rather than another. Various kinds of organization of data can be implemented on the same computer; and the reasons for preferring one to another have little to do with the machinery, but rather with properties of the organization itself. Equally different kinds of education may produce different kinds of mind; or the central control within the brain may itself result in a developed structure of thought and memory which is individual, on the lines we mentioned earlier. The distinction of convergent and divergent modes of thought, so popular amongst educationists (Hudson, 1966) may well reflect such a difference in methods of organizing and retrieving past information.

At the present stage therefore the psychologist is still discovering some facts about behaviour which will ultimately need to be explained physiologic- ally. The behavioural approach is an essential first step, since one cannot explain a phenomenon without knowing what it is; but in the end the task of the psychologist will in these areas be completed, and he can hand over to physiology. There are emerging however areas in which physiology will even in the end be irrelevant, and which will remain capable of producing new problems almost indefinitely. These are the problems of programming our own marvellously flexible computers; and of understanding the difficulties which may arise because, say, a certain system of classifying memories causes a man to react to his wife as if she was his mother.

The traditionalists are right then to insist that human psychology involves more than the dissection of a kind of clockwork mouse. They are wrong in supposing that the incredibly intricate problems of human programming can be understood intuitively, by appeal to direct experience, and using the traditional concepts of mind. The fatal flaw in such an approach is that no two people are likely to be running on exactly the same program; so that one of us cannot hope to duplicate the experience of another. Thus any analysis of mental life achieved by one man may be inappropriate for another; quite apart from the dangers of oversight and bias which pursue all human thinking. At best therefore the mentalistic approach to psychology leads to misunderstanding; at worst, to sterile conflict and polemic, because disagreement cannot be resolved.

Even in the case of computer programs, which are so much simpler than human psychology, we need to try out each program on the machine before we know that it will work; and all too often we have made a mistake, and only find it out from the behaviour of the machine. So also, those tempting problems of human psychology, which lie beyond physiology and are linked to it only as software to hardware, will require continuous and sophisticated experiments on behaviour. Without the behaviourist approach, there is no hope of understanding other people, rather than imposing upon them our own prejudices and misconceptions.

Behaviourists are sometimes criticised on the grounds that their views tend to inhumanity. One might put the criticism in this way: dealing with fellow-creatures as objects for science denies them personality, and reduces them to things. The emotional tone behind such a criticism is healthy, and we have seen the truth which certainly underlies the statements that surface behaviour is only an expression of an inner control, and that psychology is different from physiology. But even in everyday life, the man who is open and sensitive to others is the one who tries to see how they are using words, what goals they are trying to achieve, and what they are expressing by certain styles of life.

The inhuman person is rather the one who shuts himself in by thinking in terms of his own experience, and inevitably can react only by rejection and hostility to those whose experience is different.

In the philosophy of the physical world, it was the appeal to observation rather than assertion which reconciled the warring factions. Similarly in psychology it is the gradual spread of much-abused reductionism which creates a dialogue between one view and another. The content of this book serves merely as an instance of the method which science suggests for the resolution of disputes, not by words but by data. In the end, this method will give men more understanding of themselves and each other, will make them more able to do what they wish and to avoid the pain of their neighbour. The content of that ultimate knowledge we cannot yet guess; but it must be consistent with the actions of the great men of the past, if it is to be truly knowledge about human beings. We need not fear therefore some revelation that men are "really" contemptible: how can they be, to have done what some of them have done? We can, therefore, urge ourselves onward with confidence rather than recoil into the static world of a mentalistic approach. Whether the speculations of this chapter are on the right lines may well be doubted; but if they are not true, then some better thing is.

REFERENCES

Adams, J. A. (1956). Vigilance in the detection of low-intensity visual stimuli. *J. exp. Psychol.* **52**, 204-208.

Adams, J. A. and Chambers, R. W. (1962). Response to simultaneous stimulation of two sense modalities. *J. exp. Psychol.* **63**, 198-206.

Adams, J. A. and Humes, J. M. (1963). Monitoring of complex displays. IV. Training for vigilance. *Hum. Factors* **5**, 147-153.

Adams, J. A. and Boulter, L. R. (1964). Spatial and temporal uncertainty as determinants of vigilance behavior. *J. exp. Psychol.* **67**, 127-131.

Adams, J. A., Stenson, H. H. and Humes, J. M. (1961). Monitoring of complex visual displays. II. Effects of visual load and response complexity on human vigilance. *Hum. Factors* **3**, 213-221.

Adams, J. A., Humes, J. M. and Stenson, H. H. (1962). Monitoring of complex visual displays. III. Effects of repeated sessions on human vigilance. *Hum. Factors* **4**, 149-158.

Adams, J. A., Humes, J. M. and Sieveking, N. A. (1963). Monitoring of complex visual display. V. Effects of repeated sessions and heavy visual load on human vigilance. *Hum. Factors* **4**, 385-389.

Allport, D. A. (1968). Phenomenal simultaneity and the perceptual moment hypothesis. *Br. J. Psychol.* **59**, 395-406.

Alluisi, E. A., Muller, P. F. Jr. and Fitts, P. M. (1957). An information analysis of verbal and motor responses in a forced-paced serial task. *J. exp. Psychol.* **53**, 153-158.

Anderson, N. S. (1960). Post-stimulus cuing in immediate memory. *J. exp. Psychol.* **60**, 216-221.

Anderson, N. S. and Leonard, J. A. (1958). The recognition, naming, and reconstruction of visual figures as a function of contour redundancy. *J. exp. Psychol.* **56**, 262-270.

Atkinson, R. C. and Shiffrin, R. M. (1967). Human memory: a proposed system and its control processes. Tech. Rep. No. 110, Institute for Mathematical Studies in the Social Sciences, Stanford University.

Audley, R. J. (1960). A stochastic model for individual choice behaviour. *Psychol. Rev.* **67**, 1-15.

Audley, R. J. (1964). Decision-making. *Br. Med. Bull.* **20**, 27-31.

Audley, R. J. and Wallis, C. P. (1964). Response instructions and the speed of relative judgements. I. Some experiments on brightness discrimination. *Br. J. Psychol.* **55**, 59-73.

Audley, R. J. and Pike, A. R. (1965). Some alternative stochastic models of choice. *Br. J. math. statist. Psychol.* **18**, 207-225.

Averbach, E. and Coriell, A. S. (1961). Short-term memory in vision. *Bell. Sys. tech. J.* **40**, 309-328.

Baddeley, A. D. (1964a). Language-habits, S–R compatibility and verbal learning. *Am. J. Psychol.* **77**, 463-468.

Baddeley, A. D. (1964b). Immediate memory and the "perception" of letter sequences. *Q. J. exp. Psychol.* **16**, 364-367.

Baddeley, A. D. (1966a). The influence of acoustic and semantic similarity on long-term memory for word sequences. *Q. J. exp. Psychol.* **18**, 302-309.

Baddeley, A. D. (1966b). Short-term memory for word sequences as a function of acoustic, semantic and formal similarity. *Q. J. exp. Psychol.* **18**, 362-365.

Baddeley, A. D. (1966c). Influence of depth on the manual dexterity of free divers: a comparison between open sea and pressure chamber testing. *J. appl. Psychol.* **50**, 81-85.

Baddeley, A. D. (1968). How does acoustic similarity influence short-term memory? *Q. J. exp. Psychol.* **20**, 249-264.

Baddeley, A. D. and Dale, H. C. A. (1966). The effect of semantic similarity on retroactive interference in long- and short-term memory. *J. verb. Learn. verb. Behav.* **5**, 417-420.

Baddeley, A. D. and Flemming, N. C. (1967). The efficiency of divers breathing oxy-helium. *Ergonomics* **10**, 311-319.

Baddeley, A. D. and Colquhoun, W. P. (1969). Signal probability and vigilance: a reappraisal of the "signal rate" effect. *Br. J. Psychol.* **60**, 169-178.

Baddeley, A. D., Conrad, R. and Thomson, W. E. (1960). Letter structure of the English language. *Nature, Lond.* **186**, 414-416.

Baddeley, A. D., Conrad, R. and Hull, A. J. (1965). Predictability and immediate memory for consonant sequences. *Q. J. exp. Psychol.* **17**, 175-177.

Baddeley, A. D., Figueredo, J. W. de, Curtis, J. W. H. and Williams, A. N. (1968). Nitrogen narcosis and performance under water. *Ergonomics* **11**, 157-164.

Bahrick, H. P., Fitts, P. M. and Rankin, R. E. (1952). Effect of incentives upon reactions to peripheral stimuli. *J. exp. Psychol.* **44**, 400-406.

Bakan, P. (1959). Extraversion–introversion and improvement in an auditory vigilance task. *Br. J. Psychol.* **50**, 325-332.

Bakan, P. and Manley, R. (1963). Effect of visual deprivation on auditory vigilance. *Br. J. Psychol.* **54**, 115-119.

Baker, C. H. (1958). Attention to visual displays during a vigilance task, Part I, Biasing attention. *Br. J. Psychol.* **49**, 279-288.

Baker, C. H. (1959). Attention to visual displays during a vigilance task. II. Maintaining the level of vigilance. *Br. J. Psychol.* **50**, 30-36.

Baker, C. H. (1960a). Maintaining the level of vigilance by artificial signals. *J. appl. Psychol.* **44**, 336-338.

Baker, C. H. (1960b). Observing behavior in a vigilance task. *Science, N.Y.* **132**, 674-675.

Baker, C. H. (1961). Maintaining the level of vigilance by means of knowledge of results about a secondary vigilance task. *Ergonomics* **4**, 311-316.

Baker, C. H. (1962). On temporal extrapolation. *Can. J. Psychol.* **16**, 37-41.

Baker, C. H. (1963a). Further towards a theory of vigilance. *In* "Vigilance: a Symposium" (Buckner and McGrath, eds), McGraw-Hill, N.Y.

Baker, C. H. (1963b). Signal duration as a factor in vigilance tasks. *Science, N.Y.* **141**, 1196-1197.

*Baker, C. H. (1967). Target detection performance with a stationary sweep-line. *Acta Psychol.* **27**, 361-367.

Barnes, J. M. and Underwood, B. J. (1959). "Fate" of first-list associations in transfer theory. *J. exp. Psychol.* **58**, 97-105.

Acta Psychol. 27 has the same contents as "Attention and Performance" (A. F. Sanders, ed.), North Holland, Amsterdam.

Bartlett, F. C. (1932). "Remembering", Cambridge University Press, Cambridge.

Barton, M. I., Goodglass, H. and Shai, A. (1965). Differential recognition of tachistoscopically presented English and Hebrew words in right and left visual fields. *Percept. Mot. Skills.* **21**, 431-437.

Bennett, P. B., Poulton, E. C., Carpenter, A. and Catton, M. J. (1967). Efficiency of sorting cards in air and a 20 per cent oxygen–helium mixture at depths down to 100 feet and in enriched air. *Ergonomics* **10**, 53-62.

Bergum, B. O. and Lehr, D. J. (1962). Vigilance performance as a function of interpolated rest. *J. appl. Psychol.* **46**, 425-427.

Bergum, B. O. and Lehr, D. J. (1963a). Effects of authoritarianism on vigilance performance. *J. appl. Psychol.* **47**, 75-77.

Bergum, B. O. and Lehr, D. J. (1963b). End-spurt in vigilance. *J. exp. Psychol.* **66**, 383-385.

Bergum, B. O. and Lehr, D. J. (1964). Monetary incentives and vigilance. *J. exp. Psychol.* **67**, 197-198.

Berlyne, D. E., Borsa, D. M., Hamacher, J. H. and Koenig, I. D. V. (1966). Paired-associate learning and the timing of arousal. *J. exp. Psychol.* **72**, 1-6.

Bertelson, P. (1961). Sequential redundancy and speed in a serial 2-choice responding task. *J. exp. Psychol.* **13**, 90-102.

Bertelson, P. (1963). S–R relationship and reaction times to new versus repeated signals in a serial task. *J. exp. Psychol.* **65**, 478-484.

Bertelson, P. (1967). The refractory period of choice reactions with regular and irregular interstimuli intervals. *Acta Psychol.* **27**, 45-56.

Bertelson, P. and Barzeele, J. (1965). Interaction of time-uncertainty and relative signal frequency in determining choice reaction time. *J. exp. Psychol.* **70**, 448-451.

Bertelson, P. and Renkin, A. (1966). Reaction times to new *vs* repeated signals in a serial task as a function of response–signal time interval. *Acta Psychol.* **25**, 132-136.

Bertelson, P. and Tisseyre, F. (1966). Choice reaction time as a function of stimulus versus response relative frequency of occurrence. *Nature, Lond.* **212**, 1069-1070.

Bexton, W. H., Heron, W. and Scott, T. H. (1954). Effects of decreased variation in the sensory environment. *Can. J. Psychol.* **8**, 70-76.

Bills, A. G. (1931). Blocking: a new principle in mental fatigue. *Am. J. Psychol.* **43**, 230-245.

Binford, J. R. and Loeb, M. (1963). Monitoring readily detected auditory signals and detection of obscure visual signals. *Percept. Mot. Skills* **17**, 735-746.

Binford, J. R. and Loeb, M. (1966). Changes within and over repeated sessions in criterion and effective sensitivity in an auditory vigilance task. *J. exp. Psychol.* **72**, 339-345.

Birren, J. E. (ed.) (1959). "Handbook of Aging and the Individual: Psychological and Biological Aspects", University of Chicago Press, Chicago.

Blair, W. C. and Kaufman, H. M. (1959). Command Control. I. Multiple display monitoring. II. Control-display spatial arrangement. Electric Boat Tech. Rep. SPD–59–082.

Blake, M. J. F. (1967a). Time of day effects on performance in a range of tasks. *Psychon. Sci.* **9**, 349-350.

Blake, M. J. F. (1967b). Relationship between circadian rhythm of body-temperature and introversion–extraversion. *Nature, Lond.* **215**, 896-897.

Blyth, K. W. (1963). Ipsilateral confusion in 2-choice and 4-choice responses with the hands and feet. *Nature, Lond.* **199**, 1312.

Blyth, K. W. (1964). Errors in a further 4-choice reaction task with the hands and feet. *Nature, Lond.* **201**, 641.

Boer, E. de (1956). On the "residue" in hearing. Doctoral Dissertation, University of Amsterdam.

Borger, R. (1963). The refractory period and serial choice-reactions. *Q. J. exp. Psychol.* **15**, 1-12.

Boulter, L. R. and Adams, J. A. (1963). Vigilance decrement, the expectancy hypothesis and intersignal interval. *Can. J. Psychol.* **17**, 201-209.

Bowen, H. M. (1964). Vigilance as a function of signal frequency and flash rate. *Percept. Mot. Skills* **18**, 333-338.

Bowsher, J. M., Johnson, D. R. and Robinson, D. W. (1966). A further experiment on judging the noisiness of aircraft in flight. *Acustica* **17**, 245-266.

Brainard, R. W., Irby, T. S., Fitts, P. M. and Alluisi, E. A. (1962). Some variables influencing the rate of gain of information. *J. exp. Psychol.* **63**, 105-110.

Brand, H., Sakoda, J. M. and Woods, P. J. (1957). Contingent partial reinforcement and the anticipation of correct alternatives. *J. exp. Psychol.* **53**, 417-424.

Brelsford, J. W. and Atkinson, R. C. (1968). Recall of paired-associates as a function of overt and covert rehearsal procedures. *J. verb. Learn. verb. Behav.* **7**, 730-736.

Broadbent, D. E. (1950). The twenty dials test under quiet conditions. A.P.U. Report No. 130.

Broadbent, D. E. (1952a). Listening to one of two synchronous messages. *J. exp. Psychol.* **44**, 51-55.

Broadbent, D. E. (1952b). Failures of attention in selective listening. *J. exp. Psychol.* **44**, 428-433.

Broadbent, D. E. (1953). Noise, paced performance, and vigilance tasks. *Br. J. Psychol.* **44**, 295-303.

Broadbent, D. E. (1954a). Some effects of noise on visual performance. *Q. J. exp. Psychol.* **6**, 1-5.

Broadbent, D. E. (1954b). The role of auditory localization in attention and memory span. *J. exp. Psychol.* **47**, 191-196.

Broadbent, D. E. (1955). A note on binaural fusion. *Q. J. exp. Psychol.* **7**, 46-47.

Broadbent, D. E. (1956a). Listening between and during practised auditory distractions. *Br. J. Psychol.* **47**, 51-60.

Broadbent, D. E. (1956b). Successive responses to simultaneous stimuli. *Q. J. exp. Psychol.* **8**, 145-152.

Broadbent, D. E. (1957a). Effects of noises of high and low frequency on behaviour. *Ergonomics* **1**, 21-29.

Broadbent, D. E. (1957b). Immediate memory and simultaneous stimuli. *Q. J. exp. Psychol.* **9**, 1-11.

Broadbent, D. E. (1957c). Effects of noise on behaviour. *In* "Handbook of Noise Control" (Harris, C. M., ed.), Chap. 10, pp. 1-33, McGraw-Hill, New York.

Broadbent, D. E. (1958). "Perception and Communication", Pergamon Press, London.

Broadbent, D. E. (1958a). Effect of noise on an "intellectual" task. *J. acoust. Soc. Am.* **30**, 824-827.

Broadbent, D. E. (1961). Psychophysical methods and individual differences in the kinaesthetic figural after-effect. *Br. J. Psychol.* **52**, 97-104.

Broadbent, D. E. (1963a). Some recent research from the Applied Psychology Research Unit, Cambridge. *In* "Vigilance: a symposium" (Buckner and McGrath, eds), McGraw-Hill, New York.

Broadbent, D. E. (1963b). Flow of information within the organism. *J. verb. Learn. verb. Behav.* **2**, 34-39.

Broadbent, D. E. (1965a). A reformulation of the Yerkes-Dodson law. *Br. J. math. statist. Psychol.* **18**, 145-157.

Broadbent, D. E. (1965b). Perceptual defence and the engineering psychologist. *Bull. Br. psychol. Soc.* **18**, No. 60.

Broadbent, D. E. (1966). Two-state threshold model and rating-scale experiments. *J. acoust. Soc. Am.* **40**, 244-245.

Broadbent, D. E. (1967a). The relation between theory and experiment. *In* "Les modèles et la formalisation du comportment", CNRS, Paris.

Broadbent, D. E. (1967b). Word-frequency effect and response bias. *Psychol. Rev.* **74**, 1-15.

Broadbent, D. E. (1970). Stimulus set and response set: two kinds of selective attention. *In* "Attention: Contemporary Theories and Analysis" (D. Mostofsky, ed.), Appleton-Century-Crofts, New York.

Broadbent, D. E. and Ladefoged, P. (1957). On the fusion of sounds reaching different sense organs. *J. acoust. Soc. Am.* **29**, 708-710.

Broadbent, D. E. and Ladefoged, P. (1959). Auditory perception of temporal order, *J. acoust. Soc. Am.* **31**, 1539.

Broadbent, D. E. and Ladefoged, P. (1960). Vowel judgments and adaptation level. *Proc. R. Soc.* B. **151**, 384-399.

Broadbent, D. E. and Little, E. A. J. (1960). Effects of noise reduction in a work situation. *Occupational Psychol.* **34**, 133-140.

Broadbent, D. E. and Gregory, M. (1961). On the recall of stimuli presented alternately to two sense organs. *Q. J. exp. Psychol.* **13**, 103-109.

Broadbent, D. E. and Gregory, M. (1962a). Human response to classes of stimuli. *Nature, Lond.* **193**, 1315-1316.

Broadbent, D. E. and Gregory, M. (1962b). Donders' *B*- and *C*-reactions and *S–R* compatibility. *J. exp. Psychol.* **63**, 575-578.

Broadbent, D. E. and Heron, A. (1962). Effects of a subsidiary task on performance involving immediate memory by younger and older men. *Br. J. Psychol.* **53**, 189-198.

Broadbent, D. E. and Gregory, M. (1963a). Vigilance considered as a statistical decision. *Br. J. Psychol.* **54**, 309-323.

Broadbent, D. E. and Gregory, M. (1963b). Division of attention and the decision theory of signal detection. *Proc. R. Soc.* B. **158**, 222-231.

Broadbent, D. E. and Gregory, M. (1964a). Stimulus set and response set: The alternation of attention. *Q. J. exp. Psychol.* **16**, 309-317.

Broadbent, D. E. and Gregory, M. (1964b). Accuracy of recognition for speech presented to the right and left ears. *Q. J. exp. Psychol.* **16**, 359-360.

Broadbent, D. E. and Gregory, M. (1965a). Effects of noise and of signal rate upon vigilance analysed by means of decision theory. *Hum. Factors* 7, 155-162.

Broadbent, D. E. and Gregory, M. (1965b). Some confirmatory results on age differences in memory for simultaneous stimulation. *Br. J. Psychol.* **56**, 77-80.

Broadbent, D. E. and Gregory, M. (1965c). On the interaction of *S–R* compatibility with other variables affecting reaction time. *Br. J. Psychol.* **56**, 61-67.

Broadbent, D. E. and Gregory, M. (1967a). Perception of emotionally toned words. *Nature, Lond.* **215**, 581-584.

Broadbent, D. E. and Gregory, M. (1967b). Psychological refractory period and the length of time required to make a decision. *Proc. R. Soc.* B. **168**, 181-193.

Brown, C. R. and Rubenstein, H. (1961). Test of the response bias explanation of word-frequency effect. *Science, N.Y.* **133**, 280-281.

Brown, D. R. (1953). Stimulus similarity and the anchoring of subjective scales. *Am. J. Psychol.* **66**, 199-214.

Brown, J. (1954). The nature of set-to-learn and of intra-material interference in immediate memory. *Q. J. exp. Psychol.* **6**, 141-148.

Brown, J. (1955). Immediate memory. Ph.D. Thesis, University of Cambridge.

Brown, J. (1958). Some tests of the decay theory of immediate memory. *Q. J. exp. Psychol.* **10**, 12-21.

Brown, J. (1960). Evidence for a selective process during perception of tachisto-scopically presented stimuli. *J. exp. Psychol.* **59**, 176-181.

Brown, W. P. (1961). Conceptions of perceptual defence. *Br. J. Psychol. Monograph Supplements* **23**, 106.

Brunswik, E. (1939). Probability as a determiner of rat behaviour. *J. exp. Psychol.* **25**, 175-197.

Bryden, M. P. (1962). Order of report in dichotic listening. *Can. J. Psychol.* **16**, 291-299.

Bryden, M. P. (1963). Ear preference in auditory perception. *J. exp. Psychol.* **65**, 103-105.

Bryden, M. P. (1964a). The manipulation of strategies of report in dichotic listening. *Can. J. Psychol.* **18**, 126-138.

Bryden, M. P. (1964b). Tachistoscopic recognition and cerebral dominance. *Percept. Mot. Skills.* **19**, 686.

Bryden, M. P. (1965). Tachistoscopic recognition, handedness and cerebral dominance. *Neuropsychol.* **3**, 1-8.

Bryden, M. P. (1966). Short-term memory for unbalanced dichotic lists. *Psychon. Sci.* **6**, 379-380.

Bryden, M. P. and Rainey, C. A. (1963). Left-right differences in tachistoscopic recognition. *J. exp. Psychol.* **66**, 568-571.

Buck, L. (1966). Reaction time as a measure of perceptual vigilance. *Psychol. Bull.* **65**, 291-304.

Buckner, D. N. and McGrath, J. J. (1963). A comparison of performances on simple and dual sensory mode vigilance tasks. *In* "Vigilance: a Symposium" (Buckner and McGrath, eds), McGraw-Hill, New York.

Bursill, A. E. (1958). The restriction of peripheral vision during exposure to hot and humid conditions. *Q. J. exp. Psychol.* **10**, 113-129.

Caird, W. K. (1964). Reverberatory activity and memory disorder. *Nature, Lond.* **201**, 1150.

Caird, W. K. and Inglis, J. (1961). The short-term storage of auditory and visual two channel digits by elderly patients with a memory disorder. *J. ment. Sci.* **107**, 1062-1069.

Callaway, E. and Stone, G. (1960). Re-evaluating the focus of attention. *In* "Drugs and Behaviour" (L. Uhr and J. G. Miller, eds), John Wiley, New York.

Campbell, D. T., Lewis, N. A. and Hunt, W. A. (1958). Context effects with judgmental language that is absolute, extensive, and extra-experimentally anchored. *J. exp. Psychol.* **55**, 220-228.

Cardozo, B. L. and Leopold, F. F. (1963). Human code transmission. Letters and digits compared on the basis of immediate memory error rates. *Ergonomics* **6**, 133-141.

Carlton, P. L. (1963). Cholinergic mechanisms in the control of behavior by the brain. *Psychol. Rev.* **70**, 19-39.

Chapman, D. W. (1932). The relative effects of determinate and indeterminate Aufgaben. *Am. J. Psychol.* **44**, 163-174.

Cherry, E. C. (1953). Some experiments on the recognition of speech with one and two ears. *J. acoust. Soc. Am.* **25**, 975-979.

Cherry, E. C. and Taylor, W. K. (1954). Some further experiments upon the recognition of speech, with one and two ears. *J. acoust. Soc. Am.* **26**, 554-559.

Chinn, R. McC. and Alluisi, E. A. (1964). Effect of three kinds of knowledge-of-results information on three measures of vigilance performance. *Percept. Mot. Skills* **18**, 901-912.

Chomsky, N. (1968). "Language and Mind". Harcourt, Brace and World, New York.

Christie, L. S. and Luce, R. D. (1956). Decision structure and time relations in simple choice behaviour. *Bull. math. Biophys.* **18**, 89-111.

Claridge, G. (1960). The excitation-inhibition balance in neurotics. *In* "Experiments in Personality, Vol. 2, Psychodiagnostics and Psychodynamics" (H. J. Eysenck, ed.), Routledge and Kegan Paul, London.

Clarke, F. R. (1957). Constant-ratio rule for confusion matrices in speech communication. *J. acoust. Soc. Am.* **29**, 715-720.

Colquhoun, W. P. (1960). Temperament, inspection efficiency and time of day. *Ergonomics* **3**, 377-378.

Colquhoun, W. P. (1961). The effect of unwanted signals on performance on a vigilance task. *Ergonomics* **4**, 41-51.

Colquhoun, W. P. (1962a). The effects of a small dose of alcohol and of certain other factors on performance on a vigilance task. *Bulletin Cent. Étud. Rech. Psychol.* **11**, 27-44.

Colquhoun, W. P. (1962b). Effects of hyoscine and meclozine on vigilance and short-term memory. *Br. J. industr. Med.* **19**, 287-296.

Colquhoun, W. P. (1966a). Training for vigilance: a comparison of different techniques. *Hum. Factors* **8**, 7-12.

Colquhoun, W. P. (1966b). The effect of "unwanted" signals on performance in a vigilance task: a reply to Jerison. *Ergonomics* **9**, 417-419.

Colquhoun, W. P. (1967). Sonar target detection as a decision process. *J. appl. Psychol.* **51**, 187-190.

Colquhoun, W. P. and Baddeley, A. D. (1964). Role of retest expectancy in vigilance decrement. *J. exp. Psychol.* **68**, 156-160.

Colquhoun, W. P. and Corcoran, D. W. J. (1964). The effects of time of day and social isolation on the relationship between temperament and performance. *Br. J. soc. clin. Psychol.* **3**, 226-231.

Colquhoun, W. P. and Baddeley, A. D. (1967). Influence of signal probability during pre-training on vigilance decrement. *J. exp. Psychol.* **73**, 153-155.

Colquhoun, W. P., Blake, M. J. F. and Edwards, R. S. (1968). Experimental studies of shift-work, I: a comparison of "rotating" and "stabilized" 4-hour shift systems. *Ergonomics* **11**, 437-453.

Conrad, R. (1958). Accuracy of recall using a keyset and telephone dial and the effect of a prefix digit. *J. appl. Psychol.* **42**, 285-288.

Conrad, R. (1962a). Practice, familiarity and reading rate for words and nonsense syllables. *Q. J. exp. Psychol.* **14**, 71-76.

Conrad, R. (1962b). An association between memory errors and errors due to acoustic masking of speech. *Nature, Lond.* **193**, 1314-1315.

Conrad, R. (1964). Acoustic confusions in immediate memory. *Br. J. Psychol.* **55**, 75-84.

Conrad, R. (1965). Order error in immediate recall of sequences. *J. verb. Learn. verb. Behav.* **4**, 161-169.

Conrad, R. (1966). The short-term memory factor in the design of data entry keyboards: an interface between short-term memory and S–R compatibility. *J. appl. Psychol.* **50**, 353-356.

Conrad, R. and Hille, B. A. (1958). The decay theory of immediate memory and paced recall. *Can. J. Psychol.* **12**, 1-6.

Conrad, R. and Hull, A. J. (1968). Input modality and the serial position curve in short-term memory. *Psychon. Sci.* **10**, 135-136.

Cooper, F. S., Delattre, P. C., Liberman, A. M., Borst, J. M. and Gerstman, L. J. (1952). Some experiments on the perception of synthetic speech sounds. *J. acoust. Soc. Am.* **24**, 597-606.

Corballis, M. C. (1966). Rehearsal and decay in immediate recall of visually and auditorily presented items. *Can. J. Psychol.* **20**, 43-51.

Corcoran, D. W. J. (1962). Noise and loss of sleep. *Q. J. exp. Psychol.* **14**, 178-182.

Corcoran, D. W. J. (1963a). Doubling the rate of signal presentation in a vigilance task during sleep deprivation. *J. appl. Psychol.* **47**, 412-415.

Corcoran, D. W. J. (1963b). Individual differences in performance after loss of sleep. Ph.D. Thesis, University of Cambridge, Cambridge.

Corcoran, D. W. J. (1964). Changes in heart-rate and performance as a result of loss of sleep. *Br. J. Psychol.* **55**, 307-314.

Corcoran, D. W. J. (1965). Personality and the inverted-*U* relation. *Br. J. Psychol.* **56**, 267-273.

Costa, L. D., Horwitz, M. and Vaughan, H. G. Jr. (1966). Effects of stimulus uncertainty and S–R compatibility on speed of digit coding. *J. exp. Psychol.* **72**, 895-900.

Costello, C. G. (1961). Constant errors in the measurement of kinaesthetic figural after-effects. *Am. J. Psychol.* **74**, 473-474.

Craik, F. I. M. (1965). The nature of the age decrement in performance on diochotic listening tasks. *Q. J. exp. Psychol.* **17**, 228-240.

Craik, F. I. M. (1968). Two components in free recall. *J. verb. Learn. verb. Behav.* **7**, 996-1004.

Creamer, L. R. (1963). Event uncertainty, psychological refractory period, and human data processing. *J. exp. Psychol.* **66**, 187-194.

Cross, D. V., Lane, H. L. and Sheppard, W. C. (1965). Identification and discrimination functions for a visual continuum and their relation to the motor theory of speech perception. *J. exp. Psychol.* **70**, 63-74.

Crossman, E. R. F. W. (1953). Entropy and choice-time: the effect of frequency unbalance on choice response. *Q. J. exp. Psychol.* **5**, 41-51.

Crossman, E. R. F. W. (1955). The measurement of discriminability. *Q. J. exp. Psychol.* **7**, 176-195.

Crossman, E. R. F. W. (1956). The information-capacity of the human operator in symbolic and non-symbolic control processes. *In* "The Application of Information Theory to Human Operator Problems" (J. Draper, ed.), W.R.(D) Report No. 2/56 Ministry of Supply.

Crossman, E. R. F. W. (1960). Information and serial order in human immediate memory. *In* "Information Theory" (C. Cherry, ed.), Butterworth, London.

Crowder, R. G. (1967). Prefix effects in immediate memory. *Can. J. Psychol.* **21**, 450-461.

Dale, H. C. A. (1967). Familiarity and free recall. *Q. J. exp. Psychol.* **19**, 103-108.

Dale, H. C. A. (1968). Weighing evidence: an attempt to assess the efficiency of the human operator. *Ergonomics* **11**, 215-230.

Dale, H. C. A. and Baddeley, A. D. (1962). Alternatives in testing recognition memory. *Nature, Lond.* **196**, 93-94.

Dale, H. C. A. and Gregory, M. (1966). Evidence of semantic coding in short-term memory. *Psychon. Sci.* 5, 75-76.

Dale, H. C. A. and McGlaughlin, A. (1968). Acoustic similarity and RI in PAL. *Psychon. Sci.* 13, 225-226.

Dallett, K. M. (1966). Effects of within list and between list acoustic similarity on the learning and retention of paired associates. *J. exp. Psychol.* 72, 667-677.

Dardano, J. F. (1962). Relationships of intermittent noise, intersignal interval, and skin conductance to vigilance behaviour. *J. appl. Psychol.* 46, 106-114.

Darwin, C. J. (1969). The relationship between auditory perception and cerebral dominance. Ph.D. thesis, University of Cambridge.

Davidon, R. S. (1962). Relevance and category scales of judgment. *Br. J. Psychol.* 53, 373-380.

Davies, D. R. and Hockey, G. R. J. (1966). The effects of noise and doubling the signal frequency on individual differences in visual vigilance performance. *Br. J. Psychol.* 57, 381-389.

Davies, D. R., Hockey, G. R. J. and Taylor, A. (1969). Varied auditory stimulation temperament differences and vigilance performance. *Br. J. Psychol.* 60, 453-457.

Davies, D. R. and Krkovic, A. (1965). Skin-conductance, alpha activity and vigilance. *Am. J. Psychol.* 78, 304-306.

Davies, H., Silverman, S. R. and McAuliffe, D. R. (1951). Some observations on pitch and frequency. *J. acoust. Soc. Am.* 23, 40-42.

Davis, R. (1956). The limits of the "psychological refractory period". *Q. J. exp. Psychol.* 8, 24-38.

Davis, R. (1957). The human operator as a single-channel information system. *Q. J. exp. Psychol.* 9, 119-129.

Davis, R. (1959). The role of "attention" in the psychological refractory period. *Q. J. exp. Psychol.* 11, 211-220.

Davis, R. (1965). Expectancy and intermittency. *Q. J. exp. Psychol.* 17, 75-78.

Davis, R., Moray, N. and Treisman, A. M. (1961a). Imitative responses and the rate of gain of information. *Q. J. exp. Psychol.* 13, 78-89.

Davis, R., Sutherland, N. S. and Judd, B. R. (1961b). Information content in recognition and recall. *J. exp. Psychol.* 61, 422-429.

Deese, J. (1955). Some problems in the theory of vigilance. *Psychol. Rev.* 62, 359-368.

Deese, J. (1960). Frequency of usage and number of words in free recall: the role of association. *Psychol. Rep.* 7, 337-344.

Deutsch, J. A. and Deutsch, D. (1963). Attention: some theoretical considerations. *Psychol. Rev.* 70, 80-90.

Deutsch, J. A. and Deutsch, D. (1967). Comments on "selective attention: perception or response?". *Q. J. exp. Psychol.* 19, 362-363.

Dodwell, P. C. (1964). Some factors affecting the hearing of words presented dichotically. *Can. J. Psychol.* 18, 72-91.

Donders, F. C. (1868). Die Schnelligkeit psychischer Processe. *Arch. Anat. Physiol., Leipzig* 657-681.

Drew, G. C., Colquhoun, W. P. and Long, H. A. (1959). Effect of small doses of alcohol on a skill resembling driving. M.R.C. Memorandum No. 38, H.M.S.O., London.

Eason, R. G., Beardshall, A., and Jaffee, S. (1965). Performance and physiological indicants of activation in a vigilance situation. *Percept. Mot. Skills* 20, 3-13.

Easterbrook, J. A. (1959). The effect of emotion on cue utilization and the organization of behaviour. *Psychol. Rev.* 66, 183-201.

Edwards, W. (1954). The theory of decision making. *Psychol. Bull.* 51, 380-417.

Edwards, W. (1956). Reward probability, amount, and information as determiners of sequential two-alternative decisions. *J. exp. Psychol.* **52**, 177-188.

Egan, J. P. (1958). Recognition memory and the operating characteristic. Indiana University: Hearing and Communication Laboratory, Technical Note AFCRC-TN-58-51.

Egan, J. P., Carterette, E. C. and Thwing, E. J. (1954). Some factors affecting multi-channel listening. *J. acoust. Soc. Am.* **26**, 774-782.

Egan, J. P., Schulman, A. I. and Greenberg, G. Z. (1959). Operating characteristics determined by binary decisions and by ratings. *J. acoust. Soc. Am.* **31**, 768-773.

Egan, J. P., Greenberg, G. Z. and Schulman, A. I. (1961). Operating characteristics, signal detectability, and the method of free response. *J. acoust. Soc. Am.* **33**, 993-1007.

Egeth, H. (1967). Selective attention. *Psychol. Bull.* **67**, 41-57.

Elithorn, A. (1961). Central intermittency: some further observations. *Q. J. exp. Psychol.* **13**, 240-247.

Elithorn, A. and Barnett, T. J. (1967). Apparent individual differences in channel capacity. *Acta Psychol.* **27**, 75-83.

Elliott, E. (1957). Auditory Vigilance Tasks. *Adv. Sci.* **14**, 393-9.

Emmerich, D. S., Goldenbaum, D. M., Haden, D. L., Hoffman, L. S. and Treffts, J. L. (1965). Meaningfulness as a variable in dichotic hearing. *J. exp. Psychol.* **69**, 433-436.

Eriksen, C. W. and Steffy, R. A. (1964). Short-term memory and retroactive interference in visual perception. *J. exp. Psychol.* **68**, 423-434.

Falmagne, J. C. (1965). Stochastic models for choice reaction time with applications to experimental results. *J. math. Psychol.* **2**, 77-124.

Faulkner, T. W. (1962). Variability of performance in a vigilance task. *J. appl. Psychol.* **46**, 325-328.

Fitts, P. M. (1966). Cognitive aspects of information processing: III. Set for speed versus accuracy. *J. exp. Psychol.* **71**, 849-857.

Fitts, P. M. and Seeger, C. M. (1953). *S–R* compatibility: spatial characteristics of stimulus and response codes. *J. exp. Psychol.* **46**, 199-210.

Fitts, P. M. and Deininger, R. L. (1954). *S–R* compatibility: correspondence among paired elements within stimulus and response codes. *J. exp. Psychol.* **48**, 483-492.

Fitts, P. M. and Switzer, G. (1962). Cognitive aspects of information processing: I. The familiarity of *S–R* sets and subsets. *J. exp. Psychol.* **63**, 321-329.

Fitts, P. M. and Biederman, I. (1965). *S–R* compatibility and information reduction. *J. exp. Psychol.* **69**, 408-412.

Fitts, P. M., Weinstein, M., Rappaport, M., Anderson, N. S., and Leonard, J. A. (1956). Stimulus correlates of visual pattern recognition: a probability approach. *J. exp. Psychol.* **51**, 1-11.

Fitts, P. M., Peterson, J. R. and Wolpe, G. (1963). Cognitive aspects of information processing: II. Adjustments to stimulus redundancy. *J. exp. Psychol.* **65**, 423-432.

Flanagan, J. L. (1965). "Speech Analysis, Synthesis and Perception", Springer-Verlag, New York.

Fletcher, H. (1953). "Speech and Hearing in Communication", Van Nostrand, New York.

Floyd, A., Griggs, G. D. and Baker, R. A. (1961). Role of expectancy in auditory vigilance. *Percept. Mot. Skills* **13**, 131-134.

Foster, H. (1962). The operation of set in a visual search task. *J. exp. Psychol.* **63**, 74-83.

Fraisse, P. (1957). La période réfractaire psychologique (The psychological refractory period). *Ann. Psychol.* **57**, 315-328.

Fraser, D. C. (1953). The relation of an environmental variable to performance in a prolonged visual task. *Q. J. exp. Psychol.* **5**, 31-32.

Fraser, D. C. (1957). A study of vigilance and fatigue. Doctorial thesis, University of Edinburgh.

Fraser, D. C. (1958). Decay of immediate memory with age. *Nature, Lond.* **182**, 1163.

Gaito, J. and Zavala, A. (1964). Neurochemistry and learning. *Psychol. Bull.* **61**, 45-62.

Galanter, E. and Holman, G. L. (1967). Some invariances of the isosensitivity function and their implications for the utility function of money. *J. exp. Psychol.* **73**, 333-339.

Garner, W. R. (1954). Context effects and the validity of loudness scales. *J. exp. Psychol.* **48**, 218-224.

Garvey, W. D., Taylor, F. V. and Newlin, E. P. (1959). The use of artificial signals to enhance monitoring performance. U.S. Naval Res. Lab. Rep. No. 5269.

Gerard, R. W. (1963). The material basis of memory. *J. verb. Learn. verb. Behav.* **2**, 22-33.

Gerbrandt, L. K. (1965). Neural systems of response release and control. *Psychol. Bull.* **64**, 113-123.

Gill, M. B., *et al.* (1964). Falling efficiency at sorting cards during acclimatization at 19,000 ft. *Nature, Lond.* **203**, 436.

Glanzer, M. and Cunitz, A. R. (1966). Two storage mechanisms in free recall. *J. verb. Learn. verb. Behav.* **5**, 351-360.

Glucksberg, S. (1962). The influence of strength of drive on functional fixedness and perceptual recognition. *J. exp. Psychol.* **63**, 36-41.

Goggin, J. (1966). Retroactive and proactive inhibition in the short-term retention of paired associates. *J. verb. Learn. verb. Behav.* **5**, 526-535.

Goldiamond, I. and Hawkins, W. F. (1958). Vexierversuch: the log relationship between word-frequency and recognition obtained in the absence of stimulus words. *J. exp. Psychol.* **56**, 457-463.

Gray, J. A. and Wedderburn, A. A. (1960). Grouping strategies with simultaneous stimuli. *Q. J. exp. Psychol.* **12**, 180-184.

Green, B. F. and Anderson, L. K. (1956). Colour coding in a visual search task. *J. exp. Psychol.* **51**, 19-24.

Green, D. M. (1960). Psychoacoustics and detection theory. *J. acoust. Soc. Am.* **32**, 1189-1203.

Green, D. M. and Birdsall, T. G. (1964). The effect of vocabulary size on articulation score. *In* "Signal Detection and Recognition by Human Observers" (J. A. Swets, ed.), pp. 609-619, John Wiley, New York.

Green, D. M. and Swets, J. A. (1966). "Signal Detection Theory and Psychophysics", John Wiley, New York.

Green, D. M., Birdsall, T. G. and Tanner, W. P. (1957). Signal detection as a function of signal intensity and duration. *J. acoust. Soc. Am.* **29**, 523-531.

Griew, S. (1958). Information gain in tasks involving different stimulus-response relationships. *Nature, Lond.* **182**, 1819.

Gruber, A. (1964). Sensory alternation and performance in a vigilance task. *Hum. Factors* **6**, 3-12.

Haber, R. N. (1966). Nature of the effect of set on perception. *Psychol. Rev.* **73**, 335-351.

Haider, M. (1967). Vigilance, attention, expectancy and cortical evoked potentials. *Acta Psychol.* **27**, 246-252.

Hamilton, P. (1967). Selective attention in multi-source monitoring tasks. Ph.D. Thesis, University of Dundee. See also *J. exp. Psychol.* **83**, 34-37.

Hardy, G. R. and Legge, D. (1968). Cross-modal induction in changes in sensory thresholds. *Q. J. exp. Psychol.* **20**, 20-29.

Harris, C. S. and Haber, R. N. (1963). Selective attention and coding in visual perception. *J. exp. Psychol.* **65**, 328-333.

Harvey, O. J. and Campbell, D. T. (1963). Judgements of weight as affected by adaptation range, adaptation duration, magnitude of unlabeled anchor, and judgemental language. *J. exp. Psychol.* **65**, 12-21.

Hebb, D. O. (1949). "The Organization of Behaviour", John Wiley, New York.

Hebb, D. O. (1961). Distinctive features of learning in the higher animal. *In* "Brain Mechanism and Learning" (J. F. Delafresnaye, ed.), Oxford University Press, London.

Hellyer, S. (1962). Supplementary report: frequency of stimulus presentation and short-term decrement in recall. *J. exp. Psychol.* **64**, 650.

Hellyer, S. (1963). Stimulus-response coding and amount of information as determinants of reaction time. *J. exp. Psychol.* **65**, 521-522.

Helper, M. M. (1957). The effects of noise on work output and physiological activation. U.S. Army Med. Res. Lab. Report No. 270.

Helson, H. (1948). Adaptation-level as a basis for a quantitative theory of frames of reference. *Psychol. Rev.* **55**, 297-313.

Helson, H. (1964). "Adaptation-level Theory", Harper and Row, New York.

Helson, H. and Nash, M. C. (1960). Anchor, contrast and paradoxical distance effects. *J. exp. Psychol.* **59**, 113-121.

Heron, A. (1956). A two-part personality measure for use as a research criterion. *Br. J. Psychol.* **47**, 243-251.

Heron, A. and Craik, F. I. M. (1964). Age differences in cumulative learning of meaningful and meaningless material. *Scand. J. Psychol.* **5**, 209-217.

Hick, W. E. (1952). On the rate of gain of information. *Q. J. exp. Psychol.* **4**, 11-26.

Hockey, G. R. J. (1970). Signal probability and spatial location as possible bases for increased selectivity in noise. *Q. J. exp. Psychol.* **22**, 37-42.

Hodge, M. H. (1959). The effect of irrelevant information upon complex discrimination. *J. exp. Psychol.* **57**, 1-5.

Hohle, R. H. (1965). Inferred components of reaction times as functions of foreperiod duration. *J. exp. Psychol.* **69**, 382-386.

Holland, J. G. (1957). Technique for behavioural analysis of human observing. *Science, N.Y.* **125**, 348-350.

Holland, J. G. (1958). Human vigilance. *Science, N.Y.* **128**, 61-67.

Hörmann, H. and Todt, E. (1960). Lärm and lernen. (Noise and learning.) *Z. exp. angew. Psychol.* **7**, 422-426.

Hörmann, H. and Osterkamp, U. (1966). Uber den Einfluss von kontinuierlichem Lärm auf die Organisation von Gedachnisinhalten. (On the influence of continuous noise on the organization of memory contents.) *Z. exp. angew. Psychol.* **13**, 31-38.

Howe, M. J. A. (1965). Intra-list differences in short-term memory. *Q. J. exp. Psychol.* **17**, 338-342.

Hudson, L. (1966). "Contrary Imaginations", Methuen, London.

Huggins, A. W. F. (1964). Distortion of the temporal pattern of speech: interruption and alternation. *J. acoust. Soc. Am.* **36**, 1055-1064.

R

Hull, C. L. (1952). "A Behaviour System", Yale University Press, New Haven, Connecticut, U.S.A.

Hunt, E. B. (1962). "Concept Learning. An Information Processing Problem", John Wiley, New York.

Hyman, R. (1953). Stimulus information as a determinant of reaction time. *J. exp. Psychol.* **45**, 188-196.

Imai, S. and Garner, W. R. (1965). Discriminability and preference for attributes in free and constrained classification. *J. exp. Psychol.* **69**, 596-608.

Ingleby, J. D. (1969). Decision-making processes in human perception and memory. Ph.D. Thesis, University of Cambridge, Cambridge.

Inglis, J. (1964). Influence of motivation perception and attention on age-related changes in short-term memory. *Nature, Lond.* **204**, 103-104.

Inglis, J. and Sanderson, R. E. (1961). Successive responses to simultaneous stimulation in elderly patients with memory disorder. *J. abnorm. soc. Psychol.* **62**, 709-712.

Inglis, J. and Caird, W. K. (1963). Age differences in successive responses to simultaneous stimulation. *Can. J. Psychol.* **17**, 98-105.

Inglis, J. and Ankus, M. N. (1965). Effects of age on short-term storage and serial rote learning. *Br. J. Psychol.* **56**, 183-195.

Inglis, J. and Tansey, C. L. (1967a). Perception and short-term storage in dichotic listening performance. *Psychon. Sci.* **7**, 273-274.

Inglis, J. and Tansey, C. L. (1967b). Age differences and scoring differences in dichotic listening performance. *J. Psychol.* **66**, 325-332.

Jensen, A. R. and Rohwer, W. D. Jr. (1966). The Stroop Color-Word Test: A review. *Acta Psychol.* **25**, 36-93.

Jerison, H. J. (1957). Performance on a simple vigilance task in noise and quiet. *J. acoust. Soc. Am.* **29**, 1163-1165.

Jerison, H. J. (1959). Effects of noise on human performance. *J. appl. Psychol.* **43**, 96-101.

Jerison, H. J. (1966). Remarks on Colquhoun's "The effect of 'unwanted' signals on performance in a vigilance task". *Ergonomics* **9**, 413-416.

Jerison, H. J. (1967a). Activation and long term performance. *Acta Psychol.* **27**, 373-389.

Jerison, H. J. (1967b). Signal detection theory in the analysis of human vigilance. *Hum. Factors* **9**, 285-288.

Jerison, H. J. and Wallis, R. A. (1957a). Experiments on vigilance II. One-clock and three-clock monitoring. USAF WADC Tech. Rep. TR-57-206.

Jerison, H. J. and Wallis, R. A. (1957b). Experiments on vigilance III. Performance on a simple vigilance task in noise and quiet. USAF WADC Tech. Rep. TR-57-318.

Jerison, H. J. and Pickett, R. M. (1963). Vigilance: a review and re-evaluation. *Hum. Factors* **5**, 211-238.

Jerison, H. J. and Wing, J. F. (1963). Human vigilance and operant behavior. *In* "Vigilance: a Symposium" (Buckner and McGrath, eds), McGraw-Hill, New York.

Jerison, H. J. and Pickett, R. M. (1964). Vigilance: The importance of the elicited observing rate. *Science, N.Y.* **143**, 970-971.

Jerison, H. J., Pickett, R. M. and Stenson, H. H. (1965). The elicited observing rate and decision processes in vigilance. *Hum. Factors* **7**, 107-128.

Johnson, D. R. and Robinson, D. W. (1967). The subjective evaluation of sonic bangs. *Acustica* **18**, 241-258.

Johnson, E. M. and Payne, M. C. Jr. (1966). Vigilance: effects of frequency of knowledge of results. *J. appl. Psychol.* **50**, 33-34.

Johnson, R. C., Thomson, C. W. and Frincke, G. (1960). Word values, word frequency, and visual duration thresholds. *Psychol. Rev.* **67**, 332-342.

Johnston, W. A., Howell, W. C. and Goldstein, I. L. (1966). Human vigilance as a function of signal frequency and stimulus density. *J. exp. Psychol.* **72**, 736-743.

Johnston, W. A., Howell, W. C. and Zajkowski, M. M. (1967). Regulation of attention to complex displays. *J. exp. Psychol.* **73**, 481-482.

Jones, F. N. and Woskow, M. J. (1966). Some effects of context on the slope in magnitude estimation. *J. exp. Psychol.* **71**, 170-176.

Kay, H. and Poulton, E. C. (1951). Anticipation in memorizing. *Br. J. Psychol.* **42**, 34-41.

Keppel, G. (1965). Problems of method in the study of short-term memory. *Psychol. Bull.* **63**, 1-13.

Keppel, G. and Underwood, B. J. (1962). Proactive inhibition in short-term retention of single items. *J. verb. Learn. verb. Behav.* **1**, 153-161.

Kerr M., Mingay, R. and Elithorn, A. (1963). Cerebral dominance in reaction time responses. *Br. J. Psychol.* **54**, 325-336.

Kerr, M., Mingay, R. and Elithorn, A. (1965). Patterns of reaction time responses. *Br. J. Psychol.* **56**, 53-59.

Kimble, D. P. (1967). The Organization of Recall Vol. 2. Proceedings of the second conference on Learning, Remembering and Forgetting. New York Academy of Sciences, New York.

Kimble, D. P. (1968). Hippocampus and internal inhibition. *Psychol. Bull.* **70**, 285-295.

Kimura, D. (1961a). Some effects of temporal-lobe damage on auditory perception. *Can. J. Psychol.* **15**, 156-165.

Kimura, D. (1961b). Cerebral dominance and the perception of verbal stimuli. *Can. J. Psychol.* **15**, 166-171.

Kimura, D. (1963). Right temporal-lobe damage: perception of unfamiliar stimuli after damage. *Arch. Neurol. Chicago* **8**, 264-271.

Kimura, D. (1964). Left–right differences in the perception of melodies. *Q. J. exp. Psychol.* **16**, 355-358.

Kimura, D. (1966). Dual functional asymmetry of the brain in visual perception. *Neuropsychol.* **4**, 275-285.

Kimura, D. (1967). Functional asymmetry of the brain in dichotic listening. *Cortex* **3**, 163-178.

Kimura, D. (1970). Asymmetries in perception related to hemispheric differentiation. *In* "Hemispheric Asymmetry of Function" (M. Kinsbourne, ed.), Tavistock, London. (In press.)

Kintsch, W. (1968). An experimental analysis of single stimulus tests and multiple-choice tests of recognition memory. *J. exp. Psychol.* **76**, 1-6.

Kirchner, W. K. (1958). Age differences in short-term retention of rapidly changing information. *J. exp. Psychol.* **55**, 352-358.

Klein, G. S. (1964). Semantic power measured through the interference of words with colour-naming. *Am. J. Psychol.* **77**, 576-588.

Kleinsmith, L. J. and Kaplan, S. (1963). Paired associate learning as a function of arousal and interpolated interval. *J. exp. Psychol.* **65**, 190-193.

Kornblum, S. (1967). Choice reaction time for repetitions and non-repetitions: A re-examination of the information hypothesis. *Acta Psychol.* **27**, 178-187.

Koster, W. G. and Bekker, J. A. M. (1967). Some experiments on refractoriness. *Acta Psychol.* **27**, 64-70.

Ladefoged, P. and Broadbent, D. E. (1957). Information conveyed by vowels. *J. acoust. Soc. Am.* **29**, 98-104.

Laming, D. R. J. (1968). "Information Theory of Choice-Reaction Times", Academic Press, London and New York.

Lane, H. L. (1965). The motor theory of speech perception: a critical review. *Psychol. Rev.* **72**, 275-309.

Larkin, W. D. (1965). Rating scales in detection experiments. *J. acoust. Soc. Am.* **37**, 748-749.

Lawrence, D. H. and Coles, G. R. (1954). Accuracy of recognition with alternatives before and after the stimulus. *J. exp. Psychol.* **47**, 208-214.

Lawrence, D. H. and LaBerge, D. L. (1956). Relationship between recognition accuracy and order of reporting stimulus dimensions. *J. exp. Psychol.* **51**, 12-18.

Lawson, E. A. (1966). Decisions concerning the rejected channel. *Q. J. exp. Psychol.* **18**, 260-265.

Leakey, D. M., Sayers, B. M. and Cherry, E. C. (1958). Binaural fusion of low- and high-frequency sounds. *J. acoust. Soc. Am.* **30**, 222.

Lenneberg, E. (1962). Understanding language without ability to speak: a case report. *J. abnorm. soc. Psychol.* **65**, 419-425.

Leonard, J. A. (1953). Advance information in sensorimotor skills. *Q. J. exp. Psychol.* **5**, 141-149.

Leonard, J. A. (1958). Partial advance information in a choice reaction task. *Br. J. Psychol.* **49**, 89-96.

Leonard, J. A. (1959). Tactual choice reactions: I. *Q. J. exp. Psychol.* **11**, 76-83.

Levi, L. (ed.) (1967). Emotional stress. *Försvarsmedicin* 3, Suppl. 2.

Levine, J. M. (1966). The effects of values and costs on the detection and identification of signals in auditory vigilance. *Hum. Factors* **8**, 525-537.

Liberman, A. M. (1957). Some results of research on speech perception. *J. acoust. Soc. Am.* **29**, 117-123.

Liberman, A. M., Cooper, F. S., Harris, K. S., MacNeilage, P. F. and Studdert-Kennedy, M. (1967a). Some observations on a model for speech perception. *In* "Models for the Perception of Speech and Visual Form", (Weiant Wathen-Dunn, ed.), pp. 68-87, MIT Press, Cambridge, Mass., U.S.A.

Liberman, A. M., Cooper, F. S., Shankweiler, D. P. and Studdert-Kennedy, M. (1967b). Perception of the speech code. *Psychol. Rev.* **74**, 431-461.

Licklider, J. C. R. (1956). Auditory frequency analysis. *In* "Information Theory" (E. C. Cherry, ed.), Butterworths, London.

Loeb, M. and Binford, J. R. (1964). Vigilance for auditory intensity changes as a function of preliminary feedback and confidence level. *Hum. Factors* **6**, 445-458.

Loeb, M. and Jeantheau, G. (1958). The influence of noxious environmental stimuli on vigilance. *J. Appl. Psychol.* **42**, 47-49.

Loess, H. (1964). Proactive inhibition in short-term memory. *J. verb. Learn. verb. Behav.* **3**, 362-368.

Lollo, V. di (1964). Contrast effects in the judgment of lifted weights. *J. exp. Psychol.* **68**, 383-387.

Lollo, V. di and Cassedy, J. H. (1965). Graded contrast effects in the judgment of lifted weights. *J. exp. Psychol.* **70**, 234-235.

Loveless, N. E. (1957). Signal detection with simultaneous visual and auditory presentation. FPRC Report No. 1027.

Luce, R. D. (1959). "Individual Choice Behavior", John Wiley, New York.

Luce, R. D. (1960). Detection thresholds: a problem reconsidered. *Science, N.Y.* **132**, 1495.

Luce, R. D. (1963). A threshold theory for simple detection experiments. *Psychol. Rev.* **70**, 61-79.

Mackay, H. A. and Inglis, J. (1963). The effect of age on a short-term auditory storage process. *Gerontologia* **8**, 193-200.

Mackintosh, N. J. (1965). Selective attention in animal discrimination learning. *Psychol. Bull.* **64**, 124-150.

Mackworth, J. F. (1962a). Presentation rate and immediate memory. *Can. J. Psychol.* **16**, 42-47.

Mackworth, J. F. (1962b). The effect of display time upon the recall of digits. *Can. J. Psychol.* **16**, 48-54.

Mackworth, J. F. (1962c). The visual image and the memory trace. *Can. J. Psychol.* **16**, 55-59.

Mackworth, J. F. (1963a). The effect of intermittent signal probability upon vigilance. *Can. J. Psychol.* **17**, 82-89.

Mackworth, J. F. (1963b). The duration of the visual image. *Can. J. Psychol.* **17**, 62-81.

Mackworth, J. F. (1963c). The relation between the visual image and post-perceptual immediate memory. *J. verb. Learn. verb. Behav.* **2**, 75-85.

Mackworth, J. F. (1964a). The effect of true and false knowledge of results on the detectability of signals in a vigilance task. *Can. J. Psychol.* **18**, 106-117.

Mackworth, J. F. (1964b). Performance decrement in vigilance, threshold, and high-speed perceptual motor tasks. *Can. J. Psychol.* **18**, 209-223.

Mackworth, J. F. (1964c). Interference and decay in very short-term memory. *J. verb. Learn. verb. Behav.* **3**, 300-308.

Mackworth, J. F. (1964d). Auditory short-term memory. *Can. J. Psychol.* **18**, 292-303.

Mackworth, J. F. (1965a). Deterioration of signal detectability during a vigilance task as a function of background event rate. *Psychon. Sci.* **3**, 421-422.

Mackworth, J. F. (1965b). Decision interval and signal detectability in a vigilance task. *Can. J. Psychol.* **19**, 111-117.

Mackworth, J. F. and Taylor, M. M. (1963). The *d'* measure of signal detectability in vigilance-like situations. *Can. J. Psychol.* **17**, 302-325.

Mackworth, N. H. (1950). Researches in the Measurement of Human Performance. *MRC Special Report Series* No. 268, H.M. Stationery Office.

Mackworth, N. H., Kaplan, I. T. and Metlay, W. (1964). Eye movements during vigilance. *Percept. Mot. Skills* **18**, 397-402.

Malmo, R. B. and Surwillo, W. W. (1960). Sleep deprivation: changes in performance and physiological indicants of activation. *Psychol. Monogr.* **74**. (Whole No. 502.)

Maltzman, I., Kantor, W. and Langdon, B. (1966). Immediate and delayed retention, arousal and the orienting and defense reflexes. *Psychon. Sci.* **6**, 445-446.

Martin, E. (1965). Transfer of verbal paired associates. *Psychol. Rev.* **72**, 327-343.

Mathes, R. C. and Miller, R. L. (1947). Phase effects in monaural perception. *J. acoust. Soc. Am.* **19**, 780-797.

McCormack, P. D. (1962). A two-factor theory of vigilance. *Br. J. Psychol.* **53**, 357-364.

McCormack, P. D. (1967). A two-factor theory of vigilance in the light of recent studies. *Acta Psychol.* **27**, 400-409.

McGill, W. J. (1963). Stochastic Latency Mechanisms. *In* "Handbook of Mathematical Psychology" (R. D. Luce, R. R. Bush and E. Galanter, eds), Vol. 1, John Wiley, New York.

McGill, W. J. and Gibbon, J. (1965). The general gamma distribution and reaction times. *J. math. Psychol.* **2**, 1-18.

McGinnies, E. (1949). Emotionality and perceptual defense. *Psychol. Rev.* **56**, 244-251.

McGrath, J. J. (1963). Irrelevant stimulation and vigilance performance. *In* "Vigilance: a Symposium" (Buckner and McGrath, eds), McGraw-Hill, New York.

McGrath, J. J. (1965). Performance sharing in an audio-visual vigilance task. *Hum. Factors* **7**, 141-153.

McGrath, J. J. and Harabedian, A. (1963). Signal detection as a function of inter-signal interval. *In* "Vigilance: a Symposium" (Buckner and McGrath, eds), McGraw-Hill, New York.

Medawar, P. B. (1966). "The Art of the Soluble", Methuen, London.

Melton, A. W. (1963). Implications of short-term memory for a general theory of memory. *J. verb. Learn. verb. Behav.* **2**, 1-21.

Melton, A. W. and Irwin, J. McQ. (1940). The influence of degree of interpolated learning on retroactive inhibition and the overt transfer of specific responses. *Am. J. Psychol.* **53**, 173-203.

Melton, A. W. and Lackum, W. J. von (1941). Retroactive and proactive inhibition in retention: evidence for a two-factor theory of retroactive inhibition. *Am. J. Psychol.* **54**, 157-173.

Micko, H. C. (1966). Vigilance: Arousal *vs* reinforcement. *Q. J. exp. Psychol.* **18**, 39-46.

Miller, G. A. (1956). The magical number seven, plus or minus two. *Psychol. Rev.* **63**, 81-97.

Miller, G. A. and Chomsky, N. (1963). Finitary models of language users. *In* "Handbook of Mathematical Psychology" (R. D. Luce, R. R. Bush and E. Galanter, eds), Vol. 2, pp. 419-491, John Wiley, New York.

Miller, G. A., Heise, G. A. and Lichten, W. (1951). The intelligibility of speech as a function of the context of the test materials. *J. exp. Psychol.* **41**, 329-335.

Mills, C. H. G. and Robinson, D. W. (1961). The subjective rating of motor vehicle noise. *Engineer* **211**, 1070-1074.

Milner, B. (1962). Laterality effects in audition. *In* "Interhemispheric relations and cerebral dominance" (V. Mountcastle, ed.), Johns Hopkins, Baltimore, Md., U.S.A.

Minard, J. G. (1965). Response-bias interpretation of "perceptual defense": a selective review and evaluation of recent research. *Psychol. Rev.* **72**, 74-88.

Mirsky, A. F. and Rosvold, H. E. (1960). The use of psychoactive drugs as a neuro-psychological tool in studies of attention in man. *In* "Drugs and Behaviour" (L. Uhr and J. G. Miller, eds) pp. 375-392, John Wiley, New York.

Mishkin, M. and Forgays, D. (1952). Word recognition as a function of temporal locus. *J. exp. Psychol.* **43**, 43-48.

Montague, W. E. (1965). Effect of irrelevant information on a complex auditory discrimination task. *J. exp. Psychol.* **69**, 230-236.

Montague, W. E. and Webber, C. E. (1965). Effects of knowledge of results and differential monetary reward on six uninterrupted hours of monitoring. *Hum. Factors* **7**, 173-180.

Montague, W. E., Webber, C. E. and Adams, J. A. (1965). The effects of signal and response complexity on eighteen hours of visual monitoring. *Hum. Factors* **7**, 163-172.

Monty, R. A. (1962). Effects of post-detection response complexity on subsequent monitoring behavior. *Hum. Factors* **4**, 201-208.

Moray, N. (1959). Attention in dichotic listening: affective cues and the influence of instructions. *Q. J. exp. Psychol.* **11**, 56-60.

Moray, N. (1960). Broadbent's filter theory: postulate *H* and the problem of switching time. *Q. J. exp. Psychol.* **12**, 214-220.

Moray, N. (1967). Where is capacity limited? A survey and a model. *Acta Psychol.* **27**, 84-92.

Moray, N. and Barnett, T. J. (1965). Stimulus presentation and methods of scoring in short-term memory experiments. *Acta Psychol.* **24**, 253-263.

Moray, N. and Jordan, A. (1966). Practice and compatibility in two-channel short-term memory. *Psychon. Sci.* **4**, 427-428.

Moray, N. and O'Brien, T. (1967). Signal-detection theory applied to selective listening. *J. acoust. Soc. Am.* **42**, 765-772.

Moray, N., Bates, A. and Barnett, T. (1965). Experiments on the four-eared man. *J. acoust. Soc. Am.* **38**, 196-201.

Morin, R. W., Forrin, B. and Archer, W. (1961). Information processing behaviour: the role of irrelevant stimulus information. *J. exp. Psychol.* **61**, 89-96.

Morton, J. (1964). The effects of context on the visual duration of threshold for words. *Br. J. Psychol.* **55**, 165-180.

Morton, J. (1968a). A retest of the response bias explanation of the word-frequency effect. *Br. J. math. statist. Psychol.* **21**, 21-33.

Morton, J. (1968b). Selective interference in immediate recall. *Psychon. Sci.* **12**, 75-76.

Morton, J. (1969a). Categories of interference: verbal mediation and conflict in card sorting. *Br. J. Psychol.* **60**, 329-346.

Morton, J. (1969b). Interaction of information in word recognition. *Psychol. Rev.* **76**, 165-178.

Morton, J. and Broadbent, D. E. (1967). Passive versus active recognition models or is your homunculus really necessary? *In* "Models for the Perception of Speech and Visual Form" (Weiant Wathen-Dunn, ed.), pp. 103-110, Massachusetts Institute of Technology Press, Cambridge, Mass., U.S.A.

Mowbray, G. H. (1960). Choice reaction times for skilled responses. *Q. J. exp. Psychol.* **12**, 193-202.

Mowbray, G. H. and Rhoades, M. V. (1959). On the reduction of choice-reaction times with practice. *Q. J. exp. Psychol.* **11**, 16-23.

Murdock, B. B., Jr. (1960). The immediate retention of unrelated words. *J. exp. Psychol.* **60**, 222-234.

Murdock, B. B., Jr. (1961). The retention of individual items. *J. exp. Psychol.* **62**, 618-625.

Murdock, B. B., Jr. (1962). The serial position effect in free recall. *J. exp. Psychol.* **64**, 482-488.

Murdock, B. B., Jr. (1963). Short-term retention of single paired associates. *J. exp. Psychol.* **65**, 433-443.

Murdock, B. B., Jr. (1964). Proactive inhibition in short-term memory. *J. exp. Psychol.* **68**, 184-189.

Murdock, B. B., Jr. (1965a). Effects of a subsidiary task on short-term memory. *Br. J. Psychol.* **56**, 413-419.

Murdock, B. B., Jr. (1965b). Signal-detection theory and short-term memory. *J. exp. Psychol.* **70**, 443-447.

Murdock, B. B., Jr. (1966). Visual and auditory stores in short-term memory. *Q. J. exp. Psychol.* **18**, 206-211.

Murdock, B. B., Jr. (1967a). Distractor and probe techniques in short-term memory. *Can. J. Psychol.* **21**, 25-36.

Murdock, B. B., Jr. (1967b). Auditory and visual stores in short-term memory. *Acta Psychol.* **27**, 316-324.

Murray, D. J. (1966). Vocalization-at-presentation and immediate recall, with varying recall methods. *Q. J. exp. Psychol.* **18**, 9-18.

Näätänen, R. (1967). Selective attention and evoked potentials. *Ann. Acad. Sci. Fenn.* Ser. B. **151**, 1-226.

Neisser, U. (1963). Decision time without reaction time: experiments in visual scanning. *Am. J. Psychol.* **76**, 376-385.

Neisser, U. (1967). "Cognitive Psychology", Appleton-Century-Crofts, New York.

Neisser, U., Novick, R. and Lazar, R. (1963). Searching for ten targets simultaneously. *Percept. Mot. Skills* **17**, 955-961.

Newbigging, P. L. (1961a). The perceptual redintegration of frequent and infrequent words. *Can. J. Physchol.* **15**, 123-132.

Newbigging, P. L. (1961b). The perceptual redintegration of words which differ in connotative meaning. *Can. J. Psychol.* **15**, 133-142.

Newton, J. M. and Wickens, D. D. (1956). Retroactive inhibition as a function of the temporal position of interpolated learning. *J. exp. Psychol.* **51**, 149-154.

Nicely, P. E. and Miller, G. A. (1957). Some effects of unequal spatial distribution on the detectability of radar targets. *J. exp. Psychol.* **53**, 195-198.

Nickerson, R. S. (1967a). Expectancy, waiting time and the psychological refractory period. *Acta Psychol.* **27**, 23-34.

Nickerson, R. S. (1967b). Psychological refractory phase and the functional significance of signals. *J. exp. Psychol.* **73**, 303-312.

Nickerson, R. S. and Feehrer, C. E. (1964). Stimulus categorization and response time. *Percept. Mot. Skills* **18**, 785-793.

Norman, D. A. (1966). Acquisition and retention in short-term memory. *J. exp. Psychol.* **72**, 369-381.

Norman, D. A. and Wickelgren, W. A. (1965). Short-term recognition memory for single digits and pairs of digits. *J. exp. Psychol.* **70**, 479-489.

O'Hanlon, J., Jr., Schmidt, A. and Baker, C. H. (1965). Sonar doppler discrimination and the effect of a visual alertness indicator upon detection of auditory sonar signals in a sonar watch. *Hum. Factors* **7**, 129-139.

Oltman, P. K. (1964). Field dependence and arousal. *Percept. Mot. Skills* **19**, 441.

Orbach, J. (1953). Retinal locus as a factor in the recognition of visually perceived words. *Am. J. Psychol.* **65**, 555-562.

Osgood, C. E. (1949). The similarity paradox in human learning: a resolution. *Psychol. Rev.* **56**, 132-143.

Oswald, I. (1962). "Sleeping and Waking", Elsevier, Amsterdam.

Oxbury, S., Oxbury, J. and Gardiner, J. (1967). Laterality effects in dichotic listening. *Nature, Lond.* **214**, 742-743.

Paivio, A. and Steeves, R. (1963). Personal values and selective perception of speech. *Percept. Mot. Skills* **17**, 459-464.

Parducci, A. (1959). An adaptation-level analysis of ordinal effects in judgments. *J. exp. Psychol.* **58**, 239-246.

Parducci, A. (1965). Category judgment: a range-frequency model. *Psychol. Rev.* **72**, 407-418.

Parducci, A., Calfee, R. C., Marshall, L. M. and Davidson, L. (1960). Context effects in judgment: adaptation level as a function of the mean, midpoint, and median of the stimuli. *J. exp. Psychol.* **60**, 65-77.

Parducci, A., and Marshall, L. M. (1961). Context-effects in judgments of length. *Am. J. Psychol.* **74**, 576-583.

Parducci, A. and Marshall, L. M. (1962). Assimilation *vs* contrast in the anchoring of perceptual judgments of weight. *J. exp. Psychol.* **63**, 426-437.

Parducci, A. and Sandusky, A. (1965). Distribution and sequence effects in judgment. *J. exp. Psychol.* **69**, 450-459.

Park, J. F. and Payne, M. C., Jr. (1963). Effects of noise level and difficulty of task in performing division. *J. appl. Psychol.* **47**, 367-368.

Pepler, R. D. (1958). Warmth and performance: an investigation in the tropics. *Ergonomics* **2**, 63-88.

Pepler, R. D. (1959a). Warmth and lack of sleep: accuracy or activity reduced. *J. comp. physiol. Psychol.* **52**, 446-450.

Pepler, R. D. (1959b). Extreme warmth and sensorimotor coordination. *J. appl. Psychol.* **14**, 383-386.

Pepler, R. D. (1960). Warmth, glare and a background of quiet speech: a comparison of their effects on performance. *Ergonomics* **3**, 68-73.

Peterson, L. R. (1966). Short-term verbal memory and learning. *Psychol. Rev.* **73**, 193-207.

Peterson, L. R. and Peterson, M. J. (1959). Short-term retention of individual verbal items. *J. exp. Psychol.* **58**, 193-198.

Phillips, L. D. and Edwards, W. (1966). Conservatism in a simple probability inference task. *J. exp. Psychol.* **72**, 346-354.

Pierce, J. (1963). Some sources of artifact in studies of the tachistoscopic perception of words. *J. exp. Psychol.* **66**, 363-370.

Plomp, R. (1966). "Experiments on tone perception", Institute for Perception RVO-TNO, Soesterberg. (Doctoral dissertation, University of Utrecht.)

Pollack, I. (1952). The assimilation of sequentially-encoded information. 2. Effect of rate of information presentation. Human Resources Research Laboratories Memo. Report No. 25, Air Research and Development Command, U.S.A.F.

Pollack, I. (1959). On indices of signal and response discriminability. *J. acoust. Soc. Am.* **31**, 1031(L).

Pollack, I. (1960). Message uncertainty and message reception. *J. acoust. Soc. Am.* **31**, 1500-1508.

Pollack, I. (1963). Speed of classification of words into superordinate categories. *J. verb. Learn. Verb. Behav.* **2**, 159-165.

Pollack, I. (1964). Interaction of two sources of verbal context in word identification. *Lang. Speech* **7**, 1-12.

Pollack, I., Rubenstein, H., and Decker, L. (1959). Intelligibility of known and unknown message sets. *J. acoust. Soc. Am.* **31**, 273-279.

Posner, M. I. (1964). Information reduction in the analysis of sequential tasks. *Psychol. Rev.* **71**, 491-504.

Posner, M. I. (1967). Short-term memory systems in human information processing. *Acta Psychol.* **27**, 267-284.

Posner, M. I. and Rossman, E. (1965). Effect of size and location of informational transforms upon short-term retention. *J. exp. Psychol.* **70**, 496-505.

Posner, M. I. and Konick, A. F. (1966). On the role of interference in short-term retention. *J. exp. Psychol.* **72**, 221-231.

Postman, L. (1961). The present status of interference theory. *In* "Verbal Learning and Verbal Behavior" (C. F. Cofer, ed.), McGraw-Hill, New York.

Postman, L. (1964). Short-term and incidental learning. *In* "Categories of Human Learning" (A. W. Melton, ed.), Academic Press, New York and London.

Postman, L. and Phillips, L. W. (1965). Short-term temporal changes in free recall. *Q. J. exp. Psychol.* **17**, 132-138.

R*

Poulton, E. C. (1952). The basis of perceptual anticipation in tracking. *Br. J. Psychol.* **43**, 295-302.

Poulton, E. C. (1953). Two-channel listening. *J. exp. Psychol.* **46**, 91-96.

Poulton, E. C. (1956). Listening to overlapping calls. *J. exp. Psychol.* **52**, 334-339.

Poulton, E. C. (1967). Population norms of top sensory magnitudes and S. S. Stevens' exponents. *Percept. Psychophysics* **2**, 312-316.

Poulton, E. C. (1968). The new psychophysics: six models for magnitude estimation. *Psychol. Bull.* **69**, 1-19.

Poulton, E. C. and Gregory, R. L. (1952). Blinking during visual tracking. *Q. J. exp. Psychol.* **4**, 57-65.

Poulton, E. C. and Simmonds, D. C. V. (1963). Value of standard and very first variable in judgments of reflectance of grays with various ranges of available numbers. *J. exp. Psychol.* **65**, 297-304.

Poulton, E. C. and Kerslake, D. McK. (1965). Initial stimulating effect of warmth upon perceptual efficiency. *Aerospace Medicine* **36**, 29-32.

Poulton, E. C., Catton, M. J. and Carpenter, A. (1964). Efficiency at sorting cards in compressed air. *Br. J. industr. Med.* **21**, 242-245.

Poulton, E. C., Hitchings, N. B. and Brooke, R. B. (1965). Effects of cold and rain upon the vigilance of lookouts. *Ergonomics* **8**, 163-168.

Rabbitt, P. M. A. (1959). Effects of independent variations in stimulus and response probability. *Nature, Lond.* **183**, 1212.

Rabbitt, P. M. A. (1962). Short-term retention of more than one aspect of a series of stimuli. *Nature, Lond.* **195**, 102.

Rabbitt, P. M. A. (1964a). Ignoring irrelevant information. *Br. J. Psychol.* **55**, 403-414.

Rabbitt, P. M. A. (1964b). Set and age in a choice-response task. *J. Geront.* **19**, 301-306.

Rabbitt, P. M. A. (1964c). Age and time for choice between stimuli and between responses. *J. Geront.* **19**, 307-312.

Rabbitt, P. M. A. (1965). An age decrement in the ability to ignore irrelevant information. *J. Geront.* **20**, 233-238.

Rabbitt, P. M. A. (1966a). Identification of some stimuli embedded among others. Proceedings of the 18th International Congress of Psychology, Moscow 1966. North Holland Publ. Co., Amsterdam.

Rabbitt, P. M. A. (1966b). Errors and error correction in choice-response tasks. *J.. exp. Psychol.* **71**, 264-272.

Rabbitt, P. M. A. (1966c). Error correction time without external error signals. *Nature, Lond.* **212**, 438.

Rabbitt, P. M. A. (1966d). Times for transitions between hand and foot responses in a self-paced task. *Q. J. exp. Psychol.* **18**, 334-339.

Rabbitt, P. M. A. (1967a). Learning to ignore irrelevant information. *Am. J. Psychol.* **80**, 1-13.

Rabbitt, P. M. A. (1967b). Time to detect errors as a function of factors affecting choice-response time. *Acta Psychol.* **27**, 131-142.

Rabbitt, P. M. A. and Birren, J. E. (1967). Age and responses to repetitive and interruptive signals. *J. Geront.* **22**, 143-150.

Rabbitt, P. M. A. and Phillips, S. (1967). Error-detection and correction latencies as a function of S–R compatibility. *Q. J. exp. Psychol.* **19**, 37-42.

Reiter, H. H. (1963). Effects of noise on discrimination reaction time. *Percept. Mot. Skills* **17**, 418-438.

Restle, F. (1961). "The Psychology of Judgment and Choice", John Wiley, New York.

Reuck, A. V. S. de and O'Connor, M. (1964). Disorders of Language. CIBA Foundation Symposium, Churchill, London.

Robinson, D. W. (1957). The subjective loudness scale. *Acustica* 7, 217-233.

Robinson, D. W., Copeland, W. C. and Rennie, A. J. (1961). Motor vehicle noise measurement. *Engineer* 211, 493-498.

Robinson, D. W., Bowsher, J. M. and Copeland, W. C. (1963). On judging the noise from aircraft in flight. *Acustica* 13, 324-336.

Rosenzweig, M. R. (1951). Representations of the two ears at the auditory cortex. *Am. J. Physiol.* 167, 147-158.

Rubenstein, H. and Pollack, I. (1963). Word predictability and intelligibility. *J. verb. Learn. verb. Behav.* 2, 147-158.

Rubinstein, L. (1964). Intersensory and intrasensory effects in simple reaction time. *Percept. Mot. Skills* 18, 159-172.

Rushton, R. and Steinberg, H. (1963). Mutual potentiation of amphetamine and amylobarbitone measured by activity in rats. *Br. J. Pharmacol. Chemother.* 21, 295-305.

Russell, R. W., Watson, R. H. J. and Frankenhaeuser, M. (1961). Effects of chronic reductions in brain cholinesterase activity in acquisition and extinction of a conditioned avoidance response. *Scand. J. Psychol.* 2, 21-29.

Sampson, H. (1964). Immediate Memory and simultaneous visual stimulation. *Q. J. exp. Psychol.* 16, 1-10.

Sampson, H. and Spong, P. (1961a). Handedness, eye-dominance and immediate memory. *Q. J. exp. Psychol.* 13, 173-180.

Sampson, H. and Spong, P. (1961b). Binocular fixation and immediate memory. *Br. J. Psychol.* 52, 239-248.

Samuel, W. M. S. (1964). Noise and the shifting of attention. *Q. J. exp. Psychol.* 16, 264-267.

Sanders, A. F. (1961). Rehearsal and recall in immediate memory. *Ergonomics* 4, 29-34.

Sanders, A. F. (1963). The selective process in the functional visual field. Ph.D. Thesis, Utrecht University.

Sanders, A. F. (1964). Selective strategies in the assimilation of successively presented signals. *Q. J. exp. Psychol.* 16, 368-372.

Sanders, A. F. (1967a). The effect of compatibility on grouping successively presented signals. *Acta Psychol.* 26, 373-382.

Sanders, A. F. (1967b). Some aspects of reaction processes. *Acta Psychol.* 27, 115-130.

Satterfield, J. H. (1965). Evoked cortical response enhancement and attention in man. *Electroenceph. clin. Neurophysiol.* 19, 470-475.

Satz, P., Achenbach, K., Pattishall, E. and Fennel, E. (1965). Order of report, ear asymmetry and handedness in dichotic listening. *Cortex* 1, 377-396.

Savin, H. B. (1963). Word-frequency effect and errors in the perception of speech. *J. acoust. Soc. Am.* 35, 200-206.

Savin, H. B. (1967). On the successive perception of simultaneous stimuli. *Percept. Psychophysics* 2, 479-482.

Sayers, B. M. and Cherry, E. C. (1957). Mechanism of binaural fusion in the hearing of speech. *J. acoust. Soc. Am.* 29, 973-987.

Schoeffler, M. S. (1965). Theory for psychophysical learning. *J. acoust. Soc. Am.* 37, 1124-1133.

Schonfield, D. and Robertson, B. A. (1966). Memory storage and aging. *Can. J. Psychol.* 20, 228-236.

Schouten, J. F. and Bekker, J. A. M. (1967). Reaction time and accuracy. *Acta Psychol.* **27**, 143-156.

Schuell, H. and Jenkins, J. J. (1959). The nature of language deficit in aphasia. *Psychol. Rev.* **66**, 45-67.

Schuell, H., Jenkins, J. J. and Carroll, J. B. (1962). A factor analysis of the Minnesota test for differential diagnosis of aphasia. *J. speech hear. Res.* **5**, 349-369..

Senders, J. W. (1967). On the distribution of attention in a dynamic environment. *Acta Psychol.* **27**, 349-354.

Shaffer, L. H. (1965). Choice reaction with variable S–R mapping. *J. exp. Psychol.* **70**, 284-288.

Shaffer, L. H. (1966). Some effects of partial advance information on choice reaction with fixed or variable S–R mapping. *J. exp. Psychol.* **72**, 541-545.

Shaffer, L. H. (1967). Transition effects in three-choice reaction with variable S–R mapping. *J. exp. Psychol.* **73**, 101-108.

Shallice, T. (1964). The detection of change, and the perceptual moment hypothesis. *Br. J. statist. Psychol.* **17**, 113-135.

Shallice, T. and Vickers, D. (1964). Theories and experiments on discrimination times. *Ergonomics* **7**, 37-49.

Shankweiler, D. P. and Studdert-Kennedy, M. (1967). Identification of consonants and vowels presented to left and right ears. *Q. J. exp. Psychol.* **19**, 59-63.

Shepard, R. N. and Teghtsoonian, M. (1961). Retention of information under conditions approaching a steady state. *J. exp. Psychol.* **62**, 302-309.

Sherif, M., Taub, D. and Hovland, C. I. (1958). Assimilation and contrast effects of anchoring stimuli on judgments. *J. exp. Psychol.* **55**, 150-155.

Siegal, S. and Goldstein, D. A. (1959). Decision-making behaviour in a two-choice uncertain outcome situation. *J. exp. Psychol.* **57**, 37-42.

Siegal, S. and Andrews, J. M. (1962). Magnitude of reinforcement and choice behaviour in children. *J. exp. Psychol.* **63**, 337-341.

Simpson, A. (1967). "Signal Detection and Vigilance". Ph.D. thesis, University of Reading.

Skinner, B. F. (1957). "Verbal Behavior", p. 457, Appleton–Century–Crofts, New York.

Smith, S. L. (1962). Display colour coding for a visual search task. Tech. Report No. 7, Mitre Corporation, Bedford.

Snodgrass, J. G., Luce, R. D. and Galanter, E. (1967). Some experiments on simple and choice reaction time. *J. exp. Psychol.* **75**, 1-17.

Solomon, R. L. and Postman, L. (1952). Frequency of usage as a determinant of recognition threshold for words. *J. exp. Psychol.* **43**, 195-201.

Spence, J. T. (1963). Contribution of response bias to recognition thresholds. *J. abnorm. soc. Psychol.* **66**, 339-344.

Spence, K. W. (1956). "Behaviour Theory and Conditioning", Oxford University Press, London.

Sperling, G. (1960). The information available in brief visual presentation. *Psychol. Monogr.* **74** (Whole No. 498).

Sperling, G. (1963). A model for visual memory tasks. *Hum. Factors* **5**, 19-31.

Sperling, G. (1967). Successive approximations to a model for short-term memory. *Acta Psychol.* **27**, 285-292.

Spieth, W., Curtis, J. F. and Webster, J. C. (1954). Responding to one of two simultaneous messages. *J. acoust. Soc. Am.* **26**, 391-396.

Steiner, J. (1964). The reinforcing properties of discriminative stimuli. Ph.D. Thesis, University of Cambridge.

Steiner, J. (1967). Observing responses and uncertainty reduction. *Q. J. exp. Psychol.* **19**, 18-29.

Stern, R. M. (1966). Performance and physiological arousal during two vigilance tasks varying in signal presentation rate. *Percept. Mot. Skills*, **23**, 691-700.

Stevens, K. N. (1960). Toward a model for speech recognition. *J. acoust. Soc. Am.* **32**, 47-55.

Stevens, K. N. and Halle, M. (1967). Remarks on analysis by synthesis and distinctive features. *In* "Models for the Perception of Speech and Visual Form" (Weiant Wathen-Dunn, ed.), pp. 88-102, Massachusetts Institute of Technology Press, Cambridge, Mass., U.S.A.

Stevens, S. S. (1955). The measurement of loudness. *J. acoust. Soc. Am.* **27**, 815-829.

Stevens, S. S., *et al.* (1941). The effects of noise on psychomotor efficiency. U.S.O.S.R.D. Report No. 274, Harvard University.

Stevens, S. S. and Newman, E. B. (1936). The localization of actual sources of sound. *Am. J. Psychol.* **48**, 297-306.

Stone, M. (1960). Models for choice reaction time. *Psychometrika* **25**, 251-260.

Stowe, A. N., Harris, W. P. and Hampton, D. B. (1963). Signal and context components of word-recognition behaviour. *J. acoust. Soc. Am.* **35**, 639-644.

Sumby, W. H. (1963). Word frequency and serial position effects. *J. verb. Learn. verb. Behav.* **1**, 443-450.

Surwillo, W. W. and Quilter, R. E. (1965). The relation to frequency of spontaneous skin potential responses to vigilance and to age. *Psychophysiol.* **1**, 272-276.

Sutherland, N. S. (1966). Successive reversals involving two cues. *Q. J. exp. Psychol.* **18**, 97-102.

Swets, J. A. (1959). Indices of signal detectability obtained with various psychophysical procedures. *J. acoust. Soc. Am.* **31**, 511-513.

Swets, J. A. and Sewall, S. T. (1961). Stimulus *vs* response uncertainty in recognition. *J. acoust. Soc. Am.* **33**, 1586-1592.

Tannenbaum, P. H. and Williams, F. (1968). Prompted word replacement in active and passive sentences. *Lang. Speech* **11**, 220-229.

Tanner, W. P. and Swets, J. A. (1954). A decision-making theory of visual detection. *Psychol. Rev.* **61**, 401-409.

Taylor, D. H. (1965). Latency models for reaction time distributions. *Psychometrika* **30**, 157-163.

Taylor, M. M. (1965). Detectability measures in vigilance: comment on a paper by Wiener, Poock and Steele. *Percept. Mot. Skills* **20**, 1217-1221.

Taylor, M. M. (1967). Detectability theory and the interpretation of vigilance data. *Acta Psychol.* **27**, 390-399.

Taylor, M. M., Lindsay, P. H. and Forbes, S. M. (1967). Quantification of shared capacity processing in auditory and visual discrimination. *Acta Psychol.* **27**, 223-229.

Teichner, W. H., Arees, E. and Reilly, R. (1963). Noise and human performance, a psychophysiological approach. *Ergonomics* **6**, 83-97.

Thomas, O. (1966). "Transformational Grammar and the Teacher of English", Holt, Rinehart and Winston, New York.

Thorndike, E. L. and Lorge, I. (1944). "The Teacher's Word Book of 30,000 Words." Bureau of Publications, Teachers College, Columbia University, New York.

Treisman, A. M. (1960). Contextual cues in selective listening. *Q. J. exp. Psychol.* **12**, 242-248.

Treisman, A. M. (1964a). Monitoring and storage of irrelevant messages in selective attention. *J. verb. Learn. verb. Behav.* **3**, 449-459.

Treisman, A. M. (1964b). Verbal cues, language, and meaning in selective attention. *Am. J. Psychol.* **77**, 206-219.

Treisman, A. M. (1964c). Effect of irrelevant material on the efficiency of selective listening. *Am. J. Psychol.* **77**, 533-546.

Treisman, A. M. (1969). Strategies and models of selective attention. *Psychol. Rev.* **76**, 282-299.

Treisman, A. M., and Geffen, G. (1967). Selective attention: perception or response. *Q. J. exp. Psychol.* **19**, 1-17.

Treisman, M. (1964). The effect of one stimulus on the threshold for another: an application of signal detectability theory. *Br. J. statist. Psychol.* **17**, 15-35.

Tufts College (1942). The effects of loud sounds on the accuracy of azimuth tracking and of stereoscopic range-finding. U.S. National Defense Research Council Report No. 37.

Tulving, E. (1968). Theoretical issues in free recall. *In* "Verbal Behavior and General Behavior Theory" (T. R. Dixon and D. L. Horton, eds), Prentice-Hall, New Jersey.

Tulving, E. and Patkau, J. E. (1962). Concurrent effects of contextual constraint and word frequency on immediate memory and learning of verbal material. *Can. J. Psychol.* **16**, 83-95.

Tulving, E. and Arbuckle, T. Y. (1963). Sources of intra-trial interference in immediate recall of paired associates. *J. verb. Learn. verb. Behav.* **1**, 321-334.

Tulving, E. and Arbuckle, T. Y. (1966). Input and output interference in short-term associative memory. *J. exp. Psychol.* **72**, 145-150.

Tulving, E. and Pearlstone, Z. (1966). Availability versus accessibility of information in memory for words *J. verb. Learn. verb. Behav.* **5**, 381-391.

Tulving, E. and Lindsay, P. H. (1967). Identification of simultaneously presented simple visual and auditory stimuli. *Acta Psychol.* **27**, 101-109.

Tulving, E., Mandler, G. and Baumal, R. (1964). Interaction of two sources of information in tachistoscopic word recognition. *Can. J. Psychol.* **18**, 62-71.

Turvey, M. T. (1966). The effects of rehearsing analysed information upon the retrieval of unanalysed information. *Psychon. Sci.* **6**, 365-366.

Turvey, M. T. (1967). Repetition and the preperceptual information store. *J. exp. Psychol.* **74**, 289-293.

Underwood, B. J. (1957). Interference and forgetting. *Psychol. Rev.* **64**, 49-60.

Underwood, B. J. and Schulz, R. W. (1960). "Meaningfulness and Verbal Learning", Lippincott, Philadelphia, U.S.A.

Underwood, B. J., Ham, M. and Ekstrand, B. (1962). Cue selection in paired associate learning. *J. exp. Psychol.* **64**, 405-409.

Venables, P. H. (1963). The relationship between level of skin potential and fusion of paired light flashes in schizophrenic and normal subjects. *J. psychiat. Res.* **1**, 279-287.

Venables, P. H. (1964). Input dysfunction in schizophrenia. *In* "Progress in Experimental Personality Research" (B. A. Maher, ed.), Vol. 1, Academic Press, New York and London.

Verschoor, A. M. and Hoogenboom, W. (1970). Vigilance performance and skin conductance level as an index of activation. (In preparation.) (Free University, Amsterdam.)*

Vickery, B. C. (1965). "On Retrieval System Theory" (2nd Ed.), Butterworths, London.

* These results and additional work can be found more conveniently in a paper by Verschoor, A. M. and Wieringen, P. C. W. van (1970). Vigilance performance and skin conductance. *Acta Psychol.* **33**, 394-401.

Viteles, M. S. and Smith, K. R. (1946). An experimental investigation of the effect of change in atmospheric conditions and noise upon performance. *Trans. Am. Soc. Heat. Vent. Engrs.* **52**, (1291), 167-182.

Walker, E. L. and Tarte, R. D. (1963). Memory storage as a function of arousal and time with homogeneous and heterogeneous lists. *J. verb. Learn. verb. Behav.* **2**, 113-119.

Wallach, H., Newman, E. B. and Rosenzweig, M. R. (1949). The precedence effect in sound localization. *Am. J. Psychol.* **62**, 315-336.

Wallis, C. P. and Audley, R. J. (1964). Response instructions and the speed of relative judgments. II. Pitch discrimination. *Br. J. Psychol.* **55**, 121-132.

Wallis, D. and Newton, G. de C. (1957). An experiment on synthetic signal injection as a method of improving radar detection. *Dept. of Sen. Psychol., The Admiralty*, Rep. No. W2/4.

Warr, B. J. (1964). The relative importance of proactive inhibition and degree of learning in retention of paired associate items. *Br. J. Psychol.* **55**, 19-30.

Watson, C. S., Rilling, M. E. and Bourbon, W. T. (1964). Receiver-operating characteristics determined by a mechanical analog to the rating scale. *J. acoust. Soc. Am.* **36**, 283-288.

Waugh, N. C. and Norman, D. A. (1965). Primary memory. *Psychol. Rev.* **72**, 89-104.

Webber, C. E. and Adams, J. A. (1964). Effects of visual display mode on six hours of visual monitoring. *Hum. Factors* **6**, 13-20.

Webster, J. C. and Thompson, P. O. (1953). Some audio considerations in air control towers. *J. audio. Engng. Soc.* **1**, 171-175.

Webster, J. C. and Thompson, P. O. (1954). Responding to both of two overlapping messages. *J. acoust. Soc. Am.* **26**, 396-402.

Webster, J. C. and Solomon, L. N. (1955). Effects of response complexity upon listening to competing messages. *J. acoust. Soc. Am.* **27**, 1194-1198.

Webster, R. G. and Haslerud, G. M. (1964). Influence on extreme peripheral vision of attention to a visual or auditory task. *J. exp. Psychol.* **68**, 269-272.

Weiner, B. and Walker, E. L. (1966). Motivational factors in short-term retention. *J. exp. Psychol.* **71**, 190-193.

Weinstein, A. and Mackenzie, R. S. (1966). Manual performance and arousal. *Percept. Mot. Skills* **22**, 498.

Weisstein, N. (1966). Backward masking and models of perceptual processing. *J. exp. Psychol.* **72**, 232-240.

Weitzman, E. D. and Kremen, H. (1965). Auditory evoked responses during different stages of sleep in man. *Electroenceph. clin. Neurophysiol.* **18**, 65-70.

Welford, A. T. (1952). The "psychological refractory period" and the timing of high speed performance—a review and a theory. *Br. J. Psychol.* **43**, 2-19.

Welford, A. T. (1958). "Ageing and Human Skill", Oxford University Press, London.

Welford, A. T. (1960). The measurement of sensory motor performance: survey and reappraisal of 12 years' progress. *Ergonomics* **3**, 189-230.

Welford, A. T. (1962). Arousal, channel capacity, and decision. *Nature, Lond.* **194**, 365-366.

Welford, A. T. and Birren, J. E. (eds) (1965). "Behaviour, aging and the Nervous System", C. C. Thomas, Springfield, Illinois, U.S.A.

Wertheimer, M. and Leventhal, C. M. (1958). "Permanent" satiation phenomena with kinaesthetic figural after-effects. *J. exp. Psychol.* **55**, 255-257.

Weston, H. C. and Adams, S. (1932). The effect of noise on the performance of weavers. Industrial Health Research Board Report No. 65 Part II, H.M. Stationery Office.

Weston, H. C. and Adams, S. (1935). The performance of weavers under varying conditions of noise. Industrial Health Research Board Report No. 70, H.M. Stationery Office.

Wever, E. G. (1950). "Theory of Hearing", John Wiley, London.

Whitfield, I. C. (1967). Coding in the auditory nervous system. *Nature, Lond.* **213**, 756.

Wickelgren, W. A. (1965a). Acoustic similarity and retroactive interference in short-term memory. *J. verb. Learn. verb. Behav.* **4**, 53-61.

Wickelgren, W. A. (1965b). Short-term memory for phonemically similar lists. *Am. J. Psychol.* **78**, 567-574.

Wickelgren, W. A. (1966a). Phonemic similarity and interference in short-term memory for single letters. *J. exp. Psychol.* **71**, 396-404.

Wickelgren, W. A. (1966b). Short-term recognition memory for single letters and phonemic similarity of retroactive interference. *Q. J. exp. Psychol.* **18**, 55-62.

Wickelgren, W. A. and Norman, D. A. (1966). Strength models and serial position in short-term memory. *J. math. Psychol.* **3**, 316-347.

Wickens, D. D. and Eckler, G. R. (1968). Semantic as opposed to acoustic encoding in STM. *Psychon. Sci.* **12**, 63-64.

Wickens, D. D., Born, D. G. and Allen, C. K. (1963). Proactive inhibition and item similarity in short-term memory. *J. verb. Learn. verb. Behav.* **2**, 440-445.

Wiener, E. L. (1963). Knowledge of results and signal rate in monitoring: a transfer of training approach. *J. appl. Psychol.* **47**, 214-222.

Wiener, E. L. (1964). Multiple channel monitoring. *Ergonomics* **7**, 453-460.

Wiener, E. L., Poock, G. K. and Steele, M. (1964). Effect of time sharing on monitoring performance: simple mental arithmetic as a loading task. *Percept. Mot. Skills* **19**, 435-440.

Wilkinson, R. T. (1959). Rest pauses in a task affected by lack of sleep. *Ergonomics* **2**, 373-380.

Wilkinson, R. T. (1960). The effect of lack of sleep on visual watch-keeping. *Q. J. exp. Psychol.* **12**, 36-40.

Wilkinson, R. T. (1961a). Effects of sleep deprivation on performance and muscle tension. CIBA Foundation Symposium on The Nature of Sleep. (Wostenholme and O'Connor, eds), Churchill, London.

Wilkinson, R. T. (1961b). Comparison of paced, unpaced, irregular and continuous display in watchkeeping. *Ergonomics* **4**, 259-267.

Wilkinson, R. T. (1961c). Interaction of lack of sleep with knowledge of results, repeated testing and individual differences. *J. exp. Psychol.* **62**, 263-271.

Wilkinson, R. T. (1962). Muscle tension during mental work under sleep deprivation. *J. exp. Psychol.* **64**, 565-571.

Wilkinson, R. T. (1963a). Interaction of noise with knowledge of results and sleep deprivation. *J. exp. Psychol.* **66**, 332-337.

Wilkinson, R. T. (1963b). Aftereffect of sleep deprivation. *J. exp. Psychol.* **66**, 439-442.

Wilkinson, R. T. (1964a). Artificial signals as an aid to an inspection task. *Ergonomics* **7**, 63-72.

Wilkinson, R. T. (1964b). Effects of up to 60 hours' sleep deprivation on different types of work. *Ergonomics* **7**, 175-186.

Wilkinson, R. T. (1965). Sleep deprivation. *In* "The Physiology of Human Survival" (O. G. Edholm and A. L. Bacharach, eds), pp. 399-430, Academic Press, London and New York.

Wilkinson, R. T. (1967). Evoked response and reaction time. *Acta Psychol.* **27**, 234-245.

Wilkinson, R. T. (1969). Sleep deprivation: performance tests for partial and selective sleep deprivation. *In* "Progress in Clinical Psychology", Grune and Stratton Inc., U.S.A.

Wilkinson, R. T. and Morlock, H. C. (1967). Auditory evoked response and reaction time. *J. Electroenceph. clin. Neurophysiol.* **23**, 50-56.

Wilkinson, R. T. and Colquhoun, W. P. (1968). Interaction of alcohol with incentive and with sleep deprivation. *J. exp. Psychol.* **76**, 623-629.

Wilkinson, R. T., Fox, R. H., Goldsmith, R., Hampton, I. F. G. and Lewis, H. E. (1964). Psychological and physiological responses to raised body temperature. *J. appl. Physiol.* **19**, 287-291.

Wilkinson, R. T., Morlock, H. C. and Williams, H. L. (1966). Evoked cortical response during vigilance. *Psychon. Sci.* **4**, 221-222.

Willett, R. A. (1964). Experimentally induced drive and performance on a five-choice serial reaction task. *In* "Experiments in Motivation" (H. J. Eysenck, ed.), Pergamon, Oxford.

Williams, H. L., Lubin, A. and Goodnow, J. J. (1959). Impaired performance with acute sleep loss. *Psychol. Monogr.* **73** (Whole No. 484).

Williams, H. L., Kearney, O. F. and Lubin, A. (1965). Signal uncertainty and sleep loss. *J. exp. Psychol.* **69**, 401-407.

Woodhead, M. M. (1958). Effects of bursts of loud noise on a continuous visual task. *Br. J. industr. Med.* **15**, 120-125.

Woodhead, M. M. (1959). Effect of brief loud noise on decision making. *J. acoust. Soc. Am.* **31**, 1329-1331.

Woodhead, M. M. (1960). The value of ear defenders for mental work during intermittent noise. *J. acoust. Soc. Am.* **32**, 682-684.

Woodhead, M. M. (1964). The effect of bursts of noise on an arithmetic task. *Am. J. Psychol.* **77**, 627-633.

Woodhead, M. M. (1964a). Searching a visual display in intermittent noise. *J. Sound. Vib.* **1**, 157-161.

Woodhead, M. M. (1966). An effect of noise on the distribution of attention. *J. appl. Psychol.* **50**, 296-299.

Wright, P. (1969). Transformations and the understanding of sentences. *Lang Speech* **12**, 156-166.

Yntema, D. B. and Mueser, G. E. (1960). Remembering the present state of a number of variables. *J. exp. Psychol.* **60**, 18-22.

Yntema, D. B. and Mueser, G. E. (1962). Keeping track of variables that have few or many states. *J. exp. Psychol.* **63**, 391-395.

Yntema, D. B. and Trask, F. P. (1963). Recall as a search process. *J. verb. Learn. verb. Behav.* **2**, 67-74.

Yntema, D. B. and Schulman, G. M. (1967). Response selection in keeping track of several things at once. *Acta Psychol.* **27**, 325-332.

Zajonc, R. B. and Nieuwenhuyse, B. (1964). Relationship between word frequency and recognition: perceptual process or response bias? *J. exp. Psychol.* **67**, 276-285.

Zubek, J. P. (1964). Effects of prolonged sensory and perceptual deprivation. *Br. Med. Bull.* **20**, 38-42.

Zuercher, J. D. (1965). The effects of extraneous stimulation on vigilance. *Hum. Factors* **7**, 101-106.

AUTHOR INDEX

The numbers in *italics* indicate the pages on which names are mentioned in the reference list

A

Achenbach, K., 201, *501*
Adams, J. A., 27, 29, 30, 33, 43, 46, 55, 308, *480*, *483*, *496*, *505*
Adams, S., 410, *505*
Allen, C. K., 336, 346, 381, *506*
Allport, D. A., 312, *480*
Alluisi, E. A., 34, 281, 285, *480*, *483*, *486*
Anderson, L. K., 181, *490*
Anderson, N. S., 181, 182, 183, 185, 329, 358, *480*, *489*
Andrews, J. M., 452, *502*
Ankus, M. N., 207, *492*
Arbuckle, T. Y., 329, 358, *504*
Archer, W., 188, *497*
Arees, E., 414, *503*
Atkinson, R. C., 362, 363, *480*, *483*
Audley, R. J., 26, 290, 292, 318, *480*, *505*
Averbach, E., 170, 353, *480*

B

Baddeley, A. D., 38, 80, 285, 337, 341, 348, 349, 350, 351, 353, 374, 375, 382, 383, 388, 403, 423, 424, *480*, *481*, *486*, *487*
Bahrick, H. P., 431, *481*
Bakan, P., 46, 422, *481*
Baker, C. H., 26, 27, 29, 31, 32, 42, 44, 49, 56, *481*, *498*
Baker, R. A., 39, *489*
Barnes, J. M., 334, 340, *481*
Barnett, T. J., 161, 162, 315, 367, *489*, *497*
Bartlett, F. C., 271, 387, *481*
Barton, M. I., 204, *482*

Barzeele, J., 297, *482*
Bates, A., 161, 162, 367, *497*
Baumal, R., 254, *504*
Beardshall, A., 47, *488*
Bekker, J. A. M., 288, 309, 316, *493*, *501*
Bennett, P. B., 403, *482*
Bergum, B. O., 21, *482*
Berlyne, D. E., 415, *482*
Bertelson, P., 297, 302, 310, 317, *482*
Bexton, W. H., 22, *482*
Biederman, I., 188, *489*
Bills, A. G., 23, *482*
Binford, J. R., 30, 46, 77, 78, 81, 82, 84, 89, 90, 96, 102, *482*, *494*
Birdsall, T. G., 198, 199, 251, *490*
Birren, J. E., 209, *482*, *500*, *505*
Blair, W. C., 29, 42, *482*
Blake, M. J. F., 403, 420, 421, *482*, *486*
Blyth, K. W., 316, *482*, *483*
Boer, E. de, 120, *483*
Borger, R., 309, 316, *483*
Born, D. G., 336, 346, 381, *506*
Borsa, D. M., 415, *482*
Borst, J. M., 311, *487*
Boulter, L. R., 27, 29, *480*, *483*
Bourbon, W. T., 72, 73, *505*
Bowen, H. M., 20, *483*
Bowsher, J. M., 221, 222, *483*, *501*
Brainard, R. W., 285, *483*
Brand, H., 453, *483*
Brelsford, J. W., 363, *483*
Broadbent, D. E., 5, 6, 7, 8, 9, 10, 20, 21, 23, 30, 40, 42, 47, 51, 52, 60, 62, 65, 66, 77, 80, 81, 84, 89, 90, 92, 96, 97, 101, 102, 103, 105, 108, 109, 126, 127, 132, 133, 134, 135, 136, 137, 147, 149, 154,

508

SUBJECT INDEX

A

Acetylcholine, 442-446
Acoustic similarity
  acid bath theory of, 369-370
  acoustic features, 352-353
  effects of, 329-330, 347-354, 369-370,
    374-375, 381-385, 395-397
Adaptation level theory, 214-236
Adrenaline-noradrenaline, 442-446
Ageing, 139, 207-211
Air pressure, see *Arousal*
Alcohol, 424-425, 441
Amphetamine, 442-443
Anchor stimuli, 214, 215, 226, 231, 232
Anticipation, 404
Anticipatory goal response, 439-440
Apparent location, see *Channel selection*
Arousal, 440-456
  acetylcholine, see *Acetylcholine*
  adrenaline-noradrenaline, see *Adrenaline*
  air pressure, 403, 423-424
  alcohol, see *Alcohol*
  amphetamine, see *Amphetamine*
  barbiturates, see *Barbiturates*
  consolidation, 370-374
  decision theory, 447-457
  drive, 427, 434
  heat, 403, 406, 417-418, 431
  hyoscine, see *Hyoscine*
  incentive, 408-410, 429-431
  lower system of, 441, 442, 443, 444,
    446, 447
  meclozine, see *Meclozine*
  noise, see *Noise*
  over arousal, 425-437, 453, 454, 455,
    456
  paired associate learning, 415-416, 427
  personality, 421-423

physiological changes, 411-413
reserpine, see *Reserpine*
response competition, 427-431, 434-437
reticular formation, see *Reticular formation*
signal rate, 411
sleep, 411-413, 418-420
speech perception, 268, 428-431
temperature, 417-418
theory of stress, 411-413
time of day, 403, 420-421
tranquillizers, see *Tranquillizers*
upper system of, 441-447
vigilance, see *Vigilance*
Ascending and descending method of
  limits, 217-219
Attenuation, 149, 151, 158, 164, 168,
  200-201
Atropine, 443
Audition
  analysis of complex sounds, 112-118
  buffer storage, 353, 366-368
  perceptual selectivity, see *Perceptual selectivity*
  pitch perception, 114-122
  sound localization, 128-130
Authority figures, 21

B

β, see *Decision theory, vigilance and β, arousal and decision theory*
Bandwidth, see *Channel selection*
Barbiturates, 442, 443
Basilar membrane, 115-121, 124-127
Body temperature, see *Temperature*
Brain injury and speech, 205-207
Brain stem, 442

516